Leadership Approaches in Global Hospitality and Tourism

Ahmet Baytok
Afyon Kocatepe University, Turkey

Özcan Zorlu
Afyon Kocatepe University, Turkey

Ali Avan
Afyon Kocatepe University, Turkey

Engin Bayraktaroğlu
Anadolu University, Turkey

A volume in the Advances in Hospitality, Tourism, and the Services Industry (AHTSI) Book Series

Published in the United States of America by
IGI Global
Business Science Reference (an imprint of IGI Global)
701 E. Chocolate Avenue
Hershey PA, USA 17033
Tel: 717-533-8845
Fax: 717-533-8661
E-mail: cust@igi-global.com
Web site: http://www.igi-global.com

Copyright © 2023 by IGI Global. All rights reserved. No part of this publication may be reproduced, stored or distributed in any form or by any means, electronic or mechanical, including photocopying, without written permission from the publisher. Product or company names used in this set are for identification purposes only. Inclusion of the names of the products or companies does not indicate a claim of ownership by IGI Global of the trademark or registered trademark.

Library of Congress Cataloging-in-Publication Data

Names: Baytok, Ahmet, 1969- editor. | Zorlu, Özcan, 1981- editor. | Avan, Ali, editor. | Bayraktaroğlu, Engin, 1986- editor.
Title: Leadership approaches in global hospitality and tourism / edited by Ahmet Baytok, Özcan Zorlu, Ali Avan, and Engin Bayraktaroğlu.
Description: Hershey, PA : Business Science Reference, [2023] | Includes bibliographical references and index. | Summary: "This book will reveal the leadership approaches that scholars and practitioners should adopt in order to understand the crucial role of leadership and to respond to ever-changing conditions, with empirical studies, theoretical background and best practices, especially considering the hospitality and tourism industry"-- Provided by publisher.
Identifiers: LCCN 2022043713 (print) | LCCN 2022043714 (ebook) | ISBN 9781668467138 (h/c) | ISBN 9781668467145 (s/c) | ISBN 9781668467152 (eISBN)
Subjects: LCSH: Hospitality industry--Management. | Leadership.
Classification: LCC TX911.3.M27 L426 2023 (print) | LCC TX911.3.M27 (ebook) | DDC 647.94068--dc23/eng/20221021
LC record available at https://lccn.loc.gov/2022043713
LC ebook record available at https://lccn.loc.gov/2022043714

This book is published in the IGI Global book series Advances in Hospitality, Tourism, and the Services Industry (AHTSI) (ISSN: 2475-6547; eISSN: 2475-6555)

British Cataloguing in Publication Data
A Cataloguing in Publication record for this book is available from the British Library.

All work contributed to this book is new, previously-unpublished material. The views expressed in this book are those of the authors, but not necessarily of the publisher.

For electronic access to this publication, please contact: eresources@igi-global.com.

Advances in Hospitality, Tourism, and the Services Industry (AHTSI) Book Series

Maximiliano Korstanje
University of Palermo, Argentina

ISSN:2475-6547
EISSN:2475-6555

Mission

Globally, the hospitality, travel, tourism, and services industries generate a significant percentage of revenue and represent a large portion of the business world. Even in tough economic times, these industries thrive as individuals continue to spend on leisure and recreation activities as well as services.

The Advances in Hospitality, Tourism, and the Services Industry (AHTSI) book series offers diverse publications relating to the management, promotion, and profitability of the leisure, recreation, and services industries. Highlighting current research pertaining to various topics within the realm of hospitality, travel, tourism, and services management, the titles found within the AHTSI book series are pertinent to the research and professional needs of managers, business practitioners, researchers, and upper-level students studying in the field.

Coverage

- Travel Agency Management
- Casino Management
- Health and Wellness Tourism
- Sustainable Tourism
- Service Management
- Customer Service Issues
- Service Training
- Destination Marketing and Management
- International Tourism
- Leisure & Business Travel

IGI Global is currently accepting manuscripts for publication within this series. To submit a proposal for a volume in this series, please contact our Acquisition Editors at Acquisitions@igi-global.com or visit: http://www.igi-global.com/publish/.

The Advances in Hospitality, Tourism, and the Services Industry (AHTSI) Book Series (ISSN 2475-6547) is published by IGI Global, 701 E. Chocolate Avenue, Hershey, PA 17033-1240, USA, www.igi-global.com. This series is composed of titles available for purchase individually; each title is edited to be contextually exclusive from any other title within the series. For pricing and ordering information please visit http://www.igi-global.com/book-series/advances-hospitality-tourism-services-industry/121014. Postmaster: Send all address changes to above address. Copyright © 2023 IGI Global. All rights, including translation in other languages reserved by the publisher. No part of this series may be reproduced or used in any form or by any means – graphics, electronic, or mechanical, including photocopying, recording, taping, or information and retrieval systems – without written permission from the publisher, except for non commercial, educational use, including classroom teaching purposes. The views expressed in this series are those of the authors, but not necessarily of IGI Global.

Titles in this Series

For a list of additional titles in this series, please visit: www.igi-global.com/book-series/advances-hospitality-tourism-services-industry/121014

Handbook of Research on Sustainable Tourism and Hotel Operations in Global Hypercompetition
Hakan Sezerel (Anadolu University, Turkey) and Bryan Christiansen (Global Research Society, LLC, USA)
Business Science Reference • © 2023 • 677pp • H/C (ISBN: 9781668446454) • US $315.00

Handbook of Research on Urban Tourism, Viral Society, and the Impact of the COVID-19 Pandemic
Pedro Andrade (University of Minho, Portugal) and Moisés de Lemos Martins (University of Minho, Portugal)
Business Science Reference • © 2022 • 722pp • H/C (ISBN: 9781668433690) • US $315.00

Employability and Skills Development in the Sports, Events, and Hospitality Industry
Vipin Nadda (University of Sunderland in London, UK) Ian Arnott (Westminster University, UK) Wendy Sealy (University of Chichester, UK) and Emma Delaney (University of Surrey, UK)
Business Science Reference • © 2022 • 260pp • H/C (ISBN: 9781799877813) • US $215.00

Entrepreneurship Education in Tourism and Hospitality Management
Satish Chandra Bagri (Hemvati Nandan Bahuguna Garhwal University, India) R.K. Dhodi (Hemvati Nandan Bahuguna Garhwal University, India) and K.C. Junaid (Hemvati Nandan Bahuguna Garhwal University, India)
Business Science Reference • © 2022 • 313pp • H/C (ISBN: 9781799895107) • US $230.00

Global Perspectives on Strategic Storytelling in Destination Marketing
Ana Cláudia Campos (CinTurs, University of Algarve, Portugal) and Sofia Almeida (Faculty of Tourism and Hospitality, Universidade Europeia, Portugal)
Business Science Reference • © 2022 • 313pp • H/C (ISBN: 9781668434369) • US $240.00

Promoting Social and Cultural Equity in the Tourism Sector
Priscila Cembranel (Universidade Sociedade Educacional de Santa Catarina, Brazil) Jakson Renner Rodrigues Soares (Universidad da Coruña, Spain) and André Riani Costa Perinotto (Parnaíba Delta Federal University, Brazil)
Business Science Reference • © 2022 • 302pp • H/C (ISBN: 9781668441947) • US $240.00

Challenges and Opportunities for Transportation Services in the Post-COVID-19 Era
Giuseppe Catenazzo (ICN Business School, France)
Business Science Reference • © 2022 • 268pp • H/C (ISBN: 9781799888406) • US $250.00

701 East Chocolate Avenue, Hershey, PA 17033, USA
Tel: 717-533-8845 x100 • Fax: 717-533-8661
E-Mail: cust@igi-global.com • www.igi-global.com

Table of Contents

Preface xiv

Chapter 1
Conceptual Analysis of Leadership 1
    Nimet Şensoy, Ankara Yildirim Beyazit University, Turkey
    Keziban Avci, Ankara Yildirim Beyazit University, Turkey

Chapter 2
Crucial Role of Soft Skills in Challenging Times: Conceptual Analysis of Leadership Skills 23
    Bahar Urhan, Akdeniz University, Turkey

Chapter 3
Behavioral Approaches to Leadership 40
    Zehra Saltik, Cyprus International University, Turkey

Chapter 4
Laissez-Faire Leadership 61
    Muhammad Junaid Ahsan, University of Pisa, Italy
    Muhammad Hasham Khalid, Riphah International University, Pakistan

Chapter 5
Determination of the Most Suitable Leadership Type in the Hotel Industry Using Best-Worst
Method 73
    Kevser Arman, Pamukkale University, Turkey
    Arzu Organ, Pamukkale University, Turkey

Chapter 6
Charismatic Leadership in Hospitality and Tourism 91
    Gonca Aytaş, Afyon Kocatepe University, Turkey
    Fatma Doğanay Ergen, Isparta University of Applied Sciences, Turkey
    Engin Aytekin, Afyon Kocatepe University, Turkey

Chapter 7
Transformational Leadership Research in the Field of Hospitality: A Systematic Review and
Agenda for Future Research 109
 Mert Gürlek, Burdur Mehmet Akif Ersoy University, Turkey
 İlker Kılıç, Eskişehir Osmangazi University, Turkey

Chapter 8
Transformational Leadership in the Hospitality and Tourism Industry: Reflections From a Decade
of Research 129
 Seza Aksoy, Kırklareli University, Turkey
 Onur Çakır, Kırklareli University, Turkey

Chapter 9
Transformational Leadership in the Alpine Tourism Industry: Characterizing the Leadership
Dimensions Among Entrepreneurs of Small and Medium-Sized Enterprises 155
 Stefanie Haselwanter, Management Center Innsbruck, Austria
 Julia Unterlechner, Management Center Innsbruck, Austria

Chapter 10
Transforming the Hospitality and Tourism Industry: A New Paradigm Shift of Leadership
Approach 179
 Shilpi Sarna, Lloyd Business School, India
 Akansha Tyagi, IMS Ghaziabad University, India

Chapter 11
Strategic Leadership in Tourism Enterprises 199
 Zehra Yardı, Istinye University, Turkey
 Emre Ozan Aksöz, Anadolu University, Turkey

Chapter 12
Servant Leadership in the Hospitality Industry 218
 Engin Bayraktaroglu, Anadolu University, Turkey

Chapter 13
Knowledge-Oriented Leadership for Tourist Guidance Professions: A Conceptual Analysis Based
on Specialization 230
 Özcan Zorlu, Afyon Kocatepe University, Turkey
 Ali Avan, Afyon Kocatepe University, Turkey
 Engin Aytekin, Afyon Kocatepe University, Turkey
 Ahmet Baytok, Afyon Kocatepe University, Turkey

Chapter 14
Leadership in the Kitchen: Culinary Chefs 246
 Ozan Güngör, Aydın Adnan Menderes University, Turkey
 Sinan Yilmaz, Zonguldak Bülent Ecevit University, Turkey
 Hakan Yılmaz, Anadolu University, Turkey

Chapter 15
Perceived Challenges of Self-Leadership in Outdoor Recreation Activities 263
  Serhat Bingol, Bilecik Seyh Edebali University, Turkey

Compilation of References 280

About the Contributors 336

Index 340

Detailed Table of Contents

Preface xiv

Chapter 1
Conceptual Analysis of Leadership 1
    Nimet Şensoy, Ankara Yildirim Beyazit University, Turkey
    Keziban Avci, Ankara Yildirim Beyazit University, Turkey

Fast change and transformation also has a deep effect on organizations as well as their leaders and employees. Hence, if organizations want to be successful or simply stay afloat, they need effective leaders. Leadership, which can be defined as the process of influencing the behavior of individuals and groups in reaching the goals by the organization, has become more important than ever in the era of change, transformation, and ambiguity. In this context, the aim of this chapter is to examine the concept of leadership, which is one of the main determinants in the achievement of organizational goals, its historical development, prominent leadership theories, leadership competencies, the effect of personality on leadership, the effect of leadership on teams, and leadership team building.

Chapter 2
Crucial Role of Soft Skills in Challenging Times: Conceptual Analysis of Leadership Skills 23
    Bahar Urhan, Akdeniz University, Turkey

Crisis or all types of changes affect organizations and every aspect of all units' performance. Especially unexpected ones can destroy their system entirely, so it needs to be managed professionally. However, proactive measures can help to overcome either simple changes or even global crises. Become prepared for all changes, risks, and crises by investing in soft skills that can help the business world weather the storm in a sustainable manner. As one of the soft skills, leadership skill may change the destiny of organizations, especially in challenging times like the recent COVID-19 period. In this study, soft skills in general and all aspects and approaches of the leadership concept will be discussed in detail. The importance of well-designed leadership and the fact that leadership is a skill that can be developable is the focus of the study. Showing different leadership approaches in different situations, in other words using the leadership approaches as a toolbox, is underlined by referring to the literature.

Chapter 3
Behavioral Approaches to Leadership 40
    Zehra Saltik, Cyprus International University, Turkey

Leadership is one of the top subjects of study in the past, now, and in the future. Different approaches to leadership have been put forward up to the present day. As a concept, leadership has been studied with different aspects. One of these aspects is to examine leadership in terms of behaviors, which claims that it is certain types of behavior that make a leader effective or ineffective. Hence, it assumes that leaders are not born but made. According to this approach, leadership can be learned and modelled. This approach came out as a response to the inadequacies of traits approach of leadership and focused more on behaviors to define leadership. Ohio State studies, Michigan State studies, and Blake and Mouton studies are best representative of this approach.

Chapter 4
Laissez-Faire Leadership 61
Muhammad Junaid Ahsan, University of Pisa, Italy
Muhammad Hasham Khalid, Riphah International University, Pakistan

Leaders are expected to create significant impacts on their followers. The present study aims to further investigate this corollary by elaborating on the laissez-faire approach in leadership. Generally, leadership in a laissez-faire style is considered destructive. It is assumed that leaders and followers do not remain effective in laissez-faire styled leadership. Followers expect the presence and close involvement of their leader in different situations. And if they do not find their leader's presence, then it is natural that they might think about their leader as incompetent or reluctant. This may later lead them to lose confidence in their leader. In this study, the authors have used social learning theory to elaborate what could be the effects of a laissez-faire approach in leadership on team members' performance. Research has indicated that negative impacts of the laissez-faire approach in leadership are more likely to affect employees who have relatively deeper concepts about mutual relationships.

Chapter 5
Determination of the Most Suitable Leadership Type in the Hotel Industry Using Best-Worst Method 73
Kevser Arman, Pamukkale University, Turkey
Arzu Organ, Pamukkale University, Turkey

The new age requires awareness of different types of leadership. Every enterprise may need a different type of leadership for their various purposes. Determining the most suitable leadership type for a specific industry is a quite complex issue so it can be considered a decision problem. This chapter aims to determine most suitable leadership type for hotel industry using best worst method (BWM) which is one of the multi-criteria decision-making (MCDM) tools. The results have revealed that transformational leadership is the most suitable leadership in hotel industry, followed by visionary leadership and authentic leadership. It is recommended that hotel managers should adopt these three leadership types to motivate followers, create positive culture, and maximize productivity in the hotel industry. This chapter is believed to fill the literature gap since limited studies have integrated MCDM methods with this area. Moreover, the findings of the study have revealed useful insights for hotel managers.

Chapter 6
Charismatic Leadership in Hospitality and Tourism 91
Gonca Aytaş, Afyon Kocatepe University, Turkey
Fatma Doğanay Ergen, Isparta University of Applied Sciences, Turkey
Engin Aytekin, Afyon Kocatepe University, Turkey

The study is mainly focused on determining whether the managers possess a charismatic leadership style, and meanwhile, the relations of charismatic leadership with organizational performance, psychological commitment, emotional commitment, job satisfaction, corporate reputation, and work-home arrangements are examined. In this context, in this study, first of all, the concept of charismatic leadership is explained followed by a discussion of charismatic leadership in the tourism industry and hospitality businesses.

Chapter 7
Transformational Leadership Research in the Field of Hospitality: A Systematic Review and Agenda for Future Research 109
    Mert Gürlek, Burdur Mehmet Akif Ersoy University, Turkey
    İlker Kılıç, Eskişehir Osmangazi University, Turkey

Although transformational leadership is a fundamental research area of leadership literature, it has also spread to other disciplines. Transformational leadership has been a remarkable topic for the hospitality field in terms of the effects that the leader has on his/her followers. For this reason, there has been an important accumulation of knowledge about transformational leadership in the hospitality literature. However, there is no research in the literature that addresses the progress of transformational leadership research in hospitality to help researchers develop theoretical perspectives and guide practitioners' decisions. Therefore, this research aims to systematically review transformational leadership research in the hospitality field. The review included 36 studies from seven key hospitality journals. The findings basically indicate that that research on transformational leadership in the field of hospitality has not experienced sufficient development. There is a need to develop theoretical perspectives specific to the field in the field of hospitality.

Chapter 8
Transformational Leadership in the Hospitality and Tourism Industry: Reflections From a Decade of Research 129
    Seza Aksoy, Kırklareli University, Turkey
    Onur Çakır, Kırklareli University, Turkey

This study aims to examine the transformational leadership in the context of the hospitality and tourism industry. In the first part of the study, the emergence of transformational leadership, its definition, and the importance of transformational leadership in tourism and hospitality literature is discussed. In the second part, the most commonly used transformational leadership models and the sub-factors and dimensions of these models is analyzed. In the third part of the chapter, the characteristics of managers who adopt the transformational leadership style is examined. Finally, the studies conducted in the field of hospitality and tourism that were published in peer-reviewed journals in the last decade (from 2012-2022) were systematically reviewed. Transformational leadership style is found to be one of the most suitable leadership styles for both the organization, the employees, and the leaders themselves in the hospitality and tourism industry.

Chapter 9
Transformational Leadership in the Alpine Tourism Industry: Characterizing the Leadership Dimensions Among Entrepreneurs of Small and Medium-Sized Enterprises 155
    Stefanie Haselwanter, Management Center Innsbruck, Austria
    Julia Unterlechner, Management Center Innsbruck, Austria

This chapter aims to explore the topic of leadership in touristic SMEs. Effective forms of leadership, like transformational leadership, can create a high level of work engagement through setting values and direction for all involved stakeholders and pave the way for a competitive advantage for the business as well as for the destination. Building on current research on leadership and following a qualitative research approach, the authors investigate how far entrepreneurs of touristic SMEs apply notions of transformational leadership and how their leadership skills can further be characterized. Semi-structured interviews were conducted with fifteen entrepreneurs of SMEs from five different tourism subsectors in Tyrol (Austria). The objective of this chapter is to conceptualize the leadership qualities of tourism entrepreneurs and derive implications for enhancing transformational leadership abilities. This chapter adds new insights into the status-quo of leadership in tourism research and gives valuable insights for leading SMEs in the tourism sector.

Chapter 10
Transforming the Hospitality and Tourism Industry: A New Paradigm Shift of Leadership Approach 179
Shilpi Sarna, Lloyd Business School, India
Akansha Tyagi, IMS Ghaziabad University, India

Today's hospitality and tourism industry is fast becoming a technology-enabled service industry powered by the online, mobile, cloud, IoT, AI, robotics, automation, and blockchain tools and applications. Digital technology is making its way into every aspect of the industry in its operations, services, communications, revenue management, distribution, and marketing. The previous studies of hospitality leadership during the crisis have focused on the significance of leadership resilience in corporate leadership narratives. Therefore, this chapter explores the nature of such challenges and opportunities by worldwide leaders and addresses them by using various strategies with the use of technology, especially in the pre- and post-pandemic era. Additionally, this chapter also contributes to a country-wise comparison to analyze the factors that collectively play a vital role in industry activation and revitalization.

Chapter 11
Strategic Leadership in Tourism Enterprises 199
Zehra Yardı, Istinye University, Turkey
Emre Ozan Aksöz, Anadolu University, Turkey

The rapid evolution of markets today has led to globalization, competition, and technological developments, and the present classic management concept is becoming more dynamic. This has led management to adopt a more market-responsive strategic management approach. Strategic leaders are required in a wide range of institutions and organizations. There is a greater need for strategic leaders in an enterprise or an organization with larger objectives, a growth target, or high potential. Tourism businesses must remain present in this evolving environment and meet the expectations of employees, clients, partners, suppliers, government, etc. On the other hand, to ensure interaction with the external environment, exist in the market, and satisfy the aspirations of stakeholders, they must engage in managerial work towards ordinary jobs as well as activities for future and change. That requires strategic management of tourism companies. The leadership model, which has become popular in terms of strategic management, seems to be strategic leadership.

Chapter 12
Servant Leadership in the Hospitality Industry 218
Engin Bayraktaroglu, Anadolu University, Turkey

Servant leadership is a mindset structured on the leaders' desire to serve their followers. Servant leadership is not just a type of leadership; it is a paradigm, a way of life, and an ontological stance that determines the behaviour patterns of leaders. For this reason, when examining servant leadership, it is not enough to talk only about the benefits of leadership. In this study, servant leadership in service industries was evaluated. As a result of this study, which can be considered a non-systematic literature review, theoretical suggestions were made for the future of servant leadership research.

Chapter 13
Knowledge-Oriented Leadership for Tourist Guidance Professions: A Conceptual Analysis Based on Specialization 230
Özcan Zorlu, Afyon Kocatepe University, Turkey
Ali Avan, Afyon Kocatepe University, Turkey
Engin Aytekin, Afyon Kocatepe University, Turkey
Ahmet Baytok, Afyon Kocatepe University, Turkey

Combining the dimensions of knowledge-oriented leadership and tourist guidance, this chapter unequivocally renders that tourist guides could be treated as KOLs, provided that they are conscious of the value of knowledge and interpretation. A conceptual analysis was made in order to highlight a thorough comprehension of knowledge-oriented tourist guidance. Accordingly, knowledge-oriented leadership and its relationship with tourist guidance, the profession of tourist guidance and the relevance of the knowledge provided in tourist guidance, and knowledge-based leadership responsibilities of tourist guides were emphasized. This study advances the body of knowledge by demonstrating the necessity of knowledge-based tourist guidance. The researchers asserted that this chapter could benefit leaders in the hospitality and tourism industries as well as the tourist guides who stress the value of knowledge for professional development, employing it as a leadership tool while delivering tours.

Chapter 14
Leadership in the Kitchen: Culinary Chefs 246
Ozan Güngör, Aydın Adnan Menderes University, Turkey
Sinan Yilmaz, Zonguldak Bülent Ecevit University, Turkey
Hakan Yılmaz, Anadolu University, Turkey

Increased competition has made it an imperative for restaurants to have strong management in the kitchen to ensure competitive success. Being good at preparing food doesn't necessarily mean being a successful manager in the kitchen. A good kitchen manager needs to have a wide range of skills, like math and accounting for calculations associated with menu planning and cost management, managerial skills for organization, leading, and control in the kitchen, along with marketing skills for better understanding and responding to customer demands. There is continuous production in the kitchen management of the staff, and process integration requires the organizational atmosphere to be managed effectively. The performance of the kitchen staff and their workplace motivation is directly related to the leadership style of the kitchen manager. Although accepting that people who are successful at management have innate leadership skills, various research has shown education and training can develop these innate skills or form them if they are not innately possessed.

Chapter 15
Perceived Challenges of Self-Leadership in Outdoor Recreation Activities 263
Serhat Bingol, Bilecik Seyh Edebali University, Turkey

Leadership in outdoor recreation activities was mainly described with the outdoor leadership approach. However, outdoor leadership deals with group management. Therefore, it is essential to reveal the perceived challenges in outdoor recreation activities with the self-leadership approach since self-leadership strategies influence performance positively. These strategies, behavior-focused, natural reward, and constructive thought pattern strategies, motivate individuals for productive behaviors. Even though these strategies improve individuals, they still confront some challenges in leading themselves. In this context, this study aims to reveal the perceived challenges of self-leadership in camping and rock-climbing activities to help the success of participants. Since the research was planned as qualitative research to understand participants rather than explain them, the RSLQ factors were adapted as interview questions to reveal perceived challenges. Results showed that participants cope with 26 perceived challenges before, during, and after camping and rock-climbing activities.

Compilation of References 280

About the Contributors 336

Index 340

Preface

The ever-changing conditions of the present climate require leaders who can ensure adaptation between human resources and work, transform systems, and direct people to goals in a more effective and persuasive way. Leadership is very crucial and necessary in the field of tourism, as it is in all fields. Leadership has been dealt with in the historical process with situational approaches, behavioral approaches, and leadership skills; since the early 1980s, leadership approaches such as transformative, servant, spiritual, and authentic leadership have come to the fore.

Leadership Approaches in Global Hospitality and Tourism examines popular approaches to leadership in the context of tourism and contributes to the extant literature by demonstrating various aspects of the hospitality and tourism industry. It reveals the leadership approaches that scholars and practitioners should adopt to understand the crucial role of leadership and to respond to ever-changing conditions with empirical studies, theoretical backgrounds, and best practices. Covering topics such as soft skills, transformational leadership, and self-leadership, this premier reference source is an excellent resource for business executives and managers, governmental and non-governmental organization leaders, students and teaching fellows of higher education, librarians, researchers, and academicians.

Chapter 1 examines the concept of leadership, which is one of the main determinants in the achievement of organizational goals, its historical development, prominent leadership theories, leadership competencies, the effect of personality on leadership, the effect of leadership on teams and leadership team building.

Chapter 2 discusses soft skills in general and all aspects and approaches of the leadership concept in detail. The importance of well-designed leadership and the fact that leadership is a skill that can be developable is the focus of the study. Showing different leadership approaches in different situations, in other words using the leadership approaches as a toolbox underlined by referring to the literature.

Chapter 3 investigates Ohio State studies, Michigan State studies and Blake and Mouton studies as cases of behavioral approaches in leadership research.

Chapter 4 examines Laissez-Faire approach in leadership. It is assumed that leaders and followers do not remain effective in Laissez-Faire styled leadership. Followers expect the presence and close involvement of their leader in different situations. And if they do not find their leader's presence, then it is natural that they might think about their leader as incompetent or reluctant. This may later lead them to lose confidence in their leader.

Chapter 5 aims to determine most suitable leadership type for hotel industry using Best Worst Method (BWM) which is one of the Multi-Criteria Decision Making (MCDM) tools. The results have revealed that transformational leadership is the most suitable leadership in hotel industry, followed by visionary

Preface

leadership, authentic leadership. It is recommended that hotel managers should adopt these three leadership types to motivate followers, create positive culture and maximize productivity in hotel industry.

Chapter 6 discusses the concept of charismatic leadership in the tourism industry and hospitality businesses. Authors examines the relations of charismatic leadership with organizational performance, psychological commitment, emotional commitment, job satisfaction, corporate reputation, and work-home arrangements.

Chapter 7 aims to systematically review transformational leadership research in the hospitality field. The review included 36 studies from 7 key hospitality journals. The findings basically indicate that that research on transformational leadership in the field of hospitality has not experienced sufficient development. There is a need to develop theoretical perspectives specific to the field in the field of hospitality.

Chapter 8 examines the transformational leadership in the context of the hospitality and tourism industry. In the first part of the study, the emergence of transformational leadership, its definition, and the importance of transformational leadership in tourism and hospitality literature is discussed. In the second part, the most used transformational leadership models and the sub-factors and dimensions of these models is analyzed. In the third part of the chapter, the characteristics of managers who adopt the transformational leadership style is examined.

Chapter 9 aims to explore the notion of leadership in tourism SMEs. This chapter conceptualize the leadership qualities of tourism entrepreneurs and derive implications for enhancing transformational leadership abilities. In this chapter, the authors add new insights into the status-quo of leadership in tourism research and give valuable insights for leading tourism SMEs.

Chapter 10 explores the nature of the challenges and opportunities by worldwide leaders and addresses them by using various strategies with the use of technology, especially in the pre- and post-pandemic era. Additionally, this chapter also contributes to a country-wise comparison to analyze the factors which collectively play a vital role in industry activation and revitalization.

Chapter 11 discusses general means of strategic leadership in tourism businesses. There is a greater need for strategic leaders in an enterprise or an organization with larger objectives. Tourism businesses must remain present in this evolving environment and meet the expectations of stakeholders. As an outlook, the leadership model discussed in this chapter, which has structured upon strategic management, is strategic leadership.

Chapter 12, which can be considered a non-systematic literature review, discusses servant leadership in service industry. This leadership approach is a mindset structured on the leaders' desire to serve their followers. Servant leadership is not just a type of leadership, it is a paradigm, a way of life, and an ontological stance that determines the behavior patterns of leaders. For this reason, when examining servant leadership, it is not enough to talk only about the benefits of leadership.

Combining the dimensions of knowledge-oriented leadership and tourist guidance, Chapter 13 unequivocally renders that tourist guides could treat as knowledge leaders if they are conscious of the value of knowledge and interpretation. A conceptual analysis was made to highlight a thorough comprehension of knowledge-oriented tourist guidance. Accordingly, knowledge-oriented leadership and its relationship with tourist guidance, the profession of tourist guidance and the relevance of the knowledge provided in tourist guidance, and knowledge-based leadership responsibilities of tourist guides were emphasized. This study advances the body of knowledge by demonstrating the necessity of knowledge-based tourist guidance. The researchers asserted that this chapter could benefit leaders in the hospitality and tourism industries as well as the tourist guides who stress the value of knowledge for professional development, employing it as a leadership tool while delivering tours.

Chapter 14 gives an outlook to the role of leadership in food and beverage sector in terms of leadership in the kitchen. A good kitchen manager needs to have a wide range of skills, like accounting, menu planning and cost management, managerial skills for organization, leading and control in the kitchen, along with marketing skills for better understanding and responding to customer demands. Increased competition has made it imperative for restaurants to have strong management in the kitchen to ensure competitive success.

Chapter 15 discusses leadership in recreation sector via accepting outdoor leadership as a case. Outdoor leadership deals with group management. Therefore, it is essential to reveal the perceived challenges in outdoor recreation activities with the self-leadership approach since self-leadership strategies influence performance positively. These strategies, behavior-focused, natural reward, and constructive thought pattern strategies, motivate individuals for productive behaviors.

This book focuses on the popular aspects of leadership in the context of hospitality and contributes to the extant literature by demonstrating various aspects of the industry. Chapters reveal the leadership approaches that scholars and practitioners should adopt to understand the crucial role of leadership and to respond to ever-changing conditions, with empirical studies, theoretical background, and best practices, especially considering the hospitality and tourism industry. The researchers contributing to the book aim to fill the prominent gaps with their experience and perspectives in the field of leadership. As a result, the book entitled Leadership Approaches in Global Hospitality and Tourism aims to be a vade-mecum that researchers and practitioners will benefit in their future works.

Ahmet Baytok
Afyon Kocatepe University, Turkey

Özcan Zorlu
Afyon Kocatepe University, Turkey

Ali Avan
Afyon Kocatepe University, Turkey

Engin Bayraktaroğlu
Anadolu University, Turkey

Chapter 1
Conceptual Analysis of Leadership

Nimet Şensoy
https://orcid.org/0000-0001-9066-4844
Ankara Yildirim Beyazit University, Turkey

Keziban Avci
https://orcid.org/0000-0003-0998-9583
Ankara Yildirim Beyazit University, Turkey

ABSTRACT

Fast change and transformation also has a deep effect on organizations as well as their leaders and employees. Hence, if organizations want to be successful or simply stay afloat, they need effective leaders. Leadership, which can be defined as the process of influencing the behavior of individuals and groups in reaching the goals by the organization, has become more important than ever in the era of change, transformation, and ambiguity. In this context, the aim of this chapter is to examine the concept of leadership, which is one of the main determinants in the achievement of organizational goals, its historical development, prominent leadership theories, leadership competencies, the effect of personality on leadership, the effect of leadership on teams, and leadership team building.

INTRODUCTION

"Leadership is like beauty, it is difficult to define, but you can know it once you see it"

Bennis, 1999

In the early ages, human beings formed groups in order to protect themselves from wild animals and attacks by other tribes in order to survive. Humans realized that acting as a team made them stronger (Çalışal & Yücel, 2019). Besides this human always felt the need to be part of a group in order to meet basic needs, to achieve set objectives, and to satisfy desires and wishes. For a person, it is not possible to

DOI: 10.4018/978-1-6684-6713-8.ch001

maintain one's life alone and to meet all one's needs and wishes without being part of a group or community. That is why, throughout history, human beings have always had tendencies to want to belong to groups or teams in social environments and workplaces (Ayhan, 2012).

Human beings are social beings whose desire to manage others and to be managed by others came along with the desire to live in a group (Bektaş, 2016). There is a force that attracts human beings to group together, and end up directing and motivating them to unite their desires, power, and energy, thereby developing a sense of belonging among themselves resulting in them feeling part of a specific group (Özalp, 2019; Şahne & Şar, 2015). The force which makes people which attract people to a group or team is leadership. Leadership is required wherever there are at least two people who are socializing or working together. For this reason, since the early ages leaders have been found in every sphere of life. Leaders are found in all spheres of life and their presence is acknowledged in groups and society. Due to this and challenges faced in leadership, the concept of leadership attracted the attention of several researchers. To this end, leadership has become an important research topic on which a great number of studies have been conducted (Işık, 2014).

Why is leadership so much important? What kind of contributions will the understanding of leadership qualities will contribute to the efficient managing of businesses? Why are there so many analyzes made about leadership behaviors? Multitudes of studies have been conducted to find answers to these and many similar questions. The purpose of these studies has been to determine to what extent a leader can succeed in enabling the individuals or businesses to reach the determined or desired goals by influencing them to go the extra mile willingly. In this sense, it would generally be concluded that the managers are successful in whatever they do when they possess both management and leadership qualities to achieve goals and objectives at a higher rate.

The leadership is a term widely used in every field where people are involved. For this reason, it is important for all sectors of activity to understand what the present and future characteristics of leaders will entail and what leadership will be all about. On the other hand, especially in terms of the tourism sector where the characteristics of the service providers and the beneficiaries came to the fore as human beings, and the expectations and perceptions in this sector should be handled carefully, the importance of leaders has ever been increasing. For this reason, in this part of the book, we will be discussing the competency of leadership, leadership theories (leadership styles and leadership approaches), the effect of personality on leadership, the effect of leaders on teams, and leadership and team building.

BACKGROUND

Modern organizations are open systems that encounter various complexities that affect the effectiveness of the organization. Leaders and leadership are necessary for organizations to adapt to internal and external fluctuations, improve, and succeed. Leadership contributes to the ability and capacity of the organization to adapt to threats, create organizational opportunities, and boost organizational innovation. Organizations need an effective collective leadership to survive and improve. The rapidly changing turbulent environments require a collective leadership power including individual leaders who are competent in organization and human management (Douglas et al., 2022).

Leadership is one of the complex and multidimensional phenomena. Leadership which has been debated for years, is now more important than ever given how fast our world is globalizing (Benmira

& Agboola, 2020; Prastiawan et al., 2020). Leadership is an essential process for organizations and an important factor in determining organizational success or failure (Wisittigars & Siengthai, 2019).

Organizations compete to survive, to succeed, to show the desired performance, and to maintain and increase their market share. In this process, leaders play a key role in helping organizations achieve their goals as well as the employees boost their performance. Leaders' need to take risks is a well-established challenge in today's businesses (Jamalia et al., 2022). In addition, organizations are faced with the dynamism of the technological work environment, diversity of the workforce, changing customer tastes and preferences, which are among the other challenges of leadership, as well as the challenges of fierce competition. (Bosibori, 2018). Initiating and coordinating the change always requires well-developed leadership skills. Leaders need to have the right leadership competencies to do their works better and to understand and satisfy employees (Bosibori, 2018).

The COVID-19 pandemic, the Russo-Ukrainian War, the post-pandemic economic recession and chaos, complexity, and unpredictable constant change and ambiguities have brought leadership a new meaning and requirements. Major effects of ambiguous and chaotic environment on the business world have not been prevented. Leadership plays an important role in the adaptation of organizations to this situation. Therefore, not only the organization but also the leadership are changing (Stärk, 2022). The global crisis associated with the COVID-19 pandemic can be regarded as one of the turning points of the history. While most of social, economic, political and health organizations have teetered, it is impossible to know what the new world will bring. However, the future will form depending on what leaders decide now. While some are keeping pace with this situation, some are struggling to overcome the crisis, and some others are disappearing. Leadership carries particular significance during crises (Dirani et al., 2020). They make leaders out of normal people or erase them all together. Leadership is a complex phenomenon that changes with these environmental effects, constantly evolves, and requires innovation (Mashele & Alagidede, 2020). In this context, Bennis states that 'leadership is the most studied and least understood topic in the social sciences, and it never has so many labored so long to say so little' (Benmira & Agboola, 2020).

Along with the many challenges and problems leadership has encountered, the current digital age has created both opportunities and challenges for leaders in all industries (Thompson et al., 2020). The advancement of global information technology has made it necessary to adapt to today's technologies. Leaders are expected to find out to respond quickly to the problems of the society with the challenges of Industry 4.0, especially in the digital age. Hence, the digital age therefore requires leaders to be prepared to solve complex, interconnected and unpredictable problems. No matter how different interpretations of traditional leadership are today, it is no longer sufficient for the challenges leaders will face. Instead, there has been a need for leadership network, cooperation, collectivity and sensitivity along with the digital age (Raharja et al., 2019).

Definition And History of Leadership

Literature shows that leaders' characteristics and the way these are perceived have changed over time. (Özalp, 2019) In this context, in the first ages, the qualities of leaders were regarded as an innate gift bestowed by God. This is the reason why heroes and legends were considered leaders. In the first ages, the attention focused on the behaviours/attitudes and attributes leaders had to possess, and it was suggested that leadership was not inherited but rather a developed quality that could be improved upon in course of life once given the opportunity to assume a leadership role. While leadership was considered as a symbol of power and authority in the ancient times and during the Middle Ages, the concept gained prominence in business management modern times.

Though it was not specifically mentioned, leadership conceptualization as a discipline appearance in written manuscripts can be traced back to Egypt in 2300 A.D. The word "Leader" was first used at the beginning of the 14th Century. Nevertheless, the concept of leadership was not been paid much attention to until the Industrial Revolution in the 18th Century between 1760 to 1840. The increase in the number of the machines and enterprises, and the subsequent social and organizational changes brought up the issue of the greater need of how these businesses were to be managed, and this led to an increase in research on leadership. By the 20th century, the importance of research and studies on leadership had increased due to globalization, increased competition, technological developments, changes in people's needs and expectations. The need to research on leadership became more pronounced in the 1950s, because of great strides made in the developments in management sciences, and the acceleration of the modern management approaches increased the popularity of the leadership concept (Işık, 2014).

There are multiple definitions of ''leadership'' which are as old as the history of humankind. When these definitions are analyzed, it can be realized that the changes in the meaning of ''leadership'' and the characteristics attributed to leaders throughout the history of mankind are also reflected in these definitions (Eraslan, 2004). In this context, the Great Man Theory, which was dominant in the 19th Century, described a leader "as an exceptional person or hero who used his/her intelligence, wisdom, charisma and political skills to have power and influence over other people." This can be interpreted to mean that only those considered heroes became leaders (Silva, 2016). The Traits Theory, which emerged in literature as the first leadership theory of the 20th century, claims that "one person in the group stands out, among others, in the process of controlling social movements, and that person became the leader of that group" (Eraslan, 2004). In the period following the World War II, the understanding that "the leadership, rather than being an individual characteristic, was a process by which others in the group were influenced by an individual who emerged as the leader of the group" gained prominence. Thus, the Theory of Traits was replaced by the Theory of Behavior (Silva, 2016). In the early 1950s, the first experimental studies on leadership were conducted at Ohio State and Michigan Universities, and as a result, the Contingency Approaches to leadership that emerged in the 1960s and 1970s the changed the perspective on leadership (Eraslan, 2004). In 1960s and 1970s years, leadership was described as "talent very dependent on the characteristics of the people in the group and the situation to be addressed," and it was claimed that there could not be a single leadership style that applied to all situations (Katz & Kahn, 1970).

1990's is the period when new trends on leadership emerged. During this period, leadership was defined as the act of "influencing people by exhibiting active, important and integrated behaviors such as expertise and empathy to achieve a certain purpose" (Eraslan, 2004). In this scope, according to Yukl (1989, p.18), "[…] leadership […] involves a process whereby intentional influence is exerted over other people to guide, structure, and facilitate activities and relationships in a group or organization."

By 2000s, the cumulative information obtained in the literature on leadership was reflected in the definition of the leadership. In this scope, Becker et al., (2006) sees the main task of leadership as a driving force for stepping the necessary space for maneuver and motivating people to take action to achieve the set goals. Leadership primarily means that leaders influence their subordinates. It is an interaction in which the governed consciously or unconsciously affect the rulers (Becker et al., 2006). Yukl (2013), on the other hand, defined leadership as "the process of influencing others on what needs to be done and how to do it and collective efforts to achieve common goals". Likewise, Koçel (2020) defines leadership as the process in which a person influences and guides the activities of others, under certain conditions, in order to achieve certain personal or group goals. In this sense, according to Colenda (2021), leadership is the art of inspiring people's best contributions toward the common good even under extreme circumstances. As a matter of fact, leadership in this period; was described as "a process of social influence that maximizes the efforts of others to achieve a goal" (Cathy et al., 2022). When we look at this definition, it can be understood that the capacity to influence others forms the basis for leadership.

Factors such as social changes, technological developments, globalization, and international competition that we face today are of particular interest to all kinds of businesses. Changing social structures, changes in people's expectations and demands have led the companies to make changes in many areas of business operations such as the structures through which produce products and services. In this context, it is important that people in managerial positions in organizations have leadership qualities. In other words, managers besides managing, should also lead their organizations in an understanding strongly advocated for today's businesses (Şahne & Şar, 2015).

Sometimes the terms leadership and management are used interchangeably. "Manager" was the first term used to describe a person who directed, managed and influenced people. Over the centuries, the concept management was replaced by the term leadership, as the latter had not fully met the intended meaning and the scope in the face of changes in people's desires, wishes and needs, and changes in societal and organizational structures. In this respect, leadership and management do not have the same meaning even though they are very closely related concepts. In management, the task is given by others and authority comes to the fore. As to leadership, there is no need for a legal authority. Moreover, it is stated that the leader can influence individuals with his/her unique qualities, no matter what position he/she is in, and can direct people in line with the desired goals and objectives (Özalp, 2019).

Leadership Development

Today, leadership is more about creating organizations where people can succeed than making decisions or doing things individually. Managers or leaders cannot deal with every issue that needs to be performed within the organization by themselves. Besides, there are generally no situations where they can take all decisions and dictate to subordinates what needs to be done. From this point of view, ensuring that colleagues do their best is the essence of leadership. In other words, leaders engages in ensuring the growth or development of skills, knowledge and abilities in order to achieve the highest possible performance now and in the future, both for themselves and for their colleagues. Particularly, organizational stress periods are opportunities for employees in terms of development and growth. In this respect, leaders are expected to perform the following in their organizations;

- Creating an organizational environment where employees are encouraged to learn and develop
- Identifying the most important competencies that employees must develop,
- Providing employees with opportunities to develop these competencies,
- Creating individual development plans,
- Integrating development into daily activities as much as possible (Topping, 2002).

Additionally, the steps that leaders may follow in self-development are summarized below. These are;

- Step 1. Believe You Can: To lead others and being a leader is about discovering what the leader and those they lead value, why they inspire them, what is challenging and stimulating for them.

In fact, everything starts with the feelings that the people think about themselves and the feelings they have about themselves. The belief that people can lead is necessary to develop their leadership skills and abilities. In this respect, leaders should constantly strive to become a better leader. In summary, it will be possible for people to reveal their leadership qualities only when they believe that they can do it.
- Step 2. Aspire to Excel: To be a better leader, it is important to identify first the values and principles. The ability to prepare individuals for the future requires being able to imagine what the future will look like, how it will feel, and to conceive the vision of 10 or 20 years later.
- Step 3. Challenge Yourself: To become a better leader, you must go outside of your comfort zone. Opportunities for new experiences should be sought instead of doing business in traditional ways. Challenging in leadership is an important element that often brings out the skills and abilities people didn't know they had in themselves. Developing leadership abilities requires taking initiative and volunteering for tasks that go beyond the current comfort zone. Challenges are also an opportunity to develop leadership skills.
- Step 4. Engage Support: Top performers in all fields are those who know that they cannot do extraordinary things alone. You cannot be a good leader without the help and support of others, leadership requires cooperation. In this respect, the support and advice of experts is important in being an effective leader. It is also expected from the leader to create channels to provide expert support and to identify the special expert for that subject.
- Step 5. Practice Deliberately: When the environment in which people live and work provides the necessary conditions and support for their growth and development, people get the opportunity to develop. When there is a rich leadership culture in an organization, leaders emerge, grow and succeed. The best leaders know that they need to learn constantly. In this respect, leadership is a lifelong learning effort. A leader knows that no matter how high ranks they have reached, they must take a step at a time to improve themselves. Therefore, a good leader should have a mindset that supports continuous improvement" (Kouzes & Posner, 2016).

In order to increase leadership effectiveness, some behavioral changes need to be made. The main challenge here lies in actually managing to change and improve leadership behaviors. It should be known that it will take time for people to develop their abilities, so an employee should not be expected to perform at the highest level immediately (Topping, 2002).

Leadership Competencies

Competencies are a component of human capital and one of the most important assets of a business. It plays an important role in strengthening the company's position in the competitive market. Investing in the improvement of competencies boosts the organization's capability to grow and compete through innovations. In this context, it is extremely important to build competency (Hendijani & Sohrabi 2019). The concept of competency has many meanings. These differences in meaning are associated with the fact that different types of organizations and leadership styles, which have a variety of skill and knowledge needs of individuals, require different competencies. Competency refers to the skills, knowledge, behaviors, motivation, ability, attitude and other characteristics of individuals (Radwan et al., 2020). It is also possible to define competencies as the knowledge, attitudes and skills required to perform a work effectively (Gunter, 2020). Competencies are used synonymously with other terms such as knowledge, skills or competence; therefore, they are often confused with each other. Competencies are knowledge-based, created by values, emerge as skills, and are reinforced through action. Knowledge and competence are necessary prerequisites, but not sufficient for competency (Störk, 2022).

McClelland, the founder of the concept of competency, establish an iceberg model for competencies and states that the upper part of the iceberg consists of the skills and knowledge of individuals, while the hidden lower part of the iceberg consists of facts such as individuals' self-confidence, empathy, traits, motives, self-concepts and other personal characteristics. Clark (2016) developed a Leadership Competency Model with 3 steps: Core Competencies that present Personal Skills (PS), (2) Leadership Competencies that represent Required Skills (RS), and (3) Professional Competencies. (Clark, 2016). The first step of the pyramid includes communication, teamwork, interpersonal skills, self-direction, creative problem solving, management of customer relations, flexibility, financial control, formation of appropriate relationships, business intelligence, and professionalism, representing the PS of the leader. The second step of the leadership pyramid, the leadership abilities representing the RS of the leaders include team building, leading teams, implementing employee engagement strategies, creating a vision, developing conflict resolutions, managing the project, evaluating situations quickly and accurately, and training subordinates. Professional competencies, which are the last step of the leadership pyramid, include the help, skills and knowledge needed by leaders to manage the system (Radwan et al., 2020).

Studies classify human competencies into two main categories (emotional and social competencies). Emotional competencies consist of self-awareness and self-management. The category of self-awareness is related to recognizing and understanding one's own emotions. The self-management category refers to an effective self-management and consists of one's emotional self-control, achievement orientation, positive view, and adaptability. Social competencies consist of social awareness and relationship management. Social awareness refers to understanding the emotions of others and consists of two competencies, empathy and organizational mindfulness, while relationship management is related to the use of emotional understanding in one's relationships with others. Leadership also includes many competencies such as coaching and mentoring ability, conflict management, inspirational leadership, teamwork and emotional intelligence (EQ) (Hendijani & Sohrabi, 2019).

Today, new leadership roles have also changed the competencies of leaders. The changing world of VUCA (Volatility, Uncertainty, Complexity, Ambiguity) requires many competencies for leaders in order to get rid of uncertainty and ambiguity (Störk, 2022). In most of new leadership theories, researchers assume that competencies are learned. Different combinations of competencies lead to different leadership styles that are appropriate in different situations (Gunter, 2020; Nguyen et al., 2022). In today's world, where leadership is accepted as a skill that can be developed and learned, competencies can also be trained and developed and become a characteristic of the person. It is recommended that leadership programs, especially due to their dynamic and complex nature, should give more importance to the development of leadership competencies along with programs such as team leadership, leadership training and project management in order to ensure that they develop effective leadership competencies (Talu & Nazarov, 2020).

Leadership Theories

Leadership theories contain information that can be used to better understand leadership and train more successful leaders by transferring it to practice (Schyns et al., 2011). These theories used to explain leadership include trait, behavior, probability, and integrative theories. In this context, the outstanding theories in the literature will be focused on.

Trait Theory is based on the assumption that leadership comes by birth. Researchers of this theory wanted to identify a set of characteristics that distinguish leaders from followers, or effective leaders from ineffective leaders. These characteristics include physical and psychological characteristics such as high energy, good appearance, self-confidence and ability of persuasion. These characteristics will be used as a prerequisite to promote candidates to leadership positions. Leadership positions will be awarded only to candidates with all the specified qualifications.

Behavioral Leadership Theory focuses on the nature of management work. Therefore, behavioral leadership theories have sought to explain the distinctive styles used by effective leaders or to describe the nature of their work. Mintzberg's ten managerial roles are an example of behavioral leadership theory. From this point of view, the researchers of this theory are focused on finding ways to classify behaviors that would facilitate our understanding of leadership (Greve, 2013).

Contingency leadership theories have tried to explain the appropriate leadership style according to the leader, followers and situation. In other words, the answer to the question" when contingency variables are taken into consideration which characteristics or behaviors result in leadership success" was sought.

From the mid to late 1970s, integrative theories began to emerge to connect the leadership theories of that time. Integrative leadership theories attempt to combine trait, behavioral, and contingency theories to explain successful, influencing leader-follower relationships. Theories describe behaviors and characteristics that facilitate leader effectiveness and explore why the same behavior of the leader may have a different effect on followers depending on the situation (Lussier & Achua, 2014).

Traits Theory

The Traits Theory bases the reason for choosing a person as a leader and the management phenomenon was concentrated in him/her on a number of personality traits that this individual has acquired since birth, and states that the leader is different from his followers with his/her physical and individual characteristics. In this respect, it emerged in order to determine what are the qualities that differentiate a leader from another leader (Kazancıoğlu, 2018). This theory is the most basic approach that defines and explains the leader in the literature in general and argues that the characteristics of the leaders make them superior (Sayan, 2018). On the other hand, the biggest criticism of this theory is that it generalizes all the characteristics of a leader to other leaders and argues that these qualities are found in all leaders. Situations such as the fact that although there are group members who have more than the characteristics of the leader in a group or community in daily life, these people do not appear as leaders in the group and it is difficult to measure concretely the characteristics that they claim to exist in the leader have shown that this theory is insufficient (İlbars, 2022).

Behavioral Approach

It emerged in the 1950s with the realization that, contrary to Traits theory, not all leaders show the same characteristics in general (Onen & Kanayran, 2015). According to the Behavioral Approach, the characteristics that determine the leader are not personal characteristics, but the behaviors that the leader exhibits during the leadership process and that are appropriate to the characteristics of the group he represents (Kılınç, 2019). From this point of view, the behavior of leaders constitutes the focal point of the theory (Sayan, 2018).

Various researches have contributed to the development of Behavioral Leadership Theory. As a result of these studies, various leadership styles were determined and their effectiveness was investigated. Among these works are the following are involved;

- Leadership Studies of Ohio and Michigan State Universities,
- Blake and Mouton's Management Style Matrix,
- McGregor's Theory of X and Theory Y, and
- Likert's System-4 Model.

As a result of these researches, it has been found that two important factors for work and person are effective in leadership behavior. Factors related to a person are behaviors such as leaders helping employees, caring about their ideas, treating everyone equally in a group, and owning their team. Factors related to the work or task are characteristics such as the timely and complete execution of the work, the efficient work of the team, the organization of employees by the leader, the ability to communicate effectively (Dinç, 2020).

Contingency Approach

Contingency Approach developed in the period from the end of the 1950s to the 1980s, unlike other leadership theories up to that time, beyond determining the best leader characteristics or behaviors, focused on which situations the leader characteristics or behaviors could be more effective. This theory is fundamentally connected with situations and circumstances. The basic assumption of the Contingency Approach is that an effective leader is a leader who has behaviors that may differ according to circumstances, group and personal characteristics, rather than having unchangeable behavioral characteristics. In this approach, mainly there is not a single leadership behavior or style as basis, but whichever leadership behavior will be the most effective for that situation has to be applied (Kazancıoğlu, 2018). Among the main studies of Contingency approaches;

- Fiedler's Contingency Approach,
- Hersey Blanchard Model,
- Path-Purpose Approach,
- Veoom and Yetton's Normative Theory,
- Reddin's Three-Dimensional Leadership Model are involved (Balaban, 2018).

MODERN AND POSTMODERN LEADERSHIP THEORIES

By the 1990s, the developments, differences and new ways of thinking that have emerged in the world have also led to the emergence of new ideas in the field of leadership. The main approaches that stand out among these leadership styles, called modern leadership theories, are Authentic, Democratic, Charismatic, Strategic, Decadent, Laissez-Faire, Ethical Leadership and Digital Leadership.

Authentic Leadership

Authentic leadership can be defined as creating followers by adhering to their own core values. These basic values mostly consist of moral values such as honesty, openness, transparency, justice and sincerity. The authentic leader encourages the group in which he/she takes part to such values. By applying these values first, it forms a model, and the group, motivated in this way, exhibits the same characteristics following the leader. Consistency between the words and actions of Authentic Leaders is important. A relationship will be formed between the consistent leader and the followers, so that the authentic leader will be able to achieve success by showing the desired effect on the group members (Dinç, 2020).

Democratic Leadership

Democratic Leadership is one of the leadership approaches that attaches the most importance to human relations. The most distinctive feature of the democratic leadership style is that the leader uses the ideas and thoughts of subordinates in determining the goals, plans and policies. There is no central authority in this form of leadership (Balaban, 2018). In the democratic leadership style, the leader shares the management authority with the followers. Employees are informed about their work, encouraged by the democratic leader to express their thoughts and offer suggestions (Demir, Yılmaz & Çevirgen 2010).

Leader receives the opinions of the employees regarding all kinds of situations and is open to communication. During the decision-making process, employees participate in decisions. Followers may work with the people they want and the task distribution is left to the group (Sayan, 2018). The prolongation of the decision-making process due to the participation of too many people in the process is among the criticisms of this approach. This leadership approach partially fails when it is necessary to take quick decisions (Şafaklı, 2005).

Charismatic Leadership

Charismatic leadership has often considered leadership in terms of the leader's effects on followers or the relationship between leaders and followers. The focus of charismatic leadership focuses on the question "what is the basis of charisma?". This question is based on the debate over whether charisma is primarily the result of (a) the situation or social climate the leader is facing, (b) the leader's outstanding qualities, or (c) a combination of the situation and the leader's qualities. Charisma means "divine inspiration talent" in ancient Greek. The sociological literature pioneered by Weber supports this point of view by emphasizing that charismatic leadership emerges from stressful situations. In stressful situations, charismatic leaders can express sentiments that are different from the established order and also inspire others to create a vision for a better future. Proponents of this position later claim that Martin Luther King, Nelson Mandela, Adolph Hitler or Gandhi would not have emerged as charismatic leaders without the socioeconomic and political crises prevailing in their countries. On the other side of the argument, there are those who argue that charisma does not have to be born out of adversity, but is instead the result of the innate qualities of leaders. These qualities include a strong sense of vision, outstanding communication skills, strong faith, reliability, high self-esteem, intelligence, energy and a proactive orientation. Proponents of this position argue that, regardless of the situation, none of the previously mentioned leaders would deserve the label of charisma if they did not possess these qualities. From this point of view, these leadership theorists consider charisma to be the result of followers' qualities that are influenced not only by real leader characteristics and behavior, but also by the context of the situation (Lussier & Achua, 2014).

Servant Leadership

It is a leadership style that expresses that people can serve and lead both the organization and the members within the organization, ignoring their own interests. The leader has made it a principle to strive for the followers to achieve their personal goals, to find out what they need in order for them to be successful. Instead of meeting the expectations of the leader by followers, the leader tries to fulfill their wishes by determining the needs of the followers. In this way, leader aims to strengthen the organization. (Saç, 2019; Parris & Peachey, 2013). The servant leaders act by keeping the wishes and needs of their followers ahead of leader's own wishes and needs. With this point of view, they are not pursuing any personal interests. The servant leader thinks about how to influence the followers when making decisions and behaves sensitively towards them (Balaban, 2018).

The main role of the servant leader is to develop team members, authorize them, empower them and thus enable them to do their best by unlock the potential that exists in them. Today, leaders who guide others to achieve their own desires, needs, goals and interests have now been replaced by leaders who serve their followers. In achieving the set goals and solving the problems that arise, leaders also consult the opinions of their employees and share this situation with them. Thus, servant leaders who closely follow the development of their employees are happy and satisfied with their achievements. As a result of reaching the satisfaction of the employees in the servant leadership approach, it becomes easier for the organization to reach its goals and increase its profitability (Süzer & Süzen, 2019).

Ethical Leadership

Organizations and employees face moral problems, and leaders determine the ethical climate and are responsible for the ethical or unethical behavior of employees. Ethics are the standards of right and wrong that affect behavior. The right behavior is considered ethical, and the wrong behavior is considered unethical. State laws and regulations are designed to help keep business honest. But laws do not make people moral. On the other hand, organizations make arrangements to promote moral development and ethical behavior. Trust is very important among employees, and trust is built on honesty. If you are not honest with people and take advantage of them, they will not trust you and you will not have the power to influence them. Therefore, there is a direct connection between honesty and being an effective leader (Lussier & Achua, 2014). Ethical Leadership Theory consists of principles that guide how leaders behave and how morally good they are. Ethical principles are behaviors that should be found in all leaders. Attitudes and behaviors such as truthfulness, honesty, fairness, equality, which are the basis of universal ethical principles, ensure unity and justice in the organization. Ethical principles make it easier for employees to trust and respect their leaders. (Sayan, 2018). In this theory, it has been agreed that the leader should exhibit ethical behavior and be a good example to the members of the organization from a moral point of view. Characteristics such as the character of the leader, honesty, awareness, keeping the interests of the organization above their own interests, behaving with kindness and caring about the needs and rights of other people are of great importance for employees to adopt and follow the leader. Ethical leaders are considered to be people who have ethical behavior, care about personal needs, are unbiased and impartial, defend the rights of their followers and behave fairly in their practices (Saç, 2019).

Laissez-Faire (Delegative) Leadership

Laissez-faire is a French idiom that means "let go". Self-releasing leadership describes leaders who allow people to work on their own. This leadership is also defined by some researchers as the "let them do it" type of management. This leadership style, which allows complete freedom, is a form of management that allows employees to perform the job using their own methods. In this leadership style, directing subordinates is at the lowest level. The influence of the leader on the effectiveness of the organization and the productivity of the employees is almost negligible. The leader performs management functions at a minimum level and intervenes only in emergency situations. The most important advantage of laissez faire leadership for employees is that with the autonomy provided to team members, employees develop their creativity and become able to manage themselves. This situation provides high job satisfaction and productivity increase in employees (Sayan, 2018).

This approach has the benefits of increasing the independence of employees and making them feel completely free. The person who wants to solve their problems by creating a group with the people they want, when necessary, tests their new ideas and thus takes the most appropriate decisions. In this context, the main task of the leader is to provide resources and materials. The leader expresses an opinion only when asked, on any issue, but this opinion is not binding on the activities of the group members. This type of leadership is applied in the development of innovative ideas of highly qualified personnel with high knowledge, skills and expertise working in research and development departments of enterprises, in cases of professional specialization and in the work of scientists (Şafaklı, 2005). On the other hand, one of the criticisms towards this approach is that the leader does not use the authority and deprives the group of gathering in a common goal and directing it to certain goals. In addition, this type of leadership model is difficult to succeed in groups with a low level of education, without a good distribution of work and including people who do not have a sense of responsibility (Şafaklı, 2005). Moreover, the fact that the leader has a laissez faire style may negatively affect the motivation of employees. Failure of the leader to use the reward and punishment powers and lack of support for employees may reduce the performance of employees (Sayan, 2018).

Strategic Leadership

Strategic leadership can be defined as the ability of a leader to anticipate, envision, maintain flexibility, think strategically, and work with others to initiate changes that will create a viable future for an organization (Schoemaker, Krupp, & Howland, 2013). This is the process of leadership and providing leadership. The inspiration required to determine and implement an organization's vision, mission, and strategies to achieve organizational goals is the focus of strategic leadership (Salleh & Grunewald, 2013). From this point of view, strategic leadership is also a strategic management process and change management. From this point of view, strategic leadership is the responsibility of top management. Senior management will include vice-presidents of departments or strategic business units. Top management consists of those who take the lead in creating the vision, mission, core values, goals and strategies of the organization. Strategic leaders are responsible for the short-term performance of the organization, as well as for creating conditions that will ensure the long-term competitiveness of the organization (Lussier & Achua, 2014). Strategic leadership is to be able to provide rapid strategic change when necessary in a complex global competitive environment by directing to innovative and creative goals in line with the organization's vision. Since the most obvious responsibility of a strategic leader is related to maintaining the life

Conceptual Analysis of Leadership

or competitive advantage of the enterprise, it is more important than other characteristics for the leader to have future-oriented, guiding abilities and characteristics that will benefit all stakeholders. Strategic Leadership is distinguished from other leadership theories in two ways. First, strategic leadership is only about managers. Second, managers focus not only on routine tasks, but also on strategic activities. Strategic Leadership plays a key role in enabling the organization to achieve a competitive advantage and maintain its actions efficiently. In addition, it has a very important role in terms of technological transformations and keeping up with changing environmental conditions in order for the institution to make the necessary changes and developments (Balaban, 2018).

Digital Leadership

Digital technology has an impact on both information technology and how organizations are managed and leadership styles are implemented. When examining the effect of the change in technology from past to present on leadership, leadership is divided into four phases: (1) Leadership 1.0 is the old-fashioned form of management. Managers above the hierarchy give orders to subordinates who have no freedom. (2) Leadership 2.0 is the phase in which scientific management approaches are dominant. In particular, it relies on processes, methodologies and frameworks. People aren't involved, it is realized in the old-fashioned way through the sanction power of hierarchy. (3) In Leadership 3.0, people are involved in relevant works, decisions are made together, and everyone takes responsibility for achieving success. (4) Leadership 4.0 can be defined as leadership in the Industry 4.0 era. Emphasizing fast responsiveness, Leadership 4.0 also highlights openness and flexibility in the leadership structure. This type of leadership is a fast, team-oriented, cross-hierarchical and collaborative leadership model. The concept of digital leadership, as a leader model in the Industry 4.0 era, suggests that people can learn new behaviors by observing others. Leaders must have high creativity to cope with the challenges of Industry 4.0. Creative and futuristic leadership is regarded as an effective leadership style that supports a collaborative culture and encourages innovation. In today's leadership, called digital leadership, there is a strong focus on innovation (Raharja et al., 2019).

The Effects of Personality on Leadership

The word personality is derived from the Latin word 'persona'. With the word 'persona', the differences between individuals are explained. Today, as the fact that motivation has a direct relationship with the concept of personality such as willingness to develop and behavior style, managers in the organization have given more importance to the personality phenomenon in order to ensure the desired effect and success on the employees (Kazancıoğlu, 2018). The fact that behavior is an expression of personality, the existence of a relationship between the behavior people exhibit and who they are, has led to a focus on personality in literature. It has been observed that personality traits have a decisive effect on the features required for leadership such as team forming, increasing the effectiveness of the organization, reaching results in business life, managing emergencies and directing the individuals for whom they are responsible (Taşdöven, Emhan & Dönmez, 2012).

Personality can be defined as a predisposition to think, feel and act in certain ways. Personality is largely inherited. Despite this, it is not unchangeable, there are changes in personality throughout life, but this change is slow. It is important to distinguish between personality and behavior. Personality interacts with the situation faced by the individual, exerting an influence on the individual in the perception of the situation. Thus, the personality of an individual makes him/her prone to act according to situations (such as showing sincerity, acting cautiously or distrustful). Behavior, on the other hand, is all kinds of cognitive, sensory and psychomotor reactions that individuals show towards the outside world (Pendleton, Furnham & Cowell, 2021).

The behaviors shown in the group are a reflection of the personality characteristics of the individual. Individuals with different personality traits exhibit different behaviors in certain situations. The data of the researches carried out in the fields of personality and organizational behavior reveal that personality is the most important factor guiding the behavior of the individual and in this context it is related to both the organizational performance and the attitudes of the employees (Korkmaz, 2006).

It is known that a leader's personality strongly plays a role in their emergence as a leader and their success in leadership. Although studies have shown that there are correlations between personality and leadership, it is accepted that it does not show causality. Thus, it cannot be explained why personality traits are related to leadership. The authors suggest that leaders tend to be more emotionally stable. The basis of this lies in the fact that the relationship between intelligence (IQ) and leadership is not as strong as expected which was shown as a result of researched. It is stated that successful leaders have "emotional intelligence (EQ)" and this is considered more as a personality variable than anything related to intelligence (IQ). A good team leader is able to change and direct the emotions and behaviors of others and themselves appropriately by means of their emotional intelligence. It should be noted that the fact that the influence of leadership on the performance of organizations is not always direct as such, but indirect. Because leaders assume an intermediary function in the organization by creating an impact on the people they lead in order to achieve the desired behavior or success (Pendleton, Furnham & Cowell, 2021).

In addition, leadership behaviors are examined by researchers in five dimensions in order to be used to understand which personality type is effective in leadership behaviors. These are;

- Neuroticism: Includes the tendency to easily experience unpleasant emotions such as anger, anxiety, depression or vulnerability.
- Extraversion: Seen in the form of energy, positive emotions, assertiveness and a tendency to seek encouragement and the seeking others for friendship.
- Openness: It embodies the diversity of art, emotion, adventure, unusual ideas, imagination, curiosity and experience.
- Agreeableness: It is a tendency to be compassionate and cooperative rather than suspicious and antagonistic towards others.
- Conscientiousness: Includes the tendency to show self-discipline, act dutifully and aim for success (Pendleton, Furnham & Cowell, 2021).

The Impact of Leaders on Teams

It is possible to achieve the desired results and achieve success in today's enterprises not only with the efforts of managers, but also with the fact that all employees show their talents and creativity. It is possible for employees to perform their operations faster and easier, to improve their business processes and methods through teamwork that allows employees to act together. Teamwork is an important management approach that is accepted in organizations because it provides better products or services, faster presentation and cheap costs. In addition, teamwork is also used to identify and solve problems in organizations.

Conceptual Analysis of Leadership

Teamwork is beneficial not only for the productivity and success of employees, but also for the organization due to the fact that it increases communication and information sharing (Çelik & Karaca, 2017).

Leadership is now about creating the conditions for all team members to rise and building the structures and cultures that empower any team member to lead when necessary. In today's dynamic world, everyone is a potential leader. Leaders focus on developing a vision and goals and how to achieve goals together with team members, inspiring and helping team members. Leaders instill the commitment of team members to the vision developed by establishing a guiding influence on the teams and, as a result, they create the desired effect. The team leader helps members see that their individual efforts are important and that doing their best will truly be better for everyone on the team (Osborne, 2021).

Team leaders create an environment where members have differences, share a common purpose and values, and love, trust and care for each other. In this way, they assimilate the team members' belief in belonging to the team itself and make them see themselves as "one of them" and not "special or apart". It takes time for teams to become fully active and the way they work together to mature. Since diversity among members provides the foundations for team success, it becomes important that the leader has the skills to prevent conflict and maintain harmony while addressing these differences. The behaviors or practices that leaders show in their approach to teams, other challenges, or the tasks of team members differ. Some may be more people-oriented, some may be more solitary, and some may be more thoughtful. While some leaders involve themselves intensively in their teams, others are more distant. While some plan meticulously, others may prefer to be more flexible and spontaneous. While some celebrate success, others may remain unresponsive (Cathy et al., 2022).

Leaders have abilities such as managing conflicts, leading, delegating authority, assignment and solving problems, and managing teams and the effective work of the team are critical in terms of leadership (Talip, 2019). A team leader can guide teams in line with goals and objectives by providing opportunities to their members. Since team leaders have the knowledge and equipment to motivate them in realizing the desired development and change on their followers, they have a motivating function within the organization in ensuring job satisfaction of team members and achieving success (Çelik & Karaca, 2017).

Forming a Leadership Team

Teamwork occurs when it comes to creating or presenting a product or service together that cannot be created alone (Çıraklı, Çelik & Beylik, 2015). The team forming" process is a difficult process to perform. Machines can be easily managed, but it is quite difficult to manage people with different emotions, desires, expectations, mindsets and personalities. (Talip, 2019).

Especially after the 2000s, the idea that the identification of leadership with a single person is correct but incomplete has gained acceptance. The traditional one-man leadership approach, which sees and evaluates the leader as a hero, has lost its validity today, and it is argued that the organization should be managed on the basis of a participatory understanding, by distributing the leadership concept within the team instead of the one-man leadership. (Özdemir & Yirmibeş, 2016). In addition, in order for a group to turn into a real team, the team leader must give up some of the authority and orders when necessary, so that should turn to shared leadership and take some risks and form the leadership team (Talip, 2019).

The process of forming a leadership team consists of 4 stages. These are: The Stages of Forming, Storming, Norming and Performing. At the forming stage, the purpose of the team is explained to the team members so that the structure of the team is understood by everyone. The set goal should be specific to everyone. After the forming phase, the storming stage is started. At this stage, conflicts will arise.

Because team members will struggle for power, and individuals will feel uncomfortable with this. At this stage, the opinions and ideas of the members are listened, decisions and guidelines are officially formed and power struggles are ended. Managing the conflict varies according to the leader's communication skills. At the norming stage, members begin to accept their place within the team and develop common points of view. The ability of the team to move to the performing stage, which is the fourth stage, is by setting rational goals. There should be a clear goal in the team that will unleash passion and desire. Leaders will need many skills to focus on the goal and create impact (Boykins et al., 2015).

The leadership team is formed with people. It is almost impossible to think of a leadership position that does not involve groups and teams. The ability to build and maintain relationships is a must for the leadership team. Being able to establish and maintain relationships is essential for teamwork. Researchers talk about the existence of emotional intelligence (EQ) at the core of interpersonal relationships. Emotional competencies include social skills such as awareness, understanding the feelings of others, and self-esteem. By means of these skills, professional activity and success can be achieved. However, there is empirical evidence showing that these skills may be developed and learned. It seems that those who survive and achieve success are not the strongest or the smartest (IQ), but are those who adapt the fastest to change. For this reason, the ability of members to adapt and adapt to change, to demonstrate competence in learning and development becomes of great importance in the team forming process. When forming a team, it should be recognized that each of the members has their own unique shortcomings, attention should be paid to the selection of individuals with characteristics that will contribute to the organization, taking into account the team members whose abilities complement each other (Cathy et al., 2022). One of the advantages of teamwork-based work is the opportunity to distribute work between people with different and complementary perspectives and skills (Pendleton, Furnham & Cowell, 2021).

Some of the ways a leader should follow in order to form a team can be listed as follows;

- The personality characteristics of the team members should be determined.
- Differences within the team should be supported so that new ideas may emerge.
- It should be transparent to build trust within the team.
- Emotional intelligence training should be given to team members in order to enable them to reconcile with others.
- The tasks to be carried out should be made clear in order to resolve differences of opinion and different points of view among team members.
- Team members should be authorized and empowered.
- A healthy organizational culture and organizational climate should be provided for the members to show their best performance.
- Different tools and techniques should be chosen according to the needs and expectations of the team members.
- The team should not be too closely managed and controlled.
- Feedback should be provided to members so that they can analyze their strengths and concerns.
- All concerns and fears between team members should be eliminated.
- In addition to the main goal of the organization, emphasis should be placed on additional goals.
- The energy and efforts of the members should be constantly directed towards the corporate goals.
- It should be remembered that the members of the organization are human beings rather employees. (Talip, 2019).

After the leadership team is formed, it is necessary to be constantly alert in the process in order to make it sustainable. Forming a leadership team is not a one-time and definitive task. Small adjustments are often needed in the future, and sometimes major adjustments may be required. If we compare the leadership team to a garden, feeding, pruning and acting according to environmental conditions will help the team stay healthy all seasons. The team leader has a special role to play in maintaining the balance and health of the leadership team: The lead decision maker is in a position to discriminate when such corrections are necessary and decide when such changes should be made (Pendleton, Furnham & Cowell, 2021).

CONCLUSION

The concept of leadership had been initially described as individual characteristics or differences, but now it is accepted that leadership is "a shared, relational, strategic, global and complex social dynamic" (Zhao et al., 2022). Leadership in the modern age is not only based on the knowledge and skills of a person, but also requires them to work as a team. Therefore, today's leaders need to have skills such as teamwork, cooperation, professionalism, and ethical leadership as well as knowledge in order to be successful.

Leadership is defined as setting a direction and developing the necessary strategies to act in that direction, creating and realizing a vision; therefore, it is a process related to change. The primary role of a leader is to lead change. In this regard, the essence of leadership covers encouraging change, enabling others to change, and supporting change (Mei Kin et al., 2018). Leaders should be equipped with the necessary competencies in addition to technical knowledge, skills and abilities for the constantly changing and evolving business environment (Thompson et al., 2020). Because the future is full of uncertainties, a leader has to deal with all these uncertainties and environmental turmoil that can occur. Today, solving these global complexities requires a very challenging process. In this age of VUCA and even TUNA (Turbulence, Uncertainty, Innovation and Uncertainty) that we are in, who can help the organization survive and achieve its goals, a flexible and adaptable leader is needed as the world changes so quickly with the complexity, challenges and changes occurring globally. Confronting Industry 4.0 and using and developing technology is unstoppable and non-deferrable for today's organizations (Nguyen et al., 2022). Change is unpredictable but the ability to use it can be developed (Mei Kin et al., 2018).

Competencies distinguish leaders from non-leaders. Considering leadership in terms of competencies implies that leadership can be taught and learned. Many people can become better leaders by acquiring new competencies (Mei Kin et al., 2018). Because competencies are job-specific, it is necessary to differentiate the competencies needed for different management levels. Thus, the leader has the necessary competencies to deal with future uncertainties and environmental turmoil (Nguyen et al., 2022).

Consequently, leadership is a complex and constantly renewed-developing process. Being a leader requires a lifelong passion for learning and self-improvement. It is not possible for a leader to be "one size fits all" in order to gain trust, respect and support. Leadership involves cooperation between people and systems as well as between leaders and followers. Today's business life requires a leader and an effective leadership who makes plans and resolvedly implements them to achieve their goals (Saputra & Mahaputra, 2022). Organizations that have these qualities will be the leading organizations competing to be the industry leader.

Acknowledgement. This chapter was prepared from the first author's Master thesis that title is "The Mediation Effect of Innovation on the Relationship between Strategic Leadership and Quality Practices"

REFERENCES

Ayhan, Ö. (2012). *Kız teknik ve meslek liselerindeki yöneticilerin, etkili liderlik özelliklerinin araştırılması: Kocaeli ili örneği* [Investigation of effective leadership characteristics of administrators in girls' technical and vocational high schools: The case of Kocaeli province] [Master's thesis]. Maltepe University Institute of Social Sciences.

Balaban S. (2018). *Kriz yönetiminde liderlik ve liderlik özelliklerinin kriz yönetimine etkisi üzerine bir araştırma* [A research on the effect of leadership and leadership characteristics on crisis management] [Master's thesis]. Istanbul Gelisim University Institute of Social Sciences.

Becker, L., Ehrhardt, J., & Gora, W. (2006). *Führungskonzepte und Führungskompetenz*. Die Neue Führungskunst- The New Art of Leadership. Symposion Publishing GmbH.

Bektaş, Ç. (2016). Liderlik yaklaşımları ve modern liderden beklentiler [Leadership approaches and expectations from the modern leader]. *Selçuk University Akşehir Vocational School Journal of Social Sciences*, 2(7), 43–53.

Benmira, S., & Agboola, M. (2021). Evolution of leadership theory. *BMJ Leader*, 5, 3–5.

Bosibori, O. S. (2018). *Leadership Competencies on Performance of Christian Private Universities in Kenya: Case of Daystar University* [Doctoral dissertation].

Boykins, C., Campbell, S., Corey, R., Harp, M., Mason, T., & Stanton, D. (2015). Business as usual LLC: Leadership fundamentals for the small business community. *Journal of Information Technology and Economic Development*, 6(1), 58.

Çalışal, S., & Yücel, L. (2019). Hizmetkar liderlik: Refik Saydam Örneği [Servant leadership: The Example of Refik Saydam]. *Journal of Health Academics*, 6(3), 167–172.

Cathy, L., Douglas, F., Nancy, F., & Dominique, S. (2022). *How Leadership Works A Playbook for Instructional Leaders*. Corwin Press.

Çelik, A., & Karaca, A. (2017). Hemşirelerde ekip çalışması ve motivasyon arasındaki ilişkinin ve etkileyen faktörlerin değerlendirilmesi [Evaluating The Relationship Between Teamwork And Motivation İn Nurses And Affecting Factors]. *Journal of Education and Research in Nursing*, 14(4), 254–263.

Çıraklı, Ü., Çelik, Y., & Beylik, U. (2015). Etkili ekip çalışmasının sağlıktaki önemi ve faydaları: Bir literatür çalışması [The importance and benefits of effective teamwork in health care: A literature survey]. *Journal of Health Academics*, 2(3), 140–146.

Clark, D.R. (2016). *Leadership competency model*. Academic Press.

Colenda, C. D. (2021). *Leadership The Warrior's Art* (2nd ed.). Stacpole Books.

Demir, C., Yılmaz, M. K., & Çevirgen, A. (2010). Liderlik yaklaşımları ve liderlik tarzlarına ilişkin bir araştırma [A research on leadership approaches and leadership styles]. *International Journal of Alanya Business Faculty*, *2*(1), 129–152.

Dinç B. (2020). Konfüçyüs' ün otantik ve dönüşümcü liderliği [Confucius' authentic and transformational leadership]. *International Journal of Leadership Studies: Theory and Practice*, *3*(2), 109-116.

Dirani, K. M., Abadi, M., Alizadeh, A., Barhate, B., Garza, R. C., Gunasekara, N., Ibrahim, G., & Majzun, Z. (2020). Leadership competencies and the essential role of human resource development in times of crisis: A response to Covid-19 pandemic. *Human Resource Development International*, *23*(4), 380–394. doi:10.1080/13678868.2020.1780078

Douglas, S., Merritt, D., Roberts, R., & Watkins, D. (2022). Systemic leadership development: Impact on organizational effectiveness. *The International Journal of Organizational Analysis*, *30*(2), 568–588. doi:10.1108/IJOA-05-2020-2184

Eraslan, L. (2004). Liderlik olgusunun tarihsel evrimi, temel kavramlar ve yeni liderlik paradigmasının analizi (Historical evolution of leadership phenomenon, basic concepts and analysis of new leadership paradigm). *Journal of National Education*, *162*(3).

Greve, H. R. (2013). Microfoundations of management: Behavioral strategies and levels of rationality in organizational action. *The Academy of Management Perspectives*, *27*(2), 103–119. doi:10.5465/amp.2012.0091

Gunter, R. C. (2020). *Emotional intelligence and its relationship to project manager leadership competencies and project success* [Doctoral dissertation]. Saint Leo University.

Hendijani, R., & Sohrabi, B. (2019). The effect of humility on emotional and socialcompetencies: The mediating role of judgment. *Cogent Business & Management*, *6*, 2–16. doi:10.1080/23311975.2019.1641257

Işık, N. (2014). *Liderlik yaklaşımları ve hizmetkar liderliğin işgörenlerin organizasyonel bağlılıklarına etkileri* [Leadership approaches and the effects of servant leadership on employees' organizational commitment] [Doctoral dissertation]. Bahçeşehir University Institute of Social Sciences.

Jamalia, A. R., Bhutto, A., Khaskhely, M., & Sethar, W. (2022). Impact of leadership styles on faculty performance: Moderating role of organizational culture in higher education. *Management Science Letters*, *12*(1), 1–20. doi:10.5267/j.msl.2021.8.005

Katz, D., & Kahn, R. (1970). The Social Psychology of Organizations. Wiley Eastern University Edition.

Kazancıoğlu ŞC. (2018). *Eğitim kurumu yöneticilerinin kişilik özelliklerinin benimsedikleri liderlik tarzları üzerindeki rolünün incelenmesi* [Examination of the role of the personality traits of educational institution administrators on the leadership styles they adopt] [Master's thesis]. Recep Tayyip Erdogan University Institute of Social Sciences, Department of Educational Sciences.

Kılınç, E. (2019). Sivil toplum kuruluşlarında liderlik [Leadership in civil society organizations]. *Bingol University Journal of Social Sciences Institute*, *9*(18). http://busbed.bingol.edu.tr

Koçel, T. (2020). *İşletme yöneticiliği (18th ed.)*. Beta Yayınları.

Korkmaz, M. (2006). Okul yöneticilerinin kişilik özellikleri ile liderlik stilleri arasındaki ilişki [The relationship between the personality traits of school administrators and their leadership styles]. *Educational Management in Theory and Practice, 46*(46), 199–226.

Kouzes, J. M., & Posner, B. Z. (2016). *Learning leadership: The five fundamentals of becoming an exemplary leader* (1st ed.). John Wiley & Sons. doi:10.1002/9781119176725

Lussier, R.N., & Achua, C.F. (2015). *Leadership: Theory, application, & skill development*. Cengage Learning.

Mashele, W., & Alagidede, I. P. (2022). The appropriate leadership styles in times of crisis: A study of women in senior leadership positions in corporate South Africa. *Gender in Management, 37*(4), 494–508. doi:10.1108/GM-02-2021-0031

Mei Kin, T., Abdull Kareem, O., Nordin, M. S., & Wai Bing, K. (2018). Principal change leadership competencies and teacher attitudes toward change: The mediating effects of teacher change beliefs. *International Journal of Leadership in Education, 21*(4), 427–446. doi:10.1080/13603124.2016.1272719

Nguyen, L. V., Haar, J., & Smollan, R. (2022). Hospitality Leadership Competencies and Employee Commitment: New Insights From the Booming Hotel Industry in Vietnam. *Tourism and Hospitality Management, 28*(2), 419–443. doi:10.20867/thm.28.2.10

Önen, S. M., & Kanayran, H. G. (2015). Liderlik ve motivasyon: Kuramsal bir değerlendirme [Leadership and motivation: A theoretical evaluation]. *Journal of Individual and Society, 5*(10), 43–63.

Osborne, C. (2021). *Leadership (Essential Managers)*. DK Publishing.

Özalp, M. (2019). *Liderlik kuramları çerçevesinde Soğuk Savaş sonrası BM'de liderlik sorunu: Kofi Annan yılları, 1996-2007* [The problem of leadership in the UN after the Cold War within the framework of leadership theories: The years of Kofi Annan, 1996-2007] [Unpublished master thesis]. Anadolu University, Institute of Social Sciences, Eskisehir, Turkey.

Özdemir, M., & Yirmibeş, A. (2016). Okullarda liderlik ekibi uyumu ve öğretmen performansı ilişkisinde iş doyumunun aracı etkisi [The mediating effect of job satisfaction on the relationship between leadership team cohesion and teacher performance in schools]. *Journal of Gazi University Gazi Education Faculty, 36*(2), 323–348.

Parris, D. L., & Peachey, J. W. (2013). A systematic literature review of servant leadership theory in organizational contexts. *Journal of Business Ethics, 113*(3), 377–393. doi:10.100710551-012-1322-6

Pendleton, D., Furnham, A. F., & Cowell, J. (2020). *Leadership: No more heroes* (3rd ed.). Springer Nature Switzerland AG. doi:10.1007/978-3-030-60437-0

Prastiawan, A., Gunawan, I., Putra, A. P., Dewantoro, D. A., Cholifah, P. S., Nuraini, N. L. S., ... Surahman, E. (2020, December). School leadership skills in educational institutions. *6th International Conference on Education and Technology (ICET 2020)*, 438-441.

Radwan, O. A. A., Razak, A. Z. A., & Ghavifekr, S. (2020). Leadership competencies based on gender differences among academic leaders from the perspective of faculty members: A scenario from saudi higher education. *International Online Journal of Educational Leadership*, *4*(1), 18–36. doi:10.22452/iojel.vol4no1.3

Raharja, W. T., Suryanto, J. I., Suaedi, F., & Reindrawati, D. Y. (2019). Local Public Leadership Development through Social Learning to Face the Fourth Industrial Revolution. *Journal of Southwest Jiaotong University*, *54*(6), 53. doi:10.35741/issn.0258-2724.54.6.53

Saç Ö. (2019). *Liderlik tarzları ve örgütsel bağlılık arasındaki ilişki ve bu ilişkiye örgüt kültürünün aracılık etkisi: Bir kamu iktisadi teşekkülü ve bağlı işletmelerinde uygulama* [The relationship between leadership styles and organizational commitment and the mediating effect of organizational culture on this relationship: Application in a state-owned enterprise and its subsidiaries] [Doctoral dissertation]. Balikesir University Institute of Social Sciences Department of Business Administration.

Şafaklı, O. V. (2005). KKTC'deki kamu bankalarında liderlik stilleri üzerine bir çalışma [A study on leadership styles in public banks in KKTC]. *Doğuş University Journal*, *6*(1), 132–143.

Şahne, B. S., & Şar, S. (2015). Liderlik kavramının tarihçesi ve Türkiye'de ilaç endüstrisinde liderliğin önemi [The history of the concept of leadership and the importance of leadership in the pharmaceutical industry in Turkey]. *Marmara Pharmaceutical Journal*, *19*(2), 109–115.

Salleh, M., & Grunewald, D. (2013). Organizational leadership–the strategic role of the chief exec. *Journal of Leadership, Accountability and Ethics*, *10*(5), 9–20.

Saputra, F., & Mahaputra, M. R. (2022). Effect of job satisfaction, employee loyalty and employee commitment on leadership style (human resource literature study). *DIJMS Dinasti İnternational Journal of Management Science*, *3*(4), 762–772.

Sayan, İ. (2018). *Kurumsal liderlik tarzlarını algılamanın örgütsel bağlılık ve vatandaşlığa etkisinde çalışanların motivasyon seviyelerinin rolü ve bir araştırma* [The role of motivation levels of employees in the effect of perception of corporate leadership styles on organizational commitment and citizenship and a research] [Unpublished doctoral dissertation]. Istanbul Aydın University Institute of Social Sciences.

Schoemaker, P. J., Krupp, S., & Howland, S. (2013). Strategic leadership: The essential skills. *Harvard Business Review*, *91*(1), 131–134. PMID:23390746

Schyns, B., Kiefer, T., Kerschreiter, R., & Tymon, A. (2011). Teaching implicit leadership theories to develop leaders and leadership: How and why it can make a difference. *Academy of Management Learning & Education*, *10*(3), 397–408. doi:10.5465/amle.2010.0015

Silva, A. (2016). What is leadership? *Journal of Business Studies Quarterly*, *8*(1), 1. PMID:29355200

Stärk, R. (2022). *Which leadership competencies are required in the 21st century? A cross industry case study in service-providing departments in Germany on leadership competencies*. Academic Press.

Süzer, A. S., & Süzen, E. (2019). Liderlikte çağdaş yaklaşım olarak hizmetkâr liderlik [Service leadership as a modern approach in leadership]. *Turan-Sam International Scientific Refereed Journal*, *11*(43), 98–204. doi:10.15189/1308-8041

Talip, M. (2019). *Etik liderlik ve makyavelizmin ekip etkililiği üzerine etkileri: Örgüt temelli özsaygının düzenleyici rolü* [The effects of ethical leadership and machiavellianism on team effectiveness: The regulatory role of organization-based self-esteem] [Master's thesis]. Nevşehir Hacı Bektaş Veli University, Institute of Social Sciences, Department of Business Administration.

Talu, S., & Nazarov, A. D. (2020). Challenges and competencies of leadership in covid-19 pandemic. *Advances in Social Science, Education and Humanities Research, 486*, 518–524.

Taşdöven, H., Emhan, A., & Dönmez, M. (2012). Liderlik tarzı ve mizaç-karakter ilişkisi: Polis teşkilatında bir uygulama [Leadership style and temperament-character relationship: An application in the police force]. *Journal of Management and Economics, 19*(2), 165–177.

Thompson, C. L., Kuah, A. T., Foong, R., & Ng, E. S. (2020). The development of emotional intelligence, self-efficacy, and locus of control in Master of Business Administration students. *Human Resource Development Quarterly, 31*(1), 113–131. doi:10.1002/hrdq.21375

Topping, P. (2002). *Managerial leadership*. McGraw-Hill Companies.

Wisittigars, B., & Siengthai, S. (2019). Crisis leadership competencies: The facility management sector in Thailand. *Facilities, 37*(13/14), 881–896. doi:10.1108/F-10-2017-0100

Yukl, G. (1989). Managerial leadership: A review of theory and research. *Journal of Management, 15*(2), 215–289. doi:10.1177/014920638901500207

Yukl, G. (2013). *Leadership in Organizations* (8th ed.). Pearson Education Inc.

Zhao, L., Yang, M. M., & Wang, Z. (2022). Trends in the dynamic evolution of corporate social responsibility and leadership: A literature review and bibliometric analysis. *Journal of Business Ethics*, 1–23.

Chapter 2
Crucial Role of Soft Skills in Challenging Times:
Conceptual Analysis of Leadership Skills

Bahar Urhan
https://orcid.org/0000-0001-5559-9311
Akdeniz University, Turkey

ABSTRACT

Crisis or all types of changes affect organizations and every aspect of all units' performance. Especially unexpected ones can destroy their system entirely, so it needs to be managed professionally. However, proactive measures can help to overcome either simple changes or even global crises. Become prepared for all changes, risks, and crises by investing in soft skills that can help the business world weather the storm in a sustainable manner. As one of the soft skills, leadership skill may change the destiny of organizations, especially in challenging times like the recent COVID-19 period. In this study, soft skills in general and all aspects and approaches of the leadership concept will be discussed in detail. The importance of well-designed leadership and the fact that leadership is a skill that can be developable is the focus of the study. Showing different leadership approaches in different situations, in other words using the leadership approaches as a toolbox, is underlined by referring to the literature.

INTRODUCTION

The World Health Organization (WHO) defines soft skills as: "A set of socio-affective skills that are necessary for interaction with others and that make it possible to cope with everyday demands and challenging situations" (World Health Organization, 2003). According to UNICEF, one of the skills sets that needed for success is "transferable skills -also called *life skills, twenty-first-century skills, soft skills,* or *socio-emotional skills*- that allow young people to become agile learners and global citizens equipped to navigate personal, social, academic, and economic challenges. Transferable skills also help young people affected by crisis cope with trauma and build resilience. They include problem-solving, negotiation, managing emotions, empathy, and communication." (UNICEF, 2022). It is a skill package

DOI: 10.4018/978-1-6684-6713-8.ch002

related to personality development that includes communication and language skills, interpersonal communication, assertiveness, friendship, and optimism (Nitonde, 2014: 7). Soft skills are essential skills that are desired in all professions and business areas today, whose importance is increasing day by day and are known as 21st-century skills and are reshaped with digitalization and automation. These are a set of productive personality traits that characterize people's relationships in the social environment and workplace are directly related to attitudes and intuitions. In short, these skills are personality-oriented rather than competence-oriented. Although there is no complete and definitive catalog on soft skills, there are various lists that meet many common points in the literature. In Table 1. there are some examples of taking inventory are gathered by literature reviews.

According to the ULISSE project (ULISSE project aims to unveil the true meaning of soft skills by developing the concept of "Not-So-Soft-Skills" and creating a common language with respect to soft skills among the key actors involved (intermediaries, job seekers and employers) https://ulisseproject.eu/what-we-do/), which ended in 2019, the soft skills need of the companies were revealed and a new list emerged. It is composed of 17 soft skills, namely: 1. Communication 2. Conflict management 3. Creativity 4. Critical thinking 5. Decision-making 6. Diversity sensitivity 7. Emotional management 8. Flexibility 9. Focus on costumers needs 10. Leadership 11. Orientation to results 12. Planning 13. Problem-solving 14. Teamwork 15. Time management 16. Willingness to learn 17. Work ethics (Vieira, Meirinhos, Ardions, Araújo & Carvalho, 2019).

The Organization for Economic Co-operation and Development (OECD) recommended that the Sustainable Development Goal (SDG) includes and emphasizes soft skills to foster 'sustainable' lifestyles such as global citizenship, gender equality, and cultural awareness (Okolie, Igwe, Nwosu, Eneje, & Mlanga, 2019). In the aftermath of the COVID-19 pandemic, the prospects for skills needed in 2025 are for the requalification of millions of relocated workers. In this context, it is predicted that the expectations will turn into increasing the soft skills of the employees, and thus the requirements of global employability will change. By 2025, it is predicted that business world will face a 'double cut' in employment due to automation, comprehensively changing the world labor market, and the inevitable negative economic impact of Covid-19. Therefore, it is reported that 97 million new employment roles will be created in this process, and the requalification and upskilling of displaced workers should become the main target in restructured employability (World Economic Forum, 2020). Given that technology is advancing rapidly, low-skilled workers will be reassigned to tasks unsuitable for computerization, in other words, tasks that require creative and social intelligence. However, it will be necessary to have creative and social skills to win the race to share business areas with technology (Frey & Osborne, 2017, p.269).

The coronavirus disease (COVID-19) is a 'disaster of uncertainty,' and its psychological toxicity is increasing day by day. Therefore, in these challenging times, leaders have an obligation to act in a way that builds the resilience of those they lead (Everly Jr, Wu, Cumpsty-Fowler, Dang & Potash, 2020, p.767). While some call the current pandemic a 'great equalizer,' the emergence and manifestation of leadership processes have been affected more than ever, according to research on leadership and COVID-19 (Bauwens, Batistic, Kilroy, & Nijs, 2022, p.228). This pandemic is having a huge impact on how leaders connect and reach followers, especially given that remote work will remain important even after the pandemic.

Employees affected by COVID-19 were suddenly forced to work remotely, but many had never worked this way before. Depending on this situation, three groups emerged in the business world: Those who are forced to work outside their homes, those who are dismissed, or those who are on leave. To date, most research on leadership during crises has focused on organization-specific crises or times of

Table 1. Some scientific studies listing Soft Skills

Spencer & Spencer (1993)	• Achievement orientation • Concern for order, quality, and accuracy • Initiative • Information seeking • Interpersonal understanding • Customer service orientation • Impact and influence on others • Organizational awareness • Relationship building • Developing others • Directiveness • Teamwork and co-operation • Team leadership • Self-control • Self-confidence • Flexibility • Organizational commitment
Evers & Rush (1996)	Managing self: • Learning • Personal organization/Time management • Personal strengths • Problem solving/Analytic Communicating: • Interpersonal • Listening • Oral communication • Written communication Managing people and tasks: • Coordinating • Decision-making • Leadership/Influence • Managing conflict • Planning and organizing Mobilizing innovation and change: • Ability to conceptualize • Creativity/Innovation/Change • Risk-taking • Visioning
Andrews & Helen Higson (2008)	• Professionalism. • Reliability. • The ability to cope with uncertainty. • The ability to work under pressure. • The ability to plan and think strategically. • The capability to communicate and interact with others, either in teams or through networking. • Good written and verbal communication skills. • Information and Communication Technology skills. • Creativity and self-confidence. • Good self-management and time-management skills. • A willingness to learn and accept responsibility
Davies, Fidler, & Gorbis (2011)	• Sense–making • Social intelligence • Novel and adaptive thinking • Cross cultural competency • Computational thinking • New media literacy • Trans disciplinarity • Design mindset • Cognitive load management • Virtual collaboration
Robles (2012)	• Communication • Courtesy • Flexibility • Integrity • Interpersonal Skills • Positive Attitude • Professionalism • Responsibility • Teamwork • Work Ethic

continued on following page

Table 1. Continued

Succi (2018)	• Being Committed to Work • Being Professionally Ethical • Being Tolerant to Stress • Creativity/Innovation • Learning • Life Balance • Self-Awareness • Communication • Conflict Management & Negotiation • Contact Network • Culture Adaptability • Leadership • Teamwork • Adaptability to Change • Analysis • Continuous Improvement • Customer/User Orientation • Decision Making • Management • Results Orientation

Urhan T. (2019)	• Effective Communication:
	   Interpersonal communication
	   Nonverbal Communication
	   Verbal Communication
	   Listening
	   Persuasion
	   Confidence
	   Empathy
	   Intercultural Communication
	• Emotional Intelligence
	• Teamwork:
	   Task distribution
	   Conflict Management
	   Mediation
	• Problem Solving
	• Effective Presentation
	• Adaptability:
	   Curiosity
	   entrepreneurship
	   Motivation
	• Creativity
	• Work Ethic
	• Time Management
	• Stress Management
	• Leadership

war or economic downturns. While these contexts are similar to the current crisis in raising concerns and often leading to workforce shortages, different challenges have emerged in the COVID-19 crisis for businesses. Many people, who were suddenly forced to work from home due to COVID-19, have been deprived of an adequate home, therefore work, and environment to carry out their work due to the lack of technological facilities, difficulties in childcare, and perhaps other problems they have never experienced before. These difficulties are worsened by the fact that the pandemic creates extra problems (for example, anxiety and isolation) (Eichenauer, Ryan, & Alanis, 2022, p.191).

A kind of tension arises due to an unmet need, and this tension transforms the need into an impulse and encourages the individual to act. Need is an internal state that makes an outcome seem worth the effort. Simply put, the motivation process consists of five steps: First, a need arises, then tension arises for need, the release of energies and produce a particular activity provided there is a real chance that the need will be met, at last, the tension decreases as the need is met, again, a need arises. So, the cause of all behavior is an unmet need, an unmet value. Needs are internal stimuli that prepare a person for action and align them with goals. Achieving a self-determined goal is often associated with a sense of accomplishment that leads to more challenging goals, and a higher level of desire, even without external rewards. Many experienced leaders see the key to success as motivation. Often incorrectly referred to as a character trait, motivation can be broadly defined as the will or desire to perform a particular behavior or achieve a goal. Effort refers to the intensity of how hard someone works to achieve a specific goal. Effort in the corporate field only leads to increased performance when the goal is achieved. Therefore, not only the intensity but also the quality of the effort is important (Zellweger, 2004, p.180).

As a result of all these unexpected changes that occurred during Covid-19, it is seen how important it is to develop a set of competencies to motivate employees, especially in crisis times, such as communication, assertiveness, conflict management, empathy, emotional intelligence, social skills, collaboration, teamwork, flexibility, adaptability, resilience, stress tolerance. Research has revealed that the most essential skills in 2021 are adaptability, collaboration, creativity, emotional intelligence, and persuasion. Among them, emotional intelligence; self-awareness, self-management, social skills, empathy, and motivation emerged as a very important skill that is part of this category (Kovacs & Zarandne, 2021). The dynamics that have changed rapidly in recent years underline the importance of soft skills in service sectors such as accommodation, tourism and important business areas that require especially face-to-face communication. Leadership skills demonstrated in difficult times will increase the reputation of businesses as well as people who have a leadership role.

LEADERSHIP SKILL

The Leadership Concept and the Zeitgeist

For more than 2 million years, the small hunter-gatherer societies that made up human society were ruled by men and women who were skilled in hunting and were able to communicate with the supernatural world. As human societies grew larger and more permanent, members with superior communication skills were valued as leaders. In many societies, leadership was associated with being inherited or having a special relationship with gods and spirits. As societies grew and became states, the first treatises on leadership began to emerge. In ancient China, Confucius sought laws of order among leaders and subordinates. Plato described an ideal republic with philosopher kings who provided wise and sensible leadership. Plato and his colleagues founded Paideia, a leadership school in early Greece. In the sixteenth century, Italian Niccolo Machiavelli illuminated another aspect of leadership (by saying: *It is better to be loved or feared.*) that continues to receive much attention even five hundred years later and leadership has now become an interdisciplinary field. The word 'leader' first appeared in the English language in the 1300s comes from the root 'leden' meaning 'to travel' or 'to guide'. The term leadership emerged about five centuries later. Studies by leaders, especially historians and psychologists, preceded the systematic study of leadership. Scientific studies of leadership have developed primarily in the United States and recently since the beginning of the twentieth century (Christensen, Levinson, Goethals, & Sorenson, 2004). In one of these pioneering studies, Ghiselli and Brown (1948) pointed out that if managers initiate programs to increase employee comfort, safety, and satisfaction, such programs lead to higher profits in the long run. In other words, it has been demonstrated that satisfied and confident employees will tend to be more productive. A leader has the greatest influence on the motivation, energy, productivity, effectiveness, and commitment of his employees. In other words, a leader's behavior explains 25% of why people feel productive, motivated, energetic, effective, and engaged (Kouzes & Posner, 2010); also make great difference in a crisis time (Wilson, 2020).

Core leadership competencies are in the area of soft skills and refer to the knowledge of how to deal with people and make the right decisions. The emotional intelligence level is responsible for the quality

Table 2. Leadership concept before and after pandemic

Research period	Clusters	Keywords
Between 2010-2019 (Samul, 2020, p.133).	1. Leadership management 2. Performance leadership 3. Transformational leadership 4. Leader personality and behavior 5. Teamwork	1. Leadership development, competence, knowledge, education and power, values, and Identity.) 2. Innovation, creativity, competitive advantage, and firm performance. 3. Authentic leadership, empowering leadership, ethical leadership, participative leadership, paternalistic leadership, servant leadership. 4. Emotion, emotion regulation, emotional intelligence, emotional labor, and positive emotion. 5. Team effectiveness, team leadership, team performance, teamwork, virtual teams, work group diversity, collective-efficacy, group-performance, shared leadership, self-leadership, emergent leadership.
Between January 1 and November 20, 2020 (Bauwens, Batistic, Kilroy, & Nijs, 2022).	1. Leadership and employee health in pandemic times 2. Public leadership 3. Leadership in the health care sector 4. Leadership and diversity 5. Educational leadership 6. Leadership and persuasive communication	1. Anxiety, Behavior, Burnout, Covid-19 pandemic, Health care, Influenza, Lessons, Mental health, Nurses, Quality, Risk, SARS, Stress, Support, Work 2. Care, Climate change, Covid-19, Crisis management, Governance, Impact, Pandemics, Performance, Public leadership, Resilience, Satisfaction, Trust 3. Advocacy, Global health, Health policy, Nursing leadership, Pandemic, Personal protective equipment, public health, public policy, SARS-CoV-2, Sector, Surgery 4. China, Coronavirus, Culture, Diversity, Empathy, Gender, Health, Model, New Zealand, Policy, Social distancing 5. Challenges, Crisis, Education, Higher education, Leadership, Students, Survey 6. Communication, Experience, Management, Perceptions

of soft skills. Emotional intelligence depends on the individual's personality and environment. Therefore, emotional intelligence and thus, soft skills can be increased with training and practice. The earlier the training begins, the easier and faster it will be to achieve an emotionally stable personality. The basis for the formation and development of soft skills is awareness. The ability to perceive one's moods and mood nuances, as well as other people's, depends on the quality of their perception. In addition to soft skills, the term hard skills refer to the professional competence of a person, which is the basis of any professional activity. This information; is acquired through education, studies, or professional experience. Therefore, soft skills can also be defined as interdisciplinary competencies. Soft skills and hard skills together form 'key attributes' (Zellweger, 2004, p.13).

Seeing the current state and projected shortage of using some predictions has been underscored by the coronavirus pandemic process. To be proactive during the crisis regards real-time dynamic modeling. Considering the expected events, what is tomorrow's challenge, and what will materialize next week and next month? Proactivity can be realized in Kouzes and Posner's leadership commitment to 'challenging the process.' (Stoller, 2020, p.1). They found that when leaders are at their personal best are engage in The Five Practices of Exemplary Leadership:

- Model the Way (A leader must be a model of the behavior that he expects of others.)
- Inspire a Shared Vision (Leaders envision the future by imagining exciting and ennobling possibilities.)

- Challenge the Process (Leaders know well that innovation and change require them to experiment and take risks by constantly generating small wins and learning from experience.)
- Enable Others to Act (Exemplary leaders enable others to act.)
- Encourage the Heart (Leaders also celebrate the values and victories by creating a spirit of community.)

The challenge may have been developing and presenting an innovative new product or a cutting-edge service, spearheading an invigorating campaign, leading a revolutionary program, or starting up a new plant or business. Whatever the challenge, all involve a change from the status quo. All leaders break the 'business-as-usual' mold. Leaders are pioneers who are willing to step out into the unknown. They create opportunities by seizing the initiative and by looking for innovative ways to improve (Kouzes & Posner, 2012, p.14).

In order to understand the change or accordingly damage in a crisis period, two bibliometric analyses, which compile recent research on leadership, are chosen from relevant literature to reveal the changing trends in the leadership concept between the Covid-19 period and before (Table 2).

The COVID-19 crisis has clearly affected both managers and employees because crises create uncertainty and stress and therefore affect behavior. Studies on neuropsychology show that anxiety stemming from uncertainty and threat leads to a more careful, rigid, and halting behavior approach (Stoker, Garretsen, & Lammers, 2022). With the advent of a crisis, the need for successful leadership increases. The importance of necessary leadership skills becomes more evident as it brings success both in its presence and failure in its absence.

Research suggests that four factors underlie and predict effective crisis leadership: the vision for the future, decisiveness, effective communications, and moral authority. Effective leadership can enhance resilience and may be associated with a descending incidence of psychological casualties. While the 4 factors are empirically linked to perceptions of effective leadership, clear guidance on how to operationalize them is lacking. To address this gap in knowledge transfer, at Johns Hopkins, nine recommendations or guiding principles have been developed for implementing the factors in ways that enrich leadership skills in times of crisis:

1. Structure is the antidote for chaos.
2. Listen before you speak.
3. Information is an antidote for anxiety.
4. Transparent, timely, and truthful communication is essential to maintain credibility.
5. People trust actions not words.
6. Empowerment is an antidote for feeling out of control.
7. The perception of support is the antidote for isolation.
8. Cohesive groups do better with stress and challenges than non-cohesive groups.
9. The moment of absolute certainty may never arise (Everly Jr, Wu, Cumpsty-Fowler, Dang & Potash, 2020).

Duckworth (2017) conducted studies searching answers to the questions in various contexts: 'Who is successful?' and 'Why are they successful?' The results of these studies suggest that there are four essential elements for a leader to be successful:

- A burning desire to make a difference, that is, the commitment to make a significant contribution.
- Patience; looking at the work in the long term and not straying from and running away from the goal.
- Moral courage, that is, not compromising the values believed.
- Self-discipline, stubbornness, or perseverance, that is, not giving up.

As Goleman says: 'Great leadership works through the emotions' (Goleman, Boyatzis & McKee, 2002, p.3). Accordingly, it is the key factor for leaders to display soft skills in times of crisis; and to successfully manage crisis and the change that will occur afterward. A leader, who has the foresight and soft skills to evaluate the consequences of every risk that may arise, will be able to benefit enough from neither his experience nor his hard skills in the global crises that will be encountered once in a century such as Covid-19. Therefore, he will be distinguished from his counterparts by his soft skills.

Crisis Management, Change Management and Leadership Styles

Today's workforce is a far cry from what it was 100 years ago. The way to get the most out of people is for them to feel motivated, determined, and even inspired. Persuasion is required, not coercion, the promise of status and position may no longer be sufficient. Autocratic and hierarchical management systems have been replaced by much more open and democratic administrative forms. In a much more egalitarian society, increases in employee empowerment mean leaders now have to gain followers. They exhibit some critical leadership styles, with the qualities, attitudes, beliefs, and behaviors of those whose mission is to bring out the best in their people. Today, inter-organizational competition takes place not only at the level of products and services they provide but also at the level of competencies they have much deeper. And nowhere are these competencies more critical than the leadership style they have. The concept of 'leadership style' is the style that a leader adopts in their dealings with his followers (Kippenberger, 2022, p.6).

The crisis leader must fulfill two roles: to participate in authentic human actions and to convey institutional messages. In terms of authenticity, a leader should use comforting language and assume the role of a counselor to help individuals understand the crisis and reassure them about the future. At the same time, he is seen as a figure who must stand upright and firm when a crisis arises (Gigliotti 2016). Times of change, such as those created by the COVID-19 crisis, are potential triggers of psychological disorders among workers. Poor psychological health of employees can harm their productivity and performance in the long run (Paul, 2003). Guiding an effective response to a global pandemic requires leaders to demonstrate effective planning and coordination skills as well as the ability to empathically communicate clear and coherent messages. The language of communication used by leaders in times of crisis can play a critical role in shaping the behavior of individuals, and the tone of the message can instill confidence and reassure the public. Leaders are required to demonstrate a set of competencies that coach individuals through various crisis stages to successful recovery. Communication skills are a critical competency, and a leader's ability to communicate clearly, confidently, persuasively, and empathetically shapes the followers' perception of crisis and the way the leader's ability to manage the current crisis is evaluated (McGuire, Cunningham, Reynolds & MatthewsSmith, 2020). Hyvärinen and Vos (2016) argue that in the event of disasters and pandemics, the creation of a two-way communication path between institutional actors and the public may be more successful when there is a harmony of mutual interest. It is possible to strengthen the resilience of society through the action of communication in creating

Crucial Role of Soft Skills in Challenging Times

Table 3. Leadership Styles (Goethals, Sorenson & Burns, 2004)

Leadership Styles	Characteristics
Authentic Leadership	Authentic leadership includes resilience as part of its core and promotes positive organizational behavior belief states, states of hope, optimism, and self-efficacy towards the leader's self-awareness. Such values are open to change and can therefore help develop resilient leaders.
Autocratic Leadership	Autocratic leaders do not consult their followers, they just direct them. They give orders that will not be questioned, only enforced.
Democratic or Participative Leadership	Democratic leaders encourage open communication among all employees at all levels and demonstrate care and concern through empathetic listening and understanding.
Dysfunctional Leadership	Born from personality traits such as self-aggrandizement and empowerment, this shadow side of the leadership role thrives on narcissism, self-deception, and abuse of power.
E-Leadership	E-leadership is a social impact process that takes place in a corporate context, where a significant amount of work, including communication, is supported by IT.
Ethical Leadership	Ethical leaders educate their followers on ethical principles, laws, and norms as well as how they are to be applied to specific situations. Ethical leaders help resolve conflicts that arise when principles, laws, and norms contradict each other.
Eupsychian Management	Eupsychian is a management that prioritizes good psychology and creates a working environment conducive to collective psychological health. When self-actualized people work together, they promote eupsychiatry.
Innovative Leadership	Innovative leadership encourages employees to respond to competitive markets, design new products, adapt to changes in business processes as technology advances, and increase their level of expertise and organizational commitment.
Invisible Leadership	Invisible leaders are the defenders and embodiment of the common purpose. Individuals strive to achieve a common and valuable outcome, regardless of their visibility or recognition.
Laissez-Faire Leadership	Laissez-faire leaders believe in freedom of choice for their employees and leave them alone to do what they want. This style is adopted either because they believe the employees are doing their job well or because they are afraid of not being re-elected as a leader.
Leading at a Distance	In organizations, hierarchy is ubiquitous, the focus here on hierarchical distance. Social and psychological distance are additional effects.
Narcissistic Leadership	There are two completely different types of narcissism, healthy narcissism, and pathological narcissism. A person with healthy narcissism can relate to others with respect and love, have empathy, and support people. The relationships of pathological narcissists are shallow, unreliable, exploitative, and lack empathy.
Paternalistic Leadership	The paternalistic leadership style is highly status-oriented, demands a high level of involvement in the non-work lives of subordinates, and is highly directive. The leader takes on the role of a father, providing for the needs of his subordinates, guiding them, and protecting their interests. In return, they obey the wishes of their leaders and show a high level of loyalty.
Reconstructive Leadership	All leaders aim to change things. Reconstructive leadership succeeds in undertaking change to create entirely new standards of legitimate action.
Servant Leadership	In servant leadership, the leader guides, and influences others to follow; provides structure, and models risk-taking behavior. Both individuals and institutions can act as leaders serving each other to build a good society.
Shared Leadership	Shared leadership is a dynamic, interactive influence process among individuals in teams where the goal is to guide each other to achieve team goals.
Socio-Emotional Leadership	Socio-emotional leadership requires mirroring authentic emotion management based on honesty, fairness, justice, and respect. Authentic socio-emotional leaders encourage members of the organization to express their feelings without fear of retaliation, are aware of different emotional styles, and are adaptable, lively, and flexible.
Strategic Leadership	Strategic leadership involves making strategic decisions, creating, and communicating a vision of the future, developing organizational structures, maintaining an effective organizational culture, and infusing ethical value systems into the organization's own culture.
Transformational Leadership	Transformational leaders encourage their followers to rise morally to achieve something meaningful and become their own leaders. They are visionary change agents. Such leaders are morally uplifting and are more concerned with the common interests of the group, organization, and society rather than their interests.
Transactional Leadership	Transactional leaders establish relationships with followers that consist of more mundane and instrumental exchanges and such instrumental transactions form the bulk of relationships. Most leaders' and followers' relationships are transactional - to exchange one thing for another (vote for work; subsidies for contributions).
Tyrannical Leadership	Tyrants are rulers who oversee more of their interests than the welfare of their subjects and tend to employ powerful and brutal tactics in the process. A leader with -near-absolute power can become destructive to others.
Visionary Leadership	The visioner leader emphasizes the vision as the foundation of the group's identity. It embraces the necessity of collective effort to achieve their common goals, reinforcing the idea that individuals should subordinate their own needs for the sake of the larger group. A shared identity can strengthen a collective heroic drive and increase the likelihood of more altruistic and joint action necessary to achieve the vision's goals.

common meaning and understanding in crisis communication. The need for honesty in conveying good and bad news; mitigating the consequences of the crisis with fast, accurate, transparent, simple, and clear information, and describing how individuals should protect themselves and their families are related to the integrity and expertise that must be created and maintained before the crisis. For this reason, people tend to rely more on local information provided by their family and friends during their crisis and other sources they already trust, such as teachers and health professionals.

The source of the diversity of existing definitions of leadership lies in the individual perspectives of researchers and the characteristics of the phenomena with which they are concerned (Fiedler, 1971; Stodill, 1974; Yukl, 2012, p.66). On the other hand, leadership cannot happen without followers and always has situational factors to consider. Definitions and styles may also be varied depend on followers' styles. Kets de Vries (2001) says that the leadership style of leaders, that is, a synthesis of the various roles he chooses to adopt, is the complex result of the interaction of that person's inner theater and the competencies that a person has developed throughout their life, and defines leadership style as a point of interaction between three things:

- Leader's character type: values, attitudes, beliefs, positions, and experiences.
- Followers' character type: values, attitudes, beliefs, commitment as a group.
- Status: structure and culture of the organizations, the nature of the assignment, and the socio-economic and political environment.

Leaders who have mastered four or more styles tend to be most efficacious. Effective leaders screen people individually and in groups; so, they adjust their leadership styles accordingly (Goleman et al., 2002). Some studies have revealed that Transformational Leadership is linked to beneficial employee outcomes including mental health and psychological well-being, thereby successfully rescuing organizations from crises with increased job performance and effective Transformational Leadership (Zhang, Jia & Gu, 2012; Kelloway, Turner, Barling & Louhlin, 2012; Bowers, Hall & Srinivasan, 2017; Mu-Han Ma & Yang, 2020).

One of the first researchers to introduce the concept of Transformational Leadership in 1978 was James MacGregor Burns. According to Burns, the presence of transformational leadership in an organization emerges when leaders and followers help each other to progress to a more elevated moral and motivational level (Allen et al., 2016). Transformational leaders define public values that embrace people's supreme and enduring principles. These values shape and interpret the ideas behind constitutions and laws. Such values are not typically part of the everyday discourse. But in times of testing when people are faced with the possibilities and threat of great changes, strong core values are revived. They inspire and guide people in pursuing and trying to shape change. At the heart of transformative values is, determining whether leadership can truly be transformative (Burns, 2003, p.37).

Burns' original visions were augmented by Bass in 1985 to the development of the theory best known as Bass's Transformational Leadership Theory. According to Bass, a transformational leader can be characterized according to the effect he creates on his followers (Choi et al., 2016). Considering Covid-19 crisis is an urgent crisis that nobody or no organizations can react proactively, to determine a crisis reaction leadership style can be a proactive approach to urgent crises. Transformational Leadership can help organizations improve organizational performance and improve team cohesion during a crisis.

Mu-Han Ma and Yang (2020) demonstrated the positive role of Transformational Leadership on leadership effectiveness on crisis management performance under different perceptions of epidemic crisis. Shamshad and Khan's study (2020) revealed the relationship between a leader's emotional intelligence and employees' psychological well-being. Results show that the emotional intelligence of leaders, who use transformational leadership and self-efficacy as mediators, has long-term effects on employees' organizational output and future orientation (Fig. 1). Emotional intelligence is considered a particularly important feature for survival in a rapidly changing work environment due to continuous technological developments in almost every aspect of life. Especially pandemic period forced people to work, learn, chat, meet and do so many things remotely that in a way had never been experienced before.

Figure 1.

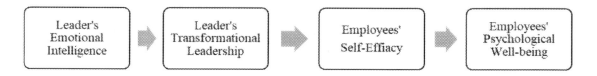

Post-Covid Leaders with Emotional Intelligence

Emotions have four basic characteristics in common:

1) Emotions always have a purpose. Something or someone triggers an emotion.
2) People do not have an unlimited number of different emotions; divided into six categories: anger, fear, joy, love, sadness, and surprise.
3) The ultimate expression of emotion is universal. People all over the world often describe the same emotions using the same facial expressions. As a result, we can recognize the emotional levels of others when we pay attention to their facial expressions.
4) Culture takes into account how and when people express their emotions. Although people all over the world express their feelings in the same way, informal standards define how acceptable it is to do so. These expectations are called cultural norms, display rules, about the proper way to express emotions (Hamid, Widodo & Buchdadi, 2022, p.29).

Salovey and Mayer, in their pioneering white paper on emotional intelligence, which examined the human ability to pay attention to and modify one's own emotions and those of others, described emotional intelligence as "The *ability to perceive and express emotion, assimilate emotion in thought, understand and reason with emotion, and regulate emotion in the self and others*" (1990, p.5). New York Times psychologist and former science writer Goleman introduced the concept of emotional intelligence to the world in his groundbreaking book Emotional Intelligence (1995).

As people's communication becomes more and more computerized in recent times, there is less interaction. Therefore, emotional intelligence is becoming increasingly necessary for the maintenance of healthy human emotional connections and relationships. Because Emotional Intelligence is a powerful indicator of long-term success (Nguyen et al. 2022). Accordingly, in a recent study, emotional intelligence was found to be positively correlated with organizational excellence (Usman, Kowalski, Andiappan & Parayitam, 2021). In Joseph and Newman's (2010) meta-analytic study, it was found that emotional perception, emotional understanding, and regulation of emotions occur in order, to influence job performance.

Growing research suggests that the way to influence and lead is to start with warmth. Warmth is an influence channel. It facilitates trust and the communication and absorption of ideas. Even with a few small nonverbal signals people can show others that they are happy to be around them and pay attention to their concerns. Prioritizing warmth helps people instantly connect with those around them, showing them that they are heard, understood, and can be trusted by them. People need to feel included, to feel a sense of belonging. Some psychologists argue that the urge to relate is among our primary needs as humans (Cuddy, Kohut & Neinger, p.44). Understanding emotions is a very valuable skill but managing and displaying emotions strategically (inside out) is a perfect sign of emotional intelligence. Groundbreaking and ever-increasing important research support the link between emotional intelligence and leadership success. Emotional intelligence was found that associated with job results achieved and ratings of effective personal behavior, the emergence of leadership in groups, annual performance appraisals, and effectiveness of leadership (Carmeli, 2003; Semadar, Robins, & Ferris, 2006; Rosete & Ciarrochi, 2005; Langhorn, 2004; Sy, Tram & O'Hara, 2006; Wong & Law, 2002; Côté, Lopes, Salovey & Miners 2010). Leaders who focus on long-term goals do not see organizations as technical tools. Leaders with high leadership skills should integrate the organization they are responsible for with social values, gain the trust of their employees and deserve their loyalty, and on the other hand, as a leader, they should make their presence appear as an important value for their followers (Türkoğlu & Çizel, 2016, p.157).

FUTURE RESEARCH DIRECTIONS

The present study did not address all aspects of soft skills and training methods but focused on leadership skills and its conceptual aspect in the context of times of crisis. Therefore, in future studies, how to develop leadership skills in times of crisis and the necessary effective and rapid training methods can be discussed.

CONCLUSION

This study focuses on soft skills which are seen as one of the most important requirements of employability in the digital age, and leadership- which is a soft skill. In this study, which deals with leadership as a skill; soft skills, that leaders should have, are also mentioned. The soft skills, that leaders will blend with emotional intelligence, will provide them with a managerial advantage- especially in times of crisis and change.

Combating a global crisis with Covid-19 and trying to manage it has been the most important challenge of the last two years. No individual or institution has been able to take proactive approaches in the management of this crisis, which has unexpected and devastating consequences. For this reason, it is recommended that leaders make the transformational leadership style a precautionary package in emergencies that may arise from now on.

The most important feature of transformational leadership is that; it requires high emotional intelligence, and therefore a skill set consisting of soft skills is needed. By making use of the most important feature of soft skills, openness to development, the way to ensure that leaders are prepared for a new crisis is possible through soft skills training. Leaders, who develop their soft skills through training and appropriately frequent practice, will demonstrate successful transformational leadership in times of crisis and also make it easier for their followers to adapt to change afterward.

REFERENCES

Andrews, J., & Higson, H. (2008). Graduate Employability, 'Soft Skills' Versus 'Hard' Business Knowledge: A European Study. *Higher Education in Europe*, *33*(4), 411–422. doi:10.1080/03797720802522627

Bauwens, R., Batistič, S., Kilroy, S., & Nijs, S. (2022). New Kids on the Block? A Bibliometric Analysis of Emerging COVID-19—Trends in Leadership Research. *Journal of Leadership & Organizational Studies*, *29*(2), 224–232. doi:10.1177/1548051821997406 PMID:35516092

Bowers, M. R., Hall, J. R., & Srinivasan, M. M. (2017). Organizational culture and leadership style: The missing combination for selecting the right leader for effective crisis management. *Business Horizons*, *60*(4), 551–563. doi:10.1016/j.bushor.2017.04.001

Burns, J. M. (2003). *Transforming Leadership: A new pursuit o happiness*. Grove Press.

Carmeli, A. (2003). The relationship between emotional intelligence and work attitudes, behavior, and outcomes: An examination among senior managers. *Journal of Managerial Psychology*, *18*(8), 788–813. doi:10.1108/02683940310511881

Christensen, K., Levinson, D., Goethals, G. R., & Sorenson, G. J. (2004). Preface. In Encyclopedia of leadership. Sage.

Côté, S., Lopes, P. N., Salovey, P., & Miners, C. T. H. (2010). Emotional intelligence and leadership emergence in small groups. *The Leadership Quarterly*, *21*(3), 496–508. doi:10.1016/j.leaqua.2010.03.012

Cuddy, A., Kohut, M., & Neinger, J. (2018). *Connect, Then Lead. In Leadership Presence*. Harvard Business Review Press.

Davies, A., Fidler, D., & Gorbis, D. (2011). *Future Work Skills 2020*. Institute for the Future for University of Phoenix Research Institute. https://www.iftf.org/uploads/media/SR1382A_UPRI_future_work_skills_sm.pdf

Duckworth, A. (2017). Grit: Why passion and resilience are the secrets to success. Ebury Publishing.

Eichenauer, C. J., Ryan, A. M., & Alanis, J. M. (2022). Leadership During Crisis: An Examination of Supervisory Leadership Behavior and Gender During COVID-19. *Journal of Leadership & Organizational Studies*, *29*(2), 190–207. doi:10.1177/15480518211010761 PMID:35516093

Everly Jr, G. S., Wu, A. W., Cumpsty-Fowler, C. J., Dang, D., & Potash, J. B. (2020). Leadership Principles to Decrease Psychological Casualties in COVID-19 and Other Disasters of Uncertainty. *Concepts in Disaster Medicine*. . doi:10.1017/dmp.2020.395

Evers, F. T., & Rush, J. C. (1996). The bases of competence: Skill development during the transition from university to work. *Management Learning*, *27*(3), 275–299. doi:10.1177/1350507696273001

Fadlun, A. (2022, September). The Influence of Transformational Leadership, Emotional Intelligence, Organizational Climate, and Teamwork, Towards Organizational Citizenship Behavior of Civil Servants. *International Journal for Applied Information Management*, 2(3), 26–39.

Fiedler, F. E. (1971). Validation and extension of the contingency model of leadership effectiveness: A review of empirical findings. *Psychological Bulletin*, 76(2), 128–148. doi:10.1037/h0031454 PMID:4942584

Frey, C. B., & Osborne, M. A. (2017). The future of employment: How susceptible are jobs to computerisation? *Technological Forecasting and Social Change*, 114(January), 254–280. doi:10.1016/j.techfore.2016.08.019

Ghiselli, E. E., & Brown, C. W. (1948). *Personnel And Industrial Psychology*. McGraw-Hill.

Gigliotti, R. A. (2016). Leader as Performer; Leader as Human: A Discursive and Retrospective Construction of Crisis Leadership. *Atlantic Journal of Communication*, 24(4), 185–200. doi:10.1080/15456870.2016.1208660

Goethals, G. R., Sorenson, G. J., & Burns, J. M. (2004). *Encyclopedia of leadership*. Sage Publications. doi:10.4135/9781412952392

Goleman, D. (1995). *Emotional intelligence*. Bantam Books.

Goleman, D., Boyatzis, R. E., & McKee, A. (2002). The New Leaders. In *Transforming the Art of Leadership into the Science of Results*. Little, Brown.

Hyvärinen, J., & Vos, M. (2016). *Communication concerning disasters and pandemics: Co-producing community resilience and crisis response. In Handbook of International Crisis Communication Research*. Wiley-Blackwell. doi:10.1002/9781118516812.ch10

Joseph, D. L., & Newman, D. A. (2010). Emotional intelligence: An integrative meta-analysis and cascading model. *The Journal of Applied Psychology*, 95(1), 54–78. doi:10.1037/a0017286 PMID:20085406

Kelloway, E. K., Turner, N., Barling, J., & Loughlin, C. (2012). Transformational leadership and employee psychological well-being: The mediating role of employee trust in leadership. *Work and Stress*, 26(1), 39–55. doi:10.1080/02678373.2012.660774

Kets de Vries, M. (2001). *The Leadership Mystique*. Financial Times Prentice Hall.

Kippenberger, T. (2002). *Leadership Styles*. Capstone Publishing.

Kouzes, J. M., & Posner, B. Z. (2010). *The truth about leadership: The no-fads, heart-of-the matter facts you need to know*. Jossey-Bass, San Francisco.

Kouzes, J. M., & Posner, B. Z. (2012). The Leadership Challenge Workbook (3rd ed.). Jossey-Bass.

Kovacs, I., & Vamosi Zarandne, K. (2022). Digital marketing employability skills in job advertisements – must-have soft skills for entry level workers: A content analysis. *Economia e Sociologia*, 15(1), 178–192. doi:10.14254/2071-789X.2022/15-1/11

Langhorn, S. (2004). How emotional intelligence can improve management performance. *International Journal of Contemporary Hospitality Management*, 16(4), 220–230. doi:10.1108/09596110410537379

Ma, M.-H., & Yang, Q.-S. (2020). How does transformational leadership work on COVID-19? Empirical evidence from China. *Journal of Innovative Studies*, *1*(2). http://www.iiinstitute.us/index.php/jis/article/view/1

McGuire, D., Cunningham, J. E. A., Reynolds, K., & Matthews-Smith, G. (2020). Beating the virus: An examination of the crisis communication approach taken by New Zealand Prime Minister Jacinda Ardern during the Covid-19 pandemic. *Human Resource Development International*, *23*(4), 361–379. doi:10.1080/13678868.2020.1779543

Nguyen, T. L., Nguyen, H. A. M., Nguyen Luu, P. T., Le, M. A., Nguyen, T. A. T., & Nguyen, N. T. (2022). Leadership and Communication Skills Towards Emotional Intelligence: A Case Study of FPT University in Vietnam. *Journal of Asian Finance, Economics and Business*, *9*(5), 53–61. doi:10.13106/jafeb.2022.vol9.no5.0053

Nitonde, R. (2014). Soft Skills and Personality Development. In *Proceedings of the National Seminar*. Shri Shivaji College.

Okolie, U. C., Igwe, P. A., Nwosu, H. E., Eneje, B. C., & Mlanga, S. (2019). Enhancing graduate employability: Why do higher education institutions have problems with teaching generic skills? *Policy Futures in Education*, *18*(2), 294–313. doi:10.1177/1478210319864824

Paul, R. J. (2003, Winter). Managing employee depression in the workplace. *Review of Business, New York*, *24*(1), 31–37.

Robles, M. (2012). Executive Perceptions of the Top 10 Soft Skills Needed in Today's Workplace. *Business Communication Quarterly*, *75*(4), 453–465. doi:10.1177/1080569912460400

Rosete, D., & Ciarrochi, J. (2005). Emotional intelligence and its relationship to workplace performance outcomes of leadership effectiveness. *Leadership and Organization Development Journal*, *26*(5), 388–399. doi:10.1108/01437730510607871

Salovey, P., & Mayer, J. D. (1990). Emotional intelligence. *Imagination, Cognition and Personality*, *9*(3), 185–211. doi:10.2190/DUGG-P24E-52WK-6CDG

Samul, J. (2020). The Research Topics of Leadership: Bibliometric Analysis from 1923 to 2019. *International Journal of Educational Leadership and Management.*, *8*(2), 116–143. doi:10.17583/ijelm.2020.5036

Semadar, A., Robins, G., & Ferris, G. R. (2006). Comparing the validity of multiple social effectiveness constructs in the prediction of managerial job performance. *Journal of Organizational Behavior*, *27*(4), 443–461. doi:10.1002/job.385

Shamshad, I. & Khan, M. K. (2020). Emotional intelligence, transformational leadership, self-efficacy for well-being: A longitudinal study using sequential mediation. *Journal of Public Affairs*, *22*(2), 506. . doi:10.1002/pa.2506

Spencer, L. M., & Spencer, S. M. (1993). *Competence at Work: Models for Superior Performance*. John Wiley & Sons.

Stogdill, R. M. (1974). *Handbook of leadership: A survey of theory and research*. Free Press.

Stoker, J. I., Garretsen, H., & Lammers, J. (2022). Leading and Working from Home in Times of COVID-19: On the Perceived Changes in Leadership Behaviors. *Journal of Leadership & Organizational Studies*, *29*(2), 208–218. doi:10.1177/15480518211007452 PMID:35516094

Stoller, J. K. (2020). *Reflections on leadership in the time of COVID-19*. BMJ Leader Published Online. doi:10.1136/leader-2020-000244

Succi, C. (2015). *Soft Skills for the Next Generation: Toward a comparison between Employers and Graduate Students' Perceptions*. Academic Press.

Sy, T., Tram, S., & O'Hara, L. A. (2006). Relation of employee and manager emotional intelligence to job satisfaction and performance. *Journal of Vocational Behavior*, *68*(3), 461–473. doi:10.1016/j.jvb.2005.10.003

Türkoğlu, N. & Çizel, B. (2016). Kurumsallaşma ve Rekabet Gücü İlişkisi Üzerine Ampirik Bir Çalışma [An Empirical Study on the Relationship between Institutionalization and Competitiveness]. *Bilgi*, (33).

UNICEF. (2022). *Adolescent education and skills: Adolescents need lifelong learning to build better futures for themselves, their families, and their communities*. Retrieved from: https://www.unicef.org/education/skills-development

Urhan, T. B. (2019). Soft Beceriler, Etkili İletişim, Liderlik [Soft Skills, Effective Communication, Leadership]. Gazi Kitabevi.

Usman, S. A., Kowalski, K. B., Andiappan, V. S., & Parayitam, S. (2021). *Effect of knowledge sharing and interpersonal trust on psychological capital and emotional intelligence in higher educational institutions in India: Gender as a moderator*. FIIB Business Review. doi:10.1177/23197145211011571

Vieira, D. A., Meirinhos, V., Ardions, A., Araújo, M. S., & Carvalho, P. (2019). *Soft skills list and Mind map*. ULISSE IO2 Soft Skills Report 2. https://ulisseproject.eu/

Wilson, S. (2020). Pandemic leadership: Lessons from New Zealand's approach to COVID-19. *Leadership*, *16*(3), 279–293. doi:10.1177/1742715020929151

Wong, C. S., & Law, K. S. (2002). The effect of leader and follower emotional intelligence on performance and attitude: An exploratory study. *The Leadership Quarterly*, *13*, 243–274. doi:10.1016/S1048-9843(02)00099-1

World Economic Forum. (2020). These are the skills employers are looking for now…right up till 2025. *Future of jobs report 2020*. Retrieved from https://www.muchskills.com/blog/skills-employers-looking-for-till-2025

World Health Organization. (2003). *Skills for Health*. https://www.who.int/school_youth_health/media/en/sch_skills4health_03.pdf

Yukl, G. A. (2012). Effective Leadership Behavior: What We Know and What Questions Need More Attention. *The Academy of Management Perspectives*, *26*(4), 66–85. Advance online publication. doi:10.5465/amp.2012.0088

Zellweger, H. (2004). *Leadership by Soft Skills Checklisten für den Führungsalltag.* Gabler. . doi:10.1007/978-3-322-82482-0

Zhang, Z., Jia, M., & Gu, L. (2012). Transformational leadership in crisis situations: Evidence from the People's Republic of China. *International Journal of Human Resource Management, 23*(19), 4085–4109. doi:10.1080/09585192.2011.639027

Background. (n.d.). ULISSE project. https://ulisseproject.eu/what-we-do/

Chapter 3
Behavioral Approaches to Leadership

Zehra Saltik
https://orcid.org/0000-0002-6329-6561
Cyprus International University, Turkey

ABSTRACT

Leadership is one of the top subjects of study in the past, now, and in the future. Different approaches to leadership have been put forward up to the present day. As a concept, leadership has been studied with different aspects. One of these aspects is to examine leadership in terms of behaviors, which claims that it is certain types of behavior that make a leader effective or ineffective. Hence, it assumes that leaders are not born but made. According to this approach, leadership can be learned and modelled. This approach came out as a response to the inadequacies of traits approach of leadership and focused more on behaviors to define leadership. Ohio State studies, Michigan State studies, and Blake and Mouton studies are best representative of this approach.

INTRODUCTION

As a term, leadership existed from the beginning of human history. The permanent settlement, co-existence and organization of communities brought along the need to manage. As, in general, people are social beings who live in groups and need each other to achieve particular aims, they need leaders who can direct these groups. Especially, in today's ever changing management mentality, the need for leaders has been dramatically increased. Today every business, including hospitality industry, regardless of their scale, needs effective leaders to succeed. A good leader is required to effectively orient business operations. Being so significant, the issue of leadership has mostly been an important field of researches. As a result, leadership is still a popular topic for different disciplines and studies.

Leadership is generally defined as the skill to convince the others on specific objectives and emphasizes the relationship between rulers and ruled. Leadership is a process which focuses on the significance of interpersonal interactions. Leadership is mostly regarded as one of the most crucial factors in the success or failure of the institutions. Being so important, leadership has been one of the top study

DOI: 10.4018/978-1-6684-6713-8.ch003

Behavioral Approaches to Leadership

area by the academic researchers and businesses. A number of leadership theories came out along with increased publications and studies. Different approaches to leadership have emerged to respond to "how leadership works, what makes leaders good, how to make leaders effective" and the like. The approaches to leadership are mainly categorized as traits approach, behavioral approach and contingency approach. Despite the fact that a considerable number of studies contributed to leadership theory, it has not been integrated yet. This is especially thought to result from new leadership theories being self-replicating of old theories (Uslu, 2019).

This chapter gives a brief historical overview of the term of leadership at the beginning. Then, it dwells on behavioral approaches to leadership. The behavioral leadership theory and the styles of behavioral leadership will be explained and discussed in detail. The behavioral leadership theory studies both in hospitality industry and other fields will be examined and the results will be evaluated. This chapter also aims to present suggestions both to business and academics.

CONCEPTUAL FRAMEWORK

A Brief Introduction to the Concept of Leadership

Being one of the world's oldest preoccupation, the study of leadership dates back to the days of the emergence of civilizations. The principles of leadership were evolved out of the study of history and philosophy and spread to all the developing social disciplines. Even today, the general characteristics of leadership are built on the in-depth analysis of competencies, development and motivation of world leaders. The earliest studies on leadership were widely concerned with theoretical issues with an emphasis on the identification of different types of leadership and their relation to the functional demands of society (Bass, 1990). All these different types of or approaches to leadership try to define and explain what leadership is.

As a concept, leadership has taken a significant and central place on the literature of management and organizational behavior for several decades. The books, articles and research papers on leadership existed in several thousands and new publications continue at a high rate (Yukl, 1989). Leadership has long been a sophisticated and confusing study field and pointed out to be one of the most studied but least understood topics in social sciences. Leadership still remains complex and obscure even after many years of effort to make it more understandable. Many definitions are still confusing and inconsistent. What it needs to be a leader still holds a wide range of ideas and researches on leadership are far from complete. Studies on leadership are thought to contain many gaps, which have not been fully investigated. An important challenge in describing leadership results from social and other changes occurred in the course of history, which impact the ideas underlying leadership concept and practices. This means that a complete understanding of leadership may vary from society to society and from time to time. Similarly, leadership perspectives may differ depending on organizational and managerial level (Avery, 2004). This has led to various leadership approaches and theories.

Though there are many different definitions of leadership based on individual perspectives of researchers and many of them are ambiguous, a sufficient similarity among definitions permits to make a rough classification. Leadership can be seen as personality characteristic, having certain behaviors, a tool to reach the goals, an effective instrument of interaction, the ability of persuasion, the courage of taking on difficult tasks, being the initiation of actions, and the combinations of definitions (Bass, 1990).

Leadership has usually been described in terms of personality traits, interaction patterns, subordinates' perceptions, role relationship, leader behavior, influence over subordinates, influence on business goals and influence on organizational culture. Most leadership definitions usually consist of an influence process (Yukl, 1989).

Today leadership is still difficult to fully comprehend (Armstrong, 2009). One of the common definitions of leadership was made by Burns (1978) who defines it as the practices of those who motivates, energize and unites the followers and actuates the institutional, political, psychological and other resources. Bennis, Bennis&Nanus (1986) developed the definition by Burns and added the concepts of transformation, participation and common vision to their definion. Another common definition is that it is the process of orienting collective or individual efforts and driving others to achieving identified goals. Leadership represents the images of powerful and dynamic individuals who leads other people and/or groups. Throughout the history, in parallel with managerial developments, leadership has played a key role in the success or failure of organizations. Leadership is stated to be a universal activity and is of great importance for organizational and social functioning (Bass, 1990; Bickes & Yılmaz, 2020). Similarly, Rue & Byars (2008) point out that leadership is to pursue leader guidance willingly or to have the ability to push others to take over a business. Wice (1995) describes leadership as a mysterious process, which has a role in almost everyone's life. He also points out that leadership is a dynamic force in national and international affairs.

In the book by Tolbert & Hall (2016), leadership is explained as to find an easy solution to whatever problems are ailing an organization. Etzioni (1965) describes leadership as a special form of power consisting of personal quality – related ability to unveil the compliance among subordinates in a broad range of matters. Yet, leadership differs from power in that leadership entails influence while power implies only that subject's preferences are held in abeyance. Meindl, Ehrlich & Dukerich (1985) state that leadership involves more than simply normal exercise of authority, which is based on a position in a company. Leadership often includes some principal personal traits. From another perspective, leadership is a body of everything a leader possesses that considerably helps to achieve the goals, to provide the wellbeing of organisation and workers (Amanchukwu, Stanley, & Ololube, 2015). In other words, leadership refers to obtaining certain objectives using available resources and ensuring a coherent organizational process.

Some theorists cut the definition of leadership down to a matter of influence, which results in employees' enthusiastic commitment, contrary to being indifferent and showing reluctant obedience. Researchers who support this point of view indicate that using authority or control as a way of rewarding or punishment to manipulate and/or force employees doesn't equal to leading them. However, those who don't agree with this view consider this definition to be too restrictive due to the fact that it doesn't include influence processes, which are fundamental for comprehending why a manager or leader is effective or not effective in a specific situation. These research group believes that the initial description of leadership shouldn't determine the answer of how to make a leader effective in advance (Yukl, 1989).

Although there are many challenges, leadership is a trending topic in various disciplines such as management, sociology, psychology and politics. The evolution of leadership approaches has also been important in hospitality industry to find out the relationship between leaders and followers. Global hospitality establishments have particularly been found to be affected by leaders' behaviors and personal characteristics (Brownell, 2010). As hospitality organizations are demanded to develop their performance, the importance of effective leadership performance comes into prominence. The leadership has dramatically been important in hospitality field (Pittaway, Carmouche, & Chell, 1998). The fundamental points for the success of hospitality firms such as the intensive competitiveness, customer needs, organizational commitment of employees enhance the significance of leadership in hospitality industry. The managers of accommodation firms continue their existence in a sophisticated environment. Therefore, it is vital to swiftly solve the problems resulting from internal and external environmrnt (Akova, 2017). Leadership and leader become very important at this point. Hospitality businesses feel obliged to adopt and implement an effective leadership style to be innovative, develope effective structures, to respond to changing consumer tendencies, to keep up with digitalization, to inspire subordinates' creavity etc. (Radwan & Radwan, 2020). Therefore, the leadership style and leader behavior choosen is of great importance in terms of hospitality industry.

Despite increased numbers of researches to build up leadership theories, there is still no an integrated leadership theory. Based on the basic assumptions, leadership theories are, in general, divided into two main categories named universal and contingency theories. Universal leadership theories consist of great man, trait and behavioral theory, which assume that leadership qualities, abilities and behaviors are valid anywhere and under any conditions. The universal theories point out that effective leadership includes some distinct behaviors and traits. Great man and trait theory emphasize that, for an effective leadership, physical, psychological and personal traits are needed; while behavioral theory draws attention to the behaviors of effective leaders (Uslu, 2019). Behavioral leadership theory is the main theme of this chapter.

Behavioral Leadership Approaches

At the beginning of the 1900s, the leadership theory of traits developed in relation to the classical management idea, which points out that to be an effective leader requires to have certain personality traits. However, in the 1940s, a neoclassical approach dominated management philosophy. Accordingly, behavioral leadership theories showed up which links the effectiveness of a leader to certain kinds of behaviors. Behavioral leadership approach came out as a response to the shortcomings of the trait theory in explaining the fundamental reasons behind an effective leader. This leadership approach focuses on specifying the most suitable types of leadership and certain behaviors of leaders (Bickes & Yılmaz, 2020). This approach seeks the answers of those questions such as: "What do leaders actually do? What behaviors make these people to be perceived as leaders? What behaviors increase leaders' success?" (WGU, 2020).

The behavioral approach of leadership comes up with the idea that "leaders are made, not born". This approach claims that leadership can be gained based on learnable behaviors (WGU, 2020). As is seen, the emphasis on personal traits and qualities shifted to the actual behaviors and actions of leaders. This approach is based on the idea that the leadership is composed of an interpersonal relationship between the leader and workers in which the behavior of the leader towards the workers is the most crucial element. According to Davis & Luthans (1979), while positive behaviors of the leader increase morale and constitute confidence between team members, the opposite will disqualify the person as a leader. According to this approach, specific behavioral patterns connect leaders and followers to reach goals. Behavioral leadership approach aims to assess the relational effects between the behavior and its consequences.

Behavioral leadership approach assumes that the effective leadership does not depend on personal characteristics, but on his/her behaviors. How a leader behaves or what he/she does is what makes a leader effective. Therefore, to be a leader is not peculiar to individual as it is mentioned in great man and trait theories. This theory acknowledges that the leader should not be independently thought of the group.

The success and effectiveness of a leader comes from his/her behaviors towards and the relationships with group members. This theory especially emphasizes that leading behaviors can highly possibly be acquired (Uslu, 2019). The behavioral leadership theory suggests that particular behaviors differentiate leaders from others. This theory refers to the idea which is based on the fact that an effective leader is the one who behaves in accordance with group productivity and psychological growth (Deshwal & Ali, 2020). As also mentioned by (Amanchukwu, Stanley, & Ololube, 2015), the behavioral leadership approach prioritizes leaders' actions. Any person can turn into a leader through training and observation.

According to the behavioral leadership perspective, the most essential predictors of effective leadership are some behaviors and abilities people could learn over time. These abilities and behaviors are developed based on personality traits (Holdford, 2003). From this point of view, leadership is defined in terms of behavioral patterns contrary to intrinsic properties or traits (Yago, 1982). The behavioral leadership patterns gather leaders and followers around specified targets and tasks. The leader's behavior can be stated as a discriminative stimulus to remind the subordinate his/her duties. The supervisor does not actually cause the subordinate's attitude, but just provides a discriminative stimulus or sets the occasion. The behavioral leadership view indicates that behaviors and the consequences are in an on-going interaction (Davis & Luthans, 1979). In other words, the leader and the subordinate are in an exchange relationship, which mutually modify or reinforce one another's behaviors.

The behavioral theory takes into consideration how the leader acts against situations. Behavioral approach describes leadership as the subset of human behavior. This theory was interpreted as a major improvement in leadership theory not only for it possessed empirical support, but also provided an easy way to make managers practice enhancing their efficiency and leadership effectiveness. Some studies on behavioral approach have mostly focused on typical behavioral patterns while some of them have determined the behavioral differences between poor and effective leaders (Seters & Field, 1990). Research findings have categorized different behavioral patterns which are labelled as styles. That's why this theory is also called style theory. Some of the early researches on understanding the impacts of leaders' behaviors were launched at Ohio State University and University of Michigan in the late 1940s. A third line of research on behavioral approach was conducted by Blake and Mouton in the early 1960s called managerial grid model. These three researches are the most well-known in this field. Four factor theory (Bowers & Seashore, 1966), theory X and Y (McGregor, 1966) and action theory (Argyris, 1976) are other behavioral theories of leadership.

Ohio State University Leadership Behavior Studies

Due to the failure of the traits approach to predict leadership, researchers turned towards leader behaviors. Leadership style effects (i.e., democratic vs. autocratic) studied on small groups, process analysis of interactions and employers' reports indicating the behavioral styles of the supervisors aimed to identify leader behavior patterns related to good morale and increased productivity. Out of these researches, one of the most extensive and effective ones on the leadership field was a number of studies released by Ohio State University. The Leader Behavior Description Questionnaire (LBDQ), the Leadership Opinion Questionnaire and the Supervisory Behavior Description Questionnaire were developed within behavior studies, all to be known under the name of Ohio State University leadership scales. The Leader Behavior Description Questionnaire (LBDQ), firstly included almost 1800 leader behaviors, then was reduced to 150 items of behavioral inventories, was applied to supervisors, subordinates, and observers both in military and industrial organizations. This questionnaire basically aims to measure the perception of

Behavioral Approaches to Leadership

subordinates over supervisory behaviors. However, the Leadership Opinion Questionnaire focuses on how the supervisor assumes he/she could behave in his/her leadership role. As for the Supervisory Behavior Description Questionnaire, it attempts to determine subordinate's perception of the supervisor's actual behavior. This scale differs from LBDQ by a number of items. Factor analysis results revealed two main clusters which could largely explain the variability in leaders' behaviors. These two clusters are labeled as *consideration* and *initiation of structure* (Chemers, 2000; Schriesheim & Kerr, 1974). As it is understood from the paragraph, the Ohio State studies not only made a considerable change in the way that leadership is measured and developed, but also identified the two most widely accepted leadership behavior categories.

Figure 1.

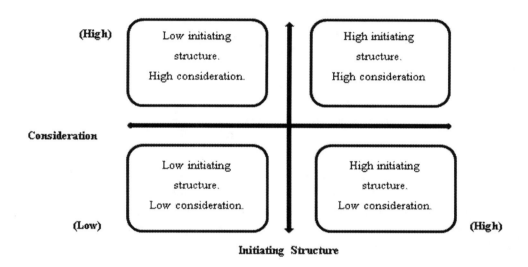

According to Figure 1, consideration and initiating structure behaviors are shaped in four different leadership styles being categorized as low initiating structure, high consideration; low initiating structure, low consideration; high initiating structure, high consideration; high initiating structure, low consideration. This means that possessing high initiating structure and high consideration behaviors bring along better outcomes for businesses. Therefore, high initiating structure and high consideration are two fundamental behaviors, which make a leader effective. In other words, these two behavior styles affect leadership performance and productivity.

According to Ohio State studies, consideration behavior refers to behaviors which emphasize employees' relationships. Leaders with consideration behavior display an employee-oriented leadership style. They care about subordinates' feelings and ideas. They prioritize mutual trust and cooperation. They observe their subordinates, try to identify their abilities and capacities, and offer some solutions to them in order to deal with work-related issues. Those who adopt a high level of this behavior style highly likely tend to provide more job satisfaction and less intention to leave the job (Griffin, Phillips, & Gully, 2016; Henkel & Bourdeau, 2018). The category *consideration* consists of behaviors such as indicating concern and/or affection for subordinates, ensuring that their viewpoints were included in decision making process, trying hard to decrease the conflicts in work environment, etc. These behaviors apparently reflect leader's intentions which back up positive morale and employees' satisfaction (Chemers, 2000).

The dimension of *consideration* pays attention to behaviors regarding wellbeing, status, promotion, contribution and comfort of the followers. Consideration behaviors consist of doing personal favors for coworkers, supporting subordinates' ideas and in their actions, approaching the followers as equals and being reachable (Li M., 2018). Consideration dimension focuses on the significance to understand human relations and is linked with employee needs (Uslu, 2019). To sum up, consideration behavior is the amount of harmony and confidence a leader creates among his/her subordinates (Khan, Nawaz, & Khan, 2016). According to Holdford (2003), employee oriented leaders prioritize the tasks less but are more concerned about their followers. These types of leaders treat their followers not as cogs in the machine but as human beings.

Initiating structure dimension refers to task-oriented leadership behavior and focuses on doing one's duties. Initiating structure behavior includes the activities related to defining, shaping and initiating the duties and targets which are expected to be achieved by the employees and groups and by the leader himself. This behavior style also consists of managing, planning and programming the activities of employees and groups, providing communication among them and implementing new ideas. Initiating structure refers to behavior pattern which backs up and help the employees to accomplish the determined objectives and display a high performance (Akova, 2017). As a strong factor, initiating structure consists of items assessing the leader's use of standard operating procedures, criticizing poor work and prioritizing high levels of performance. These behaviors seem to be linked with the leader's focus on constituting a structure to accomplish the tasks (Chemers, 2000). According to another perspective, initiating structure points out to what extent a person is likely to structure and describe his/her role and his/her followers to attain a goal (Schriesheim & Kerr, 1974). To Jago (1982), initiating structure points out to the leader's behaviors such as defining and organizing relationships among team members and building well-defined communication channels and proper ways to accomplish organizational tasks.

The two dimensions of Ohio State studies, consideration and initiating structure shouldn't be thought as two opposite ends of a single leadership behavior pattern, but as two separate and independent dimensions. Ohio State University studies are important in that they indicated a leader could have a high or low level of consideration and initiating structure behaviors (Akova, 2017). Even though LBDQ factors were found to be reliable in leader behavior ratings, they were not acknowledged to be totally successful to estimate significant outcomes linked with the effectiveness of leaders. Consideration and initiating structure behaviors were sometimes but not always predictive of employees' performance (Chemers, 2000). The shortcomings of this carefully studied and deeply searched behavior theory pushed researchers to new leadership studies. A number of studies pointed out that consideration and initiating behavior patterns may not be ideal under certain circumstances. For instance, a higher initiating structure may result in higher efficiency, yet, it may also result in a higher level of turnover and grievances. Therefore, it is not sensible to attempt to identify a universally valid leadership behavior based on these two dimensions (Jago, 1982; Schriesheim & Kerr, 1974). However, despite its disputable side, Ohio State University leadership studies are still of great importance.

Taking into consideration the behavioral leadership styles and hospitality industry, it is possible to see that certain leadership behaviors such as democratic and authocratic have been studied. The studies indicates that hospitality leaders are authocratic due to unpredictable demands and uncertainties in hospitality industry. Hospitality leaders have to manage their subordinates effectively, to achieve organizational targets, to take action as soon as possible andd to adjust the inputs and outputs as best as they can. In hospitality industry, even though democratic leadership is an efficient alternative under certain circumstances, it may need to apply authocratic leadership style to accomplish organizational goals (Raguž, 2007; Yamak & Eyüpoğlu, 2018). Leavitt (2003) points out that managers of hospitality industry have to be equipped with more skills and competencies due to fast-changing world and technology. Given the fact that tourism is sensitive and vulnerable to changes, managers of hospitality industry need to be persuasive, visionary, creative and inspirational to motivate and direct followers through displaying appropriate behaviors.

Michigan State University Leadership Studies

A group of researchers conducted leadership studies at Michigan State University Research Center under the guidance of Rensis Likert starting from 1947. They examined the relationship between behavior and productivity, the characteristic differences of group leaders with high and low productivity (Akbaba & Erenler, 2008). Michigan State leadership studies also focused on job satisfaction, employee turnover rates, absenteeism, work complainings, cost and motivation, determining the factors impacting the satisfaction of group members and efficiency and the relationship among these variables and examining the relationship between these variables and leadership styles. Leadership studies by Michigan State University categorized two leadership behaviors: job-oriented and employee-oriented. These behaviors have similarities with behavior approaches put forward by Ohio State University categorized as *"initiating structure"* and *"consideration"*. Along with this, the research findings of Michigan State University indicated that the supervision behavior of leader had an impact on subordinate's productivity. In addition, control distance was found to be effective; employees controlled at a close distance had a lower efficiency than those who were controlled at a far distance. Michigan state studies showed that effective leaders had constructive relations with their subordinates, supported them and increased their self-confidence, achieved high performance targets by applying group management and decision making techniques. (Akova, 2017).

Figure 2.

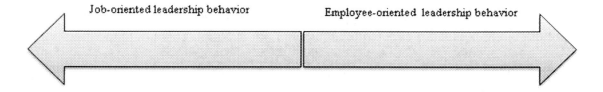

Employee-oriented leadership behavior: According to the findings of Michigan University research, employee-oriented leadership is the most effective leadership behavior. The more a leader displays employee-led behavior, the more a leader gets away from production-led behaviors (Uslu, 2019). Any leader who adopts employee-oriented behaviors gives priority to the needs of the subordinates and followers. Leaders with this behavior style regards their workplace as a social system and take more into consideration subordinates and their personal abilities. They identify performance criteria by taking followers' ideas into account. Afterwards, they make a set of goals which aims high performance. Employee performance has been found to be higher in organizations in which employee-oriented leadership behavior is adopted (Champoux, 2017). Employee oriented leadership has been widely associated with high group performance, efficiency and work satisfaction (Armandi, Oppedisano, & Sherman, 2003). As it is seen, employee-oriented leaders care about subordinates' wellbeing, are concerned about their feelings, and respect their actions and decisions. When it is thought in terms of hospitality industry and the fact that hospitality is labour-intensive, employee oriented leadership behaviors would give a rise to employee-satisfaction, productivity, organizational commitment and subordinates welfare (Nwokorie & Okechukwu, 2014). Studies indicate that an employee-oriented approach leads to high level of inspiration, persistence, enthusiasm, immersion and concentration at work and mental wellbeing. Similar results have been obtained from hospitality industry employees. It has been put forward that highly engaged employees tend to achieve better employees outcomes, enhance work satisfaction, have reduced turnover intention and display better customer service (Gemeda & Lee, 2020; Rabiul, et al., 2022; Zheng, et al., 2020). These results are consistent with consideration dimension of Ohio State University studies and employee-oriented leadership approach of Michigan State University studies.

Job-oriented leadership behavior: This dimension refers to defining tasks and roles, relationships among workers, coordinating workers' actions, identifying task performance standards and increasing workers' performance up to these standards. They use these standards to provide subordinates' commitment, productivity and motivation (Derue, Nahrgang, Wellman, & Humphrey, 2011). Job-oriented leadership behavior can be seen in servant and transactional leadership styles which have been proven to be most appropriate styles in hospitality industry as they are human service-focused. Both servant and transactional leadership styles focus on tasks through an exchange program in which organizational objectives come first. Service-oriented industries, such as accommodations, require to meet customers' satisfaction and expectations, therefore, need their employees to accomplish their tasks and deliver quality servive on time (Kaya & Karatepe, 2020; Li, et al., 2021; Rabiul, et al., 2022). To sum up, task (job) – oriented leaders direct employees to get the tasks done and make sure that the organizational goals are achieved. Leaders who adopt task-oriented behaviors can achieve more productivity, yet, employees may be less satisfied and may react negatively. It is understood that employees' needs don't come first. As tasks are prioritized and are assumed to be done on time, this can cause pressure on followers. Therefore, negative consequences such as high turnover, absenteeism, less commitment, less confidence and alike may occur.

Similar to Ohio State leadership studies, Michigan State leadership behaviors were categorized under two themes: task orientation and employee orientation. Task-oriented leadership behavior has common characteristics with initiating structure while employee-oriented behavior is close to consideration dimension. However, unlike Ohio State leadership studies, the two dimensions of leadership styles of Michigan State University are not independent (Uslu, 2019). According to these studies, the most effective leader may adopt a task-oriented approach to achieve production target, while, at the same time, he/she can care about employees' relationship to increase work satisfaction. It may be possible for a leader, even may be difficult in practical context, to possess a moderate level for both dimensions to obtain the best results for the company (Sivaruban, 2021). This considerably separates Ohio State studies from Michigan State studies.

Behavioral Approaches to Leadership

Figure 3.

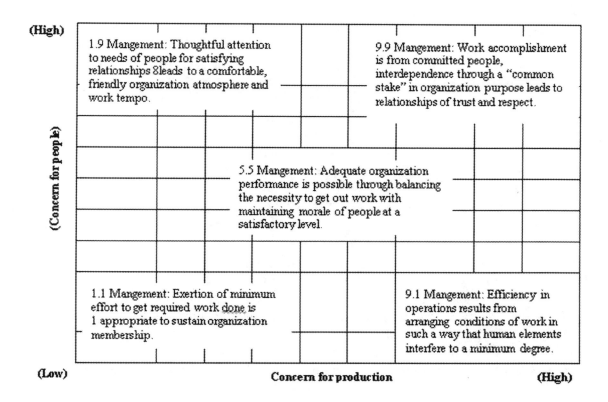

Blake and Mouton Managerial Diagram Model

Blake and Mouton (1964) defined leadership behavior and developed a behavior-based matrix to determine an ideal leader style based on the two dimensions of Ohio State leadership studies (Bertocci, 2009). Leadership matrix, previously known as manager matrix, is a practical approach which sheds light on research findings of Ohio and Michigan State Universities. This matrix is the best-known model of management behavior (Northouse, 2016) and still used in leadership development and consultation practices. This approach describes leadership behavior under two dimensions: concern for people (employee-oriented, consideration oriented, initiating structure) and concern for production (task-oriented). If these two dimensions were perfectly integrated in this Grid, then they would form a style called 'team manager' which is especially suggested for hotel managers. Participative group system has been advised to be one of the most appropriate approach for hotel managers. In hospitality industry, in most stuations, managers are given multiple tasks and have complex interrelationships. Therefore, task-oriented and/or interpersonal-oriented approach is considered to be more helpful for hotel managers to achieve better results from their subordinates (Masry, Kattara, & Demerdash, 2004). Blake and Mouton forms a 9 x 9 matrix using both dimensions and explains leadership behavior based on this matrix (Bickes & Yılmaz, 2020). This matrix uses changing gradings from 1 to 9, from least concern to the most concern. The scores obtained are then added and placed into a two-dimensional matrix. This matrix mainly reflects a team management model. It considers that productivity can increase if there is a consistency among group members. Production target is of low importance (Akova, 2017).

According to Blake and Mouton, using a 9-point scale, the degree of the two concerns of people and production constitutes a management style. A 9,9 combination of these two concerns identifies the leadership style that adopts a participative approach to management and leadership. It provides the best way to lead and manage. A 9,1 combination of two concerns refers to an authority-obedience leadership style while a 1,9 combination stands for country club management. A 1,1 degree of two concerns points out to the impoverished style, in other words, to the all poor choices and a 5,5 combination refers to the second most compromising leadership and management style (Burke, 2017). Authority-obedience leadership (9,1) displays a low concern level for people and a high level of concern for output. Leaders of this style focus on duties and tasks and almost don't care about their followers' emotions. The accomplishment of tasks always comes first. Country club leadership (combination of 1,9) is more concerned about people and less concerned about output. This leadership style prioritizes building a friendly business environment by taking into consideration people's attitudes, needs and emotions rather than work completion. Impoverished leadership (position 1,1) represents both a low level of concern for output and people. This kind of a leader is neither interested in completing task nor in building relations or networking with people which results in followers' being indifferent to achievement and making efforts. Team leadership (position 9,9), contrary to impoverished leadership, has both a high level of concern for output and people. This leadership style gives priority not only to organizational success and task completion, but also providing a friendly business environment and developing good relations among subordinates. Middle-of-the-road leadership, also labeled as organizational leadership (position 5,5), refers to moderate concern both for output and people. Such leaders aim to keep a balance between concerns for people and output (Bickes & Yılmaz, 2020).

Blake and Mouton based their ideas on social psychology. Despite Blake and Mouton having been grounded in a series of researches, theories and practices, the management grid eventually lost its popularity. The superior idea behind the grid did not make much sense. This model faced some challenges by the 1960s after understanding, once more, the significance of variations on the two functions of leadership which had already been identified by Ohio State University researchers in the 1950s: *initiating structure* and *consideration*. On the other hand, the contingency theory by Fred Fiedler identified two categories of leadership behaviors labeled as task-oriented and relationship-oriented leadership behaviors which supported Ohio State reserach results. Similarly, situational leadership theory by Hersey and Blanchard (1977) focused on two important leadership behaviors categorized as task and relationship. As a result, Managerial Grip was challenged by these three theories as it was thought to ignore different situations (Burke, 2017). Moreover, it mostly represents management style rather than leadership.

Iowa University Leadership Studies

Iowa University conducted a set of leadership studies during the 1930s under the leadership of Kurt Lewin and his friends. These studies were conducted in a controlled testing environment rather than participants' own natural environment (Akova, 2017). At the end of the researches, three leadership styles were determined which labeled as democratic leadership, autocratic leadership and laissez-faire leadership. According to these researches, a leader's effectiveness is based on his/her behavior.

Autocratic leadership refers to the centralization of power and provision of power from control of rewards, position and coercion. These researches point out that an authoritarian leader can be appropriate for job-oriented entity and disciplinary forces. On the other hand, such a leader can be effective in the short run to create successful results (Sivaruban, 2021). Yet, some researchers agree that an authoritarian leader can find certain ways to achieve organizational objectives within the time frame. But, as already mentioned, autocratic leadership was found to lead increased production volume in the short term (Billig, 2015). Similarly, according to a research assessing the impact leadership styles on employees' job satisfaction in five-star hotels, authocratic leadership is not a preferred leadership style, but sometimes is seen to be necessary. In the same study, authocratic leadership style was found not to have any impact on employees' satisfaction (Al-Ababneh, 2013). To Fouad (2019), an authocratic approach could be beneficial under some circumstances. For example it could be vital when a business faces an emergency and requires an urgent action as soon as possible. For hospitality industry, authocratic leadership represents the most common style due to unpredictable nature of the industry. While autocratic leadership provides a high level of task completion, democratic leadership was determined to possess high quality. A democratic leader displays behaviors such as being participative, employee-oriented, supporting group decisions and caring about individual differences. Iowa University studies indicated that democratic leadership was the most effective leadership style in the long term (Akova, 2017). Laissez-faire leadership refers to the avoidance and/or the absence of leadership. This style was found to be the most ineffective leadership behavior. Employees who are under the laissez-faire leadership are never intervened or interfered with (Harrison, 2018). Laissez-faire leadership approach is not also reccommended in hospitality industry. It was found that this leadership style impacted workers' job satisfaction in a negative way in the hospitality industry (Erkutlu, 2008). Laissez-faire leadership style is seen a sink-or-swim procedure in which workers either succeed on their own or fail in every task (Fouad, 2019). It can be concluded that this leadership style is not beneficial in terms of employees' performance.

Douglas McGregor's Theory X and Y

Douglas McGregor, in 1960, published a book with the name "*The Human Side of Enterprise*" which led a different path for management thinking and practices. McGregor put forward a new role for managers based on questioning a number of assumptions about human behaviors. This book was praised by many other authors as "one of the most significant and useful books" or "a book which changed organization concept and replaced it with a new idea that emphasized human potential". This book was thought to stress human potential, human growth, and human role in organizational environment. In this book, Mcgregor identified two theories named as Theory X and Y which explains the nature of humans and how they should be led (Kopelman, Prottas, & Davis, 2008).

Douglas McGregor was inspired by Dr. Mayo's studies and developed X theory based on Classical Management Theory by Tylor and Fayol. Then, McGregor criticized this theory and put forward the principles of the theory of human relations. According to this theory, assumptions about employees' behaviors are one of the most fundamental factors, which shape managers' behaviors. In other words, a manager's ideas and thoughts about human behaviors impact his/her behaviors. These assumptions, representing two ends opposite to each other, were labeled as Theory X and Y (Akova, 2017). Theory X is mostly considered as fanatical, narrow-minded and an arrogant style of management. It usually ignores human issues (Touma, 2021). According to Theory X, people are not naturally willing to work and would refrain from it if it was possible. For this reason, most people must be forced, controlled and threatened to make them work. Theory X assumes that an average person would rather be directed, keeps away from responsibility, is less ambitious and cares about security. As a result, managers feel obliged to control employees over their work environment and use influential methods which can be direct and harsh. Theory X managers acknowledge the chain of command, use "reward or punish" motivational techniques, and emphasize close supervision of subordinates' behaviors through rigid behaviors. The classical management method was described by McGregor as hindering rather than contributing to organizations to solve problems, achieve their goals and position their product in a reliable way. However, McGregor criticized this approach as he believed that, as from the 1950s, employees began to prioritize their social needs and self-esteem (Aydin, 2012). They moved beyond lower needs. This reflects changes in employees' behaviors and so does in managers' behaviors.

Theory X continues to exist not because of the nature of jobs, but because of the fact that different personalities still respond to this theory. The powerful side of Theory X is that it helps managers to understand the methods which focus on how to relate employees to work. This theory widely results in employees' dissatisfaction. It forces employees to please their managers. On the other hand, managers show no interest in human feelings and put too much pressure on workers to get the tasks done. This theory claims that the employees don't have ambition and ignore their responsibilities. They have no self-confidence and are obviously not trustworthy. Theory X has a direct impact on organization's structure where the salaries are paid based on the positions rather than qualifications of employees (Touma, 2021). It can be clearly seen that Theory X sounds more authocratic and as mentioned above, even sometimes it work, it is generally not appriciated in hospitality industry.

Theory Y was raised out of the ideologies presented by philosophers like Locke and Smith (Oluwakayode, Clinton, Stanley, & Subi, 2017). Theory Y of McGregor is based on the assumptions that employees are: (1) not inherently lazy, (2) capable of self-control and self-direction, (3) in the position of presenting significant ideas and suggestions that can improve organizational effectiveness. Therefore, through appropriate management practices, for instance, employees are given the opportunity to participate in decision making processes; organizational and personal goals can simultaneously be realized. Theory Y supports the idea of participative leadership, delegation, job enlargement and performance appraisals (Kopelman, Prottas, & Davis, 2008). In Theory Y, managers point out that employees they supervise have as much organizational commitment and are as capable of solving problems as they are themselves. Theory Y managers aim to structure the environment of an organization to let employees' goals coincide with organizational goals which is expected to result in greater productivity and creativity (Aydin, 2012).

In Theory Y, the role of manager shifts to a more democratic leadership style. Theory Y managers believe that the employees actually take responsibility in finding solutions. Theory Y managers are more participative and have better relations with team members. Teamwork is important for them and they prefer their employees to have a high capacity of creativity and imagination to determine problems and come up with proper solutions. Theory Y suggests managers to be aware that business is all about people and trusting in their employees will make them more productive and effective. Managers are assumed to share and negotiate all decisions with their followers to reach the best one. An organization can extensively achieve its targets and reach its peak as long as it promotes employees' participation in organizational process. Theory Y exists in an environment where productivity, scientific issues, problem solving and creativity are promoted. Managers' understanding and flexibility will help employees to accomplish their tasks. Theory Y management style will lead to the achievement of higher effectiveness, higher productivity, more responsibility, higher level of motivation and self – esteem (Touma, 2021). As can be understood, Theory Y managers are more democratic and liberal. Theory Y suggests a new management model which widely pays attention to human relations and feelings. As this approach is more democratic, considerate and employee-oriented, it can clearly be concluded that this approach fits in hospitality industry. However, on the other hand, this theory has some shortcomings as it assumes all employees are equal. It thinks that all employees are creative or, at least, dream to be creative. It ignores different types of personalities that can respond to Theory X management style rather than Theory Y management style under certain circumstances.

Likert's Four System of Leadership Style

In 1947, as a continuation of Michigan State University leadership studies, Rennis Likert examined how to manage employees' efforts in the best possible way to achieve performance and satisfaction targets. At the end of the reserach were determined three main variable groups that impacted the leadership-performance relationship. These three main variable groups were categorized as situational variables (organizational structure, policies, individual characteristics etc.), intermediate variables (performance goals, perception, attitudes, motivation measures, etc.) and dependent variables (productivity, service, cost, quality, earnings, etc.). (Küçüközkan, 2015).

According to Likert, leader behaviors can be categorized as "exploitative authoritative (System I), benevolent authoritative (System II), consultative (System III), and participative (System IV) (Akova, 2017). Likert's System I, labeled as exploitative authoritative leadership style, refers to a kind of system in which almost all decisions are taken by managers. There is the least level of confidence between supervisor and subordinates (Tajedin, Moradi, & Alitabrizi, 2017). Leaders apply threatening and/or punishing methods against subordinates to make them accomplish their tasks. Organizational goals and decisions are determined by executives and are hierarchically transferred from top to bottom (Akova, 2017). In the System II (benevolent authoritative), leaders supervise and control, however, subordinates are allowed to present their ideas to a certain extent. Even though the confidence between supervisor and subordinates is still low (Tajedin, Moradi, & Alitabrizi, 2017), a supervisor may trust his followers in a controlled manner. Making decision is still widely in the charge of the executives. Yet, on the other hand, certain parts of decisions were left to the subordinates in a controlled manner. Subordinates' ideas and advices are asked under some circumstances and bottom-up communication is sometimes allowed in system II (Akova, 2017). In the system III (consultative), subordinates are able to determine their goals. They are given opportunities on how to accomplish their tasks. However, essential and important decisions are still made by the executives. In this system, leaders would rather reward and encourage subordinates in order to provide their motivation (Tajedin, Moradi, & Alitabrizi, 2017). Hierarchically, leaders both use bottom-up and top-to-bottom communication methods. A leader in this system plays a consultative (advisor) role (Akova, 2017). In the final Likert system (system IV), leaders rely on subordinates and their relations are based on mutual confidence and honesty. Goals are identified and organizational decisions are made with the participation of both superiors and subordinates. Rewarding method is applied to motivate team members and to create the sense of value and importance among them (Tajedin, Moradi, & Alitabrizi, 2017). Communication is conducted, similar to system III, both top-to-bottom and bottom-up ways. In this system, the leader encourages and promotes the followers to participate in the decision making process (Akova, 2017). As can be obviously seen, the leaders of the last system and system III are more effective than the first two ones. The productivity and satisfaction of subordinates are apparently expected to be higher in system III and system IV.

SOLUTIONS AND RECOMMENDATIONS

As a profound and complex concept, leadership has been of great importance as it can considerably shape the achievement and realization of common goals of an organization. It has been defined in a different way by different theorists. Leadership has usually been defined based on individual perspectives of researchers. Stogdill (1974) points out that there are nearly as many definitions of leadership as the number of people who attempted to define the concept. The key role of leadership on organizational success has driven the attention of many researchers in different fields and led to a great number of studies. These studies, in general, aim to identify the factors and styles of what makes a leader or leadership more effective. The answers given to this question have revealed different leadership approaches and theories in parallel with the development of management approaches (Bickes & Yılmaz, 2020).

Leadership was mostly defined in terms of personal traits during classical management development. This approach claims that leaders are not made, but born. However, this approach was criticized to ignore direct measurement of leadership behaviors and influence as it was later proved that leader traits are mediated by leadership behaviors (Yukl, 1989). This new approach is called behavioral leadership and comes up with the idea that leaders are made, not born. Leadership can be modeled and learned according to behavior approach. Behavior approach focuses on the importance of behaviors to make a leader effective or ineffective. Behavioral leadership studies identified leader behaviors over subordinates in main two categories: task-oriented and people-oriented.

One of the most known behavioral leadership studies, Ohio State University leadership studies, identified two categories labeled as initiating structure and consideration. Michigan State leadership studies, in a similar way, concluded on two categories of leader behaviors called as job-oriented and employee-oriented. The other most well-known behavioral leadership research was conducted by Blake and Mouton who describe leader behaviors on a 9 x 9 managerial grid. Based on this managerial grid, leadership behaviors were explained under dimensions named as concern for production and concern for people which similarly refer to task and employee orientation. Iowa University studies determined three different leadership styles (autoratic, democratic and laissez-faire leadership) which can be interpreted in terms of task and employee orientation dimensions. Douglas McGregor explains human nature and how to effectively manage people based on the theories he developed: Theory X and Y. These two theories are based upon the priority of the completion of tasks or human relation styles that end up with task-oriented or people-oriented styles. In Likert's Four System of Leadership Style, we see a similar finding. Likert divided leaders' behaviors in four main categories as mentioned above. While taking into consideration the exploitative authoritative and benevolent authoritative leader behaviors, we can clearly see that they both prioritize the accomplishments of tasks and ignore human relations and feelings. Leaders of these styles overcontrol and underfollow subordinates to make them accomplish their tasks. Yet, on the other hand, consultative and participative leader styles are based on motivating and promoting followers. In all behavioral leadership, employee-oriented leadership style has considerably been found to be the most effective one. This behavioral leadership style improves productivity and effectiveness. Each of these behavioral leadership studies contributes to the definition of leadership and other aspects of leadership concept.

In this book chapter, behavioral leadership approaches have been explained based on different studies and views. This approach put forward the impact of behaviors on leadership effectiveness rather than personal traits. Similar to the former leadership theory (trait theory), the assumptions and principal ideas of behavioral leadership theory were analyzed with a critical perspective. This approach was followed by other leadership theories as it was determined to have shortcomings. As it is understood, this approach could not completely fullfilled the gaps in leadership studies. Later studies criticized this approach in terms of not considering situational and environmental factors (Uslu, 2019). From this point of view, it can be thought that a leader may need to adopt different approaches to be effective. As Holford (2003) suggests, having the capability to exhibit different leadership styles under different circumstances may be a better solution. On the other hand, it should not be forgotten that a balance is important both in task-oriented and employee-oriented behaviors. Too much focus on tasks may cause subordinates to feel abused while too much focus on employees may result in failure to achieve organizational goals (Holdford, 2003). Therefore, leaders are recommended to be aware of subordinates' abilities, personal characteristics and values to be more effective (Chemers, 2000). As is seen, as a concept and study field, leadership still needs to be studied more and in different perspectives. Along with the changes in technological world and organizational environment, leadership can be strongly recommended to be searched and new leadership theories should be developed to shed light on present and future researches.

FUTURE RESEARCH DIRECTIONS

As is seen from literature, leadership studies never remained limited to behavioral approaches neither previously nor afterwards. Shortcomings of each leadership theory were determined and criticized. Criticism to trait theory was followed by a behavioral leadership approach whose shortcomings were tried to be fulfilled with situational leadership theory. Continuing research indicates that leadership, as a study field, has not been completed yet. This field continues to develop based on environmental changes and improvements in management. It seems that leadership will keep its presence in academic and sector studies in the future. New leadership approaches and styles will continue to be created with further studies. Technological developments and innovations and the involvement of virtual organizations in working life (Bickes & Yılmaz, 2020) will necessitate studying what makes a leader effective in this new world. There are still unanswered questions in the relationship with leadership. With the changing times and new arising needs, it becomes important to put forward new leadership perspectives to meet the needs. Academics and researchers should go towards new contexts of leadership in order to contribute to the existing literature and shed light on future studies. In addition to leadership research, new management approaches should also be closely followed as leadership and management are two interrelated concepts. Any developments or new theories in other disciplines which leadership has a link with should also be followed as they can provide a new insight for researchers. Using different research methods also matters to better complete the missing parts of leadership. However, as Bickes and Yılmaz (2020) state, dark points in leadership will always exist, and so will the need for new approaches and views, in other words, new colors and new voices.

All these suggestions are also valid for hospitality industry. Tourism researchers and academics should follow new researches on leadership approach and theories and should contribute to leadership studies on hospitality industry. Tourism researchers can be reccommended to put forward the proper and effective leadership patterns in hospitality businesses. As hospitality industry is labour intensive and the success of hospitality sector is mostly based on customer satisfaction, leadership studies possess great importance. The gaps in the field should be listed and fullfilled for the future of hospitality industry. Behavioral approaches of leadership should be further studied to fill the gaps of this theory in terms of hospitality industry. Leader's behaviors can be studied in wider perspective. The menegerial roles and behaviors of leaders in hospitality businesses should be carefully analyzed. This will both contribute to academic and buiness world.

CONCLUSION

As mentioned under the former heading, leadership is one of the most complex and contradictory study field that has not completely been clarified yet. There is not an absolute universal consistency among leadership studies. On the other hand, leadership changes based on internal and external factors. Therefore, this concept will continue to domain the study fields. Any global and/or domestic developments mean new research for leadership and new leadership publications. Up-to-date leadership approaches and assumptions should be the field of interest of future research and researchers. Each new or existing theory and assumption can be reconsidered and/or reinterpreted by future researchers with a critical point of view. As can be seen from literature, there are still gaps in the field of leadership which need to be fulfilled. Future books, articles and any other publications should focus on any of these gaps to contribute to leadership studies.

REFERENCES

Akbaba, A., & Erenler, E. (2008). Otel İşletmelerinde Yöneticilerin Liderlik Yönelimleri ve İşletme Performansı İlişkisi. *Anatolia: Turizm Araştırmaları Dergisi*, *19*(1), 21–36.

Akova, O. (2017). *Liderlik Davranışı Örgütsel Sessizlik ve Örgütsel Performans Arasında Neddensellik Analizi: Beş Yıldızlı Otel İşletmelerinde Bir Araştırma*. Detay Yayıncılık.

Al-Ababneh, M. (2013). Leadership Style of Managers in Five-Star Hotels and its Relationship with Employee's Job Satisfaction. *International Journal of Management & Business Studies*, *3*(2), 93–98. doi:10.2139srn.3633072

Amanchukwu, R. N., Stanley, G. J., & Ololube, N. P. (2015). A Review of Leadership Theories, Principles and Styles and Their Relevance to Educational Management. *Management*, *5*(1), 6–14.

Armandi, B., Oppedisano, J., & Sherman, H. (2003). Leadership theory and practice: A "case" in point. *Management Desicion*, *41*(10), 1076–1088. doi:10.1108/00251740310509607

Armstrong, M. (2009). Armstrong's Handbook of Management and Leadership: A Guide to Managing Results (2nd ed.). New Delhi: Kogan Page.

Avery, G. C. (2004). *Understanding Leadership: Paradigms and Cases*. SAGE.

Aydin, O. T. (2012). The Impact of Theory X, Theory Y and Theory Z on Research Performance: An Empirical Study from A Turkish University. *International Journal of Advances in Management and Economics*, *1*(5), 24–30. doi:10.31270/ijame/01/05/2012/05

Bass, B. M. (1990). Bass & Stogdill's Handbook of Leadership: Theory, Research & Managerial Applications (3rd ed.). New York: The Free Press.

Bennis, W., Bennis, W. G., & Nanus, B. (1986). *Leaders: The Strategies for Taking Charge.* Harper & Row.

Bertocci, D. I. (2009). *Leadership in Organizations: There is a Difference Between Leaders and Managers.* University Press of America.

Bickes, D. M., & Yılmaz, C. (2020). Leadership Theories. In A Handbook of Leadership Styles (pp. 1-34). Cambridge Scholars Publishing.

Billig, M. (2015). Kurt Lewin's Leadership Studies and His Legacy to Social Psychology: Is There Nothing as Practical as a Good Theory? *Journal for the Theory of Social Behaviour, 45*(4), 440–460. doi:10.1111/jtsb.12074

Brownell, J. (2010). Leadership in the Service of Hospitality. *Cornell Hospitality Quarterly, 51*(3), 363–378. doi:10.1177/1938965510368651

Burke, W. W. (2017). *Robert R. Blake and Jane S. Mouton: Concern for People and Production. In The Palgrave Handbook of Organizational Change Thinkers.* Palgrave Macmillan. doi:10.1007/978-3-319-49820-1_4-1

Burns, J. M. (1978). *Leadership.* Harper & Row.

Champoux, J. E. (2017). Organizational Behavior: Integrating Individuals, Groups, and Organizations (5th ed.). New York: Routledge.

Chemers, M. M. (2000). Leadership Research and Theory: A Functional Integration. *Group Dynamics, 4*(1), 27–43. doi:10.1037/1089-2699.4.1.27

Davis, T. R., & Luthans, F. (1979). Leadership Reexamined: A Behavioral Approach. *Academy of Management Review, 4*(2), 237–248. doi:10.2307/257777 PMID:10297506

Derue, D. S., Nahrgang, J. D., Wellman, N., & Humphrey, S. E. (2011). Trait and Behavioral Theories of Leadership: An Integration and Meta-Analytic Test of Their Relative Validity. *Personnel Psychology, 64*(1), 7–52. doi:10.1111/j.1744-6570.2010.01201.x

Deshwal, V., & Ali, M. A. (2020). A Systematic Review of Various Leadership Theories. *International Journal of Commerce, 8*(1), 38–43. doi:10.34293/commerce.v8i1.916

Erkutlu, H. (2008). The impact of transformational leadership on organizational and leadership effectiveness: The Turkish case. *Journal of Management Development, 27*(7), 708–726. doi:10.1108/02621710810883616

Etzioni, A. (1965). Dual Leadership in Complex Organizations. *American Sociological Review, 30*(5), 688–698. doi:10.2307/2091137 PMID:5824934

Fouad, M. (2019). Impact of Leadership Style on Employee Job Satisfaction in the Hospitality Industry. *International Journal of Heritage, Tourism and Hospitality, 13*(1), 1–12.

Gemeda, H. K., & Lee, J. (2020). Leadership styles, work engagement and outcomes among information and communications technology professionals: A cross-national study. *Heliyon, 6*(4), 1–10. doi:10.1016/j.heliyon.2020.e03699 PMID:32280799

Griffin, R. W., Phillips, J. M., & Gully, S. M. (2016). Organizational Behavior: Managing People and Organizations (12th ed.). Boston: Cengage Learning.

Harrison, C. (2018). *Leadership Theory and Research: A Critical Approach to New and Existing Paradigms*. Palgrave Macmillan. doi:10.1007/978-3-319-68672-1

Henkel, T., & Bourdeau, D. (2018). A Field Study: An Examination Of Managers' Situational Leadership Styles. *Journal of Diversity Management*, *13*(2), 7–14. doi:10.19030/jdm.v13i2.10218

Holdford, D. A. (2003). Leadership theories and their lessons for pharmacists. *American Journal of Health-System Pharmacy*, *60*(17), 1780–1786. doi:10.1093/ajhp/60.17.1780 PMID:14503115

Jago, A. G. (1982). Leadership: Perspectives in Theory and Research. *Management Science*, *28*(3), 315–336. doi:10.1287/mnsc.28.3.315

James, R., Meindl, S. B., & Dukerich, J. M. (1985). The Romance of Leadership. *Administrative Science Quarterly*, *30*(1), 78–102. doi:10.2307/2392813

Kaya, B., & Karatepe, O. M. (2020). Does servant leadership better explain work engagement, career satisfaction and adaptive performance than authentic leadership? *International Journal of Contemporary Hospitality Management*, *32*(6), 2075–2095. doi:10.1108/IJCHM-05-2019-0438

Khan, Z. A., Nawaz, A., & Khan, I. U. (2016). Leadership Theories and Styles: A Literature Review. *Journal of Resources Development and Management*, *16*, 1–7.

Kopelman, R. E., Prottas, D. J., & Davis, A. L. (2008). Douglas McGregor's Theory X and Y: Toward a Construct-valid Measure. *Journal of Managerial Issues*, *20*(2), 255–271.

Küçüközkan, Y. (2015). Liderlik ve Motivasyon Teorileri: Kuramsal Bir Çerçeve. *Uluslararası Akademik Yönetim Bilimleri Dergisi*, *1*(2), 86–115.

Leavitt, H. J. (2003). Why Hierarchies Thrive. *Harvard Business Review*, *81*(3), 96–112. PMID:12632808

Li, M. (2018, June 8). *What Have We Learned from the 100-Year History of Leadership Research?* https://fisher.osu.edu/

Li, P., Sun, J.-M., Taris, W., Xing, L., & Peeters, M. C. W. (2021). Country differences in the relationship between leadership and employee engagement: A meta-analysis. *The Leadership Quarterly*, *32*(1), 1–14. doi:10.1016/j.leaqua.2020.101458

Masry, S. E., Kattara, H., & Demerdash, J. E. (2004). A Comparative Study on Leadership Styles Adopted by General Managers: A Case Study in Egypt. *Anatolia*, *15*(2), 109–124. doi:10.1080/13032917.2004.9687150

Northouse, P. G. (2016). Leadership: Theory and Practice (7th ed.). SAGE Publications.

Nwokorie, E. C., & Okechukwu, O. C. (2014). The Impact of Leadership Style on Effective Human Resources Management and Productivity in Hospitality Organizations. *Journal of Technical Education and Management Sciences*, *9*(2), 106–118.

Oluwakayode, O., Clinton, E., Stanley, A., & Subi, J. (2017). A Review and Application of McGregor Theory X and Theory Y in Business Research. In *1st Covenant University International Conference on Entrepreneurship* (pp. 245-256). Covenant University Press.

Pittaway, L., Carmouche, R., & Chell, E. (1998). The way forward: Leadership research in the hospitality industry. *Hospital Management, 17*(4), 407–426. doi:10.1016/S0278-4319(98)00035-8

Rabiul, M. K., Shamsudin, F. M., Yean, T. F., & Patwary, A. K. (2022). Linking leadership styles to communication competency and work engagement: Evidence from the hotel industry. *Journal of Hospitality and Tourism Insights,* 1-22.

Radwan, H., & Radwan, I. (2020). Leadership Styles in the Hotel Sector and Its Effect on Employees' Creativity and Organizational Commitment. *International Journal of Social and Business Sciences, 14*(3), 169–179.

Raguž, I. V. (2007). The interdependence between characteristics and leadership style of managers in the hospitality industry in Dubrovnik-Neretva county: Empirical research. *Management, 12*(2), 57–68.

Rue, L., & Byars, L. (2008). Management: Skills and Application (13th ed.). McGraw-Hill/Irwin.

Schriesheim, C., & Kerr, S. (1974). Psychometric properties of the Ohio state leadership scales. *Psychological Bulletin, 81*(11), 756–765. doi:10.1037/h0037277 PMID:4612572

Seters, D. A., & Field, R. H. (1990). The Evolution of Leadership Theory. *Journal of Organizational Change Management, 3*(3), 29–45. doi:10.1108/09534819010142139

Sivaruban, S. (2021). A Critical Perspective of Leadership Theories. *Business Ethics and Leadership, 5*(1), 57–65. doi:10.21272/bel.5(1).57-65.2021

Stogdill, R. M. (1974). *Handbook of leadership; A survey of theory and research.* Free Press.

Tajedin, B., Moradi, M., & Alitabrizi, M. (2017). Study of the relationship between managers leadership style and employees Satisfaction based on Likert theory. *International Journal of Human Capital in Urban Management, 2*(2), 147–154.

Tolbert, P. S., & Hall, R. H. (2016). Organisations: Structures, Processes, and Outcomes (10th ed.). Routledge.

Touma, J. (2021). Theories X and Y in Combination for Effective Change during Economic Crisis. *Journal of Human Resource and Sustainability Studies, 09*(9), 20–29. doi:10.4236/jhrss.2021.91002

Uslu, O. (2019). A General Overview to Leadership Theories From A Critical Perspective. *Marketing and Management Innovations, 1*, 161–172. doi:10.21272/mmi.2019.1-13

WGU. (2020, June 17). *Successful leadership attitudes and behaviors.* June 18, 2022 tarihinde WGU (Western Governor University): https://www.wgu.edu/blog/successful-leadership-attitudes-behaviors2006.html

WGU. (2020, April 7). *Leadership theories and styles*. June 18, 2022 tarihinde WGU: https://www.wgu.edu/blog/leadership-theories-styles2004.html#:~:text=The%20behavioral%20leadership%20theory%20focuses,created%20based%20on%20learnable%20behavior

Wice, P. B. (1995). Court Reform and Judicial Leadership: A Theoretical Discussion. *The Justice System Journal, 17*(3), 309–321. doi:10.1080/23277556.1995.10871212

Yago, A. G. (1982). Leadership: Perspectives in Theory and Research. *Management Science, 28*(3), 315–336. doi:10.1287/mnsc.28.3.315

Yamak, Ö. U., & Eyüpoğlu, Ş. Z. (2018). Leadership Styles of Hotel Managers in Northern Cyprus: Which Style is Dominant? *International Journal of Organizational Leadership, 7*(7), 1–11. doi:10.33844/ijol.2018.60202

Yukl, G. (1989). Managerial Leadership: A Review of TIneory and Research. *Journal of Management, 15*(2), 251–289. doi:10.1177/014920638901500207

Zheng, Y., Graham, L., Epitropaki, O., & Snape, E. (2020). Service Leadership, Work Engagement, and Service Performance: The Moderating Role of Leader Skills. *Group & Organization Management, 45*(1), 43-74.

Chapter 4
Laissez-Faire Leadership

Muhammad Junaid Ahsan
https://orcid.org/0000-0002-5754-8187
University of Pisa, Italy

Muhammad Hasham Khalid
Riphah International University, Pakistan

ABSTRACT

Leaders are expected to create significant impacts on their followers. The present study aims to further investigate this corollary by elaborating on the laissez-faire approach in leadership. Generally, leadership in a laissez-faire style is considered destructive. It is assumed that leaders and followers do not remain effective in laissez-faire styled leadership. Followers expect the presence and close involvement of their leader in different situations. And if they do not find their leader's presence, then it is natural that they might think about their leader as incompetent or reluctant. This may later lead them to lose confidence in their leader. In this study, the authors have used social learning theory to elaborate what could be the effects of a laissez-faire approach in leadership on team members' performance. Research has indicated that negative impacts of the laissez-faire approach in leadership are more likely to affect employees who have relatively deeper concepts about mutual relationships.

INTRODUCTION

Leaders are expected to create great impacts on their followers. Our present study aims to further investigate this corollary by elaborating on the laissez-faire approach in leadership and the history of laissez-faire. Given the widespread role expectations that leaders should handle the majority of their team's leadership responsibilities, one strategy that organizations looking to promote leadership might use is to encourage their leaders to be more passive (Wellman, Mayer, Ong, & DeRue, 2016). When supervisors perform in this way, they are referred to as laissez-faire formal leaders since they rarely take necessary action or make choices (Piccolo, Greenbaum, Hartog, & Folger, 2010). Generally, leadership in a laissez-faire style is considered destructive (Klasmeier, Schleu, Millhoff, Poethke, & Bormann, 2022; Pahi & HAMID, 2016). It is assumed that mutual trust between leader and followers does not remain effective

DOI: 10.4018/978-1-6684-6713-8.ch004

in laissez-faire styled leadership. Followers expect the presence and close involvement of their leader in different situations. In addition, if they do not find their leader's presence, then it is natural that they might think about their leader as incompetent or reluctant. This may later lead them to lose confidence in their leader (Griffin, Hanna, Smith, & Kirkman, 2022). Therefore, to keep the trust of their followers aligned with the ultimate cause, the leader must show continuous involvement in affairs with followers.

Research has indicated that negative impacts of the laissez-faire approach in leadership are more likely to affect employees, which have relatively deeper concepts about mutual relationships. The laissez-faire approach in leadership will finally result in making them feel less comfortable contributing toward the ultimate goal. Therefore, to achieve mutual goals efficiently, it is essential to provide the followers with adequate leadership, which understands them well and directs them according to different situations.

The findings in this study contribute in many significant ways. The most significant finding of our study is that team members' perceptions of their supervisors' effective leadership behavior and that the presence of leadership does not always translate into a team's members feeling the need for leadership or acting to give it.

HISTORY OF LAISSEZ FAIRE

A social system that tries to give markets rather than politics the blame for economic outcomes is known as laissez-faire. Beyond this broad interpretation, its precise meaning has remained ambiguous and contradictory. Some maintain that it pertains to a government that offers little more than minimal defenses against criminal conduct, such as in Carlyle (1885) "anarchy plus the constable" or Lassalle (1985)" night-watchman state." Few significant thinkers have adopted this extreme interpretation of the term as a reflection of their beliefs, despite its frequent use of it by critics and dogmatists. The word can refer to a government strategy that seeks to guarantee not only peace, defense, and commutative justice, but also public works that are regarded as vital and unlikely to be followed by the private sector (Viner, 1960). Others contend that the term can refer to a much wider range of activities. By adopting an unintelligibly broad interpretation of its meaning, one can regard canonical thinkers such as Smith and Copley (1995) to be proponents of laissez-faire.

Laissez-faire has been most frequently used to refer to an implicit standard of inaction to which economic and political measures might be measured, rather than a specific and highly articulated system of political philosophy, in part because of these uncertainties. In his Principles of Political Economy, Mill (1848) offered a famous expression of this philosophy, writing, "Letting alone, in short, should be the general practice: every departure from it, unless required by some enormous good, is a certain evil" (Mill, 1848, p. 865). When applied in this way, laissez-faire can serve as a principle that puts the onus of proof on those who advocate for government involvement in the market economy. Numerous economists disagree with these applications of the term, believing that they provide nothing more than a "simple handy rule of practice" that is "completely devoid of any scientific authority" (Cairnes, 1873, p. 244). However, despite forecasts of its impending demise, laissez-faire has consistently proven to be a very robust idea.

Although it did not become widely used in English until the middle of the 1800s, the phrase laissez-faire had already entered French studies of political economy more than a century earlier. Turgot (2014) traced the occurrence's beginning to an event that allegedly occurred in the late seventeenth century, when the French businessman François Legendre allegedly said, "laissez-nous faire" to Louis XIV's meddling finance minister Colbert.

Although de Boisguilbert (2014) publications later had slight variants of this formula, it wasn't until the middle of the seventeenth century that it gained more popularity. Vincent de Gournay is famously credited by Dupont de Nemours (1883) with popularizing the expression "laissez faire, laissez passer" during that time, however, Gournay left no publications to support the assertion. The Marquis d'Argenson, a contemporary of Gournay who widely disseminated his writings but only published one anonymous letter in his lifetime, used the term laissez-faire to denote an economic system for the first time.

Laissez-faire was hardly mentioned during the remainder of the eighteenth century. This idea, which was never employed by Quesnay and only twice in Turgot's writings, was not shared by the majority of Physiocrats. Smith and Copley (1995) never used the phrase either, and there has long been debate among academics over whether it applies to his worldview. Smith was a staunch supporter of free trade and consistently questioned the government's ability to sway the outcomes of the market, but he also advocated for public education, pushed for strict anti-monopoly laws, supported aggressive government action to improve the lot of the poor, and expressed concerns about the repetitive nature of mass production. The phrase "laissez-faire" cannot be retroactively applied to Smith's work without qualification, despite the fact that there are many aspects of his writings that supporters of the philosophy can respect. The term's connection to the writings of Malthus (2015); Ordoliberalism et al. has been overblown, and it is also absent from their works. Although Ordoliberalism et al. claimed that the proper "watchword of government" should be "be quiet" in the first chapter of A Manual of Political Economy, his enthusiasm for bureaucratic oversight and his careful distinction between the "Agenda" and the "Non-agenda" of government made it clear that he supported extensive interventions. Since then, market results have been justified using Malthus's negative predictions from his Essay on the Principle of Population, but Malthus himself found advantages in severe trade limitations. Although Ricardo was a well-known proponent of free trade, his work's political consequences were murky, and his theory of value ended up serving as the main argument for socialism economics.

Stuart (1901), laissez-faire finally gained widespread acceptance in the English language. Although Mill (1848) embraced laissez-faire as a starting point above which all government interference would need to be justified, he discovered that in reality there were numerous situations where such intervention was appropriate. The ideal government envisioned by Mill accepted responsibility for the maintenance of a learned class, the provision of education, the care of insane people, idiots, and children, the control of practical monopolies, and the management of business dealings that affected outsiders, and the exercise of control over practical monopolies. Cairnes (1873) and Sidgwick (1885), two of Mill (1848) supporters, were harshly critical of those who wanted to turn his qualified rule into a prescriptive philosophy.

Despite Mill (1848) objections, many people came to view the middle decades of the nineteenth century as the heyday of laissez-faire. Richard Cobden strongly promoted free trade in England and used the intransigence of what became known as "the Manchester School" to argue successfully for the removal of the Corn Laws in 1846. Herbert Spencer used cutting-edge evolutionary theories to support a system of economics that reduced redistribution to the poor. In France, Bastiat (1966) used a philosophy of natural rights to carry out the "mission of liberating the entire realm of private action from the encroachments of government" with remarkable regularity (Bastiat, 1966). Walker (1889) noted that in America, laissez-faire had turned into a litmus test for "if a guy were an economist at all" (Walker, 1889, p. 17). There was a surge of interest in "English economics" even in Germany. Support for laissez-faire economic principles started to decline across Europe in the late 1860s. A group of historical economists in Germany, led by Schmoller (1870), contended that the nation's recent adherence to an abstract market ideal had led to terrible inequities. American doctoral students who attended German institutions returned home with fresh skepticism over an economic system that many now identified with their own country. Ely (1884) stated that the new political economy "does not recognize laissez-faire as an excuse for doing nothing while people starve, nor allow the all-sufficiency of competition as a reason for grinding the poor" just a year before the American Economic Association was established (Ely, 1884, p. 64). Support for laissez-faire principles began a steady slide, even in England. British constitutional lawyer Albert Venn Dicey's 1898 Harvard Law School lectures on the relationship between law and public opinion, which were later published in 1905, contained a long lament about the rise of socialism and the ensuing "eclipse" of laissez-faire. Dicey overstated the level of support for laissez-faire among traditional economists, even though many others agreed with him that it had reached its apex. In a speech in 1906, the American economist Irving Fisher claimed that laissez-faire had "generally been abandoned" because of "the cumulative effect of experience," the need for "self-defense" against strong new commercial enterprises, and the growing "popular confidence" in governing bodies that were quickly becoming more competent and effective (Fisher, 1907, p. 18). In a paper titled "The End of Laissez-Faire," published over two decades later, John Maynard Keynes argued that the idea had devolved into a mere "copybook maxim," had no backing from academic economists, and was rapidly losing its appeal to the general public (J. Keynes, 2016; J. M. Keynes, 1927, p. 20). Laissez-faire was on the decrease, according to Fisher and Keynes, and this was a long-term trend that would finally lead to its permanent replacement.

Since the media on both sides of the Atlantic claimed that prior economic upheavals had signaled the end of the laissez-faire era, the events of the Great Depression first seemed to corroborate these predictions. Even the most renowned free trade advocates wanted to dissociate themselves from the concept. Friedrich Hayek chastised his colleagues for their dogmatic laissez-faire support and disrespect for the "positive" function of their profession to assess where and when state action was desirable in his first lecture at the London School of Economics. Later, in his 1944 article The Road to Serfdom, Hayek criticized laissez-faire as "a highly ambiguous and false formulation of the concepts on which a liberal policy is founded" (Hayek, 1944, p. 118). Then, he listed a wide range of initiatives for which he thought government action was justified, including setting work hour restrictions, providing infrastructure for transportation, outlawing harmful business practices, putting price controls on monopolies, and providing social insurance that ensured everyone had access to a minimal level of food and shelter.

Stronger words were used by Hayek's closest allies in the US to indicate their opposition to laissez-faire. Early in the 1920s, economist Frank Knight of the University of Chicago claimed that laissez-faire economists' ethical judgments were based on unfounded presumptions. He rebuked them for ignoring the following facts: knowledge was frequently constrained; humans were irrational and impulsive; desires were influenced by culture; goods were immobile or indivisible; rivals sought cooperation; transactions affected more than just the parties involved; and economic productivity did not correspond to moral desolation (Knight & Paterson, 2018). Henry Simons, a student of Knight's, promoted a "positive agenda for laissez-faire" that included a proposal for the dissolution of major businesses into many smaller economic units and a steeply progressive income tax. In urging the rejection of laissez-faire in favor of less dogmatic methods of market promotion, Knight and Simons joined Hayek. However, in the decades following World War II, several distinct communities of market advocates created innovative new arguments against government intrusion, making forecasts of the collapse or supersession of laissez-faire seem wrong. Hayek's former mentor in Vienna, Ludwig von Mises, who immigrated to the United States in 1938 and eventually accepted a chair at New York University, oversaw the development of one of these communities. According to Mises' postwar work Human Action, the discipline of economics developed through rigorous aprioristic reasoning, which proved that government involvement was only justified in situations involving the maintenance of economic freedom (Von Mises, 2002). The "Austrian" beliefs of Mises' ardent community of adherents and successors were rejected by an economics profession that grew more unfamiliar with their syllogistic logic and literary style. Ayn Rand, a Soviet émigré who wrote widely read books like The Fountainhead (1943) and Atlas Shrugged had a wider impact (published in 1957). The "Objectivism" theory of Ayn Rand justified market outcomes by pointing out a direct correlation between economic productivity and moral apathy. Mises and Rand both upheld the laissez-faire philosophy while criticizing peers who were more prepared to accept exceptions from the rule.

But Milton Friedman, an economist at the University of Chicago, was the most significant academic proponent of laissez-faire during the second half of the 20th century. Friedman created a multifaceted attack against the Keynesian consensus that many of his colleagues embraced by relying on the empirical research techniques and mathematical vocabulary of postwar economics. In several significant analytical writings, he claimed that the Great Depression was driven by ineffective monetary policy rather than market inefficiencies and that fiscal policy had not successfully boosted demand as Keynesians had predicted. Invoking the work of his colleague George Stigler, Friedman claimed that fears about monopoly advantages were mostly unfounded and that regulators frequently served the firms they were tasked with monitoring. He developed these points with the release of Capitalism and Freedom in 1962, expressing a thorough political perspective. Friedman campaigned for the elimination of government operations including licensing agencies, disaster relief, military conscription, and national parks because he believed that usually, government causes more problems than it fixes. Even his favorable ideas, such as a negative income tax and school vouchers, were meant to be workable alternatives on the way to a government without assistance or public education. Friedman's rise to prominence symbolized the revival of political interest in an extreme form of laissez-faire. His ideal state did little more than enforce contracts and perform police duties.

Laissez-faire proponents like Mises, Rand, Friedman and their adherents have long portrayed it as a very limited kind of governmental involvement in the lives of citizens. However, their detractors countered that laissez-faire did not develop naturally and that it, too, was only made feasible by considerable government interference. In The Great Transformation, Karl Polanyi argued that laissez-faire was not natural and that free markets could not have developed by simply letting events play out naturally (Polanyi, 2001, p. 145). The self-regulating market could only be preserved by regular and frequently severe interventions since it was constantly challenged by dangers ranging from monopolies to trade unions. The limitations on democracy that "neoliberal" economists and politicians have enforced to safeguard their favored systems of commercial exchange have recently been highlighted by economic sociologists. They have stressed that such regimes frequently place the economic interests of people in positions of political and financial influence ahead of political freedoms. According to these readings, the phrase "laissez-faire" is inaccurately used to describe a system in which the government carefully crafts the terms of exchange and limits the democratic right to intervene.

The phrase laissez-faire is still vague. It has been used to refer to both thinkers who want to limit government to only police responsibilities and those who support much more expansive roles consistent with those of the majority of contemporary democratic governments. It has functioned as both a normative standard and the basis for an economic worldview; as a broad moral doctrine built on a productivity-based ethos and as a specific economic doctrine centered on wealth accumulation; as a pessimistic limitation on the exercise of popular democracy and as an optimistic attempt to broaden freedom of choice. Critics have portrayed it as dependent on the ongoing use of state authority, while supporters have portrayed it as a lack of intervention. Laissez-faire remains a very important notion in discussions of political economy, regardless of its significance, rationale, and conceptual feasibility. The phrase's continued ubiquity depends on its inherent ambiguity, which permits its definition to change to suit the demands of people who use it.

LAISSEZ-FAIRE LEADERSHIP AND TEAM MEMBERS

Organizational research has long been at the forefront of leadership. Negative leadership styles have not received as much attention in studies as positive leadership styles have (Schyns & Schilling, 2013; Tepper, 2007; Tuffour, Gali, & Tuffour, 2022). The notion that "bad is stronger than good" (Baumeister, Bratslavsky, Finkenauer, & Vohs, 2001) suggests that negative leadership styles may have greater influence than positive ones. Consequently, it is surprising that there has not been much research in this area (Hinkin & Schriesheim, 2008a). Despite recent interest in destructive leadership, less active but just as harmful kinds of leadership, such as laissez-faire leadership, did not garner the same attention (Che, Zhou, Kessler, & Spector, 2017). Laissez-faire leadership, which is the most severe kind of inactivity, can nonetheless have negative impacts on workers and organizations (Hinkin & Schriesheim, 2008a; Skogstad et al., 2014). Laissez-faire refers to a strategy of influencing others in the workplace that is "hands-off, let things ride"(Squires, 2016). Laissez-faire leadership is "the absence of leadership" and "the avoidance of involvement" (Bass & Avolio, 1990; Judge, Piccolo, & Ilies, 2004, p. 756). Leaders who practice laissez-faire usually portray themselves as having abdicated their duties and responsibilities (Lewin, Lippitt, & White, 1939).

Similar to "impoverished management," which Blake and Mouton (1985) defined as a leader who exerts little effort to perform important duties and has little concern for their staff, this leadership style lacks both of these qualities (Einarsen, Aasland, & Skogstad, 2007). Lewin et al. (1939) assert that laissez-faire leaders disobey the duties and obligations placed on them, even though they have been nominated for leadership positions and possess them. So, in addition to "lack of presence," laissez-faire leadership should be seen as "zero leadership." Despite Schyns and Schilling (2013) disagreement, Einarsen et al. (2007) definition of destructive leadership includes laissez-faire leadership. Laissez-faire leadership undercuts the legitimate interests of businesses and their employees by compromising corporate goals and/or subordinates' well-being (Einarsen et al., 2007). Conversely, Bass and Avolio (1990) view passive corrective leadership as an ineffective leadership style that waits for anything to go wrong before stepping in, as well as active corrective leadership that monitors and focuses on flaws.

Laissez-faire leadership steers clear of making crucial choices and offers minimal aid in fixing problems (Piccolo et al., 2010). Under laissez-faire leadership, there is no job enhancement intervention or performance feedback follow-up (Gill, 2011). For instance, laissez-faire leadership has been associated with worse job satisfaction, leader effectiveness, satisfaction, and performance (Judge et al., 2004). Similar conclusions were reached by Skogstad et al. (2014), who found that the only (unfavorable) leadership predictor of work satisfaction over two years was laissez-faire leadership. Depending on their inclinations, people may react to laissez-faire leadership in different ways. An important personal characteristic that has been considered in previous leadership research is the self-concept (Van Knippenberg, Van Knippenberg, De Cremer, & Hogg, 2004). The way that people describe themselves is known as their self-concept, and as such, it affects how they see themselves and other people (Brewer & Gardner,

1996; Lord & Brown, 2004). It is made up of several drives, sources of one's worth, and self-awareness (Brickson, 2000). Each of the three facets of the self-concept—individual, relational, and collective—has been identified as a unique layer of the construct (Brewer & Gardner, 1996; Lord & Brown, 2004). A relational self-concept, which relates to the relevance of dyadic interactions in people's lives (Johnson & Saboe, 2011), is a conspicuous trait that may affect how employees react to leaders because leadership entails dyadic relationships between leaders and subordinates (Brewer & Gardner, 1996). Laissez-faire leadership is likely to have a greater impact on and a stronger reaction from employees with a strong relational self-concept because it threatens their objectives, needs, and identity-defining relationship (Wisse & Sleebos, 2016). Their expectation that the leader will take care of their relationship needs and work-related concerns may be violated by the lack of decisions and contact with the leader (Lord & Brown, 2001). Because of this, people with strong relational self-concepts could find laissez-faire leadership to be gloomy, which will result in negative perceptions of their managers and the business. Laissez-faire leaders also neglect to acknowledge and give feedback to their staff (Hinkin & Schriesheim, 2008b), and they frequently disregard the needs of their followers since they do not address workplace issues (Yukl, 2010). These leaders lack organizational skills when handling priorities and do not take sides in disputes (Bass, 1998). According to their poll, Aasland, Skogstad, Notelaers, Nielsen, and Einarsen (2010) found that laissez-faire leadership was the most common type of negative leadership, with 21% of employees reporting that their bosses had acted in a laissez-faire manner toward them in the preceding six months.

Neglecting one's duties as a leader is detrimental to the company and the employees (Hinkin & Schriesheim, 2008a). Laissez-faire leadership is damaging as well as ineffectual (Aasland et al., 2010; Einarsen et al., 2007; Skogstad et al., 2014). Laissez-faire leadership is associated with decreased subordinate effort, performance, work satisfaction, perceived leader effectiveness, and leader satisfaction, according to empirical data (Judge et al., 2004); increased levels of stress and interpersonal disputes (Skogstad, Einarsen, Torsheim, Aasland, & Hetland, 2007); and even greater role confusion and conflict (Skogstad et al., 2014; Skogstad et al., 2007). The typical inactivity of laissez-faire leadership, however, distinguishes it from other harmful leadership ideologies since its bad effects resulting from the absence of constructive acts rather than the presence of destructive ones (Kelloway, Mullen, & Francis, 2006; Tuffour et al., 2022). Therefore, greater study on laissez-faire leadership is required.

DISCUSSION

Numerous significant theoretical advancements are made by our findings. Our findings suggest that perceived role modeling of effective leadership may be a more accurate predictor of leadership than perceived need, and that team leadership models. Our results are comparable to past research that showed that laissez-faire leaders often had negative effects on team members' cognition, conduct, and performance in several aspects (Hinkin & Schriesheim, 2008a; Pahi & HAMID, 2016). Our findings make recommendations for how organizations could counteract the detrimental effects of such leaders. Businesses may take steps to ensure that team members have access to other leaders who follow less lenient leadership principles. This may apply to leaders in the top management group or "skip" levels, who are two to five levels above the team members (Detert & Treviño, 2010; Tuffour et al., 2022). Team members may be more inclined to overlook their immediate supervisor's laissez-faire style if they see other leaders modeling effective leadership and are exposed to less laissez-faire behavior.

Organizations could make sure that teams with less laissez-faire leaders who are opportunistic have more team members. These team members can counteract the impacts of such a leader and assist the team in maintaining high levels of task performance by continually exercising high degrees of leadership.

CONCLUSION

A further perspective on the influence of laissez-faire leaders on team task performance. We suggested that a detrimental indirect effect due to team members' perceptions of good leadership modeling. Because team members believe a laissez-faire leader models effective leadership less, they exhibit less leadership themselves. We also found that a laissez-faire leader can be more adversely related to teams.

Laissez-faire leadership tries to avoid influencing their followers, instead letting them spend their time however they wish. In the lack of direction, employees follow their professional objectives and even have the freedom to establish new objectives that are independent of the leader. Even though the leader does not directly affect the followers, they may nevertheless regard the leader as a valuable resource. Although they don't try to influence their followers, laissez-faire leaders are nonetheless in charge of the behavior and development of their flock. As a result, followers can use the leader as a sort of "safety net," enabling them to take risks while performing their jobs. The followers may expand their conception of themselves to include the leader, as they perceive this part of the leader as a significant resource for their interests and creativity.

LIMITATIONS AND DIRECTIONS FOR FUTURE RESEARCH

A more thorough understanding of who the prospective team leaders are and how their leadership behavior might be supported is crucial if businesses are to effectively fulfill the coordination expectations imposed by the modern business environment. The chapter tried to explain how laissez-faire leaders affect their team members, which adds to the growing corpus of study and theory in the field of leadership. We believe that the implications of our research will spur researchers to consider the dynamics between leaders and teams in more depth and to look further into the causes and effects of leadership behavior.

Like all research, the work described here has some restrictions. First, the decline in their social exchange relationships with team members (Cropanzano & Mitchell, 2005) the depletion of team members' resources (Hobfoll, 1989); or a lack of clarity regarding roles are other factors that may contribute to the detrimental effects of laissez-faire leaders (Skogstad et al., 2014). The validity of these and other theoretical explanations of how laissez-faire leaders impact teams might be investigated in further research. Second, we built our investigation onto the prior work that highlights the significance of leaders modeling good leadership conduct (Dragoni, Park, Soltis, & Forte-Trammell, 2014). We were able to link our mechanism with the team members' focused outcome by focusing on how effective leadership was considered to be modeled. An alternative and presumably more accurate empirically test would evaluate how team members feel their leader exhibits a laissez-faire attitude as well as how laissez-faire they are themselves. However, it would undoubtedly be useful for future research to evaluate such modeling. Further research is required to test these statements empirically.

Funding

This research received no specific grant from any funding agency in the public, commercial, or not-for-profit sectors.

REFERENCES

Aasland, M. S., Skogstad, A., Notelaers, G., Nielsen, M. B., & Einarsen, S. (2010). The prevalence of destructive leadership behaviour. *British Journal of Management*, *21*(2), 438–452.

Bass, B. M. (1998). Transformational leadership: Industrial, military, and educational impact. Academic Press.

Bass, B. M., & Avolio, B. J. (1990). *Transformational leadership development: Manual for the multifactor leadership questionnaire*. Consulting Psychologists Press.

Bastiat, F. (1966). *Economic Harmonies*. Foundation for Economic Education.

Baumeister, R. F., Bratslavsky, E., Finkenauer, C., & Vohs, K. D. (2001). Bad is stronger than good. *Review of General Psychology*, *5*(4), 323–370. doi:10.1037/1089-2680.5.4.323

Blake, R. R., & Mouton, J. S. (1985). *The managerial grid III: A new look at the classic that has boosted productivity and profits for thousands of corporations worldwide*. Gulf Publishing Company, Book Division.

Brewer, M. B., & Gardner, W. (1996). Who is this" We"? Levels of collective identity and self representations. *Journal of Personality and Social Psychology*, *71*(1), 83–93. doi:10.1037/0022-3514.71.1.83

Brickson, S. (2000). The impact of identity orientation on individual and organizational outcomes in demographically diverse settings. *Academy of Management Review*, *25*(1), 82–101. doi:10.2307/259264

Cairnes, J. E. (1873). *Essays in political economy*. Macmillan and Company.

Carlyle, T. (1885). *Latter-day pamphlets* (Vol. 5). Chapman and Hall, Limited.

Che, X. X., Zhou, Z. E., Kessler, S. R., & Spector, P. E. (2017). Stressors beget stressors: The effect of passive leadership on employee health through workload and work–family conflict. *Work and Stress*, *31*(4), 338–354. doi:10.1080/02678373.2017.1317881

Cropanzano, R., & Mitchell, M. S. (2005). Social exchange theory: An interdisciplinary review. *Journal of Management*, *31*(6), 874–900. doi:10.1177/0149206305279602

de Boisguilbert, P. (2014). *Détail de la France* [Detail of France]. Institut Coppet.

Detert, J. R., & Treviño, L. K. (2010). Speaking up to higher-ups: How supervisors and skip-level leaders influence employee voice. *Organization Science*, *21*(1), 249–270. doi:10.1287/orsc.1080.0405

Dragoni, L., Park, H., Soltis, J., & Forte-Trammell, S. (2014). Show and tell: How supervisors facilitate leader development among transitioning leaders. *The Journal of Applied Psychology*, *99*(1), 66–86. doi:10.1037/a0034452 PMID:24060160

Dupont de Nemours, P. S. (1883). Décret sur la circulation des poudres, lors de la séance du 4 juillet 1790 [Decree on the circulation of powders, during the session of July 4. 1790]. *Archives Parlementaires de la Révolution Française*, *16*(1), 694–694.

Einarsen, S., Aasland, M. S., & Skogstad, A. (2007). Destructive leadership behaviour: A definition and conceptual model. *The Leadership Quarterly*, *18*(3), 207–216. doi:10.1016/j.leaqua.2007.03.002

Ely, R. T. (1884). *The past and the present of political economy*. Johns Hopkins University. doi:10.5479il.405460.39088006748982

Fisher, I. (1907). Why has the doctrine of laissez faire been abandoned? *Science*, *25*(627), 18–27. doi:10.1126cience.25.627.18 PMID:17739703

Gill, R. (2011). Theory and practice of leadership. *Sage (Atlanta, Ga.)*.

Griffin, R. W., Hanna, A. A., Smith, T. A., & Kirkman, B. L. (2022). How Bad Leaders Impact Organizational Effectiveness. *Overcoming Bad Leadership in Organizations*, 224.

Hayek, F. (1944). *The Road to Serfdom*. G. Routledge & Sons.

Hinkin, T. R., & Schriesheim, C. A. (2008a). An examination of" nonleadership": From laissez-faire leadership to leader reward omission and punishment omission. *The Journal of Applied Psychology*, *93*(6), 1234–1248. doi:10.1037/a0012875 PMID:19025245

Hinkin, T. R., & Schriesheim, C. A. (2008b). A theoretical and empirical examination of the transactional and non-leadership dimensions of the Multifactor Leadership Questionnaire (MLQ). *The Leadership Quarterly*, *19*(5), 501–513. doi:10.1016/j.leaqua.2008.07.001

Hobfoll, S. E. (1989). Conservation of resources: A new attempt at conceptualizing stress. *The American Psychologist*, *44*(3), 513–524. doi:10.1037/0003-066X.44.3.513 PMID:2648906

Johnson, R. E., & Saboe, K. N. (2011). Measuring implicit traits in organizational research: Development of an indirect measure of employee implicit self-concept. *Organizational Research Methods*, *14*(3), 530–547. doi:10.1177/1094428110363617

Judge, T. A., Piccolo, R. F., & Ilies, R. (2004). The forgotten ones? The validity of consideration and initiating structure in leadership research. *The Journal of Applied Psychology*, *89*(1), 36–51. doi:10.1037/0021-9010.89.1.36 PMID:14769119

Kelloway, E. K., Mullen, J., & Francis, L. (2006). Divergent effects of transformational and passive leadership on employee safety. *Journal of Occupational Health Psychology*, *11*(1), 76–86. doi:10.1037/1076-8998.11.1.76 PMID:16551176

Keynes, J. (2016). *Essays in persuasion*. Springer.

Keynes, J. M. (1927). The End of Laissez-Faire (London, 1926). *Collected Writings*, 9.

Klasmeier, K. N., Schleu, J. E., Millhoff, C., Poethke, U., & Bormann, K. C. (2022). On the destructiveness of laissez-faire versus abusive supervision: A comparative, multilevel investigation of destructive forms of leadership. *European Journal of Work and Organizational Psychology, 31*(3), 406–420. doi:10.1080/1359432X.2021.1968375

Knight, B., & Paterson, F. (2018). Behavioural competencies of sustainability leaders: An empirical investigation. *Journal of Organizational Change Management, 31*(3), 557–580. doi:10.1108/JOCM-02-2017-0035

Lassalle, F. (1985). Workers' Programme On the particular connection between the present period of history andthe idea of the Workers' Estate (April 1862/January 1863). *Economy and Society, 14*(3), 337–349. doi:10.1080/03085148500000016

Lewin, K., Lippitt, R., & White, R. K. (1939). Patterns of aggressive behavior in experimentally created "social climates". *The Journal of Social Psychology, 10*(2), 269–299. doi:10.1080/00224545.1939.9713366

Lord, R., & Brown, D. (2004). *Organization and management series. Leadership processes and follower self-identity*. Lawrence Erlbaum Associates Publishers.

Lord, R. G., & Brown, D. J. (2001). Leadership, values, and subordinate self-concepts. *The Leadership Quarterly, 12*(2), 133–152. doi:10.1016/S1048-9843(01)00072-8

Malthus, T. (2015). *An essay on the principle of population and other writings*.

Mill, J. S. (1848). *Principles of Political Economy*. Prometheus Books. www. nowecantsong. org

Pahi, M. H., & Hamid, K. A. (2016). The magic of destructive leadership: Laissez-faire leadership and commitment to service quality. *International Journal of Economic Perspectives, 10*(4).

Piccolo, R. F., Greenbaum, R., Hartog, D. N., & Folger, R. (2010). The relationship between ethical leadership and core job characteristics. *Journal of Organizational Behavior, 31*(2-3), 259–278. doi:10.1002/job.627

Polanyi, K. (2001). *The great transformation: The political and economic origins of our time*. Beacon press.

Schmoller, G. (1870). *Zur Geschichte der deutschen Kleingewerbe im 19. Jahrhundert Gustav Schmoller*. Waisenhauses.

Schyns, B., & Schilling, J. (2013). How bad are the effects of bad leaders? A meta-analysis of destructive leadership and its outcomes. *The Leadership Quarterly, 24*(1), 138–158. doi:10.1016/j.leaqua.2012.09.001

Sidgwick, H. (1885). *The scope and method of economic science*. Macmillan and Company.

Skogstad, A., Aasland, M. S., Nielsen, M. B., Hetland, J., Matthiesen, S. B., & Einarsen, S. (2014). The relative effects of constructive, laissez-faire, and tyrannical leadership on subordinate job satisfaction: Results from two prospective and representative studies. *Zeitschrift für Psychologie mit Zeitschrift für Angewandte Psychologie, 222*(4), 221.

Skogstad, A., Einarsen, S., Torsheim, T., Aasland, M. S., & Hetland, H. (2007). The destructiveness of laissez-faire leadership behavior. *Journal of Occupational Health Psychology*, *12*(1), 80–92. doi:10.1037/1076-8998.12.1.80 PMID:17257068

Smith, A., & Copley, S. (1995). *Adam Smith's Wealth of nations: new interdisciplinary essays* (Vol. 1). Manchester University Press.

Squires, V. (2016). *Leadership: Theory and Practice*. Sage.

Stuart, M. J. (1901). *Principles of political economy*. Forgotten Books.

Tepper, B. J. (2007). Abusive supervision in work organizations: Review, synthesis, and research agenda. *Journal of Management*, *33*(3), 261–289. doi:10.1177/0149206307300812

Tuffour, J. K., Gali, A. M., & Tuffour, M. K. (2022). Managerial leadership style and employee commitment: Evidence from the financial sector. *Global Business Review*, *23*(3), 543–560. doi:10.1177/0972150919874170

Turgot, A.-R. (2014). *Ecrits économiques*. Calmann-Lévy.

Van Knippenberg, D., Van Knippenberg, B., De Cremer, D., & Hogg, M. A. (2004). Leadership, self, and identity: A review and research agenda. *The Leadership Quarterly*, *15*(6), 825–856. doi:10.1016/j.leaqua.2004.09.002

Viner, J. (1960). The intellectual history of laissez faire. *The Journal of Law & Economics*, *3*, 45–69. doi:10.1086/466561

Von Mises, L. (2002). *Epistemological problems of economics*. Ludwig von Mises Institute.

Walker, F. A. (1889). Recent progress of political economy in the United States. *Publications of the American Economic Association*, *4*(4), 17–40.

Wellman, N., Mayer, D. M., Ong, M., & DeRue, D. S. (2016). When are do-gooders treated badly? Legitimate power, role expectations, and reactions to moral objection in organizations. *The Journal of Applied Psychology*, *101*(6), 793–814. doi:10.1037/apl0000094 PMID:26882445

Wisse, B., & Sleebos, E. (2016). When change causes stress: Effects of self-construal and change consequences. *Journal of Business and Psychology*, *31*(2), 249–264. doi:10.100710869-015-9411-z PMID:27226696

Yukl, G. (2010). *Leadership in organizations*. Pearson.

Chapter 5
Determination of the Most Suitable Leadership Type in the Hotel Industry Using Best–Worst Method

Kevser Arman
https://orcid.org/0000-0002-4400-5976
Pamukkale University, Turkey

Arzu Organ
https://orcid.org/0000-0002-2400-4343
Pamukkale University, Turkey

ABSTRACT

The new age requires awareness of different types of leadership. Every enterprise may need a different type of leadership for their various purposes. Determining the most suitable leadership type for a specific industry is a quite complex issue so it can be considered a decision problem. This chapter aims to determine most suitable leadership type for hotel industry using best worst method (BWM) which is one of the multi-criteria decision-making (MCDM) tools. The results have revealed that transformational leadership is the most suitable leadership in hotel industry, followed by visionary leadership and authentic leadership. It is recommended that hotel managers should adopt these three leadership types to motivate followers, create positive culture, and maximize productivity in the hotel industry. This chapter is believed to fill the literature gap since limited studies have integrated MCDM methods with this area. Moreover, the findings of the study have revealed useful insights for hotel managers.

INTRODUCTION

Leadership has become a major research in management with the growing awareness of the importance of leadership (Hilton et al., 2021: 1042). Leadership has an important place in achieving the goals of the

DOI: 10.4018/978-1-6684-6713-8.ch005

enterprises. Previous studies on leadership provide strong evidence that the importance of determining the most suitable leadership type in a specific industry is too great to be ignored. Leadership is a concept as old as human history, is essential management skill that is the process of directing the activities of an organization to achieve of goals (Keklik, 2012: 75; Hilton et al., 2021: 1043). Leadership is one of the most researched management topics since it can affect many variables in terms of businesses, sectors, and countries (Çelik, 2019: 518). Today's managers should have leadership skills, regardless of the field in which they operate. At this point, the leadership qualities of the managers have gain importance (Serinkan, 2005: 86). Determining the most efficient type of leadership for an organization is closely related to the success of the organization (Zendeh & Aali, 2011: 20). Which leadership type is the most suitable for an enterprise is a very complex issue. Every enterprise may need a different type of leadership for their various purposes. At this point, determining the most suitable leadership type can be considered as a decision problem.

The World Travel and Tourism Council (WTTC, 2022) have revaled that tourism accounted for 6.1% of the World's gross domestic product (GDP) in 2021. In addition to this, tourism is growing sector in the world and it plays a major role in economic development of countries (Sandıkcı et al., 2015: 166). Similarly, as stated by Çelik (2019), tourism is a growing sector day by day and it continues to be the focus of attention of researchers. The growth of the tourism industry means the growth of the hotel industry. For this reason, hotel industry is one of the sectors that attracts the attention of both managers and academics. The purpose of this study is to evaluate leadership types and determine most suitable leadership type in the hotel industry by Best Worst Method (BWM) which is one of the Multi-Criteria Decision Making (MCDM) tools. The main question of this study is "What is the most suitable leadership type for hotel industry in Turkey?" For this reason, ten leadership types as criteria have been determined based on review of literature. However, autocratic leadership has been excluded from the among criteria because it has been found to be the least suitable type of leadership according to expert opinion and in many previous study findings. Therefore, leadership types are determined as digital leadership, democratic leadership, authentic leadership, servant leadership, transformational leadership, transactional leadership, charismatic leadership, visionary leadership, and delegative leadership. Brief descriptions of the nine leadership types handled in the study are given below.

Digital leadership is a process that brings about changes in attitudes, feelings, thoughts, and behaviors, supported by information technology. Digital leaders utilize technological tools in their leadership process (Salamzadeh et al., 2022: 198).

Democratic leadership is primarily about the decision-making. Decision making are done by the leader and the group. Democratic leaders give importance the opinions of the followers and offers them the opportunity to make contribute in the decision making process (Hilton et al., 2021: 1044).

Authentic leadership can be expressed as a process to build leader obligation by honesty, respect all the opinions from followers. Authentic leaders improve engagement and satisfaction so folllower's identity is strengthened (Purwanto et al., 2021: 3).

Servant leadership is basically based on promoting the development and well-being of its followers (Hai and Van, 2021: 247). Servant leaders have some distinct characteristics such as: honesty, humility, focus on followers' success and decentralization (Küçük & Yavuz, 2021: 83).

Transformational leadership consist of individualized consideration, intellectual stimulation, charisma, and motivation (Yukl, 1999: 286). Transformational leaders predict potential opportunities, create vision for the future, remove resistance to change (Zorlu et al., 2016: 214).

Transactional leadership can be expressed as a process in which the followers is rewarded or punished for achieving certain goals. Transactional leaders recognize behavior, needs of followers, and motivate them to their work role (Jung, 2001: 187-188).

Charismatic leadership can be defined as a leader who can lead his or her followers to behave in the way he wants with his characteristics. Charismatic leaders develop strong emotional bonds with their followers, thereby motivating them for superior performance (Fuller, 1996: 272).

Visionary leadership provides opportunities to meet an organization's needs and foster its capacity in creative ways. Visionary leaders create a clear, realistic, and compelling vision for their followers (Taylor et al., 2014: 567).

Delegative leadership can be defined as a concept in which employees have great freedom to make decisions in order to achieve the determined goals. Delegative leaders provide resources and materials, and he or she can give support when it necessary but his ideas are not binding on the activities of his followers (Yörük et al., 2011: 105).

The significance of this study can be evaluated from several aspects. A limited number of studies have used the MCDM method to select the most appropriate leadership type and it can be seen that these studies applied classical and popular MCDM methods. In addition to this, BWM has not yet been used in this area. Therefore, this study helps to provide mathematical model to determine the most suitable leadership type in hotel industry. Moreover, the perspectives of managers and academics have been not combined to evaluate leadership types in earlier studies. It is considered significant to combine these two different views to evaluation. Therefore, it is believed that this study fills the gap in the literature by presenting an integrated perspective. Furthermore, studies in the literature have generally used similar leadership types. In this study, less used leadership types such as authentic leadership, servant leadership and digital leadership etc. have also been evaluated. Consequently, the findings of the study are useful to understanding the suitable leadership types for hotel industry in Turkey. With these aspects of the study, it is expected to contribute to researchers and practitioners.

The study is planned as follows. Background presents literature review about leadership types in hotel industry and leadership selection problem using MCDM method. Then, main focus of the chapter has been handled and BWM is introduced for the application. Then, solutions and recommendations section are presented. Finally, future research directions and conclusion are given.

BACKGROUND

Definition of leadership are very hard to define. Moreover, there are many different definitions of leadership in the literature. Although leadership is one of the most studied areas, it has been one of the least agreed-upon concepts. Researchers often define leadership from their own perspective (Sandıkcı et al., 2015: 164). However, it is very significant to have a good definition of leadership since it is one of the terms most widely used in many various areas such as human activity, business, religion, politics, etc. (Silva, 2016: 1). Leadership can be considered as a process person uses to lead the followers. Leaders have a positive effect on the efficiency of the organization. That's why, it is siginificant to understand the nature of leadership types to evaluate their effect on different industry (Al-Malki & Juan, 2018: 51). In addition, many leadership types have been established in the last 30 years based on different purposes of organizations (Tang, 2018: 2590). Since, leadership types is considered as a significant subject for academics and managers (Al-Ababneh, 2013: 93). According to the Nipu and Ahmed (2019), leadership is significant for enterprises since it helps maximize productivity, bring about a positive culture and promote harmony among followers. Ahmad Shakani bin Abdullah et al. (2021) states that leadership affects many process in an organization and it is one of the main factors affect to success or failure of an organization. Therefore, it is vital to identify the suitable type of leadership for the organizations. This study aims to evaluate leadership types and determine most suitable leadership type in the hotel industry. For this reason, earlier studies on this subject are as follows.

Literature Review About Leadership Types in the Hotel Industry

Kozak and Uca (2008) have determined the factors affecting the leadership types of managers in accommodation sector. Findings indicated that democratic and laissez-faire leadership types have been adopted by managers in accommodation enterprises in Alanya, Turkey. Gill et al. (2010) studied the effect of transformational leadership and employee empowerment on hospitality industry employees job stress. The findings showed that transformational leadership and employee empowerment reduce the job stress of customer contact service employees in hospitality industry. Rothfelder et al. (2012) investigated the effect of transformational, transactional and non-leadership styles on employee job satisfaction. The outcomes showed that job satisfaction of hotel employees in Germany has been strongly affected by leadership behaviour. Al-Ababneh (2013) studied the impact of leadership types on employee job satisfaction in five-star hotels. The outcomes have revealed that democratic and laissezfaire leadership types have statically a positive and a significant impact on employees' job satisfaction. Moreover, democratic leadership has been found as dominant leadership type and employees have medium satisfied with their job. Salehzadeh et al. (2015) investigated impact of spiritual leadership on organizational performance for hotel industry. The results show that spiritual leadership have a positive and a significant impact on organizational performance. Zorlu et al. (2016) have examined the effects of transformational leadership behaviours on knowledge management processes in hotel chains. The outcomes showed that transformational leadership behaviours have a significant positive effect on knowledge management processes. Tran (2017) has examined the impact of leadership on financial performance in hospitality and tourism industry. The findings show that transformational leadership and longer-tenured CEOs with high power and affiliation motives has been related with return on equity while transactional leadership and older CEOs with high achievement motive effect return on assets. Yamak and Eyüpoglu (2018) have evaluated the dominant leadership types of managers working in 4- and 5-star hotels in Northern Cyprus. The determined four leadership types for the study are: autocratic, democratic, laissez-faire, and charismatic. The results show that charismatic leadership is the dominant leadership types. Cinnioğlu et al. (2019) have studied the effect of hotel employees perceived leadership types (employee-oriented, change-oriented, and production-oriented) on their level of burnout. According to the findings of the study, burnout levels of hotel employees are close to medium level and mostly production-oriented leadership type has been perceived. Alzoubi and Jaaffar (2020) have studied that the mediating effect of crisis management on leadership types and hotel performance. The findings indicated that transformational leadership positively affect hotel performance. Rescalvo-Martin et al. (2021) investigated the impact of paradoxical leadership on extra-role service. The outcomes of the study show that paradoxical leadership have a positive impact on extra-role service of Spanish hotels employees.

Literature Review About Leadership Types Using MCDM Tools

Zendeh and Aali (2011) handled the leadership style selection problem using Analytical Hierarchy Process (AHP) method. For the purpose of the study, four styles have been determined as selling style, telling style, participating style, and delegating style. According to the findings, telling style is the most appropriate while delegating style is the least inappropriate leadership style in Islamic Azad University. Kahya and Pabuçcu (2015) have evaluated leadership types with Fuzzy AHP method in a Turkish university. Four leadership types have been determined and these are exploitative authoritative, benevolent authoritative, consultative, and participative group. Findings have revealed that participative group are the most suitable and benevolent authoritative is the least suitable leadership type. Yılmaz et al. (2016) have determined optimal leadership style for organization structure of Airport using AHP. They have determined six alternatives as engaged leadership, directive leadership, coaching leadership, democratic leadership, affiliative leadership, and expert leadership. According to the findings, the engaged leadership is the most suitable leadership style whereas affiliative leadership is the least suitable leadership style for organization structure of Airport. Derici and Elden (2019) have determined the most appropriate leadership type for public institutions with AHP method. Five leadership types (transformational leadership, autocratic leadership, democratic leadership, charismatic leadership, and visionary leadership) have been identified and visionary leadership has been found the most preferred and autocratic leadership is the least preferred leadership type for public institutions. Doğaner et al. (2021) evaluated the leadership types in corporate organizations using the Step-Wise Weight Assessment Ratio Analysis (SWARA) method. Eleven leadership types have been determined and these are autocratic leadership, democratic leadership, laissez-faire leadership, task leadership, situational leadership, purpose-path leadership theory, vroam-yettan-jogo model, servant leadership, transformational leadership, transactional leadership, and charismatic leadership. The findings of the study show that democratic leadership is the most efficient and autocratic leadership is the least efficient type of leadership in corporate organizations. Ulucan and Yavuz Aksakal (2022) have handled a problem of leadership selection using the Fuzzy Technique for Order Preference by Similarity to Ideal Solution (TOPSIS) method in the hospitality sector from the perspectives of tourism employees. The study findings show that hospitality employees have preferred transformational leadership. It is followed by democratic leadership, charismatic leadership, transactional leadership laissez-faire leadership, and autocratic leadership.

Although the significance of leadership types has been accepted in both practice and academia, limited study has focused on to determine most suitable leadership type among various leadership types for hotel industry. Moreover, the discussed literature reveals that earlier studies have used MCDM methods to evaluate leadership types. However, they generally used classic and popular MCDM methods such as AHP, SWARA and TOPSIS. The novelty of this chapter is that BWM will be used for the first time to evaluate leadership types in hotel industry.

MAIN FOCUS OF THE CHAPTER

Tourism is one of the growing industry in the world and it contributes employment, economic development of the country, etc. Moreover, it has a significant place in Turkey's economic development. The hotel industry, on the other hand, is closely related to the tourism industry, so it attracts the attention of both managers and academics. Hotel enterprises strive to provide the best quality service to their customers. At this point, a suitable leadership selection helps the hotel management to achieve their goals and show a competitive advantage. Many leadership styles have been proposed until today. Determining the most appropriate type of leadership for a particular industry is a difficult and complex issue because the most appropriate type of leadership will vary with the purpose of the operating field, the character of internal and external customers, and even cultural differences. Therefore, this problem can be solved using MCDM methods. In this study, it is recommended to use BWM, one of the current MCDM methods, to determine the most suitable leadership type for the hotel industry in Turkey. A quite limited number of studies in the literature have used the MCDM method for this problem. Furthermore, these studies generally applied the AHP method, which is the most popular MCDM method. In this study, the BWM is proposed for this problem. In this study, one of the reason for preferring the BMW method is that the AHP method includes more pairwise comparisons than the BWM method, and this bring about the consistency problem. Furthermore, both qualitative and quantitative criteria can be integrated in BWM and it is a flexible decision methodology that can be applied in a various areas. Therefore, in this study, the BWM method has been used to determine the most appropriate leadership type for the hotel industry.

The Best - Worst Method (BWM), is a structured technique by Rezaei (2015). BWM is one of the MCDM tools to calculate the weights of the criteria in the decision-making process. Some recent studies of BWM applications in the literature is as follows: Gupta and Barua (2017) have applied the BWM and fuzzy TOPSIS to supplier selection among SMEs on the basis of their green innovation ability. Ecer (2021) have used the BWM for sustainability assessment of existing onshore wind plants in the context of triple bottom line. Arman and Organ (2021) have utilized the fuzzy BWM to determination of the importance level of digital supply chain on sustainability. Öztaş et al. (2021) have applied the BWM based approach to criteria assessment for Covid-19 vaccine selection. Khan et al. (2022) have used the BWM for investigating the barriers of blockchain technology integrated food supply chain. Jangre et al. (2022) have utilized the BWM to prioritization of factors and selection of best business practice from bio medical waste generated. Mendes et al. (2022) have applied BWM for determinants of sustainable entrepreneurship in small and medium-sized enterprises.

The following steps are considered to calculate the weights of the criteria using BWM (Rezaei, 2016: 126-127):

Step 1. Define the decision criteria $(C_1, C_2, ..., C_n)$. The pairwise comparison matrix A is obtained as follows.

$$A = \begin{pmatrix} a_{11} & a_{12} & \cdots & a_{1n} \\ a_{21} & a_{22} & \cdots & a_{2n} \\ \vdots & \vdots & \cdots & \vdots \\ a_{m1} & a_{m2} & \cdots & a_{mn} \end{pmatrix}$$

Where a_{ij} represent the relative preference of criterion i (i=1,2,...m) to criterion j (j=1,2,...n).

Step 2. Select the best and worst criteria criteria. Where the best criterion represents the most important criterion determined by the decision maker, while the worst criterion represents the least important criterion.

Step 3. Define the priority of the best criterion over all the criteria by using the Saaty (2008) 1–9 scale and best-to-others vector is defined: $A_B = (a_{B1}, a_{B2}, ..., a_{Bn})$, here a_{Bj} denotes the priority of the best criterion B over criterion j $(j = 1,2,...n)$.

Step 4. Define the priority of all the criteria over the worst criterion by using the Saaty (2008) 1–9 scale and others-to-worst vector is defined: $A_W = (a_{1W}, a_{2W}, ..., a_{nW})^T$, here a_{jW} denotes the priority of the criterion j $(j=1,2,...n)$ over the worst criterion W.

Step 5. Obtain the optimal criteria weights $(w_{c1}, w_{c2}, ..., w_{cn})$.

The purpose is to obtain the optimal weights of the criteria so that the maximum absolute gap for all j should be minimized of the following set, $\left\{ \left| \frac{w_B}{w_j} - a_{Bj} \right|, \left| \frac{w_j}{w_W} - a_{jW} \right| \right\}$. This can be translated to minimax model as follows (Rezaei, 2015: 52):

$$\operatorname{minmax}_j \left\{ \left| \frac{w_B}{w_j} - a_{Bj} \right|, \left| \frac{w_j}{w_W} - a_{jW} \right| \right\}$$

s.t.

$$\sum_j w_j = 1,$$

$$w_j \geq 0, \text{ for all j.} \tag{1}$$

Model (1) can be transferred to the linear model (Rezaei, 2016: 130):

$$\min \xi^L$$

$$\left| w_B - a_{Bj} w_j \right| \leq \xi^L, \text{ for all j}$$

$$\left| w_j - a_{jW} w_W \right| \leq \xi^L, \text{ for all j}$$

$$\sum_j w_j = 1$$

$$w_j \geq 0, \text{ for all j} \tag{2}$$

The model 2 is solved and optimal value ξ^L and the optimal weights $(w_{c1}, w_{c2}, ..., w_{cn})$ are calculated.

Step 6. Check the consistency degree of the pairwise comparisons. There are some deficiencies in original BWM to check consistency degree. The study that has been performed by Liang et al. (2020) have overcome this deficiency. Moreover, it provides immediate feedback of comparison's consistency. Input-based consistency ratio CR^I which has been presented by Liang et al. (2020) is obtained as follows (Liang et al., 2020: 3):

$$CR^I = \max_j CR^I_j$$

Where

$$CR^I_j = \begin{cases} \dfrac{|a_{Bj} a_{jW} - a_{BW}|}{a_{BW} a_{BW} - a_{BW}} & a_{BW} > 1 \\ 0 & a_{BW} = 1 \end{cases}$$

The input-based thresholds based on the number of criteria and the scales which have been developed by Liang et al. (2020) are as per in Table 1.

Table 1. Input-Based Consistency Thresholds for Different Combinations

Scales	Number of Criteria						
	3	4	5	6	7	8	9
3	0.1667	0.1667	0.1667	0.1667	0.1667	0.1667	0.1667
4	0.1121	0.1529	0.1898	0.2206	0.2527	0.2577	0.2683
5	0.1354	0.1994	0.2306	0.2546	0.2716	0.2844	0.2960
6	0.1330	0.1990	0.2643	0.3044	0.3144	0.3221	0.3262
7	0.1294	0.2457	0.2819	0.3029	0.3144	0.3251	0.3403
8	0.1309	0.2521	0.2958	0.3154	0.3408	0.3620	0.3657
9	0.1359	0.2681	0.3062	0.3337	0.3517	0.3620	0.3662

Source: Liang et al. (2020)

Issues, Controversies, Problems

Earlier studies have provided good overviews of the most suitable leadership types for specific sector. However, one of the primary constraint is that specific leadership types have been handled. Unlike other studies, this study comprehensively addresses leadership types and evaluates them from the perspective of five-star hotel managers and academics in Turkey. In addition, this study will use BWM for the first time to determine the most suitable leadership type in hotel industry. This chapter aims to determine most suitable leadership type for hotel industry. For this reason, nine criteria are determined. The nine leadership types have been determined based on earlier study findings and expert opinion. In MCDM methods, decision makers can be determined according to the purpose of the research or the preferences of the researchers. In this study, hotel managers and academics has been determined as the decision maker group. Another aspect of this study that differs from earlier studies is that it includes both managers and academics as the decision-makers. In this respect, it tries to integrate theoretical and practical views. The evaluation has been performed by seven decision makers. However, the evaluations of two decision makers that did not provide a consistent comparison were not taken into account and the evaluations of five decision makers have been used for the analysis.

SOLUTIONS AND RECOMMENDATIONS

The first phase of the BWM involves determination of the criteria. The next step is to determine the best and worst criteria. Then, the priority of the best criterion over all the criteria and also the priority of all the criteria over the worst criterion have been defined by using the 1–9 scale. The last step is to calculation of the optimal values of the criteria. A linear model has been formed to obtain weights of criteria for each decision makers based on the best-to-others and others-to-worst vectors. Consistency is significant issue in pairwise comparisons in BWM. For this reason, the consistency degrees should be checked for each decision makers. There are two evaluations which a consistency ratio above threshold so these evaluations have been excluded from the study. Moreover, all CR^I in the five evaluations are less than the thresholds developed by Liang et al. (2020). Therefore, five evaluations have been accepted.

The calculation of criteria weights using the BWM method according to the evaluations made by Decision Maker 1 (DM 1) is given below as an example. DM 1 has determined the most important leadership type is C8: Visionary Leadership and the least important leadership type is C6: Transactional Leadership. Then, best-to-others and others-to-worst vectors have been obtained and it is showed in Table 2.

Table 2. Best-to-Others and Others-to-Worst estimates

Best: C8	Best-to-Others	Worst: C6	Others-to-Worst estimates
C1	5	C1	3
C2	3	C2	5
C3	6	C3	2
C4	3	C4	5
C5	2	C5	6
C6	7	C6	1
C7	4	C7	4
C8	1	C8	7
C9	5	C9	3

According to best-to-others and others-to-worst estimates, Model 3 is obtained as follows.

$\min \xi^L$

s.t.

$$w_8 - 5*w_1 \leq \xi^L; w_8 - 5*w_1 \geq -\xi^L;$$

$$w_8 - 3*w_2 \leq \xi^L; w_8 - 3*w_2 \geq -\xi^L$$

$$w_8 - 6*w_3 \leq \xi^L; w_8 - 6*w_3 \geq -\xi^L$$

$$w_8 - 3*w_4 \leq \xi^L; w_8 - 3*w_4 \geq -\xi^L$$

$$w_8 - 2*w_5 \leq \xi^L; w_8 - 2*w_5 \geq -\xi^L$$

$$w_8 - 7*w_6 \leq \xi^L; w_8 - 7*w_6 \geq -\xi^L$$

$$w_8 - 4*w_7 \leq \xi^L; w_8 - 4*w_7 \geq -\xi^L$$

$$w_8 - 5*w_9 \leq \xi^L; w_8 - 5*w_9 \geq -\xi^L \tag{3}$$

$$w_1 - 3*w_6 \leq \xi^L; w_1 - 3*w_6 \geq -\xi^L;$$

$$w_2 - 5*w_6 \leq \xi^L; w_2 - 5*w_6 \geq -\xi^L;$$

$$w_3 - 2*w_6 \leq \xi^L; w_3 - 2*w_6 \geq -\xi^L;$$

$$w_4 - 5*w_6 \leq \xi^L; w_4 - 5*w_6 \geq -\xi^L;$$

$$w_5 - 6*w_6 \leq \xi^L; w_5 - 6*w_6 \geq -\xi^L;$$

$$w_7 - 4*w_6 \leq \xi^L; w_7 - 4*w_6 \geq -\xi^L;$$

$$w_9 - 3*w_6 \leq \xi^L; w_9 - 3*w_6 \geq -\xi^L;$$

$$\sum_{j=1}^{9} w_j = 1,$$

$w_j \geq 0$,

Model 3 is solved with Microsoft Excel Solver and the optimal weights of the criteria according to DM 1's evaluations are obtained. Similarly, the optimal weights of the criteria for each DM have been calculated. By averaging of the five evaluations, the final weights and ranking of the criteria have been presented in Table 3. Figure 1 shows the criteria weights distribution.

Table 3. Weights and Ranking of Leadership Types

Decision Maker (DM)	DM 1	DM 2	DM 3	DM 4	DM 5	Weights	Ranking
C1: Digital Leadership	0.068	0.086	0.128	0.220	0.033	0.107	4
C2: Democratic Leadership	0.114	0.086	0.096	0.071	0.131	0.100	5
C3: Authentic Leadership	0.057	0.130	0.064	0.220	0.131	0.120	3
C4: Servant Leadership	0.114	0.130	0.077	0.095	0.079	0.099	6
C5: Transformational Leadership	0.171	0.130	0.315	0.220	0.328	0.233	1
C6: Transactional Leadership	0.034	0.065	0.048	0.041	0.098	0.057	9
C7: Charismatic Leadership	0.085	0.025	0.055	0.057	0.079	0.060	7
C8: Visionary Leadership	0.288	0.219	0.192	0.057	0.066	0.164	2
C9: Delegative Leadership	0.068	0.130	0.027	0.019	0.056	0.060	8

Figure 1. Weights Distribution

According to the evaluations results, C5: Transformational Leadership is the most suitable leadership type for hotel industry, followed by C8: Visionary Leadership, C3: Authentic Leadership, C1: Digital Leadership, C2: Democratic Leadership, C4: Servant Leadership, C7: Charismatic Leadership, C9: Delegative Leadership, and C6: Transactional Leadership. It is useful to briefly explain the two leadership types that draw attention as a result of this study. Transformational leaders strive for the well being of all their followers, guide them and help them create a vision with their high motivation. It can be inferred that leadership success is expected to increase with the adoption of the transformational leadership type in the hotel industry. On the other hand, transactional leaders motivate their followers through various interest, but their followers face punishment if the objective is not achieved. Therefore, the organization mainly focuses on the achievement of the objective. However, according to five DM's evaluations, transactional leadership has been found to be the least suitable leadership type in the hotel industry.

In this study, it has been revealed that C5: Transformational Leadership is the most suitable leadership type for hotel industry, followed by C8: Visionary Leadership, C3: Authentic Leadership. The results obtained from the study agree with the results of some earlier studies. Blayney and Blotnicky (2010) have showed that visionary leadership has a significant positive effect on hotel performance as measured by revenue per available room (RevPAR). Zorlu et al. (2016) have revealed that transformational leadership behaviours have a significant positive impact on knowledge management processes in hotel chains. Tran (2017) emphasizes that return on equity has been associated with transformational leadership in hospitality and tourism industry. Singh et al. (2020) have revealed that authentic leadership has statically a positive and a significant effect on hotel employee engagement. Alzoubi and Jaaffar (2020) have found that transformational leadership positively affect hotel performance. Moreover, transactional leadership positively affect crisis management. Grudić Kvasić et al. (2021) have stated that authentic leadership has a significant positive effect on hotel employees' psychological capacities such as hope, optimism, resilience and self-efficacy. Ulucan and Yavuz Aksakal (2022) have revealed that hospitality employees have preferred to work with transformational leader. AlKayid et al. (2022) emphasizes that the creativity of the hotel employees, who work with visionary leaders, has developed.

The outcomes of this study and earlier studies clearly show that transformational leadership, visionary leadership and authentic leadership are the most suitable leadership types for the hotel industry in in different countries. It is recommended that hotel managers should demonstrate transformational leadership, visionary and authentic leadership together. Because adoption of these three leadership styles within the hotel industry, the performance of hotel enterprises will increase under constantly changing competitive conditions.

FUTURE RESEARCH DIRECTIONS

The limitations of this study are that a limited number of decision makers and leadership types have been considered. Therefore, these dimensions can be expanded in future studies. In addition, in future studies, hotel employees can be handled as the decision-makers and a comparative ranking can be obtained. Moreover, using the criteria discussed in this study, different MCDM methods can be used and the results can be compared. The literature review claim that there are many different leadership types and it can be said that the type of leadership that is suitable for one industry may not be suitable for another. It may be the same industry, but even being in a different country can change the suitable leadership type. Therefore, the future research can consider suitable leadership types in hotel industry for different countries. In addition to this, the future research can investigate the effect of specific leadership types such as: transformational leadership, visionary leadership, and authentic leadership on hotel employees' performance.

CONCLUSION

Leadership is very significant topic in the social sciences and enterprises operating in different fields may need to adopt different types of leadership to increase and sustain their success. Determining the most suitable of leadership for a specific industry is a quite complex issue and can be considered as a decision problem. In this study, it is aimed to determine the most suitable leadership types for hotel industry using BWM which is one of the MCDM tools. Furthermore, the weights of the leadership types have been obtained using BWM method for the first time in the literature. For the purpose of the study, nine leadership types as criteria have been determined according to expert opinion and earlier study findings. Decision group consist of five-star hotel managers and academics in Turkey. According to the literature review, perspectives of managers and academics have been not combined to evaluate leadership types in hotel industry. With this aspect, the study presents a new integrated perspective that combines the theory and practice to evaluate leadership types in hotel industry. That's why, this study fills the gap in the literature.

According to the outcomes of the study, the ranking of the nine leadership types is as follows. Transformational Leadership > Visionary Leadership > Authentic Leadership > Digital Leadership > Democratic Leadership > Servant Leadership > Charismatic Leadership > Delegative Leadership > Transactional Leadership. The findings of the study shows that transformational leadership is the most suitable while transactional leadership is the least suitable leadership type for hotel industry. Similarly, the findings of earlier studies show that transformational leadership is among the most suitable leadership types for different sectors. In this study, the hotel industry is specifically addressed and it has been revealed that the most appropriate leadership type is transformational leadership. In addition to that previous studies indicate that the least suitable leadership type for different sectors is autocratic leadership. For this reason, autocratic leadership type has not been handled in this study. Moreover, this study has revealed that transactional leadership is the least suitable leadership type. According to the study findings, transformational leadership, visionary and authentic leadership are the most suitable leadership types for managing hotels. It is thought that the efficiency will improve and goals will be achieved in hotel industry by adopting these leadership types.

This chapter provides further understanding leadership types for hotel industry from the perspective of five-star hotel managers and academics in Turkey. As many earlier studies about evaluate leadership types for hotel industry, this study outcomes have validated that transformational leadership is the most suitable leadership type for hotel industry in Turkey. This chapter will contribute to existing literature is two-fold. Firstly, there is a limited studies about evaluating leadership types with MCDM tools. Moreover, BWM has not been used for this area. Therefore, this chapter will use the BWM method for the first time to evaluate leadership types in the hotel industry. Secondly, hotel managers should be aware different leadership types and integrate which are suitable to their industry in order to achieve their competitiveness. The outcomes of this study present insights for researchers and a practitioners in hotel industry.

REFERENCES

Abdullah, Rahim, Jeinie, Zulkafli, & Nordin. (2021). Leadership, task load and job satisfaction: a review of special education teachers perspective. *Turkish Journal of Computer and Mathematics Education*, *12*(11), 5300-5306.

Al-Ababneh, M. M. (2013). Leadership style of managers in five-star hotels and its relationship with employee's job satisfaction. *International Journal of Management & Business Studies*, *3*(2), 93–98. doi:10.2139srn.3633072

Al-Malki, M., & Juan, W. (2018). Leadership styles and job performance: A literature review. *Journal of International Business Research and Marketing*, *3*(3), 50–59. doi:10.18775/jibrm.1849-8558.2015.33.3004

AlKayid, K., Selem, K. M., Shehata, A. E., & Tan, C. C. (2022). Leader vision, organizational inertia and service hotel employee creativity: Role of knowledge-donating. *Current Psychology*, 1–13. doi:10.100712144-022-02743-6 PMID:35125851

Alzoubi, R. H., & Jaaffar, A. H. (2020). The mediating effect of crisis management on leadership styles and hotel performance in Jordan. *International Journal of Financial Research*, *11*(4), 384–397. doi:10.5430/ijfr.v11n4p384

Arman, K., & Organ, A. (2021). A Fuzzy Best Worst approach to the determination of the importance level of digital supply chain on sustainability. *Business & Management Studies: An International Journal*, *9*(4), 1366–1379. doi:10.15295/bmij.v9i4.1901

Blayney, C., & Blotnicky, K. (2010). Leadership in the hotel industry: Evidence from Canada. *International Journal of Management and Marketing Research*, *3*(3), 53–66.

Çelik, S. (2019). Turizm alanında liderlik konusu ile ilgili hazırlanmış tezlere yönelik bibliyometrik bir analiz [A bibliometric analysis of the theses on leadership in the field of tourism]. *Journal of Academic Value Studies*, *5*(4), 516–527.

Cinnioğlu, H., Atay, L., & Karakaş, E. (2019). The influence of hotel employee's perceived leadership style on their level of burnout: Çanakkale sample. *Journal of Social Sciences of Mus Alparslan University*, *7*(6), 157–165.

Derici, S., & Elden, B. (2019). *Determining the most appropriate leadership style for public institutions in industry 4.0 by managerial abilities. In Turkey Vision: Multidisciplinary Studies*. Ekin Yayınevi.

Doğaner, M., Aydın, M. S., & İncioğlu, C. (2021). Evaluation of leadership types efficiency in corporate organizations by SWARA method. *Pamukkale University Journal of Business Research*, *8*(1), 66–81.

Ecer, F. (2021). Sustainability assessment of existing onshore wind plants in the context of triple bottom line: A best-worst method (BWM) based MCDM framework. *Environmental Science and Pollution Research International*, *28*(16), 19677–19693. doi:10.100711356-020-11940-4 PMID:33405119

Fuller, J. B., Patterson, C. E., Hester, K. I. M., & Stringer, D. Y. (1996). A quantitative review of research on charismatic leadership. *Psychological Reports*, *78*(1), 271–287. doi:10.2466/pr0.1996.78.1.271

Gill, A., Flaschner, A. B., & Bhutani, S. (2010). The impact of transformational leadership and empowerment on employee job stress. *Business and Economics Journal*, 1–11.

Grudić Kvasić, S., Nikolić, G., & Milojica, V. (2021). The impact of authentic leadership on employee psychological capital in the hospitality industry. *Poslovna Izvrsnost*, *15*(1), 9–22. doi:10.22598/pibe/2021.15.1.9

Gupta, H., & Barua, M. K. (2017). Supplier selection among SMEs on the basis of their green innovation ability using BWM and fuzzy TOPSIS. *Journal of Cleaner Production*, *152*, 242–258. doi:10.1016/j.jclepro.2017.03.125

Hai, T. N., & Van, Q. N. (2021). Servant leadership styles: A theoretical approach. *Emerging Science Journal*, *5*(2), 245–256. doi:10.28991/esj-2021-01273

Hilton, S. K., Arkorful, H., & Martins, A. (2021). Democratic leadership and organizational performance: The moderating effect of contingent reward. *Management Research Review*, *44*(7), 1042–1058. doi:10.1108/MRR-04-2020-0237

Jangre, J., Hameed, A. Z., Srivastava, M., Prasad, K., & Patel, D. (2022). Prioritization of factors and selection of best business practice from bio-medical waste generated using best–worst method. *Benchmarking*. Advance online publication. doi:10.1108/BIJ-11-2021-0698

Jung, D. I. (2001). Transformational and transactional leadership and their effects on creativity in groups. *Creativity Research Journal*, *13*(2), 185–195. doi:10.1207/S15326934CRJ1302_6

Kahya, C., & Pabuçcu, H. (2015). Evaluating leadership styles within the scope of Rensis Likerts 4-Model by using fuzzy AHP approach. *IIB International Refereed Academic Social Sciences Journal*, *6*(17), 1–23. doi:10.17364/IIB.2015179721

Keklik, B. (2012). Determination of leadership style preferred in health institutions: Example of a private hospital. *Afyon Kocatepe Üniversitesi İktisadi ve İdari Bilimler Fakültesi Dergisi*, *14*(1), 73–93.

Khan, S., Kaushik, M. K., Kumar, R., & Khan, W. (2022). Investigating the barriers of blockchain technology integrated food supply chain: A BWM approach. *Benchmarking*. Advance online publication. doi:10.1108/BIJ-08-2021-0489

Kozak, M. A., & Uca, S. (2008). Effective factors in the constitution of leadership styles: A study of Turkish hotel managers. *Anatolia*, *19*(1), 117–134. doi:10.1080/13032917.2008.9687057

Küçük, B., & Yavuz, E. (2021). Examination of the relationship between servant leadership and organizational cynicism: An application in the service industry. *Alanya Academic Review Journal*, *5*(1), 453–472.

Liang, F., Brunelli, M., & Rezaei, J. (2020). Consistency issues in the best worst method: Measurements and thresholds. *Omega*, *96*, 102175. doi:10.1016/j.omega.2019.102175

Mendes, A. C., Ferreira, F. A., Kannan, D., Ferreira, N. C., & Correia, R. J. (2022). A BWM approach to determinants of sustainable entrepreneurship in small and medium-sized enterprises. *Journal of Cleaner Production*, *371*, 133300. doi:10.1016/j.jclepro.2022.133300

Nipu, A., & Ahmed, S. (2019). Qualitative model for identifying leadership using fuzzy logic. *International Journal of Applications of Fuzzy Sets and Artificial Intelligence*, *9*, 13–29.

Öztaş, G. Z., Bars, A., Genç, V., & Erdem, S. (2021, June). Criteria Assessment for Covid-19 Vaccine Selection via BWM. In *The International Workshop on Best-Worst Method* (pp. 228-237). Springer.

Purwanto, A., Asbari, M., Hartuti, H., Setiana, Y. N., & Fahmi, K. (2021). Effect of psychological capital and authentic leadership on innovation work behavior. *International Journal of Social and Management Studies*, *2*(1), 1–13.

Rescalvo-Martin, E., Gutierrez-Gutierrez, L., & Llorens-Montes, F. J. (2021). The effect of paradoxical leadership on extra-role service in the hospitality industry. *International Journal of Contemporary Hospitality Management*, *33*(10), 3661-3684. doi:10.1108/IJCHM-02-2021-0198

Rezaei, J. (2015). Best-Worst Multi-Criteria Decision-Making Method. *Omega*, *53*, 49–57. doi:10.1016/j.omega.2014.11.009

Rezaei, J. (2016). Best-worst multi-criteria decision-making method: Some properties and a linear model. *Omega, 64*, 126–130. doi:10.1016/j.omega.2015.12.001

Rothfelder, K., Ottenbacher, M. C., & Harrington, R. J. (2012). The impact of transformational, transactional and non-leadership styles on employee job satisfaction in the German hospitality industry. *Tourism and Hospitality Research, 12*(4), 201–214. doi:10.1177/1467358413493636

Saaty, T. L. (2008). Decision making with the analytic hierarchy process. *International Journal of Services Sciences, 1*(1), 83–98. doi:10.1504/IJSSCI.2008.017590

Salamzadeh, Y., Farzad, F. S., Salamzadeh, A., & Palalić, R. (2022). Digital leadership and organizational capabilities in manufacturing industry: A study in Malaysian context. *Periodicals of Engineering and Natural Sciences, 10*(1), 195–211.

Salehzadeh, R., Pool, J. K., Lashaki, J. K., Dolati, H., & Jamkhaneh, H. B. (2015). Studying the effect of spiritual leadership on organizational performance: An empirical study in hotel industry. *International Journal of Culture, Tourism and Hospitality Research, 9*(3), 346–359. doi:10.1108/IJCTHR-03-2015-0012

Sandıkcı, M., Vural, T., & Zorlu, Ö. (2015). Otel işletmelerinde dönüştürücü liderlik davranışlarının örgüt sağlığı üzerine etkileri: Afyonkarahisar ilinde bir araştırma [The effects of transformative leadership behaviors in hotel businesses on organizational health: A study in Afyonkarahisar province]. *Yönetim Bilimleri Dergisi, 13*(25), 161–200.

Serinkan, C. (2005). İşletmelerde liderlik tarzları ve toplam kalite yönetimi ilişkisi [Relationship between leadership styles and total quality management in businesses]. *Yönetim Dergisi: İstanbul Üniversitesi İşletme Fakültesi İşletme İktisadı Enstitüsü, 16*(50), 86–103.

Silva, A. (2016). What is leadership? *Journal of Business Studies Quarterly, 8*(1), 1–6. PMID:29355200

Singh, G. K. P. A., Subramaniam, A., Mohamed, A. S. B., Mohamed, R., & Ibrahim, S. (2020). Role of authentic leadership, servant leadership and destructive leadership behaviour on employee engagement in Malaysian hospitality industry. *International Journal of Academic Research in Business & Social Sciences, 10*(9), 113–125.

Tang, H. W. V. (2018). Modeling critical leadership competences for junior high school principals: A hybrid MCDM model combining DEMATEL and ANP. *Kybernetes, 49*(11), 2589–2613. doi:10.1108/K-01-2018-0015

Taylor, C. M., Cornelius, C. J., & Colvin, K. (2014). Visionary leadership and its relationship to organizational effectiveness. *Leadership and Organization Development Journal, 35*(6), 566–583. doi:10.1108/LODJ-10-2012-0130

Tran, X. (2017). Effects of leadership styles on hotel financial performance. *Tourism and Hospitality Management, 23*(2), 163–183. doi:10.20867/thm.23.2.7

Ulucan, E., & Yavuz Aksakal, N. (2022). Leadership selection with the fuzzy topsis method in the hospitality sector in sultanahmet region. *Mathematics, 10*(13), 2195. doi:10.3390/math10132195

World Travel and Tourism Council. (2022). *Travel and Tourism Economic Impact 2022*. Retrieved from https://wttc.org/Portals/0/Documents/Reports/2022/EIR2022-Global%20Trends.pdf

Yamak, Ö. U., & Eyüpoglu, S. Z. (2018). Leadership styles of hotel managers in Northern Cyprus: Which style is dominant? *International Journal of Organizational Leadership*, 7(1), 1–11. doi:10.33844/ijol.2018.60202

Yılmaz, A. K., Tanrıverdi, G., & Durak, M. Ş. (2016). Determination of optimal leadership style for an organization: Case of Hasan Polatkan Airport. *Transport & Logistics*, 16(38/39), 1–8.

Yörük, D., Dündar, S., & Topçu, B. (2011). Türkiye'deki Belediye Başkanlarının Liderlik Tarzı ve Liderlik Tarzını Etkileyen Faktörler [Leadership Style of Mayors in Turkey and Factors Affecting Leadership Style]. *Ege Akademik Bakış*, 11(1), 103–109. doi:10.21121/eab.2011119591

Yukl, G. (1999). An evaluation of conceptual weaknesses in transformational and charismatic leadership theories. *The Leadership Quarterly*, 10(2), 285–305. doi:10.1016/S1048-9843(99)00013-2

Zendeh, A. B., & Aali, S. (2011). An AHP approach for selecting the suitable leadership style. *Management and Economics*, 25, 20–24.

Zorlu, Ö., Baytok, A., & Avan, A. (2016). The effect of transformational leadership behaviours on knowledge management practices: A study about hotel chains. *The Journal of Academic Social Science*, 4(35), 209–236. doi:10.16992/ASOS.6577

ADDITIONAL READING

Arici, H. E., & Uysal, M. (2022). Leadership, green innovation, and green creativity: A systematic review. *Service Industries Journal*, 42(5-6), 280–320. doi:10.1080/02642069.2021.1964482

Elkhwesky, Z., Salem, I. E., Ramkissoon, H., & Castañeda-García, J. A. (2022). A systematic and critical review of leadership styles in contemporary hospitality: A roadmap and a call for future research. *International Journal of Contemporary Hospitality Management*, 34(5), 1925–1958. doi:10.1108/IJCHM-09-2021-1128

Gurmani, J. K., Khan, N. U., Khalique, M., Yasir, M., Obaid, A., & Sabri, N. A. A. (2021). Do environmental transformational leadership predicts organizational citizenship behavior towards environment in hospitality industry: Using structural equation modelling approach. *Sustainability*, 13(10), 5594. doi:10.3390u13105594

Huertas-Valdivia, I., Gallego-Burín, A. R., & Lloréns-Montes, F. J. (2019). Effects of different leadership styles on hospitality workers. *Tourism Management*, 71, 402–420. doi:10.1016/j.tourman.2018.10.027

Huertas-Valdivia, I., González-Torres, T., & Nájera-Sánchez, J. J. (2022). Contemporary leadership in hospitality: A review and research agenda. *International Journal of Contemporary Hospitality Management*, 34(6), 2399–2422. doi:10.1108/IJCHM-05-2021-0658

Kourtesopoulou, A., & Chatzigianni, E. E. (2021). Gender equality and women's entrepreneurial leadership in tourism: A systematic review. In M. Valeri & V. Katsoni (Eds.), *Gender and tourism* (pp. 11–36). Emerald Publishing Limited. doi:10.1108/978-1-80117-322-320211002

Orero-Blat, M., Jordán, H. D. J., & Palacios-Marqués, D. (2022). A literature review of causal relationships in 21st century skills and digital leadership. *International Journal of Services Operations and Informatics*, *12*(1), 1–12. doi:10.1504/IJSOI.2022.123567

Rescalvo-Martin, E., Castillo, A., Moreno-Marcial, A. P., Albacete-Saez, C. A., & Llorens-Montes, F. J. (2022). Effects of empowering leadership under boundary conditions in the hospitality industry. *International Journal of Hospitality Management*, *105*, 103269. doi:10.1016/j.ijhm.2022.103269

Santo, V., Sacavã, A., dos Reis, I. P., & Sampaio, M. C. (2019). 4.0 Leadership skills in hospitality sector. *Journal of Reviews on Global Economics*, *8*, 105-117.

Vogel, B., Reichard, R. J., Batistič, S., & Černe, M. (2021). A bibliometric review of the leadership development field: How we got here, where we are, and where we are headed. *The Leadership Quarterly*, *32*(5), 101381. doi:10.1016/j.leaqua.2020.101381

KEY TERMS AND DEFINITIONS

BWM: The Best-Worst Method (BWM) has been developed by Rezaei (2015). BWM is one of the MCDM methods to obtain the weights of the criteria in the decision-making process. The BMW offers a flexible decision methodology that makes it possible to apply it in different areas.

Consistency Degree: Consistency degree is a very important issue when using MCDM methods. For this reason, consistency degree of the pairwise comparisons should be checked. If there are no consistent comparisons for some evaluations, comparisons should be made again until an acceptable degree of consistency is achieved.

Hotel Industry: The hotel industry is large subsection of the hospitality industry, and it provides accommodation services to customers. In addition, they are facilities that can include different units for various needs such as food and beverage, meetings, and events.

Leadership: Leadership can be defined as motivating followers to achieve their common goals. Leadership is very important among management topics as it provides various functions vital to the success of an organization.

Leadership Types: Leadership theories include many approaches to explain leadership and it is generally described depend on leader characteristics. Many leadership theories have been defined until today. However, in the changing world, different leadership types may be needed, and new leadership types are emerging.

MCDM: MCDM is one of the branches of operations research (OR). One of the application areas of MCDM methods is to evaluate multiple conflicting criteria in decision making. For this reason, many MCDM methods have been introduced so far and still continue to be developed.

Chapter 6
Charismatic Leadership in Hospitality and Tourism

Gonca Aytaş
Afyon Kocatepe University, Turkey

Fatma Doğanay Ergen
Isparta University of Applied Sciences, Turkey

Engin Aytekin
Afyon Kocatepe University, Turkey

ABSTRACT

The study is mainly focused on determining whether the managers possess a charismatic leadership style, and meanwhile, the relations of charismatic leadership with organizational performance, psychological commitment, emotional commitment, job satisfaction, corporate reputation, and work-home arrangements are examined. In this context, in this study, first of all, the concept of charismatic leadership is explained followed by a discussion of charismatic leadership in the tourism industry and hospitality businesses.

INTRODUCTION

It is apparent that many interpretations of leadership concentrate on issues such as influencing and persuading, initiating, directing, shaping, and interacting (Şişman, 2014: 4). Leadership is an important concept not only in social sciences but also in corporate life. A culture that supports the accomplishment of a company's goals and objectives must be established by leaders. These are the behaviors associated with the charismatic leadership style (Maher, 2017). An impressive relationship between charismatic leadership and high performance and follower satisfaction is emerging from an increasing corpus of studies. People who work for charismatic leaders are inspired to exert more effort and demonstrate greater satisfaction because they genuinely care about their leader (Nandal & Krishnan, 2000). At the same time, charismatic leadership is frequently considered to be the most productive leadership style since it motivates workers in a persuasive manner. The charismatic style also has the potential to be an

DOI: 10.4018/978-1-6684-6713-8.ch006

effective instrument for bringing about subconscious transformation and meets the strong leadership expectations of employees through vision (Biviano, 2000).

Tourism businesses have complex and difficult architecture with their distinctive business designs, diverse cultures, and business functions as well because the service sector has its own attributes. Therefore, this may lead to the emergence of a different leadership style in each business (Ersöz & Turan, 2021: 129). Thus, the managers working in tourism businesses should adopt a leadership style accordingly (Turan & Ersöz, 2021: 5). However, since the interactions between leaders and employees and between employees and customers in tourism businesses that are part of the service sector are what specify service quality and customer satisfaction, the influence of the leader on employee performance and motivation is crucial (Ersöz & Turan, 2021: 129).

People who are referred to as leaders today occupy a significant position in relation to both the people in the societies, they are a part of and the workers in the organizations they work for, and they have an impact on both groups of people. Tourism business managers who possess leadership skills are among those who contribute to the caliber of the services offered and who must make sure that the employees share their goals and objectives. In addition to the stated characteristics, managers who are self-confident, communication-oriented, attach importance to the values of society and individuals, can create a vision and have high persuasion power are also called charismatic leaders in the literature (Erkılıç, 2021: 149).

Understanding leadership styles in tourism businesses is fundamental to comprehending the topic from both a scientific and sectoral perspective, just like it is in other fields and industries (Turan & Ersöz, 2021: 5). In this context, when the literature is examined, it is clear that research has been undertaken on the subject of charismatic leadership in the tourism industry and the actors involved in effective destination management (Maher, 2017; Gerges, Kamal & Mohammed, 2017; Valente, Dredge & Lohmann, 2014; Komppula, 2016). However, in the literature, it is noteworthy that the studies in which charismatic leadership is also investigated on the employees of the hospitality business take up more space (Priastana & Mujiati, 2020; Piuchan & Prachansit, 2019; Yamak & Eyüpoğlu, 2018; Stavrinoudis & Chrysanthopoulou, 2017; Bilgin, Kuzey, Torlak & Uyar, 2015; Tromp & Blomme, 2014; Choi, 2010; Kozak & Uca, 2008). It has been noted that the studies are mainly focused on determining whether the managers possess a charismatic leadership style, and meanwhile, it is observed that the relations of charismatic leadership with organizational performance, psychological commitment, emotional commitment, job satisfaction, corporate reputation and work-home arrangements are examined. It is thought that it is important to reveal the importance of charismatic leadership in the field of tourism, especially in accommodation businesses, and to evaluate the studies on the subject. In this context, in this study, the concept of charismatic leadership is explained and followed by a discussion of charismatic leadership in the tourism industry and hospitality businesses.

BACKGROUND

The Concept of Leadership and Charismatic Leadership

Despite the fact that there are numerous definitions of leadership, in its most basic sense, leadership is the capacity to inspire people to attain objectives (Hughes, 2009). The definition of leadership is "to lead, to guide, to direct, to have the capacity for persuasion, and to be a pioneer" (Greger & Peterson, 2000: 16). However, when the many definitions and conceptualizations of leadership are explored, it becomes clear that they differ based on a) group processes, b) personalities, c) behavior d) power, e) realization of purpose, f) people's influence on each other, g) the way the leader influences the followers. These considerations have led to the definition of leadership as the practice of "influencing" others and the group to behave in accordance with shared objectives and "leading" activities (Turan, 2020: 2).

According to Edmonstone & Western (2002), the personal qualities of leaders are discussed in the literature. These qualities include having a successfully shared big picture vision and making clear, decisive decisions after evaluating the information at hand. Leaders commit to growing others' abilities and enabling them while being respectful, consultative, and willing to make challenging decisions when essential. Credibility, which is frequently accomplished by moral and open methods of operation, is at the heart of leadership. Leaders take calculated risks, when necessary, challenge the status quo, and step forward to take responsibility and show initiative when necessary (Hughes, 2009). The idea of leadership is absolutely vital for organizations as well because it is the responsibility of the leaders not to overlook the current situation, guide the organization toward its goals, and transform it into the state they desire to be in the future (Gandolfi & Stone, 2018).

The production-oriented approach in the classical period has also caused managers to have a rigid structure. Excellence is characterized not just in terms of work-related issues but also in terms of the manager's physical and mental traits. The neo-classical era used human nature and behaviors to interpret the decisions and acts of the administrators. The idea that management may evolve depending on the circumstances of the firm has gained general acceptance since the 1960s as a result of the rapid change in environmental factors (particularly the impact of technological developments on the change in enterprises). As a result, managers and leaders who can adapt to change, think critically, and have great communication and cognitive abilities have become increasingly imperative (Akoğlan Kozak, 2008: 506).

When the pertinent literature is evaluated within the framework of the research, it becomes clear that leadership approaches are divided into two categories: conventional leadership and contemporary leadership approaches. Numerous studies have been undertaken to explain the leader and leadership. Traits approaches, behavioral approaches, and contingency methods are the three categories used to categorize traditional leadership approaches. On the other hand, among the contemporary leadership styles, it is believed that charismatic leadership style, transactional (interactionist), transformational (transformational) leadership, strategic leadership approaches attract more attention today (Ergun Özler, 2013: 100; Saylı & Baytok, 2014: 40).

One of the first systematic attempts to research leadership was the trait method, which grabbed the interest of researchers during the 20th century. Early in the 20th century, researchers looked into leadership characteristics to uncover what made some people competent leaders. According to hypotheses that have been developed, only "great" people possess these traits, including best-known social, political, and military leaders like Napoleon Bonaparte, Indira Gandhi, and Abraham Lincoln (Bass, 1990; Jago, 1982: cited in Northouse, 2013: 19). In this approach, the main characteristics of the leader are physical characteristics (such as height, weight, age, health status) and personal characteristics (such as intelligence, education level, speaking ability, social relations, communication power, confidence, initiative, risk taking, courage, self-confidence) (Şişman, 2014: 6). When the distinguishing traits of leaders are evaluated, it becomes clear that honesty, truthfulness, being inspiring, assertiveness, openness to communication, and great self-confidence are the most prevalent traits. The leaders should be correct, honest, stable, consistent, extroverted, and open to communication. They also need to have self-confidence and make others feel that way, mobilize their followers and motivate them in the context of achieving goals as well as being able to pull the masses after him/her (Ergun Özler, 2013: 98). Given the fact that some academics believe it is legitimate to attribute leadership to purely personal traits, some theorists have argued that leadership cannot be explained solely by personal traits and that it is not always possible for individuals with particular traits to become leaders (Ergun Özler, 2013: 106). Besides, some inconsistencies have demonstrated that those with the listed traits make "excellent managers." In addition to these discrepancies, the rise in the number of traits assigned to leaders on a daily basis and the insufficiency of the traits or skills assigned to each period have begun to suggest that behaviors need to be looked into in the justification of the leadership process (Kozak, Gül Yılmaz & Çakır, 2017: 66).

However, it is commonly assumed that charismatic leaders captivate the audience with their own traits by making them look different. Most of the time, charismatic traits develop spontaneously in a person. There are those who contend that charismatic leadership is associated with innate personality qualities and those who assert that charismatic actions can be mastered later; both viewpoints are regarded to be valid (Ergun Özler, 2013: 106).

On the other side, the behavior of the leader has been investigated rather than the traits of the leader in the behavioral approach, which starts from the premise that there cannot be any universal generic characteristics associated with the leader. The profile of leader conduct was attempted to be ascertained via looking at the behaviors of successful leaders. The main studies in behavioral theory are studies such as Research by Ohio University, Research by Michigan University, and Managerial Grid Theory (Robert Blake and Jane Mouton) (Şişman, 2014: 6).

The understanding of the traits and behaviors of leaders has greatly benefited from behavioral leadership research. Indeed, following these studies, the connections defining how leaders in organizations should act toward their subordinates were drawn, and it became clear that the leaders had distinct behaviors depending on whether they were dealing with people or work/production. Additionally, the fundamental traits of leadership actions toward people and the workplace were thoroughly investigated. According to behavioral leadership studies, self-directed leaders may be more effective and provide greater guidance to followers. Later, this broad conclusion was questioned because it was claimed that generalizations like "individually oriented leaders will be successful" are not always applicable, and a body of research on contingency leadership about what kind of leadership would be more acceptable under certain circumstances and environments evolved (Ergun Özler, 2013: 111).

The starting point of the contingency approach is based on the understanding that "there is no valid leadership characteristic and behavior in every environment". This strategy postulates that multiple leadership behaviors exist depending on the setting and the type of group. Some approaches gathered under this title are: Path-Goal Theory of Leadership (Robert House & Martin Evans), Fiedler's Contingency Leadership Theory, Vroom and Yetton's Normative Theory, Paul Hersey and Keneth Blanchard's Situational Leadership Theory, Reddin's Three-Dimensional Grid or 3-D Leadership Theory. Some theories have also been developed under the names of leadership, based on leader characteristics, action-centered, social, situational, contextual and strategic leadership (Şişman, 2014: 6).

Along with the human relations approach in management science, leadership images have also changed, and today's leaders are required to comprehend the psychological and social needs of their workforce and take appropriate action to address those demands. (Şişman, 2014: 7).

The last quarter of the 20th century witnessed a number of drastic developments, particularly in the business world, which made it clear that the previous paradigms were less effective at producing alternatives. New issues and demands called for fresh approaches, and the old paradigm's incapacity to meet these demands made discussion of it necessary. Because of this, conventional (classical) theories have been debated for a very long period, hastening the quest for fresh ideas that are appropriate for the demands of the current era. In this process, classical theories are not completely rejected, on the contrary, the knowledge created by them facilitates the development of new theories and models (Saylı and Baytok, 2014: 111).

According to the circumstances they are in, leaders are rated in the modern approach era as being supportive, domineering, participatory, or success-oriented. Yet, in the post-modern period, leaders are understood to be those who seek to instill a sense of purpose in the organization, build strong relationships with their team members, have faith in them, aim to make a difference, and prefer to lead rather than control (Akoğlan Kozak, 2008: 506).

Leadership studies performed in recent years deal with a wider range of issues and attempt to reconceptualize leadership (Saylı & Baytok, 2014: 111). In this context, the literature display that there are many different current leadership approaches such as servant leadership, transformational, leadership, authentic leadership, spiritual leadership and ethical leadership, charismatic leadership. Therefore, charismatic leadership is one of the current leadership approaches. To put it differently, charismatic leadership is one of the most widely acknowledged leadership principles within the context of the leadership strategies that have been developed in recent years (Akoğlan Kozak, 2008: 506).

The Greek definition of the term charisma includes "gift, favor." It is used to describe the holy spirit in the Bible. Among the terms used to represent the charismatic characteristic are judgment, prophecy, teaching, duty, wisdom, and healing (Conger & Kanungo, 1987: 637).

According to Weber (1968: 358–359), the charismatic person is distinguishable from regular people and is perceived to having supernatural, superhuman, or at the very least exceptional powers and attributes that are unavailable to ordinary people but are thought to be of divine origin or divine origin. On the basis of this, the individual is treated as a leader and sets an example (Conger & Kanungo, 1994: 440).

German political economy expert and sociologist Max Weber played an important role in conceptualizing charismatic leadership and laying its theoretical foundations (Özdemir & Pektaş, 2020: 4). Therefore, the research done by Max Weber in 1964 serves as the foundation for the usage of the paradigm of charismatic leadership (Akoğlan Kozak, 2008: 497). Weber produced a substantial contribution to the conceptual growth of charismatic leadership since he included charismatic authority in his authority classification (Özdemir & Pektaş, 2020: 4). Weber conceptualized charismatic authority but did not provide a detailed description of the charismatic leader's characteristics and behaviors that differentiate the leader from other leaders (Conger & Kanungo, 1987; Saylı & Baytok: 2014: 117). Later, in the MLQ-Multifunctional Leadership Questionnaire developed by Bass, charismatic leadership as a dimension of transformational leadership was discussed (Marjosola & Takala, 2000; Akoğlan Kozak, 2008:498).

Despite the fact that charisma lacks a systematic infrastructure (Conger and Kanungo, 1987), study in this field at the organizational level has allowed us to comprehend the idea of leadership process in particular. For instance, charismatic leadership approaches have shown the remarkable effects of leaders, which could not be the focus of earlier leadership theories. The relevance of followers' emotional responses to the leader was highlighted in charismatic leadership approaches, whereas leader-follower interaction was viewed as a rational-measurable element in earlier theories. Charismatic leadership theories, which reveal how the leader can influence the followers without establishing a face-to-face relationship in bilateral relations (Yukl, 1994), drew attention to the effects of the leader's role and symbolic behaviors on the followers (Saylı & Baytok, 2014: 122).

Charismatic leadership has been conceptualized as "*a process of signaling by which a leader influences his followers to achieve effective management*" (Teng & Tsaur, 2022). At the same time, a charismatic leader is defined as "*a person who signals a leader by using values-based, symbolic and emotionally charged mechanisms*" (Antonakis, Bastardoz, Jacquart & Shamir, 2016). In a study conducted by Jung and Sosik (2006) to determine what distinguishes charismatic leaders from others, they found that charismatic leaders constantly have self-monitoring, participation in impression management, motivation to reach social power, and self-actualization motivation (Northouse, 2013: 20). Charismatic leaders are often heralded as corporate heroes by managing setbacks, initiating new ventures, participating in organizational renewal or change, and achieving outstanding performance from individuals (Howell & Avolio, 1992). Charismatic leaders thrive on change and reason. They believe strongly in their cause, vision, and making things happen. Their dreams are usually big, and their ideas are innovative (Poskas & Messer, 2015). However, charismatic leaders have great referential power and influence. Followers want to identify with them and emulate them. Followers develop intense feelings about them and above all followers trust them (Bass, 1985).

The dearth of charismatic leaders in business and industry may be due to managers' lack of the requisite abilities, although more charismatic leaders may be found in corporate settings and may be crucial to an organization's success because of their influence on their followers (Bass, 1985). Some of the impacts, such as the followers' emotional attachment to the leader, are highlighted by charismatic leadership theories. These outcomes, according to the argument, are brought about by leadership behaviors that appeal to followers' drives for self-expression, self-esteem, self-worth, and self-consistency, including self-concept. Leader behavior activates followers' self-concepts, which in turn influences followers' later motivational mechanisms. These variables and processes that come into play have a strong positive effect on the behavior and psychological state of followers (Shamir, House & Arthur, 1993).

The emergence of wise leadership appears to be influenced by charismatic leadership (McCann, Graves & Cox, 2014), which *"involves a combination of one's awareness of the workplace environment and the ability to anticipate outcomes within the workplace dynamics"* (Elbaz & Haddoud, 2017). On the other hand, charismatic leadership is at the center of the transformational leadership process (Bass, 1985). There is a common feature between charismatic leadership and transformational leadership. Both focus on charisma (Elkhwesky, Salem, Ramkissoon & Garcia, 2022). The concept of charisma is a personal leadership ability that people are born with but can learn and develop. Charisma is a natural attraction that draws people to the leader and the enthusiasm of the leader (Piuchan & Prachansit, 2019). However, in order for the charismatic influence to emerge and the followers willingly submit to the leader's influence, the leader must be accepted by the followers as he conveys the values and mission that appeal to his followers (Antonakis, Bastardoz, Jacquart & Shamir, 2016). Accordingly, in organizational settings, charisma is one of the critical aspects that sets apart the average manager from the real leader. Charisma includes a two-way process. If a leader has supporters who give him great value and personal power, that leader is thought to have charisma. When subordinates have extremely reliant personalities, this is simpler to accomplish. A charismatic leader or a leader who tries to employ emotional inspiration is less likely to persuade followers who take pride in their rationalism, skepticism, independence, concern for the rule of law, and care for the leader's example. Egalitarian, self-assured, highly educated, self-reliant, and high-status subordinates are more inclined to reject charismatic leaders (Bass, 1985).

It is established that charismatic leaders can be classified as either ethical or unethical. Many charismatic leaders incorporate their followers' goals, dreams, and aspirations in their visions. These leaders encourage critical and creative thinking in their followers, give them growth opportunities, welcome both positive and negative criticism, value other people's contributions, impart knowledge to their followers, and uphold moral principles that place a strong emphasis on the group's, organization's, or society's common interests. These leaders are viewed as "ethical charismatics". Other charismatic leaders work toward their own objectives. These charismatic leaders have the capacity to dominate and mislead their followers. They simultaneously uphold moral norms that serve their own self-interest and advocate for what is best for themselves rather than their organization. "Ethical charismatics" are the name given to these leaders (Howell & Avolio, 1992). On the other hand, when studies on the dimensions of charismatic leadership are explored, Nandal & Krishnan (2000) state that charismatic leadership consists of five factors: strategic vision, environmental awareness, sensitivity to the needs of members, personal risks, and unconventional behaviors. In addition, Shao, Feng, Hu & Liu (2009) state that there are five factors in charismatic leadership: environmental sensitivity, dynamic leadership, exemplary leadership, personal leadership, and leader expectation. Environmental sensitivity is defined as the leader's ability to make timely decisions to apply for organizational environmental change and dynamic leadership as the leader's ability to convey an exciting vision and paint an exciting picture of the organization's future. Exemplary leadership is the leader's ability to set a good example for his employees by participating in organizational activities, while personal leadership is explained as the leader's ability to encourage his employees and develop their self-confidence. Finally, it is expressed that the leader is expected to create high expectations for them and strengthen them.

One of the theories including charismatic leadership (Conger & Kanungo, 1987; Conger & Kanungo, 1988) is the "Attribution Theory of Charismatic Leadership" (Conger & Kanungo, 1994: 442). According to Conger and Kanungo (1994), the behaviors displayed by charismatic leaders are listed as setting vision, showing sensitivity to member needs, showing environmental sensitivity, taking personal risks, changing the current situation, and exhibiting extraordinary behavior.

- **Setting Vision:** Charismatic leaders differ from other leaders with their ability to formulate and express an inspiring vision, and with behavior and actions that create the impression that they and their mission are extraordinary (Conger & Kanungo, 1994: 442).
- **Showing Sensitivity to Member Needs:** Charismatic leaders are aware of their followers' requirements and feelings. They pay attention to what matters to their followers and are aware of what they want. They create an emotional connection with their followers. As a result, they merge with their followers. They take an interest in each of their followers individually, attend to their needs, and promote their personal growth. (Sincer, 2021: 25). The sensitivity of charismatic leaders to the needs of their members causes the belief that they are valued among the audience. The employees who perceive that their needs are taken care of can follow their leaders without any questions (Oktay & Gül: 2003: 409; Arıkan, Kılıç, & Becerikli (2017: 6). The needs, values, resources, and aspirations of their followers are transformed by charismatic leaders into shared interests. Because they trust their leaders and place a high value on their ideals, followers are devoted to their leaders' visions and are more motivated as a result (Akgündüz, 2020: 58).
- **Showing Environmental Sensitivity:** While defining the vision and implementing the established vision, charismatic leaders take care to set attainable goals by assessing the organizational environment, opportunities, and threats (Sincer, 2021: 25).
- **Taking Personal Risks**: Followers demonstrate emotional commitment when a charismatic leader is prepared to make some personal sacrifices for them as well as to pay a price for his own success and life (Oktay & Gül, 2003: 409). Charismatic leaders can take personal risks for the benefit of the organization. These personal risks may include possible financial loss or loss of more significant achievements, withdrawal of organizational resources, dismissal or demotion, and loss of formal or informal status, power, authority, and credibility (Conger & Kanungo, 1987: 642).

- **Changing The Current Situation:** Charismatic leaders are leaders who initiate change. The ability of these leaders to foster change by seeking innovations rather than maintaining the status quo is one of the most crucial traits of these leaders. The inclination of charismatic leaders to challenge the status quo is one of their defining characteristics. In order to achieve organizational objectives, they prefer to do things completely differently and drastically alter them as opposed to "doing things as they were done before." (Oktay & Gül, 2003: 406; Arıkan, Kılıç, & Becerikli, 2017: 6).
- **Exhibiting Extraordinary Behavior:** According to Baltaş (2000:136-137), one of the characteristics of charismatic leaders is to exhibit extraordinary behaviors. These actions do not constitute misconduct or unethical conduct. It means acting in ways that differ from the conventionally recognized patterns up until this point. These characteristics of charismatic leaders manifest in the way they use unexpected behaviors, unusual approaches, and unexpected behaviors to surprise their followers in order to accomplish the organization's objectives. According to Yukl (1994: 322-323) Conger and Kanungo, charisma is attributed to leaders who try to achieve the vision through non-traditional methods. The use of innovative strategies that are considered successful causes the leader to attribute greater mastery to his subordinates (as cited in Oktay & Gül, 2003: 406).

Conger and Kanungo (1994: 442) classified the characteristics of the behavior of charismatic leaders, and according to the authors, the characteristics include opposing and attempting to change the status quo, having an idealized vision that clearly distinguishes from the status quo, having a shared perspective and idealized vision, and viewing the person as a hero deserving of imitation. They also asserted that charismatic leaders are non-conformists who specialize in exploiting non-traditional techniques to transcend the current order and who disinterestedly maintain their cause despite suffering considerable personal risk and sacrifice. Additionally, in order to alter the status quo, these leaders must possess a high level of environmental awareness. Moreover, they are those who have a combination of future vision and motivation, and personal strength (expertise, respect, and admiration for a unique hero). Finally, they are elite, enterprising, and exemplary, and have the ability to transform people to share the radical changes advocated (Conger & Kanungo, 1987: 641) In this direction, charismatic leaders are needed in the tourism sector as well as in every sector.

MAIN FOCUS OF THE CHAPTER

Charismatic Leadership in Tourism

Tourism is turning into a well-liked option for communities looking to enhance their local economies, react to shifting social and environmental conditions, and aim for new standards as a result of the growing impact of globalization, economic diversion, and challenges. The tourism sector must, however, devise new strategies for bringing about positive, long-lasting change as a result of its own observed and accelerating changes (Poskas & Messer, 2015).

The tourist industry is one of the most significant subbranches of the service sector and is a labor-intensive industry. One of the industries most impacted by changes brought on by increased global competition is the tourism industry. The degree to which tourism businesses can react to these developments and changes will determine how competitive they are. On the other hand, employees in the tourism industry have a direct impact on the company's performance through the services they offer. Additionally, characteristics including an employee's behavior, dedication to the company, and motivation are among those that influence customer satisfaction and competitive advantage. Therefore, as in all sectors, there is a need for leaders who have a direct or indirect influence on the employees in tourism businesses, holding them together depending on the objectives of the business and affecting their performance (Turan & Ersöz, 2021: 4).

Regardless of their product and service categories, businesses in the tourism sector require teamwork in order to fulfill their aims and objectives inside an organization. The tourism industry is one where conditions change regularly and there is fierce competition, therefore they also need leaders who can make crucial judgments. It can also be said that leaders with the mentioned characteristics are also charismatic leaders in tourism businesses where leadership behaviors are effective in teamwork (Erkılıç, 2021: 155).

The loyalty of employees who are managed jointly to the aims and objectives strengthens with the good charismatic leadership behaviors that will be displayed or are displayed in tourism businesses, and they have access to a space where they may express their thoughts. When there is no need for a leader, people are also more prepared to accept responsibility and have the freedom to decide how to carry out their tasks. They believe in achieving the same goals along with the leader, by demonstrating a commitment to the values and culture of the business, along with the inspiration, excitement, and power they get from the leader (Erkılıç, 2021: 156).

As a result, it is necessary to look into the relationships between leaders and followers, and in this context, looking at the relationship between charismatic leaders and followers yields valuable information. Because they can build strong bonds with their followers, charismatic leaders can promote or encourage civic or community involvement, which is essential for the development of networks or social capital in their communities (Poskas & Messer, 2015). At the same time, thanks to the self-confidence and optimism of the charismatic leader, it will be possible to avoid bad managerial effects and to develop training programs for the management level of tourism activities (Gerges, Kamal & Mohammed, 2017).

Maher (2017) investigated how the perceptions of employees in the tourism sector about their leaders affect their thoughts and behaviors about work. In his study, it was determined that charismatic leadership in travel businesses was positively related to the psychological commitment of the employee. In the study by Gerges, Kamal, & Mohammed (2017), in which the effect of charismatic leadership behaviors of travel agency managers on organizational performance was examined, it was revealed that charismatic leadership behaviors (non-traditional behavior, strategic vision, environmental awareness, and sensitivity to the needs of organizational members) positively affect organizational performance. On the other hand, leadership is also included as a basic plan for successful destination management (Valente, Dredge & Lohmann, 2014). It is also argued that leadership in a destination is not necessarily attributed to organizations but individuals. Charismatic entrepreneurs and business managers, determined and visionary municipal officials, and influential politicians are able to take control of leadership in the destination as primary stakeholders in tourism development (Komppula, 2016).

Charismatic Leadership in Hospitality Businesses

Compared to other industries, the hospitality businesses within the tourist sector as well as the industry as a whole operate under intense competition and have a number of distinctive characteristics. Businesses must contend with rising customer demands as a result of this severe competition. Therefore, businesses must foster employee creativity and raise the caliber of their services (Bilgin, Kuzey, Torlak & Uyar,

2015; Hoang, Evered, Binney & Luu, 2021). However, hospitality business employees often need to be on the front lines and take swift action to provide good service. For this reason, the inability of the employees who come into contact with the customer to respond quickly to the unexpected situations of the service provided or the unwillingness of the employees may cause unsatisfactory service encounters for the guest (Valdivia, Burin & Montes, 2019). Therefore, hospitality businesses need employees who are seen as the key to organizational success in order to provide quality service (Weerakit & Beeton, 2018). Certain management styles can play a very important role in hospitality businesses in order to get positive results from employees as well (Valdivia, Burin & Montes, 2019). In management styles, leadership that can be an admired role model creating a positive perception and satisfaction among employees is called successful leadership, and successful leadership and supervision are important for businesses (Priastana & Mujiati, 2020; Weerakit & Beeton, 2018). Interpersonal skills are seen as the most important competency for managers as factors affecting leadership in hospitality businesses. Age, managerial experience, and hotel management types have significant effects on the importance of leadership competency levels. It has been determined that the most important leadership competencies for small and mid-level hospitality business managers are "coaching and empowerment", "intellectual encouragement", "interpersonal skills", "role modelling" and "inspirational motivation" (Weerakit & Beeton, 2018). On the other hand, it is stated that charismatic leadership can be adopted as the leadership style of an organization dealing with tourism (Aguzman, Manurung, Pradipto & Sanny, 2020).

The charismatic leadership style is reported to leave a favorable impression on the employees in the hotel departments by fostering a climate of trust and respect (Dimitrov, 2015). At the same time, it is evidenced that charismatic leadership and emotional commitment as well as charismatic leadership and job satisfaction in the hotel industry have strong positive relationships. At the same time, the relationship between charismatic leadership and organizational citizenship behavior is mediated by both job satisfaction and affective commitment. Businesses in the hotel industry are advised to pay close attention to emotional commitment and job satisfaction, and in this context, the role of charismatic leadership draws attention (Bilgin, Kuzey, Torlak & Uyar, 2015).

According to the study by Greger and Peterson (2000), the suggested profiles based on interviews with hospitality managers for leadership and business success are to have a vision and passion and the ability to communicate them to others, core values, including integrity, caring for culture, conscientiousness and accessibility, personal touch and involvement; to be an exemplary person; to have high energy and a determined work ethic, to have the ability to listen, to have imagination and creativity, to use technology effectively; always to think and act like "us".

When other studies on charismatic leadership with hospitality business employees are examined in the literature, it is seen that Kozak & Uca (2008) conducted a study with managers of five-star hospitality businesses in Alanya, Turkey, and the styles of democratic leadership, charismatic leadership, laissez-faire leadership, and autocratic leadership of the managers participating in the research were examined. It was found that 12.3% and 7.9% of managers adopted charismatic and autocratic leadership styles, respectively. Choi (2010) examined the effect of charismatic leadership and transactional leadership on organizational commitment among kitchen workers in hotel businesses, and it was determined that both leadership styles have significant positive effects on employees' organizational commitment. It has been determined that charismatic leadership has a stronger effect on organizational commitment than transactional leadership. On the other hand, it has also been revealed that job satisfaction has moderator effects between charismatic leadership and organizational commitment. The research was conducted by Bozkurt & Göral (2013) in order to determine the leadership styles of the senior managers of the hotels and the innovation strategies they prefer to follow, and it focused on the general managers and owners of four and five-star hotels operating in Ankara. As a result of the study, it was stated that the views on charismatic leadership style behaviors were more positive than other modern leadership styles. In the study by Tromp & Blomme (2014) conducted with the employees of hospitality businesses, a positive relationship was found between the transactional and charismatic leadership style and the view on the presented work-home arrangements. Transactional and charismatic leadership styles seem to have a positive effect on perceived work-home arrangements and flexibility. It has been determined that the more the employees experience the leadership style of their managers as charismatic and/or interactive, the more positive their opinions about the work-home arrangements offered. The study is considered important to reduce the negative work-home interaction among employees of human resource management policies in the hospitality industry. In another study conducted with the employees of hospitality businesses, the existence of a strong positive relationship between charismatic leadership and corporate reputation was revealed. It is concluded that the higher the charismatic leadership level, the more it strengthens the reputation of the hotel. Charismatic leadership has the greatest impact on corporate reputation, followed by leadership skills. On the other hand, leadership skills have a great impact on charismatic leadership. It is concluded that the higher the level of leadership skills, the higher the level of charismatic leadership will be (Stavrinoudis & Chrysanthopoulou, 2017). In the research conducted by Arıkan & Kılıç (2017), in which the relationship between charismatic leadership and organizational citizenship for the employees of five-star hotels in Kuşadası was determined, it was determined that there was a positive and significant relationship between the two variables. However, it was also found that there is a weak but significant relationship between charismatic leadership sub-dimensions such as setting vision, being sensitive to member needs, showing environmental sensitivity, taking personal risks, changing the current situation, and exhibiting extraordinary behavior and organizational citizenship behavior. In the study of Yamak & Eyüpoğlu (2018) in which they investigated the dominant leadership styles of 4 and 5-star hotel managers operating in the Turkish Republic of Northern Cyprus, it was determined that charismatic leadership was the dominant leadership style among autocratic, democratic, laissez-faire, and charismatic leadership styles. This means that the charismatic leadership style is perceived significantly more often compared to the remaining leadership styles. In the study of Piuchan & Prachansit (2019), they aimed to show the leadership characteristics and styles of two leading hotel operators in Asia, and it was indicated that the ability to communicate well, share dreams, and motivate people to pursue the same goals are stated as clear combinations of charismatic leadership. Thus, charismatic leadership is emphasized as an ideal leader with behavior that creates confidence in leaders respected by their followers, visionary, ability to inspire, high morale, and verbal and non-verbal communication. On the other hand, there are four widely shared characteristics of how to be successful hotel leaders in the study, and it is stated that among the defined characteristics are visionary leadership, charismatic leadership, entrepreneurial leadership, and ethical leadership. In the study conducted by Priastana and Mujiati (2020), it was revealed that charismatic leadership can affect the performance of the food and beverage department employees of the hotel business.

SOLUTIONS AND RECOMMENDATIONS

Businesses in the tourism industry should concentrate on recruiting, training, and motivating leaders to create rewarding connections with their employees. The energy and willingness of the employees to work harder are raised by charismatic leaders. Therefore, as part of their leadership development or promotion, tourism businesses should offer pertinent training. At the same time, it seems important to encourage employees to adopt charismatic leadership behavior in order to influence and improve their psychological participation (Maher, 2017). The ability to take the initiative and take personal risks on behalf of the hotel is one thing, but executives must also stand out for their unconventional behavior in order to accomplish the goals. The best leaders have excellent talents in many different areas, are attentive to the demands of their team members, and the atmosphere found in hotels (interpersonal communication, business, and leadership). Hotel management and the hotel's reputation as a whole are improved by the interaction between charismatic leadership and leader qualities (Stavrinoudis & Chrysanthopoulou, 2017). In hospitality businesses, human resources strategies are also believed to be significant for the development of leadership skills. The human resources strategy should be created to help supervisors and managers in acquiring motivating leadership abilities and to encourage them to use these skills with their staff, with a focus on training and development, performance management, and rewards. These procedures promote a productive workplace where team members can work effectively, think creatively, and realize their full potential (Weerakit & Beeton, 2018). However, there is also a requirement for clearly defined processes that center on finding managers who have leadership qualities and can, thus, exhibit charismatic leadership. These managers must be given the space, power, and trust they need to bring success. Because of this, it is essential to employ leaders in roles that will allow them to contribute to the advancement of the hotel and its services. Such approaches should be backed up by training initiatives that hone and improve the manager's leadership abilities (Stavrinoudis & Chrysanthopoulou, 2017).

Considering the positive effects of charismatic leadership style on employees in hospitality businesses, it is weighty for managers to have some basic characteristics of charismatic leadership. In this context, suggestions that are thought to contribute to the sector are presented below.

- Modern leadership styles are needed in order for hospitality businesses to meet customer demands in an intensely competitive environment, ensure customer satisfaction, and provide qualified service, thus ensuring development and continuity in the business. One of these leadership styles is charismatic leadership.
- It is considered important to have charismatic leaders in the organization who develop creativity and critical thinking in their followers and also provide them with opportunities for development. Therefore, it is thought that it is important to determine the managers who apply the charismatic leadership style in the hotel.
- Since it is seen that the charismatic leadership style contributes to the performance of the employees and the reputation of the hotel, it would be beneficial to give these people the necessary authority and responsibilities, especially training, in order to support the development of the people who show charismatic leadership behavior.
- It is crucial to guarantee employee satisfaction in hospitality businesses where the employee turnover rate is high. Therefore, it is noteworthy to lower the intention to quit and to make sure that employees are highly committed to the organization. This is based on an effective management strategy. This is based on a good management approach. For this reason, there is a need for charismatic leadership behaviors, which is one of the visionary leadership styles that will move the employees behind them.

FUTURE RESEARCH DIRECTIONS

The literature review displays that studies on charismatic leadership have been primarily conducted with employees of the hospitality industry. By conducting research on charismatic leadership with the employees of other tourism businesses, it is claimed that it will benefit both the literature and the sector. However, it can be observed that the charismatic leadership style is researched with the subjects of organizational performance, psychological commitment, emotional commitment, job satisfaction, corporate reputation, and work-home arrangements in the studies done with the employees of tourism organizations. Yet, it is thought that it is important to investigate the charismatic leadership style in subjects that have not been studied such as organizational citizenship behavior, organizational commitment, or intention to leave, and burnout.

CONCLUSION

It may be mentioned that human-based management techniques are now acceptable in hospitality businesses, where it is paramount to satisfy the requirements of both customers and employees. Managers are expected to take on a leadership role in the effective implementation of these management practices, combined with more flexible management. One of the most crucial elements in evaluating employee performance and the achievement of organizational goals is the leadership style of today's managers. This situation gains even more importance due to the fact that hotel processing is labor-intensive, and the employee turnover rate is high. In order to foster innovation and creativity, create managerial settings that result in high employee satisfaction, manage change, and establish vision, managers and leaders are required in the hospitality businesses (Akoğlan Kozak, 2008: 505; Kılıç, Gülaydın, Sürücü & Kasapoğlu, 2018: 995).

Tourism businesses have a delicate structure, and when they are severely affected by crises, the executives of those businesses are compelled to take on significant responsibilities and develop certain traits. In this manner, instead of responding quickly and in accordance with one opinion, leaders can make the business productive by taking more appropriate stages in the process and listening to other opinions with the help of subordinates and superiors. Likewise, as most tourism-related businesses require a lot of labor, it can be claimed that human-oriented leadership approaches will bring more success in today's conditions (Göktaş, 2021: 170). In other words, in order to procure a competitive edge in the rapidly expanding tourism industry, multinational companies must adopt management strategies that boost employee motivation. It has been discovered that in order to enhance employee motivation, the tourism industry, which is infamous for its lengthy work hours, low job satisfaction, low earnings, and authoritarian management models, also needs fresh leadership philosophies (Halis, 2021: 144). Charismatic leadership is one of these leadership philosophies.

Following a review of studies on charismatic leaders in the tourism industry, it was encountered that these studies primarily sought to ascertain whether the managers possessed a charismatic leadership style, while also examining the relationships between charismatic leadership and organizational performance, psychological commitment, emotional commitment, job satisfaction, corporate reputation, and work-home arrangements. In addition, it has been reported in these studies that charismatic leadership is positively related to the psychological commitment of the employee, positively affects organizational performance, has a positive relationship with organizational citizenship, and has significant positive effects on employees' organizational commitment. On the other hand, it is seen that the relationship of charismatic leadership in the field of tourism with different subjects is also examined. In Tuan's (2020) study with the employees and managers of tour companies operating in Vietnam, it was aimed to reveal the role of charismatic leadership in nurturing collective work resourcefulness and therefore team performance. The results unveiled that crafting of sales job served as a mediator for the nexus between charismatic leadership and in-role as well as extra-role performance of sales teams. Furthermore, the effect of charismatic leadership on collective job crafting was moderated by collective person-group fit. The findings underscore the magnitude of building charismatic leadership to help sales teams to promote collective job crafting and enhance their performance. Moreover, it was concluded that the higher the level of charismatic leadership, which has a strong positive relationship with corporate reputation, the more it strengthens the reputation of the hotel. As a result of the abovementioned research, it can be voiced that the service quality may improve, and customer satisfaction may be intensified considering that people who adopt charismatic leadership in the tourism sector positively impact the employees of tourism businesses.

REFERENCES

Aguzman, G., Manurung, A. H., Pradipto, Y. D., & Sanny, L. (2020). The effect of charismatic leadership on the sustainability of tourism destination with entrepreneurship orientation and community empowerment as a mediator. *Advances in Social Science, Education and Humanities Research*, 585, 691–695.

Akgündüz, Y. (2020). Örgütsel davranış [Organizational Behavior]. Nobel Yayınevi.

Akoğlan Kozak, M. (2017). Liderlik. In *Rekreasyonel liderlik ve turist rehberliği: Kavram ve kuramlar üzerinden bir analiz*. Detay Yayıncılık.

Akoğlan Kozak, M. (2008). Turizm işletmelerinde liderlik ve liderlik tarzları. [Leadership in tourism and types of leadership] In Turizm işletmelerinde çağdaş yönetim teknikleri. [Modern management techniques in Tourism Enterprises] Detay Yayıncılık.

Antonakis, J., Bastardoz, N., Jacquart, P., & Shamir, B. (2016). Charisma: An illdefined and ill-measured gift. *Annual Review of Organizational Psychology and Organizational Behavior*, 3(1), 293–319. doi:10.1146/annurev-orgpsych-041015-062305

Baltaş, A. (2000). *Değişimin içinden geleceğe doğru ekip çalışması ve liderlik* [Teamwork and leadership through change towards the future]. Remzi Kitabevi.

Bass, B. M. (1990). *Bass and Stogdill's handbook of leadership: A survey of theory and research*. Free Press.

Bass, B. M. (1985). Leadership: Good, better, best. *Organizational Dynamics*, 13(3), 26–40. doi:10.1016/0090-2616(85)90028-2

Bilgin, N., Kuzey, C., Torlak, G., & Uyar, A. (2015). An investigation of antecedents of organizational citizenship behavior in the Turkish hospitality industry: A structural equation approach. *International Journal of Culture, Tourism and Hospitality Research*, 9(2), 200–222. doi:10.1108/IJCTHR-08-2014-0072

Biviano, J. A. (2000). *Charismatic leadership: An effective instrument for cultural transformation.* RMIT Business School of Management Working Paper Series.

Bozkurt, Ö., & Göral, M. (2013). Modern liderlik tarzlarının yenilik stratejilerine etkisini belirlemeye yönelik bir çalışma [A study to determine the effect of modern leadership styles on innovation strategies]. *Anadolu Üniversitesi Sosyal Bilimler Dergisi, 13*(4), 1–14.

Choi, H. J. (2010). The effects of leadership styles on organizational commitment among cuisine employees in hotel-focused on the moderated effect of job satisfaction. *The Korean Journal of Culinary Research, 16*(5), 64–78.

Conger, J. A., & Kanungo, R. N. (1994). Charismatic leadership in organizations: Perceived behavioral attributes and their measurement. *Journal of Organizational Behavior, 15*(5), 439–452. doi:10.1002/job.4030150508

Conger, J. A., & Kanungo, R. N. (1987). Toward a behavioral theory of charismatic leadership in organizational settings. *Academy of Management Review, 12*(4), 637–647. doi:10.2307/258069

Conger, J. A., & Kanungo, R. N. (1988). Behavioral dimensions of charismatic leadership. In Charismatic Leadership. Jossey Bass.

Dimitrov, D. (2015). Leadership in a humane organization. *European Journal of Training and Development, 39*(2), 122–142. doi:10.1108/EJTD-07-2014-0051

Edmonstone, J., & Western, J. (2002). Leadership development in health care: What do we know? *Journal of Management in Medicine, 16*(1), 34–47. doi:10.1108/02689230210428616 PMID:12069350

Elbaz, A. M., & Haddoud, M. Y. (2017). The role of wisdom leadership in increasing job performance: Evidence from the Egyptian tourism sector. *Tourism Management, 63*, 66–76. doi:10.1016/j.tourman.2017.06.008

Elkhwesky, Z., Salem, I. E., Ramkissoon, H., & Garcia, J. A. C. (2022). A systematic and critical review of leadership styles in contemporary hospitality: A roadmap and a call for future research. *International Journal of Contemporary Hospitality Management, 34*(5), 1925–1958. doi:10.1108/IJCHM-09-2021-1128

Ergun Özler, D. (2013). Liderlik. In Yönetim ve oganizasyon. Anadolu Üniversitesi Açıköğretim Fakültesi Yayınları.

Erkılıç, E. (2021). Turizm işletmelerinde karizmatik liderlik. In Turizm işletmelerinde liderlik. Detay Yayıncılık.

Ersöz, G. Y., & Turan, B. (2021). Turizm işletmelerinde etkileşimci liderlik. In Turizm İşletmelerinde Liderlik. Detay Yayıncılık.

Gandolfi, F., & Stone, S. (2018). Leadership, leadership styles, and servant leadership. *Journal of Management Research, 18*(4), 261–269.

Gerges, S., Kamal, N. M., & Mohammed, H., A. (2017). The impact of charismatic leadership on the organizational performance in travel agencies. *Journal of Faculty of Tourism and Hotels-University of Sadat City, 1*(2/1), 128-150.

Göktaş, L. S. (2021). Turizm işletmelerinde kuantum liderlik. Turizm işletmelerinde hizmetkar liderlik [Quantum leadership in tourism businesses. Servant leadership in tourism businesses]. In Turizm işletmelerinde liderlik. Detay Yayıncılık.

Greger, K., R. & Peterson, J., S. (2000). Leadership profiles for the new millennium. *Cornell Hotel and Restaurant Administration Quarterly,* (1), 16-29.

Halis, M. (2021). Turizm işletmelerinde hizmetkar liderlik [Servant leadership in tourism businesses]. Detay Yayıncılık.

Hoang, G., Evered, E. W., Binney, L. L., & Luu, T. T. (2021). Empowering leadership in hospitality and tourism management: A systematic literatüre review. *International Journal of Contemporary Hospitality Management, 33*(12), 4182–4214. doi:10.1108/IJCHM-03-2021-0323

Howell, J. M., & Avolio, B. J. (1992). The ethics of charismatic leadership: Submission or liberation? *The Academy of Management Executive, 6*(2), 43–54.

Hughes, R. (2009). Time for leadership development interventions in the publice health nutrition workforce. *Public Health Nutrition, 12*(8), 1029. doi:10.1017/S1368980009990395 PMID:19570300

Jago, A. G. (1982). Leadership: Perspectives in theory and research. Management Science, 28(3), 315–336.

Jung, D., & Sosik, J. J. (2006). Who are the spellbinders? Identifying personal attributes of charismatic leaders. Journal of Leadership & Organizational Studies, 12, 12–27.

Kılıç, G., Gülaydın, M., Sürücü, Ö., & Kasapoğlu, B. (2018). Beş yıldızlı otel işletmelerinde liderlik davranışları ile örgütsel muhalefet ilişkisi [The relationship between leadership behaviors and organizational opposition in five-star hotel businesses]. *Uluslararası Sosyal Araştırmalar Dergisi, 11*(59), 994–1003.

Komppula, R. (2016). The role of different stakeholders in destination development. *Tourism Review, 71*(1), 67–76. doi:10.1108/TR-06-2015-0030

Kozak, M. A., & Uca, S. (2008). Effective factors in the constitution of leadership styles: A study of Turkish hotel managers. *Anatolia: An International Journal of Tourism and Hospitality Research, 19*(1), 117–134. doi:10.1080/13032917.2008.9687057

Maher, A. (2017). Charismatic leadership impact on employee psychological engagement: Evidence from travel companies. *Journal of Faculty Tourism and Hotels-University of Sadat City, 1*(2/1), 151-178.

Marjolosa Aaltio, I., & Takala, T. (2000). Charismatic leadership, manipulation and the complexity of organizational life. *Journal of Workplace Learning: Employee Counselling Today, 12*(4), 146–158. doi:10.1108/13665620010332750

McCann, J. T., Graves, D., & Cox, L. (2014). Servant leadership, employee satisfaction, and organizational performance in rural community hospitals. *International Journal of Business and Management, 9*(10), 28–38. doi:10.5539/ijbm.v9n10p28

Nandal, V., & Krishnam, V. (2000). Charismatic leadership and self efficacy: Importance of role clarity. *Management and Labour Studies, 25*(4), 231–243. doi:10.1177/0258042X0002500401

Oktay, E., & Gül, H. (2003). Çalışanların duygusal bağlılıklarının sağlanmasında conger ve kanungo'nun karizmatik lider özelliklerinin etkileri üzerine karaman ve aksaray emniyet müdürlüklerinde yapılan bir araştırma [A research conducted in Karaman and Aksaray Police Departments on the effects of the charismatic leader characteristics of Conger and Kanungo on the emotional commitment of employees]. *Selçuk Üniversitesi Sosyal Bilimler Enstitüsü Dergisi, 10*, 403–427.

Özdemir, M., & Pektaş, V. (2020). Conger- kanungo karizmtik liderlik ölçeğinin türk kültürüne uyarlama çalışması [An adaptation study of the Conger-kazango charismatic leadership scale to Turkish culture]. *Hacettepe Üniversitesi Sosyal Bilimler Dergisi, 2*(1), 2–18.

Piuchan, M., & Prachansit, S. (2019). Hotel pioneers' leadership styles: A case study on the founders of Oberoi Group and Soneva and Six Senses Resort and Spa. *Tourism Original Scientific Paper, 67*(4), 375–388.

Poskas, D. A. T., & Messer, C. C. (2015). Investigating leadership applications in tourism: A case study of leadership in community tourism. *Journal of Teaching in Travel & Tourism, 15*(2), 186–198. doi:10.1080/15313220.2015.1026475

Priastana, A., & Mujiati, N. W. (2020). Influence of transformational leadership style, organizational commitment and work stress on performance of employees food & beverage service division in the resort Bali hotel. *American Journal of Humanities and Social Sciences Research, 4*(5), 174–182.

Saylı, H. & Baytok, A. (2014). *Örgütlerde liderlik teori uygulama ve yeni perspektifler* [Leadership theory application and new perspectives in organizations]. Nobel Akademik Yayıncılık Eğitim Danışmanlık Tic. Ltd.

Shamir, B., House, R., & Arthur, M. B. (1993). The motivational effects of charismatic leadership: A self-concept based theory. *Organization Science, 4*(4), 577–594. doi:10.1287/orsc.4.4.577

Shao, Z., Feng, Y., Hu, Q., & Liu, Y. (2009). A conceptual model for studying the influence of charismatic leadership on ERP implementation lifecycle. *Proceedings of the 42nd Hawaii International Conference on System Sciences*, 1-9.

Sincer, S. (2021). *Öğretmen performansı, örgütsel sadakat ve karizmatik liderlik arasındaki ilişkinin incelenmesi: bir karma yöntem araştırması* [Examining the relationship between teacher performance, organizational loyalty and charismatic leadership: a mixed method research]. Haccettepe Üniversitesi Eğitim Bilimleri Enstitüsü. Eğitim Bilimleri Ana Bilim Dalı Eğitim Yönetimi Teftişi Planlaması ve Ekonomisi Programı.

Şişman, M. (2014). Öğretim liderliği [Instructional Leaderhsip]. Pegem Akademi.

Stavrinoudis, T. A., & Chrysanthopoulou, D. (2017). The role of leadership in building and managing corporate reputation of 4 and 5 star hotels. *Tourism and Hospitality Research, 17*(2), 176–189. doi:10.1177/1467358415613392

Teng, H. Y., & Tsaur, S. H. (2022). Charismatic tour-guiding: Scale development and validation. *Journal of Travel Research, 61*(7), 1495–1507. doi:10.1177/00472875211039556

Tromp, D. M., & Blomme, R. J. (2014). Leadership style and negative work-home interference in the hospitality industry. *International Journal of Contemporary Hospitality Management, 26*(1), 85–106. doi:10.1108/IJCHM-04-2012-0058

Tuan, T. L. (2020). Crafting the sales job collectively in the tourism industry: The roles of charismatic leadership and collective person-group fit. *Journal of Hospitality and Tourism Management, 45*, 245–255. doi:10.1016/j.jhtm.2020.08.003

Turan, B., & Ersöz, G. Y. (2021). Turizm işletmelerinde liderlik. [Leadership in tourism businesses]. Detay Yayıncılık.

Turan, S. (2020). Liderlik nedir? [What is leadership?]. Pegem Akademi. doi:10.14527/9786257052252.01

Valdivia, I. H., Burin, A. R. G., & Montes, J. L. (2019). Effects of different leadership styles on hospitality workers. *Tourism Management, 71*, 402–420. doi:10.1016/j.tourman.2018.10.027

Valente, F. J., Dredge, D., & Lohmann, G. (2014). Leadership capacity in two Brazilian regional tourism organisations. *Tourism Review, 69*(1), 10–24. doi:10.1108/TR-07-2013-0039

Weerakit, N., & Beeton, R. J. S. (2018). Leadership competencies for hospitality management staff in Thailand. *Journal of Human Resources in Hospitality & Tourism, 17*(3), 314–339. doi:10.1080/15332 845.2017.1406277

Yamak, Ö. (2018). Leadership styles of hotel managers in Northern Cyprus: Which style is dominant? *International Journal of Organizational Leadership, 7*(1), 1–11. doi:10.33844/ijol.2018.60202

Yukl, G. (1994). *Leadership in organizations* (3rd ed.). Prentice Hall International.

ADDITIONAL READING

Eatwell, R. (2006). The concept and theory of charismatic leadership. *Totalitarian Movements and Political Religions, 7*(2), 141–156. doi:10.1080/14690760600642156

Boerner, S., Dütschke, E., & Wied, S. (2008). Charismatic leadership and organizational citizenship behavior: Examining the role of stressors and strain. *Human Resource Development International, 11*(5), 507–521. doi:10.1080/13678860802417643

Horn, D., Mathis, C. J., Robinson, S. L., & Randle, N. (2015). Is charismatic leadership effective when workers are pressured to be good citizens. *The Journal of Psychology, 149*(8), 751–774. doi:10.1080/0 0223980.2014.978253 PMID:25491931

Chapter 7
Transformational Leadership Research in the Field of Hospitality:
A Systematic Review and Agenda for Future Research

Mert Gürlek
https://orcid.org/0000-0002-0024-7746
Burdur Mehmet Akif Ersoy University, Turkey

İlker Kılıç
Eskişehir Osmangazi University, Turkey

ABSTRACT

Although transformational leadership is a fundamental research area of leadership literature, it has also spread to other disciplines. Transformational leadership has been a remarkable topic for the hospitality field in terms of the effects that the leader has on his/her followers. For this reason, there has been an important accumulation of knowledge about transformational leadership in the hospitality literature. However, there is no research in the literature that addresses the progress of transformational leadership research in hospitality to help researchers develop theoretical perspectives and guide practitioners' decisions. Therefore, this research aims to systematically review transformational leadership research in the hospitality field. The review included 36 studies from seven key hospitality journals. The findings basically indicate that that research on transformational leadership in the field of hospitality has not experienced sufficient development. There is a need to develop theoretical perspectives specific to the field in the field of hospitality.

DOI: 10.4018/978-1-6684-6713-8.ch007

INTRODUCTION

The hospitality sector has experienced intense competition that requires exceptional understanding and skills. In line with that, environmental conditions are constantly changing and becoming more unpredictable. In such an environment, the leadership skills of hospitality managers come to the fore and transformational leaders are needed to overcome such difficult conditions (Salem, 2015; Prikshat, Rajesh, & Rajaguru, 2021). Therefore, the research on transformational leadership creates value for the hospitality industry. Leadership research has long served as a theoretical lens for the prediction of executive and employee behavior. For more than sixty years, hospitality researchers have been making efforts to identify the types of leadership that lead to higher employee and firm performance (Arici et al., 2021). Out of leadership styles, transformational leadership has particularly received more attention than other leadership styles. As a result of this, articles on transformational leadership are among the most cited leadership articles (Antonakis, Bastardoz, Liu, & Schriesheim, 2014). Huertas-Valdivia, González-Torres, & Nájera-Sánchez (2022) identified eleven main leadership research trends in the hospitality literature and revealed that transformational and servant leadership are the most widely used styles. Transformational leadership is defined as a leadership style that changes the values, ideals, morale and interests of followers of leaders, leading followers to perform better than expected (Bass, 1985; Pieterse et al., 2010). The secret behind the success of transformational leaders is often their charisma and the strong relationships they build with their followers. Such leaders develop collaborative relationships by communicating openly and clearly, supporting teamwork and creating a common vision (Brownell, 2010).

Although transformational leadership is a fundamental research area in the leadership literature, (Bass & Riggio, 2005), it has spread to many industries and disciplines, including the hospitality sector (Giddens, 2018; Elkhwesky et al., 2022). Transformational leadership has been a remarkable issue in the field of hospitality, considering the effects that the leader could have on the followers. For example, Gui, Luo, Zhang, & Deng (2020) conducted a meta-analysis study and found that transformational leadership in the field of hospitality has the strongest effect on relational perceptions, followed by attitudinal and behavioral consequences on subordinates. For this reason, an important accumulation of knowledge about transformational leadership has been formed in the hospitality literature.

However, there are no studies in the literature that address the progress regarding transformational leadership research in the field of hospitality to help researchers develop theoretical perspectives and guide field practitioners in their decision-making processes. Just single research (Gui et al., 2020) conducted a meta-analysis on transformational leadership and focused on a quantitative review of transformational leadership and its consequences. However, this research has not carried out qualitative research. Therefore, this research aims to systematically review transformational leadership research in the field of hospitality. For this purpose, this book chapter seeks answers to the following questions;

- What are the levels of development and current trends in transformational leadership studies?
- What are the consequences of transformational leadership?
- What are the research gaps and suggestions for future studies?

Since the literature on transformational leadership in the field of hospitality has arrived at a certain saturation stage (Wang, Oh, Courtright, & Colbert, 2011; Arnold, 2017), it is time to conduct an in-depth analysis of already published research. Such an analysis will help to present a holistic picture of the current literature. This study used a systematic literature review method. The Web of Science database was used to access the studies on transformational leadership. The articles published in the leading 7 journals in the field of hospitality (International Journal of Contemporary Hospitality Management International Journal of Hospitality Management, International Journal of Hospitality and Tourism Administration, Cornell Hospitality Quarterly, Journal of Hospitality Marketing & Management, Journal of Hospitality & Tourism Research Journal of Hospitality and Tourism Management) have been taken as the focus of the study.

Transformational leadership studies in the field of hospitality have been identified using the aforementioned database to find answers to the questions stated above. Then, a detailed analysis of the extant literature is presented. Finally, research gaps have been identified and suggestions for future research have been developed within the scope of the study

BACKGROUND

Transformational leadership

It is claimed that there are almost as many leadership theories as people are trying to understand the nature of leadership. Of these theories, transformational leadership theory has been one of the most popular theories catching the most interest (Bass, 1998; Newman, & Butler, 2014). Burns (1978) suggested that leadership occurs in two types: transformational and transactional. The difference between these two types of leadership comes from the value that the leaders present to their followers. Transformational leadership involves changes in the beliefs, needs and values of followers, while transactional leadership involves an exchange relationship based on the mutual exchange of a valuable resource (Kuhnert & Lewis, 1987; Jung & Avolio, 2000). This book chapter focused on transformational leadership. Transformational leadership, with the simplest definition, is the ability of a leader to motivate his followers to perform better than expected.

Although there are alternative models on transformational leadership in the literature (e.g. Bass & Avolio, 1995; Kouzes & Posner, 1995; Rafferty & Griffin, 2004), we follow Bass and Avolio's (1995) model as it is well-known and frequently used (see Siangchokyoo et al., 2020). In this context, transformational leadership consists of four dimensions idealized influence, inspirational motivation, individual consideration, and intellectual stimulation (Bass, 1999; Bass, & Avolio, 1995). The idealized effect is the degree to which the leader treats his followers in an admirable way that will allow followers to identify themselves with the leader. Inspirational motivation is the degree to which the leader puts an inspiring vision in front of his followers. Individual consideration is the degree to which the leader knows the individual characteristics of each follower and is interested in his followers' individual needs. Intellectual stimulation is the degree to which the leader can mentally mobilize his followers, support their development of ideas and stimulate their creativity. In the process of intellectual stimulation, leaders guide their followers, acting as a coach or mentor (Bass et al., 2003; Judge & Piccolo, 2004; Kara et al., 2013).

THE TRANSFORMATIONAL LEADERSHIP RESEARCH IN THE HOSPITALITY FIELD

Method

This study used the systematic literature review method. This method provides a detailed presentation of the existing literature (Dhir et al., 2020). Many studies have used this method to examine the previous literature (Guzzo, Abbott, & Madera, 2020; Madanaguli et al., 2021; Hoang et al., 2021). A good systematic literature review consists of the following stages: identification of research questions, identification of the studies to be reviewed, checking the quality of studies to be reviewed, interpretation of the obtained evidence and evaluation of the findings (Khan et al., 2003). The mentioned stages have been carefully followed in this study.

The research questions for which answers were sought in the research are as follows: What are the levels of development and current trends in transformational leadership studies? What are the consequences of transformational leadership? What are the research gaps and recommendations for future studies?

In the study, the Web of Science (WoS) database, which has a high reputation, was used to identify the studies to be reviewed. The keyword "transformational leadership" was used for scanning the database. In this context, firstly, the Hospitality Leisure Sport Tourism category was selected out of the Web of Science Categories. Secondly, journals were selected out of the titles. In this review, seven leading journals focusing on hospitality have been selected; International Journal of Contemporary Hospitality Management International Journal of Hospitality Management, International Journal of Hospitality and Tourism Administration, Cornell Hospitality Quarterly, Journal of Hospitality Marketing & Management, Journal of Hospitality & Tourism Research Journal of hospitality and Tourism Management. The review studies in the literature frequently used the seven leading journals (Aladag et al., 2020; Arici et al., 2021).

As a result of the screening conducted to find the articles on transformational leadership in leading 7 journals, a total of 138 studies published until August 1, 2022, have been accessed. In order for the researchers to determine whether the accessed articles were related to the focus of the research, they read the abstracts of all the accessed articles and coded them. Two researchers answered whether the articles matched the research focus in the coding book. In the first stage, the two researchers reached a 90% consensus on coding. In order to achieve 100% consensus, the two researchers discussed the studies again. Finally, 36 articles directly focusing on transformational leadership out of the examined research were included in the research sample.

A coding book was created for this research using Excel. The coding book consists of details such as the title of the article, year of publication, name of the publishing journal, country, theoretical perspective, industry, antecedents, consequences, analysis unit, method, data collection and data analysis. All of the articles were submitted for content analysis and then the relevant information was transferred to the coding book. Then the two researchers checked the code book separately to confirm that the book fits the purpose of the research. As a result of this control, the two researchers achieved 100% consensus on the coding process. As a result of the review of the literature conducted for the research, a total of 36 transformational leadership articles published in the field of Hospitality were identified. The titles of the accessed studies are detailed in Table 1.

Transformational Leadership Research in the Field of Hospitality

Table 1. List of transformational leadership articles

1.	Brownell, (2010). Leadership in the service of hospitality.
2.	Liang et al., (2017). Transformational leadership and employee voices in the hospitality industry.
3.	Yang et al., (2019). Transformational leadership, proactive personality and service performance: The mediating role of organizational embeddedness.
4.	Uen et al., (2012). Transformational leadership and branding behavior in Taiwanese hotels.
5.	Gui et al., (2020). A meta-analysis of transformational leadership in hospitality research.
6.	Chen & Wu, (2017). Improving the turnover intention of tourist hotel employees: Transformational leadership, leader-member exchange, and psychological contract breach.
7.	Patiar & Wang, (2016). The effects of transformational leadership and organizational commitment on hotel departmental performance.
8.	Gill et al., (2010). The relationship between transformational leadership and employee desire for empowerment.
9.	Mostafa, (2019). Transformational leadership and restaurant employees customer-oriented behaviours: The mediating role of organizational social capital and work engagement.
10.	Dai et al., (2013). Transformational vs transactional leadership: which is better? A study on employees of international tourist hotels in Taipei City.
11.	Zopiatis & Constanti, (2010). Leadership styles and burnout: is there an association?
12.	Luo et al., (2017). Linking leadership and justice to organizational commitment: The mediating role of collective identity in the hotel industry.
13.	Schuckert et al., (2018). Motivate to innovate: How authentic and transformational leaders influence employees' psychological capital and service innovation behavior.
14.	Yu et al., (2022). Robots can't take my job: antecedents and outcomes of Gen Z employees' service robot risk awareness.
15.	Buil et al., (2019). Transformational leadership and employee performance: The role of identification, engagement and proactive personality.
16.	Patiar & Mia, (2009). Transformational leadership style, market competition and departmental performance: Evidence from luxury hotels in Australia.
17.	Jaiswal & Dhar, (2015). Transformational leadership, innovation climate, creative self-efficacy and employee creativity: A multilevel study.
18.	Luo et al., (2019). Transformational leadership and service recovery performance: The mediating effect of emotional labor and the influence of culture.
19.	Li & Yuan, (2017). Both angel and devil: The suppressing effect of transformational leadership on proactive employee's career satisfaction.
20.	Lee et al., (2013). Does transformational leadership style influence employees' attitudes toward food safety practices?
21.	Yang et al., (2021). Dual-focused transformational leadership and service innovation in hospitality organisations: A multilevel investigation.
22.	Rabiul & Yean, (2021). Leadership styles, motivating language, and work engagement: An empirical investigation of the hotel industry.
23.	Luo et al., (2016). How is leadership related to employee self-concept?
24.	Kara et al., (2013). The effects of leadership style on employee well-being in hospitality.
25.	Kloutsiniotis et al., (2022). Transformational Leadership, HRM practices and burnout during the COVID-19 pandemic: The role of personal stress, anxiety, and workplace loneliness.
26.	Tosun et al., (2022). Effects of green transformational leadership on green performance of employees via the mediating role of corporate social responsibility: Reflection from North Cyprus.
27.	Kim et al., (2020). Hotels' environmental leadership and employees' organizational citizenship behavior.
28.	Lee et al., (2011). Do emotions play a mediating role in the relationship between owner leadership styles and manager customer orientation, and performance in service environment?
29.	Chang & Teng, (2017). Intrinsic or extrinsic motivations for hospitality employees' creativity: The moderating role of organization-level regulatory focus.
30.	Luo et al., (2013). Testing the structure and effects of full range leadership theory in the context of China's hotel industry.
31.	Mohamed, (2016). Assessing the effects of transformational leadership: A study on Egyptian hotel employees.
32.	Amankwaa et al., (2022). Tackling hotel employees' turnover: A moderated-mediation analysis of transformational leadership, organisational embeddedness, and community embeddedness.
33.	Kim et al., (2021). The impact of transformational leadership and commitment to change on restaurant employees' quality of work life during a crisis.
34.	Patiar & Wang, (2020). Managers' leadership, compensation and benefits, and departments' performance: Evidence from upscale hotels in Australia.
35.	Yang et al., (2021). Linking transformational leadership to team service innovation in the hospitality industry: A team-level mediation and moderation investigation.
36.	Nazarian et al., (2021). Factors affecting organizational effectiveness in independent hotels–The case of Iran.

Table 2. List of journals and number of articles

Journals	Number of articles
Cornell Hospitality Quarterly	1
International Journal of Hospitality Management	15
International Journal of Contemporary Hospitality Management	13
Journal of Hospitality and Tourism Management	6
Journal of Hospitality Marketing & Management	1
International Journal of Hospitality and Tourism Administration	0
Journal of Hospitality & Tourism Research	0

FINDINGS

Publication Channels

Table 2 shows the number of journals and publications. The articles were found to have been published in five different journals. The journal with the highest number of articles was found to be the International Journal of Hospitality Management with 15 published articles. The International Journal of Contemporary Hospitality Management (IJCHM) ranked second with 13 articles. IJCHM was followed by the Journal of Hospitality and Tourism Management with six articles. Only 5 out of 7 leading Hospitality journals were found to have published articles on transformational leadership. No transformational leadership articles have been published in the International Journal of Hospitality and Tourism Administration and the Journal of Hospitality & Tourism Research. The number of articles per journal was found to be 7.2. These findings show that although transformational leadership research has received much attention in the general management literature, it has not yet received enough attention in the field of hospitality.

The review revealed that the first article on transformational leadership was published in the International Journal of Hospitality Management in 2009 (Patiar & Mia, 2009). The details of publications are presented in Figure 1. Most articles were published in 2017 and 2021. These were followed by the years 2014, 2020 and 2022 respectively. The number of articles published in a year has not yet reached

Figure 1. Evolution of H&T transformational leadership literature

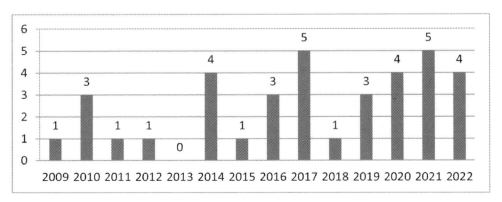

Figure 2. Regions with the greatest production

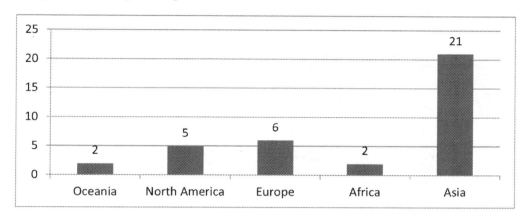

double digits. An average of 5.5 articles were found to have been published in the focused journals between the years 2009-2022.

Articles by Region

The number of articles by region is presented in Figure 2. Most publications were found to be from the Asian region with 21 articles. Europe was found to have ranked second with 6 articles. North America was found to have ranked third with 3 articles. There are an average of 7.2 articles per region.

The distribution of the articles according to the developmental levels of the countries is shown in Figure 3. The highest number of articles were found to have been published in developing countries with 19 articles. This was followed by developed countries and least developed countries, respectively.

Theoretical Perspectives

According to the findings of the literature review, the most used theories were found to be the Theory of Social Exchange (e.g. Dai et al., 2013; Buil, Martínez & Matute, 2019; Yang, Luu, & Qian, 2021) and the Full-range Leadership Theory (e.g. Buil, Martínez, & Matute, 2019; Yang, Luu, & Qian, 2021; Luo,

Figure 3. Distribution of articles according to the development level of the countries

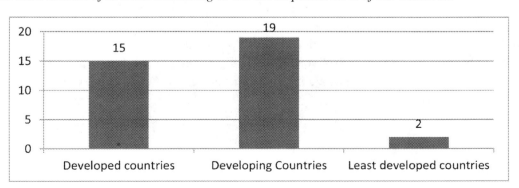

Table 3. Theoretical perspectives

Theoretical Perspective	Number of articles
1. Social information processing theory	1
2. Conservation of resources theory	2
3. Leader-member exchange theory	2
4. Full range leadership theory	3
5. Job embeddedness theory,	1
6. Ability-motivation-opportunity theory	1
7. Path–goal theory	1
8. Regulatory focus theory	1
9. Self-determination theory	1
10. Social cognitive theory	2
11. Social exchange theory	4
12. Social identity theory	1
13. Social learning theory	1
14. Speech act theory	1
15. Self-efficacy theory	1
16. Trait activation theory	1
Note: some studies have used more than one theoretical perspective.	

Wang & Marnburg, 2013; Luo et al., 2016; Nazarian et al., 2021). However, the theory use varies and a total of 16 different theories have been used. Therefore, it is difficult to claim that a certain theory is dominantly used. A distinguishable theoretical perspective was used in 24 articles. No distinguishable theoretical perspective was used in the remaining 12 articles. When the articles were examined, it was seen that no theory specific to the field of hospitality was used. The theories used are taken from other disciplines.

Research Methods

Table 4 presents the methodological details of the articles. An overwhelming majority of articles used a quantitative methodology. The most preferred data collection technique was found to be the questionnaire. About half of the research has been conducted in the hotel industry. In terms of the analysis unit, the most preferred unit was found to be the employees. The most commonly used data analysis technique was Structural Equation Modeling. In addition, some articles collected data from multiple sources (Mostafa, 2019; Yang, Luu, & Qian, 2021; Chang, & Teng, 2017; Uen et al., 2012). In such articles, Multilevel Hierarchical Linear Modeling and Hierarchical Linear Modeling were used as analysis techniques, respectively.

Transformational Leadership Research in the Field of Hospitality

Table 4. Research methods and industries

Research type	Number of articles	Data collection methods	Number of articles	Industry	Number of articles	Analysis unit	Number of articles	Data analysis	Number of articles
Quantitative	35	Survey	34	Hotel	23	Employee	18	Hierarchical linear modeling (HLM)	2
Conceptual	1	Secondary sources	2	Hospitality	8	Employee and Manager	10	One-way ANOVA	1
				Restaurant	5	Manager	6	Regression	4
						Document	2	Multilevel Hierarchical Linear Modeling	2
								Meta-analysis	1
								Multilevel SEM	2
								SEM	22
								Correlation analysis	1

Consequences of Transformational Leadership

A total of 34 consequences of transformational leadership have been identified. These consequences were gathered under four groups: performance consequences, behavioral consequences, organizational consequences and psychological consequences (Figure 4). The most obvious among these consequences are behavioral consequences. Transformational leadership encouraged organizational commitment (Luo, Marnburg & Law, 2017), green organizational citizenship behavior (Kim et al., 2020), relational identification (Liang et al., 2017), work engagement (Mostafa, 2019), commitment to change (Kim, Im, & Shin, 2021), leader-member exchange (Chen, & Wu, 2017), organizational embeddedness (Yang et al., 2020), procedural justice, distributive justice (Dai et al., 2013), deep acting, surface acting (Luo et al., 2019), employee collective identity (Luo et al.., 2017), environmental belief (Kim et al., 2020), and quality of work life (Kim, Im, & Shin, 2021), which are all to the benefit of organisations; however, it was found to have reduced the variables such as turnover intention (Chen, & Wu, 2017) and workplace loneliness (Kloutsiniotis et al., 2022), which all work against organisations.

The second obvious consequence is the organizational one. Transformational leadership not only affects individual-level employee consequences but also affects organizational consequences. As seen in Figure 4, transformational leadership encouraged organisational level variables such as organizational effectiveness (Nazarian et al., 2021), organizational brand climate (Uen et al., 2012), corporate social responsibility (Tosun et al., 2022), organizational social capital (Mostafa et al., 2019), adhocracy culture, market culture (Nazarian et al., 2021), and innovation climate (Jaiswal & Dhar, 2015).

The third prominent consequences are the performance consequence. Transformational leadership was found to have encouraged performance-related variables such as hotel departmental performance

Figure 4. Consequences of transformational leadership

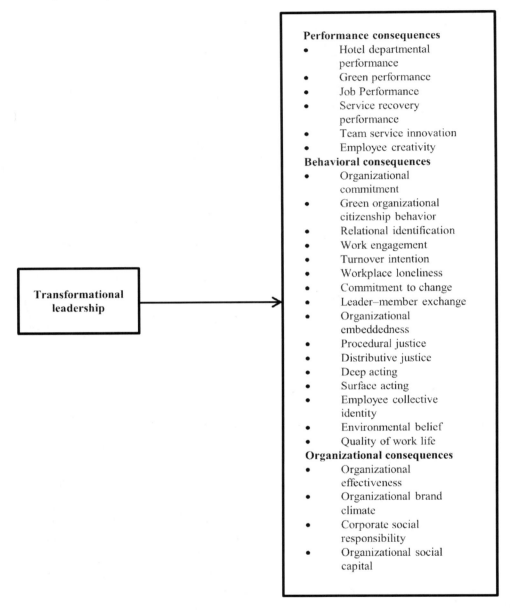

(Patiar & Wang, 2016), green performance (Tosun et al., 2022), job performance (Buil, Martínez, & Matute, 2019), service recovery performance (Luo et al., 2019), team service innovation (Yang, Luu, & Qian, 2021), employee creativity (Chang & Teng, 2017). The fourth prominent consequences are the psychological consequence. Transformational leadership were found to have reduced the negative psychological factors such as stress, anxiety (Kloutsiniotis et al., 2022) and psychological contract breach (Chen & Wu, 201); however, it was found to have increased some positive psychological factors such as positive emotion (Lee et al., 2011) and psychological capital (Schuckert et al., 2018).

SOLUTIONS AND RECOMMENDATIONS

This study reviewed the articles on transformational leadership published in the field of hospitality. Publication channels, the evolution of studies by years, the most published regions, theoretical perspectives, methods, and consequences were identified in this review. This study revealed that hospitality researchers have not paid enough attention to the studies on transformational leadership. Only 5 journals out of 7 leading journals on hospitality have published articles on transformational leadership. In addition, the number of published articles was found to be 36. Top-ranking hospitality journals could publish special issues to draw more attention to the research on transformational leadership.

It has been observed that the overwhelming majority of studies were conducted in Asian countries. It would be useful for researchers in Europe and North America to focus more on the research on transformational leadership. In this way, the meta-analysis studies to be carried out, especially in the future could make comparisons between regions. In addition, the majority of studies were found to have been conducted in developed and developing countries. The number of studies conducted in underdeveloped countries is extremely limited. Therefore, it is advisable to conduct more transformational leadership research in underdeveloped countries. No distinctive theoretical perspective was used in 12 articles out of the examined 36 articles. In addition, theoretical perspectives were found to have been taken from different fields and used in 24 articles using a theory. This finding indicates that research on transformational leadership in the field of hospitality has not experienced sufficient development. There is a need to develop theoretical perspectives specific to the field in the field of hospitality.

The overwhelming majority of the reviewed research was found to be quantitative research. When the studies are examined, hospitality researchers were found not to have gone beyond testing the leadership theories developed in the general leadership literature in the hospitality industry. In order to conduct transformational leadership research specific to the field of hospitality, it is necessary to conduct conceptual and qualitative research that allows the development of models, perspectives and theories providing the basis for empirical research (Hofer & Knight, 2022; Gürlek & Köseoglu, 2021; Gürlek, 2022). In addition, while almost all of the studies examined presented evidence regarding the consequences of transformational leadership, they did not provide enough evidence regarding its antecedents. More research is needed on the antecedents of transformational leadership.

DIRECTIONS FOR FUTURE RESEARCH

Future researchers could conduct comparative studies between regions to better understand the nature of transformational leadership. Previous studies have mostly focused on the Asian region. Hospitality researchers in the European and North American regions are recommended to pay more attention to transformational leadership. As seen in Table 4, previous studies have focused on hotels and restaurants. Future research could focus on the businesses such as travel agencies and theme parks. Besides, learning the nature of transformational leadership in SMEs and family businesses could create value for its practitioners.

The previous studies in the literature have not developed a field-specific theoretical framework for transformational leadership. The used theories are taken from general management literature. Future research could develop field-specific theoretical framework. Grounded theory methodology could be followed to develop original frameworks in the field of hospitality. Grounded theory methodology is an inductive approach that enables the development of hypotheses and theories based on qualitative data (Mehmetoglu & Altinay, 2006; Gürlek, 2022). The majority of previous research is quantitative. More qualitative research is needed in the field of hospitality to reveal the nature of transformational leadership. In addition, hospitality researchers could use mixed methods that include both qualitative and quantitative approaches. In particular, the sequential exploratory mixed-methods design could be used to identify the antecedents and consequences of transformational leadership in detail.

Although the behavioral, organizational and psychological consequences of transformational leadership have been discussed in previous studies, the relationship of transformational leadership with other areas such as HRM, strategic management, entrepreneurship, and marketing has not been discussed. Therefore, future research could focus on this gap. The previous literature has mainly focused on the consequences of transformational leadership. However, mediator and moderator variables have been neglected in the research on transformational leadership. For this reason, future research could include the mediator and moderator variables in their research models. As a result, future researchers are recommended to focus on the following research questions.

- Do the consequences of transformational leadership differ according to the region?
- Does the nature of transformational leadership differ according to the sub-industries of the hospitality industry?
- Do the relationships between transformational leadership and its consequences vary according to business types (e.g. family business, SME)?
- In which cultures does transformational leadership produce more effective consequences?
- What kinds of theories and models should be developed to explain the nature of transformational leadership in the field of hospitality?
- What are the antecedents of transformational leadership?
- What are the mediator and moderator variables that can be used in transformational leadership research?
- What is the role of transformational leaders in the formation of HRM policies?
- What is the relationship between transformational leadership and green innovation?
- What is the role of transformational leadership in the creation of a Green HRM system?
- What is the role of transformational leadership in the strategic management process?
- How can transformational leadership encourage entrepreneurship?
- What is the role of transformational leadership in determining marketing strategies?
- What are the relationships between transformational leadership and innovation types?
- What is the relationship between transformational leadership and leader trust?

CONCLUSION

The hospitality industry is one of the most labour-intensive industries. Since the hospitality industry has a dynamic, intense, fast and constantly changing work environment that requires extremely high leadership skills, the adoption of transformational leadership by managers creates value (Tuna et al., 2017; Çiftçi & Zencir, 2019). Vargas-Sevalle, Karami & Spector, 2020). Transformational leaders encourage their followers to take responsibility for realizing a vision, and they also support their followers to improve themselves (Kim, Im, & Shin, 2021) as well as higher employee motivation (Uysal, 2021). Transformational leadership consists of idealized influence, inspirational motivation, intellectual stimulation, and individual consideration (Bass, & Avolio, 1993; Bass et al., 2003). Hospitality leaders can improve the service performance of employees by applying these elements together (Yang et al., 2020). For this reason, transformational leadership is expected to be one of the main research topics for hospitality researchers.

A meta-analysis study by Gui and others (2020) has shown that transformational leadership in the field of hospitality has strong effects on its followers. This indicates that enough knowledge about transformational leadership has been accumulated. Therefore, it is time to review transformational leadership research. Based on this, this research aimed to review the research transformational leadership in the field of hospitality. In order to achieve this goal, the systematic literature review method was used. The findings of the review are summarized below.

A total of 36 articles from 7 leading hospitality journals were reached within the scope of the review. These findings indicate that although transformational leadership has received a lot of attention in the general management literature, it has not received enough attention in the field of hospitality. Most publications were found to be from the Asian region. This is another example of the rise of the Asian region, as it is in many other areas (Gürlek, 2022). When examined in terms of theory use, it has been observed that researchers used theoretical perspectives developed in other fields rather than developing field-specific theoretical drafts. In terms of the research type, quantitative research was found to have superiority.

However, it is necessary to conduct qualitative research to develop original theoretical frameworks in the field. When transformational leadership was considered from the point of view of its antecedents and consequences, the articles included in the analysis focused on the consequences of transformational leadership, but the antecedents of transformational leadership were ignored. 34 different consequences of transformational leadership were revealed in the review. The consequences of transformational leadership were collected under four groups performance consequences, behavioral consequences, organizational consequences and psychological consequences. As a result, it is possible to claim that transformational leadership in the field of hospitality has not made sufficient progress.

It should be kept in mind that the results summarized above should be evaluated within the framework of certain research limitations. Firstly, this research has focused on the articles in 7 leading hospitality journals. Secondly, this review included only articles. Thirdly, only the Web of Science database was used in the review. Fourth, filtering the search with the title, abstract and topic of the articles when scanning the database may have caused some articles to be missed out.

This research provides several contributions to the literature and practitioners. First, this research reveals the progress of transformational leadership research in the literature on hospitality. Researchers studying this review can have a holistic perspective on the topic. Secondly, this research reveals the progress in transformational leadership research and presents the research gaps to the attention of researchers. Thirdly, this research reveals the consequences of transformational leadership and contributes to practitioners' understanding of the importance of transformational leadership. It should always be remembered that systematic literature reviews have a critical value in the dissemination of evidence-based knowledge to guide practitioners in the field (Briner et al., 2009).

REFERENCES

Aladag, O. F., Köseoglu, M. A., King, B., & Mehraliyev, F. (2020). Strategy implementation research in hospitality and tourism: Current status and future potential. *International Journal of Hospitality Management*, 88, 102556. doi:10.1016/j.ijhm.2020.102556 PMID:32390680

Amankwaa, A., Seet, P. S., & Susomrith, P. (2022). Tackling hotel employees' turnover: A moderated-mediation analysis of transformational leadership, organisational embeddedness, and community embeddedness. *Journal of Hospitality and Tourism Management*, 51, 67–78. doi:10.1016/j.jhtm.2022.02.029

Antonakis, J., Bastardoz, N., Liu, Y., & Schriesheim, C. A. (2014). What makes articles highly cited? *The Leadership Quarterly*, 25(1), 152–179. doi:10.1016/j.leaqua.2013.10.014

Arici, H. E., Arici, N. C., Köseoglu, M. A., & King, B. E. M. (2021). Leadership research in the root of hospitality scholarship: 1960–2020. *International Journal of Hospitality Management*, 99, 103063. doi:10.1016/j.ijhm.2021.103063

Arnold, K. A. (2017). Transformational leadership and employee psychological well-being: A review and directions for future research. *Journal of Occupational Health Psychology*, 22(3), 381–393. doi:10.1037/ocp0000062 PMID:28150998

Bass, B. M. (1985). *Leadership and performance beyond expectations*. Free Press.

Bass, B. M. (1998). *Transformational Leadership: Industry, Military, and Educational Impact*. Lawrence Erlbaum.

Bass, B. M. (1999). Two decades of research and development in transformational leadership. *European Journal of Work and Organizational Psychology*, 8(1), 9–32. doi:10.1080/135943299398410

Bass, B. M., & Avolio, B. J. (1993). Transformational leadership and organizational culture. *Public Administration Quarterly*, 17(1), 112–121.

Bass, B. M., & Avolio, B. J. (1995). *Manual for the multifactor leadership questionnaire: Rater form (5X short)*. Mind Garden.

Bass, B. M., Avolio, B. J., Jung, D. I., & Berson, Y. (2003). Predicting unit performance by assessing transformational and transactional leadership. *The Journal of Applied Psychology*, 88(2), 207–218. doi:10.1037/0021-9010.88.2.207 PMID:12731705

Bass, B. M., & Riggio, R. E. (2005). Transformational leadership theory. *Organizational behavior I. Essential theories of motivation and leadership*, 361-385.

Bass, B. M., & Riggio, R. E. (2005). *Transformational Leadership* (2nd ed.). Psychology Press., doi:10.4324/9781410617095

Briner, R. B., Denyer, D., & Rousseau, D. M. (2009). Evidence-based management: Concept cleanup time? *The Academy of Management Perspectives*, 23(4), 19–32. doi:10.5465/AMP.2009.45590138

Brownell, J. (2010). Leadership in the service of hospitality. *Cornell Hospitality Quarterly*, 51(3), 363–378. doi:10.1177/1938965510368651

Buil, I., Martínez, E., & Matute, J. (2019). Transformational leadership and employee performance: The role of identification, engagement and proactive personality. *International Journal of Hospitality Management, 77*, 64–75. doi:10.1016/j.ijhm.2018.06.014

Burns, J. M. (1978). *Leadership*. Harper & Row.

Chang, J. H., & Teng, C. C. (2017). Intrinsic or extrinsic motivations for hospitality employees' creativity: The moderating role of organization-level regulatory focus. *International Journal of Hospitality Management, 60*, 133–141. doi:10.1016/j.ijhm.2016.10.003

Chen, T., & Wu, C. (2017). Improving the turnover intention of tourist hotel employees: Transformational leadership, leader-member exchange, and psychological contract breach. *International Journal of Contemporary Hospitality Management, 29*(7), 1914–1936. doi:10.1108/IJCHM-09-2015-0490

Çiftçi, F., & Zencir, E. (2019). Turizm sektöründeki sosyal girişim çalışanlarının sosyal girişimcilik davranışı, iş ve yaşam tatmini: Tatuta projesi Narköy örneği [Social entrepreneurial behavior, job and life satisfaction of social entrepreneurs in the tourism sector: Tatuta project Narköy example]. *Turizm Akademik Dergisi/Tourism Academic Journal, 6*(1), 131-145.

Dai, Y. D., Dai, Y. Y., Chen, K. Y., & Wu, H. C. (2013). Transformational vs transactional leadership: which is better?: A study on employees of international tourist hotels in Taipei City. *International Journal of Contemporary Hospitality Management, 25*(5), 760–778. doi:10.1108/IJCHM-Dec-2011-0223

Dhir, A., Talwar, S., Kaur, P., & Malibari, A. (2020). Food waste in hospitality and food services: A systematic literature review and framework development approach. *Journal of Cleaner Production, 270*, 122861. doi:10.1016/j.jclepro.2020.122861

Elkhwesky, Z., Salem, I. E., Ramkissoon, H., & Castañeda-García, J. A. (2022). A systematic and critical review of leadership styles in contemporary hospitality: A roadmap and a call for future research. *International Journal of Contemporary Hospitality Management, 34*(5), 1925–1958. doi:10.1108/IJCHM-09-2021-1128

Giddens, J. (2018). Transformational leadership: What every nursing dean should know. *Journal of Professional Nursing, 34*(2), 117–121. doi:10.1016/j.profnurs.2017.10.004 PMID:29703313

Gill, A., Fitzgerald, S., Bhutani, S., Mand, H., & Sharma, S. (2010). The relationship between transformational leadership and employee desire for empowerment. *International Journal of Contemporary Hospitality Management, 22*(2), 263–273. doi:10.1108/09596111011018223

Gui, C., Luo, A., Zhang, P., & Deng, A. (2020). A meta-analysis of transformational leadership in hospitality research. *International Journal of Contemporary Hospitality Management, 32*(6), 2137–2154. doi:10.1108/IJCHM-05-2019-0507

Gürlek, M. (2022). Social Entrepreneurship in Tourism, Hospitality and Events: A State of the Art. In A. Farmaki, L. Altinay, & X. Font (Eds.), *Planning and Managing Sustainability in Tourism. Tourism, Hospitality & Event Management*. Springer. doi:10.1007/978-3-030-92208-5_5

Gürlek, M., & Koseoglu, M. A. (2021). Green innovation research in the field of hospitality and tourism: The construct, antecedents, consequences, and future outlook. *Service Industries Journal*, *41*(11-12), 734–766. doi:10.1080/02642069.2021.1929930

Guzzo, R. F., Abbott, J., & Madera, J. M. (2020). A micro-level view of CSR: A hospitality management systematic literature review. *Cornell Hospitality Quarterly*, *61*(3), 332–352. doi:10.1177/1938965519892907

Hoang, G., Wilson-Evered, E., Lockstone-Binney, L., & Luu, T. T. (2021). Empowering leadership in hospitality and tourism management: A systematic literature review. *International Journal of Contemporary Hospitality Management*, *33*(12), 4182–4214. doi:10.1108/IJCHM-03-2021-0323

Hofer, K. M., & Knight, G. (2022). International services marketing: an integrative assessment of the literature [国际化服务行业市场营销: 综合文献分析]. *Service Industries Journal*, *42*(3-4), 225–248. doi:10.1080/02642069.2020.1862091

Huertas-Valdivia, I., González-Torres, T., & Nájera-Sánchez, J. J. (2022). Contemporary leadership in hospitality: a review and research agenda. *International Journal of Contemporary Hospitality Management*.

Jaiswal, N. K., & Dhar, R. L. (2015). Transformational leadership, innovation climate, creative self-efficacy and employee creativity: A multilevel study. *International Journal of Hospitality Management*, *51*, 30–41. doi:10.1016/j.ijhm.2015.07.002

Judge, T. A., & Piccolo, R. F. (2004). Transformational and transactional leadership: A meta-analytic test of their relative validity. *The Journal of Applied Psychology*, *89*(5), 755–768. doi:10.1037/0021-9010.89.5.755 PMID:15506858

Jung, D. I., & Avolio, B. J. (2000). Opening the black box: An experimental investigation of the mediating effects of trust and value congruence on transformational and transactional leadership. *Journal of Organizational Behavior*, *21*(8), 949–964. doi:10.1002/1099-1379(200012)21:8<949::AID-JOB64>3.0.CO;2-F

Kara, D., Uysal, M., Sirgy, M. J., & Lee, G. (2013). The effects of leadership style on employee well-being in hospitality. *International Journal of Hospitality Management*, *34*, 9–18. doi:10.1016/j.ijhm.2013.02.001

Khan, K., Kunz, R., Kleijnen, J., & Antes, G. (2003). Five steps to conducting a systematic review. *Journal of the Royal Society of Medicine*, *96*(3), 118–121. doi:10.1177/014107680309600304 PMID:12612111

Kim, H., Im, J., & Shin, Y. H. (2021). The impact of transformational leadership and commitment to change on restaurant employees' quality of work life during a crisis. *Journal of Hospitality and Tourism Management*, *48*, 322–330. doi:10.1016/j.jhtm.2021.07.010

Kim, W. G., McGinley, S., Choi, H. M., & Agmapisarn, C. (2020). Hotels' environmental leadership and employees' organizational citizenship behavior. *International Journal of Hospitality Management*, *87*, 102375. doi:10.1016/j.ijhm.2019.102375

Kloutsiniotis, P. V., Mihail, D. M., Mylonas, N., & Pateli, A. (2022). Transformational Leadership, HRM practices and burnout during the COVID-19 pandemic: The role of personal stress, anxiety, and workplace loneliness. *International Journal of Hospitality Management*, *102*, 103177. doi:10.1016/j.ijhm.2022.103177 PMID:35079194

Kouzes, J. M., & Posner, B. Z. (1995). *The Leadership Challenge: How to Keep Getting Extraordinary Things Done in Organizations*. Jossey-Bass.

Kuhnert, K. W., & Lewis, P. (1987). Transactional and transformational leadership: A constructive/developmental analysis. *Academy of Management Review*, *12*(4), 648–657. doi:10.2307/258070

Lee, J. E., Almanza, B. A., Jang, S. S., Nelson, D. C., & Ghiselli, R. F. (2013). Does transformational leadership style influence employees' attitudes toward food safety practices? *International Journal of Hospitality Management*, *33*, 282–293. doi:10.1016/j.ijhm.2012.09.004

Lee, Y. K., Son, M. H., & Lee, D. J. (2011). Do emotions play a mediating role in the relationship between owner leadership styles and manager customer orientation, and performance in service environment? *International Journal of Hospitality Management*, *30*(4), 942–952. doi:10.1016/j.ijhm.2011.02.002

Li, J., & Yuan, B. (2017). Both angel and devil: The suppressing effect of transformational leadership on proactive employee's career satisfaction. *International Journal of Hospitality Management*, *65*, 59–70. doi:10.1016/j.ijhm.2017.06.008

Liang, T., Chang, H., Ko, M., & Lin, C. (2017). Transformational leadership and employee voices in the hospitality industry. *International Journal of Contemporary Hospitality Management*, *29*(1), 374–392. doi:10.1108/IJCHM-07-2015-0364

Luo, A., Guchait, P., Lee, L., & Madera, J. M. (2019). Transformational leadership and service recovery performance: The mediating effect of emotional labor and the influence of culture. *International Journal of Hospitality Management*, *77*, 31–39. doi:10.1016/j.ijhm.2018.06.011

Luo, Z., Marnburg, E., & Law, R. (2017). Linking leadership and justice to organizational commitment: The mediating role of collective identity in the hotel industry. *International Journal of Contemporary Hospitality Management*, *29*(4), 1167–1184. doi:10.1108/IJCHM-08-2015-0423

Luo, Z., Wang, Y., & Marnburg, E. (2013). Testing the structure and effects of full range leadership theory in the context of China's hotel industry. *Journal of Hospitality Marketing & Management*, *22*(6), 656–677. doi:10.1080/19368623.2012.708959

Luo, Z., Wang, Y., Marnburg, E., & Øgaard, T. (2016). How is leadership related to employee self-concept? *International Journal of Hospitality Management*, *52*, 24–32. doi:10.1016/j.ijhm.2015.09.003

Madanaguli, A. T., Kaur, P., Bresciani, S., & Dhir, A. (2021). Entrepreneurship in rural hospitality and tourism. A systematic literature review of past achievements and future promises. *International Journal of Contemporary Hospitality Management*.

Mehmetoglu, M., & Altinay, L. (2006). Examination of grounded theory analysis with an application to hospitality research. *International Journal of Hospitality Management*, *25*(1), 12–33. doi:10.1016/j.ijhm.2004.12.002

Mohamed, L. M. (2016). Assessing the effects of transformational leadership: A study on Egyptian hotel employees. *Journal of Hospitality and Tourism Management*, *27*, 49–59. doi:10.1016/j.jhtm.2016.04.001

Mostafa, A. M. S. (2019). Transformational leadership and restaurant employees customer-oriented behaviours: The mediating role of organizational social capital and work engagement. *International Journal of Contemporary Hospitality Management, 31*(3), 1166–1182. doi:10.1108/IJCHM-02-2018-0123

Nazarian, A., Atkinson, P., Foroudi, P., & Edirisinghe, D. (2021). Factors affecting organizational effectiveness in independent hotels–The case of Iran. *Journal of Hospitality and Tourism Management, 46*, 293–303. doi:10.1016/j.jhtm.2021.01.002

Newman, A., & Butler, C. (2014). The influence of follower cultural orientation on attitudinal responses towards transformational leadership: Evidence from the Chinese hospitality industry. *International Journal of Human Resource Management, 25*(7), 1024–1045. doi:10.1080/09585192.2013.815250

Patiar, A., & Mia, L. (2009). Transformational leadership style, market competition and departmental performance: Evidence from luxury hotels in Australia. *International Journal of Hospitality Management, 28*(2), 254–262. doi:10.1016/j.ijhm.2008.09.003

Patiar, A., & Wang, Y. (2016). The effects of transformational leadership and organizational commitment on hotel departmental performance. *International Journal of Contemporary Hospitality Management, 28*(3), 586–608. doi:10.1108/IJCHM-01-2014-0050

Patiar, A., & Wang, Y. (2020). Managers' leadership, compensation and benefits, and departments' performance: Evidence from upscale hotels in Australia. *Journal of Hospitality and Tourism Management, 42*, 29–39. doi:10.1016/j.jhtm.2019.11.005

Pieterse, A. N., Van Knippenberg, D., Schippers, M., & Stam, D. (2010). Transformational and transactional leadership and innovative behavior: The moderating role of psychological empowerment. *Journal of Organizational Behavior, 31*(4), 609–623. doi:10.1002/job.650

Prikshat, V., Rajesh, J. I., & Rajaguru, R. (2021). The growth satisfaction in jobs among hospitality employees: The role of transformational leadership, interpersonal communication satisfaction and trust. *Journal of Human Resources in Hospitality & Tourism, 20*(1), 48–74. doi:10.1080/15332845.2020.1821427

Rabiul, M. K., & Yean, T. F. (2021). Leadership styles, motivating language, and work engagement: An empirical investigation of the hotel industry. *International Journal of Hospitality Management, 92*, 102712. doi:10.1016/j.ijhm.2020.102712

Rafferty, A. E., & Griffin, M. A. (2004). Dimensions of transformational leadership: Conceptual and empirical extensions. *The Leadership Quarterly, 15*(3), 329–354. doi:10.1016/j.leaqua.2004.02.009

Salem, I. E. B. (2015). Transformational leadership: Relationship to job stress and job burnout in five-star hotels. *Tourism and Hospitality Research, 15*(4), 240–253. doi:10.1177/1467358415581445

Schuckert, M., Kim, T., Paek, S., & Lee, G. (2018). Motivate to innovate: How authentic and transformational leaders influence employees' psychological capital and service innovation behavior. *International Journal of Contemporary Hospitality Management, 30*(2), 776–796. doi:10.1108/IJCHM-05-2016-0282

Siangchokyoo, N., Klinger, R. L., & Campion, E. D. (2020). Follower transformation as the linchpin of transformational leadership theory: A systematic review and future research agenda. *The Leadership Quarterly, 31*(1), 101341. doi:10.1016/j.leaqua.2019.101341

Tosun, C., Parvez, M. O., Bilim, Y., & Yu, L. (2022). Effects of green transformational leadership on green performance of employees via the mediating role of corporate social responsibility: Reflection from North Cyprus. *International Journal of Hospitality Management, 103,* 103218. doi:10.1016/j.ijhm.2022.103218

Tuna M., Akça İ., Tuna A. A. & Gürlek M. (2017). Perceptions of sector working conditions of tourism students and attitudes towards working in the sector: A research on vocational school, college and faculty students. *Turizm Akademik Dergisi/Tourism Academic Journal, 4*(2), 41-60.

Uen, J. F., Wu, T., Teng, H. C., & Liu, Y. S. (2012). Transformational leadership and branding behavior in Taiwanese hotels. *International Journal of Contemporary Hospitality Management, 24*(1), 26–43. doi:10.1108/09596111211197782

Uysal, D. (2021). Perceived leadership styles and employee motivation: A research in Turkish hotel context. *Journal of Ekonomi, 3*(2), 106–110.

Vargas-Sevalle, L., Karami, M., & Spector, S. (2020). Transformational Leadership in the Hospitality and Tourism Industry. In Entrepreneurial Opportunities. Emerald Publishing Limited. doi:10.1108/978-1-83909-285-520201007

Wang, G., Oh, I. S., Courtright, S. H., & Colbert, A. E. (2011). Transformational leadership and performance across criteria and levels: A meta-analytic review of 25 years of research. *Group & Organization Management, 36*(2), 223–270. doi:10.1177/1059601111401017

Yang, C., Chen, Y., Zhao, X., & Hua, N. (2020). Transformational leadership, proactive personality and service performance: The mediating role of organizational embeddedness. *International Journal of Contemporary Hospitality Management, 32*(1), 267–287. doi:10.1108/IJCHM-03-2019-0244

Yang, M., Luu, T. T., & Qian, D. (2021). Dual-focused transformational leadership and service innovation in hospitality organisations: A multilevel investigation. *International Journal of Hospitality Management, 98,* 103035. doi:10.1016/j.ijhm.2021.103035

Yang, M., Luu, T. T., & Qian, D. X. (2021). Linking transformational leadership to team service innovation in the hospitality industry: A team-level mediation and moderation investigation. *Journal of Hospitality and Tourism Management, 49,* 558–569. doi:10.1016/j.jhtm.2021.11.011

Yu, H., Shum, C., Alcorn, M., Sun, J., & He, Z. (2022). Robots can't take my job: Antecedents and outcomes of Gen Z employees' service robot risk awareness. *International Journal of Contemporary Hospitality Management, 34*(8), 2971–2988. doi:10.1108/IJCHM-10-2021-1312

Zopiatis, A., & Constanti, P. (2010). Leadership styles and burnout: Is there an association? *International Journal of Contemporary Hospitality Management, 22*(3), 300–320. doi:10.1108/09596111011035927

ADDITIONAL READING

Badrinarayan, S. P. (2003). Central conceptual issues in transformational leadership research. *Leadership and Organization Development Journal, 24*(7), 397–406. doi:10.1108/01437730310498596

Brown, D. J., & Keeping, L. M. (2005). Elaborating the construct of transformational leadership: The role of affect. *The Leadership Quarterly, 16*(2), 245–272. doi:10.1016/j.leaqua.2005.01.003

Hinkin, T. R., & Tracey, J. B. (1994). Transformational leadership in the hospitality industry. *Hospitality Research Journal, 18*(1), 49–63. doi:10.1177/109634809401800105

Popper, M., Mayseless, O., & Castelnovo, O. (2000). Transformational leadership and attachment. *The Leadership Quarterly, 11*(2), 267–289. doi:10.1016/S1048-9843(00)00038-2

Tracey, J. B., & Hinkin, T. R. (1996). How transformational leaders lead in the hospitality industry. *International Journal of Hospitality Management, 15*(2), 165–176. doi:10.1016/0278-4319(95)00059-3

Van Knippenberg, D., & Sitkin, S. B. (2013). A critical assessment of charismatic—transformational leadership research: Back to the drawing board? *The Academy of Management Annals, 7*(1), 1–60. doi:10.5465/19416520.2013.759433

Yammarino, F. J., Spangler, W. D., & Bass, B. M. (1993). Transformational leadership and performance: A longitudinal investigation. *The Leadership Quarterly, 4*(1), 81–102. doi:10.1016/1048-9843(93)90005-E

KEY TERMS AND DEFINITIONS

Consequences of Transformational Leadership: Refers to the effects of transformational leadership on individuals and organizations.

Evidence-Based Knowledge: The knowledge that is created by scientific research and guides practitioners.

Leadership: The sum of all actions used to lead an organization or a community.

Meta-Analysis: It is a type of statistical analysis that combines the findings of studies in a particular field.

Systematic Review: It is a synthesis of knowledge that comprehensively defines and evaluates previous studies in a field and expands horizons for future studies.

Theoretical Perspective: A theoretical lens that helps explain the facts.

Transformational Leadership: It is a type of leadership that enables its followers to show superior performance when influenced, inspired, showed individual attention, and acted intellectually by leaders.

Chapter 8
Transformational Leadership in the Hospitality and Tourism Industry:
Reflections From a Decade of Research

Seza Aksoy
https://orcid.org/0000-0003-2993-3499
Kırklareli University, Turkey

Onur Çakır
https://orcid.org/0000-0001-8360-0324
Kırklareli University, Turkey

ABSTRACT

This study aims to examine the transformational leadership in the context of the hospitality and tourism industry. In the first part of the study, the emergence of transformational leadership, its definition, and the importance of transformational leadership in tourism and hospitality literature is discussed. In the second part, the most commonly used transformational leadership models and the sub-factors and dimensions of these models is analyzed. In the third part of the chapter, the characteristics of managers who adopt the transformational leadership style is examined. Finally, the studies conducted in the field of hospitality and tourism that were published in peer-reviewed journals in the last decade (from 2012-2022) were systematically reviewed. Transformational leadership style is found to be one of the most suitable leadership styles for both the organization, the employees, and the leaders themselves in the hospitality and tourism industry.

INTRODUCTION

The hospitality and tourism industries are defined as a labor-intensive industry which have a high-pressure work environment. Therefore, regardless of their department, all employees play an essential role in

DOI: 10.4018/978-1-6684-6713-8.ch008

the success of the tourism businesses. In addition, compared to the other industries, the hospitality and tourism industry is more vulnerable and has a fragile structure, and it is affected more by the political, economic, environmental, technological, and socio-cultural changes or the crises that may occur in these areas (Biggs, 2011). In order to achieve high service standards, employees are often required to go beyond their job description and perform well even when industry is facing crisis such as COVID-19 pandemic. Facing with all these challenges, managers are also required to lead and guide by showing excellent leadership skills that will motivate and influence their employees to establish the success of the organization. The roles of leaders in anticipating, managing, and resolving crises that pose a danger to the survival of their organizations are crucial because crises in any corporate setting demand rapid and urgent actions. Therefore, transformational leadership style is frequently seen as a potent force behind businesses' ability to thrive in the face of threats and crises (Hannah, Uhl-Bien, Avolio, & Cavarretta, 2009).

Since the beginning of the COVID-19 pandemic, many tourism businesses have to keep up with organizational changes and transformations in order to survive. The leadership style adopted by the businesses became an important aspect of this adaptation process (Mansurova & Güney, 2018). In the literature, many studies emphasize that transformational leadership is one of the most important leadership styles for the hospitality and tourism industry, since transformational leaders have the ability to quickly adapt to crises and events when unexpected changes and transformations are required in the organization (Al Harbi, Alarifi & Mosbah, 2019). Therefore, hospitality and tourism businesses should prioritize and embrace good transformational leadership practices to avoid negative outcomes such as employee turnover, absenteeism, lower job performance, decrease in service quality etc. (Kara et al., 2013).

As for all organizations, the success of tourism businesses depends on the use of human resources' abilities and talents for organizational purposes (Armstrong & Taylor, 2020). Recent studies reveal that transformational leadership has a significant impact on both improving the individual performance of employees and increasing organizational performance of businesses. According to Bass (1990), leadership is one of the most basic tools of management. With a good leadership, managers can achieve organizational goals and productivity of employees can be increased significantly. As a matter of fact, studies show that transformational leadership, in many different types of organizations, has a significant positive effect on employees' job satisfaction, attitudes towards work, organizational citizenship behavior, commitment, effectiveness, effort and performance. Transformational leaders mostly focus on meeting the higher-order intrinsic needs of their followers by improving their personal development and commitment based on trust and meeting their expectations (Zheng et al., 2017; Wen et al., 2019). Bass et. al. (2003) states that *"transformational leadership occurs when leaders broaden and lift up the interests when they generate awareness and recognition of the purposes and mission of the group, and when they stir, they are to look beyond their self-interest for the good of the group"*.

Transformational leadership and its outcomes are considered as one of the most researched leadership topics in the last four decades. Transformational leadership is defined as a process in which leaders and followers reach a higher level of motivation together (Masood, Dani, Burns & Backhouse, 2006). Transformational leadership creates radical changes and transformations both on employees and on the entire organization (Al Harbi, Alarifi & Mosbah, 2019). One of the first studies investigating transformational leadership in the field of hospitality and tourism industry dates back to 1994 and was conducted by Hinkin and Tracey (1994). They revealed that by implementing transformational leadership style, hospitality managers may achieve several favorable results such as openness of communication, clearer roles and missions, higher satisfaction with the leadership, and ratings of leaders' effectiveness. In the recent studies, transformational leadership were also found to have a significant positive relationship with the creativity and organizational innovation of followers through psychological empowerment of employees, improving workplace relationships, supporting innovation and employee learning. Moving one step further, recent studies have also shown that transformational leadership can successfully guide organizations out of crises (Kim, Im & Shin, 2021; Ma & Yang, 2020; Bowers, et al, 2017). It is also emphasized that transformational leadership creates a radical change and transformation on individual and organizational levels (Al Harbi, Alarifi & Mosbah, 2019). Ma and Yang (2020) provided examples of how transformational leadership improved crisis management abilities of hospitality managers under various pandemic crisis perceptions.

The value of transformational leadership in tourism becomes more apparent when recent studies are examined. For instance, Chiang & Wang (2012) and Dlami et al. (2017) revealed that transformational leadership increased employees' organizational commitment. In addition, transformational leadership were found to be positively related to tourism employees' creativity (Wang et al., 2014), job performance (Yanti, Mujiati & Suwandana, 2021), and job satisfaction (Day et al., 2022). Moreover, researchers also revealed that transformational leadership significantly reduced workplace stress and burnout (Salem & Kattara, 2015) as well as turnover intentions (Ariyabuddhiphongs & Khan, 2017). In conclusion, the necessity for tourism managers to adopt transformational leadership arises due to the fragile structure of tourism industry, and due to the fact that tourism employees' commitment to the organization, job performance, job satisfaction, and stress and burnout levels becoming crucial elements for the success of any tourism business.

In this chapter, we aim to examine the transformational leadership in the context of the hospitality and tourism industry. In the first part of the study, the emergence of transformational leadership, its definition, and the importance of transformational leadership in tourism and hospitality literature will be discussed. In the second part, the most widely used transformational leadership models in the field of tourism and hospitality will be systematically analyzed, and in addition, factors and the sub- dimensions of these models will be examined in depth. In the third part of the chapter, the characteristics of managers who adopt the transformational leadership style will be examined. Finally, the chapter aims to systematically and extensively review the studies conducted in the field of hospitality and tourism which were published in peer-reviewed journals in the last decade (from 2012-2022). By this review, the chapter aims to illustrate how Transformational Leadership Theory may be a salient framework for understanding how employees and organizations should be lead especially during fast-paced changes occur in the world and in the tourism industry. By synthesizing findings from different studies, we hope to provide a better understanding and some concrete recommendations for students, professionals, and scholars on how to better utilize transformational leadership practically and theoretically.

BACKGROUND

Emergence, Definition, and Importance of the Concept of Transformational Leadership in the Tourism Sector

Transformational leadership is a process in which the individual always strives to move himself to a better point and aims to improve. James MacGregor Burns defines this situation as *"a process in which leaders and followers help each other to increase the motivation level of a group of people while working"* (Masood et al., 2006; Ballester-Miquel et al., 2017).

When the literature is examined, it is seen that the concept of transformational leadership was derived from Weber's charismatic leadership studies in 1947 (Ullah, Latif & Alam, 2018). The concept of tranforsmational leadership was first created by James V. Downton in 1973 in his book titled "Rebel Leadership". Later in 1978, in his research on political leaders titled "Depression Leadership", James MacGregor Burns expended the term transformational leadership and divided leaders into two groups as transcational leaders who lead through performance exchanges for rewards and transformational leaders who lead by inspring, stimulating, motivating (Yıldırım, 2019; Turan, 2019; Ullah, Latif, & Alam, 2018). Bass and Avolio (1985) aimed to measure the extent to which a leader has transformational leadership characteristics with the scale they developed called "Transformational Leadership Questionnaire" in their study. Although Burns laid the foundations of the concept, the concept was later spread to a wider audience from both academics and practitioners with Bass and Avolio's (1985) scale development study, since they made it easier to measure the transformational leadership (Altıntaş, 2020). Bass emphasized the need to bring a new perspective to leadership in his book titled 'Leadership and Performance Beyond Expectations' in which he examines the relationships between family traditions and variables such as maternal behavior, power, ambition, and adult behavior with transformational leadership. Kuhnert & Kewis (1987) were amongst the first who discussed 'being exemplary' as one of the characteristics of transformational leadership. With the addition of setting an example, leaders have begun to be studied as someone who is not only content with setting a vision, but also sets an example with their behaviors (Ünsal, 2019; Kuhnert & Lewis, 1987). In this case, the followers of the leader will be able to add to their own lives just by watching the leaders.

Since the early 1990s, the relationship between transformational leadership and businesses has been emphasized. This situation can be attributed to the fact that the most important element of the resources owned by the enterprises has begun to be perceived as human resources (Wang et al., 2011). House & Shamir (1993) underlines that the most important emphasis for the leaders' followers is to gain self-confidence and achieve success, and to believe that anything can be done. Thoms & Grennberger (1995) attribute the success of leaders to the fact that they act as a bridge between both the past and the future. It underlines that leaders, who are knowledgeable about the past and can plan for the future, can achieve success (Ünsal, 2019). As the number of studies increased, it began to be mentioned as an indispensable feature that leaders are transformational while talking about leadership characteristics. As transactional leaders began to lose their popularity and validity, old leadership styles remained only on paper as a kind of control expert (Phaneuf et al., 2016).

Many definitions of the concept of transformational leadership have been made since the day it was written in the literature. For example, Bass (1985) emphasizes that the leader's transformative nature is a feature that helps the followers put their individual interests aside for the benefit of the organization by raising awareness of the consequences of actions. Similarly, Roueche et. al. (1989) defines transformational leadership as the leader's ability to persuade others' attitudes, values, beliefs, and behaviors to achieve organizational goals (Ullah, Latif & Alam, 2018). From Yukl's (1989) perspective, transformational leadership is a process that starts from creating commitment to common goals and extends to empowering followers to achieve these goals. Leaders who bring about great changes are very important in the commitment of the members of the organization to the mission, goals and strategies adopted by the organization (Yukl, 1989). When the definitions of transformational leadership in the literature are examined, transformational leaders are generally defined as people who make a positive impact on their relations with their followers or employees and contribute to personal development of the employees and organizational development in general (Chen, Brian & Hou, 2015). Thomson et. al. (2016) defined transformational leadership as the most effective and most widely adopted leadership style despite its relationship and task-oriented nature. According to Chianga & Lin (2016), transformational leaders are the type of leaders that supports the development of individual employees. These leaders consist of satisfied, high-performing individuals who are fully committed to their organizations. They also have the ability and potential to persuade employees to make extraordinary efforts for the benefit of the organization (Ohunakin et al., 2019). It is known by studies that transformational leadership has a significant positive relationship with the creativity and organizational innovation of followers through psychological empowerment of employee, workplace relations, innovation support and employee learning. It is emphasized that transformational leadership is an approach that creates a radical change and transformation on employees and on the entire organization (Al Harbi, Alarifi & Mosbah, 2019).

Considering the common points of transformational leadership definitions in different disciplines; transformational leaders are individuals with willpower, determination, and optimistic character who are also risk takers, egalitarian, developed themselves internally and spiritually. With all these characteristics, it can be said that they are individuals who have positive effects on the attitudes and actions of their subordinates and have positive effects on organizational outputs, as well as have positive effects on the general morality of their subordinates or followers (Felix, Ahmad & Arshad, 2016). Transformational leaders communicate important values and a shared sense of purpose through role modeling, which enables their followers to rate their leaders highly for honesty, competence, and helpfulness. In recent studies, it has been emphasized that transformational leadership has a positive and significant effect on employees with creative process management (Mahmood, Uddin & Fan, 2019).

The tourism sector has a more fragile structure than other sectors and is more affected by political, economic, environmental, technological, and socio-cultural changes or crises that may occur in these areas (Biggs, 2011). Faced with all these challenges, managers also need to guide employees by demonstrating leadership skills. Leaders' roles in anticipating, managing, and resolving crises that pose a threat to their organizations' survival are crucial because in any corporate setting, crises require swift and immediate action. Therefore, the transformational leadership style is often seen as a powerful force behind the ability of businesses to succeed in the face of threats and crises (Hannah, Uhl-Bien, Avolio & Cavarretta, 2009). For example, many tourism businesses have had to keep up with organizational changes and transformations in order to survive, since the beginning of the COVID-19 pandemic, which has disrupted the tourism industry as well as all other sectors. The leadership style adopted by businesses has been an important dimension of this adaptation process (Mansurova & Güney, 2018). Many studies in the literature highlighted that transformational leadership is one of the most important leadership styles for the tourism industry, as it has the ability to adapt quickly to crises and events when unexpected changes and transformations in the organization are required. (Al Harbi, Alarifi & Mosbah, 2019; Güzel & Akgündüz, 2011). In line with all this information, it is possible to say that transformational leadership is a crucial aspect for the success and survival of the hospitality and tourism businesses.

Transformational Leadership Models and Sub-Dimensions

In this part of the study, it is aimed to examine the most frequently used transformational leadership models in the field of tourism and hospitality, as well as the sub-factors and dimensions of these models. It is seen that the studies examined generally include the MLQ model developed by Bass and the models derived around this model. In the research, the 5 most frequently used transformational leadership models in the literature are examined in detail. These are the Multifactor Leadership Questionnaire "MLQ" developed by Bass (1985), MLQ-5X model developed by Bass, Avolio and Jung (1999), Transformational Leadership Questionnaire (TLQ) developed by Bass and Avolio (1995), Transformational Leadership Inventory (TLI) developed by Podsakoff et al. (1990) and "A Short Measure of Transformational Leadership (TFL)" model developed by Carless, Wearing and Mann (2000) respectively (Table 1).

Table 1. Transformational Leadership Models and Sub-Dimensions

MLQ	MLQ-5X	TLQ	Transformational Leadership Inventory	TFL
Charisma	Charisma	Idealized Influence	Vision	Vision
Individual Consideration	Intellectual Stimulation	Individual Consideration	Providing the Appropriate Model	Staff Development
Inspirational Motivation	Individual Consideration	Intellectual Stimulation	Intellectual Stimulation	Supportive Leadership
Intellectual Stimulation	Contingent Reward	Inspiration Motivation	Expecting High Performance	Empowerment
Contingent Reward (transactional)	Active Management by Exception		Individual Support	Innovative Thinking
Management by Exceptions (Transactional)	Passive-Avoidance Management		Encouragement	Leading by Example
Laissez-faire Leadership (Transactional)				Charisma

MLQ Model

Developed by Bass in 1985, the model focused on the needs of the followers rather than the leader. (Başaran, 2020). According to Bass, the transformational leadership is an approach that makes employees or followers feel valued, and at the same time increases their motivation in work environments. The 'Multifactor Leadership Questionnaire MLQ Form-1' model consists of seven dimensions. These dimensions are charisma, individual consideration, inspirational motivation, intellectual stimulation, contingent reward, management by exception, and laissez-faire leadership.

Based on the work that Bass and Avolio carried out together in 1999, it was seen that the dimensions of charisma and inspiration were similar, so they could not be distinguished from each other by individuals. Thus, they were reduced to one dimension. Thus, the Multi-Factor Leadership scale had begun to be examined in six dimensions (Arslantaş & Pekdemir, 2007). The dimensions of contingent reward, management by exception, and laissez-faire leadership have been transferred to other leadership types (Doğanbaş, 2017).

Model MLQ-5X

Many authors using the multi-factor leadership model (MLQ Form-1) questionnaire have raised the question of whether the components of transformational leadership should be considered independent of contingent reward leadership or as a separate factor. Furthermore, many authors have argued that the components of transformational leadership cannot be empirically distinguished.

Additionally, Bass, Avolio, and Jung presented an updated version of the Multi-Factor Leadership model (MLQ Form 5X) in 1999 (Avolio, Bass & Jung, 1999). The model creates a single charisma dimension by combining ascribed charisma, charismatic behavior, and inspiring leadership into one factor.

- **Charisma:** With their charisma, leaders energize their followers, provide a clear sense of purpose, and set a role model for ethical behavior. Thus, followers identify more easily with their leaders.
- **Intellectual Stimulation:** Transformational leaders question the mentality of "this is how we've always done things," challenging the status quo and even veteran leaders' assumptions. They instill this mindset in their employees. This includes emphasizing new experiences, opportunities, and ways of thinking. The transformational leader eliminates the "fear factor" from work by emphasizing opportunities to grow and learn rather than focusing on the outcomes of the efforts. encourages followers to question the methods they use to develop tried and true ways of solving problems.
- **Individual Consideration:** The ability to transmit a sense of the larger culture to the individual is one of the key transformational leadership traits, giving employees a sense of ownership in company goals and independence in the workplace. They care about their employees' professional development and strive to build positive relationships with them. This includes maintaining open lines of communication, attending to employees' individual needs, mentoring them, and recognizing each person's unique contributions.
- **Contingent Reward:** Leader explains what is expected of followers and what they will receive if they perform at the expected level.
- **Active Management by Exception:** Focuses on monitoring the execution of the task for any issues that may arise and fixing them to maintain current performance levels.
- **Passive Avoidant Leadership:** Leaders frequently avoid making decisions and only react to take corrective action when problems become serious.

TLQ Model

TLQ model is a revised version of Bass's Multi-Factor Leadership Model (MLQ) developed by Bass & Avolio (1995) and includes only four dimensions of the Transformational Leadership Questionnaire (TLQ) (Avolio, Bass & Jung, 1999). Bass defines these dimensions as "the quartet of transformational leadership" (Eraslan, 2006:12).

- **Idealized Influence:** Bass & Avolio (1990) argues that followers will achieve the optimal level of performance through leaders' idealized influence. This dimension emphasizes the trust, integrity, and morality of the leader (Kirkbride, 2006). The most effective way to influence employees is to positively model it. Transformational leaders need to serve as role models for their employees in every possible way. This accompanies ethical and socially desirable behavior, being committed to work goals, and demonstrating enthusiasm for organizational goals. This influence is built on trust and respect. Employees trust and respect leaders who have developed idealized influence to make good decisions, not just "for the good of the organization," but for the good of the team and for them as individuals. With this trust, employees become followers who want to imitate and internalize their leaders' ideals.

- **Individualized Consideration:** Leader, by showing individual support, helps followers to perform higher (Bass, 1994). Followers who see that their wants and needs are noticed by their leaders are more successful in adapting to the environment and revealing their unique perspectives. Thanks to this situation, there is more sharing of ideas within the organization (Bass and Avolio, 1990: 26).
- **Intellectual Stimulation:** According to Bass & Avolio (1993), thanks to the intellectual stimulation feature of the transformational leader, the leader's use of the situations that he/she has previously experienced, and this allows them to look situations from different perspectives (Öncü, 2017).
- **Inspirational Motivation:** Bass & Avolio (1990) argued that leaders could increase the motivation and enthusiasm of their followers by giving pep talk. With such speeches, the leader wants the followers to achieve a common goal and encourages them to cooperate (Bass & Steidlmeier, 1999: 188).

TLI Model

Podsakoff et al. (1990) proposed that transformational leadership is multidimensional in their 'Transformational Leadership Behavior Inventory (TLI) Model', and based on their research, they revealed that there are six important dimensions of transformational leadership. These dimensions are vision expression, appropriate modeling, goal acceptance, high performance expectations, individual support, and intellectual stimulation (Podsakoff et al., 1990).

- **Vision:** A leader's actions should be aimed towards seeing new opportunities for the organization as well as creating, expressing, and motivating others' future visions.
- **Providing an Appropriate Model:** The behavior of the leader provides an example for followers and is congruent with the values of the leader.
- **Intellectual Stimulation:** The leader is compelled to reevaluate some of their job-related assumptions and reconsider how this might be accomplished through intellectual stimulation.
- **Expecting High Performance:** It is the leader's display of excellence, quality, or high-performance expectations from followers.
- **Individual Support:** This is the behavior that demonstrates that the leader values his followers and is concerned about their personal feelings and needs.
- **Encouragement:** It aims to encourage cooperation among the leader's employees and to enable them to work together for a common purpose.

TFL Model

Carless, Wearing & Mann introduced a new model to the literature in 2000 with their work named "A Short Measure of Transformational Leadership". The model consists of seven dimensions. Since the concept of transformational leadership in TFL model is based on the 'A Short Measure of Transformational Leadership' model in the study, its dimensions are named similarly as vision, personnel development, supportive leadership, empowerment, innovative thinking, exemplary and charisma.

- **Vision:** Making a vision or ideal goal is one aspect of transformational leadership that sets it apart from other leadership approaches (Bryman, 1992; cited in Carless, Wearing, & Mann, 2000). Leaders that are transformational create a vision for their company's future. They frequently use the appropriate language to convey to their subordinates the vision they have developed. Through the process of communicating a vision, the leader conveys a set of values that guide and motivate employees. Practically speaking, a vision gives employees a shared goal to encourage personal conduct for the firm in keeping with the leaders' principles (Conger & Kanungo, 1988; Kouzes & Posner, 1987; Tichy & Devanna, 1986; cited in Carless, Wearing & Mann, 2000). Many researchers argue that the ability to create and share a vision is the key attribute of leaders (Carless, Wearing, & Mann, 2000)
- **Staff Development:** An effective leader recognizes each employee's needs and abilities, encourages, and facilitates their personal development (Nadler & Tushman, 1990). Individual development entails delegating tasks and responsibilities to followers in order to facilitate the acquisition of new skills and to provide challenging opportunities (Bass, 1990). Through delegation, the leader conveys confidence that her/his staff will effectively demonstrate their abilities (Nadler & Tushman, 1990).
- **Supportive Leadership:** Giving positive feedback to employees and recognizing their individual accomplishments are examples of supportive leadership. Leaders express confidence in their employees' ability to perform effectively and achieve challenging goals. When challenging goals are set, it is critical for the leader to support the staff. Not only is supportive leadership important for the individual, but it is also important for the organization as a whole. (Nadler & Tushman, 1990; Yukl, 1994; cited in Carless, Wearing & Mann, 2000). Kouzes & Posner (1987) argue that successful leaders not only recognize employees' individual achivements but also gain recognition of organizational success (Carless, Wearing & Mann, 2000).
- **Empowerment:** The empowerment dimension refers to the followers' involvement in the decision-making process. These leaders encourage autonomy while sharing power and expertise with their workforce. (Conger & Kanungo, 1988; Kouzes & Posner, 1987; Larson & Lafasto, 1989; cited in Carless, Wearing & Mann, 2000; Nadler & Tushman, 1990). Leaders develop policies and procedures that involve employees in the organization's process of resolving potential problems and making important decisions empower members by delegating authority to implement policies and supporting members' decisions. Creating an atmosphere of trust, respect, open communication, and collaboration that supports a collaborative, participative group climate is another aspect of empowerment.
- **Innovative Thinking:** In the dimension of innovative thinking, leaders employ novel, occasionally unusual methods to accomplish their objectives (Conger & Kanungo, 1988; Kouzes & Posner, 1987; Tichy & Devanna, 1986; Carless, Wearing & Mann, 2000) . They are prepared to take risks to realize their goals and seize advantages of difficult situations. Similarly, by giving their employees challenging tasks, transformational leaders encourage their employees to think innovatively. Leaders see mistakes as a learning opportunity (Carless, Wearing & Mann, 2000).
- **Exemplary:** The exemplary dimension concerns the coherence of transformative leaders' professed views and actions. A strong leader makes his principles and ideas known to his team in a straightforward manner (Kouzes & Posner, 1987; Carless, Wearing & Mann, 2000; Podsakoff et al., 1990). They serve as an example for their staff by adopting the attitudes and principles they uphold. Shamir, House & Arthur (1993) summarized this behavior as "the *leader provides an*

ideal, a reference point, and focus for followers' indirect learning" (Shamir, House & Arthur, 1993:585).
- **Charisma:** According to several studies (Bass, 1992; Yammario & Bass, 1990; Carless, Wearing & Mann, 2000), one of the most crucial traits of a transformational leader is their charisma. According to Bass and colleagues, charisma is crucial for transformation. People view charismatic leaders as trustworthy, extremely skilled, and deserving of respect (Bass, 1990). High levels of motivation and performance are inspired by charismatic leadership, which supports organizational goals (Howell & Avolio, 1993). Therefore, charismatic leadership is included as a component of transformational leadership in TFL model.

CHARACTERISTICS OF TRANSFORMATIONAL LEADERS

In the globalizing and developing world, leaders have assumed entrepreneurial, motivating, guiding, inspiring and supportive roles in order to adapt to the differentiating organizational and environmental factors so that organizations can grow and survive in a competitive environment (Basaran, 2020).

According to Yukl (1999), the emphasis of the transformational leadership approach is on emotions and values. Transformational leaders give constructive feedback to their subordinates and have the capacity to influence their followers by giving up their own self-interest for the good of the whole group (Bass, 1985). Zwingmann et al. (2014) defined transformational leaders as motivators who create a persuasive vision and encourage employees to prioritize the demands of the organization. Similarly, Schmidt et al. (2014) argue that transformational leaders have motivating abilities to increase employee well-being by creating a thriving work environment (Ohunakin et al., 2019).

A transformational leader must exhibit exemplary behaviors with the vision he/she creates. This way leaders can gain followers' trust and respect. During this process, transformational leaders attach importance to intelligence, use simple language, draw attention to high-level expectations, and aim to solve problems carefully and take care of their followers directly by guiding each individual and giving stimulating ideas (Brestrich, 2000; Başaran, 2020). Mills (2007) listed the characteristics of transformational leaders as follows (cited by Gabriel et al., 2022):

- Inspiring
- Charismatic,
- Activating the intelligence of the followers,
- Establishing a safe and open communication with their followers,
- Offering different perspectives to her/his followers, challenging traditional thinking.

Similarly, Hacker & Roberts (2003: 75-76) listed transformational leadership characteristics and traits as follows:

- Transformational leaders are analytical and make predictions about the future.
- They encourage their followers to think innovatively.
- They support the empowerment of followers.
- Thanks to the vision they create, leaders inspire the development of their followers.

- They represent the transformation of both their followers and the organization they are affiliated with.
- Leaders are individuals with high psychological resilience.

In summary, transformational leadership is a leadership style that includes innovation, creativity, individual attention, building trust and relationships, and rational care.

SYSTEMATIC ANALYSIS OF TRANSFORMATIONAL LEADERSHIP STUDIES CONDUCTED BETWEEN 2012-2022

In this study, we utilized systematic literature review method. Systematic literature review is used as a statistical tool for a comprehensive review of a number of empirical studies in the literature addressing the same research topic and for providing a concise summary of the best sources to answer researchers' questions (Field & Gillett, 2010). Within the scope of the research, transformational leadership studies in the field of hospitality and tourism management which were carried out between the years of 2012-2022 were examined. The studies were accessed from online indices and academic databases such as "ScienceDirect", "Proquest", "SageJournals", "Google Scholar", "Researchgate" and "SemanticScholar" with the keywords "transformational leadership" "tourism" and "hospitality". As a result of the search, 75 studies were reached. These studies were systematically examined in terms of year, method, model, subject, sample, number of samples and their results.

Findings of the Method and Sample of Studies on the Concept of Transformational Leadership in Tourism Literature

Studies dealing with the concept of transformational leadership in the tourism literature between the years 2012-2022 are examined according to their research designs, data collection tools, models used, number of samples and research area. In terms of research methods, it was determined that almost all of the studies were designed according to quantitative research methods (93.5%), and there were very few studies designed with qualitative (2.6%) mixed (2.6%) and conceptual (1.3%) research designs. Since the quantitative research method is mostly used in the studies, the most used data collection tool were questionnaires (94.8%). It is seen that the data collected through interviews (2.6%), meta-analysis (1.3%) and literature review (1.3%) is quite scarce (Table 2).

When the studies are examined in terms of models that they utilized, MLQ (30.9%) and MLQ-5X (13.7%) models were the most preferred ones, and these models followed by TLI (12.5%), TFL (5.6%), TLQ (4.1%) and other models. Although the majority focused on 5 models, the researchers preferred sixteen different models in their studies. However, in 7 studies, the researchers did not clearly state which model they used. When the research areas of these studies were analyzed, it is seen that the majority of the studies were conducted in Asia (63.6%), followed by the Europe (18.9%) and Africa (13.5%) continents, respectively. Studies conducted in America (2.7%) and Australia (1.3%) are quite limited (Table 3).

Table 2. Research Design and the Data Collection Tools

Research Design	n	%
Quantitative	70	93.5
Qualitative	2	2.6
Mixed	2	2.6
Conceptual	1	1.3
Total	75	%100

Data collection tool	n	%
Questionnaire	71	94.8
Interview	2	2.6
Meta Analysis	1	1.3
Literature Review	1	1.3
Total	75	100.0%

Table 3. Transformational Leadership Models Utilized in the Studies and Research Areas

Models	n	%
MLQ	22	30.9
MLQ 5X	10	13.7
TFI	9	12.5
TFL	4	5.6
TLQ	3	4.1
Others	18	24.6
Not specified	7	9.6
Total	73	100.0%

Research Areas (By Continent)	n	%
Asia	46	63.6
Europe	14	18.9
Africa	10	13.5
America	2	2.7
Australia	1	1.3
Total	73	100.0%

Findings about Studies on the Concept of Transformational Leadership in Tourism Literature

In this part of the research, the studies discussed are categorized according to their subjects. Studies that investigated "organizational commitment, organizational brand climate, organizational justice, organizational trust, organizational citizenship, organizational culture, organizational success, creativity and innovation behavior, social responsibility, empowerment, operational performance, entrepreneurship, team performance, social change theory, hotel performance, organizational citizenship", "emotional commitment" and "team service" were categorized as "organization" level studies. Studies examining the effects of transformational leadership on "job satisfaction, employee well-being, emotional commitment, psychological optimism, job performance, job satisfaction, productivity, job commitment, psychological contract, motivation, customer citizenship behavior, innovative work behavior, employment contract, psychological capital, job life satisfaction, employee engagement, work stress, burnout and intention to leave" included in the "employee" category. Finally, the studies on "gender, personal characteristics, emotional intelligence, cultural intelligence and social responsibility" were discussed under the "leader" category. Although the majority of the obtained studies consisted of studies conducted on the employees (57.9%) and the organization (32.9%), there were also some studies focusing on the leaders specifically (9.2%) in the literature (Table 4).

Table 4. Subjects of Studies on the Concept of Transformational Leadership in Tourism Literature

Subjects	n	%
Worker	44	57.9
Organization	24	32.9
Leader	7	9.2
Total	**75**	**%100**

Findings on the Variables Investigated in the Studies

In this part of the chapter, the studies were categorized according to the main variables they examined. A total of 75 studies were handled in seventeen categories in total. These are commitment, trust, empowerment, citizenship, capital, satisfaction, performance, satisfaction, burnout, intention to leave, creativity, innovation, productivity, knowledge sharing, motivation, and leader characteristics (Table 5).

CONCLUSION AND RECOMMENDATIONS

There is a great need for managers who can control the negative situations and even crises in a fragile sector like tourism, and who will guide his/her followers with his/her leadership skills. Transformational leadership is a sought-after leadership style in the tourism industry, both with its vision, its openness to transformation and its efforts to develop its followers.

In this study, firstly, the emergence and definition of transformational leadership and its importance for the tourism sector are mentioned. Then, the most used models in the tourism literature were identified and examined in depth. The conceptual framework is concluded by listing the unique characteristics of a transformational leader. How transformational leadership has been handled in the tourism literature in the last decade has been analyzed using the systematic literature review technique. A total of 75 studies were reached and these studies were examined in the form of methods, analysis techniques, models used

Table 5. Variables Investigated in Studies on the Concept of Transformational Leadership in Tourism Literature

No	Variable	Result	Reflection	Sources
1	Loyalty	It has been determined that transformational leadership has a direct positive effect on organizational commitment, normative commitment, employee engagement and emotional commitment. In addition, transformational leadership indirectly increases commitment through non-financial and sustainability performance, trust, and psychological well-being.	In order to increase individual and organizational commitment, it is recommended that leaders be trained to be transformational.	Chiang & Wang (2012), Dai et, al. (2012), Newman & Butler (2014), Apfiasari et, al (2015), Patiar & Wang (2016), Liang et, al. (2017), Dlamini et, al. (2017), Sung et, al. (2019), Teguh, Devine & Wijiya (2020), Ali Shah et, al. (2020), Sobaih et, al (2020), Yuan et, al. (2021)
2	Confidence	Transformational leadership has been found to have positive effects on cognitive and emotional trust, as well as providing employees' trust. At the same time, trust, psychological well-being, and organizational culture mediate the relationship of transformational leadership on organizational commitment, and trust mediates the significant relationship between transformational leadership and follower growth satisfaction in the workplace.	It is recommended that managers adopt transformational leadership, as it is known that it provides the trust of the employees and indirectly affects the commitment positively.	Chiang & Wang (2012), Dai et, al. (2012), Apfiasari et, al (2015), Prikshat, Rajesh & Rajaguru (2020)
3	Strengthening	Structural empowerment is indirectly effective in the relationship between transformational leadership and the employment contract.	For the positive effect of empowerment, it is recommended to develop the balance scorecard application.	Ballester-Miquel et, al. (2017), Amor, Vazquez & Faina (2019)
4	Citizenship	Transformational leadership has been found to have a direct and indirect positive and significant effect on employees' citizenship behavior, and organizational citizenship behavior.	Adopting transformational leadership is advised in order to lessen emotional to improve work performance as a result of increased organizational citizenship behaviors.	Dai et, al. (2012), Buil, Martinez & Matute (2019), Khan et, al. (2020), Khan et, al. (2020), Gurmani et, al. (2021)
5	Psychological and Social Capital	It has been determined that there is a positive relationship between transformational leadership and social and psychological capital. It has a mediating effect on issues such as creativity, innovation, willingness to leave the job and sharing information.	It has been suggested that upper-level managers adopt a transformational leadership style in order to decrease the intention of employees to leave the job.	Liu (2017), Nagele & Awuor (2018), Naderi et, al. (2019), Sasmita (2019), Sürücü, Maşlakçı & Şeşen (2019), Gom et, al. (2021)
6	Satisfaction	It has been determined that transformational leadership and its sub-dimensions have a strong positive effect on job satisfaction and life satisfaction. In addition, it was concluded that job satisfaction mediated the effect of transformational leadership on turnover intention and that job satisfaction fully mediated employee performance with transformational leadership and partially mediated employee performance with job motivation.	It is recommended that managers learn to utilize transformational leadership to help employees increase their job and life satisfaction.	Spitzbart (2013), Rothfelder, Ottenbacher & Harrington (2013), Emmanuel & Hassan (2015), Chukwuba (2015), Jaiswal & Dhar (2015), Hakim & Ibrahim (2017), Prikshat, Rajesh & Rajaguru (2020)
7	Performance	It has been determined that transformational leadership can increase the performance of employees through psychological optimism, increase financial performance through organizational commitment, proactive personality will positively affect the service performance of employees through organizational resilience, increase employee performance through job satisfaction, significantly affect employee performance, and increase financial performance through employee commitment. The studies also revealed that the transformational leadership is an important antecedent of creating social value that can support corporate performance, its positive effect on team performance, it increases employee performance through job satisfaction, the higher the leader-member harmony, the higher the effect of transformational leadership on the performance of employees, and it has significant positive effects on hotel performance.	It is recommended that leaders participate in transformational leadership trainings to increase employee and organizational performance.	Chen, Wu & Wang (2015), Patiar & Wang (2016), Ullah, Latif & Alam (2017), Silitonga (2018), Nagele & Awuor (2018), Prabowo & Irawanto (2018), Buil, Martinez & Matute (2019), Yang et, al. (2019), Mishra, Mishra & Singh (2019), Teguh, Devine & Wijiya (2020), Anshori et, al. (2020), Hasib et, al. (2020), Alzuobi & Jaaffar (2020), Idris et, al. (2022)
8	Satisfaction	It has been established that transformational leadership has a positive impact on satisfaction, that there is a positive relationship between employee and guest satisfaction, and that interpersonal communication satisfaction and follower trust mediate the significant relationship between transformational leadership and follower growth satisfaction in the workplace.	It is recommended that managers working in the tourism sector adopt transformational leadership behaviors in order to ensure both employee and guest satisfaction.	Quintana, Park & Cabrera (2015), Emmanuel & Hassan (2015), Mohamed (2016), Hakim & Ibrahim (2017), Baquero et, al. (2019), Anshori et, al. (2020), Prikshat, Rajesh & Rajaguru (2020), Belias et, al. (2021), Day et, al. (2022)
9	Burnout	Transformational leadership and job burnout have been found to have a significant negative relationship.	It is recommended that leaders adopt transformational leadership in order to prevent negativities that may cause burnout in employees. In addition, emphasis was placed on strengthening citizenship behaviors in order to prevent emotional exhaustion.	Salem & Kattara (2015), Reddy & Metha (2019), Khan et, al. (2020)
10	Intention to Leave	It has been found that there is a direct negative relationship between transformational leadership and turnover intention, and that all sub-dimensions of transformational leadership significantly affect employees' turnover intention in the opposite direction.	It is recommended to adopt a transformational leadership style to reduce employees' turnover intention.	Hakim & Ibrahim (2017), Chen & Wu (2017), Reddy & Metha (2019), Ohunakin et, al. (2019), Gom et, al. (2021), Gabriel et, al. (2022)
11	Creativity	It has been determined that transformational leadership positively affects the creative self-efficacy and creativity of employees, can support an innovation climate that encourages creativity of employees, and employee service creativity significantly affects innovative behavior.	It is recommended that managers adopt transformational leadership behavior in order to achieve higher employee creativity.	Wang, Tsai & Tsai (2014), Jaiswal & Dhar (2015), Slatten & Mehmetoğlu (2015), Mohamed (2016), Liu (2017), Minh-Duc & Huu-Lam (2019)
12	Innovation	Transformational leadership and all its sub-dimensions positively affect innovative work behavior. Transformational leadership significantly affects innovative behavior, job creation behaviors mediate the effect of transformational leadership on the innovative work behavior of the employee, and there are significant differences between firm innovativeness of transformational leadership and organizational citizenship behavior.	It is underlined that the transformational leadership style is useful for understanding the role of emotional commitment on employees in order to be innovative in service delivery.	Slatten & Mehmetoğlu (2015), Asfar, Masood & Umrani (2019), Khan et, al. (2020), Ali Shah et, al. (2020), Aydın & Erkılıç (2020), Sürücü, Maşlakçı & Şeşen (2021), Gabriel et, al. (2022)
13	Productivity	Transformational leadership has a positive effect on productivity and efficiency.	Tourism and hospitality managers should adopt transformational leadership style in order to increase efficiency, productivity and service quality.	Quintana, Park & Cabrera (2015), Chen & Wu (2020)
14	Service (Standard, Quality, Innovation)	It has been found that transformational leadership improves team service through a culture of development and also increases team service innovation through the mediating role of developmental culture.		Yang, Luu & Qian (2020), Teguh, Devine & Wijiya (2020), Yang, Luu & Qian (2021), Charoenboon & Chankaew (2022)
15	Information sharing	Transformational leadership has been shown to have significant positive effects on knowledge sharing practices. Furthermore, critical mediation features that connect the relationships between knowledge sharing, transformational leadership, and creativity have been identified. Furthermore, receiving information has a positive impact on innovative work behavior.	Considering that knowledge sharing positively affects creativity and innovation, it is recommended to provide socialization and information on how to combine the understanding between leaders and employees by paying attention to what the employee needs and what the leader expects.	Baytok, Kurt & Zorlu (2014), Liu (2017), Aydın & Erkılıç (2020)
16	Motivation	Employee performance was found to be positively and significantly impacted by both transformational leadership and work motivation, and leaders should emphasize employee intrinsic motivation and good organizational citizenship behaviors.	To increase employee motivation and creativity, the managers are advised to embrace transformational leadership behavior.	Silitonga (2018), Prabowo & Irawanto (2018), Minh-Duc & Huu-Lam (2019)
17	Leader's Traits	It was found that emotional intelligence and transformational leadership were positively correlated, as were extraversion, openness, conscientiousness, and a higher level of cultural competence. There was no discernible difference between male and female leaders in transformational leadership behaviors.	People with transformational leadership qualities should be preferred in new job acquisitions.	Marinakou (2012), Zopiatis & Constanti (2012), Mohamed & Fahmy (2015), Bazazo et, al. (2016), Vasilagos, Polychroniou & Maroudas (2017), Carrion, Ramirez & Flores (2018), Asfar et, al. (2019)

in the study, the main subject of the research, mediator effects, research areas and sample characterics, and finally the results obtained.

In studies examining the effects of transformational leadership throughout the organization it has been determined that transformational leadership has both direct and indirect positive effects on organizational commitment, organizational brand climate, organizational justice, organizational trust, organizational citizenship, organizational culture, organizational success, creativity and innovation behavior, social responsibility, empowerment, operational performance, entrepreneurship, team performance, hotel performance, organizational citizenship, emotional commitment and teamwork. Researchers recommend that managers should focus on these points in order to maximize organizational benefits of transformational leadership:

- Leaders of hospitality and tourism businesses should adopt transformational leadership,
- In new job recruitments, leaders who have adopted the transformational style should be preferred in order for the organization to be more successful,
- Since the success of transformational leadership is known, managers should make transformational leadership trainings compulsory in organizations,
- Emphasizing that transformational leadership is a long-term leadership process; in addition to transformational leadership, the use of transactional leadership, which is a short-term management technique is recommended.

Secondly, in the studies examined the effects of transformational leadership at the employee level; transformational leadership was found to be positively related to job satisfaction, employee well-being, emotional commitment, psychological optimism, job performance, job satisfaction, productivity, job commitment, psychological contract, motivation, customer citizenship behavior, innovative work behavior, employment contract, psychological capital, job life satisfaction, customer satisfaction, employee commitment. On the other hand, it has been determined that transformational leadership negatively effects job stress, burnout, and intention to leave. In addition, no relationship was found between creative self-efficacy and transformational leadership.

The studies conducted on the leaders revealed that that extroversion, openness, and conscientiousness were positively related to personal characteristics and had significant effects on emotional intelligence and cultural intelligence. Researchers recommend hiring extroverted individuals who exhibit transformational leadership behaviors in recruitment, and they suggest that managers should provide coaching and support, with vision they create by embodying the transformational leadership characteristics.

As in all studies, there are some limitations in this study. Only studies published in international peer-reviewed journals and in English were examined in the study. In addition, only the studies published in the last 10 years were evaluated in the study. In future studies, the literature review can be extended to cover a longer period of time or comparative analyzes can be carried out by comparing the findings of transformational leadership and other leadership types.

When the studies are examined from a theoretical point of view, it can be seen that the vast majority of the studies conducted on transformational leadership in the tourism and hospitality industry were conducted with quantitative research design. Moreover, there is a lack of studies particularly focusing on the leaders and their characteristics. Authors may address this gap by utilizing qualitative or mixed research designs to obtain in-depth information about the leaders themselves. In addition, it is seen that the majority of the data analyzed in the studies were obtained from the Asian countries. For future studies, it is important for researchers to collect data from other areas and test the models in different cultures to obtain cross-cultural validation.

In summary, it is clearly seen that transformational leadership is one of the most suitable leadership styles for both the organization, the employees, and the leader himself in hospitality and tourism industry. It is critical that the transformational leadership style, which increases the development, satisfaction, and loyalty of the organization and the employee, and is beneficial in minimizing the negative feelings and thoughts of the organization and the employees, is more widely adopted in the hospitality and tourism industries, and that leaders are encouraged to participate in such trainings.

REFERENCES

Al Harbi, J., Alarifi, S., & Mosbah, A. (2019). Transformation leadership and creativity. *Personnel Review*, *48*(5), 1082–1090. doi:10.1108/PR-11-2017-0354

Altıntaş, D. (2020). *Dönüşümcü liderlik ve örgütsel bağlılık arasındaki ilişkinin incelenmesi: iletişim sektöründe bir araştırma* [Examining the relationship between transformational leadership and organizational commitment: A research in the communication sector] [Master Thesis]. Altınbaş University Graduate School of Education. Business Administration/Human Resources Management.

Alzoubi, R. H., & Jaaffar, A. H. (2020). The mediating effect of crisis management on leadership styles and hotel performance in Jordan. *International Journal of Financial Research*, *11*(4), 384–395. doi:10.5430/ijfr.v11n4p384

Amor, A. M., Vazquez, J. P., & Faina, J. A. (2019). Transformational leadership and work engagement: Exploring the mediating role of structural empowerment. *European Management Journal*, 1–10.

Anshori, M. Y., Karya, D. F., Muslihah, N., & Herlambang, T. (2020). Analysis of transformational leadership style for employee performance with job satisfaction as intervening variable. *International Journal of Advanced Science and Technology*, *29*(9), 3967–3973.

Apfiasari, S., Waskito, A., Ajit, A., Pertiwi, D. E., & Mukhlasin, M. (2015). The role of transformational leadership, trust, psychological well-being, and organizational culture on organizational commitment (Study on hotel employees in serang city). *Journal of Industrial Engineering & Management Research*, *2*(5), 1–12.

Ariyabuddhiphongs, V., & Kahn, S. I. (2017). Transformational leadership and turnover intention: The mediating effects of trust and job performance on café employees in Thailand. *Journal of Human Resources in Hospitality & Tourism*, *16*(2), 215–233. doi:10.1080/15332845.2016.1202730

Armstrong, M., & Taylor, S. (2020). *Armstrong's handbook of human resource management practice*. Kogan Page Publishers.

Arslantaş, C. C., & Pekdemir, I. (2007). Dönüşümcü liderlik, örgütsel vatandaşlık davranışı ve örgütsel adalet arasındaki ilişkileri belirlemeye yönelik görgül bir araştırma [An empirical research to determine the relationships between transformational leadership, organizational citizenship behavior, and organizational justice]. *Anadolu University Journal of Social Sciences*, *7*(1), 261–286.

Avolio, B., Bass, B., & Jung, D. (1999). Re-examining the components of transformational and transactional leadership using the Multifactor Leadership Questionnaire. *Journal of Occupational and Organizational Psychology*, *72*(4), 441–462. doi:10.1348/096317999166789

Aydın, E., & Erkılıç, E. (2020). Transformational leadership and innovative work behaviour: The mediating role of knowledge sharing. *Tourism and Recreation*, *2*(2), 106–117.

Ballester-Miquel, J. C., Pérez-Ruiz, P., Hernández-Gadea, J., & Palacios-Marqués, D. (2017). Implementation of the Balanced Scorecard in the hotel sector through transformational leadership and empowerment. *Multidisciplinary Journal for Education. Social and Technological Sciences*, *4*(1), 1–15.

Baquero, A., Delgado, B., Escortell, R., & Sapena, J. (2019). The influence of transformational and authentic leadership on the satisfaction of hotel customers in the Canary Islands. *Tourism and Hospitality Research*, 1–14.

Başaran, S. (2020). *Okul müdürlerinin algılanan dönüşümcü liderlik davranışlarının öğretmenlerin örgütsel sinizm düzeyine etkisi* [The effect of perceived transformational leadership behaviors of school principals on teachers' level of organizational cynicism] [Master's Thesis]. Istanbul Marmara University.

Bass, B. M. (1985). *Leadership and performance beyond expectations*. Free Press.

Bass, B. M. (1990). From transactional to transformational leadership: Learning to share the vision. *Organizational Dynamics*, *18*(3), 19–31. doi:10.1016/0090-2616(90)90061-S

Bass, B. M. (1992). Assessing the charismatic leader. In M. Syrett & C. Hogg (Eds.), *Frontiers of leadership*. Blackwell.

Bass, B. M. (1994). *Transformational leadership and team and organizational decision making, in improving organizational effectiveness through transformational leadership* (B. M. Bass & B. J. Avolio, Eds.). Sage Publications Inc.

Bass, B. M., & Avolio, B. J. (1985). *Improving organizational effectiveness through transformational leadership*. Sage.

Bass, B. M., & Avolio, B. J. (1990). Developing transformational leadership. *Journal of European Industrial Training*, *14*(5), 21–27. doi:10.1108/03090599010135122

Bass, B. M., & Avolio, B. J. (1993). Transformational leadership: A response to critiques. In M. M. Chemers & R. Ayman (Eds.), *Leadership theory and research: Perspectives and directions* (pp. 49–80). Academic Press.

Bass, B. M., & Avolio, B. J. (1995). *Multifactor leadership questionnaire: Technical report*. Mind Garden.

Bass, B. M., Avolio, B. J., & Jung, D. I. (1999). Re-examining the components of transformational and transactional leadership using the multifactor leadership questionnaire. *Journal of Occupational and Organizational Psychology*, *72*(4), 441–462. doi:10.1348/096317999166789

Bass, B. M., Avolio, B. J., Jung, I. D., & Berson, Y. (2003). Predicting unit performance by assessing transformational and transactional leadership. *The Journal of Applied Psychology*, *88*(2), 207–218. doi:10.1037/0021-9010.88.2.207 PMID:12731705

Bass, B. M., & Steidlmeier, P. (1999). Ethics, character, and authentic transformational leadership behavior. *The Leadership Quarterly, 10*(2), 181–217. doi:10.1016/S1048-9843(99)00016-8

Baytok, A., Kurt, M., & Zorlu, Ö. (2014). The role of transformational leader on knowledge sharing practices: A study about international hotel chains. *European Journal of Business and Management, 6*(7), 45–61.

Bazazo, I. K., Alayanzeh, O. A., Adas, K., & Alshawagfih, K. F. (2016). The role of the transformational leadership in enhancing the social responsibility at the five stars hotels in the Hashemite Kingdom of Jordan. *European Journal of Business and Management, 8*(23), 67–74.

Belias, D., Rossidis, I., Papademetriou, C., & Mantas, C. (2021). Job satisfaction as affected by types of leadership: A case study of Greek tourism sector. *Journal of Quality Assurance in Hospitality & Tourism*, 1–20.

Biggs, D. (2011). Understanding resilience in a vulnerable industry: The case of reef tourism in Australia. *Ecology and Society, 16*(1), art30. doi:10.5751/ES-03948-160130

Bowers, M. R., Hall, J. R., & Srinivasan, M. M. (2017). Organizational culture and leadership style: The missing combination for selecting the right leader for effective crisis management. *Business Horizons, 60*(4), 551–563. doi:10.1016/j.bushor.2017.04.001

Brestrich, E. T. (2000). *Transformational leadership from modernism to postmodernism*. Seba Publications.

Bryman, A. (1992). *Charisma and leadership in organizations*. Sage.

Buil, I., Martínez, E., & Matute, J. (2019). Transformational leadership and employee performance: The role of T identification, engagement and proactive personality. *International Journal of Hospitality Management, 77*, 64–75. doi:10.1016/j.ijhm.2018.06.014

Carless, S. A., Wearing, A., & Mann, L. (2000). A short measure of transformational leadership. *Journal of Business and Psychology, 14*(3), 389–405. doi:10.1023/A:1022991115523

Carrión, I. A., Ramírez, M. C., & Flores, J. C. (2018). Transformational ledership and gender in 4 and 5 Star Hotel in Tijuana (Mexico). *Cuadernos de Turismo, 42*, 609–612.

Charoenboon, P., & Chankaew, K. (2022). Managing strategies of transformational leadership to create service standard of boutique hotel in Thailand. *International Journal of Health Sciences, 6*(3), 6984–6994. doi:10.53730/ijhs.v6nS3.7625

Chen, A., Brian, M., & Hou, Y. (2015). Impact of transformational leadership on subordinate's EI and work performance. *Personnel Review, 44*(4), 438–453. doi:10.1108/PR-09-2012-0154

Chen, T. J., & Wu, C. M. (2017). Improving the turnover intention of tourist hotel employees: Transformational leadership, leader-member exchange, and psychological contract breach. *International Journal of Contemporary Hospitality Management, 29*(7), 1914–1936. doi:10.1108/IJCHM-09-2015-0490

Chen, T. J., & Wu, C. M. (2020). Can newcomers perform better at hotels? Examining the roles of transformational leadership, supervisor-triggered positive affect, and perceived supervisor support. *Tourism Management Perspectives, 33*, 1–15. doi:10.1016/j.tmp.2019.100587

Chen, T. J., Wu, C. M., & Wang, Y. C. (2015). Impact of transformational leadership behaviors and psychological optimism on subordinate performance in Taiwan's tourism hotel industry. *Open Journal of Social Sciences, 3*(07), 174–179. doi:10.4236/jss.2015.37028

Chiang, C. F., & Wang, Y. Y. (2012). The effects of transactional and transformational leadership on organizational commitment in hotels: The mediating effect of trust. *Hotel & Business Management, 1*(1), 3–11. doi:10.4172/2169-0286.1000103

Chianga, C., & Lin, M. (2016). Motivating organizational commitment in hotels: The relationship between leaders and employees. *Journal of Human Resources in Hospitality & Tourism, 15*(4), 462–484. doi:10.1080/15332845.2016.1148570

Chukwuba, K. (2015). *A quantitative model studying the effects of transformational leadership on job satisfaction*. College of Management and Technology, Walden University.

Conger, J. A., & Kanungo, R. N. (1988). *Charismatic leadership: The elusive factor in organizational effectiveness*. Jossey-Bass.

Dai, Y. D., Dai, Y. Y., Chen, K. Y., & Wu, H. C. (2013). Transformational vs transactional leadership: Which is better? A study on employees of international tourist hotels in Taipei City. *International Journal of Contemporary Hospitality Management, 25*(5), 760–778. doi:10.1108/IJCHM-Dec-2011-0223

Day, S. W., Lawong, D., Miles, A. K., & Effon, T. (2022). Leadership and culture in ghana's tourism and hospitality industry: The impact of transformational leadership on job satisfaction in an emerging economy. *Journal of Leadership, Accountability and Ethics, 19*(1), 127–134.

Dlamini, N., Garg, A. K., & Muchie, P. M. (2017). The impact of transformational leadership style on organizational commitment in the hospitality industry. *African Journal of Hospitality, Tourism and Leisure, 6*(3), 1–21.

Doğanbaş, Z. E. (2017). *Dönüşümcü liderlik ile iş tatmini arasındaki ilişkinin incelenmesi: kuşaklar arası farklılık* [Examining the relationship between transformational leadership and job satisfaction: Generational difference] [Master Thesis]. Çankaya University, Institute of Social Sciences.

Downton, J. V. (1973). *Rebel leadership: Commitment and charisma in the revolutionary process*. Free Press.

Emmanuel, A. O., & Hassan, Z. (2015). The effects of transformational leadership on job satisfaction: A study on four and five star hotels in Kuala Lumpur. *International Journal of Accounting, Business and Management, 3*(1), 88–98.

Eraslan, L. (2006). Liderlikte post-modern bir paradigma: Dönüşümcü liderlik [A post-modern paradigm in leadership: Transformational leadership]. *International Journal of Human Sciences*, 1–32.

Felix, C., Ahmad, A., & Arshad, R. (2016). Examining ethical reasoning and transformational leadership style in Nigeria public sector. *SAGE Open, 6*(2), 1–7. doi:10.1177/2158244016635256

Field, A. P., & Gillett, R. (2010). How to do a meta-analysis. *British Journal of Mathematical & Statistical Psychology, 63*(3), 665–694. doi:10.1348/000711010X502733 PMID:20497626

Gabriel, O. D., Alwis, C. D., Jayang, E. A., & Wai, S. L. (2022). The impact of transformational leadership on generation z employee retention and innovative behaviour: A case of Malaysian hotel industry. *International Journal of Multicultural and Multireligious Understanding*, 9(4), 35–53.

Gom, D., Lew, T. Y., Jiony, M. M., Tanakinjal, G. H., & Stephen Sondoh, J. (2021). The role of transformational leadership and psychological capital in the hotel industry: A sustainable approach to reducing turnover intention. *Sustainability*, 13(19), 1–20. doi:10.3390u131910799

Gurmani, J. K., Khan, N. U., Khalique, M., Yasir, M., Obaid, A., & Sabri, N. A. (2021). Do environmental transformational leadership predicts organizational citizenship behavior towards environment in hospitality industry: Using structural equation modeling approach. *Sustainability*, 13(10), 1–29. doi:10.3390u13105594

Güzel, T., & Akgündüz, Y. (2011). Liderlik davranışlarının orta düzey yöneticiler üzerindeki etkisi ve yöneticilerin tükenmişlik düzeyleri ile ilişkisi; Kuşadası otel işletmelerinde bir araştırma [The effects of leadership behaviors on mid-level managers and their relationship with burnout levels; a research in Kusadasi hotel businesses]. *Journal of Management Sciences*, 9(2), 280–296.

Hacker, S., & Roberts, T. (2003). *Transformational leadership: Creating organizations of meaning.* ASQ Quality, Milwaukee.

Hakim, A. H., & Ibrahim, H. M. (2017). Transformational leadership and turnover intention: Mediating role of overall job satisfaction. *Journal of Tourism. Hospitality & Culinary Arts*, 9(2), 237–248.

Hannah, S. T., Uhl-Bien, M., Avolio, B. J., & Cavarretta, F. L. (2009). A framework for examining leadership in extreme contexts. *The Leadership Quarterly*, 20(6), 897–919. doi:10.1016/j.leaqua.2009.09.006

Hasib, F. F., Eliyana, A., Arief, Z., & Pratiwi, A. A. (2020). The effect of transformational leadership on employee performance mediated by leader-member exchange (LMX). *Systematic Reviews in Pharmacy*, 11(11), 1199–1209.

Hinkin, T. R., & Tracey, J. B. (1994). Transformational leadership in the hospitality industry. *Hospitality Research Journal*, 18(1), 49–63. doi:10.1177/109634809401800105

House, R. J., & Shamir, B. (1993). Toward the integration of transformational, charismatic, and visionary theories. *Leadership Theory and Research*, 14, 81–107.

Howell, J. M., & Avolio, B. (1993). Transformational leadership, transactional leadership, locus of control and support for innovation: Key predictors of consolidated-business-unit performance. *The Journal of Applied Psychology*, 78(6), 891–902. doi:10.1037/0021-9010.78.6.891

Idris, I., Suyuti, A., Supriyanto, A. S., & As, N. (2022). transformational leadership, political skill, organizational culture, and employee performance: A case from tourism company in Indonesia. *Geo Journal of Tourism and Geosites*, 40(1), 104–110. doi:10.30892/gtg.40112-808

Jaiswal, N. K., & Dhar, R. L. (2015). Transformational leadership, innovation climate, creative self-efficacy and employee creativity: A multilevel study. *International Journal of Hospitality Management*, 51, 30–41. doi:10.1016/j.ijhm.2015.07.002

Kara, D., Uysal, M., Sirgy, M. J., & Leed, G. (2013). The effects of leadership style on employee well-being in hospitality. *International Journal of Hospitality Management, 34*, 9–18. doi:10.1016/j.ijhm.2013.02.001

Khan, A., Bibi, S., Lyu, J., Garavelli, A. C., Pontrandolfo, P., & Sanchez, M. D. (2020). Uncovering Innovativeness in Spanish Tourism Firms: The Role of Transformational Leadership, OCB, Firm Size, and Age. *Sustainability, 12*(10), 1–26. doi:10.3390u12103989

Khan, N. A., Khan, A. N., Soomro, M. A., & Khan, S. K. (2020). Transformational leadership and civic virtue behavior: Valuing act of thriving and emotional exhaustion in the hotel industry. *Asia Pacific Management Review, 25*(4), 216–225. doi:10.1016/j.apmrv.2020.05.001

Kim, H., Im, J., & Shin, Y. H. (2021). The impact of transformational leadership and commitment to change on restaurant employees' quality of work life during a crisis. *Journal of Hospitality and Tourism Management, 48*, 322–330. doi:10.1016/j.jhtm.2021.07.010

Kirkbride, P. (2006). Developing transformational leaders: The full range leadership model in action. *Industrial and Commercial Training, 38*(1), 23–32. doi:10.1108/00197850610646016

Kouzes, J. M., & Posner, B. Z. (1987). *The leadership challenge: How to get extraordinary things done in organizations*. Jossey-Bass.

Kuhnert, K. W., & Lewis, P. (1987). Transactional and transformational leadership: A constructive/developmental analysis. *Academy of Management Review, 12*(4), 648–657. doi:10.2307/258070

Larson, C. E., & Lafasto, F. (1989). *Team-work: What must go right/what can go wrong*. Sage Publications.

Liang, T. L., Chang, H. F., Ko, M. H., & Lin, C. W. (2017). Transformational leadership and employee voices in the hospitality industry. *International Journal of Contemporary Hospitality Management, 29*(1), 374–392. doi:10.1108/IJCHM-07-2015-0364

Liu, C. H. S. (2017). Remodelling progress in tourism and hospitality students' creativity through social capital and transformational leadership. *Journal of Hospitality, Leisure, Sport and Tourism Education, 21*, 69–82. doi:10.1016/j.jhlste.2017.08.003

Ma, M. H., & Yang, Q. S. (2020). How does transformational leadership work on COVID-19? An empirical evidence from China. *Journal of Innovative Studies, 1*(2).

Mahmood, M., Uddin, A., & Fan, L. (2019). The influence of transformational leadership on employees' creative process engagement. *Management Decision, 57*(3), 741–764. doi:10.1108/MD-07-2017-0707

Mansurova, S., & Güney, S. (2018). İşletmelerde dönüşümcü liderlik davranışlarının örgüt kültürüne etkisi ve bir uygulama [The effect of transformational leadership behaviors on organizational culture in businesses and an application]. *Journal of Anadolu Bil Vocational School, 13*(52), 33–54.

Marinakou, E. (2012). *An investigation of gender influences on transformational leadership style in the Greek hospitality industry* [Doctoral Thesis]. Department of Human Resources Management Strathclyde Business School University of Strathclyde.

Masood, S. A., Dani, S. S., Burns, N. D., & Backhouse, C. (2006). Transformational leadership and organizational culture: The situational strength perspective. *Proceedings of the Institution of Mechanical Engineers. Part B, Journal of Engineering Manufacture, 220*(6), 941–949. doi:10.1243/09544054JEM499

Mills, G. E. (2007). *Transformational Leadership and Employee Retention: An Exploratory Investigation of The Four Characteristic*. Capella University.

Minh-Duc, L., & Huu-Lam, N. (2019). Transformational leadership, customer citizenship behavior, employee intrinsic motivation, and employee creativity. *Journal of Asian Business and Economic Studies, 26*(2), 286–300. doi:10.1108/JABES-10-2018-0070

Mishra, N., Mishra, R., & Singh, M. K. (2019). The impact of transformational leadership on team performance: The mediating role of emotional intelligence among leaders of hospitality and tourism sector. *International Journal of Scientific & Technology Research, 8*(11), 3110–3116.

Mohamed, H. A., & Fahmy, T. M. (2015). Examining the relationship between emotional intelligence and transformational leadership (A field study of tourism managers). *Journal of Association of Arab Universities for Tourism and Hospitality, 12*(2), 97–108. doi:10.21608/jaauth.2015.67442

Mohamed, L. M. (2016). Assessing the effects of transformational leadership: A study on Egyptian hotel employees. *Journal of Hospitality and Tourism Management, 27*, 49–59. doi:10.1016/j.jhtm.2016.04.001

Naderi, A., Vosta, L. N., Ebrahimi, A., & Jalilvand, M. R. (2019). The contributions of social entrepreneurship and transformational leadership to performance Insights from rural tourism in Iran. *The International Journal of Sociology and Social Policy*, 1–19.

Nadler, D.A., & Tushman, M.L. (1990). Beyond the charismatic leader: Leadership and organizational change. *Startegs & Organization*, 77-97.

Nagele, A. D., & Awuor, E. (2018). Relationship between transformational leadership style and operational performance of hospitality industry in Kenya: A case study of star rated hotels in Nairobi county. *Stratford Peer Reviewed Journals and Book Publishing Journal of Human Resource & Leadership, 2*(4), 37–58.

Newman, A., & Butler, C. (2014). The influence of follower cultural orientation on attitudinal responses towards transformational leadership: Evidence from the Chinese hospitality industry. *International Journal of Human Resource Management, 25*(7), 1024–1045. doi:10.1080/09585192.2013.815250

Ohunakin, F., Adeniji, A. A., Oludayo, O. A., Osibanjo, A. O., & Oduyoye, O. O. (2019). Employees' retention in Nigeria's hospitality industry: The role of transformational leadership style and job satisfaction. *Journal of Human Resources in Hospitality & Tourism, 18*(4), 1–30. doi:10.1080/15332845.2019.1626795

Öncü, B. (2017). *Okul öncesi yöneticilerinin algılanan liderlik stilleri ile okul öncesi öğretmenlerinin yaşadıkları örgütsel sessizlik arasındaki ilişkinin incelenmesi (Kırklareli ili örneği)* [Investigation of the relationship between the perceived leadership styles of preschool administrators and the organizational silence experienced by preschool teachers (Kırklareli province example)] [Unpublished Master's Thesis]. Bahçeşehir University, Institute of Educational Sciences.

Patiar, K., & Wang, A. Y. (2016). The effects of transformational leadership and organizational commitment on hotel departmental performance. *International Journal of Contemporary Hospitality Management*, *38*(3), 1–40. doi:10.1108/IJCHM-01-2014-0050

Phaneuf, J., Boudrias, J., Rousseau, V., & Brunelle, E. (2016). Personality and transformational leadership: The moderating effect of organizational context. *Personality and Individual Differences*, *202*, 30–35. doi:10.1016/j.paid.2016.06.052

Podsakoff, P. M., MacKenzie, S., Moorman, R., & Fetter, R. (1990). Transformational leader behaviors and their effects on followers' trust in leader, satisfaction, and organizational citizenship behaviors. *The Leadership Quarterly*, *1*(2), 107–142. doi:10.1016/1048-9843(90)90009-7

Prabowo, T. S., & Irawanto, N. D. (2018). The influence of transformational leadership and work motivation on employee performance mediated by job satisfaction. *Journal of Applied Management*, *16*(1), 171–178. doi:10.21776/ub.jam.2018.016.01.20

Prikshat, V., Rajesh, J. I., & Rajaguru, R. (2020). The growth satisfaction in jobs among hospitality employees: The role of transformational leadership, interpersonal communication satisfaction and trust. *Journal of Human Resources in Hospitality & Tourism*, 1–28.

Quintana, T. A., Park, S., & Cabrera, Y. A. (2015). Assessing the effects of leadership styles on employees' outcomes in international luxury hotels. *Journal of Business Ethics*, *129*(2), 469–489. doi:10.100710551-014-2170-3

Reddy, A. V., & Mehta, H. N. (2019). Mediating role of transformational leadership on the relationship between burnout and intention to quit among the employees of select hotels in South India. *Organizational Psychology*, *9*(4), 8–17.

Rothfelder, K., Ottenbacher, M. C., & Harrington, R. J. (2013). The impact of transformational, transactional and non-leadership styles on employee job satisfaction in the German hospitality industry. *Tourism and Hospitality Research*, 1–14.

Roueche, J., Baker, G., & Rose, R. (1989). *Shared vision: transformational leadership in American community colleges*. Community College Press.

Salem, I., & Kattara, H. (2015). Transformational leadership: Relationship to job stress and job burnout in five-star hotels. *Tourism and Hospitality Research*, *15*(4), 1–14. doi:10.1177/1467358415581445

Sasmita, I. A. (2019). The effect of transformational leadership and psychological capital to individual readiness to change for employees in tourism development corporate. *Journal Psychodimensia*, *18*(2), 167–177. doi:10.24167/psidim.v18i2.2409

Schmidt, B., Loerbroks, A., Herr, R., Litaker, D., Wilso, M. M., Kastner, M., & Fischer, J. (2014). Psychological resources and the relationship between transformational leadership and employees' psychological strain. *Work (Reading, Mass.)*, *49*(2), 315–324. doi:10.3233/WOR-131713 PMID:24004772

Shah, S. H., Sultana, A., Gul, A., Sajjad, S., Aziz, S., Simple, A., & Qadir, A. (2020). Transformational leadership influence on innovation directly and indirectly through affective commitment in hotel industry of Malaysia. *International Review of Management and Marketing*, *10*(6), 22–28. doi:10.32479/irmm.10761

Shamir, B., House, R., & Arthur, M. (1993). The motivational effects of charismatic leadership: A self-concept based theory. *Organization Science*, *4*(4), 577–593. doi:10.1287/orsc.4.4.577

Silitonga, E. S. (2018). Employee performance analysis: Predictors of transformational leadership and work motivation (Case study at indonesian academy of tourism Jakarta). *Saudi Journal of Humanities and Social Sciences*, *3*(3), 515–523.

Slatten, T., & Mehmetoglu, M. (2015). The effects of transformational leadership and perceived creativity on innovation behavior in the hospitality industry. *Journal of Human Resources in Hospitality & Tourism*, *14*(2), 195–219. doi:10.1080/15332845.2014.955557

Sobaih, A. E., Hasanein, A. M., Aliedan, M. M., & Abdallah, H. S. (2020). The impact of transactional and transformational leadership on employee intention to stay in deluxe hotels: Mediating role of organizational commitment. *Tourism and Hospitality Research*, 1–13.

Spitzbart, I. (2013). The impact of transactional versus transformational leadership on job satisfaction in the hotel industry. *Research in Hospitality Management*, *3*(1), 69–76. doi:10.1080/22243534.2013.11828305

Sung, T. P., Joo, L. W., Rahim, I. H., & Sondoh, S. (2019). Transformational and transactional leadership styles toward organizational commitment in the hotel industry. *Journal of Tourism. Hospitality and Environment Management*, *4*(17), 34–45.

Sürücü, L., Maşlakçı, A., & Şenen, H. (2021). The influence of transformational leadership on employees' innovative behavior in the hospitality industry: The mediating role of leader member exchange. *Original Research Article*, *69*(1), 19–31.

Sürücü, L., Şenen, H., & Maşlakcı, A. (2019). On the relation between leadership and positive psychological capital in the hospitality industry. *International Journal of Business*, *24*(2), 182–197.

Teguh, E. D., Devine, D., & Wijaya, S. (2020). Transformational leadership in the hotel industry: A new look at the service-profit-chain concept. *Petra International Journal of Business Studies*, *3*(2), 98–109. doi:10.9744/ijbs.3.2.98-109

Thoms, P., & Greenberger, D. B. (1995). The relationship between leadership and time orientation. *Journal of Management Inquiry*, *4*(3), 272–292. doi:10.1177/105649269543009

Thomson, N. B. III, Rawson, J. V., Slade, C. P., & Bledsoe, M. (2016). Transformation and transformational leadership. A review of the current and relevant literature for academic radiologists. *Academic Radiology*, *23*(5), 592–599. doi:10.1016/j.acra.2016.01.010 PMID:26971043

Tichy, N. M., & Devanna, M. A. (1986). *Transformational leadership*. Wiley.

Turan, M. (2019). *Dönüşümcü liderlik ve yenilikçi iş davranışı arasındaki ilişkide kontrol odağının etkisi* [The effect of locus of control on the relationship between innovative leadership and innovative business behavior] [Master Thesis]. Recep Tayyip Erdogan University Institute of Social Sciences.

Ullah, R., Latif, K.F., & Alam, W. (2018). Role of transformational leadership style on employee job performance among high and low ranking institutions of higher education of Khyber Pakhtunkhwa. *City University Research Journal*, *8*(2).

Ünsal, A. A. (2019). *Dönüşümcü liderlik ve örgütsel vatandaşlık davranışı arasındaki ilişki* [The relationship between transformational leadership and organizational citizenship behavior] [Master Thesis]. Istanbul University Social Sciences Institute Department of Business.

Vasilagos, T., Polychroniou, P., & Maroudas, L. (2017). *Relationship between supervisor's emotional intelligence and transformational leadership in hotel organizations*. Springer.

Wang, C. J., Tsai, H. T., & Tsai, M. T. (2014). Linking transformational leadership and employee creativity in the hospitality industry: The influences of creative role identity, creative self-efficacy, and job complexity. *Tourism Management, 40*, 79–89. doi:10.1016/j.tourman.2013.05.008

Wang, G., Oh, I., Courtight, S., & Colbert, A. (2011). Transformational leadership and performance across criteria and levels: A meta-analytic review of 25 years of research. *Group & Organization Management, 36*(2), 223–270. doi:10.1177/1059601111401017

Wen, T. B., Ho, T. C., Kelana, B. W. Y., Othman, R., & Syed, O. R. (2019). Leadership styles in influencing employees' job performances. *International Journal of Academic Research in Business & Social Sciences, 9*(9), 55–65. doi:10.6007/IJARBSS/v9-i9/6269

Yammario, F. J., & Bass, B. (1990). *Long-term forecasting of transformational leadership and its effects among naval officers: Some preliminary findings*. Leadership Library of America.

Yang, C., Chen, Y., & Zhao, X., & Hua, N. (2019). Transformational leadership, proactive personality and service performance. The mediating role of organizational embeddedness. *International Journal of Contemporary Hospitality Management*.

Yang, M., Luu, T. T., & Qian, D. (2020). Dual-focused transformational leadership and service innovation in hospitality organisations: A multilevel investigation. *International Journal of Hospitality Management, 98*, 1–13.

Yanga, M., Luua, T. T., & Qiana, D. X. (2021). Linking transformational leadership to team service innovation in the hospitality industry: A team-level mediation and moderation investigation. *Journal of Hospitality and Tourism Management, 49*, 558–569. doi:10.1016/j.jhtm.2021.11.011

Yanti, N. P. R., Mujiati, N. W., & Suwandana, G. M. (2021). The influence of transformational leadership style, organizational culture, and physical work environment on employee performance in the tourism department of Bali, Indonesia. *American Journal of Humanities and Social Sciences Research, 5*(2), 363–371.

Yıldırım, S. (2019). *Sporda dönüşümcü liderlik ve performans: Bir model derlemesi* [Transformational leadership and performance in sport: A model collection] [Doctoral Thesis]. Hacettepe University Institute of Health Sciences.

Yuan, Y., Kong, H., Baum, T., Liu, Y., Liu, C., Bu, N., Wang, K., & Yin, Z. (2021). Transformational leadership and trust in leadership impacts on employee commitment. *Tourism Review, 77*(5), 1385–1399. doi:10.1108/TR-10-2020-0477

Yukl, G. (1989). Managerial leadership: A review of tineory and researct. *Journal of Management, 15*(2), 251–289. doi:10.1177/014920638901500207

Yukl, G. (1994). *Leadership in organisations* (3rd ed.). Prentice Hall.

Yukl, G. (1999). An evaluation of conceptual weaknesses in transformational and charismatic leadership theories. *The Leadership Quarterly, 10*(2), 285–300. doi:10.1016/S1048-9843(99)00013-2

Zheng, J., Wu, G., & Xie, H. (2017). Impacts of leadership on project-based organizational innovation performance: The mediator of knowledge sharing and moderator of social capital. *Sustainability, 9*(10), 1893. doi:10.3390u9101893

Zopiatis, A., & Constanti, P. (2012). Extraversion, openness and conscientiousness The route to transformational leadership in the hotel industry. *Leadership and Organization Development Journal, 33*(1), 86–104. doi:10.1108/01437731211193133

Zwingmann, I., Wegge, J., Wolf, S., Rudolf, M., Schmidt, M., & Richter, P. (2014). Is transformational leadership healthy for employees? A multilevel analysis in 16 nations. *German Journal of Research in Human Resource Management, 28*(1–2), 24–51. doi:10.1177/239700221402800103

Chapter 9
Transformational Leadership in the Alpine Tourism Industry:
Characterizing the Leadership Dimensions Among Entrepreneurs of Small and Medium-Sized Enterprises

Stefanie Haselwanter
Management Center Innsbruck, Austria

Julia Unterlechner
https://orcid.org/0000-0001-7395-6722
Management Center Innsbruck, Austria

ABSTRACT

This chapter aims to explore the topic of leadership in touristic SMEs. Effective forms of leadership, like transformational leadership, can create a high level of work engagement through setting values and direction for all involved stakeholders and pave the way for a competitive advantage for the business as well as for the destination. Building on current research on leadership and following a qualitative research approach, the authors investigate how far entrepreneurs of touristic SMEs apply notions of transformational leadership and how their leadership skills can further be characterized. Semi-structured interviews were conducted with fifteen entrepreneurs of SMEs from five different tourism subsectors in Tyrol (Austria). The objective of this chapter is to conceptualize the leadership qualities of tourism entrepreneurs and derive implications for enhancing transformational leadership abilities. This chapter adds new insights into the status-quo of leadership in tourism research and gives valuable insights for leading SMEs in the tourism sector.

INTRODUCTION

The tourism industry itself "(...) is constituted by a fast-paced, dynamic, unpredictable, and unstable

DOI: 10.4018/978-1-6684-6713-8.ch009

operating environment that requires an extraordinary leadership ability (...)" (Vargas-Sevalle et al., 2020, p. 73). Particularly in the alpine tourism industry, the small-scale structures, seasonality and a relatively high employee-turnover rate implicate tremendous challenges for entrepreneurs (Peters, 2005). Most tourism destinations in the alpine regions are dominated by small and medium-sized enterprises (SMEs) (Schwaiger & Zehrer, 2021; Weiermair, 2000). Since entrepreneurs of SMEs are usually deeply involved in daily business due to the small-scale structures, their leadership has a major influence on business performance (Peters, 2005). Particularly the notion of transformational leadership is of high relevance in the tourism industry (Farrell, 2022). Especially in SMEs, transformational leaders can create high levels of motivation and work engagement which, in turn, can result in a competitive advantage, for example in terms of service quality, service performance and customer satisfaction (Chen & Wu, 2020; Monje-Amor et al., 2020). Thus, entrepreneurs of SMEs are essential for not only driving forward their businesses but also the whole tourism industry (Haven-Tang & Jones, 2012).

The statement „*Leadership is one of the most observed and least understood phenomena on earth"* (Burns, 1978, p. 2) applies strikingly well to research on transformational leadership in SMEs in the alpine tourism industry. It is widely acknowledged that leadership in larger businesses differs from leadership in smaller companies, where special leadership qualities, abilities and characteristics are required due to the involvement of entrepreneurs in everyday business (Peters, 2005). Whereas transformational leadership in general has been studied so far, there are only few studies investigating this form of leadership among entrepreneurs of SMEs in alpine tourism destinations despite its immediate relevance for the industry, creating the need for further research in this area.

Moreover, in alpine destinations, a variety of private, public-private, and public stakeholders are producing the tourism product and offering this experience to consumers (Buhalis, 2000; Raich & Zehrer, 2010; Siller & Haselwanter, 2019). The few existing studies on transformational leadership in the tourism industry are mainly focused on hotels (Baytok et al., 2014; Hinkin & Tracey, 1994; Vargas-Sevalle et al., 2020). Other crucial stakeholders in alpine tourism destinations such as destination management organizations (DMOs), cable car companies and ski schools are often not considered in these studies. Next to that, a strong tendency towards quantitative approaches, for example in the studies by Amankwaa et al. (2019), Liang et al. (2017) and Rothfelder et al. (2013) can be identified, whereas qualitative studies in this field are rare, giving rise to the need for a more holistic and qualitative study in the field of transformational leadership arises.

Following the outlined research gaps, this contribution aims to answer the following research questions: *How do entrepreneurs of SMEs in alpine tourism destinations apply ideas of transformational leadership? Which transformational leadership dimensions and qualities do these entrepreneurs demonstrate?* In addressing the outlined research questions, our study contributes to the enhancement of research on transformational leadership of entrepreneurs in the alpine tourism industry by including all relevant stakeholder groups of alpine destinations. The aim of this research is to present a revised model of the full-range leadership model for the alpine tourism industry and to derive practical implications for leaders of SMEs in the alpine tourism industry. Hence, our study directly contributes to state-of-the-art research in leadership and expands our understanding of transformational leadership in the specific context of SMEs in alpine tourism destinations.

THEORETICAL BACKGROUND

Transformational and Transactional Leadership

Leadership is a key element for driving success, avoiding organizational failure and influencing the growth in an organisation (Madanchian & Taherdoost, 2017). Leadership in general can be defined as *"a process whereby an individual influences a group of individuals to achieve a common goal"* (Northouse, 2013, p. 15). Leaders are important for setting up values and a clear vision for the organization (Burns, 1978; Rothfelder et al., 2013) as well as for motivating and inspiring employees (Cote, 2017). Effective forms of leadership such as transactional and transformational leadership aim to create a high level of work engagement by influencing, motivating, inspiring and individually considering the employees (Burns, 1978), thus making the ability to influence, motivate and inspire people the quintessence of leadership (Bakker et al., 2022)

According to Bass and Avolio (as cited in Khan et al., 2016, p. 3), transactional leadership is *"a type of contingent-reward leadership that has active and positive exchange between leaders and followers whereby followers are rewarded or recognized for accomplishing agreed upon objectives"*. Burns (2012) states that this exchange is not aimed towards higher purposes and consequently does not necessarily foster the relationship between leader and followers. Usually this exchange results in value creation in form of rewards, recognition or promotion for the followers and commitment or loyalty towards the leader (Gosling et al., 2012). Therefore, the transactional theory is mainly focusing on the influence process between leader and followers and rather on extrinsic motivation to achieve goals (Van Seters & Field, 1990).

The transformational leadership theory on the other hand *"occurs when leaders broaden and elevate the interests of their employees, when they generate awareness and acceptance of the purpose and mission of the group, and when they stir their employees to look beyond their own self-interest for the good of the group"* (Bass, 1990, p. 21). Accordingly, transformational leadership is based on change, shared values and common goals (Sadler, 2003). Moreover, transformational leadership is concerned with the personal growth and development of followers. Their growth is stimulated and influenced by the leader and the involvement of the followers in the achievement of the vision and purpose (Liang et al., 2017).

Transformational leadership offers a broader, more integrated view on existing leadership theories by combining many aspects from earlier theoretical approaches, such as behavioural and or personality-based theories (Lang & Rybnikova, 2014). The transformational leadership approach is also characterized by including intrinsic motivation for goal achievement as well as more proactive and innovative thinking of the leader (Van Seters & Field, 1990). Since the transformational leadership theory builds on the transactional leadership theory (Bass & Avolio, 1994), it can be stated that it is more rewarding for both involved parties, as it also recognizes existing needs and brings higher levels of motivation. However, it is also more complex than the mere exchange between follower and leader (Burns, 2012).

The Full-Range Leadership Model

The full-range leadership model, originally established by Bass and Avolio (1994), helps researchers and practitioners alike to fully explore the field of leadership in more depth (Kirkbride, 2006). The model includes four dimensions of transformational leadership, three forms of transactional leadership as well as *laissez-faire* leadership. As depicted in figure 1, laissez-faire leadership is the most passive and in-

Figure 1. Full-range leadership model
Source: Adapted according to Bass & Avolio, 1994, p. 6)

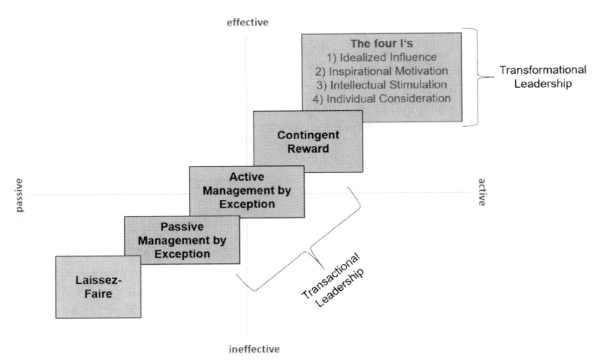

effective form, followed by transactional leadership as well as its various forms, and transformational leadership. Next to that, it visualizes that the various forms of leadership are not separate concepts as they overlap to a certain degree and thus build on each other. For example, since transactional leadership already promotes the relationship between leader and followers, it is a preliminary stage for realizing effective transformational leadership (Quintana et al., 2015).

According to this model, every leader possesses various leadership behaviours and qualities, which are used differently according to the situational and contextual settings (Sosik, 2006). Thus, a leader can express various facets of the leadership range as well as various leadership dimensions. Typically, leaders represent all mentioned styles to a certain degree (Bass & Avolio, 1994). Nevertheless, the model demonstrates that transformational leadership is the most effective and active form of leadership (Sosik, 2006).

Laissez-Faire Leadership Style

Laissez-faire leadership also known as non-leadership, marks the absence of leadership and is the most passive and ineffective form of leadership (Bass & Avolio, 1994). The laissez-faire leader is hardly available, not providing support or direction to the followers and shows very little interest in the followers (Hassan et al., 2016). Laissez-faire leaders are avoiding leadership responsibilities, decision making and problem solving (Kirkbride, 2006). Consequently, their followers also show little to no commitment, are not motivated, and demonstrate overall dissatisfaction. By limiting leadership behaviours to laissez-faire leadership, high levels of stress regarding the leader role or interpersonal conflicts may be the consequence (Hassan et al., 2016). Nonetheless, laissez-faire leadership can be effective when followers are self-motivated (Sosik, 2006). When applied in connection with other, more effective forms of leadership, laissez-faire leadership can create the opportunity for self-management of the followers (Van Eeden et al., 2008).

Dimensions of Transactional Leadership Style

Transactional leadership can further specified into contingent reward, passive and active Management-by-exception. In general, transactional leaders focus on satisfying their self-interests more than on developing their followers, for example, the latter are rarely inspired or challenged to achieve higher performance (Bass & Bass, 2009). Nonetheless, the transactional leader usually provides a clear and achievable goal set to the followers (Avolio, 2011). The dimensions of transactional leadership are outlined in the following:

Passive management-by-exception (MBE-P): The passive form of management-by-exception shows a slightly more effective behaviour of than laissez-fair behaviour (Kirkbride, 2006). The passive leader waits for things to go wrong and failures to happen; then the leader intervenes and takes corrective actions (Bass & Avolio, 1994). The passive leader deals with the effects of problems or mistakes, but does not try to prevent them in advance (Sosik, 2006). Passive management-by-exception is also characterized by sticking to the current status and avoiding changes (Kirkbride, 2006).

Active management-by-exception (MBE-A): The active form of management-by-exception includes actively monitoring the progress of accomplishing tasks by the followers (Hassan et al., 2016). In addition to retroactively correcting errors that already occurred, the active leader attempts to take corrective actions to prevent future errors (Bass & Avolio, 1994), making this approach slightly more effective and active than the passive form. However, close monitoring might lead to mistrust between leaders and followers (Sosik, 2006). However, as the goal of the leader here is reduced to assure that standards are met (Antonakis et al., 2003), followers might be discouraged from developing innovative strategies and creative ideas (Kirkbride, 2006).

Contingent reward (CR): Contingent reward leadership aims towards the achievement of a slightly higher level of development or performance while not being as active and effective as transformational leadership (Bass & Avolio, 1994). It is defined as *"providing an adequate exchange of valued resources for follower support"* (Judge & Bono, 2000, p. 752). The contingent reward form of leadership is characterized by setting a clear direction and objectives together with the followers (Kirkbride, 2006). For completing the agreed tasks and carrying out the work, the leader promises the follower a reward in exchange (Bass & Avolio, 1994). These rewards could be financial or non-financial, for example extra holidays or prestige (Burns, 2012). This form of leadership may be successful in achieving the previously set goals, but it will hardly enable higher levels or motivation of followers (Kirkbride, 2006).

Dimensions of Transformational Leadership Style

The roots of the concept of transformational leadership can be linked to several aspects of earlier studies, also including the trait theory and behavioural theory, some aspects of transformational leadership can be clearly linked to traits or are influenced by them (Judge & Bono, 2000). Through a range of mechanisms, transformational leaders can increase the performance, motivation and morale of their followers (Odumeru & Ogbonna, 2013). Thus, transformational leaders "transform" their followers and influence their work engagement in a positive way (Bakker et al., 2022). Transformational leadership enables followers to perform beyond expectations (Quintana et al., 2015) and increase their level of satisfaction (Yukl, 1999). Transformational leadership is not only positively related to satisfaction of followers, organizational commitment or increasing task performance, but also to personal benefits for the leader, like mental well-being or a positive attitude towards work. Consequently, the performance on an organizational level might improve (Gilbert et al., 2016). Overall, there are four dimensions of transformational leadership, also known as "the four Is", which stand for Idealized influence, Inspirational motivation, Intellectual stimulation and Individual consideration, will be discussed below. Transformational leaders act according to at least one of the four dimensions but may apply more or even all four Is. Applying notions of transformational leadership and working on, as well as applying the four Is can maximize leadership effectiveness (Bass & Avolio, 1994).

Idealized influence: The first "I" is referring to the leaders and their charisma as well as the perception of the followers towards the characteristics of the leader (Antonakis et al., 2003). The general target of influence is to provoke *"a change in the belief, attitude or behaviour of a person which results from the action or presence of another person"* (Raven, as cited in Krause, 2004, p. 84). By applying idealized influence, the leaders act as influence agents and role models for the followers. Thus, they gain respect and are admired, trusted or even imitated (Avolio, 2011). Followers can strongly self-identify with this leader type (Franco & Matos, 2015). By demonstrating high standards and morals as well as including the followers in the decision-making process, the leader can use power in a positive way for achieving their vision (Bass & Avolio, 1994). Idealized influence is also characterized by recognizing the achievements of the followers and empowering them. Moreover, leaders directly address problems when they occur (Kirkbride, 2006).

Inspirational motivation: Inspirational motivation is used by the leaders not only to inspire their followers but also challenge them and give meaning to their work and tasks (Bass & Avolio, 1994). Through inspirational motivation, employees are becoming aware of the company's vision and get motivated to actively commit to its achievement (Sarros & Santora, 2001). Typically, the vision is achieved by sharing optimism and team spirit, combined with clear communication of expectations and reduction of complexity. The followers get inspired by the enthusiasm as well as the shared ideas and opinion of the leader (Avolio, 2011). It is further possible to focus on setting priorities and thus being able to achieve superior performance (Kirkbride, 2006). In addition, a common ground and similar understanding of core values are achieved through interactive communication, which, in turn, forms a connection between followers and leader (Franco & Matos, 2015).

Intellectual stimulation: This dimension promotes enhancing effort, innovation and creativity of the followers by intellectually stimulating them (Bass & Bass, 2009). Finding new or alternative ways for solving problems and allowing different opinions or ideas are essential (Bass & Avolio, 1994). This is illustrated by the following quote: *"By the transformational leader's intellectual stimulation, we mean the arousal and change in followers of problem awareness and problem solving, of thought and imagination, and of beliefs and values"* (Bass, as cited in Judge & Bono, 2000, p. 751). In addition, followers are stimulated to think critically and out of the box as well as to analyse problems from different perspectives (Avolio, 2011). Intellectually stimulating leaders perceive themselves as part of an interactive and innovative process where they empower their followers to focus on things that others might overlook. Moreover, they stimulate autonomy and independence among the followers and create a relationship based on trust (Bass & Bass, 2009).

Individualized consideration: The final "I" refers to behaviours where the transformational leader acts as a coach or mentor for the followers. By actively listening, providing individual feedback and paying special attention to each follower and their individual needs, new learning possibilities can be created and higher levels of potential can be achieved (Kirkbride, 2006). It is especially important to recognize individual differences and to be aware of individual concerns (Bass & Avolio, 1994). Often leaders delegate certain tasks to their followers to individually develop them (Avolio, 2011) and value them as important contributors to the workplace (Sarros & Santora, 2001). The climate within the relationship between individually considering leaders and their followers is supportive and therefore, both sides can successfully achieve higher levels of development (Bass & Bass, 2009).

The Alpine Tourism Industry and the importance of SMEs

According to the World Tourism Organization, the tourism industry consists of *"all establishments whose main activity is a particular tourism characteristic activity that serves visitors"* (United Nations, 2010, p. 50). Pikkemaat & Zehrer (2016) explain that the tourism industry relies mainly on services and intangible products and is therefore connected with some specific characteristics. Since the tourism product generally consists of several services from different actors, one of the most important characteristic features of the tourism industry is the bundling of these services. Moreover, since the perceived quality of tourism services and products is assessed by the customers as a whole, a holistic view of the tourism industry is essential (Stickdorn & Zehrer, 2009). As stated by Siller & Haselwanter (2019), in tourism destinations several actors are engaged in the creation of the tourism product. Thus, the tourism product as a bundle of services consists of various independent actors offering goods, services, or other actions. Besides the local government, the local community, employees and visitors, the main actors in the Alpine tourism industry are the DMOs, the accommodation sector, restaurants, cable car companies, ski schools and other leisure facilities (Bausch & Gartner, 2020).

In general, the alpine regions in Europe lie in Austria, Switzerland, Germany, France, Italy, Slovenia, Liechtenstein as well as Monaco (Pechlaner & Sauerwein, 2002). In most alpine regions, tourism is an essential contributor to the economy that does not only generate jobs and wealth, but also raises the probability that individuals are able to remain in the respective areas (Zehrer, 2019). Furthermore, due to global awareness and good accessibility within the alpine regions, the tourism industry is constantly growing with currently more than 100 million travellers visiting the alpine destinations annually (Becken, as cited in Bausch & Gartner, 2020).

The alpine tourism industry is dominated by SMEs, with most of these businesses even family-run (Weiermair, 2000), which constitutes another important characteristic feature of the industry. The concept of SMEs usually involves three categories of enterprises, which are medium-sized, small and micro. These categories are formed by the number of employees and the annual turnover or the annual balance sheet total (see Table 1). In detail and according to the user guide of the European Commission, *"the category of small and medium-sized enterprises (SMEs) is made up of enterprises which employ fewer than 250 persons and which have an annual turnover not exceeding EUR 50 million, and/or an annual balance sheet total not exceeding EUR 43 million"* (European Union, 2015, p. 3).

In many European countries, SMEs form the backbone of the national economy, especially due to job creation, generation of innovation and the contribution to a dynamic competition (Hillary, 2017). About 99.6% of all businesses belong to the category of SMEs in Austria, and even 99.9% of all businesses can be classified as SMEs in the Austrian tourism industry (Austrian Institute for SME Research, 2018). The businesses falling in this definition are represented by a small scale of human resources and financial resources as well as low operating costs (Bannock, 2005). These circumstances in connection

Table 1. SME category formation

Enterprise category	Headcount: annual work unit	Annual turnover	Annual balance sheet total
medium-sized	< 250	≤ EUR 50 million	≤ EUR 43 million
small	< 50	≤ EUR 10 million	≤ EUR 10 million
micro	< 10	≤ EUR 2 million	≤ EUR 2 million

Source: European Union, 2015, p. 11

with the rather relatively low entry barriers in the tourism sector facilitate the entry for SMEs into the tourism industry (Stickdorn & Zehrer, 2009). SMEs are usually characterized by flat and less complex hierarchies, which facilitate a direct and close interaction as well as fast exchange between owner and employees (Leitch & Volery, 2017). In smaller businesses the relationship to with other stakeholders is usually closer and more interactive (Renko, 2018). In general, SMEs differ from larger organizations in terms of innovation and organizational size as well as risk and uncertainty avoidance (Leitch & Volery, 2017). Due to personal ownership, independence and a relatively small market share, SMEs are constrained in terms of market power and financial resources (Bolton, as cited in Bannock, 2005). Since the owners of SMEs are usually deeply involved in the everyday business and have a major influence on it (Peters, 2005), and carry out different tasks simultaneously, this can result in limited formal planning, especially due to time issues or a lack of knowledge (Bharati & Chaudhury, 2009).

The small-sized structure, seasonality, relatively high employee turnover rates as well as job retention implicate challenges for SMEs in the Alpine tourism industry (Farrell, 2022; Peters, 2005). However, they also foster diversification and innovation, which in turn can lead to competitive advantages such as quality and authenticity (Sandstorm & Reynolds, 2020). Some of the positive aspects of SMEs in connection to Alpine tourism destinations are for example an enhancement of destination development, resulting in value creation for the respective regions and an establishment of new ideas or innovative concepts. Moreover, the economic benefits generated by SMEs are often remaining within the region due to the collaboration with local networks such as employees and suppliers (Buhalis & Peters, 2006).

Leadership in the Context of Touristic SMEs

Leadership is a key element for driving success, avoiding organizational failure and influencing the growth of the business in SMEs (Madanchian & Taherdoost, 2017). Effective forms of leadership, like transformational leadership, can create high levels of motivation and work engagement in the employees in touristic SMEs, and lead to a competitive advantage, such as high service quality, hospitality and customer satisfaction (Chen & Wu, 2020; Monje-Amor et al., 2020). Leadership in SMEs differs from leadership in larger businesses especially in terms of leader involvement in everyday business and due to less complex hierarchical structures (Quintana et al., 2015).

Since smaller businesses generally have lower capacities to deal with various challenges, like adaption to changing markets or pressure by stakeholders, leadership is essential to motivate and train employees in order to successfully navigate future challenges (Hillary, 2017). As stated by Franco & Matos (2015) it is essential for leaders in SMEs to understand the complex and changing business environment in order to remain competitive, constantly improve processes and support employees. Since smaller tourism businesses compete on a global scale with larger corporations, the customers expect the same quality of products or services from SMEs as from larger businesses. Therefore, a leader who aligns and inspires people, and establishes a clear direction and vision is required (Franco & Matos, 2015). The target of effective leadership in SMEs is to improve performance and create a sustainable competitive advantage (Madanchian & Taherdoost, 2017).

The focus of the leadership literature in the context of leadership in SMEs is scarcely put on the tourism industry. However, here it also has been assumed that the application of one leadership style out of the full-range leadership model is commonly neither possible nor effective. An adaption to the respective situation or the SME context as well as to the different needs of the followers is required and best achieved by a balance between transactional and transformational leadership (Bass, 1999). Especially transformational leadership, which is the most active and effective form, can enable the achievement of higher goals and extraordinary business performance by motivating followers and supporting them to build up their own strengths as well as transferring common beliefs and a shared vision (Busari et al., 2019). Therefore, the present study aims to study how transformational leadership is applied by entrepreneurs of SMEs in the alpine tourism industry and works towards the identification of dimensions and qualities characterizing these entrepreneurs.

METHOD

This book chapter aims to generate new insights into transformational leadership in the alpine tourism industry and its crucial stakeholders. Based on the full-range leadership model as a theoretical foundation, the empirical part strives to further shed light on the various leadership dimensions and qualities applied in SMEs in the alpine tourism industry.

Research Methodology and Design

In order to capture the leadership approaches of entrepreneurs in touristic SMEs, a qualitative approach with semi-structured qualities was applied. This method is rooted in an explorative research approach and offers a flexible and intelligible way of capturing obvious as well as hidden facets of the participant's character and actions. The basic idea of an exploratory research approach is to derive new and differentiated insights and an adaption of theories or models as well as managerial implications (Mayring, 2007). Semi-structured interviews are useful in capturing a person's opinion about their work, actions or environment by letting them actively co-create the process of the interview (Qu & Dunmay, 2011). For the conduction of the interviews, a flexible and non-restrictive interview guideline was developed. Semi-structured interviews rely on guidelines, which are both structured and open at the same time, and where the order and formulation of questions are flexible. On the one hand, a certain amount of structure is required to cover certain topics, stick to the topic of the research and enable comparison. On the other hand, a certain degree of openness is needed to not restrict interviewees in their answers and avoid bias (Strübing, 2018). Since semi-structured interviews allow participants to actively co-create the interview process and include additional suggested topics, additional value can be created (Qu & Dunmay, 2011). It can be summarized that the capability to capture hidden facets and additional details of the participants as well as receiving access to alternative points of views are the main strengths of the qualitative interview with semi-structured qualities as a research method (Bryman, 2004).

Figure 2. Distribution of participants by industry
Source: own illustration

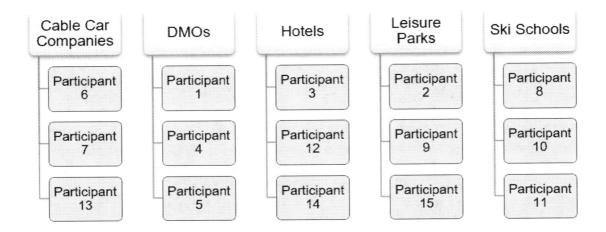

Data Collection and selection of Interview Partners

The participants of the present qualitative study were entrepreneurs of SMEs. In order to participate in the qualitative interviews, entrepreneurs had to fulfil three main requirements. First, since the present study focuses on its empirical research on the alpine tourism industry in the region of Tyrol, their business had to be based within this specific region of Austria. Second, their business had to be part of an important stakeholder group of the alpine tourism industry in Tyrol, and belong to one of the main subsectors, which are: cable car companies, DMOs, hotels, leisure parks and ski schools. Finally, the business had to be classified as an SME by the criteria defined by the European Union. In total, fifteen entrepreneurs of SMEs in the alpine tourism region of Tyrol were interviewed. As depicted in figure 2, for each of the five crucial stakeholder group, three entrepreneurs were selected. Figure 2 shows the anonymized participants of this study. Moreover, different entrepreneurs from different parts of Tyrol were interviewed to gain further insights into the leadership styles and dimensions applied in SMEs in the tourism industry.

In order to find suitable participants and information regarding their business for the study, desk research mainly refers of secondary data, available for example from a library or the internet, was conducted (Hague et al., 2004). In the case of the present study, internet sources, such as websites of the businesses of potential interview participants, were in use. The participants of the study were then directly contacted and provided the first information via e-mail. The interviews were then conducted and audio-recorded, preferably face-to-face, however, for most interviews online conferencing tools had to be used due to Covid-19 regulations. In addition to the audio recordings, notes were made in order to capture social cues and to constantly check the coverage of the topics. By sticking to previously defined topics in form of an interview guideline that was developed based on the theoretical findings, the process of interviewing could be directed to a certain degree but also left space for additional topics and open answers (Qu & Dunmay, 2011). The interviews were transcribed word-by-word from the audio recordings to depict reality as precisely as possible and potentially be able to capture additional or hidden aspects. Strong dialect was corrected to ensure understandability as well as traceability (Mayring, 2014).

Data Analysis

The qualitative content analysis according to Mayring was applied to systematically analyse and evaluate the interviews (Mayring, 1991). This analysis is described as *"an approach of empirical, methodological controlled analysis of texts within their context of communication, following content analytic rules and step by step models, without rash quantification"* (Mayring, as cited in Schilling, 2006, p. 28). The qualitative content analysis operates with categories constructed at the beginning of the analysis, or taken from previous theories, and assigns statements from the interview material to these categories (Strübing, 2018). An important point is the breakdown of the whole analysis process into individual steps, which guide the content analysis and facilitate its verification (Mayring, 1991). For the present study, the specific form of a structured content analysis with strict coding rules and a coding guideline was applied, which makes the analysis process more comprehensible (Mayring, 1991).

The first step of the structured content analysis consists of a general review of the transcripts. This step is followed by a deductive definition of the topics, which serves as a basis for the following definition and detailed description of the categories. The subsequent coding phase comprises reading the transcripts in detail, highlighting the most important phrases with MAXQDA according to the previously defined categories as well as subcategories, and bringing these findings into an order. Following this step, it may be necessary to re-examine the categories and adapt them accordingly. The concluding phase involves the description and interpretation of the results and their relevance to the research (Kohlegger et al., 2009). Despite the structured content analysis, two inductive categories were also formed during the analysis of the material by referring to the summarizing content analysis according to Mayring. Within the summarizing content analysis, categories are formed based on examples from the material as well as the following reduction, paraphrasing and generalization (Mayring, 1991). The qualitative content analysis offers several benefits, which are also represented by its structured nature, facilitating the recognition of qualitative research as a scientific approach, the comparability of the findings, the reduction of distortion and minimizing researcher bias. Moreover, the access to reality is emphasized through subjective interpretations and interpretative processes (Mayring, 2014).

FINDINGS

Through the deductive content analysis, three major topics could be derived from the interviews, namely *leadership and tourism, laissez-faire and transactional leadership* as well as *transformational leadership*. Moreover, these themes are divided into further categories and subcategories where necessary, in order to further analyse and evaluate the empirical material. The derived system of major themes, categories and subcategories is depicted in the following figure 3. The major findings are presented and interpreted in this chapter.

Figure 3. Overview of the derived category system
Source: own illustration

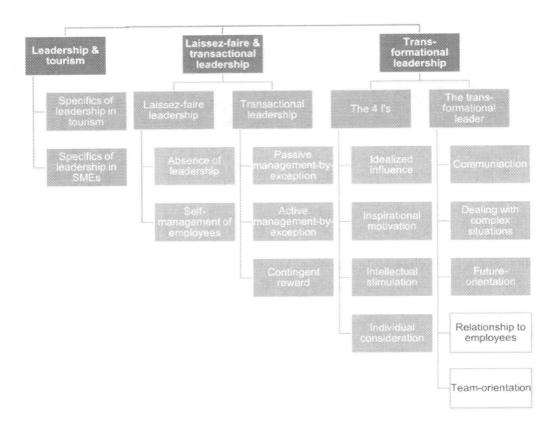

Leadership and Tourism

Category Specifics of Leadership in Tourism

Since the tourism industry mainly consists of intangible products and services (Pikkemaat & Zehrer, 2016), involves several different stakeholders (Siller & Haselwanter, 2019) and is mainly made up of SMEs, many of which are family-run (Weiermair, 2000), specific forms of leadership driving the tourism industry forward can be observed (Haven-Tang & Jones, 2012), such as entrepreneurial industry leadership (Renko, 2018). The participants of this study argued that leadership in tourism requires empathy due to the immediate contact with employees, guests, and stakeholders (P2, P4, P13), as well as flexibility due to changing market conditions, working hours or challenges like the ongoing Covid-19 pandemic (P1, P3, P7, P9, P12).

Specifics of Leadership in SMEs

Due to their small-sized structure, effective forms of leadership are especially important in SMEs. Some of the specifics of leadership in SMEs such as the high degree of leader involvement in the everyday business and flat hierarchical structures (Quintana et al., 2015) are also confirmed by the statements of the participants. Leadership in SMEs can generally be interpreted as much more personal because there is a regular contact between leader and followers including private conversations and therefore leaders are more tangible compared to the situation in larger businesses (P1, P5, P9, P13).

Laissez-faire and Transactional Leadership

Laissez-faire Leadership

Laissez-faire leadership is the least effective and least active form of leadership (Bass & Avolio, 1994), where an absence of leadership demonstrated through avoiding responsibility and not providing direction or support leads to non-motivated employees (Kirkbride, 2006). Only when combined with more effective forms of leadership such as transformational leadership, motivation can be created through self-management of employees (Van Eeden et al., 2008). In the results some degree of laissez-faire leadership is observed, marked by staying out of problems, not intervening when noticing a problem or not taking leadership responsibility (P5, P10). In some other cases, the participants supported the self-management of employees by providing them with freedom or assigning responsibility (P5, P10, P12).

Transactional Leadership

Since leadership style always depends on various factors, like the respective follower or the situation (Bass & Avolio, 1994), transactional leadership, characterized by setting a clear direction and goal or establishing rules for avoiding errors, should be applied. However, the development of employees is often neglected within this form of leadership (Avolio, 2011). Markers of passive and active management-by-exception are scarcely found in our interview, where the participants showed that they rarely attempted to avoid problems in advance or that actively monitored the work of their employees in certain contexts.

Furthermore, only two participants showed behaviour in connection to contingent-reward leadership, mentioning a bonus system and money as a motivator (P3, P7). Since the results in connection to transactional leadership are relatively low, it can be concluded that SMEs in the alpine tourism industry could benefit a more active and effective form of leadership. Furthermore, none of the DMO participants' interviews included a statement that could be linked to transactional leadership, which means they have to be classified as non-transactionally led.

Transformational Leadership

It can be stated that every leadership style is applied by the leaders at some point, but transformational leadership, when referring to the full-range leadership model, is the most effective and active form, leading to a higher performance as well as increasing personal and employee motivation (Kirkbride, 2006). When combined, especially individual consideration and intellectual stimulation are important for the considered subsectors of the Tyrolean tourism industry (Figure 4).

Figure 4. The four Is of transformational leadership
Source: own illustration

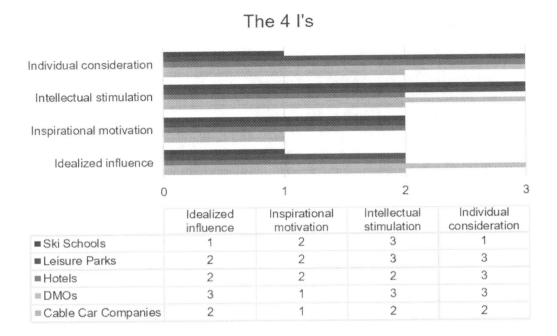

Idealized Influence

Through ideally influencing the followers by showing charisma, acting as a role model and demonstrating high morals, followers can identify with the leader and common goals can be achieved more easily (Avolio, 2011; Bass & Avolio, 1994). Within the present study, the participants ideally influence their employees by acting as a role model, taking into consideration the needs of individual employees and the team through regular meetings and conversations (P4, P5, P13).

Inspirational Motivation

In order to achieve a vision and superior performance, the motivation of followers is essential (Kirkbride, 2006). Employees are made aware of the vision and are more likely to work in the same direction through inspirational motivation, for example by sharing optimism and enthusiasm (Avolio, 2011; Franco & Matos, 2015). The participants of this study not only motivate their employees through showing passion (P5), but also by providing a clear direction (P2, P15) and offering employees a certain degree of freedom in decision-making and creativity (P4, P14). Especially ski school leaders focus on the motivation of their employees by sharing optimism and fun at work as well as by *"living the vision"* (P10), and can therefore be interpreted as inspirationally motivating.

Intellectual Stimulation

By intellectually stimulating and empowering followers through assigning responsibility or actively supporting critical thinking, leaders can create trust and facilitate new innovative solutions for problems (Bass & Bass, 2009). The participants of this study intellectually stimulated their employees by making them participate in the decision-making process, stimulating them to question processes, distributing tasks and responsibilities as well as by setting up an idea board in the employee facilities (P1, P6, P13, P14).

Individual Consideration

Leaders can uncover the whole potential of their employees by individually considering their followers and acting as a mentor (Kirkbride, 2006). This process not only helps to propagate the development of employees but can also improve the relationship between followers and leader (Bass & Bass, 2009). The results show that participants apply individual consideration through adapting the leadership style, and providing individual feedback, to individual employees. When it comes to the subsectors, especially hotels can be interpreted as individually considering by *"letting individual personalities be individual personalities"* (P3, para. 18) and individually assigning responsibility.

The Transformational Leader in the Tourism Industry

Transformational leaders can be differentiated from transactional leaders by motivating followers to achieve more than originally intended through a supportive as well as optimistic communication, individual recognition and the expression of a strong team-sprit (Bass & Bass, 2009; Chen & Wu, 2020). Through a close relationship with their employees, which is based on trust, and their orientation towards change and innovation, the transformational leader can also cope with difficult situations (Le & Lei, 2019; Sadler, 2003). When it comes to the findings, *"communication for sure is the most important thing"* (P1, para. 14), and both regular team-meetings as well as individual conversations and direct personal contact through one-on-one meetings are applied by the participants (P2, P4, P5). Furthermore, a two-sided communication with feedback from both sides at eye-level are essential for motivating employees (P6, P7).

In connection to the category of dealing with complex situations, the participants stressed the importance of communicating relevant work aspects and informing the employees about current developments: *"We also tried to pass on the information we received to the employees as soon as possible and had a kind of internal blog on the website."* (P11, para. 26). Moreover, conveying calmness in complex or stressful situations, being optimistic but realistic and taking over leadership by making fast decisions are of importance (P1, P3, P11). Furthermore, according to the participants you should be prepared for difficult situations as it is always better to look ahead and make fast decisions rather than look back and reminisce, or as one participant put it, *"it is always good to already have a plan B"* (P13, para. 26).

When it comes to future orientation, the participants are *"looking forward to the future"* (P2, para. 40) and some already expressed concrete plans, such as the construction of new additions or the incorporation of other businesses (P7, P13). Some participants brought up that they used the Covid-19 pandemic for reorganization. Next to that, some insecurities in connection to the current situation and future development of the business were also mentioned, for example due to changing customer demands or new regulations (P9).

Finally, two inductive categories were formed during the process of analysis for completeness, namely the relationship to employees and team-orientation. The relationship with employees was described with terms like "eye-level", flat hierarchies, collegial relationship or even friendship (P2, P4, P6, P9, P14). Another important aspect for the participants is team-orientation, as they highlighted the importance of a strong team spirit for increased motivation and higher performance, or perceived themselves as part of the team due to their close relationship: *"For me, it is always important that you have to make sure that the team is doing well, because then the company is also doing well."* (P4, para. 44)

DISCUSSION

Characterization of Leadership in SMEs

Transformational leadership is its most effective form because it focuses on both the development of the leader and the development of the followers (Liang et al., 2017), enabling a higher level of motivation and performance (Burns, 2012). In addition, transformational leaders share and communicate their values and goals as well as establish a common vision in accordance with the followers, towards which they work together (Sadler, 2003). The results from the interviews show that for the participants, effective leadership is characterized especially by communication, goal-orientation, and authenticity. Based on the theoretical input and the practical insights, it can be summarized that the entrepreneurs of touristic SMEs are aware of effective leadership styles and apply transformational leadership by ideally influencing, inspirationally motivating, intellectually stimulating and individually considering their employees.

For further characterizing leadership and especially transformational leadership in touristic SMEs, the full-range leadership model, as described in the theoretical part and by Bass and Avolio (1994, p. 6), is adapted to the results derived from the collected data (Figure 5). The model shows the five dimensions according to Bass and Avolio (1994): Laissez-faire leadership (LF), which is the most passive and ineffective form, passive management-by-exception (MBE-P), active management-by-exception (MBE-A) and contingent reward leadership (CR), which are progressively more effective and active, as well as transformational leadership, which is the most effective and active form. The size of the circles in Figure 5 illustrates the degree to which the leadership dimension is found among the participants (with a larger circle depicting a higher degree of presence).

In the present study, transformational leadership is more prevalent than transactional leadership and laissez-faire leadership. However, the presence of all different dimensions to a certain degree demonstrates that entrepreneurs of touristic SMEs apply a combination of leadership styles instead of only a single one. As previously mentioned and stated by Bass (1999), this result is favourable, because one single style of leadership would be neither completely effective nor possible, because it needs to be adapted according to certain circumstances. Nevertheless, it is beneficial for a high performance of the leaders, employees and businesses in SMEs in the alpine tourism industry that transformational leadership is the most widely applied style of leadership. The second-most applied leadership style is laissez-faire leadership but, as mentioned previously, when combined with more effective forms of leadership, the application of laissez-faire leadership can also help to reach a higher level of self-management of some of the employees (Van Eeden et al., 2008).

It was noticed that none of the interviewed DMO participant showed transactional leadership behaviour. When it comes to laissez-faire leadership, which not only refers to the absence of leadership but

Figure 5. Adapted full-range leadership model
Source: own illustration

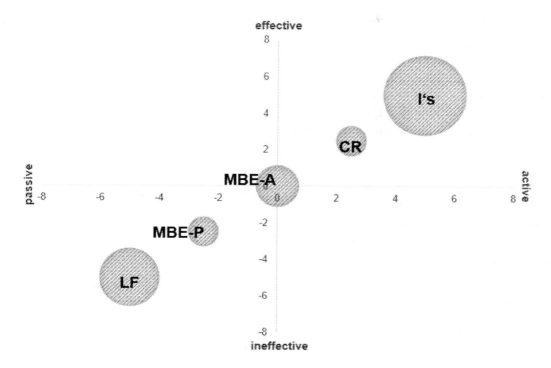

at some point also to the support of self-management of the employees (Van Eeden et al., 2008), it can be highlighted that, all interviewed ski schools made at least one statement in connection to this form of leadership. These circumstances can be taken as first indicators for varying leadership behaviour in different subsectors of the Tyrolean alpine tourism industry that warrant further investigation.

Managerial Implications

On basis of the collected data and the previous discussion on leadership dimensions, seven managerial implications can be derived for entrepreneurs of SMEs in the Alpine tourism industry r to enhance their transformational leadership qualities. The order of the implications does not reflect their importance.

Flexibility: In connection to leadership in tourism, flexibility is a key to leadership success. On the one hand, it is important to be flexible due to certain specifics of the tourism industry, like seasonality, specific working hours, limited predictability, and a high employee turnover rate as well as due to possible short-notice changes and events. On the other hand, being flexible is also recommended in problem solving, when encountering new developments and innovations as well as for keeping up with the competition and performance improvement.

Optimism: Entrepreneurs of SMEs in the tourism industry have to deal with different internal problems, like employee loyalty but also complex, insecure and stressful situations resulting from external factors or events such as pressure from other stakeholders or crises. It is essential to look ahead and stay positive in seemingly overwhelming situations. While trying to stay positive in dealing with insecure situations, it is recommended to be honest and realistic in communicating changes to the employees and take responsibility by making decisions as a leader and entrepreneur.

Two-sided communication: Both the communication with the whole team and conversations with each individual employee should be two-sided as well as on eye-level for being more effective. Therefore, it is recommended to regularly plan team-meetings for communicating the vision, targets and current developments or changes as well as for exchanging and discussing ideas, while also providing the possibility for one-on-one meetings to talk about individual issues and provide individual feedback.

Transparent vision: A clearly formulated and stated vision not only helps entrepreneurs to stay focused and help in establishing a competitive advantage, when established in accordance with the employees during regular meetings or voluntary workshops, it can also help to increase employee motivation and performance and even lead to a higher quality of the tourism product. While it is recommended to set up a clear, achievable, and future-oriented vision together with the employees, this should also be communicated to new team-members and other stakeholders like the guests.

Continuous development: The tourism industry requires a continuous development, for example, due to changing customer or stakeholder demands, employee fluctuation or new, emerging trends. It is thus recommended for entrepreneurs of touristic SMEs to focus on a constant development of business and business strategy, but also on a personal development of themselves for being able to adapt to changes and effectively lead their employees in implementing new strategies and working towards the common vision.

Leading by example: The research results show that the employees of SMEs in the alpine tourism industry are led most effectively when they are provided with freedom for developing autonomously, but on the other hand are provided with certain framework-conditions and an example set by the entrepreneur. Therefore, it is recommended to lead by supporting and setting examples in order to inspire, motivate and stimulate employees, rather than by setting up strict working guidelines and monitoring.

Adjustable leadership style: As underlined by the results, for fully uncovering the potential of each employee, it is important to provide individual, constructive feedback in eye-level conversations as well as to specifically take into consideration individual competencies, strengths and preferences of each employee. Based on that, it is recommended for entrepreneurs of SMEs in the alpine tourism industry, to be flexible in their leadership style and make adaptions according to the employee's situation and their personality, in order to improve employee satisfaction, personal relationships and business performance.

These implications can serve as a guideline for entrepreneurs of SMEs in the alpine tourism industry. Whereas the interviews showed that individual aspects of the respective businesses or certain situations can restrict the implementation of the managerial implications, derived from previous theoretical works and practical insights gained from the semi-structured interviews, are expected to result in higher leadership effectiveness and an increased personal, employee and stakeholder satisfaction.

CONCLUSION: LIMITATIONS AND FURTHER RESEARCH

Leadership, especially in smaller businesses, influences the relationship between entrepreneur and employees. Effective leadership forms like transformational leadership are positively influencing the personal performance of the entrepreneur, the employees and the business (Monje-Amor et al., 2020). Only little research exists in connection to transformational leadership in SMEs in the tourism industry. Therefore, the present study offers a first view on how entrepreneurs apply transformational leadership, and which dimensions of transformational leadership are applied, in SMEs in the alpine tourism industry. It can be concluded that entrepreneurs of SMEs in the alpine tourism industry apply aspects of transformational leadership and the four Is when leading their businesses and employees. Transactional and laissez-faire leadership behaviours are also observed, albeit to a much lower degree. During the interview and analysis process, certain qualities of the entrepreneurs of SMEs in the alpine tourism industry were recognized.

Transformational leadership is the most effective and active form of leadership (Busari et al., 2019), however, as it is shaped by a relatively strong focus on the relationship between the single follower and the leader, the relationship between the group and the leader is often neglected (Bryant, 2003). Moreover, it can be argued that the four Is of transformational leadership provide guidance, but at some point their delimitation is unclear and their description is overlapping (Yukl, 1999). Although transformational leadership has a positive impact on employee satisfaction and motivation (Rothfelder et al., 2013), critics claim that, since not every employee has the same needs, the application of this form of leadership might not always be required (Odumeru & Ogbonna, 2013).

When it comes to the methodology, it should be said that the sample size of fifteen interview participants is small for studying transformational leadership in all of Tyrol and its tourism destinations. However, as different regions of Tyrol as well as from different subsectors of the tourism industry were sampled, an initial, holistic view can be provided. Unfortunately, most of the interviews had to be conducted using online conferencing tools due to the Covid-19 situation, preventing the observation of participants in their natural setting (Hennink et al., 2020). However, since the conduction of interviews online also meant higher flexibility, it was possible to access participants who are not easily available otherwise (Janghorban et al., 2014).

The present study with its focus on transformational leadership in SMEs in the alpine tourism industry is the first of its kind in this field of research. More interesting questions for future research arise, as there are many possibilities and perspectives left to extend and expand the research in connection to transformational leadership. Since the present study is focusing on the view of tourism entrepreneurs and their leadership dimensions and behaviours, a logical extension would be to further investigate the view of the employees. A comparison between the two could then help to identify possible accordance or derivation of the views of entrepreneurs and employees. Moreover, the inclusion of more tourism industry subsectors, like restaurants, museums, congress centres or other forms of accommodation like camping sites, is another possible extension and field of future research. Similarly, studies of further alpine regions, such as other regions of Austria as well as Switzerland, Germany, France, Italy, Slovenia, Liechtenstein and Monaco would help to identify similarities or differences with leadership behaviour as encountered in SMEs of the Tyrolean alpine tourism industry.

REFERENCES

Amankwaa, A., Gyensare, M. A., & Susomrith, P. (2019). Transformational leadership with innovative behaviour: Examining multiple mediating paths with PLS-SEM. *Leadership and Organization Development Journal, 40*(1), 107–123. doi:10.1108/LODJ-10-2018-0358

Antonakis, J., Avolio, B. J., & Sivasubramaniam, N. (2003). Context and leadership: An examination of the nine-factor full-range leadership theory using the Multifactor Leadership Questionnaire. *The Leadership Quarterly, 14*(3), 261–295. doi:10.1016/S1048-9843(03)00030-4

Austrian Institute for SME Research. (2018). *SME data*. https://www.kmuforschung.ac.at/facts-and-figures/kmu-daten/?lang=en

Avolio, B. J. (2011). *Full Range Leadership Development* (2nd ed.). SAGE Publications. doi:10.4135/9781483349107

Bakker, A. B., Hetland, J., Olsen, O. K., & Espevik, R. (2022). Daily transformational leadership: A source of inspiration for follower performance? *European Management Journal*, *40*(5). Advance online publication. doi:10.1016/j.emj.2022.04.004

Bannock, G. (2005). *The economics and management of small business: An international perspective*. Routledge.

Bass, B. M. (1985). *Leadership and performance beyond expectations*. Free Press.

Bass, B. M. (1990). From transactional to transformational leadership: Learning to share the vision. *Organizational Dynamics*, *18*(3), 19–31. doi:10.1016/0090-2616(90)90061-S

Bass, B. M., & Avolio, B. J. (1989). *Manual for the multifactor leadership questionnaire*. Consulting Psychologists Press.

Bass, B. M., & Avolio, B. J. (1990). *Multifactor leadership questionnaire*. Consulting Psychologists Press.

Bass, B. M., & Avolio, B. J. (1994). *Improving organizational effectiveness through transformational leadership*. SAGE Publications.

Bass, B. M., & Bass, R. (2009). *The Bass handbook of leadership: Theory, research, and managerial applications* (4th ed.). Free Press.

Bausch, T., & Gartner, W. C. (2020). Winter tourism in the European Alps: Is a new paradigm needed? *Journal of Outdoor Recreation and Tourism*, *31*, 100297. doi:10.1016/j.jort.2020.100297

Bharati, P., & Chaudhury, A. (2009). SMEs and competitiveness: The role of information systems. *International Journal of E-Business Research*, *5*(1), I–IX.

Bryant, S. E. (2003). The role of transformational and transactional leadership in creating, sharing and exploiting organizational knowledge. *Journal of Leadership & Organizational Studies*, *9*(4), 32–44. doi:10.1177/107179190300900403

Bryman, A. (2004). Qualitative research on leadership: A critical but appreciative review. *The Leadership Quarterly*, *15*(6), 729–769. doi:10.1016/j.leaqua.2004.09.007

Buhalis, D., & Peters, M. (2006). SMEs in tourism. In D. Buhalis & C. Costa (Eds.), *Tourism management dynamics: Trends, management and tools* (pp. 116–129). Elsevier Ltd. doi:10.1016/B978-0-7506-6378-6.50023-8

Burns, J. M. (1978). *Leadership* (1st ed.). Harper & Row.

Burns, J. M. (2012). *Leadership*. Open Road Media.

Busari, A. H., Khan, S. N., Abdullah, S. M., & Mughal, Y. H. (2019). Transformational leadership style, followership, and factors of employees' reactions towards organizational change. *Journal of Asia Business Studies, 14*(2), 181–209. doi:10.1108/JABS-03-2018-0083

Chen, T.-J., & Wu, C.-M. (2020). Can newcomers perform better at hotels? Examining the roles of transformational leadership, supervisor-triggered positive affect, and perceived supervisor support. *Tourism Management Perspectives, 33*, 100587. doi:10.1016/j.tmp.2019.100587

Cote, R. (2017). A comparison of leadership theories in an organizational environment. *International Journal of Business Administration, 8*(5), 28–35. doi:10.5430/ijba.v8n5p28

Dwyer, L., & Edwards, D. (2010). Sustainable tourism planning. In J. J. Liburd & D. Edwards (Eds.), *Understanding the sustainable development of tourism* (pp. 19–44).

European Union. (2015). *User guide to the SME definition.* Publications Office of the European Union.

Farrel, K. (2022). Transformational Leadership for the Hospitality and Tourism Industry. In K. Ogunyemi, O. Ogunyemi, & E. Okoye (Eds.), *Humanistic Perspectives in Hospitality and Tourism* (pp. 273–292). Palgrave Macmillan. doi:10.1007/978-3-030-95671-4_14

Franco, M., & Matos, P. G. (2015). Leadership styles in SMEs: A mixed-method approach. *The International Entrepreneurship and Management Journal, 11*(2), 425–451. doi:10.100711365-013-0283-2

Gilbert, S., Horsman, P., & Kelloway, E. K. (2016). The motivation for transformational leadership scale: An examination of the factor structure and initial tests. *Leadership and Organization Development Journal, 37*(2), 158–180. doi:10.1108/LODJ-05-2014-0086

Gosling, J., Jones, S., Sutherland, I., & Dijkstra, J. (2012). *Key concepts in leadership.* SAGE Publications. doi:10.4135/9781473914759

Hassan, H., Asad, S., & Hoshino, Y. (2016). Determinants of leadership style in big five personality dimensions. *Universal Journal of Management, 4*(4), 161–179. doi:10.13189/ujm.2016.040402

Haven-Tang, C., & Jones, E. (2012). Local leadership for rural tourism development: A case study of Adventa, Monmouthshire, UK. *Tourism Management Perspectives, 4*, 28–35. doi:10.1016/j.tmp.2012.04.006

Hennink, M., Hutter, I., & Bailey, A. (2020). *Qualitative research methods* (2nd ed.). SAGE Publications.

Hillary, R. (Ed.). (2017). *Small and medium-sized enterprises and the environment: Business imperatives.* Routledge. doi:10.4324/9781351282840

Janghorban, R., Roudsari, R. L., & Taghipour, A. (2014). Skype interviewing: The new generation of online synchronous interview in qualitative research. *International Journal of Qualitative Studies on Health and Well-being, 9*(1), 24152. doi:10.3402/qhw.v9.24152 PMID:24746247

Judge, T. A., & Bono, J. E. (2000). Five-Factor model of personality and transformational leadership. *The Journal of Applied Psychology, 85*(5), 751–765. doi:10.1037/0021-9010.85.5.751 PMID:11055147

Khan, Z. A., Nawaz, A., & Khan, I. (2016). Leadership theories and styles: A literature review. *Journal of Resources Development and Management, 16*(1), 1–7.

Kirkbride, P. (2006). Developing transformational leaders: The full range leadership model in action. *Industrial and Commercial Training*, *38*(1), 23–32. doi:10.1108/00197850610646016

Kohlegger, M., Maier, R., & Thalmann, S. (2009). Understanding maturity models: Results of a structured content analysis [Paper presentation]. I-KNOW '09 and I-SEMANTICSConference 2009, Graz, Austria.

Krause, D. E. (2004). Influence-based leadership as a determinant of the inclination to innovate and of innovation-related behaviors: An empirical investigation. *The Leadership Quarterly*, *15*(1), 79–102. doi:10.1016/j.leaqua.2003.12.006

Lang, R., & Rybnikova, I. (2014). *Aktuelle Führungstheorien und -konzepte*. Springer Fachmedien Wiesbaden. doi:10.1007/978-3-8349-3729-2

Le, P. B., & Lei, H. (2019). Determinants of innovation capability: The roles of transformational leadership, knowledge sharing and perceived organizational support. *Journal of Knowledge Management*, *23*(3), 527–547. doi:10.1108/JKM-09-2018-0568

Leitch, C. M., & Volery, T. (2017). Entrepreneurial leadership: Insights and directions. *International Small Business Journal*, *35*(2), 147–156. doi:10.1177/0266242616681397

Liang, T.-L., Chang, H.-F., Ko, M.-H., & Lin, C.-W. (2017). Transformational leadership and employee voices in the hospitality industry. *International Journal of Contemporary Hospitality Management*, *29*(1), 374–392. doi:10.1108/IJCHM-07-2015-0364

Madanchian, M., & Taherdoost, H. (2017). Role of leadership in small and medium enterprises (SMEs). *International Journal of Economics and Management Systems*, *2*(1), 240–243.

Mayring, P. (1991). Qualitative Inhaltsanalyse. In U. Flick, E. von Kardoff, H. Keupp, L. von Rosenstiel, & S. Wolff (Eds.), *Handbuch qualitative Forschung: Grundlagen, Konzepte, Methoden und Anwendungen* [Handbook of qualitative research; Principles, concepts, methods and applications] (pp. 209–213). Beltz Psychologie-Verlags-Union.

Mayring, P. (2007). Designs in qualitativ orientierter Forschung. *Journal für Psychologie*, *15*(2), 1–10.

Mayring, P. (2014). *Qualitative content analysis: Theoretical foundation, basic procedures and software solution*. Beltz Verlag.

Monje-Amor, A., Abeal-Vázquez, J. P., & Faíña, J. A. (2020). Transformational leadership and work engagement: Exploring the mediating role of structural empowerment. *European Management Journal*, *38*(1), 169–178. doi:10.1016/j.emj.2019.06.007

Northouse, P. G. (2013). *Leadership: Theory and Practice* (6th ed.). SAGE Publications.

Odumeru, J. A., & Ogbonna, I. G. (2013). Transformational vs. transactional leadership theories: Evidence in literature. *International Review of Management and Business Research*, *2*(2), 355–361.

Pechlaner, H., & Sauerwein, E. (2002). Strategy implementation in the Alpine tourism industry. *International Journal of Contemporary Hospitality Management*, *14*(4), 157–168. doi:10.1108/09596110210427003

Pedler, M., Burgoyne, J., & Boydell, T. (2010). *A Manager's Guide to Leadership: An action learning Approach* (2nd ed.). McGraw-Hill Publishing.

Peters, M. (2005). Entrepreneurial skills in leadership and human resource management evaluated by apprentices in small tourism businesses. *Education + Training*, *47*(8/9), 575–591. doi:10.1108/00400910510633125

Pikkemaat, B., & Zehrer, A. (2016). Innovation and service experiences in small tourism family firms. *International Journal of Culture, Tourism and Hospitality Research*, *10*(4), 343–360. doi:10.1108/IJCTHR-06-2016-0064

Qu, S. Q., & Dunmay, J. (2011). The qualitative research interview. *Qualitative Research in Accounting & Management*, *8*(3), 238–264. doi:10.1108/11766091111162070

Quintana, T. A., Park, S., & Cabrera, Y. A. (2015). Assessing the effects of leadership styles on employees' outcomes in international luxury hotels. *Journal of Business Ethics*, *129*(2), 469–489. doi:10.100710551-014-2170-3

Renko, M. (2018). Entrepreneurial leadership. In J. Antonakis & D. V. Day (Eds.), *The nature of leadership* (3rd ed., pp. 381–408). SAGE Publications. doi:10.4135/9781506395029.n15

Rothfelder, K., Ottenbacher, M. C., & Harrington, R. J. (2013). The impact of transformational, transactional and non-leadership styles on employee job satisfaction in the German hospitality industry. *Tourism and Hospitality Research*, *12*(4), 201–214. doi:10.1177/1467358413493636

Sadler, P. (2003). *Leadership* (2nd ed.). Kogan Page Limited.

Sandstorm, J. K., & Reynolds, D. E. (2020). Leading a successful hotel: A look at the general manager's ability to utilize multiple leadership styles. *International Journal of Hospitality Management*, *89*, 102399. doi:10.1016/j.ijhm.2019.102399

Sarros, J. C., & Santora, J. C. (2001). The transformational-transactional leadership model in practice. *Leadership and Organization Development Journal*, *22*(8), 383–393. doi:10.1108/01437730110410107

Schilling, J. (2006). On the pragmatics of qualitative assessment: Designing the process for content analysis. *European Journal of Psychological Assessment*, *22*(1), 28–37. doi:10.1027/1015-5759.22.1.28

Schwaiger, K. M., & Zehrer, A. (2021). The COVID-19 Pandemic and Organizational Resilience in Hospitality Firms: A Qualitative Approach. In A. Zehrer, G. Glowka, K. M. Schwaiger, & V. Ranacher-Lackner (Eds.), *Resiliency Models and Addressing Future Risks for Family Firms in the Tourism Industry* (pp. 32–49). IGI Global. doi:10.4018/978-1-7998-7352-5.ch002

Siller, H., & Haselwanter, S. (2019). Leadership in Alpine Destinations: The Showcase "Stubai 2021". In P. L. Pearce & H. Oktadiana (Eds.), *Delivering Tourism Intelligence: From Analysis to Action* (pp. 15–30). Emerald Publishing. doi:10.1108/S2042-144320190000011003

Sosik, J. J. (2006). Full range leadership: Model, research, extensions and training. In R. J. Burke & C. L. Cooper (Eds.), *Inspiring leaders* (pp. 33–66). Routledge.

Stickdorn, M., & Zehrer, A. (2009). *Service design in tourism: Customer experience driven destination management* [Paper presentation]. *First Nordic Conference on Service Design and Service Information*, Oslo, Norway.

Strübing, J. (2018). *Qualitative Sozialforschung: Eine komprimierte Einführung* [Qualitative social research: A condensed introduction] (2nd ed.). De Gruyter Oldenbourg. doi:10.1515/9783110529920

Testa, M. R., & Sipe, L. (2012). Service-leadership competencies for hospitality and tourism management. *International Journal of Hospitality Management*, *31*(3), 648–658. doi:10.1016/j.ijhm.2011.08.009

United Nations. (2010). International recommendations for tourism statistics 2008 (No. 83). United Nations Publications.

Van Eeden, R., Cilliers, F., & Van Deventer, V. (2008). Leadership styles and associated personality traits: Support for the conceptualisation of transactional and transformational leadership. *South African Journal of Psychology. Suid-Afrikaanse Tydskrif vir Sielkunde*, *38*(2), 253–267. doi:10.1177/008124630803800201

Van Seters, D. A., & Field, R. H. G. (1990). The evolution of leadership theory. *Journal of Organizational Change Management*, *3*(3), 29–45. doi:10.1108/09534819010142139

Vargas-Savalle, L., Karami, M., & Spector, S. (2020). Transformational leadership in the hospitality and tourism industry. In V. Ratten (Ed.), *Entrepreneurial opportunities* (pp. 73–97). Emerald Publishing Limited. doi:10.1108/978-1-83909-285-520201007

Weiermair, K. (2000). Know-how and qualification gaps in the tourism industry: The case of Alpine tourism in Austria. *Tourism Review*, *55*(2), 45–53.

Yukl, G. (1999). An evaluation of conceptual weaknesses in transformational and charismatic leadership theories. *The Leadership Quarterly*, *10*(2), 285–305. doi:10.1016/S1048-9843(99)00013-2

Zehrer, A. (2019). Structure, significance and challenges of family firms in community-type Alpine tourism destinations. In H. Pechlaner (Ed.), *Destination und Lebensraum: Perspektiven touristischer Entwicklung* (pp. 25–38). Springer Fachmedien Wiesbaden. doi:10.1007/978-3-658-28110-6_2

Chapter 10
Transforming the Hospitality and Tourism Industry:
A New Paradigm Shift of Leadership Approach

Shilpi Sarna
Lloyd Business School, India

Akansha Tyagi
IMS Ghaziabad University, India

ABSTRACT

Today's hospitality and tourism industry is fast becoming a technology-enabled service industry powered by the online, mobile, cloud, IoT, AI, robotics, automation, and blockchain tools and applications. Digital technology is making its way into every aspect of the industry in its operations, services, communications, revenue management, distribution, and marketing. The previous studies of hospitality leadership during the crisis have focused on the significance of leadership resilience in corporate leadership narratives. Therefore, this chapter explores the nature of such challenges and opportunities by worldwide leaders and addresses them by using various strategies with the use of technology, especially in the pre- and post-pandemic era. Additionally, this chapter also contributes to a country-wise comparison to analyze the factors that collectively play a vital role in industry activation and revitalization.

INTRODUCTION

The Indian tourism and hospitality industry has emerged as one of the key drivers of growth in the services sector in India (Kumar, 2020). Tourism and hospitality in India have significant potential considering the rich cultural and historical heritage, variety in ecology, terrains, and places of natural beauty spread across the country (Prasuna, 2020). It is an important source of foreign exchange in India, similar to many other countries. The foreign exchange earnings from 2016 to 2019 grew at a CAGR of 7% but dipped in 2020 due to the COVID-19 pandemic (Nkengasong, 2020). The tourism and hospitality sectors have

DOI: 10.4018/978-1-6684-6713-8.ch010

probably been hit the hardest and have affected the Indian economy to such an extent that it will perhaps take a decade to revive (Gössling et al., 2020). As per Statista 2022, the hospitality industry involves three basic segments, such as accommodation (including hotels, motels, resorts, hostels, service apartments, etc.), food and drinks (restaurants, catering, bars, nightclubs, tea and coffee shops), travel and tourism, and even theme parks (Orîndaru et al., 2021). Thus, the hospitality industry does not restrict its services to tourists only, but also caters to the leisure needs of people other than tourists, as in the hotel industry (Bhargav, 2017).

The hotel industry of India, consisting of branded as well as hotel chains, is spread across the length and breadth of the country. It caters to approx 1.8 billion domestic tourists and 9.5 million foreign visitors to India every year (Vig & Tewary, 2022). The organized hotels in India include more than 55% of the hotels in the three-star categories or higher. The market size of the hotel industry in India (including the unorganized market) was estimated at $22 billion in 2019, growing at 8.6% until 2025 (Koukpaki et al., 2020).

The COVID-19 pandemic that hit the world in 2020 has devastatingly affected world businesses and organizations (Tourish, 2020). With travel coming to a standstill, hotels worldwide had to shut their doors to contain the pandemic (Nagaj & Žuromskaitė, 2021). The depressing picture is especially pertinent to developing countries like India where the contribution of the hotel industry to the national GDP and employment generation is substantial (Kaushal & Srivastava, 2021). One of the main ways this industry is currently looking to streamline its services is by digitalizing (Kapoor, 2021). The global leaders of the hospitality industry had several plans for digitization in the pipeline. (Gossling et al., 2020). Digitalizing hotel information, accommodation services as well as the check-in/check-out process, were just some of the main aspects that leaders were looking to digitalize (Morrone et al., 2021). Leaders have drastically transformed their procedures by adopting technology to ensure the digitalization in hotel industry (Carnevale & Hatak, 2020).

Digital advancements create entirely new expectations for leaders to change their organizational structures, procedures, business models, and strategies (Hutajulu et al., 2021; Reis et al., 2019). The pandemic has forced the Hotel industry to implement or boost digital transformation to ensure their survival (Alrawadieh et al., 2020). In this situation, leaders and their digital behavior play a crucial role in driving employees to adopt new technologies to perform better in Hotel Industry (Bartsch et al., 2020). Digitally effective leaders make sure that the hotels they are working with must be aligned with the digitally transformed system for both external and internal stakeholders (Hernandez, 2020). They drive creativity and innovation, by encouraging employees to adopt new technology. Digital leaders transform hotels by developing effective processes and new work systems with a blend of digital competency and digital culture (De Waal et al., 2016). Technical capabilities, help leaders analyze the opportunities and difficulties related to the adoption of digitalization processes in hotels (Neves et al., 2021).

Undoubtedly, the hotel industry is one of the sectors most affected by the COVID-19 pandemic. In this sense, it is one of the most important issues in the research. The strategies implemented in combating the pandemic caused a significant increase in the use of digital technologies by leaders in the hotel industry. Hence, these leaders face extensive challenges in the hotel industry due to the pandemic, which calls for increased research on this topic with a focus on dealing with the various strategies with the use of technology.

Leadership

Leadership research has traveled history for more than a century starting with Plato a philosopher of ancient Greece but it is still evolving due to constant changes in the business environment (Ham, 2021). Leadership is the ability to influence the competence and motivation of individuals and groups to achieve specific goals (Hongdao et al., 2019; Ellemers et al., 2004; Bass, 2000). It is an essential element in the organization to select, prepare, train, and influence followers (Winston & Patterson, 2006).

Previously, leadership styles began with a conventional strategy centered on controlling, competitive, and aggressive traits; however, the continually changing era has appeared new leadership styles (Lipman Blumen, 1992). The new leadership capability is needed for the organization to support its competitive advantage considering technological breakthroughs that have prompted organizational changes, such as the digitalization of the workplace (Erhan et al., 2022). Conventional leadership focuses solely on leaders and their functions, emphasizing the concept as the sum of the leaders' performance within the organization and results from the characteristics of the leaders and the environment (Barker, 2001). However, in today's new era, leaders must follow technological development and learn about the current changes in organizational structures. Moreover, these changes bring unavoidable expectations for the organization to engage in the digitalization of the business world. As a result, compared to conventional leadership, the need for digital leadership appears, as today's organization tends to transform into digital workplaces. Digital workplaces refer to the physical, cultural, and digital arrangements that simplify working life in the complex, dynamic, and often unstructured working environment (Dery et al., 2017). Staying up to date on digital advances is critical for business leaders' competitiveness and survival. Moreover, survival is critical for the business since changing technology has caused employees to adjust to their existing circumstances, and they must also be prepared to meet the various demands of consumers and stakeholders. The pandemic ravaged all sectors of the world to have fully equipped with integrated information and communication technology (ICT). Thus, leaders have played a critical role in ICT implementation because they must first understand innovative technology usage, have the personal ability in their use, and prove a culture that encourages the use of new techniques in the Hospitality and tourism sector (Arokiasamy et al., 2015).

Leadership Perspective in the Hospitality and Tourism Industry

In a scenario where India's hospitality industry is at stake along with the interests of employees, investors, and other stakeholders, there is a need to understand what key challenges the industry leaders face. The pandemic has hit the employees the hardest in terms of stress and uncertainty due to massive job losses, apart from devastating effects on all stakeholders (WHO, 2020). Against the backdrop of the present crisis, researchers discuss the need for several Leadership styles to address the concern (Chiang & Jang, 2008). The leadership factors primarily depend upon several factors-including leaders' and followers' characteristics, environment, and type of relationship between employees and leaders (Al-Ababneh, 2013). Several leadership theories are proposed by the researchers to advance the literature in the context of the hospitality industry, transformational leadership, and leader-member exchange (Boyne, 2010; Bass, 2006). Transformational leadership manifests as the follower's engagement process with leaders resulting in a positive impact on employee engagement, and motivation and influencing them to achieve organizational goals (Boerner et al., 2007). Transformational leaders are expected to lead all stakeholders toward the organizational vision through effective communication skills and displaying charisma (Fitzgerald & Schutte, 2010; Khalili, 2016). Leader-member exchange (LMX) theory, on the other hand, represents the quality of the relationship between leaders with their followers. Trust, liking, and mutual respect are some of the characteristics of LMX theory (Abdullah et al., 2020).

Compassionate leadership is another leadership style recommended by (Oruh et al., 2021) to help mitigate employee stress during challenging times like the COVID-19 pandemic. The concept of compassion in organizational settings has an overarching value beyond acknowledging the grief and moves toward helping individuals in realistic terms (Peticca-Harris, 2019). Further, the compassionate leadership style shows empathy, benevolence, and moral support (Wasylyshyn & Masterpasqua, 2018). As Hospitality and tourism migrate towards a new working system due to the COVID-19 pandemic that has posed far-reaching societal and economic implications, the commitment to diversity and inclusiveness is rising worldwide. It has become imperative for Hospitality and Tourism to promote inclusive leadership (Mehta et al., 2020; Liang et al., 2017). Inclusive leadership makes establishments acknowledge diverse customers and ideas. The COVID-19 crisis has demonstrated how leading by example with authenticity an essential leadership style is for the current uncertain times. The authentic leadership approach has flourished out of positive psychological concepts, demonstrating an ethical approach to create a fair climate so that employees have a sense of justice (Kurian & Nafukho, 2021; Sultana et al., 2020).

Several studies have demonstrated resilience as an important leadership hallmark, especially during challenging times like the COVID-19 crisis. The leadership must understand and handle the compelling harsh circumstances to bounce back, restart the business, and shape employee behavior toward achieving a specific goal (Lombardi et al., 2021). The importance of resilience has started making inroads in the literature. The pandemic is expected to impact the H & T design and practice which requires resilience at several levels (Renjen, 2021). A large part of the research in this area is devoted to establishing the relationship between employee resilience with leadership style (Sommer et al., 2016) as the issue is still in its infancy. The COVID-19 crisis has made the case strong for developing a comprehensive framework for resilience development in the industry.

As leaders receive increased attention and scrutiny during the crisis, stakeholders have lots of expectations in the form of guidance, empathy, and keeping the team informed about various developments. At the moments of crisis, therefore, on both sides of leadership hope and despair surface. In several instances, leaders who were unable to lead during the crisis and who failed in saving the organizations lost the support of stakeholders. Some exemplary leaders successfully prevented their organizations from deep crises and managed the balance between various stakeholders (Lagowska et al., 2020). It is not surprising that the COVID-19 pandemic has spotlighted leadership from whom the stakeholders have very high expectations at crucial times. Leadership styles, therefore, are researched and questioned at such times especially. Such circumstances demand leaders' developmental models that help them understand and respond to the crisis for Hospitality and Tourism.

Regardless of the situations under which organizations and going through, such leadership skills are vital however, the present crisis resulting from pandemics adds challenges and expectations (Haq & Chandio, 2017). Leaders make sense of uncertain events by collecting information coming from various sources-they also need to take individual biases into account. Several decisive measures have been shown to signal leadership concern and reflect management support toward employees. Successful leaders remain composed during a crisis and adapt to make necessary adjustments.

The hotel industry is highly customer-oriented and faces times of intense competition (McManus, 2013). The complex and changing environment of the hospitality industry presents a tremendous set of incentives, pressures, and demands that have proven to be stressful, especially for frontline personnel (Kara et al., 2013). A key element of success for a hospitality company is the employee's motivation to reach their maximum potential, be engaged, embrace, change and make good technical decisions by leaders (Bennett, 2009; Nguyen et al., 2022). The industry has been forced to turn due to Covid 19 to effective leadership transformation as a way of ensuring employees' performance to achieve the desired results in a more dynamic and digital business environment (Huertas-Valdivia et al., 2019). For fostering innovation, generating in-depth knowledge, and educating people about digital transformation, a leadership role is critical (Güldenberg & Langhof, 2021). The definition of leadership has evolved significantly over the last few decades, with the most recent approaches focusing on the transformational aspect of the work of the leader (Brownell, 2010). Strong leaders, according to several studies, can boost the performance of their people and businesses. A leader has to be more creative and innovative to bring about new improvements in a changing setting. Because of the COVID-19 pandemic, the sudden shift to a digital environment necessitates leadership transformation to achieve workers' work performance in a virtual environment (Grint, 2020). However, digital and leadership digitalization is the new components that are successfully implementing different leadership styles all over the world. Digital technology drives change in an organization, whereas digital leadership transformation is the system to provide effective processes.

Digital Leadership

Digital is a household name these days. It has a different meaning for different people, for some, it refers to technology for others it is a way of reaching the customer and there is nothing wrong with it. But due to a lack of clear definition, it is hard to lead with a clear vision (Dörner & Edelman, 2015). Here comes a question what is the meaning of Digital Leadership? In the leadership literature the terms "Digital Leaders", "Digital Leadership", and "e-leadership" are used interchangeably. The term e-leadership defined by Avolio (2000, p. 616) and Digital Leadership by 2002 pioneered by Fisk (2002, p. 43).

A digital leader should have digital skills as well as human skills so that he can lead digital transformation through the people of the organization (Sagnas & Erdogan, 2022). According to De Waal et al. (2016) digital leadership refers to the combination of transformational leadership styles and digital technology usage during employees performing their duties. The ***Digital Leadership is leadership that is responsible for the digital transformation in an organization*** and has ability to lead people towards digital transformation in a rapidly evolving digital context (Sagnas & Erdogan, 2022; Karippur & Balaramachandran, 2022). There are many studies have undertaken to examine the association between leadership styles and performance outcomes (Erhan et al., 2021). Several authors have explored distinct leadership styles with innovative work behavior, such as transformational leadership, participative leadership ethical leadership, instructional leadership, transactional leadership, distributed leadership, supportive leadership, and directive leadership styles which are shown many principals to use in different industry (Iqbal et al., 2020; Fatima et al., 2014). Hardly few studies found related to digital leadership with digital transformation in Hospitality and tourism industry. (Elkhwesky et al., 2022; Huertas-Valdivia et al., 2022; Fenitra et al., 2018; Sharma & Sharma, 2021)

Definition of Digital Leadership

Despite the increasing academic interest in leadership styles and based on the importance to describe a comprehensive review of the Digital Leadership styles in the hospitality industry, the prior studies have approached and investigated this topic in following ways.

RESEARCH AGENDA

The significance of leadership resilience in corporate leadership narratives has been the focus of earlier studies in the field of hospitality leadership throughout the crisis. This hypothetical situation explains pandemic problems, forecasts a post-pandemic era, and supports organisational digitization by digital leaders. This chapter also contributes to a comparison of countries in order to assess the elements that jointly are crucial for industrial activation and revitalization in the post-pandemic era.

DIGITAL LEADERSHIP IN HOSPITALITY AND TOURISM

Digital transformation is increasing exponentially in volume, variety, and practices to impact every industry like Hospitality. The dynamic change and required innovation in the hotel industries move on digital technologies adaptation for delivering better results and requires a continuous digital leadership approach in work design. The rapid growth of digital transformation in this sector requires employee skills and a mindset. Today's digital leaders are dedicated to researching, creating, and applying technological methods that can modify the structure as well as the work design of personnel, allowing the organization to work effectively. Due to the COVID-19 epidemic, the concept of digital leadership has lately evolved against the backdrop of rapid digitization in many enterprises. Some of the terms used to address leadership and digitalization are digital experts, digital leaders, and e-leadership (Torre & Sarti, 2020; Cortellazzo et al., 2019). A leader's potential to create a precise, comprehensive vision for digitalization structure, as well as their ability to implement methods to accomplish that vision, is referred to as digital leadership (Larjovuori et al., 2016). The digital transformation adaptation by the leaders and hotel industries has become the most critical factor in determining employee and organizational performance. Organizations and leaders who are driving superior growth in the contemporary arena are always given new wings and directions by digital leadership. The new or enhanced capabilities required by H&T to respond to the digital transformation imperative have important implications for all. The leaders must play crucial roles in change efforts to build and sustain these capabilities, like knowledge, skills, abilities, and other characteristics that leaders require to effectively do their digital transformations (Busulwa et al., 2022; Oberländer et al., 2020). Therefore, this study explores the nature of Digital leadership in Hospitality and tourism and how such challenges are met by leaders using various strategies for industry activation and revitalisation during pandemic and post-pandemic era (Shukla et al., 2022).

REFORMS IN THE HOSPITALITY AND TOURISM INDUSTRY BY DIGITAL LEADERSHIP

Tourism has always been highly vulnerable and prone to various risks. The impact of unforeseen events usually starts with a reduction in the number of tourists and finally impacts the national and global economy. The present COVID19 crisis also ravaged the global tourism sector by 60–80% in 2020. Additionally, it is pervasive worldwide and destroying the global economy (WTO, 2020). Therefore, leaders are expected to manage people's expectations, guarantee ethical decision-making and ensure communication with stakeholders (Stephens et al., 2020; Ongsakul et al., 2022). The significant digital leadership determinants of success during pandemic crisis by effective decision-making to full fill the expectations (D'Auria & De Smet, 2020).

Table 1. Digital Leadership Challenges. Source: (Author Own Work)

Author	Definition	Explanation
Avolio (2000)	Stage of social change mediated by Advanced Information Technology to produce a change in attitude, emotion, thought, behavior, and/or performance with individuals, groups, and/or organizations.	Digital Leader is managing a change due to advancements in Information and Technology and subsequent behavioral changes in individuals, groups, and organizations.
Peter Fisk (2002)	Digital Leader is imaginative, pushing for change, capable of uniting the organization's ideas and objectives, and capable of connecting firms through partnerships/joint ventures/outsourcing and creating new opportunities for them.	Imaginative, pushing for change, connecting ideas and objectives as well as firms.
Wilson (2004)	Leadership in the basic sectors of the Information Society and its contributions to the transition to the information society.	Able to manage the change which is enforced by a change in information and technology.
Duan (2005)	Leadership in key sectors of information technology (internet service providers, internet content providers, internet application providers, and other technology-based areas such as computing, communications, and content.	Digital Leadership is leadership in Information and Technology and its application in the area of content, computing, and communication.
Kurubacak (2006)	Maintaining strong partnerships of power sufficient for their purpose, respecting civic democratic practices, ensuring that their policies are ostensibly consistent so that they can be represented and play independent roles in their online interactions, interacting with multicultural unions, and engaging with various inquiries into the complex nature of digital youth leaderships. It is a form of leadership that has the task of representing the diversity of its ideologies.	A digital leader ensures having sufficient power to warrant the responsibilities, create policies, and interact with the unions as well as answer the queries of youth.
Borrins (2010)	A leadership style with a mix of channel (Virtual World) selection, IT (Information Technology) procurement, and organizational integration of its.	Digital Leadership is a mix of leadership styles with the virtual world, and procurement of IT.
Sheninger (2014)	Being able to establish relationships to set direction, influence others, and initiate sustainable change through access to information and anticipate changes necessary for future school success.	It is a proactive leadership style not only to institute a sustainable change but also to foresee a future change and also set future directions.
Altınay (2016)	Managers defined a digital leaders as organizers who follow modern technology to reconstruct knowledge	Digital Leader uses technological development for the construction of Knowledge.
Van Wart (2016)	Ability to effectively select and use Information Communication Technologies to achieve personal and corporate goals	The ability to use Information and Communication Technologies effectively and achieve personal and organizational goals.
Narbona (2016)	Leadership style applied with digital tools in the virtual world.	A combination of leadership style with digital tools.
Larjovuori (2016)	The ability to involve all members of the organization in the digitization process and to recognize and develop the skills and abilities needed to achieve it.	The ability to enhance the skills and abilities of the organizational members and involve the process of digitalization.
El Sawy (2016)	To exhibit the right behaviors to ensure the digitalization of the business and business ecosystem strategically.	The right behavior is necessary for bringing digital transformation.
Zhong (2017)	Inspiring and leading its digital transformation, creating and maintaining a digital learning culture, supporting and developing technology-based professional development, and providing and maintaining digital organization management	Ensuring digital transformation, creating digital culture, and managing a digital organization.
Oberer, Erkollar (2018)	A fast, cross-hierarchical, team-oriented, and collaborative approach with a strong focus on innovation.	A team composed of cross-cultural members for innovation.
Tanniru (2018)	A process is necessary to develop and maintain a culture of innovation by rapidly bringing ideas to life using agile Information Technology and business architecture.	It is a process necessary to create a culture of innovation and bring new ideas using Business Architecture and Information Technology
Stana (2018)	A process of social influence mediated by technology that can occur at any hierarchical level in an organization and bring about a change in attitude, emotion, thought, behavior, and/or performance in individuals, groups, and/or organizations.	A change in the attitude, emotions, thoughts, and behavior of individuals, groups, and/or organizations due to social influence which is mediated by technology
Mihardjo (2019)	A combination between digital culture and digital competence.	A combination of digital culture and digital competence.
Antonopoulou (2019)	To reach a goal related to Information Communication Technologies in line with the use of human resources and Information Communication Technologies.	Using Human Resource and Information Communication Technologies to reach the goals of Information Communication Technologies.
Schiuma (2021)	Competence that leaders need to develop in today's digital age.	The competencies which are necessary for a leader in a digital age.
Peng (2021)	In the age of digital technology, individuals or organizations can guide teams, entire organizations, and employees to fully embrace digital thinking, using digital insight, digital decision-making, digital implementation, and digital guidance to ensure their goals are met.	Someone who can guide the digital transformation in an organization.

Technological Investment- The leaders' investment in technologies in the hotels to survive the ongoing crisis due to Covid19. The minimum human interaction was considered a latent solution to restoring the customer and employee concern for safety and Hygiene Leaders, therefore, must take cognizance of the changing circumstances whereby technology is going to shape the future of the hospitality industry. Over the years, even before the pandemic, the experts always recommended technology to address various operational and strategic issues in the hospitality Industry. The calls for the use of advanced technology in the form of "service robots" and "artificial intelligence" (Wirtz et al., 2018, p. 908) were prominent. Adopting technology in hospitality firms improves operation efficiency and effectiveness and co-creates customer experiences (Buhalis & Leung, 2018). The Huang and Rust (2021) demonstrated how associations of A.I. and service robots could replace human labor for specific hospitality tasks. However, at the same time, there is a concern among organizations to decide whether service robots and other technologies can replace employees or they must invest in a rational choice like human-robot systems (Reis et al., 2019)

Customers and Employees Safety- Making customers and employees feel safe emerged as a prominent for leaders to develop. The importance of health and safety is discussed widely in tourism and hospitality literature (Soon et al., 2021). Such measures are desperately required for a country like India because of many infection cases after the second wave of April 2021. The high number of cases has led to an increase in purchasing packaged precooked foods and other similar products (Pinto et al., 2021). The recovering from the first wave and arrival of the second wave had a devastating effect on customer confidence led to implement the customer safety by leaders.

Optimizing operations- Optimising operations emerged as another top theme from the analysis. The Digital leaders believe in adopting optimization strategies to recover from the crisis and restore stakeholder confidence, leading to an improved scorecard. Several studies have already reported hotels deploying a range of such strategies as team optimization, flexible scheduling, redefining employees' tasks and how they are performed, and staffing to actual service levels (de Lucas et al., 2021).

Agile leaders- Around the globe, organizational agility has become imperative for companies to remain competitive and is equally relevant in today's business environment. The organizations stress agility in strategic, operational, and leadership functions. Digital Leadership agility, however, plays in creating agile organizations and must be given due attention (Joiner, 2019). Organizations can benefit by embracing agility in the backdrop of a volatile, uncertain, complex, and ambiguous world. Agile organizations are ideally suited to respond to uncertainties like the ones triggered by pandemics, and financial and other environmental crises. The strong communication among tourism and hospitality stakeholders with UNWTO and WTTC is deemed vital for tackling global crisis as such (Jamal & Budke, 2020)

Crisis Management- The COVID-19 crisis is taken very seriously by all the industry. Hospitality Leaders need to demonstrate seriousness in handling the crisis visibly by bringing changes in employee behavior in performance (Canhoto & Wei, 2021). Such measures can be ensured by the induction process for all staff on enforcing hygiene and physical distancing measures by effective use of technology. Additionally, these initiatives shall have a cascading effect by increasing confidence amongst the workforce and making individual employee responsibilities clear. Formulating crisis management strategies requires constant evaluation of the systems to keep organizations ready for such events that can have devastating effects (Ghaharian et al., 2021).

Demonstrating Empathy- Showing empathy towards employees emerged as an essential theme. The employees also how leaders can be role models and compassionate during moments of crisis. For setting up a stage for the recovery of businesses, leaders are expected to show empathy toward employees. Additionally, leaders must demonstrate compassionate leadership in the face of unfolding human tragedy

Resilience- The study Handscomb et al. (2021) revealed that agile organizations witness the most extensive changes to survive the COVID-19 crisis. Our analysis shows digital leadership resilience is critical attribute stakeholders expect from leaders. A resilient digital leader treats failures as temporary setbacks from which they hope to recover quickly. Such leaders possess a positive attitude and commitment towards employees and the organization during pressing times. The importance of resilience as an individual and a leadership trait has been emphasized in hospitality industry (Newman & Newman, 2021; Andersson et al., 2019).

Involving employees in decision-making- During uncertainty, leaders can feel the urge to centralize the decisions making process; however, involving employees, and encouraging different views and debates are recommended. Since many employees have left hospitality organizations, leaving a handful of the employees behind-the leadership must empower such employees to make them feel valuable and facilitate safe decision-making. Such a digital leadership approach can lead to smarter decisions and enhance employee satisfaction during stressful times (Alexander et al., 2021).

Maintain the balance between stakeholders- Maintaining balance with all other stakeholders was another dominant factor emerging for digital leadership. The pandemic has highlighted the necessity of all stakeholders for organizational survival. The board members, along with senior management of agile organizations ensure the safety of various stakeholders (Paine, 2021).

Managing employee stress- The inability of leaders to deal with employee stress and trauma can have dire consequences for Hospitality during covid. Such industries are constrained to be innovative and are unable to handle a crisis with leadership approach (Nielsen et al., 2021).

Maintaining cash reserves- Maintaining cash reserves is vital for industry to survive crucial times. The study, Crespi-Cladera et al. (2021) predicts that when revenues drop by 80%, it could result in the solvency of up to 32% of organizations. Several leaders had a strong opinion about maintaining cash reserves for dealing with the crisis. The availability of cash reserves out of the balance sheet is one major factor that could help the firms navigate the crisis. A robust empirical investigation has done by digital leaders have maintained cash reserves during the pandemic in the backdrop of its significance of being an organizational lifeline during challenging times.

COMPARATIVE ANALYSIS OF ASIAN COUNTRIES

The spread of Covid-19 has led to a global problem in all aspects of life, including the Hospitality and tourism sector which directly affects the hotel industry (Chon et al., 2020). Asia as a continent with many countries that rely most of their revenue on tourism suffers a severe blow. The Asian continent consists of several regions such as East Asia, South Asia, West Asia, Southeast Asia, and Central Asia. In the hotel industry, Asia has a huge role in the growth of the continent. Unfortunately, the spread of Covid-19 across the globe makes hotel industries in Asian countries deeply shaken. This condition has directly affected hotel occupancy rates in Asia because a lot of countries around the world have implemented a travel ban, physical distancing, and quarantine to stop the spread of the deadly virus. In East Asia, especially in China, the rate of hotel occupancy has declined by 75% from 14 January 2020 (Hotel News Now, 2020). It is because a lot of domestic and international airlines cancel their flights to China and make the hotel room occupancy affected (Hoque et al., 2020). The counties like Srilanka, the hotel occupancy is below 10% because a lot of visitors cancel and refund their booking as caused by the spread of Covid-19 (Nikkei Asian Review, 2020). In Bangladesh, the hotel occupancy hits around 30 to

Figure 1. Reforms in the Hospitality and Tourism Industry by Digital Leadership
Source: (Author Own Work)

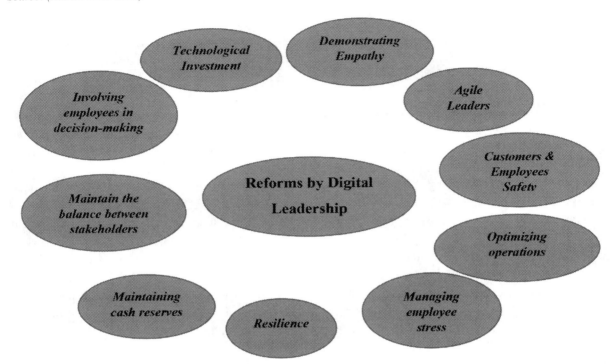

40% of the cancelation of arrival visa. Similarly, hotel occupancy in India has decreased by 43% (Str, 2020). Indonesia had fallen from 30 to 40% with Bali, Manado, Jakarta, Sulawesi, and Riau Islands. The Singapore, decreases by above 50% because flight cancellation and quarantine (ET Hospitality World, 2020). Then, in Saudi Arabia, the hotel occupancy dropped by 22%. This is the lowest performance in the pandemic makes the industry in Saudi Arabia paralyzed (Hotelier ME, 2020). Furthermore, in Central Asia for example Uzbekistan, the rate of hotel occupancy was below 25% (Eurasia net, 2021). Meanwhile, for the other countries in Central Asia, such as Kazakhstan, Turkmenistan, Tajikistan, and Kyrgyzstan, there are no confirmed cases of Covid-19 because since the first of the spread corona virus the entry and the exit access in those regions were closed (Kalpak Travel, 2020).

The decline of hotel occupancy also impacted employment in the hotel industry. Indonesia, more than 150,000 employees have been laid off (The Jakarta Post, 2020). Malaysia, around 4% of hotel industry workers have been laid off with pay cuts and unpaid leave. Hotels in India implement a pay cut off up to 40 to 60 percent for the employees and paid voluntary resignation for many employees. The total job losses in Asia have reached 63.4 million, as most of their income comes from tourism, they suffer a loss of around US$ 1.041 million (World Travel & Tourism Council, 2020).

The Asia-Pacific region has revolutionized itself into a beloved traveller hub for all types of tourists. The region has forged a reputation as being the in-trend destination for holiday goers, boasting must-see attractions and idyllic, natural landscapes. Not only does the industry provide monetary value to many countries, but it has made a significant contribution to employment. However, unprecedented events like pandemic led to huge blows to the hotel sectors throughout the entire Asia-Pacific region. Therefore, the sustainable leadership approach has brought significant changes in the survival of this sector.

CONCLUSION

In today's uncertain times a digital leader can sail through some key skills like Empathy, Resilience, involving employees in decision-making, Maintaining the balance between stakeholders, and Managing employee stress. In Asia young countries like Malaysia, Indonesia, Thailand, Vietnam, and India are young, technologically progressive have better avenues of growth in the area of travel and tourism. This study tries to highlight the strategies or operational changes by digital leader in Asian region. Additionally, this study also tries to explore the digital transformation in the post-COVID era, as most of the hotels have transformed their services for customer's affective loyalty for better result (Fenitra et al., 2022).

Hotel facilities mainly refer to the tangible facilities that hotels are providing nowadays to attract customers, like, complementary breakfasts, room services, extra services, etc (Abrudan et al., 2020). In the post-COVID era, customers are looking for better digital facilities that will reduce their risk of staying in the hotels. Hotels around the world are trying to bring changes in tangibles like, technology, arrangements, and appearance (Fatima & Razzaque, 2014) of hotels to attract customers and demonstrate that they are maintaining proper safety and security with digital transformation (Parzych & Brkic-Veimelka, 2020).

Conflict of Interest

The authors declare that they have no conflict of interest.

Funding

This is self-sponsored research in which no funding has been granted/taken/ sponsored from any organization.

ACKNOWLEDGMENT

The authors would like to thank the fellow researcher for her contribution and reviewers for their comments and suggestions that significantly helped improve this paper.

REFERENCES

Abdullah, K. H., Hashim, M. N., & Abd Aziz, F. S. (2020). A 39 years (1980-2019) bibliometric analysis of safety leadership research. *TEST Engineering and Management, 83*, 4526–4542.

Abrudan, I. N., Pop, C. M., & Lazăr, P. S. (2020). Using a general ordered logit model to explain the influence of hotel facilities, general and sustainability-related, on customer ratings. *Sustainability, 12*(21), 9302. doi:10.3390u12219302

Al-AbabnehM. M. (2013). Leadership style of managers in five-star hotels and its relationship with employee's job satisfaction. *Available at* SSRN 3633072. doi:10.2139/ssrn.3633072

Alexander, A., De Smet, A., & Weiss, L. (2021). *Decision making in uncertain times.* Retrieved 2 June 2021, from https://www.mckinsey.com/business functions/organization/our insights/decision-making-in-uncertain-times

Alrawadieh, Z., Alrawadieh, Z., & Cetin, G. (2020). Digital transformation and revenue management: Evidence from the hotel industry. *Tourism Economics.* Advance online publication. doi:10.1177/13548166209019

Altınay, F. A. (2016). Are headmasters digital leaders in school culture? *Education in Science, 40*(182), 77–86. doi:10.15390/EB.2015.4534

Andersson, T., Cäker, M., Tengblad, S., & Wickelgren, M. (2019). Building traits for organizational resilience through balancing organizational structures. *Scandinavian Journal of Management, 35*(1), 36–45. doi:10.1016/j.scaman.2019.01.001

Antonopoulou, H., Halkiopoulos, C., Barlou, O., & Beligiannis, G. N. (2019), Transformational leadership and digital skills in higher education institutes: during the COVID-19 pandemic. *Emerging Science Journal, 5*(1), 1-15.

Arokiasamy, A. R. A., Abdullah, A. G. K., & Ismail, A. (2015). Correlation between cultural perceptions, leadership style and ICT usage by school principals in Malaysia. *Procedia: Social and Behavioral Sciences, 176,* 319–332. doi:10.1016/j.sbspro.2015.01.478

Avolio, B. J., Kahai, S., & Dodge, G. E. (2000). E-leadership: Implications for theory, research, and practice. *The Leadership Quarterly, 11*(4), 615–668. doi:10.1016/S1048-9843(00)00062-X

Barker, R. A. (2001). The nature of leadership. *Human Relations, 54*(4), 469–494. doi:10.1177/0018726701544004

Bartsch, S., Weber, E., Büttgen, M., & Huber, A. (2020). Leadership matters in crisis-induced digital transformation: How to lead service employees effectively during the COVID-19 pandemic. *Journal of Service Management, 32*(1), 71–85. Advance online publication. doi:10.1108/JOSM-05-2020-0160

Bass, B. M. (2000). The Future of Leadership in Learning Organizations. *The Journal of Leadership Studies, 7*(3), 19–40. doi:10.1177/107179190000700302

Bass, B. M., & Riggio, R. E. (2006). *Transformational Leadership* (2nd ed.). Lawrence Erlbaum Associates, Inc. doi:10.4324/9781410617095

Bhargav, S. (2017). A study on marketing mix of hospitality industry. *International Journal of Management. IT & Engineering, 7*(9), 253–265.

Boerner, S., Eisenbeiss, S., & Griesser, D. (2007). Followers' behaviour and organizational performance: The impact of transformational leaders. *Journal of Leadership & Organizational Studies, 13*(3), 15–26. doi:10.1177/10717919070130030201

Borins, S. F. (2010). Digital state 2.0. In M. J. Prince, G. B. Doern, L. A. Pal, & G. Toner (Eds.), *Policy from Ideas to Implementation: In Honour of Professor G. Bruce Doern* (pp. 177–206). McGill-Queen's University Press.

Boyne, S. (2010). Leadership research in hospitality: A critical review. *Education, 17*, 20–27.

Brownell, J. (2010). Leadership in the service of hospitality. *Cornell Hospitality Quarterly, 51*(3), 363–378. doi:10.1177/1938965510368651

Buhalis, D., & Leung, R. (2018). Smart hospitality—Interconnectivity and interoperability towards an ecosystem. *International Journal of Hospitality Management, 71*, 41–50. doi:10.1016/j.ijhm.2017.11.011

Busulwa, R., Pickering, M., & Mao, I. (2022). Digital transformation and hospitality management competencies: Toward an integrative framework. *International Journal of Hospitality Management, 102*, 103132. doi:10.1016/j.ijhm.2021.103132

Canhoto, A. I., & Wei, L. (2021). Stakeholders of the world, unite!: Hospitality in the time of COVID-19. *International Journal of Hospitality Management, 95*, 102922. doi:10.1016/j.ijhm.2021.102922 PMID:36540681

Carnevale, J. B., & Hatak, I. (2020). Employee adjustment and well-being in the era of COVID-19: Implications for human resource management. *Journal of Business Research, 116*, 183–187. doi:10.1016/j.jbusres.2020.05.037 PMID:32501303

Chiang, C. F., & Jang, S. (2008). The Antecedents and Consequences of Psychological Empowerment: The Case of Taiwan's Hotel Companies. *Journal of Hospitality & Tourism Research (Washington, D.C.), 32*(1), 40–61. doi:10.1177/1096348007309568

Chon, K., Park, E., & Zoltan, J. (2020). The Asian paradigm in hospitality and tourism. *Journal of Hospitality & Tourism Research (Washington, D.C.), 44*(8), 1183–1202. doi:10.1177/1096348020945370

Cortellazzo, L., Bruni, E., & Zampieri, R. (2019). The role of leadership in a digitalized world: A review. *Frontiers in Psychology, 10*, 1938. doi:10.3389/fpsyg.2019.01938 PMID:31507494

Crespí-Cladera, R., Martín-Oliver, A., & Pascual-Fuster, B. (2021). Financial distress in the hospitality industry during the Covid-19 disaster. *Tourism Management, 85*, 104301. doi:10.1016/j.tourman.2021.104301

D'Auria, G., & De Smet, A. (2020). Leadership in a crisis: Responding to the coronavirus outbreak and future challenges. *Psychology (Irvine, Calif.), 22*(2), 273–287.

de Lucas Ancillo, A., del Val Núñez, M. T., & Gavrila, S. G. (2021). Workplace change within the COVID-19 context: A grounded theory approach. *Economic Research-Ekonomska Istraživanja, 34*(1), 2297–2316. doi:10.1080/1331677X.2020.1862689

De Waal, B., van Outvorst, F., & Ravesteyn, P. (2016). Digital leadership: The objective-subjective dichotomy of technology revisited. In *12th European Conference on Management, Leadership and Governance ECMLG 2016* (p. 52). Academic Press.

Dery, K., Sebastian, I. M., & van der Meulen, N. (2017). The digital workplace is key to digital innovation. *MIS Quarterly Executive, 16*(2).

Dörner, K., & Edelman, D. (2015). *What 'digital' really means*. McKinsey & company.

Duan, Q. (2005). *China's IT Leadership*. University of Maryland, Philosophy Graduate School.

El Sawy, O. A., Kraemmergaard, P., Amsinck, H., & Vinther, A. L. (2016). How Lego Built the Foundations and Enterprise Capabilities for Digital Leadership. *MIS Quarterly Executive*, *15*(2), 141–166.

Elkhwesky, Z., Salem, I. E., Ramkissoon, H., & Castañeda-García, J. A. (2022). A systematic and critical review of leadership styles in contemporary hospitality: A roadmap and a call for future research. *International Journal of Contemporary Hospitality Management*, *34*(5), 1925–1958. doi:10.1108/IJCHM-09-2021-1128

Ellemers, N., De Gilder, D., & Haslam, S. A. (2004). Motivating individuals and groups at work: A social identity perspective on leadership and group performance. *Academy of Management Review*, *29*(3), 459–478. doi:10.2307/20159054

Erhan, T., Uzunbacak, H. H., & Aydin, E. (2022). From conventional to digital leadership: Exploring digitalization of leadership and innovative work behavior. *Management Research Review*, *45*(11), 1524–1543. Advance online publication. doi:10.1108/MRR-05-2021-0338

Eurasianet. (n.d.). Retrieved June 3, 2021 from: https://eurasianet.org/uzbekistan-top-tier-hotels-linger-on-market.

Fatima, J. K., & Razzaque, M. A. (2014). Service quality and satisfaction in the banking sector. *International Journal of Quality & Reliability Management*, *31*(4), 367–379. Advance online publication. doi:10.1108/IJQRM-02-2013-0031

Fenitra, R. M., Abbas, A., Ekowati, D., & Suhairidi, F. (2022). Strategic Intent and Strategic Leadership: A Review Perspective for Post-COVID-19 Tourism and Hospitality Industry Recovery. The Emerald handbook of destination recovery in tourism and hospitality, 23-44.

Fisk, P. (2002). The making of a digital leader. *Business Strategy Review*, *13*(1), 43–50. doi:10.1111/1467-8616.00201

Fitzgerald, S., & Schutte, N. S. (2010). Increasing transformational leadership through enhancing self-efficacy. *Journal of Management Development*, *29*(5), 495–505. Advance online publication. doi:10.1108/02621711011039240

Ghaharian, K., Abarbanel, B., Soligo, M., & Bernhard, B. (2021). *Crisis management practices in the hospitality and gambling industry during COVID-19*. International Hospitality Review., doi:10.1108/IHR-08-2020-0037

Gössling, S., Scott, D., & Hall, C. M. (2020). Pandemics, tourism and global change: A rapid assessment of COVID-19. *Journal of Sustainable Tourism*, *29*(1), 1–20. doi:10.1080/09669582.2020.1758708

Grint, K. (2020). Leadership, management and command in the time of the Coronavirus. *Leadership*, *16*(3), 314–319. doi:10.1177/1742715020922445

Güldenberg, S., & Langhof, J. G. (2021). Digital Leadership and Technology. In *Managing Work in the Digital Economy* (pp. 157–173). Springer. doi:10.1007/978-3-030-65173-2_10

Hall, J., Johnson, S., Wysocki, A., & Kepner, K. (2008). *Transformational Leadership: The Transformational of Managers and Associates*. University of Florida.

Ham, H. (2021). Leadership: A Journey to Enacting Change. *Journal of Youth Development, 16*(1), 1–6. doi:10.5195/jyd.2021.1115

Handscomb, C., Mahadevan, D., Schor, L., Sieberer, M., Naidoo, E., & Srinivasan, S. (2021). *An operating model for the next normal: Lessons from agile organisations in the crisis*. Retrieved June 2, 2021, from: https://www.mckinsey.com/business-functions/organization/our insights/an-operating-model-for-the-next-normal-lessons-from -agile-organizations-in-the-crisis

Haq, S., & Chandio, J. (2017). Transactional Leadership and its Impact on the Organizational Performance: A Critical Analysis. *International Journal of Trend in Scientific Research and Development, 2*(1), 135–139. doi:10.31142/ijtsrd2499

Hernandez, J. (2020, August 17). *Who or what is driving digital transformation at your organization?* KPMG.

Hongdao, Q., Bibi, S., Khan, A., Ardito, L., & Nurunnabi, M. (2019). Does what goes around really comes around? The mediating effect of CSR on the relationship between transformational leadership and employee's job performance in law firms. *Sustainability, 11*(12), 3366. doi:10.3390u11123366

Hoque, A., Shikha, F. A., Hasanat, M. W., Arif, I., & Hamid, A. B. A. (2020). The effect of Coronavirus (COVID-19) in the tourism industry in China. *Asian Journal of Multidisciplinary Studies, 3*(1), 52–58.

Hospitality World, E. T. (n.d.). Retrieved April 21, 2020, From: https://hospitality.economictimes.indiatimes.com/news/hotels /covid-19-impacts-hotel-occupancy-in-the-asean-region/752675 21

Hotel News Now. (n.d.). Retrieved February 4, 2020, from: http://hotelnewsnow.com/

Hotelier, M. E. (n.d.). Retrieved May 12, 2020, from: https://www.hoteliermiddleeast.com/ business/117482-report-jeddah-hotel-occupancy-levels-falls-to-22

Huang, M. H., & Rust, R. T. (2021). A strategic framework for artificial intelligence in marketing. *Journal of the Academy of Marketing Science, 49*(1), 30–50. doi:10.100711747-020-00749-9

Huertas-Valdivia, I., González-Torres, T., & Nájera-Sánchez, J. J. (2022). Contemporary leadership in hospitality: a review and research agenda. *International Journal of Contemporary Hospitality Management*. doi:10.5281/zenodo.6602327

Huertas-Valdivia, I., Llorens-Montes, F. J., & Ruiz-Moreno, A. (2018). Achieving engagement among hospitality employees: A serial mediation model. *International Journal of Contemporary Hospitality Management, 30*(1), 217–241. doi:10.1108/IJCHM-09-2016-0538

Hutajulu, R. S., Susita, D., & Eliyana, A. (2021). The effect of digitalization and virtual leadership on organizational innovation during the COVID-19 pandemic crisis: A case study in Indonesia. *The Journal of Asian Finance. Economics and Business*, *8*(10), 57–64.

Iqbal, Z. A., Abid, G., Contreras, F., Hassan, Q., & Zafar, R. (2020). Ethical leadership and innovative work behavior: The mediating role of individual attributes. *Journal of Open Innovation*, *6*(3), 68. doi:10.3390/joitmc6030068

Jamal, T., & Budke, C. (2020). Tourism in a world with pandemics: local-global responsibility and action. *Journal of Tourism Futures*, *6*(2), 181-188.

Joiner, B. (2019). Leadership agility for organizational agility. *Journal of Creating Value*, *5*(2), 139–149. doi:10.1177/2394964319868321

Kapoor, R., & Kapoor, K. (2021). The transition from traditional to digital marketing: A study of the evolution of e-marketing in the Indian hotel industry. *Worldwide Hospitality and Tourism Themes*, *13*(2), 199–213. Advance online publication. doi:10.1108/WHATT-10-2020-0124

Kara, D., Uysal, M., Sirgy, M., & Leed, G. (2013). The effects of leadership style on employee well-being in hospitality. *International Journal of Hospitality Management*, *34*, 9–18. doi:10.1016/j.ijhm.2013.02.001

Karippur, N. K., & Balaramachandran, P. R. (2022). Antecedents of Effective Digital Leadership of Enterprises in the Asia Pacific. *AJIS. Australasian Journal of Information Systems*, *26*. Advance online publication. doi:10.3127/ajis.v26i0.2525

Kaushal, V., & Srivastava, S. (2021). Hospitality and tourism industry amid COVID-19 pandemic: Perspectives on challenges and learnings from India. *International Journal of Hospitality Management*, *92*, 102707. doi:10.1016/j.ijhm.2020.102707 PMID:33024348

Khalili, A. (2016). Linking transformational leadership, creativity, innovation, and innovation-supportive climate. *Management Decision*, *54*(9), 2277–2293. doi:10.1108/MD-03-2016-0196

Koukpaki, A.S.F., Adams, K., & Oyedijo, A. (2020). The contribution of human resource development managers to organisational branding in the hotel industry in India and South East Asia (ISEA): A dynamic capabilities perspective. *Employee Relations: The International Journal*. doi:10.1108/ER-09-2019-0375

Kumar, V. (2020). Indian tourism industry and COVID-19: Present scenario. *Journal of Tourism and Hospitality Education*, *10*, 179–185. doi:10.3126/jthe.v10i0.28768

Kurian, D., & Nafukho, F. M. (2021). *Can authentic leadership influence the employees' organizational justice perceptions? A study in the hotel context*. International Hospitality Review. doi:10.1108/IHR-08-2020-0047

Kurubacak, G. (2006). Reflections on The Digital Youth Leadership for Social Justice Activism: Understanding Silent Dialogues through Critical Pedagogy. *I-manager's Journal on School Educational Technology*, *2*(2), 44–51. doi:10.26634/jsch.2.2.860

Lagowska, U., Sobral, F., & Furtado, L. M. G. P. (2020). Leadership under crises: A research agenda for the post-Covid-19 Era. *BAR - Brazilian Administration Review*, *17*(2), 17. doi:10.1590/1807-7692bar2020200062

Larjovuori, R. L., Bordi, L., Mäkiniemi, J. P., & Heikkilä-Tammi, K. (2016). The role of leadership and employee well-being in organizational digitalization. *Tiziana Russo-Spenaand Cristina Mele, 1159*.

Liang, T. L., Chang, H. F., Ko, M. H., & Lin, C. W. (2017). Transformational leadership and employee voices in the hospitality industry. *International Journal of Contemporary Hospitality Management*, *29*(1), 374–392. doi:10.1108/IJCHM-07-2015-0364

Lipman-Blumen, J. (1992). Connective leadership: Female leadership styles in the 21st-century workplace. *Sociological Perspectives*, *35*(1), 183–203. doi:10.2307/1389374

Lombardi, S., Cunha, M. P., & Giustiniano, L. (2021). Improvising resilience: The unfolding of resilient leadership in COVID-19 times. *International Journal of Hospitality Management*, *95*, 102904. doi:10.1016/j.ijhm.2021.102904 PMID:36540683

McManus, L. (2013). Customer accounting and marketing performance measures in the hotel industry: Evidence from Australia. *International Journal of Hospitality Management*, *33*, 140–152. doi:10.1016/j.ijhm.2012.07.007

Mehta, M., Sarvaiya, H., & Chandani, A. (2020). Community engagement through responsible leadership in managing pandemic: Insight from India using netnography. *The International Journal of Sociology and Social Policy*. Advance online publication. doi:10.1108/IJSSP-06-2020-0214

Mihardjo, L., Sasmoko, S., Alamsjah, F., & Elidjen, E. (2019). Digital leadership role in developing business model innovation and customer experience orientation in industry 4.0. *Management Science Letters*, *9*(11), 1749–1762. doi:10.5267/j.msl.2019.6.015

Morrone, D., Raimo, N., Tarulli, A., & Vitolla, F. (2021). Digitalisation in the hospitality industry: Motivations, effects and role of COVID-19. *International Journal of Digital Culture and Electronic Tourism*, *3*(3-4), 257–270. doi:10.1504/IJDCET.2021.116475

Nagaj, R., & Žuromskaitė, B. (2021). Tourism in the Era of Covid-19 and Its Impact on the Environment. *Energies*, *14*(7), 2000. doi:10.3390/en14072000

Narbona, J. (2016). Digital leadership, Twitter and Pope Francis. *Church Communication and Culture*, *1*(1), 90–109. doi:10.1080/23753234.2016.1181307

Neves, P., Pires, D., & Costa, S. (2021). Empowering to Reduce Intentions to Resist Future Change: Organization-Based Self-esteem as a Boundary Condition. *British Journal of Management*, *32*(3), 872–891. doi:10.1111/1467-8551.12436

Newman, N., & Newman, D. (2021). Leadership behind masked faces: From uncertainty to resilience at a Jamaican academic library. *Journal of Academic Librarianship*, *47*(5), 102377. doi:10.1016/j.acalib.2021.102377

Nguyen, L. V., Haar, J., & Smollan, R. (2022). Hospitality Leadership Competencies and Employee Commitment: New Insights From the Booming Hotel Industry in Vietnam. *Tourism and Hospitality Management*, *28*(2), 419–443. doi:10.20867/thm.28.2.10

Nielsen, N., D'Auria, G., & Zolley, S. (2021). *Tuning in, turning outward: cultivating compassionate leadership in a crisis.* Retrieved June 2 2021, from: https://www.mckinsey.com/businessfunctions/organization/our-insights/tuning-in-turning-outward-cultivating-compassionat eleadership-in-a-crisis

Nikei Asian Review. (n.d.). Retrieved April 1 2020, from: https://asia.nikkei.com/: https://asia.nikkei.com/Spotlight/Cor onavirus/Empty-hotels-in-Sri-Lanka-and-Nepal-point-to-lengthy-economic-hit

Nkengasong, J. (2020). China's response to a novel coronavirus stands in stark contrast to the 2002 SARS outbreak response. *Nature Medicine, 26*(3), 310–311. doi:10.103841591-020-0771-1 PMID:31988464

Oberer, B., & Erkollar, A. (2018). Leadership 4.0: Digital leaders in the age of industry 4.0. *International Journal of Organizational Leadership.*

Oberländer, M., Beinicke, A., & Bipp, T. (2020). Digital competencies: A review of the literature and applications in the workplace. *Computers & Education, 146*, 103752. doi:10.1016/j.compedu.2019.103752

Ongsakul, V., Kajla, T., Raj, S., Khoa, T. T., & Ahmed, Z. U. (2022). Changing tourists' preferences in the hotel industry amid COVID-19 pandemic. *Journal of Hospitality and Tourism Technology, 13*(2), 295–313. Advance online publication. doi:10.1108/JHTT-07-2020-0179

Orîndaru, A., Popescu, M. F., Alexoaei, A. P., Căescu, Ș. C., Florescu, M. S., & Orzan, A. O. (2021). Tourism in a post-COVID-19 era: Sustainable strategies for industry's recovery. *Sustainability, 13*(12), 6781. doi:10.3390u13126781

Oruh, E. S., Mordi, C., Dibia, C. H., & Ajonbadi, H. A. (2021). Exploring compassionate managerial leadership style in reducing employee stress level during COVID-19 crisis: the case of Nigeria. *Employee Relations: The International Journal.* doi:10.1108/ER-06-2020-0302

Paine, L. (2021). *Covid-19 is rewriting the rules of corporate governance.* Retrieved June 2, 2021, from: https://hbr.org/2020/10/covid-19-is-rewriting-the-rules-of-corporate-governance

Parzych, K., & Brkić-Vejmelka, J. (2020). Guests' assessment of hotel facilities and services: Zadar case study. *European Journal of Tourism, Hospitality and Recreation, 10*(3), 241–250. doi:10.2478/ejthr-2020-0021

Peng, B. (2021). Digital leadership: State governance in the era of digital technology. *Cultura e Scuola, 1-5.* Advance online publication. doi:10.1177/2096608321989

Peticca-Harris, A. (2019). Managing compassionately? Managerial narratives about grief and compassion. *Human Relations, 72*(3), 588–612. doi:10.1177/0018726718779666

Pinto, L., Bonifacio, M. A., De Giglio, E., Santovito, E., Cometa, S., Bevilacqua, A., & Baruzzi, F. (2021). Biopolymer hybrid materials: Development, characterization, and food packaging applications. *Food Packaging and Shelf Life, 28*, 100676. doi:10.1016/j.fpsl.2021.100676

Prasuna, C. (2020). Government to promote tourism and hospitality in India. *International Journal of Multidisciplinary Educational Research, 9*(11), 34.

Reis, J., Amorim, M., Melão, N., Cohen, Y., & Rodrigues, M. (2019, July). Digitalization: A literature review and research agenda. In *International Joint conference on industrial engineering and operations management* (pp. 443-456). Springer. 10.1177/2096608321989835

Renjen, P. (2020). *The essence of resilient leadership: Business recovery from COVID-19*. Deloitte. Retrieved June 30 June 5 Available from: https://www2. deloitte. com/global/en/insights/economy/covid -19/guide-to-organizational-recovery-for-senior-executives-h eart-of-resilient-leadership. html

Sağbaş, M., & Erdoğan, F. A. (n.d.). Digital Leadership: A Systematic Conceptual Literature Review. *İstanbul Kent Üniversitesi İnsan ve Toplum Bilimleri Dergisi, 3*(1), 17-35.

Schiuma, G., Schettini, E., Santarsiero, F., & Carlucci, D. (2021). The transformative leadership compass: six competencies for digital transformation entrepreneurship. *International Journal of Entrepreneurial Behavior & Research*.

Sharma, J., & Sharma, A. (2021). *Leadership in the Hospitality Industry*. Academic Press.

Sheninger, E. (2014). Pillars of digital leadership. International Center for Leadership in Education.

Shukla, B., Sufi, T., Joshi, M., & Sujatha, R. (2022). Leadership challenges for Indian hospitality industry during COVID-19 pandemic. *Journal of Hospitality and Tourism Insights*. doi:10.1108/JHTI-08-2021-0217

Sommer, S. A., Howell, J. M., & Hadley, C. N. (2016). Keeping positive and building strength: The role of affect and team leadership in developing resilience during an organizational crisis. *Group & Organization Management, 41*(2), 172–202. doi:10.1177/1059601115578027

Soon, J. M., Vanany, I., Wahab, I. R. A., Hamdan, R. H., & Jamaludin, M. H. (2021). Food safety and evaluation of intention to practice safe eating out measures during COVID-19: Cross sectional study in Indonesia and Malaysia. *Food Control, 125*, 107920. doi:10.1016/j.foodcont.2021.107920 PMID:35668872

Stana, R., Fischer, L. H., & Nicolajsen, H. W. (2018). Review for future research in digital leadership. Information Systems Research Conference in Scandinavia (IRIS41), 1-15

Stephens, K. K., Jahn, J. L., Fox, S., Charoensap-Kelly, P., Mitra, R., Sutton, J., Waters, E. D., Xie, B., & Meisenbach, R. J. (2020). Collective sensemaking around COVID-19: Experiences, concerns, and agendas for our rapidly changing organizational lives. *Management Communication Quarterly, 34*(3), 426–457. doi:10.1177/0893318920934890

str. (2020, April 1). *Noudettu osoitteesta str*. https://str.com/data-insights- blog/covid-19-india-hotel-performance-impact

Sultana, U. S., Tarofder, A. K., Darun, M. R., Haque, A., & Sharief, S. R. (2020). Authentic leadership effect on pharmacists job stress and satisfaction during COVID-19 pandemic: Malaysian perspective. *Journal of Talent Development and Excellence, 12*(3s), 1824–1841.

Tanniru, M. R. (2018). Digital Leadership. In M. Pomffyova (Ed.), *Management of information systems* (pp. 93–109). IntechOpen.

The Jakarta Post. (n.d.). Retrieved April 2, 2020, from: https://www.thejakartapost.com/: https://www.thejakartapost.com/trave l/2020/04/02/covid-19-almost-700- hotels-in-indonesia-shut-down.html

Torre, T., & Sarti, D. (2020). The "way" toward e-leadership: Some evidence from the field. *Frontiers in Psychology, 11*, 554253. doi.org/10.3389/fpsyg.2020.55425

Tourish, D. (2020). Introduction to the special issue: Why the coronavirus crisis is also a crisis of leadership. *Leadership, 16*(3), 261–272.

Travel, K. (n.d.). Retrieved June 1, 2020, from: https://kalpak-travel.com/blog/coronavirus-central- asia/

Van Wart, M., Roman, A., Wang, X., & Liu, C. (2016). Integrating ICT Adoption Issues into (e-)Leadership Theory. *Telematics and Informatics, 34*(5), 527–537.

Vig, S., & Tewary, T. (2022). Resilience of the Hotel Industry in COVID-19: The Indian Context. In *COVID-19 Pandemic Impact on New Economy Development and Societal Change* (pp. 251–263). IGI Global. doi:10.4018/978-1-6684-3374-4.ch012

Wasylyshyn, K. M., & Masterpasqua, F. (2018). Developing self-compassion in leadership development coaching: A practice model and case study analysis. *International Coaching Psychology Review, 13*(1), 21–34.

Wilson, E. J. III. (2004). Leadership in the Digital Age. In G. R. Goethals, G. Sorenson, & J. Mac Gregor (Eds.), *Encyclopedia of Leadership* (pp. 859–862). Sage.

Winston, B. E., & Patterson, K. (2006). An integrative definition of leadership. *International Journal of Leadership Studies, 1*(2), 6–66.

Wirtz, J., Patterson, P. G., Kunz, W. H., Gruber, T., Lu, V. N., Paluch, S., & Martins, A. (2018). Brave new world: Service robots in the frontline. *Journal of Service Management, 29*(5), 907–931.

World Health Organization. (2020). Clinical management of severe acute respiratory infection (SARI) when COVID-19 disease is suspected: interim guidance, 13 March 2020 (No. WHO/2019-nCoV/clinical/2020.4). World Health Organization.

World Travel & Tourism Council. (n.d.). Retrieved May 12, 2020, from: https://wttc.org/News-Article/WTTC-now-estimates-over-100-million-jobs-losses-in-the-Travel-&-Tourism-sector-and-alerts-G20-countries-to- the-scale-of-the-crisis

Zhong, L. (2017). Indicators of digital leadership in the context of K-12 education. *Journal of Educational Technology Development and Exchange, 10*(1), 27–40.

Chapter 11
Strategic Leadership in Tourism Enterprises

Zehra Yardı
Istinye University, Turkey

Emre Ozan Aksöz
https://orcid.org/0000-0002-4109-8847
Anadolu University, Turkey

ABSTRACT

The rapid evolution of markets today has led to globalization, competition, and technological developments, and the present classic management concept is becoming more dynamic. This has led management to adopt a more market-responsive strategic management approach. Strategic leaders are required in a wide range of institutions and organizations. There is a greater need for strategic leaders in an enterprise or an organization with larger objectives, a growth target, or high potential. Tourism businesses must remain present in this evolving environment and meet the expectations of employees, clients, partners, suppliers, government, etc. On the other hand, to ensure interaction with the external environment, exist in the market, and satisfy the aspirations of stakeholders, they must engage in managerial work towards ordinary jobs as well as activities for future and change. That requires strategic management of tourism companies. The leadership model, which has become popular in terms of strategic management, seems to be strategic leadership.

INTRODUCTION

Leadership has emerged as an impressive social concept and has influenced societies that have no nationality, culture, or country. Since ancient times, philosophers have been found in societies giving guidance, and sometimes these rulers have been ascribed to divine features. Leaders have been around since people first met as social groups, but the explanations for what they wanted to say have changed over time (Gelatt, 2002).

DOI: 10.4018/978-1-6684-6713-8.ch011

History is often recounted through the lives of famous leaders (Howell & Costley 2006). Some leaders have been able to spread great desire and enthusiasm around, some leaders have built great empires, and some leaders have been able to mobilize quite ordinary people with great power. Questions about the work of how it all happened have long been the subject of debate. In the 20th century, leadership was the focus of scientific research. The determinants of leadership effectiveness lie at the heart of many studies. Sociologists strive to find traits, abilities, behaviors, sources of power, and situational conditions that determine how a leader can influence the audience and their group goals (Yukl, 2002).

Leadership is probably something that has been written, researched, and much discussed compared to many other issues. Nonetheless, despite widespread interest, leadership remained an enigmatic concept (Luthans, 1981). Thousands of studies have provided important information about what leadership is and isn't, but there are still many unknowns on the subject (Ivancevich & Matteson, 2002).

There is a different theoretical basis for leadership. The Great Man Theory asserts that he will be born a leader. This Great Man Theory is based on the assumption that some people were born with certain characteristics that would enable them to become leaders in the life process into which they were born. The Great Man Theory has prompted a quest for a theory that bears more realistic qualities for leadership. In the following process, the Property Theory was introduced. In this theory, unlike the first theory, the fact that leadership traits can be gained through learning and experience is not entirely innate. Other studies in this field have explored the universal characteristics of leaders (Luthans, 1981). Since this theory is considered inadequate to identify successful leadership characteristics, researchers have included different factors in their research. They have also begun investigating the leader's behavior and actions. Thus came the Behavioral Leadership Theory (Griffin, 2002). The basis for this theory, which seeks to explain the leadership process, is that it is not the characteristics of the leader that make the leader successful and effective. The leader's behavior while leading has been a major focus of this theory.

BACKGROUND

Modern Leadership Approaches

Due to advancements and changes from the past to the present, the idea of leadership has had to go through numerous structural changes. Traditional leadership theories are no longer valid in today's risky and uncertain world. As a result, directing and influencing people is not as simple as it once was. All of these changes have resulted in the development of modern approaches to the concept of leadership. Examining some important modern leadership theories; leadership types such as strategic leadership, servant leadership, transformational leadership, transactional leadership, charismatic leadership, authentic leadership and paternalistic leadership are encountered.

To summarize all of these modern leadership theories;

- Servant leaders are leaders who help their followers discover their own potential by meeting their needs and desires and communicating with them one-on-one to ensure that they achieve their goals (Liden et al., 2008). Being a good listener, empathizing, covering the faults of others, exhibiting conscious behaviors, having strong persuasiveness, being forward-thinking, protective, helping people develop, and creating unity are all qualities (Russell & Stone, 2002).

- Transformational leadership is defined as the process of influencing significant changes in followers' attitudes, beliefs, and values to the point where an organization's goals and the leader's vision are internalized and achieve performances beyond their followers (Gomes, 2014). It is a leadership that is ready for transformation and flexible, transformative creativity, forward-thinking, open to different ideas, people-oriented, intellectually awakening the followers, motivating, changing, and changing according to the necessary situations.
- Transactional leadership is defined as leadership that meets the expectations of the leaders and the needs of the followers in the form of recognition, exchange, or rewards after reaching the predetermined goals (Hussain et al., 2017). It defines the duties and roles of employees, assists them in reaching their goals, provides feedback, and rewards them. Certain sanctions are imposed if the goal is not met.
- Paternalistic leadership is defined as a leadership style that combines strong discipline, authority, and paternalistic intent in a personalized environment (Farh & Cheng, 2000). Paternalistic leadership assumes that managers are exact copies of the "father," a symbol of authority for individuals in the workplace (Sinha, 1990). There are three dimensions to it: paternalistic leadership, authoritarianism, benevolence, and morality (Farh & Cheng, 2000).
- Charismatic leadership approach proposed by Max Weber describes how followers attribute extraordinary qualities (charisma) to leaders. Strong personal characteristics of leaders who use this style include self-assurance, bravery, instilling envy in the audience, the ability to persuade, and motivation (Robbins & Judge, 2013).
- Authentic leadership; The concept of authenticity refers to the fact that the individual has personal experiences, feelings, thoughts, needs, desires, or beliefs and acts with genuine feelings in harmony with his own internal structure. They are self-aware, balanced and impartial, have an internalized moral understanding, and are transparent (Walumbwa et al., 2008).

The following are some of the shortcomings of modern leadership approaches:

- Transformational leadership theory; In order for business processes to be effective, leaders must be able to deceive employees by using transformational leadership elements, provide consistent motivation and feedback, and be able to perform tasks without employee approval.
- Servant Leadership Theory has some weaknesses. There are not many pioneering leaders or managers who have grown up with this philosophy; decisions are skipped due to the involvement of employees in the decision-making process and results are reached in a long time; in crisis situations, personnel often expect leaders to take control and make quick decisions; employees lack confidence or ability to move the business forward.
- Transactional leadership; It has weaknesses such as not being able to provide team spirit due to its individual personality, difficult goals causing disappointment among team members, employees not viewing the leader as a partner or friend, the relationships are unquestionably too professional, and the innovation process is abandoned or reduced if the tasks are too limited.
- Charismatic leadership; The main disadvantage of charismatic leadership is that followers are completely dependent on the leader and are left in the dark after the leader leaves the organization (Ojokuku, Odetayo & Sajuyigbe, 2012).
- Authentic leadership has drawbacks such as being a relatively new approach, the moral components of the approach may result in conflicting goals within the organization, the leader's values

are not always compatible with the organization or its shareholders, and it may impede the organization's ability to make quick decisions.
- Paternalistic leadership has drawbacks such as the inclusion of its employees in their lives being perceived as a violation of privacy, the leaders sometimes having to scold the staff using ineffective methods, and the leader's bad decisions causing high staff dissatisfaction.

Strategic leaders, on the other hand, are visionary leaders with strong stakeholder relationships. In other words, they are leaders who value collaboration in order to effect change that will benefit the organization in the long run. Strategic leaders can rely on anyone who has overall and detailed responsibility for the entire organization. Strategic leadership can be defined as a manager who thinks strategically, collaborates with members of the organization, has a vision, is adaptable, and can create value for the organization's future.

The emergence of Strategic Leadership

In the 1960s and early 1970s, the situation and conditions that businesses faced were thought of as fundamental determinants of managerial behavior and organizational output. In other words, the environmental conditions and amenities of the enterprises were considered sufficient to explain the performance of the business. Compared to the impact of the domestic and international environment of businesses, the directors of the businesses were deemed not to have sufficient skills to make decisions that would affect company performance (Ireland & Hitt 2005).

In addition, the study of leadership between the 1950s and 1980s shows that the supervisors and middle managers of organizations were investigated (Yukl 2002). After the 1980s, the direction of leadership research changed, especially after the mid-1980s when strategic leadership work and senior managers were taken up rather than managerial leadership work (Boal & Hooijberg 2000; Yukl, 2002).

This change in leadership research can be said to have first occurred in Hambrick & Mason's (1984) Upper Echelon Theory. According to Hambrick & Mason (1984), senior executives' age, education, experience, and demographics also influence the strategic decisions they make and the organization's performance. Strategic leadership theory was inspired and developed by the Upper Echelon Theory (Boal & Hooijberg 2000; Vera & Crossan 2004).

Strategic leadership theory treats organizations as a reflection of senior executives, especially the Chief Executive Officer. Many CEOs working in organizations have accepted strategic leadership responsibilities on their own. As strategic leaders of organizations, CEOs' main task is to choose a vision for their organization and create the conditions for achieving that vision. Especially when these choices have had financial successes, these strategic leaders have become known as the heroes of companies. As a result of the globalization of the 21st century, the stagnant and predictable environmental conditions that organizations are in have changed dramatically. While the shift in industries over the past century has taken place in a linear and predictable direction, the competitors of organizations are often local companies, not global ones. The new competitive structure of the global economy has prevented organizations from determining their direction from a single individual's perspective. It has therefore differentiated the structure of 21st-century organizations and strategic leadership practices. The concept of strategic leadership focuses on the people who take full responsibility for the organization. It has grown to include not only title-holder leaders but also senior management teams, dominant groups within the organization (Boal & Hooijberg 2000), board members, and members such as department general managers (Hitt et al., 2007).

Different individuals who will be responsible for building the future of the business are put in the position of strategic leadership in organizations. At this point, senior management teams in particular take on an important role. Senior management teams are small groups of executives (3 to 10 people). The global economy and today's new competitive structure make a common mind to be built by senior management teams necessary for strategic leadership applications. Senior management teams should create a group that will accommodate particularly different qualities within them, and its members should have different knowledge and skills. CEOs will use this different knowledge and skills to successfully manage the organization (Ireland & Hitt, 2005). Of course, the main responsibility for effective strategic leadership will remain at the top, especially with CEOs (Hitt et al., 2007; Swayne et al., 2006).

Concept of Strategic Leadership

The concept of strategic leadership can be explained in the form that the leadership behavior of managers is used in the process of evaluating the strategies of organizations and developing a vision (Birasnav & Biensctok, 2019). It is also seen as strategic leadership, achieving targeted strategic and organizational objectives, inspiring the team leader to carry out operating activities, engaging and commissioning the team in decision-making, and ensuring their motivation (Nyong'a & Maina, 2019). According to Elenkov, Judge & Wright (2006), strategic leadership is a vision for the future; that the leader can relate to his team; the leader's ability to encourage and motivate his followers and organize strategy-backed mutual exchanges between teammates and employees.

According to Jooste & Fourie (2009), strategic leadership refers to the organization's ability to integrate into both the domestic and external environment and manage this complex information process. Furthermore, driven by the notion that strategic leadership is a component of exploring new directions, it is considered to be aware of and exploit opportunities to create value as a result of influential strategic leaders adopting such a thinking structure (Covin & Slevin, 2017).

Nowadays, unlike traditional types of leadership, it brings many benefits for organizations to have managers who have strategic leadership qualities. Strategic leadership appears to have come to the forefront as an important concept that will allow companies to achieve their projected, desired, or intended goals and realize their vision. Therefore, this current concept will attract more attention in the future. In this respect, strategic leadership refers to the ability to integrate the organization's internal and external environment and manage the multifaceted information process (Palladan, Abdulkadir & Chong, 2016). At the same time, a strategic leader qualifies individuals who can communicate effectively with individuals around him and expect high performance from his team (Redmond, 2015). According to Thomas, Schermerhorn, & Dienhart (2004), strategic leaders responsible for "initiating changes" also embrace the goals of building an ethical organizational climate and sustaining it.

On the other hand, a strategic leader becomes an individual who engages in leadership behavior with great desire, as opposed to being led by and dependent on others (Zia-ud-Din, Shabbir, Asif, Bilal, & Raza, 2017). The strategic leader refers to individuals who can see the future and set a greater goal going forward by understanding the current state of the organization. In addition, strategic leaders can connect their strategic orientation with everyday activities and long-term objectives, goals, and concepts (Davies, 2003). As stated by Tone-Hosmer (1982), the strategic leader should create a strategic map of the organization's strategic architecture for the future. Furthermore, the strategic leader must dominate the stages of the implementation of strategies. It should revert from these stages to the backward stages and try to re-implement these strategies by the structure of the environment and the resources the organization has. In a similar vein, as Davies & Davies (2004) highlighted, strategic leaders, can translate strategy into action and form the optimal strategy for the organization.

Strategic leadership by Ireland & Hitt (2005) is defined as the ability to see the future, build vision, ensure flexibility, think strategically and work with others to initiate changes that will create a realizable future for the organization.

Rowe (2001) describes strategic leadership as maintaining short-term financial stability but also the ability to influence others to make the right day-to-day decisions that will enhance the sustainability of the company's existence over the long period. This definition differs from the definition of Ireland & Hitt (2005) in terms of willingness to make decisions and focus on the future until now. According to Sullivan & Harper (1997), strategic leadership is to manage and oversee a sensible and well-thought-out action that exists in the most basic sense of the organization, such as purpose, culture, strategy, core identities, and critical processes.

Guillot (2003) describes strategic leadership as the ability of an experienced senior executive with a mind to create a vision and make important decisions in a complex and uncertain strategic environment.

Hambrick and Pettigrew (2001) mark the two differences between leadership and strategic leadership. Strategic leadership is about people at the senior level of the organization, while leadership is about leaders at all levels of the organization. While leadership is mainly focused on the relationships between the leader and those watching, strategic leadership is more macro-dimensionally not only interested in these relational activities but also focusing on strategic activities.

Hosmer (1982) describes the strategic leader as the person responsible for the organization's strategic management processes (from building strategies to implementing and evaluating and rebuilding performance) based on regularly adapting to changes in environmental, organizational, and managerial attitudes.

Swayne and others (2006) summarize the characteristics of a strategic leader as follows:

- Sets and explains an exciting vision for the future.
- Engages people from all levels of the organization with different experiences in strategic management processes.
- Rules tomorrow more than today.
- The strategic leader devotes time to his employees and tries to understand their problems and talks to them at regular intervals.
- Allows people to make mistakes. Innovation in products, services, and management processes depends on employees taking risks. Sometimes people make mistakes, but it is necessary to strive for success.
- Develops leaders all over the organization. Senior executives encourage their audience to take responsibility for directing the organization and motivating employees.
- Instead of controlling everything to its smallest detail, it relies on others in the organization to make the best decisions.
- It gives time for things to work out.
- The strategic leader sets an example through his behavior.
- Empowers employees to solve problems.

According to Ireland and Hitt (2005), a strategic leader must fulfill the following characteristics:

- Setting the purpose and vision of the organization.
- Uncover and maintain the organization's core skills.
- Developing human resources.
- Maintain an effective organizing culture.
- Highlighting ethical practices.
- Establishing a balanced organizational control.

Figure 1. Strategic Leadership Implementation
Source: Hitt, Ireland and Hiskosson (2007)

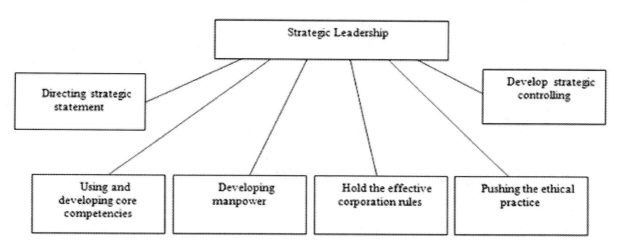

Types of Strategic Leadership

In strategic leadership literature, four key types of strategic leadership are notable; strategic leadership types appear to consist of visionary leadership, directive leadership, incubator leadership, and collaborative leadership (Olson & Simerson, 2015).

Visionary Leadership

Visionary leadership is seen as an effective way to mobilize and motivate followers by persuading individuals to contribute to the future of an organization (Van Knippenberg & Stam, 2014). In this respect, visionary leadership is a dynamic, interactive phenomenon as opposed to a one-way process. Action and communication take place simultaneously (Westley & Mintzberg, 1989). Visionary leadership consists of three key ingredients- creative thinking, self-reliance, and inspiring others (Olson & Simerson, 2015). Within this framework, visionary leaders have high imagination; visionary leaders are individuals who communicate with their team based on their empathy and intuition. Thus, it qualifies individuals who create synergies within the organization while the other hand, who have a good sense of the importance of organizational culture, and who contribute to the sustainability of the organization. While they are proactive and creative, they believe that the decisions they make will make a difference and impact both within the organization and within the organization's external environment. They strive to shape the future and invest in human resources and innovations for this purpose (Redmond, 2015). From this point of view, visionary leaders, one of the strategic leadership types, are individuals who observe environmental developments, can set forth predictions for the future, are creative and can develop solution methods, adapt to environmental changes and developments, and can ensure that both stakeholders and their followers are included in their perspective (Olson & Simerson, 2015).

Directive Leadership

Directive leadership plays an active role in solving problems and in decision-making; in line with decisions taken by the respective leaders, followers are expected to take up positions (Bass & Bass, 2009). In this respect, directive leadership consists of a combination of three key capabilities, critical thinking, organizing by planning, and motivating (Olson & Simerson, 2015). Directive behavior refers to the fact that the duties of the leader's teammates within the team are determined by the leader and delegate relevant duties and powers. In this respect, a directive leader determines how subordinates perform their duties, and then closely follows all stages and outcomes of actual implementation (Muczyk & Reimann, 1987). In this context, the directive leader is to determine the direction of the organization by leveraging the right option to move the organization forward among the alternatives; be able to build a good governance infrastructure by managing roles and processes within the organization to engage the strategy; encourage and motivate members of the team to achieve the expected contribution; predicted against possible developments and risks, and observing performance; (Olson & Simerson, 2015).

Incubator Leadership

Incubator leadership consists of three key components. It covers capabilities that can accurately evaluate the expectations of customers and consumers, value thoughts from different angles and benefit from them to the maximum, and act in a supportive direction of individuals' successful work (Olson & Simerson, 2015). As noted by Schoemaker, Krupp & Howland (2013), is open to innovations and collaborations that are important elements of strategic leadership, and being able to effectively evaluate environmental developments appears to be at the forefront of this type of strategic leadership. In this context, incubator leaders refer to individuals who can network between in-house and out-of-house, carefully evaluate potential risks and opportunities, and contribute to the performance development of individuals included in the team (Olson & Simerson, 2015).

Collaborative Leadership

Collaborative leadership involves effectively attracting, engaging, and guiding individuals or suppliers, customers, partners, and communities in other parts of the organization to achieve common goals (Ibarra & Hansen, 2011). On the other hand, collaborative leadership consists of a combination of three key abilities, the ability to think synthetically, listen effectively, and manage organizational relationships (Olson & Simerson, 2015). The focus of the concept of collaborative leadership is the word "collaboration," which highlights the process of working together. At this point, it refers to a type of strategic leadership based on mutual interaction (Markle-Reid, Dykeman, Ploeg, Stradiotto, Andrews, Bonomo, & Salker, 2017). In this context, collaborative leaders can establish effective relationships with teammates within the institution, be good listener and interpret events through the eyes of others; by meeting a common denominator, enabling individuals to do more than they can on their own; identifies individuals who can share power and authority with teammates and create an environment of trust by empowering people (Olson & Simerson, 2015).

Contributions of Strategic Leadership to Institutions

Strategic leadership is to ensure continuity and harmonious operation of the strategic management process. To maintain a long-term competitive edge, create higher customer value, and achieve the highest levels of profitability, employees at all levels of the institution need to adopt strategic leadership attitudes and behaviors. Strategic leadership contributes to a business at three key points. These are; effectiveness, strategic flexibility, and competitive advantage in the strategic management process.

Effectiveness in the Strategic Management Process:

The change in the competitive field requires continuous consideration of the organizational structure of existing strategic activities, communication systems, organization culture, asset distribution, and investment strategies, in short, all factors that may affect operating activities and long-term health. This change can cause businesses to continue to exist or disappear. That's why the process that determines decisions and actions is important to businesses. This process is called strategic management (Besler, 2004).

Ülgen & Mirze (2004) went to a dual classification of the strategic leadership process, hard elements, and soft elements. Strategic analysis and strategic selection issues have been considered hard elements as they require an objective perspective through analytical analysis. But the process of strategic management is not just made up of hard elements. There is also a human aspect. Those who make, select, and execute strategies are people who have different values, thoughts, and characteristics. They also considered human-related elements in the strategic management process as soft elements. To supporters of this view, the importance of analytical analysis is undeniable. The analysis is crucial to uncover, improve processes and identify options. However, only the analytical approach is not important for success. Large-scale strategies are often the product of different and creative brains. That is why the role of the leader in the strategic management process is so important. The successful execution of the strategic management process requires strategic leadership. Through effective strategic leadership, institutions can successfully conduct the strategic management process. As strategic leaders, senior managers are guided in the stages of determining the vision and mission of the institution. Then these leaders struggle to facilitate the development of appropriate strategic activities. By deciding how to implement the set strategies, they reach the last point where competitive supremacy and above-average revenues are earned (Besler, 2004).

Strategic Flexibility

Today's competitive environment is more dynamic and more complex compared to the 20th century. The ability of institutions to manage these unpredictable changes and uncertainties depends on having the flexibility to adapt quickly to change. The structure of the world's rapidly changing external environment; requires flexibility, speed, and innovation. The greatest contribution to the effectiveness of institutions in both the public and private sectors in this competitive area in the 21st century will be to have a flexible organizational structure. This is partially possible with downsizing. Strategic flexibility is the capacity of institutions to anticipate changing competitive conditions, respond instantly to these conditions, and gain a competitive edge based on them (Hitt, 1999). The dynamic and complex nature of the environment in which the institutions operate mandates that the product or service be delivered to the customer at great speed. Increased competition and growing demands from consumers require institutions to be faster at responding to their competitors. Therefore, through a strategic leadership approach, institutions can develop new products, ensure continuity, and thus gain more market share. Strategic leadership is one of the most important factors that can give an institution the desired flexibility. Through strategic leadership, an institution can adapt its activities to change and exploit different growth opportunities (Besler, 2004).

Competitive Advantage

In the strategy model developed by Michael Porter, one of the world's best-known strategic thinkers, there are fundamentally 5 factors affecting a firm's profitability. These are; competition in the industry, the potential of new entrants into the industry, the power of suppliers, the power of customers, and the threat of substitute products. These five forces together constitute both the profitability of the firm and the structure of the industry. Businesses should examine these factors, which will affect their profitability over the long period, and build competitive strategies accordingly. Porter's competing strategies consist of cost leadership, differentiation, and focusing strategies. The strategic leader's role is crucial to the success of the differentiation strategy, one of Porter's proposed strategies to gain the upper hand in competition (Porter, 1985). In an emerging technology and growing competitive environment, it is not possible for businesses to compete, only with their concentration on enabling their existing activities. Taking advantage by providing the same product or service as current competitors is unlikely in today's competitive environment. Efforts to increase operational effectiveness such as process management, exchange engineering, and benchmarking are necessary but not sufficient to gain the upper hand in the competition. Businesses have to make a difference to be superior to the competition. Those who make, choose, and implement strategies can be leaders with different values, thoughts, and characteristics. So it can be said that strategic leadership is the core function that will enable businesses to thrive in competition by creating a difference. As a result, if the strategic leadership process is hard to understand and emulated by competitors, the business will have achieved its competitive edge. Being superior to the competition and being able to keep it going is the universal goal for all businesses. That strategic leadership can be properly implemented in the competitive space making it easier for the business to generate a very high return on its investments. It is therefore necessary for senior managers to carry out effective strategic leadership practices.

Strategic Leadership in Tourism Enterprises

The tourism product provided by the tourism industry is typically intangible. The consumer has to travel to the area where the tourist product is before they can get it or see it. This is a feature of the tourism product's guiding principles, either synchronicity or non-separation. In this respect, potential visitors who want to experience these products travel to the region, catering businesses, travel businesses, hospitality businesses, transportation businesses, entertainment, sports, and recreational businesses, etc., benefit from facilities such as a positive or negative experience (Gevşek, 2019). These businesses often provide services according to human power. Successful implementation of these services can be achieved through the development of organizational structures and processes within companies in the context of quality of service. As a result, the best way to establish a successful organizational goal can be through the adoption of new applications to improve employer performance. Leadership is the best tool to achieve that goal. The impact that tourism business leaders have on employees is significant for the organization.

Develop leadership skills, as well as develop and implement strategies for gaining customers, gaining a competitive advantage, and delighting investors. Competitive advantage is difficult to obtain in the rapidly changing hospitality industry. Strategic leadership in hospitality necessitates a thorough understanding of the market as well as the ability to develop, evaluate, and implement competitive strategies.

The concept of Leadership influences issues such as understanding the team leader of employees, being efficient leadership, and good behavior of employees and their performance (Çalışkan, 2009). In this respect, employers who are the most important actors in tourism businesses can be successful with an effective team leader with a good quality of service (Güzel, 2009).

Businesses in the tourism sector cannot be isolated from their domestic and international environment. This is why the need to learn about events in their external environment and develop mechanisms for interpreting the events in question is becoming more important every day. For a tourism business to exist in a particular environment, it needs to carefully assess the changes and environmental conditions occurring in this environment. Because the environment of tourism businesses is in rapid change. Advances in technology bring new demands from customers and employees, pressures of globalization are being felt, and tourism products are becoming increasingly diverse. In line with these developments, it will no longer be enough for tourism businesses to be operated through traditional management practices. The life of the business depends on the elements that will support those who run it to be able to sustain life in the long term to the business. These elements depend on managers' environmental adaptation capabilities, environmental analyses, decisions and practices, and, briefly, strategic management skills.

Nowadays, the modern tourism industry aims to improve the structure and processes of organizations according to the quality of service. As such, it is important to try out new management formats to improve employee performance and service quality to create a successful organizational objective in an increasingly competitive environment. Leadership is one of the most critical elements for doing so.

In tourism businesses, leaders' impact on employees, the ability of business employees to understand the leader, the behavior and performance of employees, and the effectiveness of the leader, have shown many organizational outcomes. Employees are the most effective part of the service process in tourism businesses. With the guidance of an effective leader, employees are more successful. An interactivity-oriented perspective in leadership has a key place in the alignment of individual and organizational objectives. Depending on the business, leadership requires different leadership styles to be implemented based on the structure and culture of the business. For example, in small facilities where the culture of efficiency and cost applies, task-context leadership behavior is sufficient for success. In more luxurious facilities, the best approach to improving quality is to build rapport behavior, as a high level of service is expected (Testa, 2008). Appropriate implementation of the required leadership styles within tourism businesses ensures leadership and member engagement. This also helps employees improve their job satisfaction and commitment to the organization. Increasing employee satisfaction reduces the speed of work, which is one of the main problems of the tourism industry, and provides customer satisfaction as a natural cycle.

Tourism businesses try to take advantage of modern management methods and models. So they can address their shortcomings in the financial framework, improve the level of service and performance offered by their businesses, adapt to changes in tourism business environments, and achieve their targeted progress and success. As a result of the literature review, studies on strategic leadership in the tourism sector are also limited. For example, in a study of how high-level managers in the hospitality industry have carried out strategic leadership practices, the academics in tourism have been examined from their perspective. According to academics, it was concluded that executives in the hospitality industry have been successful in effectively utilizing new technologies, one of the practices of strategic leadership. The study was carried out using the survey technique (Kılınç & Agras, 2007).

Vukotic and Vojnovic (2016) have indicated that comprehensive tourism development in the modern age is largely aimed at tourists, customers, and customer satisfaction. So they argued that tourism is one of the world's most profitable industries and has great economic significance for countries. The higher the level of development of countries, the more important the location and role of tourism in the service industry. Therefore, it requires the adoption of a strategic management approach to gain a competitive advantage over other countries.

Strategic management is analyzes factors that influence the internal and external environment of organizations. This will give you a competitive advantage or increase your business benefits. It is one of the leading modern management models today as an organized process that includes assessment, planning, and applications designed accordingly. At this stage, strategic leadership plays an important role in the organization's activities as it contributes to the creation of a suitable organizational climate that affects employee satisfaction. It also contributes to a management environment that helps create individual, group, and organizational goals. The concept of leadership requires an understanding that needs attention to the development of individuals, groups, and the entire organization, as it is a factor that affects the effectiveness and performance of the organization (Zhang & Li, 2013).

To gain a competitive advantage in the tourism industry,

- identify the points intended for future arrival,
- planning,
- support for business strengths
- the elimination of business weaknesses,
- potential opportunities or potential hazards that the business has need to be exposed to.

Strategic leadership differs from other types of leadership in two different ways. The first style of strategic leadership is limited to top executives. Second, managers focus on strategic activities rather than just routine tasks. Hotel executives must have conceptual skills because strategic leadership necessitates them. However, as is well known, the strategy will remain a strategy for as long as it is kept secret. In other words, once the strategy is announced, it loses its ability to function as a strategy. As a result, strategic leadership is critical in the hotel industry.

Strategic leadership provides a competitive advantage in the hotel industry. It also contributes significantly to the effective and efficient execution of activities. At the same time, the strategic leader conducts his operations while keeping changing technology and environmental conditions in mind.

In their study measuring the success of leadership practices implemented in hotels in Canada, Blayney & Blotnicky (2010) discovered that strategic leadership styles are the most effective in raising RevPAR (revenue per available room), which is a critical issue in the tourism industry during an economic downturn.

Hotel leadership styles are important for businesses during a pandemic that affects the entire world. During this time, hotel executives were careful to develop a strategy and vision. Hıdıroglu (2020) stated in his research that the strategic leadership style is the most appropriate leadership style for businesses during the pandemic process, emphasizing the importance of creating a strategy and vision for businesses in particular. In their study, Al Thani & Obeidat (2020) stated that managers should exhibit strategic leadership behaviors in order for businesses to be successful during crisis processes.

Agyapong & Boamah (2013) investigated the direct and interactive effects of business strategies and strategic leadership on the performance of family hotels. According to his research, family hotels in Ghana require strategic leadership in order to thrive in highly competitive business environments by implementing sound business strategies. It also demonstrates that strategic leadership provides family businesses with the ability to "anticipate, envision, maintain flexibility, and empower others to create strategic change as needed." (Hitt et al.., 2005).

Tourism planners must consider unpredictable conditions and unpredictable restrictions when creating strategic plans (Ketchen & Short, 2011). According to Harrington and Ottenbacher (2013), the importance of strategic management and strategic thinking should be taken to assess current and future challenges and opportunities in the tourism industry, and create strategic solutions, to cope with increasing turmoil in the global environment. Studies in the tourism sector are seen to be done in leadership and leadership theories in general rather than in strategic leadership. However, when addressing issues related to the tourism industry, the work on leadership has been seen to be particularly relevant to transformational leadership, which has been a modern leadership approach in recent years. Strategic leadership is seen as a new topic in the tourism sector, where research is being directed.

SOLUTIONS AND RECOMMENDATIONS

The concept of leadership in tourism, a service-intensive industry, can be addressed in a variety of ways for employees, customers, and industry stakeholders. Market conditions that have changed from the past to the present have altered the concept of leadership in tourism over time. To adapt to changing conditions, tourism businesses today strive to improve the efficiency and effectiveness of their employers within their respective organizations. The most important factor in this is the attitude of managers or team leaders toward their employees (Filipova, 2013). Many businesses today, particularly in the tourism industry, require strong leadership. It is predicted that this demand will persist in the future. These businesses will be unable to maintain their continuity unless they adopt a leadership style or approach. Within the business, the concepts of leadership and leadership are more important in this context (Tengilimoglu, 2005). Managers in tourism businesses should exercise strategic leadership to achieve targeted strategic and organizational objectives, as well as to inspire the team by carrying out business activities and incorporating and motivating the team in decision-making. This approach allows business vision workers to develop, focus on the company's vision and mission, develop their creativity, build trust in employers, maintain healthy business communications, and meet the employers' requirements. This also enables employees to be more satisfied with their jobs (Tengilimoglu, 2005). In tourism businesses, it is important to remember that the culture of the organization is frequently made up of leadership styles (Gurdoan & Yavuz, 2013). As a result, managers should adopt a strategic leadership style to foster a culture of a more qualified and interacting organization.

FUTURE RESEARCH DIRECTIONS

The tourism industry encompasses a wide range of activities. This situation should be considered in studies that investigate the concept of strategic leadership in tourism. It is critical to thoroughly investigate strategic leadership not only in the lodging industry, but also in transportation, food and beverage, and travel agencies. At the same time, the future can be conducted to determine which management approach should be used by taking into account the different types of leadership.

CONCLUSION

The concept of strategic leadership, in general, has been examined in this chapter, as has the significance of this leadership for tourism businesses. After the mid-1980s, the process that started with the realization of leadership studies towards strategic leadership studies and senior managers has been examined. The concept of strategic leadership involves conducting business activities to achieve targeted strategic and organizational objectives. The strategic leader inspires the team, puts the team into the decision-making process, and empowers the team to be motivated. In this context, strategic leadership is divided into a variety of things like visionary leadership, directive leadership, incubator leadership, and collaborative leadership. With all of these varieties, strategic leadership has been identified as contributing to organizations in the strategic management process, such as efficiency, strategic flexibility, and competitive advantage. In the tourism industry, studies are seen in the field of leadership and leadership theories in general rather than strategic leadership. Strategic leadership is seen as a new topic in the tourism sector, where research is being directed. However, the implementation of strategic leadership practices in tourism businesses is important in terms of contributing to the establishment of a suitable organizational climate that affects employee satisfaction. It also contributes to a management environment that helps create individual, group, and organizational goals. Strategic leadership has an impact on the effectiveness or performance of individuals, groups, and the entire organization. As a result, businesses require an understanding of the importance of developing the concept of strategic leadership.

REFERENCES

Agyapong, A., & Boamah, R. B. (2013, March/April). Business Strategies And Competitive Advantage Of Family Hotel Businesses In Ghana: The Role Of Strategic Leadership. *Journal of Applied Business Research*, 29(2), 531–544. doi:10.19030/jabr.v29i2.7654

Al Thani, F. B. H., & Obeidat, A. M. (2020). The Impact of Strategic Leadership on Crisis Management. *International Journal of Asian Social Science*, 10(6), 307–326. doi:10.18488/journal.1.2020.106.307.326

Bass, B. M., & Bass, R. (2009). *The Bass Handbook of Leadership: Theory, Research, and Managerial Applications*. Simon and Schuster.

Besler, S. (2004). *İşletmelerde Stratejik Liderlik* [Strategic leadership in Business]. Beta Yay.

Birasnav, M., & Bienstock, J. (2019). Supply Chain Integration, Advanced Manufacturing Technology, and Strategic Leadership: An empirical study. *Computers & Industrial Engineering*, *130*, 142–157. doi:10.1016/j.cie.2019.01.021

Blayney, C., & Blotnicky, K. (2010). Leadership In The Hotel Industry: Evidence From Canada. *International Journal of Management and Marketing Research*, *3*(3), 53–66.

Boal, K. B., & Hooijberg, R. (2000). Strategic Leadership Research: Moving On. *The Leadership Quarterly*, *11*(4), 515–549. doi:10.1016/S1048-9843(00)00057-6

Çalışkan, S. C. (2009). Turizm İşletmelerinde Liderlik Tarzları ve Lider-Üye Etkileşimi Kalitesi (LÜE) Üzerine Bir Çalışma [A Study on Leadership Styles and Leader-Member Interaction Quality (LPI) in Tourism Businesses]. *Trakya Üniversitesi Sosyal Bilimler Dergisi*, *11*(2), 219–241.

Covin, J. G., & Slevin, D. P. (2017). The Entrepreneurial Imperatives of Strategic Leadership. *Strategic Entrepreneurship: Creating a New Mindset*, 307-327.

Davies, B. J., & Davies, B. (2004). Strategic Leadership. *School Leadership & Management*, *24*(1), 29–38. doi:10.1080/1363243042000172804

Elenkov, D. S., Judge, W., & Wright, P. (2005). Strategic Leadership And Executive Innovation Influence: An International Multi-Cluster Comparative Study. *Strategic Management Journal*, *26*(7), 665–682. doi:10.1002mj.469

Farh, J.-L., & Cheng, B.-S. (2000). *A cultural analysis of paternalistic leadership in Chinese organizations. In Management and organizations in the Chinese context*. Palgrave Macmillan.

Filipova, M. (2013). Management style in tourism. *Romanian Economic Business Review*, 1–6.

Gelatt, J. P. (2002). Leadership. In The Development of Management Theory and Practice in The United States (pp. 65-86). Pearson Custom Publishing.

Gevşek, B. (2019). Turizm İşletmelerinde Yönetimin Planlama Fonksiyonunun Önemi [The Importance of the Planning Function of Management in Tourism Businesses]. *Aydın Gastronomy*, *3*(2), 129–135.

Gomes, A. R. (2014). Transformational Leadership: Theory, Research and Application to Sports. In Contemporary Topics and Trends in the Psychology of Sports. Nova Science Publishers.

Griffin, R. W. (2002). *Management*. Houghton Mifflin Company.

Guillot, C. W. (2003). Strategic Leadership: Defining the Challenge. *Air & Space Power Journal*, (Winter), 67–75.

Gürdoğan, A., & Yavuz, E. (2013). Turizm işletmelerinde örgüt kültürü ve liderlik davranışı etkileşimi: Muğla ili'nde bir araştırma [Organizational culture and leadership behavior interaction in tourism businesses: A research in Muğla province]. *Turizm Araştırmaları Dergisi*, *24*(1), 57–69.

Güzel, T. (2009). Turizm İşletmelerinde Liderlik. In Turizm İşletmelerinde Örgütsel Davranış (pp. 121-135). Marmara Kitap Merkezi.

Hambrick, D., & Mason, P. (1984). Upper Echelons: Organization as A Reflection of its Top Managers. *Academy of Management Review, 9*(2), 193–206. doi:10.2307/258434

Harrington, R., Chathoth, P., Ottenbacher, M., & Altinay, B. (2011). *Strategic management research in hospitality and tourism: Past, present, and future.* Academic Press.

Hıdıroğlu, D. (2020). Strategic leadership: Best Practical Leadership Style to Business Strategies in The Period of Covid-19 Epidemic. *Turkish Studies - Social, 15*(4). 1945-1955.

Hitt, M. (Ed.). (1999). *Strategic Management: Competitiveness and Globalization: Concepts and Cases.* South-Western College Pub.

Hitt, M. A., Hoskisson, R. E., & Ireland, R. D. (2007). *Management of Strategy (International Student Edition).* Thomson South-Western.

Hitt, M. A., Ireland, R. D., & Hoskisson, R. E. (2012). *Strategic Management Cases: Competitiveness and Globalization.* South-Western Pub.

Hosmer, L. T. (1982). The Importance of Strategic Leadership. *The Journal of Business Strategy, 3*(2), 47–57. doi:10.1108/eb038966 PMID:10299154

Howel, J. P., & Costley, D. L. (2006). *Understanding Behaviors for Effective Leadership (2.bs.).* Pearson Prentice Hall.

Hussain, S.T., Abbas, J., Lei, S., Haider, M.J., & Akram, T. (2017). Transactional Leadership and Organizational Creativity: Examining the Mediating Role of Knowledge Sharing Behavior. *Cogent Business & Management, 3.*

Ireland, R. D., & Hitt, M. A. (2005). Achieving and Maintaining Strategic Competitiveness in the 21st. Century: The Role of Strategic Leadership. *The Academy of Management Executive, 19*(4), 63–74. doi:10.5465/ame.2005.19417908

Ivancevich, J. M., & Matteson, M. T. (2002). *Organizational Behavior and Management.* McGraw-Hill Irvin.

Jackson, T. (2016). Paternalisticleadership: Themissing link in cross-cultural leadership studies? *International Journal of Cross Cultural Management, 16*(1), 3–7. doi:10.1177/1470595816637701

Jooste, C., & Fourie, B. (2009). The Role of Strategic Leadership in Effective Strategy Implementation: Perceptions of South African Strategic Leaders. *Southern African Business Review, 13*(3), 51–68.

Ketchen, D., & Short, J. (2011). *Mastering Strategic Management. Paperback, December.* Centre for Open Education.

Liden, R. C., Wayne, S. J., Zhao, H., & Henderson, D. (2008). Servant Leadership: Development of a Multidimensional Measure and Multi-Level Assessment. *The Leadership Quarterly, 19*(2), 163. doi:10.1016/j.leaqua.2008.01.006

Luthans, F. (1981). *Organizational Behavior.* McGraw-Hill Book Company.

Markle-Reid, M., Dykeman, C., Ploeg, J., Stradiotto, C. K., Andrews, A., Bonomo, S., & Salker, N. (2017). Collaborative Leadership and the Implementation of Community-based Fall Prevention Initiatives: A Multiple Case Study of Public Health Practice Within Community Groups. *BMC Health Services Research*, *17*(141), 1–12. doi:10.118612913-017-2089-3 PMID:28209143

McGee, J., Thomas, H., & Wilson, D. C. (2010). *Strategy: Analysis and Practice*. McGraw-Hill.

Muczyk, J. P., & Reimann, B. C. (1987). The Case for Directive Leadership. *The Academy of Management Perspectives*, *1*(4), 301–311. doi:10.5465/ame.1987.4275646

Nyong'a, T. M., & Maina, R. (2019). Influence of Strategic Leadership on Strategy Implementation at Kenya Revenue Authority, Southern Region in Kenya. *International Academic Journal of Human Resource and Business Administration*, *3*(5), 128–159.

Ojokuku, R. M., Odetayo, T. A., & Sajuyigbe, A. S. (2012). Impact of leadership style on organizational performance: A case study of Nigerian banks. *American Journal of Business and Management*, *1*(4), 202–207.

Olson, A. K., & Simerson, B. K. (2015). *Leading With Strategic Thinking: Four Ways Effective Leaders Gain Insight, Drive Change, and Get Results. The Oxford Handbook of Leadership*. Oxford University Press. doi:10.1002/9781119153818

Palladan, A. A., Abdulkadir, K. B., & Chong, Y. W. (2016). The Effect of Strategic Leadership, Organization Innovativeness, Information Technology Capability on Effective Strategy Implementation: A Study of Tertiary Institutions in Nigeria. *Journal of Business and Management*, *18*(9), 109–115.

Porter, M. E. (1985). *The Competitive Advantage: Creating and Sustaining Superior Performance*. Free Press.

Redmond, J. (2015). Strategy and the Importance of Strategic Leadership. *Certified Public Accountants*, 1-9.

Robbins, S., & Judge, T. (2013). *Örgütsel Davranış*. Nobel Akademik Yayıncılık.

Rowe, W. G. (2001). Creating Wealth in Organizations: The Role of Strategic Leadership. *The Academy of Management Executive*, *15*(1), 81–94. doi:10.5465/ame.2001.4251395

Russell, R. F., & Stone, A. G. (2002). A Review of Servant Leadership Attributes: Developing A Practical Model. *Leadership and Organization Development Journal*, *23*(3), 146. doi:10.1108/01437730210424

Sammut-Bonnici, T. (2010). Information economy strategies in the mobile telecommunications industry. In S. Segal-Horn & D. Faulkner (Eds.), *Understanding Global Strategy*. Thomson Learning.

Schoemaker, P. J., Krupp, S., & Howland, S. (2013). Strategic leadership: The essential skills. *Harvard Business Review*, *91*(1), 131–134. PMID:23390746

Sinha, J.B.P. (1990). *Work culture in the Indian context*. SAGE Publications Pvt. Limited.

Swayne, L. E., Duncan, W. J., & Ginter, P. M. (2006). *Strategic Management of Health Care Organizations*. Blackwell Publishing.

Tengilimoğlu, D. (2005). Hizmet işletmelerinde liderlik davranışları ile iş doyumu arasındaki ilişkinin belirlenmesine yönelik bir araştırma [A study to determine the relationship between leadership behaviors and job satisfaction in service businesses]. *Gazi Üniversitesi Ticaret ve Turizm Eğitim Fakültesi Dergisi*, (1), 23–45.

Testa, R. M. (2007). A Deeper Look At National Culture and Leadership in the Hospitality Industry. *Hospital Management*, *26*(2), 468–484. doi:10.1016/j.ijhm.2006.11.001

Thomas, T., Schermerhorn, J. R. Jr, & Dienhart, J. W. (2004). Strategic Leadership of Ethical Behavior in Business. *The Academy of Management Perspectives*, *18*(2), 56–66. doi:10.5465/ame.2004.13837425

Tone Hosmer, L. (1982). The Importance of Strategic Leadership. *The Journal of Business Strategy*, *3*(2), 47–57. doi:10.1108/eb038966 PMID:10299154

Ülgen, H., & Mirze, S. K. (2013). İşletmelerde Stratejik Yönetim [Strategic management in Business]. Beta Yay.

Van Knippenberg, D., & Stam, D. (2014). Visionary leadership. In D. V. Day (Ed.), *The Oxford handbook of leadership and organizations* (pp. 241–259). Oxford University Press.

Vera, D., & Crossan, M. (2004). Strategic Leadership and Organizational Learning. *Academy of Management Review*, *29*(2), 222–240. doi:10.2307/20159030

Vukotić, S., & Vojnović, B. (2016). The role and importance of strategic plans in the development of tourism. *International Scientific Conference*, 118-134.

Walumbwa, F., Avolio, B., Gardner, W., Wernsing, T., & Peterson, S. (2008). Authentic Leadership: Development and Validation of a Theory-Based Measure. *Journal of Management*, *34*(1), 95. doi:10.1177/0149206307308913

Westley, F., & Mintzberg, H. (1989). Visionary Leadership and Strategic Management. *Strategic Management Journal*, *10*(S1), 17–32. doi:10.1002mj.4250100704

Yukl, G. (2002). *Leadership in Organization*. Prentice-Hall International, Inc.

Zhang, X., & Li, B. (2013). Organizational Culture and Employee Satisfaction: An Exploratory Study. *International Journal of Trade, Economics, and Finance*, *4*(1), 48–54. doi:10.7763/IJTEF.2013.V4.259

Zia-ud-Din, M., Shabbir, M. A., Asif, S. B., Bilal, M., & Raza, M. (2017). Impact of Strategic Leadership on Employee Performance. *International Journal of Academic Research in Business & Social Sciences*, *7*(6), 8–22. doi:10.6007/IJARBSS/v7-i6/2938

KEY TERMS AND DEFINITIONS

Collaborative Leadership: It is leadership that involves effectively attracting, involving, and directing individuals or suppliers, customers, partners, and communities from other parts of the organization to achieve common goals.

Directive Leadership: It is a leadership style that sets the work to be done, distributes it to its subordinates, explains what it expects of them, sets standards that set the principles of the work to be done, and instructs its subordinates to comply with standard rules and regulations.

Incubator Leadership: It covers capabilities that can accurately evaluate the expectations of customers and consumers, value thoughts from different angles and benefit from them to the maximum, and act in a supportive direction of individuals' successful work.

Strategic Leadership: It is an application where managers develop a vision by using different management styles and facilitating their adaptation to the changing economic and technological climate of their organizations.

Strategic Management: The planned use of a business's resources to achieve the company's goals and objectives.

Strategy: To drive the business and ensure competitive advantage, it is the process of continuously analyzing the business and its environment to determine the objectives that will adapt, plan activities, and re-organize the necessary tools and resources.

Tourism Enterprises: It is defined as economic units that enable the production and marketing of goods and services to meet travel and accommodation needs for a temporary period and other related needs.

Visionary Leadership: It is the ability to create and express a realistic, reliable, attractive future vision for all or a part of the organization.

Chapter 12
Servant Leadership in the Hospitality Industry

Engin Bayraktaroglu
https://orcid.org/0000-0002-9956-2593
Anadolu University, Turkey

ABSTRACT

Servant leadership is a mindset structured on the leaders' desire to serve their followers. Servant leadership is not just a type of leadership; it is a paradigm, a way of life, and an ontological stance that determines the behaviour patterns of leaders. For this reason, when examining servant leadership, it is not enough to talk only about the benefits of leadership. In this study, servant leadership in service industries was evaluated. As a result of this study, which can be considered a non-systematic literature review, theoretical suggestions were made for the future of servant leadership research.

INTRODUCTION

The concept of servant leadership was first used by Greenleaf in leadership research (Spears, 1996; Singfiel, 2018). Greenleaf combines the roles of the servant and the leader in a single concept, emphasizing that every leader is also a follower. In this concept, the servant role outweighs the leadership, and for this reason, the desire to serve lies at the basis of servant leadership (1977). Theories other than servant leadership do not involve leaders' serving desire to their subordinates. The concept of service is used to define a framework: the leader supports his subordinates and struggles in every matter in their favour. Servant leadership includes suggestions to meet subordinates' needs and leaders' support for subordinates to participate in decision-making. Servant leaders start from service behaviour, which is a different way of describing the leader's responsibilities (Vargas & Hanlon, 2007; Savage-Austin & Honeycutt, 2011). Servant leaders have the instinct to serve, and consciously choose to lead (Bass, 2000).

Servant leadership is a new-generation leadership approach that brings about serious changes in the roles of the leaders (Yıldırım, 2019). While many other leadership models focus primarily on the mission and then on empowering followers to achieve that mission, servant leaders focus primarily on developing the abilities of individuals. The success of the mission is put on focus after the empowerment

DOI: 10.4018/978-1-6684-6713-8.ch012

of individuals (Gandolfi & Stone, 2018). Servant leaders are more able to identify the primary needs of their followers and put more effort into meeting them (Farling et al., 1999). Apart from the desire to serve, the servant leader has other remarkable features such as taking initiative, listening, understanding, imagination, acceptance, empathy, intuition, foresight, awareness, perception, persuasion, conceptualization, and community-building skills (Joseph & Winston, 2005). In addition to these, features such as creating a vision, being honest, acting ethically, empowering staff, altruism, emotional healing, and helping the development and success of followers are also attributed to servant leaders (Wong & Page 2003; Patterson 2003; Winston 2003; Liden et al., 2008; Baldonado, 2017).

Individuals are affected by the attitudes, thoughts, and behaviours of the ones they take as role models and internalize their positive behaviours (Bandura, 1977). Servant leaders can influence their followers by acting as role models in the workplace (Hunter et al., 2013), and followers can internalize their leaders' behaviour by modelling them (Liden et al., 2014). There is scientific evidence that a leader-follower relationship that emerges as a result of servant leadership increases employee satisfaction, performance and organizational commitment (Liden et al., 2014; Muller et al., 2018; Schwarz et al., 2016). Servant leaders are influential throughout the organization, affecting both individuals and groups (Hu & Liden, 2011).

In this section, the concept of servant leadership will be examined under the headings of servant leadership dimensions, the characteristics of servant leaders and servant leadership in the hospitality industry. Thus, it is aimed to give an overview of the servant leadership practices encountered in hospitality businesses.

DIMENSIONS OF SERVANT LEADERSHIP

Considering the dimensions of servant leadership, it has been seen that various approaches have been used by different researchers. Eva et al., (2019) identified 16 different measurement tools that included the dimensions of servant leadership. Within the scope of this study, the nine-dimensional structure used by Liden et al., (2008) and Liden et al., (2015); and the six-dimensional structure used by Sendjaya et al., (2008), Sendjaya & Cooper (2011), and Sendjaya et al., (2019) were evaluated.

Liden et al., (2008) interpreted some of the taxonomies made before [such as Page & Wong (2000), Spears & Lawrence (2002), and Barbuto & Wheeler (2006)], and defined servant leadership under 9 dimensions. These dimensions are; (1) emotional healing, (2) creating value for the community, (3) conceptual skills, (4) empowering, (5) helping subordinates grow and succeed, (6) putting subordinates first, (7) behaving ethically, (8) relationships and, (9) servanthood. *The emotional healing* dimension is defined as the act of showing sensitivity to the personal concerns of other individuals. *Creating value for the community* dimension is the leaders' conscious, genuine concern for helping the community. *Empowering* dimension is the act of encouraging and facilitating others in identifying and solving problems while determining how to complete tasks. *Helping subordinates grow and succeed* is the dimension that defines a leader's genuine concern for others' career development by providing support and mentoring. The dimension of *putting subordinates first* can be defined as leaders' use of actions and words to make it clear to others that satisfying their work needs is a priority. *Behaving ethically* dimension expresses how open, fair, and honest are leaders in their relationships with others. *The relationships* dimension can be defined as the genuine efforts of leaders to know, understand, and support others in the organization, with an emphasis on building long-term relationships. *The servanthood* dimension is defined as the way of being marked by one's self-categorization and desire to be characterized by others as someone who serves others first, even when self-sacrifice is required.

Sendjaya et al., (2008), Sendjaya & Cooper (2011), and Sendjaya et al., (2019) structured servant leadership under six dimensions via quantitative studies. These dimensions are; (1) voluntary subordination, (2) authentic self, (3) covenantal relationship, (4) responsible morality, (5) transcendental spirituality and, (6) transforming influence. *Voluntary subordination* refers to the services performed for others without any self-interest with a sincere desire. Servant leaders place the interests and needs of their followers above their own. Servant leaders serve their subordinates voluntarily, not out of necessity, but on their own impulses. Being a servant and acts of service are the sub-components of this dimension. *The authentic self* is the dimension refers that to servant leaders' openness to criticism. Servant leaders respond to criticism positively rather than defensively. Being honest with oneself, humility, integrity, accountability, security, and vulnerability are also among the components of this dimension. *Covenantal relationship* refers to the atmosphere that forms around servant leaders and enables the creation of strong interpersonal relationships. Servant leaders approach their subordinates as equal partners. Subcomponents of this dimension are acceptance, availability, equality, and collaboration. *Responsible morality* expresses the high moral values that servant leaders represent. Thus, it is aimed to accept and follow strong moral values within the organization. Moral reasoning and moral actions are subcomponents of this dimension. *Transcendental spirituality* refers to the leadership characteristics that enable employees to balance their inner worlds and external environments, and in this way find a purpose in their lives through a healthy workplace. Interconnectedness, sense of mission, wholeness and religiousness can be accepted subcomponents of this dimension. *Transforming influence* expresses servant leaders' tendency to minimize barriers that may be resistance to the change they want to make to their followers and organizations. The subcomponents of this dimension are vision, modelling, mentoring, trust, and empowerment.

CHARACTERISTICS OF SERVANT LEADERS

Servant leaders have one-on-one, strong and long-term relations with employees. They define employees' potentials, wishes, needs, and goals, thus helping employees to feel confident and motivated (Sendjaya & Sarros, 2002; Liden et al., 2008). Moral values are the core elements of servant leadership. Servant leaders are more based on moral values such as altruism, humility, and respect (Parolini et al., 2008). Servant leaders' values not only reveal observable traits but also affect their organizations. Personal leadership values such as honesty and integrity play a primary role in establishing interpersonal and organizational trust (Russell, 2001).

Servant leaders care about their followers and desire their empowerment (Vargas & Hanlon, 2007; Gandolfi & Stone, 2018; Eva et. al. 2019). The wants and needs of their followers are important to servant leaders. They also have purposes such as creating a mission and vision in organizations and helping society. These are leaders who adhere to ethical rules, have conceptual abilities, and can empathize (Farling et al., 1999; Page & Wong, 2000; Russell & Stone, 2002; Barbuto & Wheeler, 2006; Spears, 2002; Baykal et al., 2018).

Servant leaders are assertive individuals. They have competent communication and listening skills. They also have strong imaginations and intuition. They are leaders who know to retreat, when necessary, have common sense, have high awareness, and have persuasion ability (Joseph & Winston, 2004).

High conceptual skills contribute to the formation of shared mental frameworks on a team basis. Thus, it becomes easier to focus on common goals (Zaccaro et al, 2001; Baldonado, 2017; Lee et al., 2019).

In addition to these, features such as a tendency to share power, care for group work, reliability and integrity in leadership, and concern for the well-being of subordinates are also attributed to servant leaders (Washington et al., 2006). Undoubtedly, a servant leader who leads to high-performance outputs must be goal-oriented, create a commitment, handle different personality types within the team, and increase the harmony between team members (Mahambe & Engelbrecht, 2014).

SERVANT LEADERSHIP IN HOSPITALITY BUSINESSES

The nature of the hospitality industry is to serve. Therefore, the industry itself is heavily labour-intensive and the relationships formed between leaders and followers (Hemmington, 2007), and the success of these relationships are the very critical elements of the goals (Bavik, 2020). From this point of view, it can be said that servant leadership values overlap significantly with the hospitality industry (Baytok & Ergen, 2013). There has been a rapid increase in servant leadership studies in the last decade. In addition, there are well-structured and recently published review articles (Chon & Zoltan, 2019; Bavik, 2020; Gui et al., 2020). In this part of the study, internal reflections on servant leadership in the hospitality industry will be discussed. In this context, an evaluation was made within the framework of the concepts of service climate, psychological capital, organizational commitment, work engagement, satisfaction, turnover, service quality, performance, organizational citizenship behaviour and creativity. These concepts are also categorized by Gui et al., (2020) as the outcomes of servant leader - follower relationships.

A *service climate*, in which good service is important, is critical for hospitality businesses to achieve their organizational goals (He et al., 2011). Studies show that servant leadership positively affects the service climate within service units (Walumbwa et al., 2010). It is also known that servant leadership positively affects customer service performance (Linuesa-Langreo et al., 2017), firm performance (Huang et al., 2016), and organizational citizenship behaviour (Elche et al., 2020) in the hospitality businesses through the service climate.

Psychological capital refers to the positive psychological attributes of the employee towards the job (Safavi & Bouzari, 2020). There are studies in the literature showing that servant leadership increases the positive psychological capital of hospitality employees (Hsiao et al., 2015; Bouzari & Karatepe, 2017).

Organizational commitment is defined as positive attitudes that bind/attach employees to organizations because of their positive evaluations of work and the workplace (Mottaz, 1988). Research shows that servant leadership affects hospitality employees' commitment to their organizations positively (Jang & Kandampully, 2018). The main reason for this attitude is that employees' commitment to their servant leaders lets them remain in the organization. (Bouzari & Karatepe, 2017).

Work engagement refers to employees' attachment to work physically, emotionally, and cognitively (Shaufeli et al., 2002). It is known that the effective use of servant leadership increases the work engagement of hospitality employees (Ling et al., 2017; Kaya & Karatepe, 2020; Zia et al., 2022). Because hospitality employees are more committed to work, realizing that their servant leader does not put his/her own needs before theirs (Huertas-Valdivia et al., 2021).

Job satisfaction is the pleasurable emotional state that occurs when the job meets the relevant expectations of the employee (Locke, 1969). Research shows that servant leadership increases the job satisfaction of hospitality employees (Ilkhanizadeh & Karatepe, 2018; Karatepe et al., 2019; Fitzgibbon, 2021).

Turnover intention refers to employees' awareness of quitting from his/her organization soon (Mowday et al., 1982). The high labour turnover rate is accepted as one of the most important problems of hospitality businesses (Pelit & Ak, 2018). Research shows that servant leadership and employees' turnover intention has a significant negative relationship (Jang & Kandampully, 2018; Zhang et al., 2019; Karatepe et al., 2019).

Service quality is "defined as the extent to which the service fulfils the needs or expectations of the customers" (Al-Ababneh, 2017). Research from different samples such as Bangladesh, China, South Korea, Turkey etc. shows that servant leadership affects hospitality service quality significantly positively (Koyuncu et al., 2014; Kwak & Kim, 2015; Ling et al., 2016; Qiu & Dooley, 2019; Qiu et al., 2020; Rabiul et al., 2022).

Firm performance refers to the positive or negative outputs that arise as a result of business activities. Research shows that servant leadership behaviours of CEOs have a significant positive effect on hospitality firm performance (Simons & Robertson, 2003; Huang et al., 2016; Ruiz-Palomino et al., 2021). In addition, there is evidence that environmentally specific servant leaders, who are seen as role models of green values, also contribute to the sustainability of organizations (Luu, 2018).

Organizational citizenship behaviour is voluntary behaviour that is not included in the official reward system but is formed by incentives that enable the organization to carry out its activities effectively and exhibited beyond the employment contract and determining job descriptions (Organ, 1997). Research shows that servant leadership has a positive influence on the organizational leadership behaviour of hospitality employees (Ergen, 2013; Baytok & Ergen, 2013; Wu et al., 2013; Kaplan & Uzun, 2017; Qiu & Dooley, 2019; Beğenirbaş & Can Yalçın, 2020; Zia et al., 2022). In addition, there is evidence that it also affects the reduction of negative attitudes that may harm organizational citizenship behaviour, such as presenteeism (Arslaner & Boylu, 2015; Özdemir & Gül Yılmaz, 2019).

Employee creativity refers to the production of novel and useful ideas in the workplace (Tierney et al., 1999). Research show that servant leadership has a positive influence on employee creativity in hospitality enterprises (Linuesa-Langreo et al., 2016; Ye et al., 2018; Ruiz-Palomino & Zoghbi-Manrique-de-Lara, 2020). In addition, there is evidence that top-level servant leadership also helps middle-level managers to demonstrate their own servant-leadership potential (Ling et al., 2016). Nevertheless, it is known that there is a link between environmentally-specific servant leadership and green creativity (Luu, 2020a; Luu, 2020b).

CONCLUSION

Within the scope of this study, servant leadership was defined, the dimensions of servant leadership were examined and the reflections of servant leadership in the hospitality industry were evaluated. At this point, it can be said that it is difficult to define servant leadership as a separate leadership style. From this point of view, it is possible to accept servant leadership as one of the sub-sets used in defining leadership in general means. "Servant leadership is a mindset, a paradigm, a way of leading. It is a way of engaging in an intentional change process through which leaders and followers, joined by a shared purpose, initiate action to pursue a common vision (Laub, 2004: 9). Servant leaders believe in their employees, they coach, teach, inspire, and listen to them (Berry et al., 1994). In the hospitality industry, the leader-employee relationship is stronger as servant leaders support their employees in difficult times (Chung et al., 2010). Servant leadership improves the work performance of hospitality employees (Qiu et al.,

2020). Furthermore, servant leaders increase the skills of frontline employees, which is especially very important to the hospitality industry (Connell, 2001). Thus, servant leadership also leads to increasing firm performance (Huang et al., 2016) by creating desired business outputs such as high-quality customer service (Kwak & Kim, 2015).

In this study, servant leadership has been examined in various dimensions in the context of hospitality industry. Confirmation of the studies conducted in this context on different samples should also be welcomed in terms of the validity of the information obtained. In addition, the consideration of servant leadership within the scope of theories such as social learning theory and social exchange theory has also strengthened the theoretical background in general. However, despite all the results mentioned in the study, more relationships can be tested by diversifying the variables that mediate the effects of servant leadership. Even though as far as author's knowledge, there is no study which links servant leadership with meme theory and memetics. This can be seen as a gap in the literature. Addressing servant leadership with a memetic approach, such as defining servant leader's memeplex or identifying mentoring memes, can provide new horizons in theory.

REFERENCES

Al-Abahneh, M. (2017). Service Quality in the Hospitality Industry. *Journal of Tourism & Hospitality, 6*(1), 1000e133.

Arslaner, E., & Boylu, Y. (2015). İş Hayatında Presenteeism: Otel İşletmeleri Açısından Bir Değerlendirme [Presenteeism in Work Life: An Evaluation in Hotel Industry]. *İşletme Araştırmaları Dergisi, 7*(4), 123-136.

Baldonado, A. M. (2017). Servant Leadership: Learning from Servant Leaders of the Past and Their Impact to the Future. *International Journal of Management Sciences and Business Research, 6*(1), 53–57.

Bandura, A. (1977). Self-efficacy: Toward a unifying theory of behavioral change. *Psychological Review, 84*(2), 191–215. doi:10.1037/0033-295X.84.2.191 PMID:847061

Barbuto, J. E. Jr, & Wheeler, D. W. (2006). Scale Development and Construct Clarification of Servant Leadership. *Group & Organization Management, 31*(3), 300–326. doi:10.1177/1059601106287091

Bass, B. M. (2000). The Future of Leadership in the Learning Organization. *The Journal of Leadership Studies, 7*(3), 18–38. doi:10.1177/107179190000700302

Baykal, E., Zehir, C., & Köle, M. (2018). Effects of Servant Leadership on Gratitude, Empowerment, Innovativeness and Performance: Turkey Example. *Journal of Economy Culture and Society, 57,* 29–52. doi:10.26650/JECS390903

Baytok, A., & Ergen, F.D. (2013). Hizmetkâr Liderliğin Örgütsel Vatandaşlık Davranışına Etkisi: İstanbul ve Afyonkarahisar'daki Beş Yıldızlı Otel İşletmelerinde Bir Araştırma [The Effect of Servant Leadership on Organizational Citizenship Behavior: A Study in Five Star Hotel Enterprisesin İstanbul and Afyonkarahisar]. *İşletme Araştırmaları Dergisi, 5*(4), 105-132.

Beğenirbaş, M., & Can Yalçın, R. (2020). Hizmetkâr Liderlik Algısının Duygusal Emek Üzerine Etkileri: Hizmet Çalışanları Üzerinde Bir Araştırma [The Effects of Servant Leadership Perception on Emotional Labor: A Research on Service Employees]. *Savunma Bilimleri Dergisi., 19*(1), 159–194.

Berry, L. L., Parasuraman, A., & Zeithaml, V. A. (1994). Improving service quality in America: Lessons learned. *The Academy of Management Executive*, 8(2), 32–52. doi:10.5465/ame.1994.9503101072

Bouzari, M., & Karatepe, O. M. (2017). Test of a mediation model of psychological capital among hotel salespeople. *International Journal of Contemporary Hospitality Management*, 29(8), 2178–2197. doi:10.1108/IJCHM-01-2016-0022

Chon, K., & Zoltan, J. (2019). Role of servant leadership in contemporary hospitality. *International Journal of Contemporary Hospitality Management*, 31(8), 3371–3394. doi:10.1108/IJCHM-11-2018-0935

Chung, J. Y., Chang, S. J., Kyle, G. T., & James, P. F. (2010). Justice in the U.S. National Park Service: The Antecedents of Job Satisfaction. *Journal of Park and Recreation Administration*, 28(3), 1–15.

Connell, J. (2001). Growing the right skills through five-star management. *Australian Journal of Hospitality Management*, 8(1), 1–14.

Elche, D., Ruiz-Palomino, P., & Linuesa-Langreo, J. (2020). Servant leadership and organizational citizenship behavior: The mediating effect of empathy and service climate. *International Journal of Contemporary Hospitality Management*, 32(6), 2035–2053. doi:10.1108/IJCHM-05-2019-0501

Ergen, D. (2013). *Hizmetkar Liderliğin Örgütsel Vatandaşlık Davranışına Etkisi: İstanbul ve Afyonkarahisar'daki Beş Yıldızlı Otel İşletmelerinde Bir Araştırma* [The effect of servant leadership on organizational citizenship behavior: A study in five-star hotel enterprises in Istanbul and Afyonkarahisar] [Unpublished Master's Thesis]. Kocatepe Üniversitesi Sosyal Bilimler Enstitüsü, Afyonkarahisar.

Eva, N., Robin, M., Sendjaya, S., Dierendonck, D. V., & Liden, R. C. (2019). Servant Leadership: A Systematic Review and Call for Future Research. *The Leadership Quarterly*, 30(1), 111–132. doi:10.1016/j.leaqua.2018.07.004

Farling, M. L., Stone, A. G., & Winston, B. E. (1999). Servant Leadership: Setting the Stage for Empirical Research. *The Journal of Leadership Studies*, 6(1/2), 49–72. doi:10.1177/107179199900600104

Fitzgibbon, M. (2021). *The Moderating Effect of Self-Esteem on Servant Leadership and Job Outcomes in the Hospitality Industry* [Unpublished Doctoral Dissertation]. Walden University College of Social and Behavioral Sciences, Minneapolis, MN, United States.

Gandolfi, F., & Stone, S. (2018). Leadership, Leadership Styles, and Servant Leadership. *Journal of Management Research*, 18(4), 261–269.

Greenleaf, R. K. (1977). *Servant Leadership: A Journey into The Nature of Legitimate Power and Greatness*. Paulist Press.

Gui, C., Zhang, P., Zou, R., & Ouyang, X. (2021). Servant leadership in hospitality: A meta-analytic review. *Journal of Hospitality Marketing & Management*, 30(4), 438–458. doi:10.1080/19368623.2021.1852641

He, Y., Li, W., & Lai, K. K. (2011). Service climate, employee commitment and customer satisfaction. Evidence from the hospitality industry in China. *International Journal of Contemporary Hospitality Management*, 23(5), 592–607. doi:10.1108/09596111111143359

Hemmington, N. (2007). From service to experience: Understanding and defining the hospitality business. *Service Industries Journal*, *27*(6), 747–755. doi:10.1080/02642060701453221

Hsiao, C., Lee, Y.-H., & Chen, W.-J. (2015). The effect of servant leadership on customer value co-creation: A cross-level analysis of key mediating roles. *Tourism Management*, *49*, 45–57. doi:10.1016/j.tourman.2015.02.012

Hu, J., & Liden, R. (2011). Antecedents of team potency and team effectiveness: An examination of goal and process clarity and servant leadership. *The Journal of Applied Psychology*, *96*(4), 851–862. doi:10.1037/a0022465 PMID:21319877

Huang, J., Li, W., Qiu, C., Yim, F. H., & Wan, J. (2016). The impact of CEO servant leadership on firm performance in the hospitality industry. *International Journal of Contemporary Hospitality Management*, *28*(5), 945–968. doi:10.1108/IJCHM-08-2014-0388

Huertas-Valdivia, I., Gallego-Burín, A. R., Castillo, A., & Ruiz, L. (2021). Why don't high-performance work systems always achieve superior service in hospitality? The key is servant leadership. *Journal of Hospitality and Tourism Management*, *49*, 152–163. doi:10.1016/j.jhtm.2021.09.007

Hunter, E. M., Neubert, M. J., Perry, S. J., Witt, L. A., Penney, L. M., & Weinberger, E. (2013). Servant leaders inspire servant followers: Antecedents and outcomes for employees and the organization. *The Leadership Quarterly*, *24*(2), 316–331. doi:10.1016/j.leaqua.2012.12.001

Ilkhanizadeh, S., & Karatepe, O. M. (2018). Does trust in organization mediate the influence of servant leadership on satisfaction outcomes among flight attendants? *International Journal of Contemporary Hospitality Management*, *30*(10), 3555–3573. doi:10.1108/IJCHM-09-2017-0586

Jang, J., & Kandampully, J. (2018). Reducing employee turnover intention through servant leadership in the restaurant context: A mediation study of affective organizational commitment. *International Journal of Hospitality & Tourism Administration*, *19*(2), 125–141. doi:10.1080/15256480.2017.1305310

Joseph, E. E., & Winston, B. E. (2005). A Correlation of Servant Leadership, Leader Trust, and Organizational Trust. *Leadership and Organization Development Journal*, *26*(1), 6–22. doi:10.1108/01437730510575552

Kaplan, M., & Uzun, A. (2017). Hizmetkar Liderlik Algılamalarının Tükenmişlik Üzerindeki Etkisi: Otel İşletmelerinde Bir Araştırma [The Effect of Perceptions of Servant Leadership on Burnout: A Case of Study in Hotel Businesses]. *Nevşehir Hacı Bektaş Veli Üniversitesi SBE Dergisi*, *7*(1), 14–26.

Karatepe, O. M., Ozturk, A., & Kim, T. T. (2019). Servant leadership, organizational trust, and bank employee outcomes. *Service Industries Journal*, *39*(2), 86–108. doi:10.1080/02642069.2018.1464559

Kaya, B., & Karatepe, O. M. (2020). Does servant leadership better explain work engagement, career satisfaction and adaptive performance than authentic leadership? *International Journal of Contemporary Hospitality Management*, *32*(6), 2075–2095. doi:10.1108/IJCHM-05-2019-0438

Koyuncu, M., Burke, R. J., Astakhova, M., Eren, D., & Cetin, H. (2014). Servant leadership and perceptions of service quality provided by front-line service workers in hotels in Turkey: Achieving competitive advantage. *International Journal of Contemporary Hospitality Management*, *26*(7), 1083–1099. doi:10.1108/IJCHM-06-2013-0238

Kwak, W. J., & Kim, H. (2015). Servant Leadership and Customer Service Quality at Korean Hotels: Multilevel Organizational Citizenship Behavior as a Mediator. *Social Behavior and Personality*, *43*(8), 1287–1298. doi:10.2224bp.2015.43.8.1287

Laub, J. A. (2004). Defining Servant Leadership: A Recommended Typology for Servant Leadership Studies. School of Leadership Studies, Regent University. In *Proceedings of the 2004 Servant Leadership Research Roundtable*. Regent University.

Lee, A., Lyubovnikova, J., Tian, A. W., & Knight, C. (2019). Servant leadership: A meta-analytic examination of incremental contribution, moderation, and mediation. *Journal of Occupational and Organizational Psychology*, *93*(1), 1–44. doi:10.1111/joop.12265

Liden, R. C., Sandy, J. W., Meuser, J. D., Hu, J., Wu, J., & Liao, C. (2015). Servant Leadership: Validation of A Short Form of the SL-28. *The Leadership Quarterly*, *26*(2), 254–269. doi:10.1016/j.leaqua.2014.12.002

Liden, R. C., Sandy, J. W., Zhao, H., & Henderson, D. (2008). Servant Leadership: Development of A Multidimensional Measure and Multi-Level Assessment. *The Leadership Quarterly*, *19*(2), 161–177. doi:10.1016/j.leaqua.2008.01.006

Liden, R. C., Wayne, S. J., Liao, C., & Meuser, J. D. (2014). Servant leadership and serving culture: Influence on individual and unit performance. *Academy of Management Journal*, *57*(5), 1434–1452. doi:10.5465/amj.2013.0034

Liden, R. C., Wayne, S. J., Meuser, J. D., Hu, J., Wu, J., & Liao, C. (2015). Servant leadership: Validation of a short form of the SL-28. *The Leadership Quarterly*, *26*(2), 254–269. doi:10.1016/j.leaqua.2014.12.002

Ling, Q., Lin, M., & Wu, X. (2016). The trickle-down effect of servant leadership on frontline employee service behaviors and performance: A multilevel study of Chinese hotels. *Tourism Management*, *52*, 341–368. doi:10.1016/j.tourman.2015.07.008

Linuesa-Langreo, J., Ruiz-Palomino, P., & Elche, D. (2016). Servant leadership, empowerment climate, and group creativity: A case study in the hospitality industry. *Ramon Llull Journal of Applied Ethics*, *7*, 9–36.

Locke, E. A. (1969). What is job satisfaction? *Organizational Behavior and Human Performance*, *4*(4), 309–336. doi:10.1016/0030-5073(69)90013-0

Luu, T. T. (2018). Activating tourists' citizenship behavior for the environment: The roles of CSR and frontline employees' citizenship behavior for the environment. *Journal of Sustainable Tourism*, *26*(7), 1178–1203. doi:10.1080/09669582.2017.1330337

Luu, T. T. (2020a). Environmentally-specific servant leadership and green creativity among tourism employees: Dual mediation paths. *Journal of Sustainable Tourism*, *28*(1), 86–109. doi:10.1080/09669582.2019.1675674

Luu, T. T. (2020b). Integrating green strategy and green human resource practices to trigger individual and organizational green performance: The role of environmentally-specific servant leadership. *Journal of Sustainable Tourism*, *28*(8), 1193–1222. doi:10.1080/09669582.2020.1729165

Mahembe, B., & Engelbrecht, A. S. (2014). The relationship between servant leadership, organisational citizenship behaviour and team effectiveness. *SA Journal of Industrial Psychology*, *40*(1), 1–10. doi:10.4102ajip.v40i1.1107

Mottaz, C. J. (1988). Determinants of Organizational Commitment. *Human Relations*, *41*(6), 467–482. doi:10.1177/001872678804100604

Mowday, R. T., Porter, L. W., & Steers, R. M. (1982). *Employee-Organization Linkages: The Psychology of Commitment, Absenteeism and Turnover*. Academic Press.

Muller, R., Smith, E., & Lillah, R. (2018). Perceptions Regarding the Impact of Servant Leadership on Organizational Performance in The Eastern Cape. *International Journal of Business and Management Studies*, *10*(1), 56–62.

Organ, W. D. (1997). Organizational Citizenship Behavior: It's Construct Clean-Up Time. *Human Performance*, *10*(2), 85–97. doi:10.120715327043hup1002_2

Özdemir, N., & Yılmaz, E. (2019). Algılanan Hizmetkâr Liderliğin Presentizm (Edimsizlik) Üzerindeki Etkisi: Frigya Bölgesi [The Effects of Perceived Servant Leadership on Presenteeism: Phrygia Region]. *Anatolia: Turizm Araştırmaları Dergisi*, *30*(3), 198–209.

Page, D., & Wong, P. T. P. (2000). A Conceptual Framework for Measuring Servant-Leadership. In S. Adjgibolosoo (Ed.), *The Human Factor in Shaping the Course of History and Development* (pp. 69–109). University Press of America, Inc.

Parolini, J., Patterson, K., & Winston, B. (2009). Distinguishing Between Transformational and Servant Leadership. *Leadership and Organization Development Journal*, *30*(3), 274–291. doi:10.1108/01437730910949544

Patterson, A. K. (2003). Servant Leadership: A Theoretical Model. In *Proceedings of the 2003 Servant Leadership Research Roundtable*. Regent University.

Pelit, E., & Ak, S. (2018). İnsan Kaynakları Yönetimi İşlevi Olarak Personel Bulma, Seçme ve Personeli İşe Yerleştirme ile İlgili Sorunlar: Turizm İşletmeleri Örneğinde Teorik Bir İnceleme [Problems in the Processes of Personnel Recruitment, Selection and Placement as a Function of Human Resources Management: A Theoric Research in the case of Tourism Enterprises]. *İstanbul Aydın Üniversitesi Dergisi*, *10*(2), 39-74.

Qiu, S., & Dooley, L. (2019). Servant leadership: Development and validation of a multidimensional measure in the Chinese hospitality industry. *Leadership and Organization Development Journal*, *40*(2), 193–212. doi:10.1108/LODJ-04-2018-0148

Qiu, S., Dooley, L. M., & Xie, L. (2020). How servant leadership and self-efficacy interact to affect service quality in the hospitality industry: A polynomial regression with response surface analysis. *Tourism Management*, *78*, 104051. doi:10.1016/j.tourman.2019.104051

Rabiul, M. K., Patwary, A. K., Mohamed, A. E., & Rashid, H. (2022). Leadership Styles, Psychological Factors, and Employee Commitment to Service Quality in the Hotel Industry. *Journal of Quality Assurance in Hospitality & Tourism*, *23*(4), 853–881. doi:10.1080/1528008X.2021.1913695

Ruiz-Palomino, P., Gutiérrez-Broncano, S., Jiménez-Estévez, P., & Hernandez-Perlines, F. (2021). CEO servant leadership and strategic service differentiation: The role of high-performance work systems and innovativeness. *Tourism Management Perspectives*, *40*, 100891. doi:10.1016/j.tmp.2021.100891

Ruiz-Palomino, P., & Zoghbi-Manrique-de-Lara, P. (2020). How and when servant leaders fuel creativity: The role of servant attitude and intrinsic motivation. *International Journal of Hospitality Management*, *89*, 102537. doi:10.1016/j.ijhm.2020.102537

Russell, R. F., & Stone, G. A. (2002). A Review of Servant Leadership Attributes: Developing A Practical Model. *Leadership and Organization Development Journal*, *23*(3), 145–157. doi:10.1108/01437730210424

Safavi, H. P., & Bouzari, M. (2020). How can leaders enhance employees' psychological capital? Mediation effect of person-group and person-supervisor fit. *Tourism Management Perspectives*, *33*, 100626. doi:10.1016/j.tmp.2019.100626

Savage-Austin, A. R., & Honeycutt, A. (2011). Servant Leadership: Phenomenological Study of Practices, Experiences, Organizational Effectiveness and Barriers. *Journal of Business & Economics Research*, *9*(1), 49–54. doi:10.19030/jber.v9i1.939

Schaufeli, W. B., Salanova, M., Gonzalez-Roma, V., & Bakker, A. B. (2002). The measurement of engagement and burnout: A two sample confirmatory factor analytic approach. *Journal of Happiness Studies*, *3*(1), 71–92. doi:10.1023/A:1015630930326

Schwarz, G., Newman, A., Cooper, B., & Eva, N. (2016). Servant Leadership and Follower Job Performance: The Mediating Effect of Public Service Motivation. *Public Administration*, *94*(4), 1025–1041. doi:10.1111/padm.12266

Sendjaya, S. (2015). *Personal and organizational excellence through servant leadership: Learning to serve, serving to lead, leading to transform*. Springer. doi:10.1007/978-3-319-16196-9

Sendjaya, S., & Cooper, B. (2011). Servant Leadership Behaviour Scale: A hierarchical model and test of construct validity. *European Journal of Work and Organizational Psychology*, *20*(3), 416–436. doi:10.1080/13594321003590549

Sendjaya, S., Eva, N., Butar Butar, I., Robin, M., & Castles, S. (2019). SLBS-6: Validation of a short form of the servant leadership behavior scale. *Journal of Business Ethics*, *156*(4), 941–956. doi:10.100710551-017-3594-3

Sendjaya, S., & Sarros, J. C. (2002). Servant leadership: Its origin, development, and application in organizations. *Journal of Leadership & Organizational Studies*, *9*(2), 57–64. doi:10.1177/107179190200900205

Sendjaya, S., Sarros, J. C., & Santora, J. C. (2008). Defining and Measuring Servant Leadership Behaviour in Organizations. *Journal of Management Studies*, *45*(2), 402–424. doi:10.1111/j.1467-6486.2007.00761.x

Simons, T., & Robertson, Q. (2003). Why managers should care about fairness: The effects of aggregate justice perceptions on organizational outcomes. *The Journal of Applied Psychology*, *88*(3), 432–443. doi:10.1037/0021-9010.88.3.432 PMID:12814293

Singfiel, J. (2018). When Servant Leaders Appear Laissez-Faire: The Effect of Social Identity Prototypes on Christian Leaders. *The Journal of Applied Christian Leadership*, *12*(1), 64–77.

Spears, L. C. (2002). Introduction: Tracing, the Past, Present and Future of Servant Leadership. In L. C. Spears & M. Lawrence (Eds.), *Focus on Leadership: Servant-Leadership for The Twenty-First Century* (pp. 1–18). John Wiley & Sons.

Spears, L. C., & Lawrence, M. (2002). *Focus on Leadership: Servant-Leadership for the 21st Century*. John Wiley & Sons.

Tierney, P., Farmer, S. M., & Graen, G. B. (1999). An Examination of Leadership and Employee Creativity: The Relevance of Traits and Relationships. *Personnel Psychology*, *52*(3), 591–620. doi:10.1111/j.1744-6570.1999.tb00173.x

Vargas, P. A., & Hanlon, J. (2007). Celebrating a Profession: The Servant Leadership Perspective. *The Journal of Research Administration*, *38*(1), 45–49.

Walumbwa, F. O., Hartnell, C. A., & Oke, A. (2010). Servant leadership, procedural justice climate, service climate, employee attitudes, and organizational citizenship behavior: A cross-level investigation. *The Journal of Applied Psychology*, *95*(3), 517–529. doi:10.1037/a0018867 PMID:20476830

Washington, R. R., Sutton, C. D., & Feild, H. S. (2006). Individual differences in servant leadership: The roles of values and personality. *Leadership and Organization Development Journal*, *27*(8), 700–716. doi:10.1108/01437730610709309

Winston, B. (2003). Extending Patterson's servant leadership model: Explaining how leaders and follower interact in a circular model. In *Proceedings of the 2003 Servant Leadership Research Roundtable*. Regent University.

Wong, P. T. P., & Page, D. (2003). Servant Leadership: An Opponent-Process Model and The Revised Servant Leadership Profile. In *Proceedings of the 2003 Servant Leadership Research Roundtable*. Regent University.

Wu, L.-Z., Tse, E. C.-Y., Fu, P., Kwan, H. K., & Liu, J. (2013). The Impact of Servant Leadership on Hotel Employees' "Servant Behavior. *Cornell Hospitality Quarterly*, *54*(4), 383–395. doi:10.1177/1938965513482519

Ye, Y., Lyu, Y., & He, Y. (2019). Servant leadership and proactive customer service performance. *International Journal of Contemporary Hospitality Management*, *31*(3), 1330–1347. doi:10.1108/IJCHM-03-2018-0180

Yıldırım, K.E. (2019). Hizmetkâr Liderlik ve Çalışan Davranışlarındaki Rolü: Kırgızistan'da Bir Alan Araştırması [Servant Leadership and Its Role in Employee Behavior: A Field Study in Kyrgyzstan]. *İşletme Araştırmaları Dergisi*, *11*(3), 2242-2256.

Zaccaro, S. J. (2001). *The Nature of Executive Leadership: A Conceptual and Empirical Analysis of Success*. American Psychological Association. doi:10.1037/10398-000

Zia, M. Q., Naveed, M., Bashir, M. A., & Iqbal, A. (2022). The influence of servant leadership on employees' outcomes via job embeddedness in hospitality industry. *Journal of Hospitality and Tourism Insights*, *5*(3), 612–628. doi:10.1108/JHTI-01-2021-0003

Chapter 13
Knowledge-Oriented Leadership for Tourist Guidance Professions:
A Conceptual Analysis Based on Specialization

Özcan Zorlu
https://orcid.org/0000-0003-3533-1945
Afyon Kocatepe University, Turkey

Ali Avan
https://orcid.org/0000-0003-4510-3962
Afyon Kocatepe University, Turkey

Engin Aytekin
Afyon Kocatepe University, Turkey

Ahmet Baytok
https://orcid.org/0000-0002-5826-7694
Afyon Kocatepe University, Turkey

ABSTRACT

Combining the dimensions of knowledge-oriented leadership and tourist guidance, this chapter unequivocally renders that tourist guides could be treated as KOLs, provided that they are conscious of the value of knowledge and interpretation. A conceptual analysis was made in order to highlight a thorough comprehension of knowledge-oriented tourist guidance. Accordingly, knowledge-oriented leadership and its relationship with tourist guidance, the profession of tourist guidance and the relevance of the knowledge provided in tourist guidance, and knowledge-based leadership responsibilities of tourist guides were emphasized. This study advances the body of knowledge by demonstrating the necessity of knowledge-based tourist guidance. The researchers asserted that this chapter could benefit leaders in the hospitality and tourism industries as well as the tourist guides who stress the value of knowledge for professional development, employing it as a leadership tool while delivering tours.

DOI: 10.4018/978-1-6684-6713-8.ch013

Knowledge-Oriented Leadership for Tourist Guidance Professions

INTRODUCTION

One of the most fundamental aspects of tourism services that involves a high level of engagement in terms of knowledge exchange is the profession of tourist guidance, which necessitates a multidisciplinary approach. Because of its power to influence followers, the tourist guide profession shares characteristics with leadership. Both leaders and tourist guides inspire their followers with qualities like charisma, transcendental spirituality, trust, humility, visionary behaviors, idealized influence, individualized consideration, and other qualities. Furthermore, the origin of leadership is very closely related to tourist guidance. Because, the term "leadership" is derived from the Anglo-Saxon word leadare which means "to take people on a journey" (Kets de Vries, 1995). Although the concept of leadership is typically addressed in the context of business organizations or work teams, leadership characteristics can be readily recognized in any social group that has a shared objective that needs to be accomplished together. Almost every tourist group needs a leader in order to ensure that the trip is memorable and enjoyable. The reason for this is that a leader has the power to captivate an audience with his or her charm, behaviors, and oddly convincing justifications. A tourist guide today occupies a major function due to his or her skills in tour administration, group inspiration, and knowledge transfer. Therefore, virtually all tourist guides work fervently to persuade their followers that they are ambassadors of the destination. Nonetheless, a participant (tourist) in a group prefers to listen to engaging presentations that contain fresh, original, practical, and topical information. In other words, they require well-versed guides, namely called knowledge leaders.

A knowledge-oriented leader functions the best when he/she effectively shares knowledge throughout the organization. When a leader efficiently spreads knowledge throughout the organization, that leader is most effective. As a result, he or she is widely acknowledged as a source of useful information that advances the goals of the organization. As a result, being a leader and acting in an instructive manner is the first characteristic of knowledge-oriented leaders. Then, they act as role models for everyone in the group and foster an environment that is conducive to learning, supporting the process on both an individual and group level. They successfully address the knowledge as a response. They are thus the system's experts in knowledge flow. Even though the majority of pertinent studies on knowledge-oriented leadership concentrate on business management, these leaders are visible in practically every social group due to their exceptional knowledge level and proficiency in knowledge presentation. The social groups that seek knowledge leaders in terms of their thirst for learning are those that take part in daily trips or package tours. Since tourist guides are the leaders and information sources for tourist trips, knowledge-oriented leadership should be considered in this circumstance. WFTGA, an umbrella organization for tourist guidance worldwide, clearly expresses the knowledge role of tourist guides with the following definition "… *interprets the cultural and natural heritage of an area which person normally possesses an area-specific qualification….*". Supporting this definition, tourist guides take the lead by discussing valuable information, providing explanations of natural, historical, archaeological, and cultural resources, and fostering a learning environment in the group by serving as knowledge facilitators. In this regard, they can exhibit traits that are also present in knowledge-oriented leaders, such as intellectual stimulation and knowledge sharing. This study will emphasize knowledge-oriented leadership and knowledge-based tourist guiding as a result. In light of this, the first heading of the study will provide conceptual foundations for leadership, knowledge-oriented leadership, and particular characteristics of those leaders. On the basis of earlier literature, the profession of tourist guidance and the relevance of the knowledge provided in tourist guidance will next be reviewed. The third heading will focus on the knowledge-based leadership responsibilities of tourist guides. The relationship between knowledgeable tourist guides and specializations will be covered after this heading. Finally, it will showcase a thorough comprehension of knowledge-oriented tourist guidance. The researchers asserted that this chapter could benefit leaders in the hospitality and tourism industries as well as the tourist guides who stress the value of knowledge for professional development, employing it as a leadership tool while delivering tours.

KNOWLEDGE AND KNOWLEDGE ORIENTED LEADERSHIP

Knowledge is viewed as "justified true belief" by Plato (Gao, Li & Clarke, 2008: 4), and a broad and abstract notion discussed for centuries in western philosophy (Alavi & Leidner, 2001: 107). Although knowledge has many multiple interpretations and conceptualizations, it can be summed up as the ordered integration of different data collected by a set of rules and/or processes. It is the techniques formulated through practice and experience (Bhatt, 2001: 70). On the other hand, knowledge is worthless unless it is effectively communicated or transferred during the exchange of messages and responses during communication. People exchange or communicate both explicit and implicit knowledge with others during the communication process, particularly during an interaction. In this context, explicit knowledge is formal, objective knowledge contained in written documents, whereas implicit knowledge is expertise expressed via practices and experiences. Implicit knowledge is inseparable from people, involves competence, and is attained by directed activities and experience (Kane, Ragsdell & Oppenheim, 2006: 142). People exchange this implicit and explicit knowledge in many circumstances during communication or interaction. Additionally, this is the reciprocal sharing of explicit and implicit knowledge in organizational and business environments (Lee et al., 2010: 474). Communicating implicit knowledge from a sender to a receiver or receivers typically marks the beginning of the communication process, which is the socialization of knowledge in an organizational context (Holsapple & Joshi, 1999: 3), and this implicit knowledge is made up of the sympathized knowledge of receivers (Nonaka & Takeuchi, 1995: 72).

Knowledge is one of the most effective ways to attract the target audience and may become invaluable if it is correctly communicated or conveyed. Who can affect the audience more, one would wonder in this situation? One of the ideal responses might be "a leader," as leadership is primarily an influence process, and this implicit knowledge helps people understand what you are saying (Lord & Brown, 2004: 7). Although Bertocci (2009: 70) attempts to create this power as expert power in an organizational context and claims that a leader derives this power from specialized knowledge or advanced education and influences others with this qualification, leaders should have a power that is closely linked to knowledge. As is commonly known, leaders possess a variety of skills that set them apart and are crucial to their followers. Accordingly, when leaders employ the power of knowledge considerably more, they are referred to as knowledge leaders or knowledge-oriented leaders. Hence, knowledge leadership is *an attitude or action – joint or individual, observed, or imputed – that prompts new and important knowledge to be created, shared and utilized* (Mabey, Kulich & Lorenzi-Cioldi, 2012: 2451).

Knowledge leaders, also known as knowledge-oriented leaders (KOLs), blend transformational and transactional leadership styles with elements of motivation and communication (Donate & de Pablo, 2015: 313). Consequently, especially in knowledge-intensive businesses, they are the catalysts and drivers of creative learning. However, it needs to be highlighted that knowledge-oriented leadership is a comparatively modern area of research (Gürlek & Çemberci, 2020: 2820) with increasing attention in recent years (Rehman & Iqbal, 2020: 1733). Furthermore, by performing the study in a business/organizational environment, the majority of knowledge-oriented leadership (KOL) research has centered on the role of those leaders in knowledge management or innovation (Donate & de Pablo, 2015; Sadeghi & Rad, 2018; Shariq, Mukhtar & Anwar, 2018; Naqshbandi & Jasimuddin, 2018; Shehzad, Davis & Shakil, 2021 and so). Therefore, currently, the KOL approach is being discussed within organization management regarding its potential-positive outcomes on the effectiveness of knowledge management and creative innovation.

Nowadays, scholars are highlighting KOLs' capacity for knowledge attraction as they analyze KOLs' stimulating function among the components of intellectual capital, one of the basic strengths of business organizations (Sadeghi & Rad, 2018: 153). Hence, KOLs substantially promote knowledge management channels and initiatives to explore and exploit knowledge throughout the organization through appropriate motivation, effective communication, and strategic staffing (Donate & de Pablo, 2015: 363). Three aspects are adopted by Chuan-Chun et al. (2011: 4400) to characterize KOL behaviors: ideal character and behavior, encouragement and sensible inspiration, and special care. They also highlight the significance of KOLs in organizations in spreading the knowledge management ethos through employee acceptance, respect, and mutual trust. KOLs improve learning in this way by utilizing a variety of tools and distinctive behaviors.

Figure 1. Main dimensions of knowledge-oriented leadership
Source: Viitala, 2004: 537.

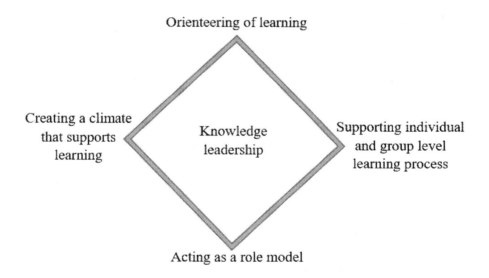

As may be seen in Figure 1, orienting learning, serving as a role model, facilitating the learning process, and creating a supportive climate for learning are four separate elements of KOLs (Viitala, 2004: 534). KOLs, on the other side, should possess interpersonal, leadership, change agent, motivational, and creative qualities. Interpersonal skills here denote effective communication and good relationships with others; leadership skills refer to visionary leadership; change agent skills indicate creating a culture of knowledge sharing; motivational skills delineate inspiring others to recognize the value of and take part in knowledge sharing; and, finally, creativity skills relate to knowledge mapping initiatives and acting as a trailblazer for knowledge transfer (Croteau & Dfouni, 2008: 57-58). With these qualities and abilities,

KOLs can inspire and reward their followers' actions that involve substantial use of knowledge management systems, encourage them in overcoming challenges, and foster interpersonal interactions (Donate et al., 2022: 582). Additionally, they serve as advisors, encourage effective communication regarding the expectations of their followers, inspire people to seek out and share crucial knowledge without concern for penalties, and significantly affect the results of innovation in organizations (Naqshbandi & Jasimuddin, 2018: 709).

It is obvious from the aforementioned justifications that KOLs are essential for implementing knowledge management strategies. This does not, however, imply that KOLs are restricted to businesses. KOLs, on the other hand, can be encountered in any team or organization that is looking for valuable incoming knowledge and needs a boost in communication between team members. Although each group member has unique qualities and personal objectives, they all work for the same objective. Additionally, if a social group communicates well and upholds a common value, they can be prosperous and/or happy. While this is going on, leadership becomes increasingly important when these social groupings are united by shared objectives like enjoyment, lifelong learning, and discovering new communities and cultures. Because these groups generally come together via a special event or social program rather than on a friendly footing, and typically someone who is the outsider leads these groups. In a social setting, a leader can achieve leading function thanks to creating a group atmosphere, giving togetherness, enabling active interaction and communication among members, behaving as a role model, and sharing new and attractive knowledge with group members. Thus, an old-hand leader could enhance the learning atmosphere, stimulate group members to seek new ways of learning, and show an appropriate pattern of behavior to achieve the group's shared goals. Within this context, leaders of social groups have some common characteristics and distinctive features like KOLs. Thus, this point of view provides us with a new insight that asserts KOLs can also be found both in business organizations and in social groups. So, the KOL approach must be searched in the business setting and other aspects.

TOURIST GUIDE AS A LEADER

An essential part of a professional tour, a tourist guide is *a person who guides visitors in the language of their choice and interprets the cultural and natural heritage of an area which person normally possesses an area-specific qualification usually issued and/or recognized by the appropriate authority* (WFTGA, 2003). A tourist guide is an expert who introduces and interprets an area that is attractive to visitors. Although sometimes, tourist guide and tour manager terms are used interchangeably, tourist guide comes to the forefront with his/her specific knowledge while tour manager deals with tour administration (Manning, 2016). Thus, a tourist guide is a professional that finds meaning in some specific traits. Pond (1993: 105-107) summarizes some of these traits as follows:

- *Enthusiasm*: Simply it pertains to a tourist guide's passion for affability and generosity. If a tourist guide is enthusiastic, he/she is inclined to become more knowledgeable about the area that he/she interprets.
- *An outgoing and affable nature*: Due to the fact that they greet, welcome, and provide services to tourists who are unfamiliar with the location, tourist guides are expected to be personable, open, and at ease in a diverse range of situations.

- *Self-confidence*: A self-confident tourist guide should be able to carry out his/her duties effectively, put people at ease, and create enjoyable experiences for the tourist groups.
- *A proactive nature*: Tourist guides must find quick and amenable solutions in case of unpredictable and challenging situations since they are the anchors for tourist groups.
- *Sensitivity*: The best tourist guides are those who can identify with tourists' requirements and comprehend their viewpoints. In particular, they are considerate, tactful, considerate, and perceptive in how they handle the profession.
- *Flexibility*: Tourist guides are both flexible and patient in unpredictable situations and are able to induce tourist groups flexible and patient in these types of situations as well.
- *Authenticity*: Tourist guides need to be professionals who are sincere, and honest and are able to embrace the group with their aura.
- *A pleasant, professional appearance*: Tourist guides must positively impress tourist groups within the first few seconds both with their physical appearance including posture, weight, and stylishness.
- *Sense of humour*: Tourist guides are those who bring humour to the experience and are likely to impress tourist groups in a positive way.
- *Knowledge*: Tourist guides are those who have a comprehensive body of knowledge about not only the visiting area but also the travel industry, cross-cultural understanding, speaking techniques, and marketing.
- *Good communication skills*: The fundamentals of effective communication for tourist guides include a clear speaking voice, eye contact, natural gestures, and articulation. It should be kept in mind that a tourist guide may not be successful in his or her career unless they have excellent communication skills in addition to being knowledgeable and sensitive individuals.
- *Organization*: Because of their diligent preparation, cautious time management, and thorough attention to detail, successful tourist guides carry out a range of tour management-related tasks competently.
- *Decisiveness*: Tourist guides are those who can make appropriate quick and difficult decisions for the achievement of tour programs and customer satisfaction.
- In addition to the key characteristics mentioned above, tourist guides frequently act as charismatic leaders for the tourist group. As a responsible individual, a tourist guide also takes morality and ethics into account in all facets of his or her career.

As was mentioned earlier, leaders of teams or groups that operate within business organizations must possess several characteristics that are also necessary for the tourist guidance profession. Well beyond that, a person with high interpersonal skills who is extroverted, sensitive, feeling, intuitive, resourceful, spontaneous, and outgoing makes a great tourist guide (Manning, 2016). Likewise, they guide tourist groups along the entire itinerary while maintaining constant contact with the visitors. Consequently, tour participants are greatly impacted by the tourist guides (Salha & Ulama, 2019: 184). They serve as a mentor and a pathfinder so that they take on four various leadership responsibilities, including instrumental, social, interactionary, and communicative duties. The crucial function of tourist guides reflects both leading the way and challenging leadership duties including locating and presenting the way, gaining access to the area, influencing guests' actions, and effectively managing the group. The ability to foster group cohesion and morale demonstrates the social function of tourist guides. Tension management, integration, morale, and animation are additional factors that need to be taken into account in relation to social roles. The interactionary role, which is the third function of the tourist guide, entails serving as a liaison between the visitor and locals, landmarks, organizations, and tourist attractions. In terms of interactional duties, tourist guides typically make use of their organizational and representational abilities. The final but most important leadership function of a tourist guide is the communication role. The communicative role includes four principal elements listed below and makes a tourist guide a culture broker (Cohen, 1985: 11-13).

a) Selection: To discover the objects of interest and to pull groups' attention to this.
b) Information: To disseminate the correct and precise knowledge
c) Interpretation: To meet the visitors' expectations and preconceptions about the destination
d) Fabrication: To present souvenirs and other touristic supplies in a manner intended to convince its members that it is the one promised in the program.

Cohen's classification of tourist guides identifies four leadership roles, while Tsaur & Teng's (2017) more thorough investigation uncovered 12 guiding styles, which indicate six distinct leadership roles (Fig. 2). The instrumental role, social role, interactional role, communicative role, dealing with the emergency role, and caring role are the distinguishing leadership functions of tourist guides. The guiding techniques used in the context of the instrumental role include continuous reminders and being completely prepared while being amusing and compassionate. Tourist guides prioritize group members as part of their interactional roles, function as cultural ambassadors, and are articulate and detailed in their communicative roles. The tasks associated with handling emergencies are represented by quick-witted and responsible tourist guides. Finally, the care role of tourist guides basically refers to considering the group members and being customer-oriented during tours (Tsaur & Teng, 2017: 443-444). It is clear from both Cohen's and Tsaur & Teng's conceptualizations that tourist guides exhibit a variety of interconnected leadership responsibilities. Moreover, researchers place a lot more emphasis on the linguistic, social, and instrumental responsibilities played by tourist guides. We can thus argue that these three leadership responsibilities make up the fundamental skills of tourist guides.

Because of the plethora of tasks that go into operating a tour—meeting participants, giving presentations, organizing activities, and looking after the group—tourist guides often multitask in their line of work. They unavoidably act as a leader while providing guidance and display a range of actions related to the four pillars of leadership identified by Cohen in 1985. Güdü Demirbulat (2020: 69), referring to Tetik-Dinç's study in 2019, subsumes under leadership behaviors of tourist guides into two categories as instrumental leadership component and social leadership component (Table 1).

Tourist guides, the vital interface between the destination community and the visitors, functions as a mediator and culture broker. Therefore, they play a cutting-edge role in enhancing the tourism experience of the visitors at the destination in addition to contributing to the cultural understanding of the visitors of the host community of the destination (Ap & Wong, 2001: 551-552). Due to the fact that visitors are alien to the destination, culture, events, artifacts, cuisine, and behaviors of the locals, they are incapable of interpreting this alien world or they will have a less rich or incorrect experience. Yet, if they appropriately and successfully evaluate the information provided by the tourist guides, they may obtain fresh perspectives and a deeper comprehension of the place, its people, and its surroundings (Reisinger & Steiner, 2006: 485-487). At this stage, it starts to matter more and more how a tourist guide shares, disseminates and transfers his or her body of knowledge. El-Sharkawy (2007: 90) asserts that tourist guides can broaden their knowledge base by paying attention to the individual experiences of other tourist guides and travelers, investigating, and researching the local environment, and keeping up with

Figure 2. Distinctive Leadership Roles
Source: Tsaur & Teng, 2017.

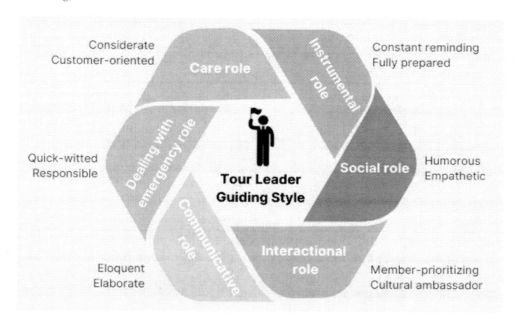

local, national, and international news through the media Thus, in order to conduct tours professionally and appeal to tourist groups, tourist guides must constantly seek out new information. Furthermore, it is accurate that tourist guides cannot develop their expertise unless they pursue specialized information. According to Manning (2016), two sorts of knowledge are necessary to become an expert in tourist guidance. All tourist guides must first be familiar with important information, such as the history of the place, the top attractions, the location of exchange offices, and so forth. Since everyone assumes that a tourist guide is familiar with this quantity of knowledge, if they do not possess it, people will not see them as a tourist guide. In addition to this, tourist guides are required that they be equipped with the information referred to as "small stuff that makes difference for the guiding profession." Small stuff knowledge mostly consists of true, genuine, and fascinating local tales or knowledge for tourists. But tourist guides should track down local storytellers and speak with them to obtain in-depth local accounts in order to obtain all these materials.

They can also use social media to connect with the appropriate person who has the necessary information, museum staff, or both. The accomplishment of guiding in practice will be aided by both significant and minute details. Tourist guides' knowledge of the local area should be enhanced to include general information about the area, the best places to eat, where to go in the evening, and other neighboring attractions (Manning, 2016).

SPECIALIZATION IN TOURIST GUIDANCE

Different people are guided by diverse tourist guides according to their nationality, line of work, degree of education, gender, marital status, and interests. Plus, they guide diversified tours, which are based

Table 1. Tourist Guides' behaviors in the context of leadership

Instrumental leadership component	Social leadership component
• To review and crosscheck the details before the tour • To inform group members of tour type, tour equipment, and the clothes fitted for tour type in advance • To enable the services and deliver them appropriately by making effective time management in advance • To ensure that all documents about the tour are ready and technical issues are solved before departure • To inform group members daily program • To review the weather forecast and other extra conditions (such as controlling the site whether open or closed to visiting) before the tour • To inform group members of safety issues and the potential safety risks • To inform group members of health risks and to have first-aid knowledge • To have knowledge about the potable waters and edible plant species provision for the potential illnesses and poisoning • To make provisions for potential dangers • To explain the tour rules that must be observed both in route and destination. • To inform group members of regulations and prohibitions • To control the group continually in order to keep them together during walking or sightseeing • To use the microphone on the coach • To get the group's opinion about common activities • To make warnings about the products or materials which are prohibited to trade and taken abroad • To have knowledge about procedures and regulations in international tours	• To know the cultural characteristics of the group members • To make short conversations with group members before starting the tour • To behave in a polite manner and flash a smile while communicating with the group members • To behave fair and equal to group members and to keep social distance • To accept critics and concerned feedback • To observe and consider the needs and expectations of group members • To create an ideal atmosphere for the participants that enhance communication and shred social experiences • To create an enjoyable atmosphere for improving the socialization among the members • To crack jokes properly at the right times and places • To improve the socialization of the members with various plays and competitions • To enable equal participation of the members to tour activities • To not pressure group members to make shopping • To avoid polemical and delicate subjects and to change the topic in case of those situations. • To mediate the communication between tour staff and the tourists • To behave preventive about potential conflicts among group members or between the group members and other parties. • To make some surprises to please tourists such as a birthday celebration

Source: Adapted from Güdü Demirbulat (2020: 69)

on tour content. Nevertheless, as a professional, a tourist guide should know each relevant subject. Yet, there are situations when they involve more than just expertise, particularly for specialized tours. Only when a tourist guide possesses the necessary professional knowledge, abilities, and experiences does this specialization become a reality. By reading books, articles, and essays, conducting online searches, and following blogs, tourist guides should attempt to fully comprehend every element within this context (Tanrısever, 2020: 89–90). To fulfill guidance responsibilities and roles at best, a deep and thorough body of knowledge is required for the specialization in tourist guidance. The tourist groups will not be satisfied with a tourist guide who does not broaden his knowledge and is ignorant of current events. In this circumstance, he or she will be a regular tourist guide who adheres to the minimum requirements. The self-development of tourist guides is, however, constrained by a number of factors, including inadequate training and knowledge, a lack of experience, issues with interaction and communication, and issues with leadership (Tanrısever, 2020: 95-97). The first step toward specialization involves self-development. However, there are a large number of opportunities for personal growth in tourist guidance. Some areas of self-development and specialization for tourist guides comprise archeology, history of art, iconography, mythology, history of religions, history of civilizations (Tanrısever, 2020: 95), theology, ethnology, culture, folklore, and architecture (Şahin, 2020: 53). Next, specializing in tourist guidance entails developing an expertise in a particular area, such as the history of Christianity, the local flora, bird migration, or a certain event, like surfing, hunting, diving, or trekking (Köroğlu & Güdü Demirbulat, 2017: 62). From one country to the next, the expertise in tourist guidance takes on distinctive meanings. In addition, despite all of that, expertise is still regarded as a competitive advantage among tourist guides. It has become more accessible (Aslan, 2018: 120). Tourist guides who get the necessary knowledge and use it successfully tend to expand themselves in specialized areas. Following is a summary of these regions by Körolu (2020: 127):

- Specialization in culture-art guidance,
- Specialization in the field of culture route groups,
- Specialization in faith tourism guidance,
- Specialization in museum guidance,
- Specialization in gastronomy tourism guidance,
- Specialization in battlefields tourism guidance,
- Specialization in adventure tourism guidance,
- Specialization in nature tourism guidance,
- Specialization in health tourism guidance,
- Specialization in urban tourism guidance,
- Specialization in overseas tours,
- Specialization in guiding event groups,
- Specialization in guiding cruise groups,
- Specialization in the field of protocol guidance.

As the list put forward, the field of specialization also delivers a broad and deep body of knowledge. The specialization in tourist guidance occurs in several circumstances. For instance, a specialist in faith tourism would need to be well-versed in the religions of the Hittites, Urartians, and Phrygians, as well as Judaism, Christianity, and Islam. Similar to this, a tourist guide should incorporate comprehensive information about regional cuisines, their ingredients, common misconceptions about local foods and cuisine, geographically indicated local foods, and cooking utensils used in the local cuisine. To put it differently, specialist tourist guides should always look for fresh, useful information that sets them apart from other tourist guides. Furthermore, the wealth of knowledge held by specialized tourist guides will support their leadership role and knowledge will be essential to providing advice service.

TOURIST GUIDE AS A KNOWLEDGE-ORIENTED LEADER

As is common knowledge, individuals go on touristic holidays for a number of reasons and anticipate certain results, like rest and relaxation, seeing new locations, healing, and other things. For this reason, tourist experiences provide a brand-new, unusual, distinctive, and thrilling condition for tourists (Rabotic, 2010). Although the expected consequences of vacations can vary depending on the vacation's focus, practically every trip results in increased knowledge and acculturation. In other words, the primary benefit of the tourism experience is discovering and appreciating new cultures. Within this context, people expect to hear genuine and useful information when they experience and enjoy touristic attractions of a destination since they are not acknowledged of the destination's culture, social structure, history, customs, regulations, artifacts, and other touristic assets. For this reason, they are eager to participate in day trips or multi-day excursions organized by licensed individuals known as tourist guides. Because,

Figure 3. A Model for Knowledge-Oriented Tourist Guide

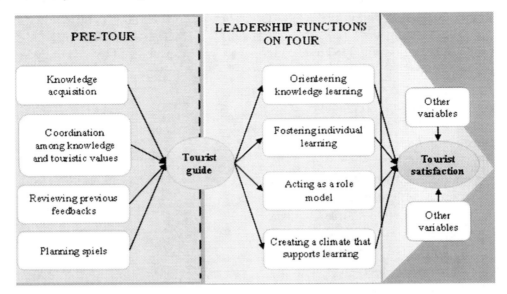

in general, tourist guides are perceived as the sole reliable knowledge sources since they interpret destination attractions and other cultural issues during the tour. Thus, a tourist guide plays a vital role in tourist satisfaction through knowledge sharing and fostering the learning process of tourists. Here, we can assume that, as shown in Figure 3, tourist guides also conduct KOL-like behaviors.

Combining the KOL and tourist guidance aspects, Figure 3 demonstrates unequivocally how tourist guides can act like KOLs so long as they are conscious of the importance of knowledge and interpretation. However, a tourist guide must previously prepare for the tour and possess the necessary knowledge management skills. He or she must therefore arrange some activities before the tour and plan ahead of it. He or she must look for the information in this environment that will be applied to the spiels and conversations. As was already indicated, the amount of knowledge employed in the spiels and conversations varies in terms of the tour's particular subject. Nonetheless, knowledge of regional traditions, culture, destination history, architectural structures, mythologies, and other issues are critical for the big majority of tours. That information can be gathered by tourist guides via websites, books, journals, documentaries, TV shows, and locals. Subsequently, they can grasp this corpus of knowledge from their more experienced co-workers. The content of general spiels and the explanations for each tourist attraction must be decided at this time, which is a major concern. For instance, tourist guides must plan in advance what they will convey on the bus and how they would showcase an ancient theatre or local cuisine. In particular, tourist guides are required to plan their speaking topics and organize their knowledge base. Outstanding and prosperous tourist guides furthermore always take into account earlier reviews. Finally, in order to properly impart knowledge, tourist guides must plan out the topic of their speeches. Although tourist guides have a distinct speaking style for their spiels, each spiel needs to be designed to methodically communicate essential information. The spiel should therefore be organized into paragraphs for the introduction, body, and conclusion, with each paragraph generally relevant to the previous paragraph.

A guided tour becomes precious if only a qualified and specialized tourist guide creates an enjoyable atmosphere for the tourists. On the other hand, this atmosphere makes group members familiar with each other while the tourist guide makes the group willing for learning. Additionally, tourist guides emphasize gaining new knowledge via instructing the group on a certain topic. They act like KOLs as a result without even realizing it. Because one of the fundamental functions of KOLs is to orient learners to new information, just like tourist guides do. Members of the group may wish to hear from the tourist guide more and more as soon as they are willing to discover something new and intriguing. In this instance, the tourist guides may play a supportive role by imparting their invaluable knowledge to members of the group. Here, we may presume that tourist guides encourage personal learning among KOLs, even if this learning process is acknowledged as being transitory. The tourist guide and the tourists instinctively appreciate each other during this learning process. Due to the rules of service, tourist guides always pay respect to the people of their group. They also gain respect through their explanations and demeanour during the service interaction. They serve as role models for tourists because they communicate relevant and new information, demonstrate how to assess a tourism asset, and impart knowledge about how to preserve the environment, culture, and historical artifacts. More noticeably, tourist guides accomplish this primarily by drawing on their extensive knowledge. By the way, it is crucial to state that, tourist guides simultaneously show their instrumental, social, communicative, and care leadership roles in creating a learning atmosphere, fostering learning, and acting as role models. In addition, with rare exceptions, it is worth pointing out that tourist guides inherently foster a learning-friendly environment in groups. As a result, explanations of the roles of tourist guides before and during tours suggest that they frequently exhibit KOL behaviors, and specialization becomes increasingly crucial to providing high-quality services and ensuring the satisfaction of visitors.

CONCLUSION

The weight they hold and the genuine ambiance in such locations are what differentiates experiences and places from one another. The intellectual knowledge communicated about the pertinent experience and destination may allow the meaning to become enduring. Tourists look for authenticity in their experiences and desire to gain knowledge about other cultures, and acquire new and original information, while still seeing and discovering tourist attractions. By serving as a source of knowledge, an interpreter of the natural world, and a cultural ambassador (Ap & Wong, 2001), tourist guides may ensure visitors have unforgettable moments through their knowledge-oriented leadership skills. Acting as knowledge facilitators, tourist guides enhance the learning environment in the group by discussing pertaining facts, analysing natural, historical, archaeological, and cultural assets, and communicating other important information. Consequently, they can also behave as intellectual catalysts for knowledge-sharing, which is a quality of knowledge-oriented leaders. Combining the dimensions of KOL and tourist guidance, this study unequivocally illustrates that tourist guides could treat as KOLs, provided that they are conscious of the value of knowledge and interpretation. The following inferences were drawn according to the viewpoints presented in this study:

- A knowledge-oriented tourist guide should get ready for the tour and be skilful about how to use knowledge efficiently.
- Tourist guides need to pre-decide the content of their spiels for effectively sharing of knowledge.

- Tourist guides should call attention to learning new information and canalize the group on specific knowledge.
- Tourist guides must always respect their group members due to the service rules, while they also earn respect through their explanations and behaviors in the service encounter.
- Tourist guides need to show their instrumental, social, communicative, and care leadership roles simultaneously in creating a learning atmosphere, fostering learning, and acting as role models.

This study advances the body of knowledge by illustrating the necessity of knowledge-based tourist guidance. By implementing a knowledge-oriented leadership attitude, tourist guides may transform into intellectual stimulators of knowledge sharing and through encouraging travellers to learn and seek out new information. A knowledge-oriented tourist guide should plan what knowledge he or she will need for intellectual knowledge transfer before embarking on the tour, establish their spiels on knowledge of regional customs, culture, destination history, architectural structures, myths, and other issues, and consider the previous feedback. Additionally, tourist guides can use the KOL approach's foundations to furnish a rewarding tour in all of its components by supporting tourist-centred learning, orienteering knowledge learning, acting as role models, and establishing a learning environment.

LIMITATIONS AND FUTURE RESEARCH

Though this study comprehensively discusses tourist guides' KOL role, the absence of qualitative or quantitative research methods still constitutes a limitation. The conceptual analysis approach used in this research restricts both revealing potential detailed info from tourist guides and discussing the results of possible findings obtained from data analysis. Also, in the body of the text, other types of leadership styles of tourist guides could have not been discussed in detail, thus correlations among tourist guides' different leadership roles and their potential effect on KOL could not be discussed. The authors also assume that the lack of an extended body of literature focused on the KOL roles of tourist guides limits the comparison of the current findings of this study in more detail.

By considering the limitations of this study, studies consisting of both qualitative and quantitative research methods or at least one of them could be conducted in the future. Additionally, in terms of the KOL of tourist guides, comparative studies that have data from different destinations or different types of tourist guidance could be made. Further, researchers could concentrate on the sub-dimensions of the KOL of tourist guides or investigate the subject with different aspects of tour satisfaction. Finally, the effects of KOL behaviours of tourist guides on experiential tourism, enhancing methods of KOL feature of tourist guides, potential outcomes of KOL behaviours of tourist guides on destination image and destination personality could be research in the future studies.

REFERENCES

Alavi, M., & Leidner, D. E. (2001). Knowledge management and knowledge management systems: Conceptual foundations and research issues. *Management Information Systems Quarterly*, 25(1), 107–136. doi:10.2307/3250961

Ap, J., & Wong, K. K. (2001). Case study on tour guiding: Professionalism, issues, and problems. *Tourism Management*, *22*(5), 551–563. doi:10.1016/S0261-5177(01)00013-9

Aslan, A. (2018). Turist rehberliği ve uzmanlık alanları [Tourist guiding and specialities]. In S. Eser, S. Şahin, & C. Çakıcı (Eds.), *Turist rehberliği* [Tourist guiding] (pp. 119–136). Detay Yayıncılık.

Bertocci, D. I. (2009). *Leadership in organizations: There is a difference between leaders and managers*. University Press of America.

Bhatt, G. D. (2001). Knowledge management in organizations: Examining the interaction between technologies, techniques, and people. *Journal of Knowledge Management*, *5*(1), 68–75. doi:10.1108/13673270110384419

Chuan-Chun, W., Chien-Hsing, W., Chang-Chun, L., & Teng-Hang, H. (2011). Drivers of organizational knowledge management. *African Journal of Business Management*, *5*(11), 4388–4402. doi:10.5897/AJBM10.1415

Cohen, E. (1985). The tourist guide: The origins, structure, and dynamics of a role. *Annals of Tourism Research*, *12*(1), 5–29. doi:10.1016/0160-7383(85)90037-4

Croteau, A. M., & Dfouni, M. (2008). Knowledge management leaders' top issues. In Knowledge management and business strategies: Theoretical frameworks and empirical research (pp. 47-68). IGI Global.

Donate, M. J., & de Pablo, J. D. S. (2015). The role of knowledge-oriented leadership in knowledge management practices and innovation. *Journal of Business Research*, *68*(2), 360–370. doi:10.1016/j.jbusres.2014.06.022

Donate, M. J., González-Mohíno, M., Appio, F. P., & Bernhard, F. (2022). Dealing with knowledge hiding to improve innovation capabilities in the hotel industry: The unconventional role of knowledge-oriented leadership. *Journal of Business Research*, *144*, 572–586. doi:10.1016/j.jbusres.2022.02.001

El-Sharkawy. (2007). Exploring knowledge and skills for tourist guides evidence from Egypt. *Tourismos: An International Multidisciplinary Journal of Tourism*, *2*(2), 77–94.

Gao, F., Li, M., & Clarke, S. (2008). Knowledge, management, and knowledge management in business operations. *Journal of Knowledge Management*, *12*(2), 3–17. doi:10.1108/13673270810859479

Güdü Demirbulat, Ö. (2020). Turist rehberlerinin iş yaşamındaki rolleri ve görevleri [Roles and duties of tourist guides in business life]. In E. Düzgün (Ed.), *Örnek olaylarla turist rehberliği* [*Tourist guidance with case studies*] (pp. 65–85). Detay Yayıncılık.

Gürlek, M., & Çemberci, M. (2020). Understanding the relationships among knowledge-oriented leadership, knowledge management capacity, innovation performance and organizational performance: A serial mediation analysis. *Kybernetes*, *49*(11), 2819–2846. doi:10.1108/K-09-2019-0632

Holsapple, C. W., & Joshi, K. D. (1999). Description and analysis of existing knowledge management frameworks. In *Proceedings of the 32nd Hawaii International Conference on System Sciences* (vol. 1, pp. 1072). 10.1109/HICSS.1999.772796

Kane, H., Ragsdell, G., & Oppenheim, C. (2006). Knowledge management methodologies. *Electronic Journal of Knowledge Management, 4*(2), 141–152.

Kets & de Vries. (1995). *Organizational paradoxes: Clinical approach to management* (2nd ed.). London: Routledge.

Köroğlu, Ö. (2020). *Turist rehberliğinde mesleki gelişim* [Professional development in tourist guidance]. Detay Yayıncılık.

Köroğlu, Ö., & Güdü Demirbulat, Ö. (2017). Rehberlikte sertifikasyon, kalifikasyon ve uzmanlaşma [Certification, qualification and specialization in guidance]. In F. Ö. Güzel, V. Altıntaş, & İ. Şahin (Eds.), *Turist rehberliği araştırmaları: Öngörüler ve uygulamalar* [Tourist guiding research: Insights and applications] (pp. 49–80). Detay Yayıncılık.

Lee, Y., Tao, W., Li, J. Y. Q., & Sun, R. (2020). Enhancing employees' knowledge sharing through diversity-oriented leadership and strategic internal communication during the COVID-19 outbreak. *Journal of Knowledge Management, 25*(6), 1526–1549. doi:10.1108/JKM-06-2020-0483

Lord, R. G., & Brown, D. J. (2004). *Leadership processes and follower self-identity*. Lawrence Erlbaum Associates, Inc.

Mabey, C., Kulich, C., & Lorenzi-Cioldi, F. (2012). Knowledge leadership in global scientific research. *International Journal of Human Resource Management, 23*(12), 2450–2467. doi:10.1080/09585192.2012.668386

Manning, N. (2016). *How to be a tour guide: The Essential manual for tour managers and tour guides*. Nick Manning.

Men, C., & Jia, R. (2021). Knowledge-oriented leadership, team learning, and team creativity: The roles of task interdependence and task complexity. *Leadership and Organization Development Journal, 42*(6), 882–898. doi:10.1108/LODJ-11-2020-0506

Naqshbandi, M. M., & Jasimuddin, S. M. (2018). Knowledge-oriented leadership and open innovation: Role of knowledge management capability in France-based multinationals. *International Business Review, 27*(3), 701–713. doi:10.1016/j.ibusrev.2017.12.001

Nonaka, I., & Takeuchi, H. (1995). *The Knowledge-Creating Company: How Japanese companies create the dynamics of innovation*. Oxford University Press.

Pond, K. L. (1993). *The professional guide: Dynamics of tour guiding*. Van Nostrand Reinhold Company.

Rabotic, B. (2010). *Professional tourist guiding: the importance of interpretation for tourist experiences*. In *20th Biennial International Congress: New Trends in Tourism and Hotel Management*, Opatija, Croatia.

Rehman, U. U., & Iqbal, A. (2020). Nexus of knowledge-oriented leadership, knowledge management, innovation, and organizational performance in higher education. *Business Process Management Journal, 26*(6), 1731–1758. doi:10.1108/BPMJ-07-2019-0274

Reisinger, Y., & Steiner, C. (2006). Reconceptualising interpretation: The role of tour guides in authentic tourism. *Current Issues in Tourism, 9*(6), 481–498. doi:10.2167/cit280.0

Sadeghi, A., & Rad, F. (2018). The role of knowledge-oriented leadership in knowledge management and innovation. *Management Science Letters, 8*(3), 151–160. doi:10.5267/j.msl.2018.1.003

Şahin, S. (2020). Turist rehberinin yetkinlikleri [Competencies of the tourist guide]. In S. Eser, S. Şahin, & C. Çakıcı (Eds.), *Turist rehberliği* [Tourist guidance] (pp. 47–76). Detay Yayıncılık.

Salha, H., & Ulama, Ş. (2019). Turist rehberliğinde liderlik [Leadership in tourist guiding]. In B. Zengin, G. Erkol Bayram, & O. Batman (Eds.), *Turist rehberliği mesleği (dünü-bugünü-yarını)* [Tourist guiding profession (yesterday-today-tomorrow)] (pp. 171–192). Detay Yayıncılık.

Shariq, S. M., Mukhtar, U., & Anwar, S. (2018). Mediating and moderating the impact of goal orientation and emotional intelligence on the relationship of knowledge oriented leadership and knowledge sharing. *Journal of Knowledge Management, 23*(2), 332–350. doi:10.1108/JKM-01-2018-0033

Shehzad, M. U., Davis, K., & Shakil A. M. (2021). Knowledge-oriented leadership and open innovation: the mediating role of knowledge process and infrastructure capability. *International Journal of Innovation Management, 25*(3). doi:10.1142/S1363919621500286

Tanrısever, C. (2020). Turist rehberliğinde kişisel gelişim [Personal development in tourist guidance]. In E. Düzgün (Ed.), *Örnek olaylarla turist rehberliği* [Tourist guidance with case studies] (pp. 65–85). Detay Yayıncılık.

Tsaur, S.-H., & Teng, H.-Y. (2017). Exploring tour guiding styles: The perspective of tour leader roles. *Tourism Management, 59*, 438–448. doi:10.1016/j.tourman.2016.09.005

Viitala, R. (2004). Towards knowledge leadership. *Leadership and Organization Development Journal, 25*(6), 528–544. doi:10.1108/01437730410556761

WFTGA. (2003). *What is a tourist guide?* https://wftga.org/about-us/what-is-a-tourist-guide/

Chapter 14
Leadership in the Kitchen:
Culinary Chefs

Ozan Güngör
Aydın Adnan Menderes University, Turkey

Sinan Yilmaz
Zonguldak Bülent Ecevit University, Turkey

Hakan Yılmaz
https://orcid.org/0000-0002-8512-2757
Anadolu University, Turkey

ABSTRACT

Increased competition has made it an imperative for restaurants to have strong management in the kitchen to ensure competitive success. Being good at preparing food doesn't necessarily mean being a successful manager in the kitchen. A good kitchen manager needs to have a wide range of skills, like math and accounting for calculations associated with menu planning and cost management, managerial skills for organization, leading, and control in the kitchen, along with marketing skills for better understanding and responding to customer demands. There is continuous production in the kitchen management of the staff, and process integration requires the organizational atmosphere to be managed effectively. The performance of the kitchen staff and their workplace motivation is directly related to the leadership style of the kitchen manager. Although accepting that people who are successful at management have innate leadership skills, various research has shown education and training can develop these innate skills or form them if they are not innately possessed.

INTRODUCTION

Increased competition has made it an imperative for restaurants to have strong management in the kitchen to ensure competitive success. Being good at preparing food doesn't necessarily mean being a successful manager in the kitchen. A good kitchen manager needs to have a wide range of skills, like math and

DOI: 10.4018/978-1-6684-6713-8.ch014

accounting for calculations associated with menu planning and cost management, managerial skills for organization, leading and control in the kitchen, along with marketing skills for better understanding and responding to customer demands. Since there is continuous production in the kitchen management of the staff and process integration requires the organizational atmosphere to be managed effectively. The performance of the kitchen staff and their workplace motivation is directly related to the leadership style of the kitchen manager. Although accepting that people who are successful at management have innate leadership skills, various research has shown education and training can develop these innate skills or form them if they are not innately possessed.

LEADERSHIP

The need for a leader, someone to guide and coordinate is the direct result of the social nature of humans. In primitive settings this person can be expected to be the strongest of the group, while in a relatively more advanced stage persons with most knowledge and wisdom, usually the elderly fulfilled this role. Today though, leadership requires much more than physical strength, knowledge, and wisdom. Since the end of the Cold War, globalization and associated diffusion of capital has increased the material welfare of many people around the world, while at the same time altering traditional lifestyles and replacing it with modern alternatives that are global in nature. This has resulted in people having less time and/or desire for meal preparation at home. Also, the higher levels of income, eating out has transformed from mere nourishment to a mechanism for socialization and even experience. This in turn has transformed an industry that was traditionally dominated by small local businesses into a large industry.

DEFINING LEADERSHIP

Social structures created by humans require people who take place in these structures cooperate among themselves in attaining the common goals that underlie these structures. Social structures of all sizes from the family all the way the nation state is built upon members performing their roles and responsibilities in accordance with the common goals. This in turn makes it inevitable that some organization members need to take over the responsibility of directing and managing the other group members and in general keeping them aligned to organizations objectives (Özel, 1998:9). This is in essence the management function labeled leading. Although the act itself is timeless the term leader is relatively new, going back to about 1300s, and the term leadership is much more novel, only appearing in the English language during the first half of the 19th century (Stogdill & Bass, 1981:7).

Owing to the popularity and importance of the topic there is an almost endless variety of definitions for leadership. As Stogdill (1974) puts it there are almost as many different definitions of leadership as there are people who've attempted to define it. Some of the more remarkable of these are, leadership:

"… is the art of influencing (Copeland, 1942), "… consists of relationship between an individual and a group (Knicerbocker, 1948), "… is the process of influencing the activities of an organized group in its effort toward goal setting and goal achievement (Stogdill, 1950)", "… induces a subordinate to behave in a desired manner (Bennis, 1959)", "… is an individual's effort to change the behavior of others (Bass, 1961), "… is interpersonal influence toward the attainment of a special goal or goals (Tannenbaum, 1961)", "… transforms followers, creates visions of the goals that may be attained and articulates for the followers ways to attain these goals. Leadership persons mobilize resources to arouse, engage and satisfy the motives of followers (Burns, 1978)", "… is an interaction and leaders are agents of change whose acts affect other people more than people's acts affect them (Bass, 1994)", "… needs a leader. The only definition of a leader is someone who has followers (Drucker, 19888)", "… refers to a potential or capacity to influence others (Vroom & Jago, 2007)".

Various researchers, in their effort to come up with a general definition of leadership have analyzed the existing definitions to determine common features. Yukl & Gardner (2020), Antonakis & Day (2017) and Northouse (2021) have concluded that the various definitions of leadership agree that; leadership is a process, it is a way of influencing, it needs a group context, and lastly, it aims at reaching a defined goal. Hence it can be said that leadership is the process of influencing the actions of group members towards a specific goal.

Since leadership is based on leading, which itself is a management function, it is inevitable that the concepts of leadership and management are related. Although leading, and what leadership does, is a part of the process of management, the two concepts are not synonymous, i.e., leaders and managers are two distinct type of organization members and there are distinct differences between what leadership and management covers.

IMPORTANCE AND POSITION OF LEADERSHIP IN MANAGEMENT

The necessity for leaders and managers in the management literature centralizes around common themes. The world is undergoing a period of rapid change in political, economic, and social domains. It has become ever more imperative to make efficient use of time, respond to societal demands, ensure motivation in organizations and fulfill management functions. This in turn requires a good management system headed by managers who are effective "leader-managers". These, so labeled, leader managers combine a leader's charisma, managerial skills, expressiveness, strong intuition, far-sightedness, and ability to exploit opportunities and administer people. Recent developments taking place in light of increased globalization make having these characteristics a prerequisite for effective managers (Hakan & Bulut, 2004:154). The increased importance of leadership in the business world can be summarized below (Selimoğlu, 2004):

- The need to adapt to change resulting from the transformation to knowledge societies and synchronizing organization members to these changes, persuading those that resist innovations is an increasingly important skill.
- Being able to take the initiative for speed and flexibility in response to bureaucratic obstacles is becoming an ever more important ability.
- The number of successful managers who are not just able to effectively function in group settings but are also able to persuade other workers that they are an important part of a team and support their innovative and enterprising ideas is increasing in numbers.

Commonly cited as one of the most important functions or components of management, leadership occupies a central place in the topic of management. The behavior exhibited by managers in directing their subordinates towards common goals is a preeminent and indispensable part of their leadership roles (Taşkıran, 2005:39). Both leadership and management involve; conceptualizing what needs to be done, aligning people and resources, taking an active role and creating success (Young & Dulwicz, 2007). There's been a long-running debate on the importance and source of leadership skills. It was traditionally held that people successful in management had innate leadership skills and qualities. Although now accepted to be partially true, much research points out that innate leadership skills can be developed, and nonexistent leadership skills can be acquired over time through training and education (Taşkıran, 2005: 41).

DIFFERENCES BETWEEN LEADERSHIP AND MANAGEMENT

Overtime numerous researchers have examined leadership and management from a multitude of approaches. It has even been suggested that leadership has been studied more extensively than any other domain of human behavior (Kets de Vries, 2001). The current hypercompetitive business environment, along with; recent deformation of formal organizational structures, increasing importance of information and communication, importance of teamwork in project-based workflows, increased customer expectations and product diversification, and frequency of crises have caused to advance leadership as one of the most important topics in organizations (Akyürek, 2020:19). Although management and leadership are frequently used synonymously and often confused for each other, they are intermeshed to a degree and closely related while being two distinct concepts (Uğur, 2014:130).

Although leading is often cited as a function of management, some management scholars choose to distinguish this function as directing. In this manner a clearer distinction between a leader, who motivates and influences people to willingly put forth the effort to obtain organizational goals, and a manager whose authority the workers respond to by putting forth the effort can be made that in most cases while managers can achieve compliance, leaders can achieve performance above and beyond organizational roles require (Clayton W. Barrows Tom Powers & Dennis Reynolds, 2012: 640). Authority by itself does not a leader make. Hence, leadership is seen more as an art.

In specific situations requiring decision-making, managers tend to stick to the roles they've assumed while leaders place more emphasis on thoughts. Managers focus on how things are done, leaders focus on what events and decisions mean for workers. People who've had management training may not be a strong leader, also the corollary that all strong leaders may not be good managers may hold true. Nonetheless, each have their own unique characteristics and functions. In the business world, both leadership and management are indispensable requirements (Özen, 2006:164).

Function wise, both managers and leaders decide what needs to be done and establish necessary transactions with people to ensure this gets done. However, they perform distinct roles in an organization. Managers sustain and control organizations while leaders attempt to shape and change them (Chamoux, 2011:287). This, above all requires vision. The managers task, that of sustaining and controlling the organization implies that they determine and plan for organizational goals, establish and organization chart, staff the positions with appropriate human resources, communicate the plans effectively, delegate authority and establish effective control systems. The leaders task requires getting to know the people, evaluate them, develop them and ensuring that they are placed in appropriate positions (Acar, 2002:107-108).

While management is concerned with ensuring that organizational plans, programs and activities are applied leadership is more concerned with forming a vision and motivating people (Çetin, 2008:25). For success leaders need to communicate a vision and also convince followers to embrace the vision, motivate and encourage them to strive towards the said vision. The only way a leader has of attaining a vision Is by motivating and inspiring people. In short, while leadership is a process of establishing a vision and inspiring, while management is a process more concerned with solving organizational problems (Acar, 2002:108).

There is no guarantee that successful managers will make good leaders, on the other hand successful leaders could very well be mediocre managers. Although both roles have similar characteristics; directing human and organizational resources, they are not the same. As expressed by Warren Bennis & Burt Nanus in 1985 and often cited by others since; "the manager does things right; the leader does the right thing". Or, as Marcouse (2014:68) put it, leaders strive to success in competition through vision and strategy, and it's the manager's job to effectively implement these strategies.

CHEF LEADERSHIP

The question "what makes a leader" has been answered by people in various ways. This results in a variety of efforts to define and explain leadership. In brief, the leader is "the person that influences others' behavior towards certain objectives" (Sabuncuoğlu ve Tüz, 2003). Leadership can be defined as influencing and directing activities of others, under certain conditions, towards attainment of personal or group goals (Koçel, 2007). The leader is a person that influences others and is as old as humanity (Hodgkinson, 1996: 85). When efficiency and effectiveness of groups are considered the need for a leader to unite and coordinate individuals' efforts becomes clearer (Eren, 2008: 525). The trend towards spread of liberalism and globalization since the 1980's has brough into light the need for novel approaches in many areas, resulting in innovation in many areas, among them leadership, where new concepts and trends have appeared since (Saylı & Baytok, 2014). Although the term leader is still widely used to refer to people who perform leadership, novel titles like mentor and coach are also making inroads (Koçel, 2007). Being a good leader requires certain qualities. The common characteristics of good leaders can be listed as (Zengin, Yurdakul, Bayram, Sakarya, & Bağcı: 2021):

- The leader assumes responsibility for the place they work and workers,
- The leader needs to be effective in decision making,
- The leader motivates workers and helps them attain the set goals,
- The leader must have a clear awareness of the environment and a strong vision,
- The leader must be able to decide quickly,
- The leader must be able to form effective teams to ensure success,
- The leader must be able to motivate teamwork,
- The leader must ensure a flexible organizational design,
- The leader must establish balance among workers,
- The leader must seek long-term / sustainable solutions to problem arising in the organization
- The leader needs to mitigate organizational risks as they arise,
- The leader must be able to turn crisis into opportunities and exploit opportunities.

Today it may be incorrect to automatically assume that the kitchen manager of a successful culinary establishment would be a successful master chef. Being a successful kitchen manager requires a range of skills and knowledge. Knowledge of accounting is necessary for menu planning and cost management, management skills are necessary for organization and administration in the kitchen, marketing skills are necessary to develop a deep understanding of customer behavior and satisfaction (Güngör & Atay, 2019:997). Inferior ingredients, inadequate equipment, lack of appropriate working conditions, delay in wages, seasonal employment are just some of the factors that can effect culinary workers performance. Even under such adverse conditions ability in managing a kitchen and exhibiting leadership successfully is directly related to correct leadership style. Also, having a master-apprentice type of staff development mechanism in the kitchen differentiates it from other departments on culinary businesses. The principles of the relationship between apprentice and master are discipline and respect. In kitchens where tolerance for error is low, success results from harmonious teamwork. This in turn is dependent on competency in planning and management which require experience and knowledge of the kitchen.

The famous chef Escoffier states that a chef in a managerial position must be a good organizer, administrator and purchaser. Additionally, it is mentioned that they need to be well informed on diet and nutrition, use this information to design menus, direct personnel in preparation of the food and possess basic mathematical knowledge and must be able to decide quickly and certainly. Ann Cooper, further states that chef must have sills like resiliency, coordination, memory and timing, in addition to being able to consistently apply cooking techniques and taste under stress. (İnce, 2016:419).

HIERARCHY IN THE KITCHEN

Hierarchies form in organization in order to make them manageable. What an organizations hierarchy looks like depend on a number of factors including; their structure, size, number of personnel and size of customer base. Hierarchy serves many functions for organizations. Foremost, the hierarchy in an organization helps establish discipline and enables workers to know their task boundaries. Also, hierarchy indicates the various positions and ranks in the organization and through these workers are able to determine the various superior-subordinate relationships and recognize their responsibilities. By having clear boundaries in task responsibilities as denoted by the hierarchical position's workers are able to be more efficient, also, the existence of superior hierarchical positions to which they can be promoted to can serve to motivate workers. The top position in organizational hierarchy is usually occupied by the proprietor in small businesses, while in medium and large enterprises this position is often staffed by a professional manager (Madenci, 2020:175). Restaurants are special places where delicacies prepared meticulously in professional kitchens are presented. These special places are presented to customers with carefully planned internal design, skilled teams of workers and quality equipment. The main objectives when hosting customers is for everything to be presented perfectly and customers to leave satisfied. These objectives raise the expectations from the team preparing different parts and pieces of the menu in the kitchen while also contributing to the responsibility and power of the kitchen chef who oversees this whole process. The kitchen chef, who occupies the highest position in the restaurant hierarchy, is responsible for the technical equipment, food, including where and how much is sourced, staff, the coordination of all these factors and the budget. Therefore, chefs are expected to be good strategists, organizational planners and leaders (İnce, 2016:419). The professional who is responsible for the administration and management of activities performed in the kitchen is the kitchen chef.

As an example, the kitchen department of a five-star accommodation business would be organized into sections based on the services performed. The hot kitchen section would be responsible for cooking and preparing soups, main courses, warm sauces, rice, pasta and other sides. The butchers section would be responsible for processing meat products and getting them ready to be cooked, the cold kitchen would be responsible for preparing appetizers, salads, cold sauces, cold cuts and kitchen decorations, the patisserie would be responsible for deserts, pastries, breads and fruits. The breakfast section would perform the tasks associated with preparing and serving breakfast, the snack bar would be preparing convenience foods like hamburgers, pizzas and sandwiches, lastly the banquet kitchen would prepare for and cater special events. The processes associated with production and service of food and beverages in an average accommodation business is indeed complex and require a well-planned hierarchy for efficient and effective operation.

During the late 19th century, Aguste Escoffier developed the "Classical Kitchen Hierarchy System" to eliminate the complexity of the tasks performed in the kitchen and establish job definitions. This system organized the kitchen into departments and classified chefs according to these departments, and forms the basis of kitchen organization. According to this system the kitchen is divided into departments and chefs according to the type of food prepared, preparation method employed and equipment used. Escoffier established the hierarchy by putting the whole kitchen under the responsibility of a master chef with subordinate assistant chefs responsible for each of the departments (Kazankodu, 2021:43). Over time there have been much discussion about the importance and sources of leadership skills. Also, different leadership styles are determined by the management model adopted.

Figure 1 represents the general hierarchy in a generic kitchen setting. Thanks to French chefs who have had immense contributions to the field most terminology is also French in origin and has diffused throughout the world in either original or a modified form. In French the person who manages and administrates over the whole kitchen is the "Chef de Cuisine", also the English language title "Executive Chef" is used to denote the same position. The assistant, or second in line to the "Chef de Cuisine" is called the "Sous Chef". Master Chefs who hold responsibility and authority over departmental areas like warm, cold, pastry, butchery or breakfast etc., are called the "Chef de Partie". Chefs who are moving towards becoming master chefs in their career development are called "Demi Chef", while those who are new in the profession and are training as apprentices are called "Apprenti". There are also high school and university students who take part in the kitchen as part of their professional education in the capacity of interns and they are called "Trainess". Depending on the size of the culinary business and the skill level and diversity employed the horizontal extent of the organizational hierarchy can expand to allow for a greater number of departments and specialties.

TYPES OF POWER IN THE KITCHEN AND LEADERSHIP

Power is the ability to influence others. Leaders use power and effective leaders know how to use power (Ataman, 2001:455). Power can arise from extraordinary talent, seniority in the organization, proximity and relationship with others in power, along with many other factors (Hicks & Gullet, 1981:46). Power does not necessarily mean the coercion of subordinates, but rather an opportunity for leaders to influence and motivate people (Hogg, 2001:186). French and Raven (1959) identify five bases of power in their seminal work. These bases of power also form the taxonomy of power types used by leaders to influence, direct, reward or punish. The five power types identified are; legitimate power, reward power, coercive power, referent power, and expert power.

Legitimate Power: This power is also known as "positional power" because it's based on the individual's relative position in the organizational hierarchy and the duties associated with the position (Ataman, 2001:455). This power is used to ensure attainment of organizational goals (Holdford, 2003).

Leadership in the Kitchen

Figure 1. General Kitchen Hierarchy Used Today

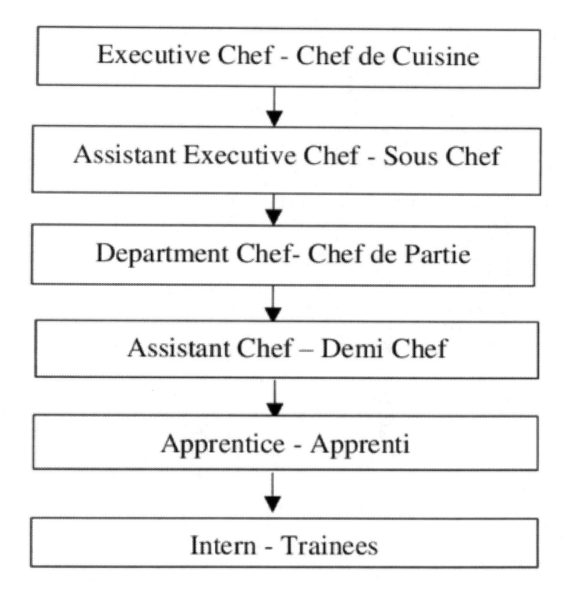

For example, the power held by a kitchen chef in an accommodation business is usually more effective than those of other department managers.

Reward Power: This power derives from the leader's ability to confer valued material needs and satisfy followers needs. In other words, this power manifests itself in workers following managers instructions because they feel they'll receive a reward for doing what's demanded of them (Ataman, 2001:455).

The ability to influence promotion in rank, controlling work schedules, issuance of bonuses etc. make kitchen chefs powerful from workers perspectives.

Coercive Power: This is the converse of reward power; it arises from the ability to demote or withhold rewards. The desire for rewards and/or fear of losing them influences or motivates the follower towards a certain behavior. This heading can be used to cover just about everything that causes fear among the group members (Koçel, 2007:543). In the kitchen the ability to warn, dock pay and terminate employment are some of the methods the chef can use as punishment.

Expert Power: Expert power is the individuals power driving from their skill, expertise, or experience. If the subordinates perceive the leader to be highly skilled, knowledgeable, or experienced they become more willing to be influenced (Ataman, 2001:455). Problem solving behavior tend to make kitchen chef more effective from the workers perspectives.

Charismatic Power: This refers to the power or ability of individuals to influence others through characteristic features like charisma (Taşkıran, 2005:51). Referent power is a form of reverence gained as a result of interpersonal relationship skills and traits that makes the power holder attractive to others. In leadership charisma excites followers and forms the basis of the leaders' effects (Kets de Vries, 2007:238). The distinct costume of the kitchen chef can serve as an example of a charismatic feature by new apprentices.

In respect to a kitchen chef, legitimate, reward and coercive powers are powers bestowed by the employer. Expert and charismatic powers are innate powers. Using these powers the leader rewards, directs or in case of infringements punishes workers. Kitchen chefs who learn to effectively use these forces are more successful in their careers and over time can build solid follower base.

FACTOR EFFECTING LEADERSHIP STYLE CHOICE IN THE KITCHEN

Although the internal dynamics of each kitchen tend to be unique, they all have a common shared point. Even across diverse geographies what makes a kitchen strong is respect for the master. Despite the fact that culinary professions are built upon master-apprentice relationship each chef is likely to have a unique leadership style. What enriches these styles are the leader's personality, live view, communication with subordinates, work environment, workers' expectations from the chef, among other variables that ultimately shape different leadership and managerial styles exhibited by different chefs.

Managerial leadership styles tend to be a conscious choice. A number of criteria weigh in on the choice (Warner, 1993:111-112):

Personality of the Manager: Managers, who are a product of their experiences, are inclined to certain types of behavior while having difficulty or uncomfortable with other certain types of behavior.

Manager's Philosophy of Life: The life philosophy embraced by the manager will serve to guide their beliefs, values, and behavior. Morally strict may be able to do things that a sensitive person may not even consider.

Characteristics of Work Group: The manager needs to be aware of individual distinct characteristics of team members.

Manager-Subordinate Relationship: The interactions between leader and followers require special approach.

Managers Influence on People with Organizational Authority: To ensure that leadership efforts are not wasted organizational authority needs to stand behind decisions and important organization members support is necessary.

Manager's Relations with other Departments: In complex enterprises, negotiation and conformance are among daily tasks.

Task Requirements and Work Environment: Available resources and challenges faced by effective leadership vary by conditions.

Organizations Requirements: Organizational philosophy and climate effect leadership style.

Leadership Style Desired by the Group: The leader and the manager survive according to the wishes of team members.

Working environment generally effects workers' expectations from the leader in addition to the leadership style choice of the leader. Effective leaders take into consideration workers' expectations and establishes a management style that will ensure maximum effectiveness.

TRADITIONAL LEADERSHIP STYLES IN THE KITCHEN

Continuum of Leadership is a concept that has its roots in Robert Tannenbaum and Warren H. Schmidt's research in Harvard University in the 1950s. Acording to this concept the leadership style of leader takes place on a continuum ranging from autocratic to laissez faire type of leadership with democratic leadership somewhere in the middle. The continuum suggests that the level of freedom that a manager gives to a team and the level of authority are inversely related. As the team's freedom increases the managers authority decreases and vice versa (Başaran, 1998). Kitchen chefs who have classical managerial views tend to reflect this in their leadership styles and exhibit one of these three leadership styles.

Autocratic Leadership: This is the style of leadership utilized by managers who prefer an oppressive style to make sure absolute compliance to their decisions by subordinates (Akat, 1984). Autocratic leaders prefer to take all decisions themselves and all courses of actions are also determined by the leader. Since all these decisions courses are at the leader's prerogative, followers face much uncertainty about the course of action to be taken at any point in the future beyond what has been communicated to them. All the tasks and collaborations of each follower are determined by the leader (Avcı & Yaşar, 2016:192). These managers issue command without consulting the group, often fail to communicate effectively with the group and make all decisions unilaterally (Özkalp, 1988). More often than not these types of managers are focused on their self-interests and tend to constantly oppress their subordinates (Akat, 1984). Kitchen chefs who embrace this leadership style tend not to like it when subordinates respond or talk back at ahem. They want whatever they say to be done. They do not like to delegate and have little communication with their subordinates. They resort to legitimate and coercive powers to ensure workers performance. In these types of situations the workers' performance tend to be low while the likelihood of then making errors tend to be high. The kitchens run by these types of chefs do not foster team spirit or teamwork, workers rarely stray out of their expected roles and hardly ever use initiative and seek responsibility. Since all work is performed under the chain of command no one dares to challenge the chef.

Democratic Leadership: The popularity of this leadership style increased parallel to the diffusion of neo-classical management which places emphasis on human relations (Bakan et al., 2013). This type of leader shares authority with group members (Eren, 2003), consults the group before acting and respects group members opinions (Özkalp, 1988), and lets decisions be influenced and shaped by group members' opinions (Başaran, 1998). Democratic leadership is seen as a favorable leadership style since it creates a positive organizational climate and motivates subordinates by including them in decisions. Democratic leaders increase subordinates' engagement and enthusiasm through delegation of authority. This type of leadership behavior also contributes to subordinates' training while at the same time freeing up more time for themselves to focus on principle issues by delegating authority and decision making to subordinates (Arıkan, 2002:242). Although kitchen chefs who subscribe to this leadership style have more communication with their subordinates, they are rarely open to change and innovation. Frequently these chefs experienced autocratic chefs in their apprenticeships and do not see their experience as being "right". Chefs who listen to and demonstrate their appreciation of subordinates, delegate authority and responsibility to ensure their development. Although they tend to respect the team's decisions the final say rests with them. The tend to protect subordinates' rights and try to act with justice.

Laissez-faire leadership: Also known as hands off leadership, is where leaders don't overhold authority and delegate all authority to the followers (Eren, 2003). This style, while flexible, expressive, motivating and encouraging innovation, can also cause negative outcomes like incoordination, goal ambiguity, lack of control and low level of cooperation (Taşkıran, 2005). Hands off leaders give complete freedom to followers. In doing so, they tend to avoid followers' questions and don't give input to their decisions. Organizations with this type of leadership often have many structural problems, are often ineffective and followers' satisfaction levels tend to be low. Work output both quantitatively and qualitatively tend to be low. Hands management style is generally cited as the management style with lowest level of satisfaction and inefficient. Followers are usually isolated from leaders who take very little part, if any in decision-making. Allowing freedom in organizations may result in lack of control and organizational sanctions allowing personal objectives superseding organizational ones (Oğuz, 2011:383). Kitchen chefs who adopt this leadership style are usually relaxed and open. They fully support their subordinates and employ their ideas and skills. Since they are open to all subordinates opinions there usually is no singular objective in the team. Since these types of leaders don't like to tackle problems they useullay avoid problems and leave them to sort themselves out. Although most subordinates tend to like chefs with this leadership approach in critical times these leaders can cause discord and arguments in the team by not being clear and leaving decisions to subordinates.

MODERN LEADERSHIP STYLES IN THE KITCHEN

New leadership concepts and approaches have supplemented and, in some cases, replaced traditional ones. Highly educated, expressive, empathetic, rational kitchen chefs who employ modern managerial and leadership styles are given preference by workers over those employing traditional styles. Depending on their personal characteristics they are beginning to embrace transformational, transactional, and charismatic leadership styles.

Transformative Leadership: According to Burns, transformative leadership happens when one or a few people inspire each other or followers to a higher motivation or morality (Yavuz, 2000:52). Transformative leadership is a leadership style that enables rapid and effective change in an organization. This leadership is more geared towards enabling learning and innovation than control and coordination of internal environment of an organization (Buluç, 2009:13). Transformational leadership rewards workers through intrinsic motivation that is not connected to material value. It bases reward on personal values like justice, order, fairness, etc. (Erkuş & Günlü, 2008:190). Transformational leaders aim to improve efficiency by discovering and developing followers skills, and increasing their motivations (Sabuncuoğlu & Tüz, 2003). They imprint a sense of mission and vision on their followers. They convince followers that by being aware of their potential they can do a better job (Eren, 2003). Most chefs with this leadership style tend to be better educated and informed, perhaps as a result of leadership training. They tend to like researching and innovation. They try to keep the team active and busy at all times. They assist their subordinates in setting and attaining career goals while also contributing to their professional and personal development.

Transactional Leadership: This type of leadership understands the followers' expectations and offers a clearly defined reward contingent on attaining the expected level of performance (Yavuz & Tokmak, 2009). In transactional leadership the leader gives the followers what they want in return for the performance the leader expects. The relationship between them is characterized by reciprocity. For the followers meeting the leaders demands is very important since reward, or punishment, is contingent on meeting expectations. On the other hand, the leader too, must frequently satisfy the followers demands. Transactional leaderships success depends on the leader's ability to keep track of and adopt to changing follower needs (Eraslan, 2006:6). Transactional leadership depends on the legitimate authority of the leaders afforded to them due to their positions in the organizational hierarchy. This type of leader emphasizes work standards, predetermined tasks, and work goals (Taşkıran, 2005). Transactional leadership is based on reciprocal interaction between leaders and followers. This proves provides for satisfaction of followers needs contingent on their exhibiting the expected performance (Wofford, 1998). Managers who adopt transactional leadership style use their authority to motivate and reward followers for higher performance through contingent rewards such as money or status (Eren, 2003). These leaders focus on tax completion and trust the system of reward and punishment in the organization to effect followers' performance (Taşkıran, 2005). Kitchen chefs who embrace this leadership style place great emphasis on rules. They have a professional approach to management and rarely get their emotions involved. They work in a goal-performance focused manner. Their communications with subordinates are usually simple and open. Since they rarely involve emotions in work, as far as they're concerned reward and punishment are mere tools.

Charismatic Leadership: The charismatic leader is the person that can use their charismatic traits to influence others to behave in the manner they want and motivate them to higher performance (Koçel, 2007). Charismatic leaders transform followers' needs, values, aspirations, and resources from individual interests to collective interest. In response the followers form a sincere commitment to the leader's mission. Followers trust their leaders, place great importance on values and increase their motivation. Another definition describes charismatic leaders as guides who inspire and reassure, venerable, arousing optimism about the future, facilitate followers see what really matters in their lives, narrate a sense of mission, exhibit motivating behavior (Oktay & Gül, 2003:405). Charismatic leaders are successful alliance builders, capable of empathy with their followers, makes time to listen to followers regardless of how busy they may be, make them feel valued and arouse feelings of comfort and peace of being heard (Kets de Vries, 2007). Kitchen chefs demonstrating this type of leadership tend to use all their powers well. Even in meting out punishment to their subordinates they're afforded understanding by the subordinates. Their teams tend to perform without objection. They are also good role models for their workers. They act in accordance with their team and this in turn strengthens the team. The tend to fully trust their subordinates. These types of leaders who tend to have excellent observation shills follow their subordinates closely and are able to predict what they think and how they feel and as a result is able to help them. They don't dwell on problems, instead focusing on solutions.

CONCLUSION

The history of the kitchen which has been a part of human society from the first seeds of civilization is as old as that of humanity. In addition to being a place that satiates people's hunger and provide daily energy needs it's held number of missions. From the great feasts preceding a societies mobilization for war to grand tables where peace terms are discussed, communal meals marking important milestones from the arrival of a baby to wedding feasts where joy is shared, to even sharing of grief after the passing of a loved one, all the culinary traditions of civilizations require a kitchen for the preparations. The management of the said kitchen and the leadership in the said setting raises curiosity when viewed from this perspective.

The people who prepare meals in the kitchen are called cooks, or chefs. The titles applied towards these people, namely master and chef denote two different set and levels of skills. Although generically, people who prepare food are called cooks, those who know how meals are prepared, what each ingredient is, the various cooking methods and can teach how each dish is prepared is a master. The cook who knows why dishes are prepared in the manner they are prepared, the business operations of the kitchen and can teach this is called a chef. Hence the question of how to become a chef, what skills are necessary to be a chef and how leadership in the kitchen works become pertinent questions in culinary science.

Becoming a kitchen chef requires knowing how a kitchen is managed and having the various additional skills that help in managing a kitchen. A good chef knows their staff, is able to motivate them to work effectively and efficiently under pressure, can manage crises, able to maintain discipline in the kitchen while being considered as reliable, honest, fair and respectable by subordinates. If the work environment is multicultural, cultural literacy and knowledge of a common switch language is also necessary.

The kitchen chef needs to be able to contribute to both professional and personal development of his staff and for this, in addition to the necessary professional knowledge, they need to have necessary general knowledge to inspire and guide their subordinates. They need the skill necessary to ensure that the menus they prepare contribute to professional development of their staff while at the same time meet the customers' demands. They need to have mastery of kitchen mathematics, be competent in the purchasing processes, and the necessary accounting and managerial skills to be able to adequately report kitchen operations to higher up executives in the organization. A person well rounded in all these areas and can build confidence in the organization is a kitchen chef.

Kitchen operations comprise several processes. Being able to use time effectively, being able to manage the process efficiently are skills that arise from experience, which is gained gradually. A very important proverb of the kitchen is that one cannot be the master of what they have not apprenticed in. This implies that the necessary body of knowledge and experience is built over time, step by step. Therefore, being a successful chef and leader in the kitchen requires patience and internalizing each of the positions of the organizational hierarchy.

REFERENCES

Acar, B. (2002). *Ekip Çalışması ve Liderlik*. Remzi Kitabevi.

Akat, İ. (1984). *İşletme Yönetimi*. İzmir: Üç el dağıtımcılık.

Akyürek, M. İ. (2020). İnovasyon ve Liderlik. *Uluslararası Liderlik Çalışmaları Dergisi. Kuram ve Uygulama, 3*(1), 5–24.

Antonakis, J., & Day, V. D. (2017). *The Nature of Leadership*. Academic Press.

Arıkan, S. (2001). Otoriter ve Demokratik Liderlik Tarzları Açısından Atatürk'ün Liderlik Davranışlarının Değerlendirilmesi. *H.Ü. İktisadi ve İdari Bilimler Fakültesi Dergisi, 19*(1), 231-257.

Ataman, G. (2001). *İşletme Yönetimi-Temel Kavramalar-Yeni Yaklaşımlar*. Türkmen Kitapevi.

Avcı, Ö., & Yaşar, Y. (2016). Bir Kamu Kuruluşunda Çalışanların Liderlik Algıları: Olgubilimsel Bir Yaklaşım. *Akademik İncelemeler Dergisi, 11*(1), 187–205. doi:10.17550/aid.52620

Bakan, İ., & Bulut, Y. (2004). Yöneticilerin Uyguladıkları Liderlik Yaklaşımlarına Yönelik Algılamalar. *İstanbul Üniversitesi Siyasal Bilimler Fakültesi Dergisi, 31*, 151-176.

Bakan, İ., Büyükbeşe, T., Erşahan, B. & Kefe, İ. (2013). Kadın Çalışanların Yöneticilere İlişkin Algıları: Bir Alan Çalışması. *Çankırı Karatekin Üniversitesi İktisadi ve İdari Bilimler Fakültesi Dergisi, 3*(2),71-84.

Barrows, Powers, & Reynolds. (2012). Introduction to Management in the Hospitality Industry (10th ed.). John Wiley & Sons.

Başaran, İ. E. (1998). *Yönetimde İnsan İlişkileri-Yönetsel Davranış*. Nobel Yayınevi.

Bass, B. M. (1961). Some aspects of attempted, successful and effective leadership. *The Journal of Applied Psychology, 45*(2), 120–122. doi:10.1037/h0049166

Bass, B. M. (1994). *Improving organizational effectiveness through transformational leadership*. Sage Publications.

Bennis, W. G. (1959). Leadership theory and administrative behavior: The problems of authority. *Administrative Science Quarterly, 4*(3), 259–301. doi:10.2307/2390911

Buluç, B. (2009). Sınıf Öğretmenlerinin Algılarına Göre Okul Müdürlerinin Liderlik Stilleri ile Örgütsel Bağlılık Arasındaki İlişki. *Kuram ve Uygulamada Eğitim Yönetimi, 15*(57), 5–34.

Burns, J. M. (1978). *Leadership*. Harper & Row.

Can, H., Akgün, A., & Kavuncubası, Ş. (2001). Kamu ve Özel Kesimde & İnsan Kaynakları Yönetimi. Ankara: Siyasal Kitabevi.

Çetin, C. (2008). *Yöneticilerin liderlik stilleri, değişim yönetimi ve ekip çalışması arasındaki ilişkilerin çok yönlü olarak değerlendirilmesi*. İstanbul: İTO yayınları.

Champous, J. E. (2011). *Organizational Behavior: Integrating Individuals, Groups and Organizations*. Routledge.

Copeland, N. (1942). *Psychology and the soldier*. Military Service Publication.

Drucker, P. F. (1998). *The Leader of the Future*. Jossey Bass.

Eraslan, L. (2004). Liderlik Olgusunun Tarihsel Evrimi, Temel Kavramlar ve Yeni Liderlik Paradigmasının Analizi. *Milli Eğitim Dergisi, 162*.

Eraslan, L. (2006). *Liderlikte post-modern bir paradigma: dönüşümcü liderlik*. Uslararası İnsan Bilimleri Dergisi.

Eren, E. (2003). *Yönetim ve Organizasyon (Çağdaş ve Küresel Yaklaşımlar)*. Beta Yayınevi.

Eren, E. (2004). Stratejik Yönetim. T.C. Anadolu Üniversitesi Yayını, 1491.

Eren, E. (2008). *Yönetim ve organizasyon (Çağdaş ve Küresel Yaklaşımlar)*. Beta Yayınevi.

Erkuş, A., & Günlü, E. (2008). Duygusal Zekanın Dönüşümcü Liderlik Üzerine Etkileri. *İşletme Fakültesi Dergisi, 9*(2), 187-209.

French, J. R. P., & Raven, B. (1959). The bases of social power. In D. Cartwright (Ed.), *Studies in Social Power* (pp. 259–269). University of Michigan Press.

Gülertekin, S. (2013). Duygu İklimi ve Liderlik Tarzının İşten Ayrılma Niyetine Etkileri: Alanya'daki Turizm İşletmelerine Yönelik Bir Araştırma. *T.C. Çanakkale On sekiz Mart Üniversitesi Sosyal Bilimler Enstitüsü Turizm İşletmeciliği Anabilim Dalı*.

Güney, S. (2012). *Liderlik*. Nobel Yayınevi.

Güngör, O. (2019). Otel İşletmelerinin Mutfak Departmanında Örgütsel İklim ve Liderlik Stilleri İlişkisinin İncelenmesi: Bir Zincir Otel İşletmesi Örneği. *Türk Turizm Araştırmaları Dergisi, 3*(4), 995–1011. doi:10.26677/TR1010.2019.224

Hicks, H., & Gullett, C. R. (1981). Organizasyonlar, Teori ve Davranış (Çeviri Besim Baykal). İstanbul: İşletme Bilimleri Enstitüsü Yayınları No:1.

Hodgkinson, C. (1996). *Yönetim felsefesi*. İstanbul: Beta yayınevi.

Hogg, A. M. (2001). A Social Identity Theory of Leadership. *Personality and Social Psychology, 5*(3), 184–200. doi:10.1207/S15327957PSPR0503_1

Holdford, D. A. (2003). Leadership Theories and Their Lessons for Pharmacists. *American Journal of Health-System Pharmacy, 60*(17), 1780–1786. doi:10.1093/ajhp/60.17.1780 PMID:14503115

İbicioğlu, H., & Özmen, H. İ., & Taş, S. (2009). Liderlik Davranışı ve Toplumsal Norm İlişki: Ampirik Bir Çalışma. *Süleyman Demirel Üniversitesi İktisadi ve İdari Bilimler Fakültesi Dergisi, 14*(2), 1–23.

İnce, Ş. (2016). *Şeflerin Savaşı: Profesyonel Mutfaklarda Erkek ve Kadın Şefler*. Moment Dergi, Cinema and Politics.

Kazkondu, İ. (2021). Mutfak Örgütlenmesi. In Mutfak Yönetimi. Ankara: Detay yayıncılık.

Kets de Vries, M. (2001). *The Leadership Mystique*. Prentice Hall.

Kets de Vries, M. (2007). Liderliğin Gizemi. İstanbul: MESS Yayın No:25.

Knickerbocker, I. (1948). Leadership: A Conception and Some Implications. *The Journal of Social Issues, 4*(3), 23–40. doi:10.1111/j.1540-4560.1948.tb01508.x

Koçel, T. (2007). *İşletme Yöneticiliği*. Arıkan Basım Yayım.

Madenci, A. B. (2020). Yiyecek İçecek İşletmelerinin Örgütsel Yapısı ve Hiyerarşisi Üzerine Bir Araştırma: Konya İli Örneği. *Gastroia: Journal of Gastronomy and Travel Research, 4*(2), 173–184.

Marcouse, I. (2014). İşletme Kitabı (Çeviri T. Göbekçin). İstanbul: Alfa yayınları. Mumford, E., (1906-907). The Origins of Leadership. *American Journal of Sociology, 12*, 216–240.

Northouse, P. G. (2021). *Leadership: Theory and Practice*. Sage.

Oğuz, E. (2011). Öğretmenlerin Örgütsel Vatandaşlık Davranışları ile Yöneticilerin Liderlik Stilleri Arasındaki İlişki. *Kuram ve Uygulamada Eğitim Yönetimi, 17*(3), 377–403.

Oktay, E., & Gül, H. (2003). Çalışanların Duygusal Bağlılıklarının Sağlanmasında Conger ve Kanungo'nun Karizmatik Lider Özelliklerinin Etkileri Üzerine Karaman ve Aksaray Emniyet Müdürlüklerinde Yapılan Bir Araştırma. *Sosyal Bilimler Enstitüsü Dergisi*.

Ören, A. S. (2006). *Günümüzün Liderlik Profili; Transformasyonel (Dönüştürücü) Liderlik Antalya Bölgesinde Bulunan Beş Yıldızlı Otel İşletmelerinde Bir Araştırma*. Akdeniz Üniversitesi Sosyal Bilimler Enstitüsü Turizm işletmeciliği ve Otelcilik Anabilim Dalı Yüksek Lisans Tezi.

Özel, M. (1998). *Liderlik Sanatı*. İz Yayıncılık.

Özkalp, E. (1988). *Örgütsel Davranış*. Eskişehir: Anadolu Üniversitesi Açık öğretim Fakültesi Yayınları No:40.

Sabuncuoğlu, Z., & Tüz, M. (2003). *Örgütsel Psikoloji*. Bursa: Alfa kitap, Aktüel baskı yayıncılık.

Saylı, H., & Baytok, A. (2014). Örgütlerde Liderlik Teori Uygulama ve Yeni Perspektifler. Ankara: Nobel Yayınevi.

Selimoğlu, E. (2004). Günümüzde Liderlik Anlayışı. *Endüstri İlişkileri ve İnsan Kaynakları Dergisi, 6*(2), 9–232.

Şişman, M. (2004). *Öğretim Liderliği*. Pegem A Yayıncılık.

Stogdill, R. M. (1974). *Handbook of leadership*. Free Press.

Stogdill, R. M., & Bass, B. M. (1981). *Stogdill's Handbook of Leadership*. The Free Press.

Tannenbaum, R. J. (1961). *Leadership and Organizations, A Behavioral Science Approach*. McGraw Hill.

Taşkıran, E. (2005). *Otel İşletmelerinde Liderlik ve Yöneticilerin Liderlik Yönelimleri: İstanbul'daki Beş Yıldızlı Otel İşletmelerinde Bir Araştırma*. T.C Abant İzzet Baysal Üniversitesi Sosyal Bilimler Enstitüsü Turizm ve Otel İşletmeciliği Anabilim Dalı, Yüksek Lisans Tezi.

Uğur, S. S. (2014). Yöneticilik ve Liderlik Kişisel Farklılıkların Rolü. *Organizasyon ve Yönetim Bilimleri Dergisi, 6*(1), 122–136.

Vroom, V. H., & Jago, A. G. (2007). The role of the Situation in Leadership. *The American Psychologist, 62*(1), 17–24. doi:10.1037/0003-066X.62.1.17 PMID:17209676

Werner, I. (1993). Leadership Skills For Executives. İstanbul: Rota Yayınları.

Yavuz, E. (2009). İş görenlerin Dönüşümcü Liderlik ve Örgütsel Bağlılık ile İlgili Tutumlarına Yönelik Bir Araştırma. *İşletme Araştırmaları Dergisi, 1*(2), 51-69.

Yavuz, E., & Tokmak, C. (2009). İş görenlerin Etkileşimci Liderlik ve Örgütsel Bağlılık ile İlgili Tutumlarına Yönelik Bir Araştırma. *International Journal of Economic and Administrative Studies, 1*(2), 17–35.

Yılmaz, H. (2008). Stratejik Liderlik. İstanbul: Kum Saati Yayınları.

Young, M., & Dulewicz, V. (2007). Similarities and Differences Between Leadership and Management: High-Performance Competencies in the British Royal Navy. *British Journal of Management, 19*(1), 17–32. doi:10.1111/j.1467-8551.2007.00534.x

Yukl, G., & Gardner, W. L. (2020). *Leadership in Organizations*. Pearson.

Zel, U. (2001). *Kişilik ve Liderlik*. Seçkin Yayıncılık.

Zengin, Y., Yurdakul, S., Bayram, N., Sakarya, M., & Bağcı, M. (2021). Yöneticilerin Liderlik Özelliklerinin Psikolojik Sahiplenme ve İş Stresi ile İlişkisi. *Turkish Business Journal, 2*(4), 56–75.

Chapter 15
Perceived Challenges of Self-Leadership in Outdoor Recreation Activities

Serhat Bingol
https://orcid.org/0000-0001-9312-4552
Bilecik Seyh Edebali University, Turkey

ABSTRACT

Leadership in outdoor recreation activities was mainly described with the outdoor leadership approach. However, outdoor leadership deals with group management. Therefore, it is essential to reveal the perceived challenges in outdoor recreation activities with the self-leadership approach since self-leadership strategies influence performance positively. These strategies, behavior-focused, natural reward, and constructive thought pattern strategies, motivate individuals for productive behaviors. Even though these strategies improve individuals, they still confront some challenges in leading themselves. In this context, this study aims to reveal the perceived challenges of self-leadership in camping and rock-climbing activities to help the success of participants. Since the research was planned as qualitative research to understand participants rather than explain them, the RSLQ factors were adapted as interview questions to reveal perceived challenges. Results showed that participants cope with 26 perceived challenges before, during, and after camping and rock-climbing activities.

INTRODUCTION

Bennis (1994) defines leadership as doing the right things since leadership means success (Smith, 2011). A leader is a person who organizes plans consistent with the needs of the individual (Enoksen & Lynch, 2018). Leaders provide experiences and opportunities for group members to apply what they have learned through their experiences. They ask questions to encourage movement through the experiential learning cycle (Wolfe, 2014). Therefore, "before stepping into a leadership role, people should begin the journey toward self-discovery. They should engage in pursuit to discover who they are, what they care about,

DOI: 10.4018/978-1-6684-6713-8.ch015

and what motivates them... This is of particular significance to leaders in the recreation, whose job is to guide..." (O'Connell, Cuthbertson & Goins, 2014: 1).

Self-leadership, an interaction through which people use self-influence to their beliefs, feelings, and behaviors, is a process as a fundamental construct (Harari et al., 2021). However, "self-leadership is not easily defined or described. Making the right decisions at the right time is complicated. Being an effective leader feels more like an art since self-leadership is a dynamic process..." (Cuthbertson, 2014: 20). Therefore, an understanding of the self is essential for effective leadership since the concepts of self-leadership relate to personality, beliefs, values, and emotions.

The self-leadership approach is a way of leading that differs from the traditional leadership perspective, which is based on external influence and control within a hierarchy of authority. In the self-leadership approach, everyone is a leader and follower. Individuals lead and influence themselves. In other words, the roles of leader and follower are regarding the individual. To be an efficient self-leader, it is vital to have coordinated efforts among individuals. Therefore, a holistic approach is necessary to effectively address the question (Neck & Manz, 1996).

Self-leadership is also characterized as a method of self-influence that people act through self-direction and motivation to do their responsibilities (Manz, 1986: 589; Manz & Neck, 1999). In the self-leadership approach, individuals manage their behaviors to achieve current standards and goals. It also evaluates standards or changes existing ones. The answers to the questions of what and why should be done are also determined. Therefore, self-leadership is not an individual, autonomous approach designed independently of the group or organization. It encourages individuals in a way that creates interaction in their identity.

Recreation activities provide unique places in which to assess human interaction, communication, and leadership. The outdoor recreation leadership literature first focuses on leadership effectiveness and competencies (Graham, 1997; Martin, et al., 2006; Smith, 2011). Competencies are mostly about decision-making skills (Gerbers & Marchand, 2021). Furthermore, Martin et al. (2006: 6) explain leadership skills as "*technical ability, safety and risk management, program management, environmental stewardship, teaching and facilitation, judgment and decision-making, foundational knowledge, self-awareness, and awareness of professional conduct.*" On the other hand, outdoor recreation leaders ensure to protect of the natural environment and improve the quality of outdoor experiences. Depending on the environment, outdoor recreation leaders maintain a level of responsibility and are a driving force behind the decision-making (Van Bussel, 2014).

Leaders need to be prepared to identify the differences among themselves (O'Connell, Cuthbertson & Goins, 2014). They should do self-analysis since leadership begins with self and self-leadership is primarily about self-management (Pinnow, 2011: 238). Therefore, understanding the self is essential for effective self-leadership in outdoor recreation activities because individuals should spend the time and attempt to obtain an accurate image of who they are (Cuthbertson, 2014). In this context, this study explores the self-leadership concept of participants in outdoor recreation activities. The study aims to reveal the perceived challenges of self-leadership in camping and rock-climbing activities. Thus, organizations can support recreationists who tend to enhance their skills, improving their performance more successful via self-leadership.

SELF-LEADERSHIP

Self-leadership is explained as a fundamental process in empowerment (Manz, 1992a; Anderson & Prussia, 1997) and the effective application of self-management groups (Manz, 1990; Neck, Stewart, & Manz, 1996). Self-leadership is an efficient set of approaches in which individuals lead themselves to get better efficiency (Manz & Neck, 1999). This leadership approach offers a process through which individuals motivate themselves to perform the self-management required (Manz & Neck, 1999). Therefore, self-leadership applies behavioral and cognitive strategies to structure individuals' performing outcomes (Houghton, Neck & Manz, 2003).

Manz (1986) depicted self-leadership as a broad concept of self-influence. Therefore, self-leadership also involves behavior-focused strategies of self-management. It indicates cognitive strategies obtained from intrinsic motivation theories (Deci & Ryan, 1985), social cognitive theory (Bandura, 1986, 1991), and clinical cognitive psychology (Ellis, 1977; Beck et al., 1979). Therefore, self-leadership characterizes self-influence strategies that are theorized to affect individuals' behavior positively. Furthermore, self-leadership requires that people struggle with themselves to accomplish the self-motivation and self-direction to perform constructive practices (Manz, 1992b). Consequently, self-leadership strategies consist of *behavior-focused strategies, natural reward strategies, and constructive thought pattern strategies* (Anderson & Prussia, 1997).

Behavior-focused strategies involve analyzing individuals' behaviors to improve self-awareness (Mahoney & Arnkoff, 1978, 1979). The main goal of these strategies is to enhance self-awareness and control behaviors (Manz & Neck, 1999). On the other hand, natural reward strategies concentrate positive experiences of responsibilities to be succeeded. These strategies involve dedication and pleasure of the job or activity for its value and improving relate to the pleasant characteristics of the task (Manz, 1992a, 1992b; Anderson & Prussia, 1997). Finally, *constructive thought pattern strategies* relate to creating and adjusting thinking patterns in desired behaviors. Therefore, these strategies vary thinking patterns and improve self-leadership (Anderson & Prussia, 1997).

Neck and Houghton (2006: 271) summarize self-leadership research literature focus on, "*a historical overview of how the concept was created and expanded as well as a detailed look at more recent self-leadership research trends and directions*." The authors (2006: 273-274) provide evidence of the self-leadership literature by research subjects and explored the following topics in self-leadership research for twenty years: "*spirituality in the work, performance appraisals, organizational change, total quality management, self-leading teams, entrepreneurship, diversity management, job satisfaction, non-profit management, goal setting/goal performance, the United States army, team performance, team sustainability, and ethics.*" While different researchers contributed to these subjects, this is how the basic structures emerged (Goldsby et al., 2021).

While Neck & Houghton's (2006) study offered a summary of subjects in self-leadership, Stewart, Courtright, & Manz's (2011) study analyzed outcomes of the performing of self-leadership at both team and individual levels. The authors found that "*at the individual level, studies consistently show that increased self-leadership corresponds with better affective responses and improved work performance. Findings are not as consistent at the team level.*" The study also classified studies on internal and external forces that affect self-leadership. Even if some subjects were as Neck and Houghton's (2006) study, Stewart et al. (2011) offered further forces such as "*productivity quality, creativity and self-efficacy, psychological empowerment and job satisfaction, organizational commitment, absenteeism, turnover, stress/anxiety, and career success.*"

Additionally, Stewart et al. (2011) analyzed the internal forces of self-leadership underlining the cognitive and emotional characteristics. According to this study, internal forces occur as follows: *"natural rewards (individual level), thought self-leadership (individual level), emotional regulation (individual level), personality (individual level), team composition (team level), cognitive ability and personality, task characteristics (team level), shared mental models (team level), cohesion (team level), conflict (team level)."* On the other hand, external forces of self-leadership were established approaches to traditional external leadership. Stewart et al. (2011) mention that individuals who perform self-leadership will affect the external leadership they have with others. They classified external forces as follows: *"training (individual level), leadership (individual level), national culture (individual level), external team leadership (team level), reward systems (team level), organizational structure/culture (team level), national culture (team level)."*

Many new subjects appeared in the research field of self-leadership in recent years. Goldsby et al. (2021) apply the previous structure to review subjects as follows: *"education-specific, scale/measurement, and sales/service leadership."* Additionally, self-leadership has also been used as an approach in various research (Megheirkouni, 2018; Proios, 2019; Proios et al., 2020). Recently, Harari et al. (2021) used another perspective on self-leadership with the Five-Factor Model (FFM) of personality. Harari et al. (2021) suggest that the personality factor with a theoretical link to self-leadership is conscientiousness. As a result of trends related to instinct control in the pursuit of long-term objectives, conscientious individuals may be to apply the behavioral strategies that are distinctive of self-leaders. Personality factors also have constructive attention as underlined in constructive thought strategies.

The classification of fundamental behaviors presented by the FFM has been established since the FFM is effective across time, cultures, and research fields (Digman, 1990). According to Connelly, Ones, and Hulsheger (2018: 325) FFM indicates *"a useful delineation of traits that will provide adequate coverage across the personality spectrum."* The FFM consists of extraversion, emotional stability, agreeableness, conscientiousness, and openness. These behaviors play significant roles in the motivation process (Judge & Ilies, 2002). They are also related to intrinsic motivation, which is essential to self-leadership (Houghton et al., 2004; Hart et al., 2007; McCrae & Löckenhoff, 2010).

PERCEIVED CHALLENGES AND OUTDOOR RECREATION

Following the stress appraisal theory (Lazarus & Folkman, 1984), once stress occurs, difficult experiences begin to appear. Stress consists of *threat, challenge, and harm*. Threat refers to the possibility of loss and risk, challenge refers to growth, or the potential to win, and harm refers to damage. Different individuals may make different evaluations when they are exposed to similar stress (Lazarus & Folkman, 1984). The experience of challenge, therefore, depends not only on the inherent challenges but also on the participant's perspective. Once individuals evaluate the same condition, they may experience a variety of feelings that lead to different behaviors that will have different outcomes.

Baird & Penna (1996) claimed that challenge contains both sensory and cognitive factors. Once effort is enough to overcome challenges, there is a perception that a goal can be achieved through the challenge. While individuals are faced with a problem and accept the risks involved in this problem, they experience fears that enable them to think about the outcome and its positive and negative consequences (Carnicelli-Filho et al., 2010). Hence, contrary to the perception of threat and harm, it can cause more satisfying feelings such as challenge, excitement, arousal, and self-confidence. That is, the ability to overcome challenges enables stress to turn into excitement and a sense of achievement. Therefore, outdoor recreation leadership is characterized as leadership competencies (Priest & Gass, 2005; Martin et al., 2006; Smith, 2011).

The research on outdoor recreation leadership competencies sought to explain the most recognized behaviors by tasks (Buell, 1981; Priest, 1984, 1986; Raiola, 1986). In his well-known study, Priest (1987) specified twelve core competencies: *"technical skills, safety skills, environmental skills, organizational skills, instructional skills, facilitation skills, flexible leadership style, communication, professional ethics, decision making, problem-solving, and sound judgment."* Furthermore, Raiola and Sugerman's (1999) outdoor leadership development cycle is appraised for its capacity in describing the development from beginner to expert.

Enoksen and Lynch (2018) discovered factors shaping leadership experiences. Authors noticed that becoming an outdoor recreation leader requires changes that can be complex to the learning background. Research continued to determine the recognized competencies list. But the extensive range in which outdoor leadership competencies are identified offers a dilemma for studies looking to describe meaningful behaviors (Gabriel, Sklar & Monu, 2020). While early research discovered technical, interpersonal, and conceptual skills as the key skills (Priest, 1987; Swiderski, 1987), Shooter, Sibthorp, & Paisley (2009) revealed that no common competencies set can be determined because of the change in the leadership required in distinctive environments. Outdoor recreation leadership offers learners prospects to improve their personal leadership capacity. Therefore, leadership skills that are applied to multiple career paths (Anderson & Prussia, 1997).

As can be seen in the studies, participants in outdoor recreation activities were mostly considered by the outdoor leadership approach. However, outdoor leadership deals with group management rather than the individual. Therefore, the self-leadership approach is also necessary to overcome the activities individually and to achieve a sense of achievement. At this point, it is essential to reveal the perceived challenges in outdoor recreation activities with the self-leadership approach.

METHOD

Designed as a qualitative research method with the phenomenological approach, the research intends to determine the perceived challenges of self-leadership in camping and rock-climbing activities. The phenomenological approach concerns the shared meaning of individuals' experiences with a phenomenon or concept (Creswell, 2017). Phenomenology aims to reduce individual experiences of a spectacle to an explanation of a universal nature. Qualitative researchers first define the phenomenon. Then, they collect data from participants who experience the phenomenon and explain what distinguishes the principle of all individuals' experiences (Creswell, 2017). This description consists of what and how the participants experienced. Therefore, participants in recreational activities are suitable research fields for the phenomenological approach as they deal with real experiences (Pernecky & Jamal, 2010).

The research data is obtained using the semi-structured interview technique via in-depth interviews. The universe of the study is all participating in camping and rock-climbing activities in Turkey. The sample of the study is outdoor recreationists who travel to participate in rock climbing and camping activities in İzmir. The research was conducted in *İzmir Kaynaklar Climbing Garden* for two months covering June-July 2022. In this context, the researcher conducts in-depth interviews with 48 participants.

The Revised Self-Leadership Questionnaire (Houghton & Neck, 2002) was chosen to create interview questions. The questionnaire consists of nine factors, demonstrating three self-leadership dimensions. Self-leadership dimensions include *behavior-focused strategies, natural reward strategies, and constructive thought pattern strategies* (Anderson & Prussia, 1997). While behavior-focused strategies consist of self-observation, self-goal setting, self-reward, self-punishment, and self-cueing, natural reward strategies consist of just one factor. On the other hand, the constructive thought strategies consist of visualizing successful performance, self-talk, and evaluating beliefs and assumptions. The Revised Self-Leadership Questionnaire (RSLQ) distinguishes individuals who have weak self-leadership abilities in recreation activities. The instrument proposed reliability and construct validity in various research (Houghton et al., 2004; Proios, 2019; Proios et al., 2020).

The research was conducted as qualitative research since in-depth interviews with camp and rock-climbing participants in their environment are more valuable to understand. Qualitative research understands individuals rather than explain them (Neuman, 2014). Therefore, self-observation, self-goal setting, self-reward, self-punishment, self-cueing, natural reward, visualizing successful performance, self-talk, and evaluating beliefs and assumptions factors from the RSLQ are adapted as interview questions.

Successful coding is the key phase of the analysis in qualitative research (Patton, 2002: 463). Therefore, through the coding process, the researcher evaluated the data and then examined it attentively. Afterward, content and descriptive analysis techniques are conducted to analyze the data by the NVIVO program. The data were analyzed to generate categories via combining the data. This process emphasizes the notions, notes, and concepts, and ultimately creates relations between themes. Through the coding process, common themes were reached. Thus, themes were created with expressions of the significance given by participants' experiences. The process was continued until it reached data saturation (Charmaz, 2006; Fusch & Ness, 2015).

FINDINGS

As the study plans to reveal the perceived challenges of self-leadership in camping and rock-climbing activities, the transcripts of the interviews were systematically examined and analyzed within the framework of the experiences of the participants. But firstly, the demographic characteristic of participants was presented in this chapter.

Demographic Characteristics

Firstly, Table 1 was presented to give comprehensive statistics about the demographic characteristics of the participants. Afterward, a broad assessment opportunity was offered about the demographic characteristics of 48 rock-climbing and camping participants. According to the data, the age range of the outdoor recreationists appeared as 19-42. But the majority is between 19 and 35. Furthermore, the number of males is higher than females in these activities. The occupations of outdoor recreationists vary, but students are the majority and all students study at a university. Finally, the number of rock-climbers is 19, the number of campers is 15, and the number of those doing both activities is 14.

Perceived Challenges of Self-Leadership in Rock-Climbing and Camping

Perceived challenges are handled with behavior-focused, natural reward, and constructive thought pattern strategies in this study. Behavior-focused strategies improve self-awareness and enable self-management to compulsory tasks which are not pleasant (Houghton & Neck, 2002). Behavior-focused strategies consist of *self-observation, self-goal setting, self-reward, self-punishment, and self-cueing* factors (Neck & Houghton, 2006). That is, these strategies aim to promote constructive behaviors that trigger effective outcomes, while controlling destructive behaviors that may cause failure. On the other hand, natural reward strategies help individuals to construct pleasant elements in activities with no external influence (Houghton et al., 2004). These strategies aim to create a performance-improving influence in the daily life, work, and activities-related behaviors of individuals and to create competence, work, and determination to succeed in the mission. Finally, constructive thought pattern strategies help continuous ways of considering that positively influence performance by *visualizing successful performance, self-talk, and evaluating beliefs and assumptions*. These strategies involve creating and maintaining a functional model of consistent thinking (Neck & Houghton, 2006: 272).

Self-Observation Challenges

Self-observation requires improving awareness of why and when an individual demonstrates specific behavior. This awareness is an essential move to eliminating or changing ineffective and unproductive behaviors (Manz & Neck, 1999: 21-35). Self-observation includes the systematic collection of information about the individual's behavior and thus provides a basis for self-evaluation. Therefore, it aims to increase the awareness of individuals by performing certain behaviors.

"What are the challenges in self-observation during the activity?" was the first question of the research. The question was asked to reveal the challenges experienced by the participants in self-observation. According to descriptive and content analysis, focusing on activity, integrating with the activity, and evaluating personal development were the main perceived challenges. A 24-year-old female participant had the following thoughts about perceived self-observation challenges:

"First, I need to focus on the activity so that I can have a chance to observe myself. But I am having serious challenges. I have very frequent disconnections. I look around and think of everything. Once the focus is lost, it is very difficult to wrap up because without focus I cannot manage myself. So, it is not easy for me to observe myself all the time"

Self-Goal Setting Challenges

Individuals who have correct indication about their present behaviors and performance levels establish objectives for themselves more effectively (Manz & Neck, 1999) since self-goal settings that are specific and not easy for individuals to accomplish their performance and motivation levels (Neck & Houghton, 2006: 271). Having such information about current behavior and performance level, individuals will be more successful in establishing personal objectives that will lead to better performance levels. Thus, individuals plan in line with their goals and organize their behavior accordingly.

"What are the main challenges when setting personal goals?" question was asked to determine the perceived self-goal setting challenges. Accordingly, self-doubt, unawareness, and economic problems

Table 1. Demographic Characteristics

Participants (T=48)	Age	Gender	Marital Status	Education	Profession Sector	Recreation Activity
P1	19	Male	Single	Bachelor-O	Student	Both
P2	31	Female	Married	Bachelor	Advocacy	Camping
P3	34	Male	Married	Bachelor	Engineering	Camping
P4	32	Female	Single	Bachelor	Education	Camping
P5	31	Male	Single	Bachelor	Not working	Rock-Climbing
P6	42	Male	Single	H. School	Worker	Camping
P7	29	Female	Married	Bachelor	Education	Camping
P8	33	Male	Married	Graduate	Education	Camping
P9	24	Female	Single	Bachelor	Not working	Camping
P10	30	Female	Married	Bachelor	Administration	Camping
P11	32	Male	Married	Bachelor	Freelance	Camping
P12	25	Male	Single	Bachelor	Not Working	Both
P13	24	Female	Single	Bachelor	Trade	Rock-Climbing
P14	22	Female	Single	Bachelor-O	Student	Rock-Climbing
P15	21	Male	Single	Bachelor-O	Student	Rock-Climbing
P16	20	Female	Single	Bachelor-O	Student	Rock-Climbing
P17	36	Male	Single	Graduate	Art	Both
P18	31	Female	Single	Bachelor	Art	Camping
P19	33	Male	Single	Bachelor	Engineering	Rock-Climbing
P20	35	Male	Married	Bachelor	Education	Rock-Climbing
P21	25	Male	Single	Bachelor	Medicine	Rock-Climbing
P22	23	Male	Single	Bachelor-O	Student	Both
P23	20	Female	Single	Bachelor	Student	Rock-Climbing
P24	22	Female	Single	Bachelor	Student	Both
P25	23	Male	Single	Bachelor	Student	Both
P26	28	Female	Single	Bachelor	Service	Camping
P27	37	Female	Married	Bachelor	Trade	Camping
P28	29	Male	Single	Bachelor	Trade	Camping
P29	27	Male	Single	Graduate	Engineering	Both
P30	30	Female	Single	Bachelor	Education	Both
P31	30	Male	Single	Bachelor	Freelance	Both
P32	29	Male	Single	Bachelor	Worker	Rock-Climbing
P33	32	Female	Single	Bachelor	Medicine	Rock-Climbing
P34	22	Male	Single	Bachelor-O	Student	Rock-Climbing
P35	26	Male	Single	Bachelor-O	Student	Both
P36	36	Male	Single	Bachelor	Advocacy	Rock-Climbing
P37	39	Female	Single	Graduate	Advocacy	Rock-Climbing
P38	25	Male	Single	Bachelor	Trade	Rock-Climbing
P39	19	Male	Single	Bachelor-O	Student	Both
P40	32	Male	Single	H. School	Worker	Both
P41	30	Male	Married	Graduate	Education	Camping
P42	28	Female	Single	Bachelor	Sport	Rock-Climbing
P43	19	Female	Single	Bachelor-O	Student	Rock-Climbing
P44	19	Male	Single	Bachelor-O	Student	Rock-Climbing
P45	26	Male	Single	Bachelor	Not Working	Camping
P46	25	Female	Single	Bachelor	Sport	Rock-Climbing
P47	24	Male	Single	Bachelor	Sport	Both
P48	20	Male	Single	Bachelor-O	Student	Both

emerged as key perceived challenges of participants. A 25-year-old male participant who is both a rock-climber and camper expressed himself as follows:

"I guess my biggest challenge is that I cannot be sure of my performance. Sometimes, I overestimate myself, and sometimes the other way around. I feel like I cannot do what I am supposed to do. Also, when setting goals, I definitely look at my money and budget. This is the big problem because I need money to go somewhere to do activities..."

Self-Reward Challenges

The individual's self-reward can add an asset to the power necessary to fulfill their goals (Manz & Neck, 1999: 21-35). The reward may also be in a simple or abstract sense. After successfully fulfilling an important and difficult task, individuals may congratulate themselves. This behavior may encourage them even more, or the reward may appear in the form of physically ordering something that the individual enjoys (Neck & Houghton, 2006: 271). So, it is individuals' determination of rewards following their goals. This includes being able to act and gather the necessary energy.

"What are the challenges for you to reward yourself after completing the activity?" question was about the perceived challenges that emerged on self-reward. Perceived challenges have emerged as tiredness and physical weakness. A 24-year-old rock climber expresses the following opinions about challenges:

"I personally take the biggest reward as a sense of success. I can say that my biggest reward is psychological. But once I put in the extra effort to achieve, I feel tired and have a physical weakness. After that, I have no expectations. When I am tired, I want to rest, revive, and drink alcohol. So, that is enough for me. Sometimes, even if want to reward myself I do not have enough energy..."

Excessive Self-Punishment

Like self-reward, self-punishment aims to efficiently rearrange desired behaviors. Reviewing undesirable behaviors or declines in performance may be more effective in improving performance. Excessive self-punishment, including criticism, can negatively affect an individual's performance, and overdoing should be avoided (Houghton & Neck, 2002: 673; Neck & Houghton, 2006: 272). That is, it is like self-reward behaviors and focuses directly on individual consequences.

Since excessive self-punishment is considered one of the sources of perceived challenges, "what causes excessive self-punishment?" question was directly asked. Accordingly, *failure, wrong decisions, and learning challenges* emerged as the reasons of self-punishment. Described himself as an adventure recreationist, a 29-year-old male explained himself as follows:

"When I fail in the activity, I get very angry with myself and feel guilty because I think I have not done enough effort. Therefore, I make wrong decisions. But sometimes, no matter what I do, I feel like it is my failure I could learn from everywhere before..."

Self-Cueing Challenges

Rehearsing the desired behavior before performing ensures that possible problems are corrected, and mistakes are avoided. This contributes positively to performance. In addition, existing cues in the environment can improve constructive behaviors and reduce destructive behaviors (Manz & Neck, 1999: 21-35). To-do lists or reminders can be examples of external cues used to help focus attention and achieve a set goal. Therefore, it includes acting in the direction of increasing constructive behaviors.

"What are the challenges to finding ways for self-cueing before an activity?" was another question that was asked to reveal participants' perceived challenges. Accordingly, the perceived challenges emerged as *not planning, rehearsing, and making a to-do list*. A participant, who stated that these challenges were mostly instant, states as follows:

"Even though I plan what I will do in my mind, not making a to-do list affects me a lot. It is easy to make a simple audio recording or write on phone. Everything will be easier if I create an outline and steps in order. That is how I see my progress. But out of laziness or habit, I always start the same way, and I cannot do most of the things I have planned in my mind at that moment."

Challenges of Focusing on Natural Reward

Natural rewards are based on the approach of revealing the pleasurable side of a job or activity. This motivates or rewards people (Neck & Houghton, 2006: 272). Natural rewards emerge within the task being performed, thus increasing the motivation level and being rewarded. Naturally, rewarding has a positive effect on high-level competency, self-control, and goal setting (Manz & Neck, 1999: 43). It means focusing on the natural reward, instead of thinking about undesirable circumstances to shape their perceptions.

"What are the challenges to focusing thoughts on natural reward?" was another question to determine perceived challenges. Challenges to the natural reward emerged as *the difficulty of the activity, sense of fear, the risk of injury, and unexpected experiences*. The 29-year-old female participant described her experience as follows:

"It is not always possible to focus on positive thoughts. The activity is already difficult and risky. While thinking about it, once you see that someone is having a problem, the fear begins, even if it is a small injury. That is why it is very difficult to manage myself. So, even though I know I will gain a big sense of success, sometimes fear does not let me focus on it"

Challenges of Visualizing Successful Performance

With mental imagery, it can generate and symbolically experience behavioral results before physical performance appears. The method is described with mental practices and symbolic rehearsal (Houghton & Neck, 2002: 674). Individuals who apply the mental description method mentally imagine that they feel successful before a job or activity. They also demonstrate positive performance when they are physically confronted. It involves visualizing the successful performance and rehearsing their activities before starting a job.

Perceived Challenges of Self-Leadership in Outdoor Recreation Activities

"What are the challenges for a successful performance" question aims to reveal the challenges that visual successful performance. Accordingly, *skill weakness and risky places* are challenges to visualizing successful performance. A 26-year-old male described these challenges for himself as follows:

"As much as I love rock climbing, it takes time to feel ready for it. Each place and route require a different skill. I must believe that I can do the route to feel completely ready for it. Unfortunately, I do not always feel sufficient in this both psychologically and skill"

Destructive Self-Talk

As negative self-talk causes destructive behaviors it should be changed with positive self-talk for success. Thus, individuals should take an essential step in their inner world. Self-talk is an individual's secret speech to themselves (Neck & Houghton, 2006: 272). Self-talk appears when people assess, guide, and mentally respond to themselves (Houghton & Neck, 2002). It means replacing destructive self-talk with constructive self-talk.

"What kind of challenges do you face when you talk with yourself?" was the next question to determine what destructive self-talk of participants while talking to themselves. Accordingly, it emerged in the *self-anger, negative talk, and quitting activity*. A participant who stated that he talked to himself a lot during the activity states as follows:

"I talk to myself to deal with challenges. But the activity is often challenging. Talking to myself means getting angry with myself after a while. This sometimes causes me to quit the activity instead of motivating myself..."

Irrational Evaluating Beliefs and Assumptions

Cognitive distortion, which represents a broad and severe obstacle in terms of personal performance, occurs from beliefs and assumptions that appear due to challenging conditions (Neck et al., 1997: 196). With a self-analysis process, individuals distinguish these beliefs, and assumptions, and change them with better ones (Neck & Houghton, 2006: 272). It involves examining an individual's current thought patterns and changing their irrational beliefs and assumptions.

The last question was "which beliefs and assumptions cause challenges for you?" The question was about the expectations of the participants from activities and other participants. Accordingly, *prejudices, conflicts, and self-interest* emerged as the main challenges. A 23-year-old female felt there is a relationship between activities and assumptions:

"Actually, prejudices about the activity are compelling and I guess I am too childish. I thought that people who do such activities have the same opinions. But when I spend time with them, I am just shocked... I guess that is why these activities usually start with very large groups and then the number of people in the group decreases. So, the assumption before activity does not match during or after."

DISCUSSION AND CONCLUSION

Self-leadership strategies are effective strategies for individuals to manage themselves and ensure their continuous development. It has been observed that performance increases with self-observation, self-goal setting, self-reward, self-punishment, self-cueing, natural reward, visualizing successful performance, self-talk, and evaluating beliefs and assumptions (Anderson & Prussia, 1997; Houghton et al., 2004; Proios, 2019; Proios et al., 2020). Therefore, these factors are perhaps the most encouraging approaches in terms of maintaining self-leadership skills in the long run. However, this study explored perceived challenges of self-leadership rather than effective of self-leadership strategies. In this context, the factors were retitled and adapted to both qualitative research and the purpose of the research. Therefore, the research was conducted in this framework to understand outdoor recreationists' challenges.

The first question revealed that self-observation challenges was affected by internal challenges such as focusing on activity, integrating with the activity, and evaluating personal development. Therefore, taking precautions will contribute to the practice of self-leadership by increasing the development and success of the participant. On the other hand, self-doubt, unawareness, and economic problems have emerged as key self-goal setting challenges. While self-doubt and unawareness are caused by internal challenges, economic problems are caused by external challenges.

Tiredness and physical weakness have emerged as *self-reward challenges*. Therefore, participants should achieve self-reward as soon as the activity ends, with the energy of that moment. Failure, wrong decisions, and learning challenges have emerged as excessive *self-punishment*. Thus, it may be helpful for outdoor recreationists to participate in education programs for their constant progress. *Self-cueing* challenges have emerged as not planning, rehearsing, and making a to-do list. Accordingly, all challenges were related to procrastinating and preparing.

Challenges of focusing on natural reward have emerged as the difficulty of the activity, sense of fear, the risk of injury, and unexpected experiences. Therefore, all the challenges are about at the core of the activity. Overcoming these challenges will lead to natural rewards. *Challenges in visualizing successful performance* have emerged as skill weaknesses and risky places. Outdoor recreationists should visualize and rehearse activities before to enhance performance.

Destructive self-talk has emerged as self-anger, negative talk, and quitting activity. While self-talk has a positive effect in general, its destructive transformation may initiate the process starting from anger to quitting the activity. *Irrational evaluating beliefs and assumptions* have emerged as prejudices, conflicts, and self-interest. These challenges are all about communication and psychology. Therefore, outdoor recreationists should take courses about these topics.

According to studies, self-leadership strategies enhance self-efficacy (Prussia, Anderson & Manz, 1998; Neck & Manz, 2007) and correlates with well-being and life satisfaction (Neck et al., 2017). On the contrary, this study focused on the reasons that prevent or reduce self-leadership strategies' effects. Therefore, it is hard to compare the research results since there is not any study about self-leadership challenges. Although there are studies about the perceived challenges of outdoor recreationists (Ewert & Hollenhorst, 1994; Tsaur, Lin & Liu, 2013; Bingöl, 2021) these studies do not include self-leadership and perceived challenges of self-leadership.

Internal challenge, interpersonal challenge, activity challenge, environmental challenge and lack of equipment are the main challenges in outdoor recreation (Ewert & Hollenhorst, 1994; Tsaur, Lin, & Liu, 2013; Tsaur, Lin, & Cheng, 2015; Bingöl, 2021). Though these studies were not conducted in the context of perceived challenges of self-leadership, the research results overlap with several challenges, particularly internal challenges. For instance, Bingöl (2021) revealed that internal challenges are physical weakness and lack of confidence which have similarities with this study. However, since this study is related to self-leadership, there are many differences. Therefore, it is essential to evaluate the results and discussions within this framework.

The 26 perceived challenges that emerge with nine different factors represent the challenges that outdoor recreation participants may encounter, even if they use self-leadership strategies. However, the study does not concern about whether participants used self-leadership strategies. The researcher applied these strategies to reveal the challenges participants encountered. Therefore, research results should be considered in this context. Furthermore, it should be noted that the results are only for campers and rock-climber in Izmir. Since this study does not generalize the results, other researchers should research outdoor recreationists in different destinations to understand and compare results. Consequently, the study will help recreationists to prevent themselves from challenges.

REFERENCES

Anderson, J. S., & Prussia, G. E. (1997). The self-leadership questionnaire: Preliminary assessment of construct validity. *The Journal of Leadership Studies*, *4*(2), 119–143. doi:10.1177/107179199700400212

Baird, J. R., & Penna, C. (1996). Challenge in learning and teaching science. *Research in Science Education*, *26*(3), 257–269. doi:10.1007/BF02356938

Bandura, A. (1986). *Social foundations of thought and action: A social cognitive theory*. Prentice-Hall.

Bandura, A. (1991). Social cognitive theory of self-regulation. *Organizational Behavior and Human Decision Processes*, *50*(2), 248–287. doi:10.1016/0749-5978(91)90022-L

Beck, A. T., Rush, A. J., Shaw, B. F., & Emery, G. (1979). *Cognitive theory of depression*. Guilford Press.

Buell, L. H. (1981). *The identification of outdoor adventure leadership competencies for entry-level and experienced-level personnel* [Unpublished doctoral dissertation]. University of Massachusetts, Amherst.

Bennis, W. (1994). *On becoming a leader*. Addison-Wesley.

Bingöl, S. (2021). Macera rekreasyonunda algılanan zorluklar: Doğa yürüyüşü ve kaya tırmanışı [Perceived challenges in adventure recreation: hiking and rock climbing]. *Journal Of Recreation and Tourism Research*, *8*(2), 247–267. doi:10.31771/jrtr.2021.100

Carnicelli-Filho, S., Schwartz, G. M., & Tahara, A. K. (2010). Fear and adventure tourism in Brazil. *Tourism Management*, *31*(6), 953–956. doi:10.1016/j.tourman.2009.07.013

Charmaz, K. (2006). *Constructing grounded theory: A practical guide through qualitative research*. Sage Publications.

Connelly, B. S., Ones, D. S., & Hulsheger, U. R. (2018). Personality in industrial, work, and organizational psychology: Theory measurement and applications. In D. S. Ones, N. Anderson, C. Viswesvaran, & H. K. Sinangil (Eds.), *The Sage handbook of industrial, work, and organizational psychology* (pp. 320–365). Sage.

Creswell, J. W., & Creswell, J. D. (2017). *Research design: Qualitative, quantitative, and mixed methods approaches*. Sage publications.

Cuthbertson, B. (2014). Self-Leadership. In *Leadership in Recreation and Leisure Services*. Human Kinetics.

Deci, E. L., & Ryan, R. M. (1985). *Intrinsic motivation and self-determination in human behavior*. Plenum. doi:10.1007/978-1-4899-2271-7

Digman, J. M. (1990). Personality structure: Emergence of the five-factor model. *Annual Review of Psychology*, *41*(1), 417–440. doi:10.1146/annurev.ps.41.020190.002221

Ellis, A. (1977). *The basic clinical theory of rational-emotive therapy*. Springer.

Enoksen, E., & Lynch, P. (2018). Learning leadership: Becoming an outdoor leader. *Journal of Adventure Education and Outdoor Learning*, *18*(2), 176–188. doi:10.1080/14729679.2017.1391105

Ewert, A., & Hollenhorst, S. (1994). Individual and setting attributes of the adventure recreation experience. *Leisure Sciences*, *16*(3), 177–199. doi:10.1080/01490409409513229

Fusch, P. I., & Ness, L. R. (2015). Are we there yet? Data saturation in qualitative research. *Qualitative Report*, *20*(9), 1408–1416. doi:10.46743/2160-3715/2015.2281

Gabriel, J., Sklar, S., & Monu, J. (2020). Teaching and learning servant-leadership in the outdoors. *The International Journal of Servant-Leadership*, *14*(1), 217–248. doi:10.33972/ijsl.30

Gerbers, K., & Marchand, G. (2021). Social class considerations in outdoor leadership education. *New Directions for Student Leadership*, *2021*(169), 93–101. doi:10.1002/yd.20425 PMID:33871947

Goldsby, M. G., Goldsby, E. A., Neck, C. B., Neck, C. P., & Mathews, R. (2021). Self-leadership: A four-decade review of the literature and trainings. *Administrative Sciences*, *11*(1), 25. doi:10.3390/admsci11010025

Graham, J. (1997). *Outdoor leadership: Technique, common sense & self-confidence*. Mountaineers.

Harari, M. B., Williams, E. A., Castro, S. L., & Brant, K. K. (2021). Self-leadership: A meta-analysis of over two decades of research. *Journal of Occupational and Organizational Psychology*, *94*(4), 890–923. doi:10.1111/joop.12365

Hart, J. W., Stasson, M. F., Mahoney, J. M., & Story, P. (2007). The Big Five and achievement motivation: Exploring the relationship between personality and a two-factor model of motivation. *Individual Differences Research*, *5*, 267–274.

Houghton, J. D., & Neck, C. P. (2002). The Revised Self-Leadership Questionnaire: Testing a hierarchical factor structure for self-leadership. *Journal of Managerial Psychology*, *17*(8), 672–692. doi:10.1108/02683940210450484

Houghton, J. D., Neck, C. P., & Manz, C. C. (2003). Self-leadership and superleadership: The heart and art of creating shared leadership in teams. In Shared leadership: Reframing the hows and whys of leadership (pp. 123-140). Academic Press.

Houghton, J. D., Bonham, T. W., Neck, C. P., & Singh, K. (2004). The relationship between self-leadership and personality. *Journal of Managerial Psychology, 19*(4), 427–441. doi:10.1108/02683940410537963

Judge, T. A., & Ilies, R. (2002). Relationship of personality to performance motivation: A meta-analytic review. *The Journal of Applied Psychology, 87*(4), 797–807. doi:10.1037/0021-9010.87.4.797 PMID:12184582

Lazarus, R. S., & Folkman, S. (1984). *Stress, appraisal, and coping*. Springer.

Mahoney, M. J., & Arnkoff, D. B. (1978). Cognitive and self-control therapies. In S. L. Garfield & A. E. Borgin (Eds.), *Handbook of psychotherapy and therapy change* (pp. 689–722). Wiley.

Mahoney, M. J., & Arnkoff, D. B. (1979). Self-management: Theory, research, and application. In J. P. Brady & D. Pomerleau (Eds.), *Behavioral medicine: Theory and practice* (pp. 75–96). Williams and Williams.

Manz, C. C. (1986). Self-leadership: Toward an expanded theory of self-influence processes in organizations. *Academy of Management Review, 11*(3), 585–600. doi:10.2307/258312

Manz, C. C. (1990). Beyond self-managing work teams: Toward self-leading teams in the workplace. In R. Woodman & W. Pasmore (Eds.), *Research in organizational change and development* (pp. 273–299). JAI Press.

Manz, C. C. (1992a). Self-leadership…The heart of empowerment. *Journal for Quality and Participation, 15*(4), 80–89.

Manz, C. (1992b). *Mastering Self-Leadership: Empowering yourself for personal excellence*. Prentice Hall.

Manz, C. C., & Neck, C. P. (1999). *Mastering self-leadership: Empowering yourself for personal excellence*. Prentice Hall.

Martin, B., Cashel, C., Wagstaff, M., & Breuning, M. (2006). *Outdoor leadership: Theory and practice*. Human Kinetics.

McCrae, R. R., & Lökenhoff, C. E. (2010). Self-regulation and the five-factor model of personality traits. In R. H. Hoyle (Ed.), *Handbook of personality and self-regulation* (pp. 145–168). Wiley-Blackwell. doi:10.1002/9781444318111.ch7

Megheirkouni, M. (2018). Self-leadership strategies and career success: Insight on sports organizations. *Sport, Business and Management, 8*(4), 393–409. doi:10.1108/SBM-02-2018-0006

Neck, C. P., Stewart, G. L., & Manz, C. C. (1996). Self-leaders within self-leading teams: Toward an optimal equilibrium. In M. Beyerlein (Ed.), *Advances in Interdisciplinary Studies of Work Teams* (pp. 43–65). JAI Press.

Neck, C. P., & Houghton, J. D. (2006). Two decades of Self-leadership Theory and research. *Journal of Managerial Psychology, 21*(4), 270–295. doi:10.1108/02683940610663097

Neck, C. P., & Manz, C. C. (2007). *Mastering self-leadership: Empowering yourself for personal excellence* (4th ed.). Prentice-Hall.

Neck, C. P., Manz, C. C., & Houghton, J. D. (2017). Self-leadership: The definitive guide to personal excellence. CA. *Sage (Atlanta, Ga.)*.

Neuman, W. L. (2014). *Social research methods: Qualitative and quantitative approaches*. Pearson Education Limited.

Patton, M. Q. (2002). *Qualitative research and evaluation methods*. Sage Publications.

Pernecky, T., & Jamal, T. (2010). Hermeneutic phenomenology in tourism studies. *Annals of Tourism Research, 37*(4), 1055–1075. doi:10.1016/j.annals.2010.04.002

Pinnow, D. F. (2011). *Leadership-What really matters: A handbook on systemic leadership*. Springer. doi:10.1007/978-3-642-20247-6

Priest, S. (1984). Effective outdoor leadership: A survey. *Journal of Experiential Education, 7*(3), 34–36. doi:10.1177/105382598400700310

Priest, S. (1986). *Outdoor leadership preparation in five nations* [Unpublished doctoral dissertation]. University of Oregon, Eugene.

Priest, S. (1987). *Preparing effective outdoor pursuit leaders*. Institute of Recreation Research and Service.

Priest, S., & Gass, M. A. (2005). *Effective leadership in adventure programming* (2nd ed.). Human Kinetics.

Proios, I. (2019). Factor validity and reliability of the Revised Self-Leadership Questionnaire in a Greek sample. *Journal of Physical Education and Sport Management, 6*(2), 41–48.

Proios, I., Fotiadou, E., Doganis, G., Batsiou, S., & Proios, M. (2020). Influence of Self-Leadership Strategies on the Beliefs of General Self-Efficacy. *The Journal of Social Sciences Research, 6*(5), 531–535. doi:10.32861/jssr.65.531.535

Prussia, G. E., Anderson, J. S., & Manz, C. C. (1998). Self-leadership and performance outcomes: The mediating influence of self-efficacy. *Journal of Organizational Behavior, 19*(5), 523–538. doi:10.1002/(SICI)1099-1379(199809)19:5<523::AID-JOB860>3.0.CO;2-I

Raiola, E. O. (1986). *Outdoor wilderness education: A leadership curriculum* [Unpublished doctoral dissertation]. Unity College, ME.

Raiola, E., & Sugerman, D. (1999). Outdoor leadership curricula. In J. Miles & S. Priest (Eds.), *Adventure programming* (pp. 241–245). Venture Publishing.

O'Connell, T. S., Cuthbertson, B., & Goins, T. J. (2014). *Leadership in recreation and leisure services*. Human Kinetics.

Shooter, W., Sibthorp, J., & Paisley, K. (2009). Outdoor leadership skills: A program perspective. *Journal of Experiential Education, 32*(1), 1–13. doi:10.1177/105382590903200102

Smith, H. A. (2011). *Extraordinary outdoor leaders: An Australian case* [Unpublished doctoral dissertation]. University of Wollongong, Australia.

Stewart, G. L., Courtright, S. H., & Manz, C. C. (2011). Self-leadership: A multilevel review. *Journal of Management, 37*(1), 185–222. doi:10.1177/0149206310383911

Swiderski, M. (1987). Soft and conceptual skills: The often-overlooked components of outdoor leadership. In G. Robb (Ed.), *Proceedings of the Coalition for Education in the Outdoor Research Symposium.* Academic Press.

Tsaur, S. H., Lin, W. R., & Liu, J. S. (2013). Sources of challenge for adventure tourists: Scale development and validation. *Tourism Management, 38*, 85–93. doi:10.1016/j.tourman.2013.03.004

Van Bussel, M. (2014). Direct Leadership in Recreation, Leisure, Hospitality, and Tourism. In *Leadership in Recreation and Leisure Services*. Human Kinetics.

Wolfe, B. (2014). Facilitating Group Experiences. In *Leadership in Recreation and Leisure Services*. Human Kinetics.

Compilation of References

Aasland, M. S., Skogstad, A., Notelaers, G., Nielsen, M. B., & Einarsen, S. (2010). The prevalence of destructive leadership behaviour. *British Journal of Management*, *21*(2), 438–452.

Abdullah, Rahim, Jeinie, Zulkafli, & Nordin. (2021). Leadership, task load and job satisfaction: a review of special education teachers perspective. *Turkish Journal of Computer and Mathematics Education*, *12*(11), 5300-5306.

Abdullah, K. H., Hashim, M. N., & Abd Aziz, F. S. (2020). A 39 years (1980-2019) bibliometric analysis of safety leadership research. *TEST Engineering and Management*, *83*, 4526–4542.

Abrudan, I. N., Pop, C. M., & Lazăr, P. S. (2020). Using a general ordered logit model to explain the influence of hotel facilities, general and sustainability-related, on customer ratings. *Sustainability*, *12*(21), 9302. doi:10.3390u12219302

Acar, B. (2002). *Ekip Çalışması ve Liderlik*. Remzi Kitabevi.

Aguzman, G., Manurung, A. H., Pradipto, Y. D., & Sanny, L. (2020). The effect of charismatic leadership on the sustainability of tourism destination with entrepreneurship orientation and community empowerment as a mediator. *Advances in Social Science, Education and Humanities Research*, *585*, 691–695.

Agyapong, A., & Boamah, R. B. (2013, March/April). Business Strategies And Competitive Advantage Of Family Hotel Businesses In Ghana: The Role Of Strategic Leadership. *Journal of Applied Business Research*, *29*(2), 531–544. doi:10.19030/jabr.v29i2.7654

Akat, İ. (1984). *İşletme Yönetimi*. İzmir: Üç el dağıtımcılık.

Akbaba, A., & Erenler, E. (2008). Otel İşletmelerinde Yöneticilerin Liderlik Yönelimleri ve İşletme Performansı İlişkisi. *Anatolia: Turizm Araştırmaları Dergisi*, *19*(1), 21–36.

Akgündüz, Y. (2020). *Örgütsel davranış [Organizational Behavior]*. Nobel Yayınevi.

Akoğlan Kozak, M. (2008). Turizm işletmelerinde liderlik ve liderlik tarzları. In *Turizm işletmelerinde çağdaş yönetim teknikleri*. Detay Yayıncılık.

Akoğlan Kozak, M. (2017). Liderlik. In *Rekreasyonel liderlik ve turist rehberliği: Kavram ve kuramlar üzerinden bir analiz*. Detay Yayıncılık.

Akova, O. (2017). *Liderlik Davranışı Örgütsel Sessizlik ve Örgütsel Performans Arasında Neddensellik Analizi: Beş Yıldızlı Otel İşletmelerinde Bir Araştırma*. Detay Yayıncılık.

Akyürek, M. İ. (2020). İnovasyon ve Liderlik. Uluslararası Liderlik Çalışmaları Dergisi. *Kuram ve Uygulama*, *3*(1), 5–24.

Al Harbi, J., Alarifi, S., & Mosbah, A. (2019). Transformation leadership and creativity. *Personnel Review*, *48*(5), 1082–1090. doi:10.1108/PR-11-2017-0354

Compilation of References

Al Thani, F. B. H., & Obeidat, A. M. (2020). The Impact of Strategic Leadership on Crisis Management. *International Journal of Asian Social Science*, *10*(6), 307–326. doi:10.18488/journal.1.2020.106.307.326

Al-Ababneh, M. (2013). Leadership Style of Managers in Five-Star Hotels and its Relationship with Employee's Job Satisfaction. *International Journal of Management & Business Studies*, *3*(2), 93–98. doi:10.2139srn.3633072

Al-Abahneh, M. (2017). Service Quality in the Hospitality Industry. *Journal of Tourism & Hospitality*, *6*(1), 1000e133.

Aladag, O. F., Köseoglu, M. A., King, B., & Mehraliyev, F. (2020). Strategy implementation research in hospitality and tourism: Current status and future potential. *International Journal of Hospitality Management*, *88*, 102556. doi:10.1016/j.ijhm.2020.102556 PMID:32390680

Alavi, M., & Leidner, D. E. (2001). Knowledge management and knowledge management systems: Conceptual foundations and research issues. *Management Information Systems Quarterly*, *25*(1), 107–136. doi:10.2307/3250961

Alexander, A., De Smet, A., & Weiss, L. (2021). *Decision making in uncertain times*. Retrieved 2 June 2021, from https://www.mckinsey.com/business functions/organization/our insights/decision-making-in-uncertain-times

AlKayid, K., Selem, K. M., Shehata, A. E., & Tan, C. C. (2022). Leader vision, organizational inertia and service hotel employee creativity: Role of knowledge-donating. *Current Psychology*, 1–13. doi:10.100712144-022-02743-6 PMID:35125851

Al-Malki, M., & Juan, W. (2018). Leadership styles and job performance: A literature review. *Journal of International Business Research and Marketing*, *3*(3), 50–59. doi:10.18775/jibrm.1849-8558.2015.33.3004

Alrawadieh, Z., Alrawadieh, Z., & Cetin, G. (2020). Digital transformation and revenue management: Evidence from the hotel industry. *Tourism Economics*. Advance online publication. doi:10.1177/13548166209019

Altınay, F. A. (2016). Are headmasters digital leaders in school culture? *Education in Science*, *40*(182), 77–86. doi:10.15390/EB.2015.4534

Altıntaş, D. (2020). *Dönüşümcü liderlik ve örgütsel bağlılık arasındaki ilişkinin incelenmesi: iletişim sektöründe bir araştırma* [Examining the relationship between transformational leadership and organizational commitment: A research in the communication sector] [Master Thesis]. Altınbaş University Graduate School of Education. Business Administration/Human Resources Management.

Alzoubi, R. H., & Jaaffar, A. H. (2020). The mediating effect of crisis management on leadership styles and hotel performance in Jordan. *International Journal of Financial Research*, *11*(4), 384–397. doi:10.5430/ijfr.v11n4p384

Amanchukwu, R. N., Stanley, G. J., & Ololube, N. P. (2015). A Review of Leadership Theories, Principles and Styles and Their Relevance to Educational Management. *Management*, *5*(1), 6–14.

Amankwaa, A., Gyensare, M. A., & Susomrith, P. (2019). Transformational leadership with innovative behaviour: Examining multiple mediating paths with PLS-SEM. *Leadership and Organization Development Journal*, *40*(1), 107–123. doi:10.1108/LODJ-10-2018-0358

Amankwaa, A., Seet, P. S., & Susomrith, P. (2022). Tackling hotel employees' turnover: A moderated-mediation analysis of transformational leadership, organisational embeddedness, and community embeddedness. *Journal of Hospitality and Tourism Management*, *51*, 67–78. doi:10.1016/j.jhtm.2022.02.029

Amor, A. M., Vazquez, J. P., & Faina, J. A. (2019). Transformational leadership and work engagement: Exploring the mediating role of structural empowerment. *European Management Journal*, 1–10.

Anderson, J. S., & Prussia, G. E. (1997). The self-leadership questionnaire: Preliminary assessment of construct validity. *The Journal of Leadership Studies*, *4*(2), 119–143. doi:10.1177/107179199700400212

Andersson, T., Cäker, M., Tengblad, S., & Wickelgren, M. (2019). Building traits for organizational resilience through balancing organizational structures. *Scandinavian Journal of Management*, *35*(1), 36–45. doi:10.1016/j.scaman.2019.01.001

Andrews, J., & Higson, H. (2008). Graduate Employability, 'Soft Skills' Versus 'Hard' Business Knowledge: A European Study. *Higher Education in Europe*, *33*(4), 411–422. doi:10.1080/03797720802522627

Anshori, M. Y., Karya, D. F., Muslihah, N., & Herlambang, T. (2020). Analysis of transformational leadership style for employee performance with job satisfaction as intervening variable. *International Journal of Advanced Science and Technology*, *29*(9), 3967–3973.

Antonakis, J., & Day, V. D. (2017). *The Nature of Leadership*. Academic Press.

Antonakis, J., Avolio, B. J., & Sivasubramaniam, N. (2003). Context and leadership: An examination of the nine-factor full-range leadership theory using the Multifactor Leadership Questionnaire. *The Leadership Quarterly*, *14*(3), 261–295. doi:10.1016/S1048-9843(03)00030-4

Antonakis, J., Bastardoz, N., Jacquart, P., & Shamir, B. (2016). Charisma: An illdefined and ill-measured gift. *Annual Review of Organizational Psychology and Organizational Behavior*, *3*(1), 293–319. doi:10.1146/annurev-orgpsych-041015-062305

Antonakis, J., Bastardoz, N., Liu, Y., & Schriesheim, C. A. (2014). What makes articles highly cited? *The Leadership Quarterly*, *25*(1), 152–179. doi:10.1016/j.leaqua.2013.10.014

Antonopoulou, H., Halkiopoulos, C., Barlou, O., & Beligiannis, G. N. (2019), Transformational leadership and digital skills in higher education institutes: during the COVID-19 pandemic. *Emerging Science Journal*, *5*(1), 1-15.

Apfiasari, S., Waskito, A., Ajit, A., Pertiwi, D. E., & Mukhlasin, M. (2015). The role of transformational leadership, trust, psychological well-being, and organizational culture on organizational commitment (Study on hotel employees in serang city). *Journal of Industrial Engineering & Management Research*, *2*(5), 1–12.

Ap, J., & Wong, K. K. (2001). Case study on tour guiding: Professionalism, issues, and problems. *Tourism Management*, *22*(5), 551–563. doi:10.1016/S0261-5177(01)00013-9

Arici, H. E., Arici, N. C., Köseoglu, M. A., & King, B. E. M. (2021). Leadership research in the root of hospitality scholarship: 1960–2020. *International Journal of Hospitality Management*, *99*, 103063. doi:10.1016/j.ijhm.2021.103063

Arıkan, S. (2001). Otoriter ve Demokratik Liderlik Tarzları Açısından Atatürk'ün Liderlik Davranışlarının Değerlendirilmesi. *H.Ü. İktisadi ve İdari Bilimler Fakültesi Dergisi*, *19*(1), 231-257.

Ariyabuddhiphongs, V., & Kahn, S. I. (2017). Transformational leadership and turnover intention: The mediating effects of trust and job performance on café employees in Thailand. *Journal of Human Resources in Hospitality & Tourism*, *16*(2), 215–233. doi:10.1080/15332845.2016.1202730

Armandi, B., Oppedisano, J., & Sherman, H. (2003). Leadership theory and practice: A "case" in point. *Management Desicion*, *41*(10), 1076–1088. doi:10.1108/00251740310509607

Arman, K., & Organ, A. (2021). A Fuzzy Best Worst approach to the determination of the importance level of digital supply chain on sustainability. *Business & Management Studies: An International Journal*, *9*(4), 1366–1379. doi:10.15295/bmij.v9i4.1901

Armstrong, M. (2009). *Armstrong's Handbook of Management and Leadership: A Guide to Managing Results* (2nd ed.). New Delhi: Kogan Page.

Compilation of References

Armstrong, M., & Taylor, S. (2020). *Armstrong's handbook of human resource management practice*. Kogan Page Publishers.

Arnold, K. A. (2017). Transformational leadership and employee psychological well-being: A review and directions for future research. *Journal of Occupational Health Psychology*, 22(3), 381–393. doi:10.1037/ocp0000062 PMID:28150998

Arokiasamy, A. R. A., Abdullah, A. G. K., & Ismail, A. (2015). Correlation between cultural perceptions, leadership style and ICT usage by school principals in Malaysia. *Procedia: Social and Behavioral Sciences*, 176, 319–332. doi:10.1016/j.sbspro.2015.01.478

Arslaner, E., & Boylu, Y. (2015). İş Hayatında Presenteeism: Otel İşletmeleri Açısından Bir Değerlendirme [Presenteeism in Work Life: An Evaluation in Hotel Industry]. *İşletme Araştırmaları Dergisi*, 7(4), 123-136.

Arslantaş, C. C., & Pekdemir, I. (2007). Dönüşümcü liderlik, örgütsel vatandaşlık davranışı ve örgütsel adalet arasındaki ilişkileri belirlemeye yönelik görgül bir araştırma[An empirical research to determine the relationships between transformational leadership, organizational citizenship behavior, and organizational justice]. *Anadolu University Journal of Social Sciences*, 7(1), 261–286.

Aslan, A. (2018). Turist rehberliği ve uzmanlık alanları [Tourist guiding and specialities]. In S. Eser, S. Şahin, & C. Çakıcı (Eds.), *Turist rehberliği* [Tourist guiding] (pp. 119–136). Detay Yayıncılık.

Ataman, G. (2001). *İşletme Yönetimi-Temel Kavramlar-Yeni Yaklaşımlar*. Türkmen Kitapevi.

Austrian Institute for SME Research. (2018). *SME data*. https://www.kmuforschung.ac.at/facts-and-figures/kmu-daten/?lang=en

Avcı, Ö., & Yaşar, Y. (2016). Bir Kamu Kuruluşunda Çalışanların Liderlik Algıları: Olgubilimsel Bir Yaklaşım. *Akademik İncelemeler Dergisi*, 11(1), 187–205. doi:10.17550/aid.52620

Avery, G. C. (2004). *Understanding Leadership: Paradigms and Cases*. SAGE.

Avolio, B. J. (2011). *Full Range Leadership Development* (2nd ed.). SAGE Publications. doi:10.4135/9781483349107

Avolio, B. J., Kahai, S., & Dodge, G. E. (2000). E-leadership: Implications for theory, research, and practice. *The Leadership Quarterly*, 11(4), 615–668. doi:10.1016/S1048-9843(00)00062-X

Avolio, B., Bass, B., & Jung, D. (1999). Re-examining the components of transformational and transactional leadership using the Multifactor Leadership Questionnaire. *Journal of Occupational and Organizational Psychology*, 72(4), 441–462. doi:10.1348/096317999166789

Aydın, E., & Erkılıç, E. (2020). Transformational leadership and innovative work behaviour: The mediating role of knowledge sharing. *Tourism and Recreation*, 2(2), 106–117.

Aydın, O. T. (2012). The Impact of Theory X, Theory Y and Theory Z on Research Performance: An Empirical Study from A Turkish University. *International Journal of Advances in Management and Economics*, 1(5), 24–30. doi:10.31270/ijame/01/05/2012/05

Background. (n.d.). ULISSE project. https://ulisseproject.eu/what-we-do/

Baird, J. R., & Penna, C. (1996). Challenge in learning and teaching science. *Research in Science Education*, 26(3), 257–269. doi:10.1007/BF02356938

Bakan, İ., & Bulut, Y. (2004). Yöneticilerin Uyguladıkları Liderlik Yaklaşımlarına Yönelik Algılamalar. *İstanbul Üniversitesi Siyasal Bilimler Fakültesi Dergisi*, 31, 151-176.

Bakan, İ., Büyükbeşe, T., Erşahan, B. & Kefe, İ. (2013). Kadın Çalışanların Yöneticilere İlişkin Algıları: Bir Alan Çalışması. *Çankırı Karatekin Üniversitesi İktisadi ve İdari Bilimler Fakültesi Dergisi, 3*(2), 71-84.

Bakker, A. B., Hetland, J., Olsen, O. K., & Espevik, R. (2022). Daily transformational leadership: A source of inspiration for follower performance? *European Management Journal, 40*(5). Advance online publication. doi:10.1016/j.emj.2022.04.004

Baldonado, A. M. (2017). Servant Leadership: Learning from Servant Leaders of the Past and Their Impact to the Future. *International Journal of Management Sciences and Business Research, 6*(1), 53–57.

Ballester-Miquel, J. C., Pérez-Ruiz, P., Hernández-Gadea, J., & Palacios-Marqués, D. (2017). Implementation of the Balanced Scorecard in the hotel sector through transformational leadership and empowerment. *Multidisciplinary Journal for Education. Social and Technological Sciences, 4*(1), 1–15.

Baltaş, A. (2000). *Değişimin içinden geleceğe doğru ekip çalışması ve liderlik* [Teamwork and leadership through change towards the future]. Remzi Kitabevi.

Bandura, A. (1977). Self-efficacy: Toward a unifying theory of behavioral change. *Psychological Review, 84*(2), 191–215. doi:10.1037/0033-295X.84.2.191 PMID:847061

Bandura, A. (1986). *Social foundations of thought and action: A social cognitive theory.* Prentice-Hall.

Bandura, A. (1991). Social cognitive theory of self-regulation. *Organizational Behavior and Human Decision Processes, 50*(2), 248–287. doi:10.1016/0749-5978(91)90022-L

Bannock, G. (2005). *The economics and management of small business: An international perspective.* Routledge.

Baquero, A., Delgado, B., Escortell, R., & Sapena, J. (2019). The influence of transformational and authentic leadership on the satisfaction of hotel customers in the Canary Islands. *Tourism and Hospitality Research,* 1–14.

Barbuto, J. E. Jr, & Wheeler, D. W. (2006). Scale Development and Construct Clarification of Servant Leadership. *Group & Organization Management, 31*(3), 300–326. doi:10.1177/1059601106287091

Barker, R. A. (2001). The nature of leadership. *Human Relations, 54*(4), 469–494. doi:10.1177/0018726701544004

Barrows, Powers, & Reynolds. (2012). Introduction to Management in the Hospitality Industry (10th ed.). John Wiley & Sons.

Bartsch, S., Weber, E., Büttgen, M., & Huber, A. (2020). Leadership matters in crisis-induced digital transformation: How to lead service employees effectively during the COVID-19 pandemic. *Journal of Service Management, 32*(1), 71–85. Advance online publication. doi:10.1108/JOSM-05-2020-0160

Başaran, S. (2020). *Okul müdürlerinin algılanan dönüşümcü liderlik davranışlarının öğretmenlerin örgütsel sinizm düzeyine etkisi* [The effect of perceived transformational leadership behaviors of school principals on teachers' level of organizational cynicism] [Master's Thesis]. Istanbul Marmara University.

Başaran, İ. E. (1998). *Yönetimde İnsan İlişkileri-Yönetsel Davranış.* Nobel Yayınevi.

Bass, B. M. (1990). Bass & Stogdill's Handbook of Leadership: Theory, Research & Managerial Applications (3rd ed.). New York: The Free Press.

Bass, B. M. (1998). Transformational leadership: Industrial, military, and educational impact. Academic Press.

Bass, B. M., & Riggio, R. E. (2005). Transformational leadership theory. *Organizational behavior I. Essential theories of motivation and leadership,* 361-385.

Compilation of References

Bass, B. M. (1961). Some aspects of attempted, successful and effective leadership. *The Journal of Applied Psychology*, *45*(2), 120–122. doi:10.1037/h0049166

Bass, B. M. (1985). *Leadership and performance beyond expectations*. Free Press.

Bass, B. M. (1985). Leadership: Good, better, best. *Organizational Dynamics*, *13*(3), 26–40. doi:10.1016/0090-2616(85)90028-2

Bass, B. M. (1990). *Bass and Stogdill's handbook of leadership: A survey of theory and research*. Free Press.

Bass, B. M. (1990). From transactional to transformational leadership: Learning to share the vision. *Organizational Dynamics*, *18*(3), 19–31. doi:10.1016/0090-2616(90)90061-S

Bass, B. M. (1992). Assessing the charismatic leader. In M. Syrett & C. Hogg (Eds.), *Frontiers of leadership*. Blackwell.

Bass, B. M. (1994). *Transformational leadership and team and organizational decision making, in improving organizational effectiveness through transformational leadership* (B. M. Bass & B. J. Avolio, Eds.). Sage Publications Inc.

Bass, B. M. (1998). *Transformational Leadership: Industry, Military, and Educational Impact*. Lawrence Erlbaum.

Bass, B. M. (1999). Two decades of research and development in transformational leadership. *European Journal of Work and Organizational Psychology*, *8*(1), 9–32. doi:10.1080/135943299398410

Bass, B. M. (2000). The Future of Leadership in Learning Organizations. *The Journal of Leadership Studies*, *7*(3), 19–40. doi:10.1177/107179190000700302

Bass, B. M., & Avolio, B. J. (1985). *Improving organizational effectiveness through transformational leadership*. Sage.

Bass, B. M., & Avolio, B. J. (1989). *Manual for the multifactor leadership questionnaire*. Consulting Psychologists Press.

Bass, B. M., & Avolio, B. J. (1990). Developing transformational leadership. *Journal of European Industrial Training*, *14*(5), 21–27. doi:10.1108/03090599010135122

Bass, B. M., & Avolio, B. J. (1990). *Multifactor leadership questionnaire*. Consulting Psychologists Press.

Bass, B. M., & Avolio, B. J. (1990). *Transformational leadership development: Manual for the multifactor leadership questionnaire*. Consulting Psychologists Press.

Bass, B. M., & Avolio, B. J. (1993). Transformational leadership and organizational culture. *Public Administration Quarterly*, *17*(1), 112–121.

Bass, B. M., & Avolio, B. J. (1993). Transformational leadership: A response to critiques. In M. M. Chemers & R. Ayman (Eds.), *Leadership theory and research: Perspectives and directions* (pp. 49–80). Academic Press.

Bass, B. M., & Avolio, B. J. (1995). *Manual for the multifactor leadership questionnaire: Rater form (5X short)*. Mind Garden.

Bass, B. M., & Avolio, B. J. (1995). *Multifactor leadership questionnaire: Technical report*. Mind Garden.

Bass, B. M., Avolio, B. J., Jung, D. I., & Berson, Y. (2003). Predicting unit performance by assessing transformational and transactional leadership. *The Journal of Applied Psychology*, *88*(2), 207–218. doi:10.1037/0021-9010.88.2.207 PMID:12731705

Bass, B. M., & Bass, R. (2009). *The Bass handbook of leadership: Theory, research, and managerial applications* (4th ed.). Free Press.

Bass, B. M., & Bass, R. (2009). *The Bass Handbook of Leadership: Theory, Research, and Managerial Applications*. Simon and Schuster.

Bass, B. M., & Riggio, R. E. (2005). *Transformational Leadership* (2nd ed.). Psychology Press., doi:10.4324/9781410617095

Bass, B. M., & Steidlmeier, P. (1999). Ethics, character, and authentic transformational leadership behavior. *The Leadership Quarterly*, *10*(2), 181–217. doi:10.1016/S1048-9843(99)00016-8

Bastiat, F. (1966). *Economic Harmonies*. Foundation for Economic Education.

Baumeister, R. F., Bratslavsky, E., Finkenauer, C., & Vohs, K. D. (2001). Bad is stronger than good. *Review of General Psychology*, *5*(4), 323–370. doi:10.1037/1089-2680.5.4.323

Bausch, T., & Gartner, W. C. (2020). Winter tourism in the European Alps: Is a new paradigm needed? *Journal of Outdoor Recreation and Tourism*, *31*, 100297. doi:10.1016/j.jort.2020.100297

Bauwens, R., Batistič, S., Kilroy, S., & Nijs, S. (2022). New Kids on the Block? A Bibliometric Analysis of Emerging COVID-19—Trends in Leadership Research. *Journal of Leadership & Organizational Studies*, *29*(2), 224–232. doi:10.1177/1548051821997406 PMID:35516092

Baykal, E., Zehir, C., & Köle, M. (2018). Effects of Servant Leadership on Gratitude, Empowerment, Innovativeness and Performance: Turkey Example. *Journal of Economy Culture and Society*, *57*, 29–52. doi:10.26650/JECS390903

Baytok, A., & Ergen, F.D. (2013). Hizmetkâr Liderliğin Örgütsel Vatandaşlık Davranışına Etkisi: İstanbul ve Afyonkarahisar'daki Beş Yıldızlı Otel İşletmelerinde Bir Araştırma [The Effect of Servant Leadership on Organizational Citizenship Behavior: A Study in Five Star Hotel Enterprisesin İstanbul and Afyonkarahisar]. *İşletme Araştırmaları Dergisi*, *5*(4), 105-132.

Baytok, A., Kurt, M., & Zorlu, Ö. (2014). The role of transformational leader on knowledge sharing practices: A study about international hotel chains. *European Journal of Business and Management*, *6*(7), 45–61.

Bazazo, I. K., Alayanzeh, O. A., Adas, K., & Alshawagfih, K. F. (2016). The role of the transformational leadership in enhancing the social responsibility at the five stars hotels in the Hashemite Kingdom of Jordan. *European Journal of Business and Management*, *8*(23), 67–74.

Beck, A. T., Rush, A. J., Shaw, B. F., & Emery, G. (1979). *Cognitive theory of depression*. Guilford Press.

Beğenirbaş, M., & Can Yalçın, R. (2020). Hizmetkâr Liderlik Algısının Duygusal Emek Üzerine Etkileri: Hizmet Çalışanları Üzerinde Bir Araştırma[The Effects of Servant Leadership Perception on Emotional Labor: A Research on Service Employees]. *Savunma Bilimleri Dergisi.*, *19*(1), 159–194.

Belias, D., Rossidis, I., Papademetriou, C., & Mantas, C. (2021). Job satisfaction as affected by types of leadership: A case study of Greek tourism sector. *Journal of Quality Assurance in Hospitality & Tourism*, 1–20.

Bennis, W. (1994). *On becoming a leader*. Addison-Wesley.

Bennis, W. G. (1959). Leadership theory and administrative behavior: The problems of authority. *Administrative Science Quarterly*, *4*(3), 259–301. doi:10.2307/2390911

Bennis, W., Bennis, W. G., & Nanus, B. (1986). *Leaders: The Strategies for Taking Charge*. Harper & Row.

Berry, L. L., Parasuraman, A., & Zeithaml, V. A. (1994). Improving service quality in America: Lessons learned. *The Academy of Management Executive*, *8*(2), 32–52. doi:10.5465/ame.1994.9503101072

Compilation of References

Bertocci, D. I. (2009). *Leadership in organizations: There is a difference between leaders and managers*. University Press of America.

Bertocci, D. I. (2009). *Leadership in Organizations: There is a Difference Between Leaders and Managers*. University Press of America.

Besler, S. (2004). *İşletmelerde Stratejik Liderlik* [Strategic leadership in Business]. Beta Yay.

Bharati, P., & Chaudhury, A. (2009). SMEs and competitiveness: The role of information systems. *International Journal of E-Business Research*, *5*(1), I–IX.

Bhargav, S. (2017). A study on marketing mix of hospitality industry. *International Journal of Management. IT & Engineering*, *7*(9), 253–265.

Bhatt, G. D. (2001). Knowledge management in organizations: Examining the interaction between technologies, techniques, and people. *Journal of Knowledge Management*, *5*(1), 68–75. doi:10.1108/13673270110384419

Bickes, D. M., & Yılmaz, C. (2020). Leadership Theories. In A Handbook of Leadership Styles (pp. 1-34). Cambridge Scholars Publishing.

Biggs, D. (2011). Understanding resilience in a vulnerable industry: The case of reef tourism in Australia. *Ecology and Society*, *16*(1), art30. doi:10.5751/ES-03948-160130

Bilgin, N., Kuzey, C., Torlak, G., & Uyar, A. (2015). An investigation of antecedents of organizational citizenship behavior in the Turkish hospitality industry: A structural equation approach. *International Journal of Culture, Tourism and Hospitality Research*, *9*(2), 200–222. doi:10.1108/IJCTHR-08-2014-0072

Billig, M. (2015). Kurt Lewin's Leadership Studies and His Legacy to Social Psychology: Is There Nothing as Practical as a Good Theory? *Journal for the Theory of Social Behaviour*, *45*(4), 440–460. doi:10.1111/jtsb.12074

Bingöl, S. (2021). Macera rekreasyonunda algılanan zorluklar: Doğa yürüyüşü ve kaya tırmanışı[Perceived challenges in adventure recreation: hiking and rock climbing]. *Journal Of Recreation and Tourism Research*, *8*(2), 247–267. doi:10.31771/jrtr.2021.100

Birasnav, M., & Bienstock, J. (2019). Supply Chain Integration, Advanced Manufacturing Technology, and Strategic Leadership: An empirical study. *Computers & Industrial Engineering*, *130*, 142–157. doi:10.1016/j.cie.2019.01.021

Biviano, J. A. (2000). *Charismatic leadership: An effective instrument for cultural transformation*. RMIT Business School of Management Working Paper Series.

Blake, R. R., & Mouton, J. S. (1985). *The managerial grid III: A new look at the classic that has boosted productivity and profits for thousands of corporations worldwide*. Gulf Publishing Company, Book Division.

Blayney, C., & Blotnicky, K. (2010). Leadership In The Hotel Industry: Evidence From Canada. *International Journal of Management and Marketing Research*, *3*(3), 53–66.

Blayney, C., & Blotnicky, K. (2010). Leadership in the hotel industry: Evidence from Canada. *International Journal of Management and Marketing Research*, *3*(3), 53–66.

Boal, K. B., & Hooijberg, R. (2000). Strategic Leadership Research: Moving On. *The Leadership Quarterly*, *11*(4), 515–549. doi:10.1016/S1048-9843(00)00057-6

Boerner, S., Eisenbeiss, S., & Griesser, D. (2007). Followers' behaviour and organizational performance: The impact of transformational leaders. *Journal of Leadership & Organizational Studies*, *13*(3), 15–26. doi:10.1177/10717919070130030201

Borins, S. F. (2010). Digital state 2.0. In M. J. Prince, G. B. Doern, L. A. Pal, & G. Toner (Eds.), *Policy from Ideas to Implementation: In Honour of Professor G. Bruce Doern* (pp. 177–206). McGill-Queen's University Press.

Bouzari, M., & Karatepe, O. M. (2017). Test of a mediation model of psychological capital among hotel salespeople. *International Journal of Contemporary Hospitality Management*, 29(8), 2178–2197. doi:10.1108/IJCHM-01-2016-0022

Bowers, M. R., Hall, J. R., & Srinivasan, M. M. (2017). Organizational culture and leadership style: The missing combination for selecting the right leader for effective crisis management. *Business Horizons*, 60(4), 551–563. doi:10.1016/j.bushor.2017.04.001

Boyne, S. (2010). Leadership research in hospitality: A critical review. *Education*, 17, 20–27.

Bozkurt, Ö., & Göral, M. (2013). Modern liderlik tarzlarının yenilik stratejilerine etkisini belirlemeye yönelik bir çalışma[A study to determine the effect of modern leadership styles on innovation strategies]. *Anadolu Üniversitesi Sosyal Bilimler Dergisi*, 13(4), 1–14.

Brestrich, E. T. (2000). *Transformational leadership from modernism to postmodernism*. Seba Publications.

Brewer, M. B., & Gardner, W. (1996). Who is this" We"? Levels of collective identity and self representations. *Journal of Personality and Social Psychology*, 71(1), 83–93. doi:10.1037/0022-3514.71.1.83

Brickson, S. (2000). The impact of identity orientation on individual and organizational outcomes in demographically diverse settings. *Academy of Management Review*, 25(1), 82–101. doi:10.2307/259264

Briner, R. B., Denyer, D., & Rousseau, D. M. (2009). Evidence-based management: Concept cleanup time? *The Academy of Management Perspectives*, 23(4), 19–32. doi:10.5465/AMP.2009.45590138

Brownell, J. (2010). Leadership in the Service of Hospitality. *Cornell Hospitality Quarterly*, 51(3), 363–378. doi:10.1177/1938965510368651

Bryant, S. E. (2003). The role of transformational and transactional leadership in creating, sharing and exploiting organizational knowledge. *Journal of Leadership & Organizational Studies*, 9(4), 32–44. doi:10.1177/107179190300900403

Bryman, A. (1992). *Charisma and leadership in organizations*. Sage.

Bryman, A. (2004). Qualitative research on leadership: A critical but appreciative review. *The Leadership Quarterly*, 15(6), 729–769. doi:10.1016/j.leaqua.2004.09.007

Buell, L. H. (1981). *The identification of outdoor adventure leadership competencies for entry-level and experienced-level personnel* [Unpublished doctoral dissertation]. University of Massachusetts, Amherst.

Buhalis, D., & Leung, R. (2018). Smart hospitality—Interconnectivity and interoperability towards an ecosystem. *International Journal of Hospitality Management*, 71, 41–50. doi:10.1016/j.ijhm.2017.11.011

Buhalis, D., & Peters, M. (2006). SMEs in tourism. In D. Buhalis & C. Costa (Eds.), *Tourism management dynamics: Trends, management and tools* (pp. 116–129). Elsevier Ltd. doi:10.1016/B978-0-7506-6378-6.50023-8

Buil, I., Martínez, E., & Matute, J. (2019). Transformational leadership and employee performance: The role of identification, engagement and proactive personality. *International Journal of Hospitality Management*, 77, 64–75. doi:10.1016/j.ijhm.2018.06.014

Buluç, B. (2009). Sınıf Öğretmenlerinin Algılarına Göre Okul Müdürlerinin Liderlik Stilleri ile Örgütsel Bağlılık Arasındaki İlişki. *Kuram ve Uygulamada Eğitim Yönetimi*, 15(57), 5–34.

Compilation of References

Burke, W. W. (2017). *Robert R. Blake and Jane S. Mouton: Concern for People and Production. In The Palgrave Handbook of Organizational Change Thinkers*. Palgrave Macmillan. doi:10.1007/978-3-319-49820-1_4-1

Burns, J. M. (1978). *Leadership*. Harper & Row.

Burns, J. M. (2003). *Transforming Leadership: A new pursuit o happiness*. Grove Press.

Busari, A. H., Khan, S. N., Abdullah, S. M., & Mughal, Y. H. (2019). Transformational leadership style, followership, and factors of employees' reactions towards organizational change. *Journal of Asia Business Studies, 14*(2), 181–209. doi:10.1108/JABS-03-2018-0083

Busulwa, R., Pickering, M., & Mao, I. (2022). Digital transformation and hospitality management competencies: Toward an integrative framework. *International Journal of Hospitality Management, 102*, 103132. doi:10.1016/j.ijhm.2021.103132

Cairnes, J. E. (1873). *Essays in political economy*. Macmillan and Company.

Çalışkan, S. C. (2009). Turizm İşletmelerinde Liderlik Tarzları ve Lider-Üye Etkileşimi Kalitesi (LÜE) Üzerine Bir Çalışma[A Study on Leadership Styles and Leader-Member Interaction Quality (LPI) in Tourism Businesses]. *Trakya Üniversitesi Sosyal Bilimler Dergisi, 11*(2), 219–241.

Can, H., Akgün, A., & Kavuncubaşı, Ş. (2001). Kamu ve Özel Kesimde & İnsan Kaynakları Yönetimi. Ankara: Siyasal Kitabevi.

Canhoto, A. I., & Wei, L. (2021). Stakeholders of the world, unite!: Hospitality in the time of COVID-19. *International Journal of Hospitality Management, 95*, 102922. doi:10.1016/j.ijhm.2021.102922 PMID:36540681

Carless, S. A., Wearing, A., & Mann, L. (2000). A short measure of transformational leadership. *Journal of Business and Psychology, 14*(3), 389–405. doi:10.1023/A:1022991115523

Carlyle, T. (1885). *Latter-day pamphlets* (Vol. 5). Chapman and Hall, Limited.

Carmeli, A. (2003). The relationship between emotional intelligence and work attitudes, behavior, and outcomes: An examination among senior managers. *Journal of Managerial Psychology, 18*(8), 788–813. doi:10.1108/02683940310511881

Carnevale, J. B., & Hatak, I. (2020). Employee adjustment and well-being in the era of COVID-19: Implications for human resource management. *Journal of Business Research, 116*, 183–187. doi:10.1016/j.jbusres.2020.05.037 PMID:32501303

Carnicelli-Filho, S., Schwartz, G. M., & Tahara, A. K. (2010). Fear and adventure tourism in Brazil. *Tourism Management, 31*(6), 953–956. doi:10.1016/j.tourman.2009.07.013

Carrión, I. A., Ramírez, M. C., & Flores, J. C. (2018). Transformational ledership and gender in 4 and 5 Star Hotel in Tijuana (Mexico). *Cuadernos de Turismo, 42*, 609–612.

Çelik, S. (2019). Turizm alanında liderlik konusu ile ilgili hazırlanmış tezlere yönelik bibliyometrik bir analiz[A bibliometric analysis of the theses on leadership in the field of tourism]. *Journal of Academic Value Studies, 5*(4), 516–527.

Çetin, C. (2008). *Yöneticilerin liderlik stilleri, değişim yönetimi ve ekip çalışması arasındaki ilişkilerin çok yönlü olarak değerlendirilmesi*. İstanbul: İTO yayınları.

Champous, J. E. (2011). *Organizational Behavior: Integrating Individuals, Groups and Organizations*. Routledge.

Champoux, J. E. (2017). Organizational Behavior: Integrating Individuals, Groups, and Organizations (5th ed.). New York: Routledge.

Chang, J. H., & Teng, C. C. (2017). Intrinsic or extrinsic motivations for hospitality employees' creativity: The moderating role of organization-level regulatory focus. *International Journal of Hospitality Management*, *60*, 133–141. doi:10.1016/j.ijhm.2016.10.003

Charmaz, K. (2006). *Constructing grounded theory: A practical guide through qualitative research*. Sage Publications.

Charoenboon, P., & Chankaew, K. (2022). Managing strategies of transformational leadership to create service standard of boutique hotel in Thailand. *International Journal of Health Sciences*, *6*(3), 6984–6994. doi:10.53730/ijhs.v6nS3.7625

Chemers, M. M. (2000). Leadership Research and Theory: A Functional Integration. *Group Dynamics*, *4*(1), 27–43. doi:10.1037/1089-2699.4.1.27

Chen, A., Brian, M., & Hou, Y. (2015). Impact of transformational leadership on subordinate's EI and work performance. *Personnel Review*, *44*(4), 438–453. doi:10.1108/PR-09-2012-0154

Chen, T. J., & Wu, C. M. (2020). Can newcomers perform better at hotels? Examining the roles of transformational leadership, supervisor-triggered positive affect, and perceived supervisor support. *Tourism Management Perspectives*, *33*, 1–15. doi:10.1016/j.tmp.2019.100587

Chen, T. J., Wu, C. M., & Wang, Y. C. (2015). Impact of transformational leadership behaviors and psychological optimism on subordinate performance in Taiwan's tourism hotel industry. *Open Journal of Social Sciences*, *3*(07), 174–179. doi:10.4236/jss.2015.37028

Chen, T., & Wu, C. (2017). Improving the turnover intention of tourist hotel employees: Transformational leadership, leader-member exchange, and psychological contract breach. *International Journal of Contemporary Hospitality Management*, *29*(7), 1914–1936. doi:10.1108/IJCHM-09-2015-0490

Che, X. X., Zhou, Z. E., Kessler, S. R., & Spector, P. E. (2017). Stressors beget stressors: The effect of passive leadership on employee health through workload and work–family conflict. *Work and Stress*, *31*(4), 338–354. doi:10.1080/02678373.2017.1317881

Chianga, C., & Lin, M. (2016). Motivating organizational commitment in hotels: The relationship between leaders and employees. *Journal of Human Resources in Hospitality & Tourism*, *15*(4), 462–484. doi:10.1080/15332845.2016.1148570

Chiang, C. F., & Jang, S. (2008). The Antecedents and Consequences of Psychological Empowerment: The Case of Taiwan's Hotel Companies. *Journal of Hospitality & Tourism Research (Washington, D.C.)*, *32*(1), 40–61. doi:10.1177/1096348007309568

Chiang, C. F., & Wang, Y. Y. (2012). The effects of transactional and transformational leadership on organizational commitment in hotels: The mediating effect of trust. *Hotel & Business Management*, *1*(1), 3–11. doi:10.4172/2169-0286.1000103

Choi, H. J. (2010). The effects of leadership styles on organizational commitment among cuisine employees in hotel-focused on the moderated effect of job satisfaction. *The Korean Journal of Culinary Research*, *16*(5), 64–78.

Chon, K., Park, E., & Zoltan, J. (2020). The Asian paradigm in hospitality and tourism. *Journal of Hospitality & Tourism Research (Washington, D.C.)*, *44*(8), 1183–1202. doi:10.1177/1096348020945370

Chon, K., & Zoltan, J. (2019). Role of servant leadership in contemporary hospitality. *International Journal of Contemporary Hospitality Management*, *31*(8), 3371–3394. doi:10.1108/IJCHM-11-2018-0935

Christensen, K., Levinson, D., Goethals, G. R., & Sorenson, G. J. (2004). Preface. In Encyclopedia of leadership. Sage.

Compilation of References

Chuan-Chun, W., Chien-Hsing, W., Chang-Chun, L., & Teng-Hang, H. (2011). Drivers of organizational knowledge management. *African Journal of Business Management*, *5*(11), 4388–4402. doi:10.5897/AJBM10.1415

Chukwuba, K. (2015). *A quantitative model studying the effects of transformational leadership on job satisfaction*. College of Management and Technology, Walden University.

Chung, J. Y., Chang, S. J., Kyle, G. T., & James, P. F. (2010). Justice in the U.S. National Park Service: The Antecedents of Job Satisfaction. *Journal of Park and Recreation Administration*, *28*(3), 1–15.

Çiftçi, F., & Zencir, E. (2019). Turizm sektöründeki sosyal girişim çalışanlarının sosyal girişimcilik davranışı, iş ve yaşam tatmini: Tatuta projesi Narköy örneği [Social entrepreneurial behavior, job and life satisfaction of social entrepreneurs in the tourism sector: Tatuta project Narköy example]. *Turizm Akademik Dergisi/Tourism Academic Journal*, *6*(1), 131-145.

Cinnioğlu, H., Atay, L., & Karakaş, E. (2019). The influence of hotel employee's perceived leadership style on their level of burnout: Çanakkale sample. *Journal of Social Sciences of Mus Alparslan University*, *7*(6), 157–165.

Cohen, E. (1985). The tourist guide: The origins, structure, and dynamics of a role. *Annals of Tourism Research*, *12*(1), 5–29. doi:10.1016/0160-7383(85)90037-4

Conger, J. A., & Kanungo, R. N. (1988). Behavioral dimensions of charismatic leadership. In Charismatic Leadership. Jossey Bass.

Conger, J. A., & Kanungo, R. N. (1987). Toward a behavioral theory of charismatic leadership in organizational settings. *Academy of Management Review*, *12*(4), 637–647. doi:10.2307/258069

Conger, J. A., & Kanungo, R. N. (1988). *Charismatic leadership: The elusive factor in organizational effectiveness*. Jossey-Bass.

Conger, J. A., & Kanungo, R. N. (1994). Charismatic leadership in organizations: Perceived behavioral attributes and their measurement. *Journal of Organizational Behavior*, *15*(5), 439–452. doi:10.1002/job.4030150508

Connell, J. (2001). Growing the right skills through five-star management. *Australian Journal of Hospitality Management*, *8*(1), 1–14.

Connelly, B. S., Ones, D. S., & Hulsheger, U. R. (2018). Personality in industrial, work, and organizational psychology: Theory measurement and applications. In D. S. Ones, N. Anderson, C. Viswesvaran, & H. K. Sinangil (Eds.), *The Sage handbook of industrial, work, and organizational psychology* (pp. 320–365). Sage.

Copeland, N. (1942). *Psychology and the soldier*. Military Service Publication.

Cortellazzo, L., Bruni, E., & Zampieri, R. (2019). The role of leadership in a digitalized world: A review. *Frontiers in Psychology*, *10*, 1938. doi:10.3389/fpsyg.2019.01938 PMID:31507494

Cote, R. (2017). A comparison of leadership theories in an organizational environment. *International Journal of Business Administration*, *8*(5), 28–35. doi:10.5430/ijba.v8n5p28

Côté, S., Lopes, P. N., Salovey, P., & Miners, C. T. H. (2010). Emotional intelligence and leadership emergence in small groups. *The Leadership Quarterly*, *21*(3), 496–508. doi:10.1016/j.leaqua.2010.03.012

Covin, J. G., & Slevin, D. P. (2017). The Entrepreneurial Imperatives of Strategic Leadership. *Strategic Entrepreneurship: Creating a New Mindset*, 307-327.

Crespí-Cladera, R., Martín-Oliver, A., & Pascual-Fuster, B. (2021). Financial distress in the hospitality industry during the Covid-19 disaster. *Tourism Management*, *85*, 104301. doi:10.1016/j.tourman.2021.104301

Creswell, J. W., & Creswell, J. D. (2017). *Research design: Qualitative, quantitative, and mixed methods approaches.* Sage publications.

Cropanzano, R., & Mitchell, M. S. (2005). Social exchange theory: An interdisciplinary review. *Journal of Management*, *31*(6), 874–900. doi:10.1177/0149206305279602

Croteau, A. M., & Dfouni, M. (2008). Knowledge management leaders' top issues. In Knowledge management and business strategies: Theoretical frameworks and empirical research (pp. 47-68). IGI Global.

Cuddy, A., Kohut, M., & Neinger, J. (2018). *Connect, Then Lead. In Leadership Presence.* Harvard Business Review Press.

Cuthbertson, B. (2014). Self-Leadership. In *Leadership in Recreation and Leisure Services.* Human Kinetics.

D'Auria, G., & De Smet, A. (2020). Leadership in a crisis: Responding to the coronavirus outbreak and future challenges. *Psychology (Irvine, Calif.)*, *22*(2), 273–287.

Dai, Y. D., Dai, Y. Y., Chen, K. Y., & Wu, H. C. (2013). Transformational vs transactional leadership: which is better?: A study on employees of international tourist hotels in Taipei City. *International Journal of Contemporary Hospitality Management*, *25*(5), 760–778. doi:10.1108/IJCHM-Dec-2011-0223

Davies, A., Fidler, D., & Gorbis, D. (2011). *Future Work Skills 2020.* Institute for the Future for University of Phoenix Research Institute. https://www.iftf.org/uploads/media/SR1382A_UPRI_future_work_skills_sm.pdf

Davies, B. J., & Davies, B. (2004). Strategic Leadership. *School Leadership & Management*, *24*(1), 29–38. doi:10.1080/1363243042000172804

Davis, T. R., & Luthans, F. (1979). Leadership Reexamined: A Behavioral Approach. *Academy of Management Review*, *4*(2), 237–248. doi:10.2307/257777 PMID:10297506

Day, S. W., Lawong, D., Miles, A. K., & Effon, T. (2022). Leadership and culture in ghana's tourism and hospitality industry: The impact of transformational leadership on job satisfaction in an emerging economy. *Journal of Leadership, Accountability and Ethics*, *19*(1), 127–134.

de Boisguilbert, P. (2014). *Détail de la France* [Detail of France]. Institut Coppet.

de Lucas Ancillo, A., del Val Núñez, M. T., & Gavrila, S. G. (2021). Workplace change within the COVID-19 context: A grounded theory approach. *Economic Research-Ekonomska Istraživanja*, *34*(1), 2297–2316. doi:10.1080/1331677X.2020.1862689

De Waal, B., van Outvorst, F., & Ravesteyn, P. (2016). Digital leadership: The objective-subjective dichotomy of technology revisited. In *12th European Conference on Management, Leadership and Governance ECMLG 2016* (p. 52). Academic Press.

Deci, E. L., & Ryan, R. M. (1985). *Intrinsic motivation and self-determination in human behavior.* Plenum. doi:10.1007/978-1-4899-2271-7

Derici, S., & Elden, B. (2019). *Determining the most appropriate leadership style for public institutions in industry 4.0 by managerial abilities. In Turkey Vision: Multidisciplinary Studies.* Ekin Yayınevi.

Derue, D. S., Nahrgang, J. D., Wellman, N., & Humphrey, S. E. (2011). Trait and Behavioral Theories of Leadership: An Integration and Meta-Analytic Test of Their Relative Validity. *Personnel Psychology*, *64*(1), 7–52. doi:10.1111/j.1744-6570.2010.01201.x

Dery, K., Sebastian, I. M., & van der Meulen, N. (2017). The digital workplace is key to digital innovation. *MIS Quarterly Executive*, *16*(2).

Deshwal, V., & Ali, M. A. (2020). A Systematic Review of Various Leadership Theories. *International Journal of Commerce*, *8*(1), 38–43. doi:10.34293/commerce.v8i1.916

Detert, J. R., & Treviño, L. K. (2010). Speaking up to higher-ups: How supervisors and skip-level leaders influence employee voice. *Organization Science*, *21*(1), 249–270. doi:10.1287/orsc.1080.0405

Dhir, A., Talwar, S., Kaur, P., & Malibari, A. (2020). Food waste in hospitality and food services: A systematic literature review and framework development approach. *Journal of Cleaner Production*, *270*, 122861. doi:10.1016/j.jclepro.2020.122861

Digman, J. M. (1990). Personality structure: Emergence of the five-factor model. *Annual Review of Psychology*, *41*(1), 417–440. doi:10.1146/annurev.ps.41.020190.002221

Dimitrov, D. (2015). Leadership in a humane organization. *European Journal of Training and Development*, *39*(2), 122–142. doi:10.1108/EJTD-07-2014-0051

Dlamini, N., Garg, A. K., & Muchie, P. M. (2017). The impact of transformational leadership style on organizational commitment in the hospitality industry. *African Journal of Hospitality, Tourism and Leisure*, *6*(3), 1–21.

Doğanbaş, Z. E. (2017). *Dönüşümcü liderlik ile iş tatmini arasındaki ilişkinin incelenmesi: kuşaklar arası farklılık* [Examining the relationship between transformational leadership and job satisfaction: Generational difference] [Master Thesis]. Çankaya University, Institute of Social Sciences.

Doğaner, M., Aydın, M. S., & İncioğlu, C. (2021). Evaluation of leadership types efficiency in corporate organizations by SWARA method. *Pamukkale University Journal of Business Research*, *8*(1), 66–81.

Donate, M. J., & de Pablo, J. D. S. (2015). The role of knowledge-oriented leadership in knowledge management practices and innovation. *Journal of Business Research*, *68*(2), 360–370. doi:10.1016/j.jbusres.2014.06.022

Donate, M. J., González-Mohíno, M., Appio, F. P., & Bernhard, F. (2022). Dealing with knowledge hiding to improve innovation capabilities in the hotel industry: The unconventional role of knowledge-oriented leadership. *Journal of Business Research*, *144*, 572–586. doi:10.1016/j.jbusres.2022.02.001

Dörner, K., & Edelman, D. (2015). *What 'digital' really means*. McKinsey & company.

Downton, J. V. (1973). *Rebel leadership: Commitment and charisma in the revolutionary process*. Free Press.

Dragoni, L., Park, H., Soltis, J., & Forte-Trammell, S. (2014). Show and tell: How supervisors facilitate leader development among transitioning leaders. *The Journal of Applied Psychology*, *99*(1), 66–86. doi:10.1037/a0034452 PMID:24060160

Drucker, P. F. (1998). *The Leader of the Future*. Jossey Bass.

Duan, Q. (2005). *China's IT Leadership*. University of Maryland, Philosophy Graduate School.

Duckworth, A. (2017). Grit: Why passion and resilience are the secrets to success. Ebury Publishing.

Dupont de Nemours, P. S. (1883). Décret sur la circulation des poudres, lors de la séance du 4 juillet 1790[Decree on the circulation of powders, during the session of July 4. 1790]. *Archives Parlementaires de la Révolution Française*, *16*(1), 694–694.

Dwyer, L., & Edwards, D. (2010). Sustainable tourism planning. In J. J. Liburd & D. Edwards (Eds.), *Understanding the sustainable development of tourism* (pp. 19–44).

Ecer, F. (2021). Sustainability assessment of existing onshore wind plants in the context of triple bottom line: A best-worst method (BWM) based MCDM framework. *Environmental Science and Pollution Research International*, *28*(16), 19677–19693. doi:10.100711356-020-11940-4 PMID:33405119

Edmonstone, J., & Western, J. (2002). Leadership development in health care: What do we know? *Journal of Management in Medicine*, *16*(1), 34–47. doi:10.1108/02689230210428616 PMID:12069350

Eichenauer, C. J., Ryan, A. M., & Alanis, J. M. (2022). Leadership During Crisis: An Examination of Supervisory Leadership Behavior and Gender During COVID-19. *Journal of Leadership & Organizational Studies*, *29*(2), 190–207. doi:10.1177/15480518211010761 PMID:35516093

Einarsen, S., Aasland, M. S., & Skogstad, A. (2007). Destructive leadership behaviour: A definition and conceptual model. *The Leadership Quarterly*, *18*(3), 207–216. doi:10.1016/j.leaqua.2007.03.002

El Sawy, O. A., Kraemmergaard, P., Amsinck, H., & Vinther, A. L. (2016). How Lego Built the Foundations and Enterprise Capabilities for Digital Leadership. *MIS Quarterly Executive*, *15*(2), 141–166.

Elbaz, A. M., & Haddoud, M. Y. (2017). The role of wisdom leadership in increasing job performance: Evidence from the Egyptian tourism sector. *Tourism Management*, *63*, 66–76. doi:10.1016/j.tourman.2017.06.008

Elche, D., Ruiz-Palomino, P., & Linuesa-Langreo, J. (2020). Servant leadership and organizational citizenship behavior: The mediating effect of empathy and service climate. *International Journal of Contemporary Hospitality Management*, *32*(6), 2035–2053. doi:10.1108/IJCHM-05-2019-0501

Elenkov, D. S., Judge, W., & Wright, P. (2005). Strategic Leadership And Executive Innovation Influence: An International Multi-Cluster Comparative Study. *Strategic Management Journal*, *26*(7), 665–682. doi:10.1002mj.469

Elkhwesky, Z., Salem, I. E., Ramkissoon, H., & Garcia, J. A. C. (2022). A systematic and critical review of leadership styles in contemporary hospitality: A roadmap and a call for future research. *International Journal of Contemporary Hospitality Management*, *34*(5), 1925–1958. doi:10.1108/IJCHM-09-2021-1128

Ellemers, N., De Gilder, D., & Haslam, S. A. (2004). Motivating individuals and groups at work: A social identity perspective on leadership and group performance. *Academy of Management Review*, *29*(3), 459–478. doi:10.2307/20159054

Ellis, A. (1977). *The basic clinical theory of rational-emotive therapy*. Springer.

El-Sharkawy. (2007). Exploring knowledge and skills for tourist guides evidence from Egypt. *Tourismos: An International Multidisciplinary Journal of Tourism*, *2*(2), 77–94.

Ely, R. T. (1884). *The past and the present of political economy*. Johns Hopkins University. doi:10.5479 il.405460.39088006748982

Emmanuel, A. O., & Hassan, Z. (2015). The effects of transformational leadership on job satisfaction: A study on four and five star hotels in Kuala Lumpur. *International Journal of Accounting, Business and Management*, *3*(1), 88–98.

Enoksen, E., & Lynch, P. (2018). Learning leadership: Becoming an outdoor leader. *Journal of Adventure Education and Outdoor Learning*, *18*(2), 176–188. doi:10.1080/14729679.2017.1391105

Eraslan, L. (2004). Liderlik Olgusunun Tarihsel Evrimi, Temel Kavramlar ve Yeni Liderlik Paradigmasının Analizi. *Milli Eğitim Dergisi, 162*.

Eraslan, L. (2006). *Liderlikte post-modern bir paradigma: dönüşümcü liderlik*. Uslararası İnsan Bilimleri Dergisi.

Eraslan, L. (2006). Liderlikte post-modern bir paradigma: Dönüşümcü liderlik[A post-modern paradigm in leadership: Transformational leadership]. *International Journal of Human Sciences*, 1–32.

Compilation of References

Eren, E. (2004). *Stratejik Yönetim*. T.C. Anadolu Üniversitesi Yayını, 1491.

Eren, E. (2003). *Yönetim ve Organizasyon (Çağdaş ve Küresel Yaklaşımlar)*. Beta Yayınevi.

Eren, E. (2008). *Yönetim ve organizasyon (Çağdaş ve Küresel Yaklaşımlar)*. Beta Yayınevi.

Ergen, D. (2013). *Hizmetkar Liderliğin Örgütsel Vatandaşlık Davranışına Etkisi: İstanbul ve Afyonkarahisar'daki Beş Yıldızlı Otel İşletmelerinde Bir Araştırma* [The effect of servant leadership on organizational citizenship behavior: A study in five-star hotel enterprises in Istanbul and Afyonkarahisar] [Unpublished Master's Thesis]. Kocatepe Üniversitesi Sosyal Bilimler Enstitüsü, Afyonkarahisar.

Ergun Özler, D. (2013). Liderlik. In *Yönetim ve oganizasyon*. Anadolu Üniversitesi Açıköğretim Fakültesi Yayınları.

Erhan, T., Uzunbacak, H. H., & Aydin, E. (2022). From conventional to digital leadership: Exploring digitalization of leadership and innovative work behavior. *Management Research Review*, 45(11), 1524–1543. Advance online publication. doi:10.1108/MRR-05-2021-0338

Erkılıç, E. (2021). Turizm işletmelerinde karizmatik liderlik. In *Turizm işletmelerinde liderlik*. Detay Yayıncılık.

Erkuş, A., & Günlü, E. (2008). Duygusal Zekanın Dönüşümcü Liderlik Üzerine Etkileri. *İşletme Fakültesi Dergisi*, 9(2), 187-209.

Erkutlu, H. (2008). The impact of transformational leadership on organizational and leadership effectiveness: The Turkish case. *Journal of Management Development*, 27(7), 708–726. doi:10.1108/02621710810883616

Ersöz, G. Y., & Turan, B. (2021). Turizm işletmelerinde etkileşimci liderlik. In *Turizm İşletmelerinde Liderlik*. Detay Yayıncılık.

Etzioni, A. (1965). Dual Leadership in Complex Organizations. *American Sociological Review*, 30(5), 688–698. doi:10.2307/2091137 PMID:5824934

Eurasianet. (n.d.). Retrieved June 3, 2021 from: https://eurasianet.org/uzbekistan-top-tier-hotels-linger-on-market.

European Union. (2015). *User guide to the SME definition*. Publications Office of the European Union.

Eva, N., Robin, M., Sendjaya, S., Dierendonck, D. V., & Liden, R. C. (2019). Servant Leadership: A Systematic Review and Call for Future Research. *The Leadership Quarterly*, 30(1), 111–132. doi:10.1016/j.leaqua.2018.07.004

Everly Jr, G. S., Wu, A. W., Cumpsty-Fowler, C. J., Dang, D., & Potash, J. B. (2020). Leadership Principles to Decrease Psychological Casualties in COVID-19 and Other Disasters of Uncertainty. *Concepts in Disaster Medicine.*. doi:10.1017/dmp.2020.395

Evers, F. T., & Rush, J. C. (1996). The bases of competence: Skill development during the transition from university to work. *Management Learning*, 27(3), 275–299. doi:10.1177/1350507696273001

Ewert, A., & Hollenhorst, S. (1994). Individual and setting attributes of the adventure recreation experience. *Leisure Sciences*, 16(3), 177–199. doi:10.1080/01490409409513229

Fadlun, A. (2022, September). The Influence of Transformational Leadership, Emotional Intelligence, Organizational Climate, and Teamwork, Towards Organizational Citizenship Behavior of Civil Servants. *International Journal for Applied Information Management*, 2(3), 26–39.

Farh, J.-L., & Cheng, B.-S. (2000). *A cultural analysis of paternalistic leadership in Chinese organizations. In Management and organizations in the Chinese context*. Palgrave Macmillan.

Farling, M. L., Stone, A. G., & Winston, B. E. (1999). Servant Leadership: Setting the Stage for Empirical Research. *The Journal of Leadership Studies*, *6*(1/2), 49–72. doi:10.1177/107179199900600104

Farrel, K. (2022). Transformational Leadership for the Hospitality and Tourism Industry. In K. Ogunyemi, O. Ogunyemi, & E. Okoye (Eds.), *Humanistic Perspectives in Hospitality and Tourism* (pp. 273–292). Palgrave Macmillan. doi:10.1007/978-3-030-95671-4_14

Fatima, J. K., & Razzaque, M. A. (2014). Service quality and satisfaction in the banking sector. *International Journal of Quality & Reliability Management*, *31*(4), 367–379. Advance online publication. doi:10.1108/IJQRM-02-2013-0031

Felix, C., Ahmad, A., & Arshad, R. (2016). Examining ethical reasoning and transformational leadership style in Nigeria public sector. *SAGE Open*, *6*(2), 1–7. doi:10.1177/2158244016635256

Fenitra, R. M., Abbas, A., Ekowati, D., & Suhairidi, F. (2022). Strategic Intent and Strategic Leadership: A Review Perspective for Post-COVID-19 Tourism and Hospitality Industry Recovery. The Emerald handbook of destination recovery in tourism and hospitality, 23-44.

Fiedler, F. E. (1971). Validation and extension of the contingency model of leadership effectiveness: A review of empirical findings. *Psychological Bulletin*, *76*(2), 128–148. doi:10.1037/h0031454 PMID:4942584

Field, A. P., & Gillett, R. (2010). How to do a meta-analysis. *British Journal of Mathematical & Statistical Psychology*, *63*(3), 665–694. doi:10.1348/000711010X502733 PMID:20497626

Filipova, M. (2013). Management style in tourism. *Romanian Economic Business Review*, 1–6.

Fisher, I. (1907). Why has the doctrine of laissez faire been abandoned? *Science*, *25*(627), 18–27. doi:10.1126cience.25.627.18 PMID:17739703

Fisk, P. (2002). The making of a digital leader. *Business Strategy Review*, *13*(1), 43–50. doi:10.1111/1467-8616.00201

Fitzgerald, S., & Schutte, N. S. (2010). Increasing transformational leadership through enhancing self-efficacy. *Journal of Management Development*, *29*(5), 495–505. Advance online publication. doi:10.1108/02621711011039240

Fitzgibbon, M. (2021). *The Moderating Effect of Self-Esteem on Servant Leadership and Job Outcomes in the Hospitality Industry* [Unpublished Doctoral Dissertation]. Walden University College of Social and Behavioral Sciences, Minneapolis, MN, United States.

Fouad, M. (2019). Impact of Leadership Style on Employee Job Satisfaction in the Hospitality Industry. *International Journal of Heritage, Tourism and Hospitality*, *13*(1), 1–12.

Franco, M., & Matos, P. G. (2015). Leadership styles in SMEs: A mixed-method approach. *The International Entrepreneurship and Management Journal*, *11*(2), 425–451. doi:10.100711365-013-0283-2

French, J. R. P., & Raven, B. (1959). The bases of social power. In D. Cartwright (Ed.), *Studies in Social Power* (pp. 259–269). University of Michigan Press.

Frey, C. B., & Osborne, M. A. (2017). The future of employment: How susceptible are jobs to computerisation? *Technological Forecasting and Social Change*, *114*(January), 254–280. doi:10.1016/j.techfore.2016.08.019

Fuller, J. B., Patterson, C. E., Hester, K. I. M., & Stringer, D. Y. (1996). A quantitative review of research on charismatic leadership. *Psychological Reports*, *78*(1), 271–287. doi:10.2466/pr0.1996.78.1.271

Fusch, P. I., & Ness, L. R. (2015). Are we there yet? Data saturation in qualitative research. *Qualitative Report*, *20*(9), 1408–1416. doi:10.46743/2160-3715/2015.2281

Compilation of References

Gabriel, J., Sklar, S., & Monu, J. (2020). Teaching and learning servant-leadership in the outdoors. *The International Journal of Servant-Leadership*, *14*(1), 217–248. doi:10.33972/ijsl.30

Gabriel, O. D., Alwis, C. D., Jayang, E. A., & Wai, S. L. (2022). The impact of transformational leadership on generation z employee retention and innovative behaviour: A case of Malaysian hotel industry. *International Journal of Multicultural and Multireligious Understanding*, *9*(4), 35–53.

Gandolfi, F., & Stone, S. (2018). Leadership, leadership styles, and servant leadership. *Journal of Management Research*, *18*(4), 261–269.

Gandolfi, F., & Stone, S. (2018). Leadership, Leadership Styles, and Servant Leadership. *Journal of Management Research*, *18*(4), 261–269.

Gao, F., Li, M., & Clarke, S. (2008). Knowledge, management, and knowledge management in business operations. *Journal of Knowledge Management*, *12*(2), 3–17. doi:10.1108/13673270810859479

Gelatt, J. P. (2002). Leadership. In The Development of Management Theory and Practice in The United States (pp. 65-86). Pearson Custom Publishing.

Gemeda, H. K., & Lee, J. (2020). Leadership styles, work engagement and outcomes among information and communications technology professionals: A cross-national study. *Heliyon*, *6*(4), 1–10. doi:10.1016/j.heliyon.2020.e03699 PMID:32280799

Gerbers, K., & Marchand, G. (2021). Social class considerations in outdoor leadership education. *New Directions for Student Leadership*, *2021*(169), 93–101. doi:10.1002/yd.20425 PMID:33871947

Gerges, S., Kamal, N. M., & Mohammed, H., A. (2017). The impact of charismatic leadership on the organizational performance in travel agencies. *Journal of Faculty of Tourism and Hotels-University of Sadat City*, *1*(2/1), 128-150.

Gevşek, B. (2019). Turizm İşletmelerinde Yönetimin Planlama Fonksiyonunun Önemi[The Importance of the Planning Function of Management in Tourism Businesses]. *Aydın Gastronomy*, *3*(2), 129–135.

Ghaharian, K., Abarbanel, B., Soligo, M., & Bernhard, B. (2021). *Crisis management practices in the hospitality and gambling industry during COVID-19*. International Hospitality Review., doi:10.1108/IHR-08-2020-0037

Ghiselli, E. E., & Brown, C. W. (1948). *Personnel And Industrial Psychology*. McGraw-Hill.

Giddens, J. (2018). Transformational leadership: What every nursing dean should know. *Journal of Professional Nursing*, *34*(2), 117–121. doi:10.1016/j.profnurs.2017.10.004 PMID:29703313

Gigliotti, R. A. (2016). Leader as Performer; Leader as Human: A Discursive and Retrospective Construction of Crisis Leadership. *Atlantic Journal of Communication*, *24*(4), 185–200. doi:10.1080/15456870.2016.1208660

Gilbert, S., Horsman, P., & Kelloway, E. K. (2016). The motivation for transformational leadership scale: An examination of the factor structure and initial tests. *Leadership and Organization Development Journal*, *37*(2), 158–180. doi:10.1108/LODJ-05-2014-0086

Gill, A., Fitzgerald, S., Bhutani, S., Mand, H., & Sharma, S. (2010). The relationship between transformational leadership and employee desire for empowerment. *International Journal of Contemporary Hospitality Management*, *22*(2), 263–273. doi:10.1108/09596111011018223

Gill, A., Flaschner, A. B., & Bhutani, S. (2010). The impact of transformational leadership and empowerment on employee job stress. *Business and Economics Journal*, 1–11.

Gill, R. (2011). Theory and practice of leadership. *Sage (Atlanta, Ga.)*.

Goethals, G. R., Sorenson, G. J., & Burns, J. M. (2004). *Encyclopedia of leadership*. Sage Publications. doi:10.4135/9781412952392

Göktaş, L. S. (2021). Turizm işletmelerinde kuantum liderlik. Turizm işletmelerinde hizmetkar liderlik [Quantum leadership in tourism businesses. Servant leadership in tourism businesses]. In Turizm işletmelerinde liderlik. Detay Yayıncılık.

Goldsby, M. G., Goldsby, E. A., Neck, C. B., Neck, C. P., & Mathews, R. (2021). Self-leadership: A four-decade review of the literature and trainings. *Administrative Sciences*, *11*(1), 25. doi:10.3390/admsci11010025

Goleman, D. (1995). *Emotional intelligence*. Bantam Books.

Goleman, D., Boyatzis, R. E., & McKee, A. (2002). The New Leaders. In *Transforming the Art of Leadership into the Science of Results*. Little, Brown.

Gom, D., Lew, T. Y., Jiony, M. M., Tanakinjal, G. H., & Stephen Sondoh, J. (2021). The role of transformational leadership and psychological capital in the hotel industry: A sustainable approach to reducing turnover intention. *Sustainability*, *13*(19), 1–20. doi:10.3390u131910799

Gomes, A. R. (2014). Transformational Leadership: Theory, Research and Application to Sports. In Contemporary Topics and Trends in the Psychology of Sports. Nova Science Publishers.

Gosling, J., Jones, S., Sutherland, I., & Dijkstra, J. (2012). *Key concepts in leadership*. SAGE Publications. doi:10.4135/9781473914759

Gössling, S., Scott, D., & Hall, C. M. (2020). Pandemics, tourism and global change: A rapid assessment of COVID-19. *Journal of Sustainable Tourism*, *29*(1), 1–20. doi:10.1080/09669582.2020.1758708

Graham, J. (1997). *Outdoor leadership: Technique, common sense & self-confidence*. Mountaineers.

Greenleaf, R. K. (1977). *Servant Leadership: A Journey into The Nature of Legitimate Power and Greatness*. Paulist Press.

Greger, K., R. & Peterson, J., S. (2000). Leadership profiles for the new millennium. *Cornell Hotel and Restaurant Administration Quarterly*, (1), 16-29.

Griffin, R. W., Hanna, A. A., Smith, T. A., & Kirkman, B. L. (2022). How Bad Leaders Impact Organizational Effectiveness. *Overcoming Bad Leadership in Organizations*, 224.

Griffin, R. W., Phillips, J. M., & Gully, S. M. (2016). Organizational Behavior: Managing People and Organizations (12th ed.). Boston: Cengage Learning.

Griffin, R. W. (2002). *Management*. Houghton Mifflin Company.

Grint, K. (2020). Leadership, management and command in the time of the Coronavirus. *Leadership*, *16*(3), 314–319. doi:10.1177/1742715020922445

Grudić Kvasić, S., Nikolić, G., & Milojica, V. (2021). The impact of authentic leadership on employee psychological capital in the hospitality industry. *Poslovna Izvrsnost*, *15*(1), 9–22. doi:10.22598/pi-be/2021.15.1.9

Güdü Demirbulat, Ö. (2020). Turist rehberlerinin iş yaşamındaki rolleri ve görevleri [Roles and duties of tourist guides in business life]. In E. Düzgün (Ed.), *Örnek olaylarla turist rehberliği* [*Tourist guidance with case studies*] (pp. 65–85). Detay Yayıncılık.

Gui, C., Luo, A., Zhang, P., & Deng, A. (2020). A meta-analysis of transformational leadership in hospitality research. *International Journal of Contemporary Hospitality Management*, *32*(6), 2137–2154. doi:10.1108/IJCHM-05-2019-0507

Compilation of References

Gui, C., Zhang, P., Zou, R., & Ouyang, X. (2021). Servant leadership in hospitality: A meta-analytic review. *Journal of Hospitality Marketing & Management*, *30*(4), 438–458. doi:10.1080/19368623.2021.1852641

Guillot, C. W. (2003). Strategic Leadership: Defining the Challenge. *Air & Space Power Journal*, (Winter), 67–75.

Güldenberg, S., & Langhof, J. G. (2021). Digital Leadership and Technology. In *Managing Work in the Digital Economy* (pp. 157–173). Springer. doi:10.1007/978-3-030-65173-2_10

Gülertekin, S. (2013). Duygu İklimi ve Liderlik Tarzının İşten Ayrılma Niyetine Etkileri: Alanya'daki Turizm İşletmelerine Yönelik Bir Araştırma. *T.C. Çanakkale On sekiz Mart Üniversitesi Sosyal Bilimler Enstitüsü Turizm İşletmeciliği Anabilim Dalı*.

Güney, S. (2012). *Liderlik*. Nobel Yayınevi.

Güngör, O. (2019). Otel İşletmelerinin Mutfak Departmanında Örgütsel İklim ve Liderlik Stilleri İlişkisinin İncelenmesi: Bir Zincir Otel İşletmesi Örneği. *Türk Turizm Araştırmaları Dergisi*, *3*(4), 995–1011. doi:10.26677/TR1010.2019.224

Gupta, H., & Barua, M. K. (2017). Supplier selection among SMEs on the basis of their green innovation ability using BWM and fuzzy TOPSIS. *Journal of Cleaner Production*, *152*, 242–258. doi:10.1016/j.jclepro.2017.03.125

Gürdoğan, A., & Yavuz, E. (2013). Turizm işletmelerinde örgüt kültürü ve liderlik davranışı etkileşimi: Muğla ili'nde bir araştırma [Organizational culture and leadership behavior interaction in tourism businesses: A research in Muğla province]. *Turizm Araştırmaları Dergisi*, *24*(1), 57–69.

Gürlek, M. (2022). Social Entrepreneurship in Tourism, Hospitality and Events: A State of the Art. In A. Farmaki, L. Altinay, & X. Font (Eds.), *Planning and Managing Sustainability in Tourism. Tourism, Hospitality & Event Management*. Springer. doi:10.1007/978-3-030-92208-5_5

Gürlek, M., & Çemberci, M. (2020). Understanding the relationships among knowledge-oriented leadership, knowledge management capacity, innovation performance and organizational performance: A serial mediation analysis. *Kybernetes*, *49*(11), 2819–2846. doi:10.1108/K-09-2019-0632

Gürlek, M., & Koseoglu, M. A. (2021). Green innovation research in the field of hospitality and tourism: The construct, antecedents, consequences, and future outlook. *Service Industries Journal*, *41*(11-12), 734–766. doi:10.1080/02642069.2021.1929930

Gurmani, J. K., Khan, N. U., Khalique, M., Yasir, M., Obaid, A., & Sabri, N. A. (2021). Do environmental transformational leadership predicts organizational citizenship behavior towards environment in hospitality industry: Using structural equation modeling approach. *Sustainability*, *13*(10), 1–29. doi:10.3390u13105594

Güzel, T. (2009). Turizm İşletmelerinde Liderlik. In *Turizm İşletmelerinde Örgütsel Davranış* (pp. 121-135). Marmara Kitap Merkezi.

Güzel, T., & Akgündüz, Y. (2011). Liderlik davranışlarının orta düzey yöneticiler üzerindeki etkisi ve yöneticilerin tükenmişlik düzeyleri ile ilişkisi; Kuşadası otel işletmelerinde bir araştırma[The effects of leadership behaviors on mid-level managers and their relationship with burnout levels; a research in Kusadasi hotel businesses]. *Journal of Management Sciences*, *9*(2), 280–296.

Guzzo, R. F., Abbott, J., & Madera, J. M. (2020). A micro-level view of CSR: A hospitality management systematic literature review. *Cornell Hospitality Quarterly*, *61*(3), 332–352. doi:10.1177/1938965519892907

Hacker, S., & Roberts, T. (2003). *Transformational leadership: Creating organizations of meaning*. ASQ Quality, Milwaukee.

Hai, T. N., & Van, Q. N. (2021). Servant leadership styles: A theoretical approach. *Emerging Science Journal*, 5(2), 245–256. doi:10.28991/esj-2021-01273

Hakim, A. H., & Ibrahim, H. M. (2017). Transformational leadership and turnover intention: Mediating role of overall job satisfaction. *Journal of Tourism. Hospitality & Culinary Arts*, 9(2), 237–248.

Halis, M. (2021). Turizm işletmelerinde hizmetkar liderlik [Servant leadership in tourism businesses]. Detay Yayıncılık.

Hall, J., Johnson, S., Wysocki, A., & Kepner, K. (2008). *Transformational Leadership: The Transformational of Managers and Associates*. University of Florida.

Hambrick, D., & Mason, P. (1984). Upper Echelons: Organization as A Reflection of its Top Managers. *Academy of Management Review*, 9(2), 193–206. doi:10.2307/258434

Ham, H. (2021). Leadership: A Journey to Enacting Change. *Journal of Youth Development*, 16(1), 1–6. doi:10.5195/jyd.2021.1115

Handscomb, C., Mahadevan, D., Schor, L., Sieberer, M., Naidoo, E., & Srinivasan, S. (2021). *An operating model for the next normal: Lessons from agile organisations in the crisis*. Retrieved June 2, 2021, from: https://www.mckinsey.com/business-functions/organization/our insights/an-operating-model-for-the-next-normal-lessons-from -agile-organizations-in-the-crisis

Hannah, S. T., Uhl-Bien, M., Avolio, B. J., & Cavarretta, F. L. (2009). A framework for examining leadership in extreme contexts. *The Leadership Quarterly*, 20(6), 897–919. doi:10.1016/j.leaqua.2009.09.006

Haq, S., & Chandio, J. (2017). Transactional Leadership and its Impact on the Organizational Performance: A Critical Analysis. *International Journal of Trend in Scientific Research and Development*, 2(1), 135–139. doi:10.31142/ijtsrd2499

Harari, M. B., Williams, E. A., Castro, S. L., & Brant, K. K. (2021). Self-leadership: A meta-analysis of over two decades of research. *Journal of Occupational and Organizational Psychology*, 94(4), 890–923. doi:10.1111/joop.12365

Harrington, R., Chathoth, P., Ottenbacher, M., & Altinay, B. (2011). *Strategic management research in hospitality and tourism: Past, present, and future*. Academic Press.

Harrison, C. (2018). *Leadership Theory and Research: A Critical Approach to New and Existing Paradigms*. Palgrave Macmillan. doi:10.1007/978-3-319-68672-1

Hart, J. W., Stasson, M. F., Mahoney, J. M., & Story, P. (2007). The Big Five and achievement motivation: Exploring the relationship between personality and a two-factor model of motivation. *Individual Differences Research*, 5, 267–274.

Hasib, F. F., Eliyana, A., Arief, Z., & Pratiwi, A. A. (2020). The effect of transformational leadership on employee performance mediated by leader-member exchange (LMX). *Systematic Reviews in Pharmacy*, 11(11), 1199–1209.

Hassan, H., Asad, S., & Hoshino, Y. (2016). Determinants of leadership style in big five personality dimensions. *Universal Journal of Management*, 4(4), 161–179. doi:10.13189/ujm.2016.040402

Haven-Tang, C., & Jones, E. (2012). Local leadership for rural tourism development: A case study of Adventa, Monmouthshire, UK. *Tourism Management Perspectives*, 4, 28–35. doi:10.1016/j.tmp.2012.04.006

Hayek, F. (1944). *The Road to Serfdom*. G. Routledge & Sons.

Hemmington, N. (2007). From service to experience: Understanding and defining the hospitality business. *Service Industries Journal*, 27(6), 747–755. doi:10.1080/02642060701453221

Compilation of References

Henkel, T., & Bourdeau, D. (2018). A Field Study: An Examination Of Managers' Situational Leadership Styles. *Journal of Diversity Management*, *13*(2), 7–14. doi:10.19030/jdm.v13i2.10218

Hennink, M., Hutter, I., & Bailey, A. (2020). *Qualitative research methods* (2nd ed.). SAGE Publications.

Hernandez, J. (2020, August 17). *Who or what is driving digital transformation at your organization?* KPMG.

He, Y., Li, W., & Lai, K. K. (2011). Service climate, employee commitment and customer satisfaction. Evidence from the hospitality industry in China. *International Journal of Contemporary Hospitality Management*, *23*(5), 592–607. doi:10.1108/09596111111143359

Hicks, H., & Gullett, C. R. (1981). Organizasyonlar, Teori ve Davranış (Çeviri Besim Baykal). İstanbul: İşletme Bilimleri Enstitüsü Yayınları No:1.

Hıdıroğlu, D. (2020). Strategic leadership: Best Practical Leadership Style to Business Strategies in The Period of Covid-19 Epidemic. *Turkish Studies - Social*, *15*(4). 1945-1955.

Hillary, R. (Ed.). (2017). *Small and medium-sized enterprises and the environment: Business imperatives*. Routledge. doi:10.4324/9781351282840

Hilton, S. K., Arkorful, H., & Martins, A. (2021). Democratic leadership and organizational performance: The moderating effect of contingent reward. *Management Research Review*, *44*(7), 1042–1058. doi:10.1108/MRR-04-2020-0237

Hinkin, T. R., & Schriesheim, C. A. (2008a). An examination of" nonleadership": From laissez-faire leadership to leader reward omission and punishment omission. *The Journal of Applied Psychology*, *93*(6), 1234–1248. doi:10.1037/a0012875 PMID:19025245

Hinkin, T. R., & Schriesheim, C. A. (2008b). A theoretical and empirical examination of the transactional and nonleadership dimensions of the Multifactor Leadership Questionnaire (MLQ). *The Leadership Quarterly*, *19*(5), 501–513. doi:10.1016/j.leaqua.2008.07.001

Hinkin, T. R., & Tracey, J. B. (1994). Transformational leadership in the hospitality industry. *Hospitality Research Journal*, *18*(1), 49–63. doi:10.1177/109634809401800105

Hitt, M. (Ed.). (1999). *Strategic Management: Competitiveness and Globalization: Concepts and Cases*. South-Western College Pub.

Hitt, M. A., Hoskisson, R. E., & Ireland, R. D. (2007). *Management of Strategy (International Student Edition)*. Thomson South-Western.

Hitt, M. A., Ireland, R. D., & Hoskisson, R. E. (2012). *Strategic Management Cases: Competitiveness and Globalization*. South-Western Pub.

Hoang, G., Evered, E. W., Binney, L. L., & Luu, T. T. (2021). Empowering leadership in hospitality and tourism management: A systematic literatüre review. *International Journal of Contemporary Hospitality Management*, *33*(12), 4182–4214. doi:10.1108/IJCHM-03-2021-0323

Hobfoll, S. E. (1989). Conservation of resources: A new attempt at conceptualizing stress. *The American Psychologist*, *44*(3), 513–524. doi:10.1037/0003-066X.44.3.513 PMID:2648906

Hodgkinson, C. (1996). *Yönetim felsefesi*. İstanbul: Beta yayınevi.

Hofer, K. M., & Knight, G. (2022). International services marketing: an integrative assessment of the literature [国际化服务行业市场营销: 综合文献分析]. *Service Industries Journal*, *42*(3-4), 225–248. doi:10.1080/02642069.2020.1862091

Hogg, A. M. (2001). A Social Identity Theory of Leadership. *Personality and Social Psychology*, *5*(3), 184–200. doi:10.1207/S15327957PSPR0503_1

Holdford, D. A. (2003). Leadership theories and their lessons for pharmacists. *American Journal of Health-System Pharmacy*, *60*(17), 1780–1786. doi:10.1093/ajhp/60.17.1780 PMID:14503115

Holsapple, C. W., & Joshi, K. D. (1999). Description and analysis of existing knowledge management frameworks. In *Proceedings of the 32nd Hawaii International Conference on System Sciences* (vol. 1, pp. 1072). 10.1109/HICSS.1999.772796

Hongdao, Q., Bibi, S., Khan, A., Ardito, L., & Nurunnabi, M. (2019). Does what goes around really comes around? The mediating effect of CSR on the relationship between transformational leadership and employee's job performance in law firms. *Sustainability*, *11*(12), 3366. doi:10.3390u11123366

Hoque, A., Shikha, F. A., Hasanat, M. W., Arif, I., & Hamid, A. B. A. (2020). The effect of Coronavirus (COVID-19) in the tourism industry in China. *Asian Journal of Multidisciplinary Studies*, *3*(1), 52–58.

Hosmer, L. T. (1982). The Importance of Strategic Leadership. *The Journal of Business Strategy*, *3*(2), 47–57. doi:10.1108/eb038966 PMID:10299154

Hospitality World, E. T. (n.d.). Retrieved April 21, 2020, From: https://hospitality.economictimes.indiatimes.com/news/hotels/covid-19-impacts-hotel-occupancy-in-the-asean-region/75267521

Hotel News Now. (n.d.). Retrieved February 4, 2020, from: http://hotelnewsnow.com/

Hotelier, M. E. (n.d.). Retrieved May 12, 2020, from: https://www.hoteliermiddleeast.com/ business/117482-report-jeddah-hotel-occupancy-levels-falls-to-22

Houghton, J. D., Neck, C. P., & Manz, C. C. (2003). Self-leadership and superleadership: The heart and art of creating shared leadership in teams. In Shared leadership: Reframing the hows and whys of leadership (pp. 123-140). Academic Press.

Houghton, J. D., Bonham, T. W., Neck, C. P., & Singh, K. (2004). The relationship between self-leadership and personality. *Journal of Managerial Psychology*, *19*(4), 427–441. doi:10.1108/02683940410537963

Houghton, J. D., & Neck, C. P. (2002). The Revised Self-Leadership Questionnaire: Testing a hierarchical factor structure for self-leadership. *Journal of Managerial Psychology*, *17*(8), 672–692. doi:10.1108/02683940210450484

House, R. J., & Shamir, B. (1993). Toward the integration of transformational, charismatic, and visionary theories. *Leadership Theory and Research*, *14*, 81–107.

Howel, J. P., & Costley, D. L. (2006). *Understanding Behaviors for Effective Leadership (2.bs.)*. Pearson Prentice Hall.

Howell, J. M., & Avolio, B. (1993). Transformational leadership, transactional leadership, locus of control and support for innovation: Key predictors of consolidated-business-unit performance. *The Journal of Applied Psychology*, *78*(6), 891–902. doi:10.1037/0021-9010.78.6.891

Howell, J. M., & Avolio, B. J. (1992). The ethics of charismatic leadership: Submission or liberation? *The Academy of Management Executive*, *6*(2), 43–54.

Hsiao, C., Lee, Y.-H., & Chen, W.-J. (2015). The effect of servant leadership on customer value co-creation: A cross-level analysis of key mediating roles. *Tourism Management*, *49*, 45–57. doi:10.1016/j.tourman.2015.02.012

Compilation of References

Huang, J., Li, W., Qiu, C., Yim, F. H., & Wan, J. (2016). The impact of CEO servant leadership on firm performance in the hospitality industry. *International Journal of Contemporary Hospitality Management*, 28(5), 945–968. doi:10.1108/IJCHM-08-2014-0388

Huang, M. H., & Rust, R. T. (2021). A strategic framework for artificial intelligence in marketing. *Journal of the Academy of Marketing Science*, 49(1), 30–50. doi:10.100711747-020-00749-9

Huertas-Valdivia, I., González-Torres, T., & Nájera-Sánchez, J. J. (2022). Contemporary leadership in hospitality: a review and research agenda. *International Journal of Contemporary Hospitality Management*.

Huertas-Valdivia, I., González-Torres, T., & Nájera-Sánchez, J. J. (2022). Contemporary leadership in hospitality: a review and research agenda. *International Journal of Contemporary Hospitality Management*. doi:10.5281/zenodo.6602327

Huertas-Valdivia, I., Gallego-Burín, A. R., Castillo, A., & Ruiz, L. (2021). Why don't high-performance work systems always achieve superior service in hospitality? The key is servant leadership. *Journal of Hospitality and Tourism Management*, 49, 152–163. doi:10.1016/j.jhtm.2021.09.007

Huertas-Valdivia, I., Llorens-Montes, F. J., & Ruiz-Moreno, A. (2018). Achieving engagement among hospitality employees: A serial mediation model. *International Journal of Contemporary Hospitality Management*, 30(1), 217–241. doi:10.1108/IJCHM-09-2016-0538

Hughes, R. (2009). Time for leadership development interventions in the publice health nutrition workforce. *Public Health Nutrition*, 12(8), 1029. doi:10.1017/S1368980009990395 PMID:19570300

Hu, J., & Liden, R. (2011). Antecedents of team potency and team effectiveness: An examination of goal and process clarity and servant leadership. *The Journal of Applied Psychology*, 96(4), 851–862. doi:10.1037/a0022465 PMID:21319877

Hunter, E. M., Neubert, M. J., Perry, S. J., Witt, L. A., Penney, L. M., & Weinberger, E. (2013). Servant leaders inspire servant followers: Antecedents and outcomes for employees and the organization. *The Leadership Quarterly*, 24(2), 316–331. doi:10.1016/j.leaqua.2012.12.001

Hussain, S.T., Abbas, J., Lei, S., Haider, M.J., & Akram, T. (2017). Transactional Leadership and Organizational Creativity: Examining the Mediating Role of Knowledge Sharing Behavior. *Cogent Business & Management, 3*.

Hutajulu, R. S., Susita, D., & Eliyana, A. (2021). The effect of digitalization and virtual leadership on organizational innovation during the COVID-19 pandemic crisis: A case study in Indonesia. *The Journal of Asian Finance. Economics and Business*, 8(10), 57–64.

Hyvärinen, J., & Vos, M. (2016). *Communication concerning disasters and pandemics: Co-producing community resilience and crisis response. In Handbook of International Crisis Communication Research*. Wiley-Blackwell. doi:10.1002/9781118516812.ch10

İbicioğlu, H., & Özmen, H. İ., & Taş, S. (2009). Liderlik Davranışı ve Toplumsal Norm İlişki: Ampirik Bir Çalışma. *Süleyman Demirel Üniversitesi İktisadi ve İdari Bilimler Fakültesi Dergisi*, 14(2), 1–23.

Idris, I., Suyuti, A., Supriyanto, A. S., & As, N. (2022). transformational leadership, political skill, organizational culture, and employee performance: A case from tourism company in Indonesia. *Geo Journal of Tourism and Geosites*, 40(1), 104–110. doi:10.30892/gtg.40112-808

Ilkhanizadeh, S., & Karatepe, O. M. (2018). Does trust in organization mediate the influence of servant leadership on satisfaction outcomes among flight attendants? *International Journal of Contemporary Hospitality Management*, 30(10), 3555–3573. doi:10.1108/IJCHM-09-2017-0586

İnce, Ş. (2016). *Şeflerin Savaşı: Profesyonel Mutfaklarda Erkek ve Kadın Şefler*. Moment Dergi, Cinema and Politics.

Iqbal, Z. A., Abid, G., Contreras, F., Hassan, Q., & Zafar, R. (2020). Ethical leadership and innovative work behavior: The mediating role of individual attributes. *Journal of Open Innovation*, *6*(3), 68. doi:10.3390/joitmc6030068

Ireland, R. D., & Hitt, M. A. (2005). Achieving and Maintaining Strategic Competitiveness in the 21st. Century: The Role of Strategic Leadership. *The Academy of Management Executive*, *19*(4), 63–74. doi:10.5465/ame.2005.19417908

Ivancevich, J. M., & Matteson, M. T. (2002). *Organizational Behavior and Management*. McGraw-Hill Irvin.

Jackson, T. (2016). Paternalisticleadership: Themissing link in cross-cultural leadership studies? *International Journal of Cross Cultural Management*, *16*(1), 3–7. doi:10.1177/1470595816637701

Jago, A. G. (1982). Leadership: Perspectives in theory and research. Management Science, 28(3), 315–336.

Jago, A. G. (1982). Leadership: Perspectives in Theory and Research. *Management Science*, *28*(3), 315–336. doi:10.1287/mnsc.28.3.315

Jaiswal, N. K., & Dhar, R. L. (2015). Transformational leadership, innovation climate, creative self-efficacy and employee creativity: A multilevel study. *International Journal of Hospitality Management*, *51*, 30–41. doi:10.1016/j.ijhm.2015.07.002

Jamal, T., & Budke, C. (2020). Tourism in a world with pandemics: local-global responsibility and action. *Journal of Tourism Futures*, *6*(2), 181-188.

James, R., Meindl, S. B., & Dukerich, J. M. (1985). The Romance of Leadership. *Administrative Science Quarterly*, *30*(1), 78–102. doi:10.2307/2392813

Janghorban, R., Roudsari, R. L., & Taghipour, A. (2014). Skype interviewing: The new generation of online synchronous interview in qualitative research. *International Journal of Qualitative Studies on Health and Well-being*, *9*(1), 24152. doi:10.3402/qhw.v9.24152 PMID:24746247

Jang, J., & Kandampully, J. (2018). Reducing employee turnover intention through servant leadership in the restaurant context: A mediation study of affective organizational commitment. *International Journal of Hospitality & Tourism Administration*, *19*(2), 125–141. doi:10.1080/15256480.2017.1305310

Jangre, J., Hameed, A. Z., Srivastava, M., Prasad, K., & Patel, D. (2022). Prioritization of factors and selection of best business practice from bio-medical waste generated using best–worst method. *Benchmarking*. Advance online publication. doi:10.1108/BIJ-11-2021-0698

Johnson, R. E., & Saboe, K. N. (2011). Measuring implicit traits in organizational research: Development of an indirect measure of employee implicit self-concept. *Organizational Research Methods*, *14*(3), 530–547. doi:10.1177/1094428110363617

Joiner, B. (2019). Leadership agility for organizational agility. *Journal of Creating Value*, *5*(2), 139–149. doi:10.1177/2394964319868321

Jooste, C., & Fourie, B. (2009). The Role of Strategic Leadership in Effective Strategy Implementation: Perceptions of South African Strategic Leaders. *Southern African Business Review*, *13*(3), 51–68.

Joseph, D. L., & Newman, D. A. (2010). Emotional intelligence: An integrative meta-analysis and cascading model. *The Journal of Applied Psychology*, *95*(1), 54–78. doi:10.1037/a0017286 PMID:20085406

Joseph, E. E., & Winston, B. E. (2005). A Correlation of Servant Leadership, Leader Trust, and Organizational Trust. *Leadership and Organization Development Journal*, *26*(1), 6–22. doi:10.1108/01437730510575552

Judge, T. A., & Bono, J. E. (2000). Five-Factor model of personality and transformational leadership. *The Journal of Applied Psychology*, *85*(5), 751–765. doi:10.1037/0021-9010.85.5.751 PMID:11055147

Compilation of References

Judge, T. A., & Ilies, R. (2002). Relationship of personality to performance motivation: A meta-analytic review. *The Journal of Applied Psychology*, *87*(4), 797–807. doi:10.1037/0021-9010.87.4.797 PMID:12184582

Judge, T. A., & Piccolo, R. F. (2004). Transformational and transactional leadership: A meta-analytic test of their relative validity. *The Journal of Applied Psychology*, *89*(5), 755–768. doi:10.1037/0021-9010.89.5.755 PMID:15506858

Judge, T. A., Piccolo, R. F., & Ilies, R. (2004). The forgotten ones? The validity of consideration and initiating structure in leadership research. *The Journal of Applied Psychology*, *89*(1), 36–51. doi:10.1037/0021-9010.89.1.36 PMID:14769119

Jung, D., & Sosik, J. J. (2006). Who are the spellbinders? Identifying personal attributes of charismatic leaders.Journal of Leadership & Organizational Studies, 12, 12–27.

Jung, D. I. (2001). Transformational and transactional leadership and their effects on creativity in groups. *Creativity Research Journal*, *13*(2), 185–195. doi:10.1207/S15326934CRJ1302_6

Jung, D. I., & Avolio, B. J. (2000). Opening the black box: An experimental investigation of the mediating effects of trust and value congruence on transformational and transactional leadership. *Journal of Organizational Behavior*, *21*(8), 949–964. doi:10.1002/1099-1379(200012)21:8<949::AID-JOB64>3.0.CO;2-F

Kahya, C., & Pabuçcu, H. (2015). Evaluating leadership styles within the scope of Rensis Likerts 4-Model by using fuzzy AHP approach. *IIB International Refereed Academic Social Sciences Journal*, *6*(17), 1–23. doi:10.17364/IIB.2015179721

Kane, H., Ragsdell, G., & Oppenheim, C. (2006). Knowledge management methodologies. *Electronic Journal of Knowledge Management*, *4*(2), 141–152.

Kaplan, M., & Uzun, A. (2017). Hizmetkar Liderlik Algılamalarının Tükenmişlik Üzerindeki Etkisi: Otel İşletmelerinde Bir Araştırma[The Effect of Perceptions of Servant Leadership on Burnout: A Case of Study in Hotel Businesses]. *Nevşehir Hacı Bektaş Veli Üniversitesi SBE Dergisi*, *7*(1), 14–26.

Kapoor, R., & Kapoor, K. (2021). The transition from traditional to digital marketing: A study of the evolution of e-marketing in the Indian hotel industry. *Worldwide Hospitality and Tourism Themes*, *13*(2), 199–213. Advance online publication. doi:10.1108/WHATT-10-2020-0124

Kara, D., Uysal, M., Sirgy, M. J., & Lee, G. (2013). The effects of leadership style on employee well-being in hospitality. *International Journal of Hospitality Management*, *34*, 9–18. doi:10.1016/j.ijhm.2013.02.001

Karatepe, O. M., Ozturk, A., & Kim, T. T. (2019). Servant leadership, organizational trust, and bank employee outcomes. *Service Industries Journal*, *39*(2), 86–108. doi:10.1080/02642069.2018.1464559

Karippur, N. K., & Balaramachandran, P. R. (2022). Antecedents of Effective Digital Leadership of Enterprises in the Asia Pacific. *AJIS. Australasian Journal of Information Systems*, *26*. Advance online publication. doi:10.3127/ajis.v26i0.2525

Kaushal, V., & Srivastava, S. (2021). Hospitality and tourism industry amid COVID-19 pandemic: Perspectives on challenges and learnings from India. *International Journal of Hospitality Management*, *92*, 102707. doi:10.1016/j.ijhm.2020.102707 PMID:33024348

Kaya, B., & Karatepe, O. M. (2020). Does servant leadership better explain work engagement, career satisfaction and adaptive performance than authentic leadership? *International Journal of Contemporary Hospitality Management*, *32*(6), 2075–2095. doi:10.1108/IJCHM-05-2019-0438

Kazkondu, İ. (2021). Mutfak Örgütlenmesi. In Mutfak Yönetimi. Ankara: Detay yayıncılık.

Keklik, B. (2012). Determination of leadership style preferred in health institutions: Example of a private hospital. *Afyon Kocatepe Üniversitesi İktisadi ve İdari Bilimler Fakültesi Dergisi*, *14*(1), 73–93.

Kelloway, E. K., Mullen, J., & Francis, L. (2006). Divergent effects of transformational and passive leadership on employee safety. *Journal of Occupational Health Psychology*, *11*(1), 76–86. doi:10.1037/1076-8998.11.1.76 PMID:16551176

Kelloway, E. K., Turner, N., Barling, J., & Loughlin, C. (2012). Transformational leadership and employee psychological well-being: The mediating role of employee trust in leadership. *Work and Stress*, *26*(1), 39–55. doi:10.1080/02678373.2012.660774

Ketchen, D., & Short, J. (2011). *Mastering Strategic Management. Paperback, December*. Centre for Open Education.

Kets & de Vries. (1995). *Organizational paradoxes: Clinical approach to management* (2nd ed.). London: Routledge.

Kets de Vries, M. (2001). *The Leadership Mystique*. Financial Times Prentice Hall.

Kets de Vries, M. (2007). Liderliğin Gizemi. İstanbul: MESS Yayın No:25.

Kets de Vries, M. (2001). *The Leadership Mystique*. Prentice Hall.

Keynes, J. M. (1927). The End of Laissez-Faire (London, 1926). *Collected Writings, 9*.

Keynes, J. (2016). *Essays in persuasion*. Springer.

Khalili, A. (2016). Linking transformational leadership, creativity, innovation, and innovation-supportive climate. *Management Decision*, *54*(9), 2277–2293. doi:10.1108/MD-03-2016-0196

Khan, A., Bibi, S., Lyu, J., Garavelli, A. C., Pontrandolfo, P., & Sanchez, M. D. (2020). Uncovering Innovativeness in Spanish Tourism Firms: The Role of Transformational Leadership, OCB, Firm Size, and Age. *Sustainability*, *12*(10), 1–26. doi:10.3390u12103989

Khan, K., Kunz, R., Kleijnen, J., & Antes, G. (2003). Five steps to conducting a systematic review. *Journal of the Royal Society of Medicine*, *96*(3), 118–121. doi:10.1177/014107680309600304 PMID:12612111

Khan, N. A., Khan, A. N., Soomro, M. A., & Khan, S. K. (2020). Transformational leadership and civic virtue behavior: Valuing act of thriving and emotional exhaustion in the hotel industry. *Asia Pacific Management Review*, *25*(4), 216–225. doi:10.1016/j.apmrv.2020.05.001

Khan, S., Kaushik, M. K., Kumar, R., & Khan, W. (2022). Investigating the barriers of blockchain technology integrated food supply chain: A BWM approach. *Benchmarking*. Advance online publication. doi:10.1108/BIJ-08-2021-0489

Khan, Z. A., Nawaz, A., & Khan, I. (2016). Leadership theories and styles: A literature review. *Journal of Resources Development and Management*, *16*(1), 1–7.

Khan, Z. A., Nawaz, A., & Khan, I. U. (2016). Leadership Theories and Styles: A Literature Review. *Journal of Resources Development and Management*, *16*, 1–7.

Kılıç, G., Gülaydın, M., Sürücü, Ö., & Kasapoğlu, B. (2018). Beş yıldızlı otel işletmelerinde liderlik davranışları ile örgütsel muhalefet ilişkisi[The relationship between leadership behaviors and organizational opposition in five-star hotel businesses]. *Uluslararası Sosyal Araştırmalar Dergisi*, *11*(59), 994–1003.

Kim, H., Im, J., & Shin, Y. H. (2021). The impact of transformational leadership and commitment to change on restaurant employees' quality of work life during a crisis. *Journal of Hospitality and Tourism Management*, *48*, 322–330. doi:10.1016/j.jhtm.2021.07.010

Kim, W. G., McGinley, S., Choi, H. M., & Agmapisarn, C. (2020). Hotels' environmental leadership and employees' organizational citizenship behavior. *International Journal of Hospitality Management*, *87*, 102375. doi:10.1016/j.ijhm.2019.102375

Compilation of References

Kippenberger, T. (2002). *Leadership Styles*. Capstone Publishing.

Kirkbride, P. (2006). Developing transformational leaders: The full range leadership model in action. *Industrial and Commercial Training*, *38*(1), 23–32. doi:10.1108/00197850610646016

Klasmeier, K. N., Schleu, J. E., Millhoff, C., Poethke, U., & Bormann, K. C. (2022). On the destructiveness of laissez-faire versus abusive supervision: A comparative, multilevel investigation of destructive forms of leadership. *European Journal of Work and Organizational Psychology*, *31*(3), 406–420. doi:10.1080/1359432X.2021.1968375

Kloutsiniotis, P. V., Mihail, D. M., Mylonas, N., & Pateli, A. (2022). Transformational Leadership, HRM practices and burnout during the COVID-19 pandemic: The role of personal stress, anxiety, and workplace loneliness. *International Journal of Hospitality Management*, *102*, 103177. doi:10.1016/j.ijhm.2022.103177 PMID:35079194

Knickerbocker, I. (1948). Leadership: A Conception and Some Implications. *The Journal of Social Issues*, *4*(3), 23–40. doi:10.1111/j.1540-4560.1948.tb01508.x

Knight, B., & Paterson, F. (2018). Behavioural competencies of sustainability leaders: An empirical investigation. *Journal of Organizational Change Management*, *31*(3), 557–580. doi:10.1108/JOCM-02-2017-0035

Koçel, T. (2007). *İşletme Yöneticiliği*. Arıkan Basım Yayım.

Kohlegger, M., Maier, R., & Thalmann, S. (2009). Understanding maturity models: Results of a structured content analysis [Paper presentation]. I-KNOW '09 and I-SEMANTICSConference 2009, Graz, Austria.

Komppula, R. (2016). The role of different stakeholders in destination development. *Tourism Review*, *71*(1), 67–76. doi:10.1108/TR-06-2015-0030

Kopelman, R. E., Prottas, D. J., & Davis, A. L. (2008). Douglas McGregor's Theory X and Y: Toward a Construct-valid Measure. *Journal of Managerial Issues*, *20*(2), 255–271.

Köroğlu, Ö. (2020). *Turist rehberliğinde mesleki gelişim* [Professional development in tourist guidance]. Detay Yayıncılık.

Köroğlu, Ö., & Güdü Demirbulat, Ö. (2017). Rehberlikte sertifikasyon, kalifikasyon ve uzmanlaşma [Certification, qualification and specialization in guidance]. In F. Ö. Güzel, V. Altıntaş, & İ. Şahin (Eds.), *Turist rehberliği araştırmaları: Öngörüler ve uygulamalar* [Tourist guiding research: Insights and applications] (pp. 49–80). Detay Yayıncılık.

Koukpaki, A.S.F., Adams, K., & Oyedijo, A. (2020). The contribution of human resource development managers to organisational branding in the hotel industry in India and South East Asia (ISEA): A dynamic capabilities perspective. *Employee Relations: The International Journal*. doi:10.1108/ER-09-2019-0375

Kouzes, J. M., & Posner, B. Z. (2012). The Leadership Challenge Workbook (3rd ed.). Jossey-Bass.

Kouzes, J. M., & Posner, B. Z. (1987). *The leadership challenge: How to get extraordinary things done in organizations*. Jossey-Bass.

Kouzes, J. M., & Posner, B. Z. (1995). *The Leadership Challenge: How to Keep Getting Extraordinary Things Done in Organizations*. Jossey-Bass.

Kouzes, J. M., & Posner, B. Z. (2010). *The truth about leadership: The no-fads, heart-of-the matter facts you need to know*. Jossey-Bass, San Francisco.

Kovacs, I., & Vamosi Zarandne, K. (2022). Digital marketing employability skills in job advertisements – must-have soft skills for entry level workers: A content analysis. *Economia e Sociologia*, *15*(1), 178–192. doi:10.14254/2071-789X.2022/15-1/11

Koyuncu, M., Burke, R. J., Astakhova, M., Eren, D., & Cetin, H. (2014). Servant leadership and perceptions of service quality provided by front-line service workers in hotels in Turkey: Achieving competitive advantage. *International Journal of Contemporary Hospitality Management*, *26*(7), 1083–1099. doi:10.1108/IJCHM-06-2013-0238

Kozak, M. A., & Uca, S. (2008). Effective factors in the constitution of leadership styles: A study of Turkish hotel managers. *Anatolia*, *19*(1), 117–134. doi:10.1080/13032917.2008.9687057

Krause, D. E. (2004). Influence-based leadership as a determinant of the inclination to innovate and of innovation-related behaviors: An empirical investigation. *The Leadership Quarterly*, *15*(1), 79–102. doi:10.1016/j.leaqua.2003.12.006

Küçük, B., & Yavuz, E. (2021). Examination of the relationship between servant leadership and organizational cynicism: An application in the service industry. *Alanya Academic Review Journal*, *5*(1), 453–472.

Küçüközkan, Y. (2015). Liderlik ve Motivasyon Teorileri: Kuramsal Bir Çerçeve. *Uluslararası Akademik Yönetim Bilimleri Dergisi*, *1*(2), 86–115.

Kuhnert, K. W., & Lewis, P. (1987). Transactional and transformational leadership: A constructive/developmental analysis. *Academy of Management Review*, *12*(4), 648–657. doi:10.2307/258070

Kumar, V. (2020). Indian tourism industry and COVID-19: Present scenario. *Journal of Tourism and Hospitality Education*, *10*, 179–185. doi:10.3126/jthe.v10i0.28768

Kurian, D., & Nafukho, F. M. (2021). *Can authentic leadership influence the employees' organizational justice perceptions? A study in the hotel context*. International Hospitality Review. doi:10.1108/IHR-08-2020-0047

Kurubacak, G. (2006). Reflections on The Digital Youth Leadership for Social Justice Activism: Understanding Silent Dialogues through Critical Pedagogy. *I-manager's Journal on School Educational Technology*, *2*(2), 44–51. doi:10.26634/jsch.2.2.860

Kwak, W. J., & Kim, H. (2015). Servant Leadership and Customer Service Quality at Korean Hotels: Multilevel Organizational Citizenship Behavior as a Mediator. *Social Behavior and Personality*, *43*(8), 1287–1298. doi:10.2224bp.2015.43.8.1287

Lagowska, U., Sobral, F., & Furtado, L. M. G. P. (2020). Leadership under crises: A research agenda for the post-Covid-19 Era. *BAR - Brazilian Administration Review*, *17*(2), 17. doi:10.1590/1807-7692bar2020200062

Langhorn, S. (2004). How emotional intelligence can improve management performance. *International Journal of Contemporary Hospitality Management*, *16*(4), 220–230. doi:10.1108/09596110410537379

Lang, R., & Rybnikova, I. (2014). *Aktuelle Führungstheorien und -konzepte*. Springer Fachmedien Wiesbaden. doi:10.1007/978-3-8349-3729-2

Larjovuori, R. L., Bordi, L., Mäkiniemi, J. P., & Heikkilä-Tammi, K. (2016). The role of leadership and employee well-being in organizational digitalization. *Tiziana Russo-Spenaand Cristina Mele*, *1159*.

Larson, C. E., & Lafasto, F. (1989). *Team-work: What must go right / what can go wrong*. Sage Publications.

Lassalle, F. (1985). Workers' Programme On the particular connection between the present period of history and the idea of the Workers' Estate (April 1862/January 1863). *Economy and Society*, *14*(3), 337–349. doi:10.1080/03085148500000016

Laub, J. A. (2004). Defining Servant Leadership: A Recommended Typology for Servant Leadership Studies. School of Leadership Studies, Regent University. In *Proceedings of the 2004 Servant Leadership Research Roundtable*. Regent University.

Lazarus, R. S., & Folkman, S. (1984). *Stress, appraisal, and coping*. Springer.

Compilation of References

Leavitt, H. J. (2003). Why Hierarchies Thrive. *Harvard Business Review*, *81*(3), 96–112. PMID:12632808

Lee, A., Lyubovnikova, J., Tian, A. W., & Knight, C. (2019). Servant leadership: A meta-analytic examination of incremental contribution, moderation, and mediation. *Journal of Occupational and Organizational Psychology*, *93*(1), 1–44. doi:10.1111/joop.12265

Lee, J. E., Almanza, B. A., Jang, S. S., Nelson, D. C., & Ghiselli, R. F. (2013). Does transformational leadership style influence employees' attitudes toward food safety practices? *International Journal of Hospitality Management*, *33*, 282–293. doi:10.1016/j.ijhm.2012.09.004

Lee, Y. K., Son, M. H., & Lee, D. J. (2011). Do emotions play a mediating role in the relationship between owner leadership styles and manager customer orientation, and performance in service environment? *International Journal of Hospitality Management*, *30*(4), 942–952. doi:10.1016/j.ijhm.2011.02.002

Lee, Y., Tao, W., Li, J. Y. Q., & Sun, R. (2020). Enhancing employees' knowledge sharing through diversity-oriented leadership and strategic internal communication during the COVID-19 outbreak. *Journal of Knowledge Management*, *25*(6), 1526–1549. doi:10.1108/JKM-06-2020-0483

Leitch, C. M., & Volery, T. (2017). Entrepreneurial leadership: Insights and directions. *International Small Business Journal*, *35*(2), 147–156. doi:10.1177/0266242616681397

Le, P. B., & Lei, H. (2019). Determinants of innovation capability: The roles of transformational leadership, knowledge sharing and perceived organizational support. *Journal of Knowledge Management*, *23*(3), 527–547. doi:10.1108/JKM-09-2018-0568

Lewin, K., Lippitt, R., & White, R. K. (1939). Patterns of aggressive behavior in experimentally created "social climates". *The Journal of Social Psychology*, *10*(2), 269–299. doi:10.1080/00224545.1939.9713366

Li, M. (2018, June 8). *What Have We Learned from the 100-Year History of Leadership Research?* https://fisher.osu.edu/

Liang, F., Brunelli, M., & Rezaei, J. (2020). Consistency issues in the best worst method: Measurements and thresholds. *Omega*, *96*, 102175. doi:10.1016/j.omega.2019.102175

Liang, T., Chang, H., Ko, M., & Lin, C. (2017). Transformational leadership and employee voices in the hospitality industry. *International Journal of Contemporary Hospitality Management*, *29*(1), 374–392. doi:10.1108/IJCHM-07-2015-0364

Liden, R. C., Sandy, J. W., Meuser, J. D., Hu, J., Wu, J., & Liao, C. (2015). Servant Leadership: Validation of A Short Form of the SL-28. *The Leadership Quarterly*, *26*(2), 254–269. doi:10.1016/j.leaqua.2014.12.002

Liden, R. C., Wayne, S. J., Liao, C., & Meuser, J. D. (2014). Servant leadership and serving culture: Influence on individual and unit performance. *Academy of Management Journal*, *57*(5), 1434–1452. doi:10.5465/amj.2013.0034

Liden, R. C., Wayne, S. J., Zhao, H., & Henderson, D. (2008). Servant Leadership: Development of a Multidimensional Measure and Multi-Level Assessment. *The Leadership Quarterly*, *19*(2), 163. doi:10.1016/j.leaqua.2008.01.006

Li, J., & Yuan, B. (2017). Both angel and devil: The suppressing effect of transformational leadership on proactive employee's career satisfaction. *International Journal of Hospitality Management*, *65*, 59–70. doi:10.1016/j.ijhm.2017.06.008

Ling, Q., Lin, M., & Wu, X. (2016). The trickle-down effect of servant leadership on frontline employee service behaviors and performance: A multilevel study of Chinese hotels. *Tourism Management*, *52*, 341–368. doi:10.1016/j.tourman.2015.07.008

Linuesa-Langreo, J., Ruiz-Palomino, P., & Elche, D. (2016). Servant leadership, empowerment climate, and group creativity: A case study in the hospitality industry. *Ramon Llull Journal of Applied Ethics*, *7*, 9–36.

Li, P., Sun, J.-M., Taris, W., Xing, L., & Peeters, M. C. W. (2021). Country differences in the relationship between leadership and employee engagement: A meta-analysis. *The Leadership Quarterly*, *32*(1), 1–14. doi:10.1016/j.leaqua.2020.101458

Lipman-Blumen, J. (1992). Connective leadership: Female leadership styles in the 21st-century workplace. *Sociological Perspectives*, *35*(1), 183–203. doi:10.2307/1389374

Liu, C. H. S. (2017). Remodelling progress in tourism and hospitality students' creativity through social capital and transformational leadership. *Journal of Hospitality, Leisure, Sport and Tourism Education*, *21*, 69–82. doi:10.1016/j.jhlste.2017.08.003

Locke, E. A. (1969). What is job satisfaction? *Organizational Behavior and Human Performance*, *4*(4), 309–336. doi:10.1016/0030-5073(69)90013-0

Lombardi, S., Cunha, M. P., & Giustiniano, L. (2021). Improvising resilience: The unfolding of resilient leadership in COVID-19 times. *International Journal of Hospitality Management*, *95*, 102904. doi:10.1016/j.ijhm.2021.102904 PMID:36540683

Lord, R. G., & Brown, D. J. (2001). Leadership, values, and subordinate self-concepts. *The Leadership Quarterly*, *12*(2), 133–152. doi:10.1016/S1048-9843(01)00072-8

Lord, R. G., & Brown, D. J. (2004). *Leadership processes and follower self-identity*. Lawrence Erlbaum Associates, Inc.

Lord, R., & Brown, D. (2004). *Organization and management series. Leadership processes and follower self-identity*. Lawrence Erlbaum Associates Publishers.

Luo, A., Guchait, P., Lee, L., & Madera, J. M. (2019). Transformational leadership and service recovery performance: The mediating effect of emotional labor and the influence of culture. *International Journal of Hospitality Management*, *77*, 31–39. doi:10.1016/j.ijhm.2018.06.011

Luo, Z., Marnburg, E., & Law, R. (2017). Linking leadership and justice to organizational commitment: The mediating role of collective identity in the hotel industry. *International Journal of Contemporary Hospitality Management*, *29*(4), 1167–1184. doi:10.1108/IJCHM-08-2015-0423

Luo, Z., Wang, Y., & Marnburg, E. (2013). Testing the structure and effects of full range leadership theory in the context of China's hotel industry. *Journal of Hospitality Marketing & Management*, *22*(6), 656–677. doi:10.1080/19368623.2012.708959

Luo, Z., Wang, Y., Marnburg, E., & Øgaard, T. (2016). How is leadership related to employee self-concept? *International Journal of Hospitality Management*, *52*, 24–32. doi:10.1016/j.ijhm.2015.09.003

Luthans, F. (1981). *Organizational Behavior*. McGraw-Hill Book Company.

Luu, T. T. (2018). Activating tourists' citizenship behavior for the environment: The roles of CSR and frontline employees' citizenship behavior for the environment. *Journal of Sustainable Tourism*, *26*(7), 1178–1203. doi:10.1080/09669582.2017.1330337

Luu, T. T. (2020a). Environmentally-specific servant leadership and green creativity among tourism employees: Dual mediation paths. *Journal of Sustainable Tourism*, *28*(1), 86–109. doi:10.1080/09669582.2019.1675674

Luu, T. T. (2020b). Integrating green strategy and green human resource practices to trigger individual and organizational green performance: The role of environmentally-specific servant leadership. *Journal of Sustainable Tourism*, *28*(8), 1193–1222. doi:10.1080/09669582.2020.1729165

Compilation of References

Mabey, C., Kulich, C., & Lorenzi-Cioldi, F. (2012). Knowledge leadership in global scientific research. *International Journal of Human Resource Management*, *23*(12), 2450–2467. doi:10.1080/09585192.2012.668386

Madanaguli, A. T., Kaur, P., Bresciani, S., & Dhir, A. (2021). Entrepreneurship in rural hospitality and tourism. A systematic literature review of past achievements and future promises. *International Journal of Contemporary Hospitality Management*.

Madanchian, M., & Taherdoost, H. (2017). Role of leadership in small and medium enterprises (SMEs). *International Journal of Economics and Management Systems*, *2*(1), 240–243.

Madenci, A. B. (2020). Yiyecek İçecek İşletmelerinin Örgütsel Yapısı ve Hiyerarşisi Üzerine Bir Araştırma: Konya İli Örneği. *Gastroia: Journal of Gastronomy and Travel Research*, *4*(2), 173–184.

Mahembe, B., & Engelbrecht, A. S. (2014). The relationship between servant leadership, organisational citizenship behaviour and team effectiveness. *SA Journal of Industrial Psychology*, *40*(1), 1–10. doi:10.4102ajip.v40i1.1107

Maher, A. (2017). Charismatic leadership impact on employee psychological engagement: Evidence from travel companies. *Journal of Faculty Tourism and Hotels-University of Sadat City*, *1*(2/1), 151-178.

Mahmood, M., Uddin, A., & Fan, L. (2019). The influence of transformational leadership on employees' creative process engagement. *Management Decision*, *57*(3), 741–764. doi:10.1108/MD-07-2017-0707

Mahoney, M. J., & Arnkoff, D. B. (1978). Cognitive and self-control therapies. In S. L. Garfield & A. E. Borgin (Eds.), *Handbook of psychotherapy and therapy change* (pp. 689–722). Wiley.

Mahoney, M. J., & Arnkoff, D. B. (1979). Self-management: Theory, research, and application. In J. P. Brady & D. Pomerleau (Eds.), *Behavioral medicine: Theory and practice* (pp. 75–96). Williams and Williams.

Malthus, T. (2015). *An essay on the principle of population and other writings*.

Ma, M. H., & Yang, Q. S. (2020). How does transformational leadership work on COVID-19? An empirical evidence from China. *Journal of Innovative Studies*, *1*(2).

Ma, M.-H., & Yang, Q.-S. (2020). How does transformational leadership work on COVID-19? Empirical evidence from China. *Journal of Innovative Studies*, *1*(2). http://www.iiinstitute.us/index.php/jis/article/view/1

Manning, N. (2016). *How to be a tour guide: The Essential manual for tour managers and tour guides*. Nick Manning.

Mansurova, S., & Güney, S. (2018). İşletmelerde dönüşümcü liderlik davranışlarının örgüt kültürüne etkisi ve bir uygulama[The effect of transformational leadership behaviors on organizational culture in businesses and an application]. *Journal of Anadolu Bil Vocational School*, *13*(52), 33–54.

Manz, C. (1992b). *Mastering Self-Leadership: Empowering yourself for personal excellence*. Prentice Hall.

Manz, C. C. (1986). Self-leadership: Toward an expanded theory of self-influence processes in organizations. *Academy of Management Review*, *11*(3), 585–600. doi:10.2307/258312

Manz, C. C. (1990). Beyond self-managing work teams: Toward self-leading teams in the workplace. In R. Woodman & W. Pasmore (Eds.), *Research in organizational change and development* (pp. 273–299). JAI Press.

Manz, C. C. (1992a). Self-leadership…The heart of empowerment. *Journal for Quality and Participation*, *15*(4), 80–89.

Manz, C. C., & Neck, C. P. (1999). *Mastering self-leadership: Empowering yourself for personal excellence*. Prentice Hall.

Marcouse, I. (2014). İşletme Kitabı (Çeviri T. Göbekçin). İstanbul: Alfa yayınları. Mumford, E., (1906-907). The Origins of Leadership. *American Journal of Sociology*, *12*, 216–240.

Marinakou, E. (2012). *An investigation of gender influences on transformational leadership style in the Greek hospitality industry* [Doctoral Thesis]. Department of Human Resources Management Strathclyde Business School University of Strathclyde.

Marjolosa Aaltio, I., & Takala, T. (2000). Charismatic leadership, manipulation and the complexity of organizational life. *Journal of Workplace Learning: Employee Counselling Today, 12*(4), 146–158. doi:10.1108/13665620010332750

Markle-Reid, M., Dykeman, C., Ploeg, J., Stradiotto, C. K., Andrews, A., Bonomo, S., & Salker, N. (2017). Collaborative Leadership and the Implementation of Community-based Fall Prevention Initiatives: A Multiple Case Study of Public Health Practice Within Community Groups. *BMC Health Services Research, 17*(141), 1–12. doi:10.118612913-017-2089-3 PMID:28209143

Martin, B., Cashel, C., Wagstaff, M., & Breuning, M. (2006). *Outdoor leadership: Theory and practice*. Human Kinetics.

Masood, S. A., Dani, S. S., Burns, N. D., & Backhouse, C. (2006). Transformational leadership and organizational culture: The situational strength perspective. *Proceedings of the Institution of Mechanical Engineers. Part B, Journal of Engineering Manufacture, 220*(6), 941–949. doi:10.1243/09544054JEM499

Masry, S. E., Kattara, H., & Demerdash, J. E. (2004). A Comparative Study on Leadership Styles Adopted by General Managers: A Case Study in Egypt. *Anatolia, 15*(2), 109–124. doi:10.1080/13032917.2004.9687150

Mayring, P. (1991). Qualitative Inhaltsanalyse. In U. Flick, E. von Kardoff, H. Keupp, L. von Rosenstiel, & S. Wolff (Eds.), *Handbuch qualitative Forschung: Grundlagen, Konzepte, Methoden und Anwendungen* [Handbook of qualitative research; Principles, concepts, methods and applications] (pp. 209–213). Beltz Psychologie-Verlags-Union.

Mayring, P. (2007). Designs in qualitativ orientierter Forschung. *Journal für Psychologie, 15*(2), 1–10.

Mayring, P. (2014). *Qualitative content analysis: Theoretical foundation, basic procedures and software solution*. Beltz Verlag.

McCann, J. T., Graves, D., & Cox, L. (2014). Servant leadership, employee satisfaction, and organizational performance in rural community hospitals. *International Journal of Business and Management, 9*(10), 28–38. doi:10.5539/ijbm.v9n10p28

McCrae, R. R., & Lökenhoff, C. E. (2010). Self-regulation and the five-factor model of personality traits. In R. H. Hoyle (Ed.), *Handbook of personality and self-regulation* (pp. 145–168). Wiley-Blackwell. doi:10.1002/9781444318111.ch7

McGee, J., Thomas, H., & Wilson, D. C. (2010). *Strategy: Analysis and Practice*. McGraw-Hill.

McGuire, D., Cunningham, J. E. A., Reynolds, K., & Matthews-Smith, G. (2020). Beating the virus: An examination of the crisis communication approach taken by New Zealand Prime Minister Jacinda Ardern during the Covid-19 pandemic. *Human Resource Development International, 23*(4), 361–379. doi:10.1080/13678868.2020.1779543

McManus, L. (2013). Customer accounting and marketing performance measures in the hotel industry: Evidence from Australia. *International Journal of Hospitality Management, 33*, 140–152. doi:10.1016/j.ijhm.2012.07.007

Megheirkouni, M. (2018). Self-leadership strategies and career success: Insight on sports organizations. *Sport, Business and Management, 8*(4), 393–409. doi:10.1108/SBM-02-2018-0006

Mehmetoglu, M., & Altinay, L. (2006). Examination of grounded theory analysis with an application to hospitality research. *International Journal of Hospitality Management, 25*(1), 12–33. doi:10.1016/j.ijhm.2004.12.002

Mehta, M., Sarvaiya, H., & Chandani, A. (2020). Community engagement through responsible leadership in managing pandemic: Insight from India using netnography. *The International Journal of Sociology and Social Policy*. Advance online publication. doi:10.1108/IJSSP-06-2020-0214

Compilation of References

Men, C., & Jia, R. (2021). Knowledge-oriented leadership, team learning, and team creativity: The roles of task interdependence and task complexity. *Leadership and Organization Development Journal*, *42*(6), 882–898. doi:10.1108/LODJ-11-2020-0506

Mendes, A. C., Ferreira, F. A., Kannan, D., Ferreira, N. C., & Correia, R. J. (2022). A BWM approach to determinants of sustainable entrepreneurship in small and medium-sized enterprises. *Journal of Cleaner Production*, *371*, 133300. doi:10.1016/j.jclepro.2022.133300

Mihardjo, L., Sasmoko, S., Alamsjah, F., & Elidjen, E. (2019). Digital leadership role in developing business model innovation and customer experience orientation in industry 4.0. *Management Science Letters*, *9*(11), 1749–1762. doi:10.5267/j.msl.2019.6.015

Mill, J. S. (1848). *Principles of Political Economy*. Prometheus Books. www. nowecantsong. org

Mills, G. E. (2007). *Transformational Leadership and Employee Retention: An Exploratory Investigation of The Four Characteristic*. Capella University.

Minh-Duc, L., & Huu-Lam, N. (2019). Transformational leadership, customer citizenship behavior, employee intrinsic motivation, and employee creativity. *Journal of Asian Business and Economic Studies*, *26*(2), 286–300. doi:10.1108/JABES-10-2018-0070

Mishra, N., Mishra, R., & Singh, M. K. (2019). The impact of transformational leadership on team performance: The mediating role of emotional intelligence among leaders of hospitality and tourism sector. *International Journal of Scientific & Technology Research*, *8*(11), 3110–3116.

Mohamed, H. A., & Fahmy, T. M. (2015). Examining the relationship between emotional intelligence and transformational leadership (A field study of tourism managers). *Journal of Association of Arab Universities for Tourism and Hospitality*, *12*(2), 97–108. doi:10.21608/jaauth.2015.67442

Mohamed, L. M. (2016). Assessing the effects of transformational leadership: A study on Egyptian hotel employees. *Journal of Hospitality and Tourism Management*, *27*, 49–59. doi:10.1016/j.jhtm.2016.04.001

Morrone, D., Raimo, N., Tarulli, A., & Vitolla, F. (2021). Digitalisation in the hospitality industry: Motivations, effects and role of COVID-19. *International Journal of Digital Culture and Electronic Tourism*, *3*(3-4), 257–270. doi:10.1504/IJDCET.2021.116475

Mostafa, A. M. S. (2019). Transformational leadership and restaurant employees customer-oriented behaviours: The mediating role of organizational social capital and work engagement. *International Journal of Contemporary Hospitality Management*, *31*(3), 1166–1182. doi:10.1108/IJCHM-02-2018-0123

Mottaz, C. J. (1988). Determinants of Organizational Commitment. *Human Relations*, *41*(6), 467–482. doi:10.1177/001872678804100604

Mowday, R. T., Porter, L. W., & Steers, R. M. (1982). *Employee-Organization Linkages: The Psychology of Commitment, Absenteeism and Turnover*. Academic Press.

Muczyk, J. P., & Reimann, B. C. (1987). The Case for Directive Leadership. *The Academy of Management Perspectives*, *1*(4), 301–311. doi:10.5465/ame.1987.4275646

Muller, R., Smith, E., & Lillah, R. (2018). Perceptions Regarding the Impact of Servant Leadership on Organizational Performance in The Eastern Cape. *International Journal of Business and Management Studies*, *10*(1), 56–62.

Naderi, A., Vosta, L. N., Ebrahimi, A., & Jalilvand, M. R. (2019). The contributions of social entrepreneurship and transformational leadership to performance Insights from rural tourism in Iran. *The International Journal of Sociology and Social Policy*, 1–19.

Nadler, D.A., & Tushman, M.L. (1990). Beyond the charismatic leader: Leadership and organizational change. *Startegs & Organization*, 77-97.

Nagaj, R., & Žuromskaitė, B. (2021). Tourism in the Era of Covid-19 and Its Impact on the Environment. *Energies*, *14*(7), 2000. doi:10.3390/en14072000

Nagele, A. D., & Awuor, E. (2018). Relationship between transformational leadership style and operational performance of hospitality industry in Kenya: A case study of star rated hotels in Nairobi county. *Stratford Peer Reviewed Journals and Book Publishing Journal of Human Resource & Leadership*, *2*(4), 37–58.

Nandal, V., & Krishnam, V. (2000). Charismatic leadership and self efficacy: Importance of role clarity. *Management and Labour Studies*, *25*(4), 231–243. doi:10.1177/0258042X0002500401

Naqshbandi, M. M., & Jasimuddin, S. M. (2018). Knowledge-oriented leadership and open innovation: Role of knowledge management capability in France-based multinationals. *International Business Review*, *27*(3), 701–713. doi:10.1016/j.ibusrev.2017.12.001

Narbona, J. (2016). Digital leadership, Twitter and Pope Francis. *Church Communication and Culture*, *1*(1), 90–109. doi:10.1080/23753234.2016.1181307

Nazarian, A., Atkinson, P., Foroudi, P., & Edirisinghe, D. (2021). Factors affecting organizational effectiveness in independent hotels–The case of Iran. *Journal of Hospitality and Tourism Management*, *46*, 293–303. doi:10.1016/j.jhtm.2021.01.002

Neck, C. P., & Houghton, J. D. (2006). Two decades of Self-leadership Theory and research. *Journal of Managerial Psychology*, *21*(4), 270–295. doi:10.1108/02683940610663097

Neck, C. P., Manz, C. C., & Houghton, J. D. (2017). *Self-leadership: The definitive guide to personal excellence*. CA. Sage (Atlanta, Ga.).

Neck, C. P., Stewart, G. L., & Manz, C. C. (1996). Self-leaders within self-leading teams: Toward an optimal equilibrium. In M. Beyerlein (Ed.), *Advances in Interdisciplinary Studies of Work Teams* (pp. 43–65). JAI Press.

Neuman, W. L. (2014). *Social research methods: Qualitative and quantitative approaches*. Pearson Education Limited.

Neves, P., Pires, D., & Costa, S. (2021). Empowering to Reduce Intentions to Resist Future Change: Organization-Based Self-esteem as a Boundary Condition. *British Journal of Management*, *32*(3), 872–891. doi:10.1111/1467-8551.12436

Newman, A., & Butler, C. (2014). The influence of follower cultural orientation on attitudinal responses towards transformational leadership: Evidence from the Chinese hospitality industry. *International Journal of Human Resource Management*, *25*(7), 1024–1045. doi:10.1080/09585192.2013.815250

Newman, N., & Newman, D. (2021). Leadership behind masked faces: From uncertainty to resilience at a Jamaican academic library. *Journal of Academic Librarianship*, *47*(5), 102377. doi:10.1016/j.acalib.2021.102377

Nguyen, T. L., Nguyen, H. A. M., Nguyen Luu, P. T., Le, M. A., Nguyen, T. A. T., & Nguyen, N. T. (2022). Leadership and Communication Skills Towards Emotional Intelligence: A Case Study of FPT University in Vietnam. *Journal of Asian Finance, Economics and Business*, *9*(5), 53–61. doi:10.13106/jafeb.2022.vol9.no5.0053

Nguyen, L. V., Haar, J., & Smollan, R. (2022). Hospitality Leadership Competencies and Employee Commitment: New Insights From the Booming Hotel Industry in Vietnam. *Tourism and Hospitality Management*, *28*(2), 419–443. doi:10.20867/thm.28.2.10

Nielsen, N., D'Auria, G., & Zolley, S. (2021). *Tuning in, turning outward: cultivating compassionate leadership in a crisis*. Retrieved June 2 2021, from: https://www.mckinsey.com/businessfunctions/ organization/our-insights/tuning-in-turning-outward-cultivating-compassionat eleadership-in-a-crisis

Nikei Asian Review. (n.d.). Retrieved April 1 2020, from: https://asia.nikkei.com/: https://asia.nikkei.com/Spotlight/Cor onavirus/Empty-hotels-in-Sri-Lanka-and-Nepal-point-to-lengthy-economic-hit

Nipu, A., & Ahmed, S. (2019). Qualitative model for identifying leadership using fuzzy logic. *International Journal of Applications of Fuzzy Sets and Artificial Intelligence*, *9*, 13–29.

Nitonde, R. (2014). Soft Skills and Personality Development. In *Proceedings of the National Seminar*. Shri Shivaji College.

Nkengasong, J. (2020). China's response to a novel coronavirus stands in stark contrast to the 2002 SARS outbreak response. *Nature Medicine*, *26*(3), 310–311. doi:10.103841591-020-0771-1 PMID:31988464

Nonaka, I., & Takeuchi, H. (1995). *The Knowledge-Creating Company: How Japanese companies create the dynamics of innovation*. Oxford University Press.

Northouse, P. G. (2016). Leadership: Theory and Practice (7th ed.). SAGE Publications.

Nwokorie, E. C., & Okechukwu, O. C. (2014). The Impact of Leadership Style on Effective Human Resources Management and Productivity in Hospitality Organizations. *Journal of Technical Education and Management Sciences*, *9*(2), 106–118.

Nyong'a, T. M., & Maina, R. (2019). Influence of Strategic Leadership on Strategy Implementation at Kenya Revenue Authority, Southern Region in Kenya. *International Academic Journal of Human Resource and Business Administration*, *3*(5), 128–159.

O'Connell, T. S., Cuthbertson, B., & Goins, T. J. (2014). *Leadership in recreation and leisure services*. Human Kinetics.

Oberer, B., & Erkollar, A. (2018). Leadership 4.0: Digital leaders in the age of industry 4.0. *International Journal of Organizational Leadership*.

Oberländer, M., Beinicke, A., & Bipp, T. (2020). Digital competencies: A review of the literature and applications in the workplace. *Computers & Education*, *146*, 103752. doi:10.1016/j.compedu.2019.103752

Odumeru, J. A., & Ogbonna, I. G. (2013). Transformational vs. transactional leadership theories: Evidence in literature. *International Review of Management and Business Research*, *2*(2), 355–361.

Oğuz, E. (2011). Öğretmenlerin Örgütsel Vatandaşlık Davranışları ile Yöneticilerin Liderlik Stilleri Arasındaki İlişki. *Kuram ve Uygulamada Eğitim Yönetimi*, *17*(3), 377–403.

Ohunakin, F., Adeniji, A. A., Oludayo, O. A., Osibanjo, A. O., & Oduyoye, O. O. (2019). Employees' retention in Nigeria's hospitality industry: The role of transformational leadership style and job satisfaction. *Journal of Human Resources in Hospitality & Tourism*, *18*(4), 1–30. doi:10.1080/15332845.2019.1626795

Ojokuku, R. M., Odetayo, T. A., & Sajuyigbe, A. S. (2012). Impact of leadership style on organizational performance: A case study of Nigerian banks. *American Journal of Business and Management*, *1*(4), 202–207.

Okolie, U. C., Igwe, P. A., Nwosu, H. E., Eneje, B. C., & Mlanga, S. (2019). Enhancing graduate employability: Why do higher education institutions have problems with teaching generic skills? *Policy Futures in Education*, *18*(2), 294–313. doi:10.1177/1478210319864824

Oktay, E., & Gül, H. (2003). Çalışanların Duygusal Bağlılıklarının Sağlanmasında Conger ve Kanungo'nun Karizmatik Lider Özelliklerinin Etkileri Üzerine Karaman ve Aksaray Emniyet Müdürlüklerinde Yapılan Bir Araştırma. *Sosyal Bilimler Enstitüsü Dergisi*.

Oktay, E., & Gül, H. (2003). Çalışanların duygusal bağlılıklarının sağlanmasında conger ve kanungo'nun karizmatik lider özelliklerinin etkileri üzerine karaman ve aksaray emniyet müdürlüklerinde yapılan bir araştırma[A research conducted in Karaman and Aksaray Police Departments on the effects of the charismatic leader characteristics of Conger and Kanungo on the emotional commitment of employees]. *Selçuk Üniversitesi Sosyal Bilimler Enstitüsü Dergisi*, *10*, 403–427.

Olson, A. K., & Simerson, B. K. (2015). *Leading With Strategic Thinking: Four Ways Effective Leaders Gain Insight, Drive Change, and Get Results. The Oxford Handbook of Leadership*. Oxford University Press. doi:10.1002/9781119153818

Oluwakayode, O., Clinton, E., Stanley, A., & Subi, J. (2017). A Review and Application of McGregor Theory X and Theory Y in Business Research. In *1st Covenant University International Conference on Entrepreneurship* (pp. 245-256). Covenant University Press.

Öncü, B. (2017). *Okul öncesi yöneticilerinin algılanan liderlik stilleri ile okul öncesi öğretmenlerinin yaşadıkları örgütsel sessizlik arasındaki ilişkinin incelenmesi (Kırklareli ili örneği)* [Investigation of the relationship between the perceived leadership styles of preschool administrators and the organizational silence experienced by preschool teachers (Kırklareli province example)] [Unpublished Master's Thesis]. Bahçeşehir University, Institute of Educational Sciences.

Ongsakul, V., Kajla, T., Raj, S., Khoa, T. T., & Ahmed, Z. U. (2022). Changing tourists' preferences in the hotel industry amid COVID-19 pandemic. *Journal of Hospitality and Tourism Technology*, *13*(2), 295–313. Advance online publication. doi:10.1108/JHTT-07-2020-0179

Ören, A. S. (2006). *Günümüzün Liderlik Profili; Transformasyonel (Dönüştürücü) Liderlik Antalya Bölgesinde Bulunan Beş Yıldızlı Otel İşletmelerinde Bir Araştırma*. Akdeniz Üniversitesi Sosyal Bilimler Enstitüsü Turizm işletmeciliği ve Otelcilik Anabilim Dalı Yüksek Lisans Tezi.

Organ, W. D. (1997). Organizational Citizenship Behavior: It's Construct Clean-Up Time. *Human Performance*, *10*(2), 85–97. doi:10.120715327043hup1002_2

Orîndaru, A., Popescu, M. F., Alexoaei, A. P., Căescu, Ş. C., Florescu, M. S., & Orzan, A. O. (2021). Tourism in a post-COVID-19 era: Sustainable strategies for industry's recovery. *Sustainability*, *13*(12), 6781. doi:10.3390u13126781

Oruh, E. S., Mordi, C., Dibia, C. H., & Ajonbadi, H. A. (2021). Exploring compassionate managerial leadership style in reducing employee stress level during COVID-19 crisis: the case of Nigeria. *Employee Relations: The International Journal*. doi:10.1108/ER-06-2020-0302

Özdemir, M., & Pektaş, V. (2020). Conger- kanungo karizmtik liderlik ölçeğinin türk kültürüne uyarlama çalışması[An adaptation study of the Conger-kazango charismatic leadership scale to Turkish culture]. *Hacettepe Üniversitesi Sosyal Bilimler Dergisi*, *2*(1), 2–18.

Özdemir, N., & Yılmaz, E. (2019). Algılanan Hizmetkâr Liderliğin Presentizm (Edimsizlik) Üzerindeki Etkisi: Frigya Bölgesi[The Effects of Perceived Servant Leadership on Presenteeism: Phrygia Region]. *Anatolia: Turizm Araştırmaları Dergisi*, *30*(3), 198–209.

Özel, M. (1998). *Liderlik Sanatı*. İz Yayıncılık.

Compilation of References

Özkalp, E. (1988). *Örgütsel Davranış*. Eskişehir: Anadolu Üniversitesi Açık öğretim Fakültesi Yayınları No:40.

Öztaş, G. Z., Bars, A., Genç, V., & Erdem, S. (2021, June). Criteria Assessment for Covid-19 Vaccine Selection via BWM. In *The International Workshop on Best-Worst Method* (pp. 228-237). Springer.

Page, D., & Wong, P. T. P. (2000). A Conceptual Framework for Measuring Servant-Leadership. In S. Adjgibolosoo (Ed.), *The Human Factor in Shaping the Course of History and Development* (pp. 69–109). University Press of America, Inc.

Pahi, M. H., & Hamid, K. A. (2016). The magic of destructive leadership: Laissez-faire leadership and commitment to service quality. *International Journal of Economic Perspectives*, *10*(4).

Paine, L. (2021). *Covid-19 is rewriting the rules of corporate governance*. Retrieved June 2, 2021, from: https://hbr.org/2020/10/covid-19-is-rewriting-the-rules-of-corporate-governance

Palladan, A. A., Abdulkadir, K. B., & Chong, Y. W. (2016). The Effect of Strategic Leadership, Organization Innovativeness, Information Technology Capability on Effective Strategy Implementation: A Study of Tertiary Institutions in Nigeria. *Journal of Business and Management*, *18*(9), 109–115.

Parolini, J., Patterson, K., & Winston, B. (2009). Distinguishing Between Transformational and Servant Leadership. *Leadership and Organization Development Journal*, *30*(3), 274–291. doi:10.1108/01437730910949544

Parzych, K., & Brkić-Vejmelka, J. (2020). Guests' assessment of hotel facilities and services: Zadar case study. *European Journal of Tourism, Hospitality and Recreation*, *10*(3), 241–250. doi:10.2478/ejthr-2020-0021

Patiar, A., & Mia, L. (2009). Transformational leadership style, market competition and departmental performance: Evidence from luxury hotels in Australia. *International Journal of Hospitality Management*, *28*(2), 254–262. doi:10.1016/j.ijhm.2008.09.003

Patiar, A., & Wang, Y. (2016). The effects of transformational leadership and organizational commitment on hotel departmental performance. *International Journal of Contemporary Hospitality Management*, *28*(3), 586–608. doi:10.1108/IJCHM-01-2014-0050

Patiar, A., & Wang, Y. (2020). Managers' leadership, compensation and benefits, and departments' performance: Evidence from upscale hotels in Australia. *Journal of Hospitality and Tourism Management*, *42*, 29–39. doi:10.1016/j.jhtm.2019.11.005

Patterson, A. K. (2003). Servant Leadership: A Theoretical Model. In *Proceedings of the 2003 Servant Leadership Research Roundtable*. Regent University.

Patton, M. Q. (2002). *Qualitative research and evaluation methods*. Sage Publications.

Paul, R. J. (2003, Winter). Managing employee depression in the workplace. *Review of Business, New York*, *24*(1), 31–37.

Pechlaner, H., & Sauerwein, E. (2002). Strategy implementation in the Alpine tourism industry. *International Journal of Contemporary Hospitality Management*, *14*(4), 157–168. doi:10.1108/09596110210427003

Pedler, M., Burgoyne, J., & Boydell, T. (2010). *A Manager's Guide to Leadership: An action learning Approach* (2nd ed.). McGraw-Hill Publishing.

Pelit, E., & Ak, S. (2018). İnsan Kaynakları Yönetimi İşlevi Olarak Personel Bulma, Seçme ve Personeli İşe Yerleştirme ile İlgili Sorunlar: Turizm İşletmeleri Örneğinde Teorik Bir İnceleme [Problems in the Processes of Personnel Recruitment, Selection and Placement as a Function of Human Resources Management: A Theoric Research in the case of Tourism Enterprises]. *İstanbul Aydın Üniversitesi Dergisi*, *10*(2), 39-74.

Peng, B. (2021). Digital leadership: State governance in the era of digital technology. *Cultura e Scuola, 1-5*. Advance online publication. doi:10.1177/2096608321989

Pernecky, T., & Jamal, T. (2010). Hermeneutic phenomenology in tourism studies. *Annals of Tourism Research, 37*(4), 1055–1075. doi:10.1016/j.annals.2010.04.002

Peters, M. (2005). Entrepreneurial skills in leadership and human resource management evaluated by apprentices in small tourism businesses. *Education + Training, 47*(8/9), 575–591. doi:10.1108/00400910510633125

Peticca-Harris, A. (2019). Managing compassionately? Managerial narratives about grief and compassion. *Human Relations, 72*(3), 588–612. doi:10.1177/0018726718779666

Phaneuf, J., Boudrias, J., Rousseau, V., & Brunelle, E. (2016). Personality and transformational leadership: The moderating effect of organizational context. *Personality and Individual Differences, 202*, 30–35. doi:10.1016/j.paid.2016.06.052

Piccolo, R. F., Greenbaum, R., Hartog, D. N., & Folger, R. (2010). The relationship between ethical leadership and core job characteristics. *Journal of Organizational Behavior, 31*(2-3), 259–278. doi:10.1002/job.627

Pieterse, A. N., Van Knippenberg, D., Schippers, M., & Stam, D. (2010). Transformational and transactional leadership and innovative behavior: The moderating role of psychological empowerment. *Journal of Organizational Behavior, 31*(4), 609–623. doi:10.1002/job.650

Pikkemaat, B., & Zehrer, A. (2016). Innovation and service experiences in small tourism family firms. *International Journal of Culture, Tourism and Hospitality Research, 10*(4), 343–360. doi:10.1108/IJCTHR-06-2016-0064

Pinnow, D. F. (2011). *Leadership-What really matters: A handbook on systemic leadership*. Springer. doi:10.1007/978-3-642-20247-6

Pinto, L., Bonifacio, M. A., De Giglio, E., Santovito, E., Cometa, S., Bevilacqua, A., & Baruzzi, F. (2021). Biopolymer hybrid materials: Development, characterization, and food packaging applications. *Food Packaging and Shelf Life, 28*, 100676. doi:10.1016/j.fpsl.2021.100676

Pittaway, L., Carmouche, R., & Chell, E. (1998). The way forward: Leadership research in the hospitality industry. *Hospital Management, 17*(4), 407–426. doi:10.1016/S0278-4319(98)00035-8

Piuchan, M., & Prachansit, S. (2019). Hotel pioneers' leadership styles: A case study on the founders of Oberoi Group and Soneva and Six Senses Resort and Spa. *Tourism Original Scientific Paper, 67*(4), 375–388.

Podsakoff, P. M., MacKenzie, S., Moorman, R., & Fetter, R. (1990). Transformational leader behaviors and their effects on followers' trust in leader, satisfaction, and organizational citizenship behaviors. *The Leadership Quarterly, 1*(2), 107–142. doi:10.1016/1048-9843(90)90009-7

Polanyi, K. (2001). *The great transformation: The political and economic origins of our time*. Beacon press.

Pond, K. L. (1993). *The professional guide: Dynamics of tour guiding*. Van Nostrand Reinhold Company.

Porter, M. E. (1985). *The Competitive Advantage: Creating and Sustaining Superior Performance*. Free Press.

Poskas, D. A. T., & Messer, C. C. (2015). Investigating leadership applications in tourism: A case study of leadership in community tourism. *Journal of Teaching in Travel & Tourism, 15*(2), 186–198. doi:10.1080/15313220.2015.1026475

Prabowo, T. S., & Irawanto, N. D. (2018). The influence of transformational leadership and work motivation on employee performance mediated by job satisfaction. *Journal of Applied Management, 16*(1), 171–178. doi:10.21776/ub.jam.2018.016.01.20

Prasuna, C. (2020). Government to promote tourism and hospitality in India. *International Journal of Multidisciplinary Educational Research*, *9*(11), 34.

Priastana, A., & Mujiati, N. W. (2020). Influence of transformational leadership style, organizational commitment and work stress on performance of employees food & beverage service division in the resort Bali hotel. *American Journal of Humanities and Social Sciences Research*, *4*(5), 174–182.

Priest, S. (1986). *Outdoor leadership preparation in five nations* [Unpublished doctoral dissertation]. University of Oregon, Eugene.

Priest, S. (1984). Effective outdoor leadership: A survey. *Journal of Experiential Education*, *7*(3), 34–36. doi:10.1177/105382598400700310

Priest, S. (1987). *Preparing effective outdoor pursuit leaders*. Institute of Recreation Research and Service.

Priest, S., & Gass, M. A. (2005). *Effective leadership in adventure programming* (2nd ed.). Human Kinetics.

Prikshat, V., Rajesh, J. I., & Rajaguru, R. (2021). The growth satisfaction in jobs among hospitality employees: The role of transformational leadership, interpersonal communication satisfaction and trust. *Journal of Human Resources in Hospitality & Tourism*, *20*(1), 48–74. doi:10.1080/15332845.2020.1821427

Proios, I. (2019). Factor validity and reliability of the Revised Self-Leadership Questionnaire in a Greek sample. *Journal of Physical Education and Sport Management*, *6*(2), 41–48.

Proios, I., Fotiadou, E., Doganis, G., Batsiou, S., & Proios, M. (2020). Influence of Self-Leadership Strategies on the Beliefs of General Self-Efficacy. *The Journal of Social Sciences Research*, *6*(5), 531–535. doi:10.32861/jssr.65.531.535

Prussia, G. E., Anderson, J. S., & Manz, C. C. (1998). Self-leadership and performance outcomes: The mediating influence of self-efficacy. *Journal of Organizational Behavior*, *19*(5), 523–538. doi:10.1002/(SICI)1099-1379(199809)19:5<523::AID-JOB860>3.0.CO;2-I

Purwanto, A., Asbari, M., Hartuti, H., Setiana, Y. N., & Fahmi, K. (2021). Effect of psychological capital and authentic leadership on innovation work behavior. *International Journal of Social and Management Studies*, *2*(1), 1–13.

Qiu, S., & Dooley, L. (2019). Servant leadership: Development and validation of a multidimensional measure in the Chinese hospitality industry. *Leadership and Organization Development Journal*, *40*(2), 193–212. doi:10.1108/LODJ-04-2018-0148

Qiu, S., Dooley, L. M., & Xie, L. (2020). How servant leadership and self-efficacy interact to affect service quality in the hospitality industry: A polynomial regression with response surface analysis. *Tourism Management*, *78*, 104051. doi:10.1016/j.tourman.2019.104051

Quintana, T. A., Park, S., & Cabrera, Y. A. (2015). Assessing the effects of leadership styles on employees' outcomes in international luxury hotels. *Journal of Business Ethics*, *129*(2), 469–489. doi:10.100710551-014-2170-3

Qu, S. Q., & Dunmay, J. (2011). The qualitative research interview. *Qualitative Research in Accounting & Management*, *8*(3), 238–264. doi:10.1108/11766091111162070

Rabiul, M. K., Shamsudin, F. M., Yean, T. F., & Patwary, A. K. (2022). Linking leadership styles to communication competency and work engagement: Evidence from the hotel industry. *Journal of Hospitality and Tourism Insights*, 1-22.

Rabiul, M. K., Patwary, A. K., Mohamed, A. E., & Rashid, H. (2022). Leadership Styles, Psychological Factors, and Employee Commitment to Service Quality in the Hotel Industry. *Journal of Quality Assurance in Hospitality & Tourism*, *23*(4), 853–881. doi:10.1080/1528008X.2021.1913695

Rabiul, M. K., & Yean, T. F. (2021). Leadership styles, motivating language, and work engagement: An empirical investigation of the hotel industry. *International Journal of Hospitality Management, 92*, 102712. doi:10.1016/j.ijhm.2020.102712

Rabotic, B. (2010). *Professional tourist guiding: the importance of interpretation for tourist experiences*. In 20th Biennial International Congress: New Trends in Tourism and Hotel Management, Opatija, Croatia.

Radwan, H., & Radwan, I. (2020). Leadership Styles in the Hotel Sector and Its Effect on Employees' Creativity and Organizational Commitment. *International Journal of Social and Business Sciences, 14*(3), 169–179.

Rafferty, A. E., & Griffin, M. A. (2004). Dimensions of transformational leadership: Conceptual and empirical extensions. *The Leadership Quarterly, 15*(3), 329–354. doi:10.1016/j.leaqua.2004.02.009

Raguž, I. V. (2007). The interdependence between characteristics and leadership style of managers in the hospitality industry in Dubrovnik-Neretva county: Empirical research. *Management, 12*(2), 57–68.

Raiola, E. O. (1986). *Outdoor wilderness education: A leadership curriculum* [Unpublished doctoral dissertation]. Unity College, ME.

Raiola, E., & Sugerman, D. (1999). Outdoor leadership curricula. In J. Miles & S. Priest (Eds.), *Adventure programming* (pp. 241–245). Venture Publishing.

Reddy, A. V., & Mehta, H. N. (2019). Mediating role of transformational leadership on the relationship between burnout and intention to quit among the employees of select hotels in South India. *Organizational Psychology, 9*(4), 8–17.

Redmond, J. (2015). Strategy and the Importance of Strategic Leadership. *Certified Public Accountants*, 1-9.

Rehman, U. U., & Iqbal, A. (2020). Nexus of knowledge-oriented leadership, knowledge management, innovation, and organizational performance in higher education. *Business Process Management Journal, 26*(6), 1731–1758. doi:10.1108/BPMJ-07-2019-0274

Reisinger, Y., & Steiner, C. (2006). Reconceptualising interpretation: The role of tour guides in authentic tourism. *Current Issues in Tourism, 9*(6), 481–498. doi:10.2167/cit280.0

Reis, J., Amorim, M., Melão, N., Cohen, Y., & Rodrigues, M. (2019, July). Digitalization: A literature review and research agenda. In *International Joint conference on industrial engineering and operations management* (pp. 443-456). Springer. 10.1177/2096608321989835

Renjen, P. (2020). *The essence of resilient leadership: Business recovery from COVID-19*. Deloitte. Retrieved June 30 June 5 Available from: https://www2. deloitte. com/global/en/insights/economy/covid -19/guide-to-organizational-recovery-for-senior-executives-h eart-of-resilient-leadership. html

Renko, M. (2018). Entrepreneurial leadership. In J. Antonakis & D. V. Day (Eds.), *The nature of leadership* (3rd ed., pp. 381–408). SAGE Publications. doi:10.4135/9781506395029.n15

Rescalvo-Martin, E., Gutierrez-Gutierrez, L., & Llorens-Montes, F. J. (2021). The effect of paradoxical leadership on extra-role service in the hospitality industry. *International Journal of Contemporary Hospitality Management, 33*(10), 3661–3684. doi:10.1108/IJCHM-02-2021-0198

Rezaei, J. (2015). Best-Worst Multi-Criteria Decision-Making Method. *Omega, 53*, 49–57. doi:10.1016/j.omega.2014.11.009

Rezaei, J. (2016). Best-worst multi-criteria decision-making method: Some properties and a linear model. *Omega, 64*, 126–130. doi:10.1016/j.omega.2015.12.001

Robbins, S., & Judge, T. (2013). *Örgütsel Davranış*. Nobel Akademik Yayıncılık.

Compilation of References

Robles, M. (2012). Executive Perceptions of the Top 10 Soft Skills Needed in Today's Workplace. *Business Communication Quarterly*, *75*(4), 453–465. doi:10.1177/1080569912460400

Rosete, D., & Ciarrochi, J. (2005). Emotional intelligence and its relationship to workplace performance outcomes of leadership effectiveness. *Leadership and Organization Development Journal*, *26*(5), 388–399. doi:10.1108/01437730510607871

Rothfelder, K., Ottenbacher, M. C., & Harrington, R. J. (2012). The impact of transformational, transactional and non-leadership styles on employee job satisfaction in the German hospitality industry. *Tourism and Hospitality Research*, *12*(4), 201–214. doi:10.1177/1467358413493636

Roueche, J., Baker, G., & Rose, R. (1989). *Shared vision: transformational leadership in American community colleges*. Community College Press.

Rowe, W. G. (2001). Creating Wealth in Organizations: The Role of Strategic Leadership. *The Academy of Management Executive*, *15*(1), 81–94. doi:10.5465/ame.2001.4251395

Rue, L., & Byars, L. (2008). Management: Skills and Application (13th ed.). McGraw-Hill/Irwin.

Ruiz-Palomino, P., Gutiérrez-Broncano, S., Jiménez-Estévez, P., & Hernandez-Perlines, F. (2021). CEO servant leadership and strategic service differentiation: The role of high-performance work systems and innovativeness. *Tourism Management Perspectives*, *40*, 100891. doi:10.1016/j.tmp.2021.100891

Ruiz-Palomino, P., & Zoghbi-Manrique-de-Lara, P. (2020). How and when servant leaders fuel creativity: The role of servant attitude and intrinsic motivation. *International Journal of Hospitality Management*, *89*, 102537. doi:10.1016/j.ijhm.2020.102537

Russell, R. F., & Stone, A. G. (2002). A Review of Servant Leadership Attributes: Developing A Practical Model. *Leadership and Organization Development Journal*, *23*(3), 146. doi:10.1108/01437730210424

Saaty, T. L. (2008). Decision making with the analytic hierarchy process. *International Journal of Services Sciences*, *1*(1), 83–98. doi:10.1504/IJSSCI.2008.017590

Sabuncuoğlu, Z., & Tüz, M. (2003). *Örgütsel Psikoloji*. Bursa: Alfa kitap, Aktüel baskı yayıncılık.

Sadeghi, A., & Rad, F. (2018). The role of knowledge-oriented leadership in knowledge management and innovation. *Management Science Letters*, *8*(3), 151–160. doi:10.5267/j.msl.2018.1.003

Safavi, H. P., & Bouzari, M. (2020). How can leaders enhance employees' psychological capital? Mediation effect of person-group and person-supervisor fit. *Tourism Management Perspectives*, *33*, 100626. doi:10.1016/j.tmp.2019.100626

Sağbaş, M., & Erdoğan, F. A. (n.d.). Digital Leadership: A Systematic Conceptual Literature Review. *İstanbul Kent Üniversitesi İnsan ve Toplum Bilimleri Dergisi*, *3*(1), 17-35.

Şahin, S. (2020). Turist rehberinin yetkinlikleri [Competencies of the tourist guide]. In S. Eser, S. Şahin, & C. Çakıcı (Eds.), *Turist rehberliği* [Tourist guidance] (pp. 47–76). Detay Yayıncılık.

Salamzadeh, Y., Farzad, F. S., Salamzadeh, A., & Palalić, R. (2022). Digital leadership and organizational capabilities in manufacturing industry: A study in Malaysian context. *Periodicals of Engineering and Natural Sciences*, *10*(1), 195–211.

Salehzadeh, R., Pool, J. K., Lashaki, J. K., Dolati, H., & Jamkhaneh, H. B. (2015). Studying the effect of spiritual leadership on organizational performance: An empirical study in hotel industry. *International Journal of Culture, Tourism and Hospitality Research*, *9*(3), 346–359. doi:10.1108/IJCTHR-03-2015-0012

Salem, I. E. B. (2015). Transformational leadership: Relationship to job stress and job burnout in five-star hotels. *Tourism and Hospitality Research*, *15*(4), 240–253. doi:10.1177/1467358415581445

Salha, H., & Ulama, Ş. (2019). Turist rehberliğinde liderlik [Leadership in tourist guiding]. In B. Zengin, G. Erkol Bayram, & O. Batman (Eds.), *Turist rehberliği mesleği (dünü-bugünü-yarını)* [Tourist guiding profession (yesterday-today-tomorrow)] (pp. 171–192). Detay Yayıncılık.

Salovey, P., & Mayer, J. D. (1990). Emotional intelligence. *Imagination, Cognition and Personality, 9*(3), 185–211. doi:10.2190/DUGG-P24E-52WK-6CDG

Sammut-Bonnici, T. (2010). Information economy strategies in the mobile telecommunications industry. In S. Segal-Horn & D. Faulkner (Eds.), *Understanding Global Strategy*. Thomson Learning.

Samul, J. (2020). The Research Topics of Leadership: Bibliometric Analysis from 1923 to 2019. *International Journal of Educational Leadership and Management., 8*(2), 116–143. doi:10.17583/ijelm.2020.5036

Sandıkcı, M., Vural, T., & Zorlu, Ö. (2015). Otel işletmelerinde dönüştürücü liderlik davranışlarının örgüt sağlığı üzerine etkileri: Afyonkarahisar ilinde bir araştırma[The effects of transformative leadership behaviors in hotel businesses on organizational health: A study in Afyonkarahisar province]. *Yönetim Bilimleri Dergisi, 13*(25), 161–200.

Sandstorm, J. K., & Reynolds, D. E. (2020). Leading a successful hotel: A look at the general manager's ability to utilize multiple leadership styles. *International Journal of Hospitality Management, 89*, 102399. doi:10.1016/j.ijhm.2019.102399

Sarros, J. C., & Santora, J. C. (2001). The transformational-transactional leadership model in practice. *Leadership and Organization Development Journal, 22*(8), 383–393. doi:10.1108/01437730110410107

Sasmita, I. A. (2019). The effect of transformational leadership and psychological capital to individual readiness to change for employees in tourism development corporate. *Journal Psychodimensia, 18*(2), 167–177. doi:10.24167/psidim.v18i2.2409

Savage-Austin, A. R., & Honeycutt, A. (2011). Servant Leadership: Phenomenological Study of Practices, Experiences, Organizational Effectiveness and Barriers. *Journal of Business & Economics Research, 9*(1), 49–54. doi:10.19030/jber.v9i1.939

Saylı, H. & Baytok, A. (2014). *Örgütlerde liderlik teori uygulama ve yeni perspektifler* [Leadership theory application and new perspectives in organizations]. Nobel Akademik Yayıncılık Eğitim Danışmanlık Tic. Ltd.

Saylı, H., & Baytok, A. (2014). Örgütlerde Liderlik Teori Uygulama ve Yeni Perspektifler. Ankara: Nobel Yayınevi.

Schaufeli, W. B., Salanova, M., Gonzalez-Roma, V., & Bakker, A. B. (2002). The measurement of engagement and burnout: A two sample confirmatory factor analytic approach. *Journal of Happiness Studies, 3*(1), 71–92. doi:10.1023/A:1015630930326

Schilling, J. (2006). On the pragmatics of qualitative assessment: Designing the process for content analysis. *European Journal of Psychological Assessment, 22*(1), 28–37. doi:10.1027/1015-5759.22.1.28

Schiuma, G., Schettini, E., Santarsiero, F., & Carlucci, D. (2021). The transformative leadership compass: six competencies for digital transformation entrepreneurship. *International Journal of Entrepreneurial Behavior & Research*.

Schmidt, B., Loerbroks, A., Herr, R., Litaker, D., Wilso, M. M., Kastner, M., & Fischer, J. (2014). Psychological resources and the relationship between transformational leadership and employees' psychological strain. *Work (Reading, Mass.), 49*(2), 315–324. doi:10.3233/WOR-131713 PMID:24004772

Schmoller, G. (1870). *Zur Geschichte der deutschen Kleingewerbe im 19. Jahrhundert Gustav Schmoller*. Waisenhauses.

Schoemaker, P. J., Krupp, S., & Howland, S. (2013). Strategic leadership: The essential skills. *Harvard Business Review, 91*(1), 131–134. PMID:23390746

Compilation of References

Schriesheim, C., & Kerr, S. (1974). Psychometric properties of the Ohio state leadership scales. *Psychological Bulletin*, *81*(11), 756–765. doi:10.1037/h0037277 PMID:4612572

Schuckert, M., Kim, T., Paek, S., & Lee, G. (2018). Motivate to innovate: How authentic and transformational leaders influence employees' psychological capital and service innovation behavior. *International Journal of Contemporary Hospitality Management*, *30*(2), 776–796. doi:10.1108/IJCHM-05-2016-0282

Schwaiger, K. M., & Zehrer, A. (2021). The COVID-19 Pandemic and Organizational Resilience in Hospitality Firms: A Qualitative Approach. In A. Zehrer, G. Glowka, K. M. Schwaiger, & V. Ranacher-Lackner (Eds.), *Resiliency Models and Addressing Future Risks for Family Firms in the Tourism Industry* (pp. 32–49). IGI Global. doi:10.4018/978-1-7998-7352-5.ch002

Schwarz, G., Newman, A., Cooper, B., & Eva, N. (2016). Servant Leadership and Follower Job Performance: The Mediating Effect of Public Service Motivation. *Public Administration*, *94*(4), 1025–1041. doi:10.1111/padm.12266

Schyns, B., & Schilling, J. (2013). How bad are the effects of bad leaders? A meta-analysis of destructive leadership and its outcomes. *The Leadership Quarterly*, *24*(1), 138–158. doi:10.1016/j.leaqua.2012.09.001

Selimoğlu, E. (2004). Günümüzde Liderlik Anlayışı. *Endüstri İlişkileri ve İnsan Kaynakları Dergisi*, *6*(2), 9–232.

Semadar, A., Robins, G., & Ferris, G. R. (2006). Comparing the validity of multiple social effectiveness constructs in the prediction of managerial job performance. *Journal of Organizational Behavior*, *27*(4), 443–461. doi:10.1002/job.385

Sendjaya, S. (2015). *Personal and organizational excellence through servant leadership: Learning to serve, serving to lead, leading to transform.* Springer. doi:10.1007/978-3-319-16196-9

Sendjaya, S., & Cooper, B. (2011). Servant Leadership Behaviour Scale: A hierarchical model and test of construct validity. *European Journal of Work and Organizational Psychology*, *20*(3), 416–436. doi:10.1080/13594321003590549

Sendjaya, S., Eva, N., Butar Butar, I., Robin, M., & Castles, S. (2019). SLBS-6: Validation of a short form of the servant leadership behavior scale. *Journal of Business Ethics*, *156*(4), 941–956. doi:10.100710551-017-3594-3

Sendjaya, S., & Sarros, J. C. (2002). Servant leadership: Its origin, development, and application in organizations. *Journal of Leadership & Organizational Studies*, *9*(2), 57–64. doi:10.1177/107179190200900205

Sendjaya, S., Sarros, J. C., & Santora, J. C. (2008). Defining and Measuring Servant Leadership Behaviour in Organizations. *Journal of Management Studies*, *45*(2), 402–424. doi:10.1111/j.1467-6486.2007.00761.x

Serinkan, C. (2005). İşletmelerde liderlik tarzları ve toplam kalite yönetimi ilişkisi[Relationship between leadership styles and total quality management in businesses]. *Yönetim Dergisi: İstanbul Üniversitesi İşletme Fakültesi İşletme İktisadı Enstitüsü*, *16*(50), 86–103.

Seters, D. A., & Field, R. H. (1990). The Evolution of Leadership Theory. *Journal of Organizational Change Management*, *3*(3), 29–45. doi:10.1108/09534819010142139

Shah, S. H., Sultana, A., Gul, A., Sajjad, S., Aziz, S., Simple, A., & Qadir, A. (2020). Transformational leadership influence on innovation directly and indirectly through affective commitment in hotel industry of Malaysia. *International Review of Management and Marketing*, *10*(6), 22–28. doi:10.32479/irmm.10761

Shamir, B., House, R., & Arthur, M. B. (1993). The motivational effects of charismatic leadership: A self-concept based theory. *Organization Science*, *4*(4), 577–594. doi:10.1287/orsc.4.4.577

Shamshad, I. & Khan, M. K. (2020). Emotional intelligence, transformational leadership, self-efficacy for well-being: A longitudinal study using sequential mediation. *Journal of Public Affairs, 22*(2), 506. . doi:10.1002/pa.2506

Shao, Z., Feng, Y., Hu, Q., & Liu, Y. (2009). A conceptual model for studying the influence of charismatic leadership on ERP implementation lifecycle. *Proceedings of the 42nd Hawaii International Conference on System Sciences*, 1-9.

Shariq, S. M., Mukhtar, U., & Anwar, S. (2018). Mediating and moderating the impact of goal orientation and emotional intelligence on the relationship of knowledge oriented leadership and knowledge sharing. *Journal of Knowledge Management*, 23(2), 332–350. doi:10.1108/JKM-01-2018-0033

Sharma, J., & Sharma, A. (2021). *Leadership in the Hospitality Industry*. Academic Press.

Shehzad, M. U., Davis, K., & Shakil A. M. (2021). Knowledge-oriented leadership and open innovation: the mediating role of knowledge process and infrastructure capability. *International Journal of Innovation Management*, 25(3). doi:10.1142/S1363919621500286

Sheninger, E. (2014). Pillars of digital leadership. International Center for Leadership in Education.

Shooter, W., Sibthorp, J., & Paisley, K. (2009). Outdoor leadership skills: A program perspective. *Journal of Experiential Education*, 32(1), 1–13. doi:10.1177/105382590903200102

Shukla, B., Sufi, T., Joshi, M., & Sujatha, R. (2022). Leadership challenges for Indian hospitality industry during COVID-19 pandemic. *Journal of Hospitality and Tourism Insights*. doi:10.1108/JHTI-08-2021-0217

Siangchokyoo, N., Klinger, R. L., & Campion, E. D. (2020). Follower transformation as the linchpin of transformational leadership theory: A systematic review and future research agenda. *The Leadership Quarterly*, 31(1), 101341. doi:10.1016/j.leaqua.2019.101341

Sidgwick, H. (1885). *The scope and method of economic science*. Macmillan and Company.

Silitonga, E. S. (2018). Employee performance analysis: Predictors of transformational leadership and work motivation (Case study at indonesian academy of tourism Jakarta). *Saudi Journal of Humanities and Social Sciences*, 3(3), 515–523.

Siller, H., & Haselwanter, S. (2019). Leadership in Alpine Destinations: The Showcase "Stubai 2021". In P. L. Pearce & H. Oktadiana (Eds.), *Delivering Tourism Intelligence: From Analysis to Action* (pp. 15–30). Emerald Publishing. doi:10.1108/S2042-144320190000011003

Silva, A. (2016). What is leadership? *Journal of Business Studies Quarterly*, 8(1), 1–6. PMID:29355200

Simons, T., & Robertson, Q. (2003). Why managers should care about fairness: The effects of aggregate justice perceptions on organizational outcomes. *The Journal of Applied Psychology*, 88(3), 432–443. doi:10.1037/0021-9010.88.3.432 PMID:12814293

Sincer, S. (2021). *Öğretmen performansı, örgütsel sadakat ve karizmatik liderlik arasındaki ilişkinin incelenmesi: bir karma yöntem araştırması* [Examining the relationship between teacher performance, organizational loyalty and charismatic leadership: a mixed method research]. Hacettepe Üniversitesi Eğitim Bilimleri Enstitüsü. Eğitim Bilimleri Ana Bilim Dalı Eğitim Yönetimi Teftişi Planlaması ve Ekonomisi Programı.

Singfiel, J. (2018). When Servant Leaders Appear Laissez-Faire: The Effect of Social Identity Prototypes on Christian Leaders. *The Journal of Applied Christian Leadership*, 12(1), 64–77.

Singh, G. K. P. A., Subramaniam, A., Mohamed, A. S. B., Mohamed, R., & Ibrahim, S. (2020). Role of authentic leadership, servant leadership and destructive leadership behaviour on employee engagement in Malaysian hospitality industry. *International Journal of Academic Research in Business & Social Sciences*, 10(9), 113–125.

Sinha, J.B.P. (1990). *Work culture in the Indian context*. SAGE Publications Pvt. Limited.

Şişman, M. (2014). Öğretim liderliği [Instructional Leaderhsip]. Pegem Akademi.

Compilation of References

Şişman, M. (2004). *Öğretim Liderliği*. Pegem A Yayıncılık.

Sivaruban, S. (2021). A Critical Perspective of Leadership Theories. *Business Ethics and Leadership*, 5(1), 57–65. doi:10.21272/bel.5(1).57-65.2021

Skogstad, A., Aasland, M. S., Nielsen, M. B., Hetland, J., Matthiesen, S. B., & Einarsen, S. (2014). The relative effects of constructive, laissez-faire, and tyrannical leadership on subordinate job satisfaction: Results from two prospective and representative studies. *Zeitschrift für Psychologie mit Zeitschrift für Angewandte Psychologie*, 222(4), 221.

Skogstad, A., Einarsen, S., Torsheim, T., Aasland, M. S., & Hetland, H. (2007). The destructiveness of laissez-faire leadership behavior. *Journal of Occupational Health Psychology*, 12(1), 80–92. doi:10.1037/1076-8998.12.1.80 PMID:17257068

Slatten, T., & Mehmetoglu, M. (2015). The effects of transformational leadership and perceived creativity on innovation behavior in the hospitality industry. *Journal of Human Resources in Hospitality & Tourism*, 14(2), 195–219. doi:10.1080/15332845.2014.955557

Smith, H. A. (2011). *Extraordinary outdoor leaders: An Australian case* [Unpublished doctoral dissertation]. University of Wollongong, Australia.

Smith, A., & Copley, S. (1995). *Adam Smith's Wealth of nations: new interdisciplinary essays* (Vol. 1). Manchester University Press.

Sobaih, A. E., Hasanein, A. M., Aliedan, M. M., & Abdallah, H. S. (2020). The impact of transactional and transformational leadership on employee intention to stay in deluxe hotels: Mediating role of organizational commitment. *Tourism and Hospitality Research*, 1–13.

Sommer, S. A., Howell, J. M., & Hadley, C. N. (2016). Keeping positive and building strength: The role of affect and team leadership in developing resilience during an organizational crisis. *Group & Organization Management*, 41(2), 172–202. doi:10.1177/1059601115578027

Soon, J. M., Vanany, I., Wahab, I. R. A., Hamdan, R. H., & Jamaludin, M. H. (2021). Food safety and evaluation of intention to practice safe eating out measures during COVID-19: Cross sectional study in Indonesia and Malaysia. *Food Control*, 125, 107920. doi:10.1016/j.foodcont.2021.107920 PMID:35668872

Sosik, J. J. (2006). Full range leadership: Model, research, extensions and training. In R. J. Burke & C. L. Cooper (Eds.), *Inspiring leaders* (pp. 33–66). Routledge.

Spears, L. C. (2002). Introduction: Tracing, the Past, Present and Future of Servant Leadership. In L. C. Spears & M. Lawrence (Eds.), *Focus on Leadership: Servant-Leadership for The Twenty-First Century* (pp. 1–18). John Wiley & Sons.

Spears, L. C., & Lawrence, M. (2002). *Focus on Leadership: Servant-Leadership for the 21st Century*. John Wiley & Sons.

Spencer, L. M., & Spencer, S. M. (1993). *Competence at Work: Models for Superior Performance*. John Wiley & Sons.

Spitzbart, I. (2013). The impact of transactional versus transformational leadership on job satisfaction in the hotel industry. *Research in Hospitality Management*, 3(1), 69–76. doi:10.1080/22243534.2013.11828305

Squires, V. (2016). *Leadership: Theory and Practice*. Sage.

Stana, R., Fischer, L. H., & Nicolajsen, H. W. (2018). Review for future research in digital leadership. Information Systems Research Conference in Scandinavia (IRIS41), 1-15

Stavrinoudis, T. A., & Chrysanthopoulou, D. (2017). The role of leadership in building and managing corporate reputation of 4 and 5 star hotels. *Tourism and Hospitality Research*, 17(2), 176–189. doi:10.1177/1467358415613392

Stephens, K. K., Jahn, J. L., Fox, S., Charoensap-Kelly, P., Mitra, R., Sutton, J., Waters, E. D., Xie, B., & Meisenbach, R. J. (2020). Collective sensemaking around COVID-19: Experiences, concerns, and agendas for our rapidly changing organizational lives. *Management Communication Quarterly*, *34*(3), 426–457. doi:10.1177/0893318920934890

Stewart, G. L., Courtright, S. H., & Manz, C. C. (2011). Self-leadership: A multilevel review. *Journal of Management*, *37*(1), 185–222. doi:10.1177/0149206310383911

Stickdorn, M., & Zehrer, A. (2009). *Service design in tourism: Customer experience driven destination management* [Paper presentation].*First Nordic Conference on Service Design and Service Information*, Oslo, Norway.

Stogdill, R. M. (1974). *Handbook of leadership*. Free Press.

Stogdill, R. M. (1974). *Handbook of leadership: A survey of theory and research*. Free Press.

Stogdill, R. M. (1974). *Handbook of leadership; A survey of theory and research*. Free Press.

Stogdill, R. M., & Bass, B. M. (1981). *Stogdill's Handbook of Leadership*. The Free Press.

Stoker, J. I., Garretsen, H., & Lammers, J. (2022). Leading and Working from Home in Times of COVID-19: On the Perceived Changes in Leadership Behaviors. *Journal of Leadership & Organizational Studies*, *29*(2), 208–218. doi:10.1177/15480518211007452 PMID:35516094

Stoller, J. K. (2020). *Reflections on leadership in the time of COVID-19*. BMJ Leader Published Online. doi:10.1136/leader-2020-000244

str. (2020, April 1). *Noudettu osoitteesta str*. https://str.com/data-insights-blog/covid-19-india-hotel-performance-impact

Strübing, J. (2018). *Qualitative Sozialforschung: Eine komprimierte Einführung* [Qualitative social research: A condensed introduction] (2nd ed.). De Gruyter Oldenbourg. doi:10.1515/9783110529920

Stuart, M. J. (1901). *Principles of political economy*. Forgotten Books.

Succi, C. (2015). *Soft Skills for the Next Generation: Toward a comparison between Employers and Graduate Students' Perceptions*. Academic Press.

Sultana, U. S., Tarofder, A. K., Darun, M. R., Haque, A., & Sharief, S. R. (2020). Authentic leadership effect on pharmacists job stress and satisfaction during COVID-19 pandemic: Malaysian perspective. *Journal of Talent Development and Excellence*, *12*(3s), 1824–1841.

Sung, T. P., Joo, L. W., Rahim, I. H., & Sondoh, S. (2019). Transformational and transactional leadership styles toward organizational commitment in the hotel industry. *Journal of Tourism. Hospitality and Environment Management*, *4*(17), 34–45.

Sürücü, L., Maşlakçı, A., & Şenen, H. (2021). The influence of transformational leadership on employees' innovative behavior in the hospitality industry: The mediating role of leader member exchange. *Original Research Article*, *69*(1), 19–31.

Sürücü, L., Şenen, H., & Maşlakcı, A. (2019). On the relation between leadership and positive psychological capital in the hospitality industry. *International Journal of Business*, *24*(2), 182–197.

Swayne, L. E., Duncan, W. J., & Ginter, P. M. (2006). *Strategic Management of Health Care Organizations*. Blackwell Publishing.

Swiderski, M. (1987). Soft and conceptual skills: The often-overlooked components of outdoor leadership. In G. Robb (Ed.), *Proceedings of the Coalition for Education in the Outdoor Research Symposium*. Academic Press.

Compilation of References

Sy, T., Tram, S., & O'Hara, L. A. (2006). Relation of employee and manager emotional intelligence to job satisfaction and performance. *Journal of Vocational Behavior*, *68*(3), 461–473. doi:10.1016/j.jvb.2005.10.003

Tajedin, B., Moradi, M., & Alitabrizi, M. (2017). Study of the relationship between managers leadership style and employees Satisfaction based on Likert theory. *International Journal of Human Capital in Urban Management*, *2*(2), 147–154.

Tang, H. W. V. (2018). Modeling critical leadership competences for junior high school principals: A hybrid MCDM model combining DEMATEL and ANP. *Kybernetes*, *49*(11), 2589–2613. doi:10.1108/K-01-2018-0015

Tannenbaum, R. J. (1961). *Leadership and Organizations, A Behavioral Science Approach*. McGraw Hill.

Tanniru, M. R. (2018). Digital Leadership. In M. Pomffyova (Ed.), *Management of information systems* (pp. 93–109). IntechOpen.

Tanrısever, C. (2020). Turist rehberliğinde kişisel gelişim [Personal development in tourist guidance]. In E. Düzgün (Ed.), *Örnek olaylarla turist rehberliği* [Tourist guidance with case studies] (pp. 65–85). Detay Yayıncılık.

Taşkıran, E. (2005). *Otel İşletmelerinde Liderlik ve Yöneticilerin Liderlik Yönelimleri: İstanbul'daki Beş Yıldızlı Otel İşletmelerinde Bir Araştırma*. T.C Abant İzzet Baysal Üniversitesi Sosyal Bilimler Enstitüsü Turizm ve Otel İşletmeciliği Anabilim Dalı, Yüksek Lisans Tezi.

Taylor, C. M., Cornelius, C. J., & Colvin, K. (2014). Visionary leadership and its relationship to organizational effectiveness. *Leadership and Organization Development Journal*, *35*(6), 566–583. doi:10.1108/LODJ-10-2012-0130

Teguh, E. D., Devine, D., & Wijaya, S. (2020). Transformational leadership in the hotel industry: A new look at the service-profit-chain concept. *Petra International Journal of Business Studies*, *3*(2), 98–109. doi:10.9744/ijbs.3.2.98-109

Teng, H. Y., & Tsaur, S. H. (2022). Charismatic tour-guiding: Scale development and validation. *Journal of Travel Research*, *61*(7), 1495–1507. doi:10.1177/00472875211039556

Tengilimoğlu, D. (2005). Hizmet işletmelerinde liderlik davranışları ile iş doyumu arasındaki ilişkinin belirlenmesine yönelik bir araştırma[A study to determine the relationship between leadership behaviors and job satisfaction in service businesses]. *Gazi Üniversitesi Ticaret ve Turizm Eğitim Fakültesi Dergisi*, (1), 23–45.

Tepper, B. J. (2007). Abusive supervision in work organizations: Review, synthesis, and research agenda. *Journal of Management*, *33*(3), 261–289. doi:10.1177/0149206307300812

Testa, M. R., & Sipe, L. (2012). Service-leadership competencies for hospitality and tourism management. *International Journal of Hospitality Management*, *31*(3), 648–658. doi:10.1016/j.ijhm.2011.08.009

Testa, R. M. (2007). A Deeper Look At National Culture and Leadership in the Hospitality Industry. *Hospital Management*, *26*(2), 468–484. doi:10.1016/j.ijhm.2006.11.001

The Jakarta Post. (n.d.). Retrieved April 2, 2020, from: https://www.thejakartapost.com/: https://www.thejakartapost.com/trave l/2020/04/02/covid-19-almost-700- hotels-in-indonesia-shut-down.html

Thomas, T., Schermerhorn, J. R. Jr, & Dienhart, J. W. (2004). Strategic Leadership of Ethical Behavior in Business. *The Academy of Management Perspectives*, *18*(2), 56–66. doi:10.5465/ame.2004.13837425

Thomson, N. B. III, Rawson, J. V., Slade, C. P., & Bledsoe, M. (2016). Transformation and transformational leadership. A review of the current and relevant literature for academic radiologists. *Academic Radiology*, *23*(5), 592–599. doi:10.1016/j.acra.2016.01.010 PMID:26971043

Thoms, P., & Greenberger, D. B. (1995). The relationship between leadership and time orientation. *Journal of Management Inquiry*, *4*(3), 272–292. doi:10.1177/105649269543009

Tichy, N. M., & Devanna, M. A. (1986). *Transformational leadership*. Wiley.

Tierney, P., Farmer, S. M., & Graen, G. B. (1999). An Examination of Leadership and Employee Creativity: The Relevance of Traits and Relationships. *Personnel Psychology*, *52*(3), 591–620. doi:10.1111/j.1744-6570.1999.tb00173.x

Tolbert, P. S., & Hall, R. H. (2016). Organisations: Structures, Processes, and Outcomes (10th ed.). Routledge.

Torre, T., & Sarti, D. (2020). The "way" toward e-leadership: Some evidence from the field. *Frontiers in Psychology*, *11*, 554253. doi.org/10.3389/fpsyg.2020.55425

Tosun, C., Parvez, M. O., Bilim, Y., & Yu, L. (2022). Effects of green transformational leadership on green performance of employees via the mediating role of corporate social responsibility: Reflection from North Cyprus. *International Journal of Hospitality Management*, *103*, 103218. doi:10.1016/j.ijhm.2022.103218

Touma, J. (2021). Theories X and Y in Combination for Effective Change during Economic Crisis. *Journal of Human Resource and Sustainability Studies*, *09*(9), 20–29. doi:10.4236/jhrss.2021.91002

Tourish, D. (2020). Introduction to the special issue: Why the coronavirus crisis is also a crisis of leadership. *Leadership*, *16*(3), 261–272.

Tran, X. (2017). Effects of leadership styles on hotel financial performance. *Tourism and Hospitality Management*, *23*(2), 163–183. doi:10.20867/thm.23.2.7

Travel, K. (n.d.). Retrieved June 1, 2020, from: https://kalpak-travel.com/blog/coronavirus-central- asia/

Tromp, D. M., & Blomme, R. J. (2014). Leadership style and negative work-home interference in the hospitality industry. *International Journal of Contemporary Hospitality Management*, *26*(1), 85–106. doi:10.1108/IJCHM-04-2012-0058

Tsaur, S. H., Lin, W. R., & Liu, J. S. (2013). Sources of challenge for adventure tourists: Scale development and validation. *Tourism Management*, *38*, 85–93. doi:10.1016/j.tourman.2013.03.004

Tsaur, S.-H., & Teng, H.-Y. (2017). Exploring tour guiding styles: The perspective of tour leader roles. *Tourism Management*, *59*, 438–448. doi:10.1016/j.tourman.2016.09.005

Tuan, T. L. (2020). Crafting the sales job collectively in the tourism industry: The roles of charismatic leadership and collective person-group fit. *Journal of Hospitality and Tourism Management*, *45*, 245–255. doi:10.1016/j.jhtm.2020.08.003

Tuffour, J. K., Gali, A. M., & Tuffour, M. K. (2022). Managerial leadership style and employee commitment: Evidence from the financial sector. *Global Business Review*, *23*(3), 543–560. doi:10.1177/0972150919874170

Tuna M., Akça İ., Tuna A. A. & Gürlek M. (2017). Perceptions of sector working conditions of tourism students and attitudes towards working in the sector: A research on vocational school, college and faculty students. *Turizm Akademik Dergisi/Tourism Academic Journal*, *4*(2), 41-60.

Turan, B., & Ersöz, G. Y. (2021). Turizm işletmelerinde liderlik. [Leadership in tourism businesses]. Detay Yayıncılık.

Turan, M. (2019). *Dönüşümcü liderlik ve yenilikçi iş davranışı arasındaki ilişkide kontrol odağının etkisi* [The effect of locus of control on the relationship between innovative leadership and innovative business behavior] [Master Thesis]. Recep Tayyip Erdogan University Institute of Social Sciences.

Turan, S. (2020). Liderlik nedir? [What is leadership?]. Pegem Akademi. doi:10.14527/9786257052252.01

Turgot, A.-R. (2014). *Ecrits économiques*. Calmann-Lévy.

Türkoğlu, N. & Çizel, B. (2016). Kurumsallaşma ve Rekabet Gücü İlişkisi Üzerine Ampirik Bir Çalışma [An Empirical Study on the Relationship between Institutionalization and Competitiveness]. *Bilgi,* (33).

Uen, J. F., Wu, T., Teng, H. C., & Liu, Y. S. (2012). Transformational leadership and branding behavior in Taiwanese hotels. *International Journal of Contemporary Hospitality Management, 24*(1), 26–43. doi:10.1108/09596111211197782

Uğur, S. S. (2014). Yöneticilik ve Liderlik Kişisel Farklılıkların Rolü. *Organizasyon ve Yönetim Bilimleri Dergisi, 6*(1), 122–136.

Ülgen, H., & Mirze, S. K. (2013). İşletmelerde Stratejik Yönetim [Strategic management in Business]. Beta Yay.

Ullah, R., Latif, K.F., & Alam, W. (2018). Role of transformational leadership style on employee job performance among high and low ranking institutions of higher education of Khyber Pakhtunkhwa. *City University Research Journal, 8*(2).

Ulucan, E., & Yavuz Aksakal, N. (2022). Leadership selection with the fuzzy topsis method in the hospitality sector in sultanahmet region. *Mathematics, 10*(13), 2195. doi:10.3390/math10132195

UNICEF. (2022). *Adolescent education and skills: Adolescents need lifelong learning to build better futures for themselves, their families, and their communities.* Retrieved from: https://www.unicef.org/education/skills-development

United Nations. (2010). International recommendations for tourism statistics 2008 (No. 83). United Nations Publications.

Ünsal, A. A. (2019). *Dönüşümcü liderlik ve örgütsel vatandaşlık davranışı arasındaki ilişki* [The relationship between transformational leadership and organizational citizenship behavior] [Master Thesis]. Istanbul University Social Sciences Institute Department of Business.

Urhan, T. B. (2019). Soft Beceriler, Etkili İletişim, Liderlik [Soft Skills, Effective Communication, Leadership]. Gazi Kitabevi.

Uslu, O. (2019). A General Overview to Leadership Theories From A Critical Perspective. *Marketing and Management Innovations, 1,* 161–172. doi:10.21272/mmi.2019.1-13

Usman, S. A., Kowalski, K. B., Andiappan, V. S., & Parayitam, S. (2021). *Effect of knowledge sharing and interpersonal trust on psychological capital and emotional intelligence in higher educational institutions in India: Gender as a moderator.* FIIB Business Review. doi:10.1177/23197145211011571

Uysal, D. (2021). Perceived leadership styles and employee motivation: A research in Turkish hotel context. *Journal of Ekonomi, 3*(2), 106–110.

Valdivia, I. H., Burin, A. R. G., & Montes, J. L. (2019). Effects of different leadership styles on hospitality workers. *Tourism Management, 71,* 402–420. doi:10.1016/j.tourman.2018.10.027

Valente, F. J., Dredge, D., & Lohmann, G. (2014). Leadership capacity in two Brazilian regional tourism organisations. *Tourism Review, 69*(1), 10–24. doi:10.1108/TR-07-2013-0039

Van Bussel, M. (2014). Direct Leadership in Recreation, Leisure, Hospitality, and Tourism. In *Leadership in Recreation and Leisure Services.* Human Kinetics.

Van Eeden, R., Cilliers, F., & Van Deventer, V. (2008). Leadership styles and associated personality traits: Support for the conceptualisation of transactional and transformational leadership. *South African Journal of Psychology. Suid-Afrikaanse Tydskrif vir Sielkunde, 38*(2), 253–267. doi:10.1177/008124630803800201

Van Knippenberg, D., & Stam, D. (2014). Visionary leadership. In D. V. Day (Ed.), *The Oxford handbook of leadership and organizations* (pp. 241–259). Oxford University Press.

Van Knippenberg, D., Van Knippenberg, B., De Cremer, D., & Hogg, M. A. (2004). Leadership, self, and identity: A review and research agenda. *The Leadership Quarterly*, *15*(6), 825–856. doi:10.1016/j.leaqua.2004.09.002

Van Wart, M., Roman, A., Wang, X., & Liu, C. (2016). Integrating ICT Adoption Issues into (e-)Leadership Theory. *Telematics and Informatics*, *34*(5), 527–537.

Vargas, P. A., & Hanlon, J. (2007). Celebrating a Profession: The Servant Leadership Perspective. *The Journal of Research Administration*, *38*(1), 45–49.

Vargas-Sevalle, L., Karami, M., & Spector, S. (2020). Transformational Leadership in the Hospitality and Tourism Industry. In Entrepreneurial Opportunities. Emerald Publishing Limited. doi:10.1108/978-1-83909-285-520201007

Vasilagos, T., Polychroniou, P., & Maroudas, L. (2017). *Relationship between supervisor's emotional intelligence and transformational leadership in hotel organizations*. Springer.

Vera, D., & Crossan, M. (2004). Strategic Leadership and Organizational Learning. *Academy of Management Review*, *29*(2), 222–240. doi:10.2307/20159030

Vieira, D. A., Meirinhos, V., Ardions, A., Araújo, M. S., & Carvalho, P. (2019). *Soft skills list and Mind map*. ULISSE IO2 Soft Skills Report 2. https://ulisseproject.eu/

Vig, S., & Tewary, T. (2022). Resilience of the Hotel Industry in COVID-19: The Indian Context. In *COVID-19 Pandemic Impact on New Economy Development and Societal Change* (pp. 251–263). IGI Global. doi:10.4018/978-1-6684-3374-4.ch012

Viitala, R. (2004). Towards knowledge leadership. *Leadership and Organization Development Journal*, *25*(6), 528–544. doi:10.1108/01437730410556761

Viner, J. (1960). The intellectual history of laissez faire. *The Journal of Law & Economics*, *3*, 45–69. doi:10.1086/466561

Von Mises, L. (2002). *Epistemological problems of economics*. Ludwig von Mises Institute.

Vroom, V. H., & Jago, A. G. (2007). The role of the Situation in Leadership. *The American Psychologist*, *62*(1), 17–24. doi:10.1037/0003-066X.62.1.17 PMID:17209676

Vukotić, S., & Vojnović, B. (2016). The role and importance of strategic plans in the development of tourism. *International Scientific Conference*, 118-134.

Walker, F. A. (1889). Recent progress of political economy in the United States. *Publications of the American Economic Association*, *4*(4), 17–40.

Walumbwa, F. O., Hartnell, C. A., & Oke, A. (2010). Servant leadership, procedural justice climate, service climate, employee attitudes, and organizational citizenship behavior: A cross-level investigation. *The Journal of Applied Psychology*, *95*(3), 517–529. doi:10.1037/a0018867 PMID:20476830

Walumbwa, F., Avolio, B., Gardner, W., Wernsing, T., & Peterson, S. (2008). Authentic Leadership: Development and Validation of a Theory-Based Measure. *Journal of Management*, *34*(1), 95. doi:10.1177/0149206307308913

Wang, C. J., Tsai, H. T., & Tsai, M. T. (2014). Linking transformational leadership and employee creativity in the hospitality industry: The influences of creative role identity, creative self-efficacy, and job complexity. *Tourism Management*, *40*, 79–89. doi:10.1016/j.tourman.2013.05.008

Wang, G., Oh, I. S., Courtright, S. H., & Colbert, A. E. (2011). Transformational leadership and performance across criteria and levels: A meta-analytic review of 25 years of research. *Group & Organization Management*, *36*(2), 223–270. doi:10.1177/1059601111401017

Washington, R. R., Sutton, C. D., & Feild, H. S. (2006). Individual differences in servant leadership: The roles of values and personality. *Leadership and Organization Development Journal*, *27*(8), 700–716. doi:10.1108/01437730610709309

Wasylyshyn, K. M., & Masterpasqua, F. (2018). Developing self-compassion in leadership development coaching: A practice model and case study analysis. *International Coaching Psychology Review*, *13*(1), 21–34.

Weerakit, N., & Beeton, R. J. S. (2018). Leadership competencies for hospitality management staff in Thailand. *Journal of Human Resources in Hospitality & Tourism*, *17*(3), 314–339. doi:10.1080/15332845.2017.1406277

Weiermair, K. (2000). Know-how and qualification gaps in the tourism industry: The case of Alpine tourism in Austria. *Tourism Review*, *55*(2), 45–53.

Wellman, N., Mayer, D. M., Ong, M., & DeRue, D. S. (2016). When are do-gooders treated badly? Legitimate power, role expectations, and reactions to moral objection in organizations. *The Journal of Applied Psychology*, *101*(6), 793–814. doi:10.1037/apl0000094 PMID:26882445

Wen, T. B., Ho, T. C., Kelana, B. W. Y., Othman, R., & Syed, O. R. (2019). Leadership styles in influencing employees' job performances. *International Journal of Academic Research in Business & Social Sciences*, *9*(9), 55–65. doi:10.6007/IJARBSS/v9-i9/6269

Werner, I. (1993). Leadership Skills For Executives. İstanbul: Rota Yayınları.

Westley, F., & Mintzberg, H. (1989). Visionary Leadership and Strategic Management. *Strategic Management Journal*, *10*(S1), 17–32. doi:10.1002mj.4250100704

WFTGA. (2003). *What is a tourist guide?* https://wftga.org/about-us/what-is-a-tourist-guide/

WGU. (2020, April 7). *Leadership theories and styles*. June 18, 2022 tarihinde WGU: https://www.wgu.edu/blog/leadership-theories-styles2004.html#:~:text=The%20behavioral%20leadership%20theory%20focuses,created%20based%20on%20learnable%20behavior

WGU. (2020, June 17). *Successful leadership attitudes and behaviors*. June 18, 2022 tarihinde WGU (Western Governor University): https://www.wgu.edu/blog/successful-leadership-attitudes-behaviors2006.html

Wice, P. B. (1995). Court Reform and Judicial Leadership: A Theoretical Discussion. *The Justice System Journal*, *17*(3), 309–321. doi:10.1080/23277556.1995.10871212

Wilson, E. J. III. (2004). Leadership in the Digital Age. In G. R. Goethals, G. Sorenson, & J. Mac Gregor (Eds.), *Encyclopedia of Leadership* (pp. 859–862). Sage.

Wilson, S. (2020). Pandemic leadership: Lessons from New Zealand's approach to COVID-19. *Leadership*, *16*(3), 279–293. doi:10.1177/1742715020929151

Winston, B. (2003). Extending Patterson's servant leadership model: Explaining how leaders and follower interact in a circular model. In *Proceedings of the 2003 Servant Leadership Research Roundtable*. Regent University.

Winston, B. E., & Patterson, K. (2006). An integrative definition of leadership. *International Journal of Leadership Studies*, *1*(2), 6–66.

Wirtz, J., Patterson, P. G., Kunz, W. H., Gruber, T., Lu, V. N., Paluch, S., & Martins, A. (2018). Brave new world: Service robots in the frontline. *Journal of Service Management*, *29*(5), 907–931.

Wisse, B., & Sleebos, E. (2016). When change causes stress: Effects of self-construal and change consequences. *Journal of Business and Psychology, 31*(2), 249–264. doi:10.100710869-015-9411-z PMID:27226696

Wolfe, B. (2014). Facilitating Group Experiences. In *Leadership in Recreation and Leisure Services*. Human Kinetics.

Wong, C. S., & Law, K. S. (2002). The effect of leader and follower emotional intelligence on performance and attitude: An exploratory study. *The Leadership Quarterly, 13*, 243–274. doi:10.1016/S1048-9843(02)00099-1

Wong, P. T. P., & Page, D. (2003). Servant Leadership: An Opponent-Process Model and The Revised Servant Leadership Profile. In *Proceedings of the 2003 Servant Leadership Research Roundtable*. Regent University.

World Economic Forum. (2020). These are the skills employers are looking for now…right up till 2025. *Future of jobs report 2020*. Retrieved from https://www.muchskills.com/blog/skills-employers-looking-for-till-2025

World Health Organization. (2003). *Skills for Health*. https://www.who.int/school_youth_health/media/en/sch_skills4health_03.pdf

World Health Organization. (2020). Clinical management of severe acute respiratory infection (SARI) when COVID-19 disease is suspected: interim guidance, 13 March 2020 (No. WHO/2019-nCoV/clinical/2020.4). World Health Organization.

World Travel & Tourism Council. (n.d.). Retrieved May 12, 2020, from: https://wttc.org/News-Article/WTTC-now-estimates-over-100-million-jobs-losses-in-the-Travel-&-Tourism-sector-and-alerts-G20-countries-to-the-scale-of-the-crisis

World Travel and Tourism Council. (2022). *Travel and Tourism Economic Impact 2022*. Retrieved from https://wttc.org/Portals/0/Documents/Reports/2022/EIR2022-Global%20Trends.pdf

Wu, L.-Z., Tse, E. C.-Y., Fu, P., Kwan, H. K., & Liu, J. (2013). The Impact of Servant Leadership on Hotel Employees' "Servant Behavior. *Cornell Hospitality Quarterly, 54*(4), 383–395. doi:10.1177/1938965513482519

Yamak, Ö. U., & Eyüpoğlu, Ş. Z. (2018). Leadership Styles of Hotel Managers in Northern Cyprus: Which Style is Dominant? *International Journal of Organizational Leadership, 7*(7), 1–11. doi:10.33844/ijol.2018.60202

Yammario, F. J., & Bass, B. (1990). *Long-term forecasting of transformational leadership and its effects among naval officers: Some preliminary findings*. Leadership Library of America.

Yang, C., Chen, Y., & Zhao, X., & Hua, N. (2019). Transformational leadership, proactive personality and service performance. The mediating role of organizational embeddedness. *International Journal of Contemporary Hospitality Management*.

Yang, C., Chen, Y., Zhao, X., & Hua, N. (2020). Transformational leadership, proactive personality and service performance: The mediating role of organizational embeddedness. *International Journal of Contemporary Hospitality Management, 32*(1), 267–287. doi:10.1108/IJCHM-03-2019-0244

Yang, M., Luu, T. T., & Qian, D. (2021). Dual-focused transformational leadership and service innovation in hospitality organisations: A multilevel investigation. *International Journal of Hospitality Management, 98*, 103035. doi:10.1016/j.ijhm.2021.103035

Yang, M., Luu, T. T., & Qian, D. X. (2021). Linking transformational leadership to team service innovation in the hospitality industry: A team-level mediation and moderation investigation. *Journal of Hospitality and Tourism Management, 49*, 558–569. doi:10.1016/j.jhtm.2021.11.011

Compilation of References

Yanti, N. P. R., Mujiati, N. W., & Suwandana, G. M. (2021). The influence of transformational leadership style, organizational culture, and physical work environment on employee performance in the tourism department of Bali, Indonesia. *American Journal of Humanities and Social Sciences Research*, *5*(2), 363–371.

Yavuz, E. (2009). İş görenlerin Dönüşümcü Liderlik ve Örgütsel Bağlılık ile İlgili Tutumlarına Yönelik Bir Araştırma. *İşletme Araştırmaları Dergisi*, *1*(2), 51-69.

Yavuz, E., & Tokmak, C. (2009). İş görenlerin Etkileşimci Liderlik ve Örgütsel Bağlılık ile İlgili Tutumlarına Yönelik Bir Araştırma. *International Journal of Economic and Administrative Studies*, *1*(2), 17–35.

Ye, Y., Lyu, Y., & He, Y. (2019). Servant leadership and proactive customer service performance. *International Journal of Contemporary Hospitality Management*, *31*(3), 1330–1347. doi:10.1108/IJCHM-03-2018-0180

Yıldırım, K.E. (2019). Hizmetkâr Liderlik ve Çalışan Davranışlarındaki Rolü: Kırgızistan'da Bir Alan Araştırması [Servant Leadership and Its Role in Employee Behavior: A Field Study in Kyrgyzstan]. *İşletme Araştırmaları Dergisi*, *11*(3), 2242-2256.

Yıldırım, S. (2019). *Sporda dönüşümcü liderlik ve performans: Bir model derlemesi* [Transformational leadership and performance in sport: A model collection] [Doctoral Thesis]. Hacettepe University Institute of Health Sciences.

Yılmaz, H. (2008). Stratejik Liderlik. İstanbul: Kum Saati Yayınları.

Yılmaz, A. K., Tanrıverdi, G., & Durak, M. Ş. (2016). Determination of optimal leadership style for an organization: Case of Hasan Polatkan Airport. *Transport & Logistics*, *16*(38/39), 1–8.

Yörük, D., Dündar, S., & Topçu, B. (2011). Türkiye'deki Belediye Başkanlarının Liderlik Tarzı ve Liderlik Tarzını Etkileyen Faktörler[Leadership Style of Mayors in Turkey and Factors Affecting Leadership Style]. *Ege Akademik Bakış*, *11*(1), 103–109. doi:10.21121/eab.2011119591

Young, M., & Dulewicz, V. (2007). Similarities and Differences Between Leadership and Management: High-Performance Competencies in the British Royal Navy. *British Journal of Management*, *19*(1), 17–32. doi:10.1111/j.1467-8551.2007.00534.x

Yuan, Y., Kong, H., Baum, T., Liu, Y., Liu, C., Bu, N., Wang, K., & Yin, Z. (2021). Transformational leadership and trust in leadership impacts on employee commitment. *Tourism Review*, *77*(5), 1385–1399. doi:10.1108/TR-10-2020-0477

Yu, H., Shum, C., Alcorn, M., Sun, J., & He, Z. (2022). Robots can't take my job: Antecedents and outcomes of Gen Z employees' service robot risk awareness. *International Journal of Contemporary Hospitality Management*, *34*(8), 2971–2988. doi:10.1108/IJCHM-10-2021-1312

Yukl, G. (2010). Leadership in organizations. Pearson.

Yukl, G. (1989). Managerial Leadership: A Review of TIneory and Research. *Journal of Management*, *15*(2), 251–289. doi:10.1177/014920638901500207

Yukl, G. (1994). *Leadership in organisations* (3rd ed.). Prentice Hall.

Yukl, G. (1994). *Leadership in organizations* (3rd ed.). Prentice Hall International.

Yukl, G. (1999). An evaluation of conceptual weaknesses in transformational and charismatic leadership theories. *The Leadership Quarterly*, *10*(2), 285–305. doi:10.1016/S1048-9843(99)00013-2

Yukl, G. (2002). *Leadership in Organization*. Prentice-Hall International, Inc.

Yukl, G. A. (2012). Effective Leadership Behavior: What We Know and What Questions Need More Attention. *The Academy of Management Perspectives, 26*(4), 66–85. Advance online publication. doi:10.5465/amp.2012.0088

Yukl, G., & Gardner, W. L. (2020). *Leadership in Organizations*. Pearson.

Zaccaro, S. J. (2001). *The Nature of Executive Leadership: A Conceptual and Empirical Analysis of Success*. American Psychological Association. doi:10.1037/10398-000

Zehrer, A. (2019). Structure, significance and challenges of family firms in community-type Alpine tourism destinations. In H. Pechlaner (Ed.), *Destination und Lebensraum: Perspektiven touristischer Entwicklung* (pp. 25–38). Springer Fachmedien Wiesbaden. doi:10.1007/978-3-658-28110-6_2

Zellweger, H. (2004). *Leadership by Soft Skills Checklisten für den Führungsalltag*. Gabler. . doi:10.1007/978-3-322-82482-0

Zel, U. (2001). *Kişilik ve Liderlik*. Seçkin Yayıncılık.

Zendeh, A. B., & Aali, S. (2011). An AHP approach for selecting the suitable leadership style. *Management and Economics, 25*, 20–24.

Zengin, Y., Yurdakul, S., Bayram, N., Sakarya, M., & Bağcı, M. (2021). Yöneticilerin Liderlik Özelliklerinin Psikolojik Sahiplenme ve İş Stresi ile İlişkisi. *Turkish Business Journal, 2*(4), 56–75.

Zhang, X., & Li, B. (2013). Organizational Culture and Employee Satisfaction: An Exploratory Study. *International Journal of Trade, Economics, and Finance, 4*(1), 48–54. doi:10.7763/IJTEF.2013.V4.259

Zhang, Z., Jia, M., & Gu, L. (2012). Transformational leadership in crisis situations: Evidence from the People's Republic of China. *International Journal of Human Resource Management, 23*(19), 4085–4109. doi:10.1080/09585192.2011.639027

Zheng, Y., Graham, L., Epitropaki, O., & Snape, E. (2020). Service Leadership, Work Engagement, and Service Performance: The Moderating Role of Leader Skills. *Group & Organization Management, 45*(1), 43-74.

Zheng, J., Wu, G., & Xie, H. (2017). Impacts of leadership on project-based organizational innovation performance: The mediator of knowledge sharing and moderator of social capital. *Sustainability, 9*(10), 1893. doi:10.3390u9101893

Zhong, L. (2017). Indicators of digital leadership in the context of K-12 education. *Journal of Educational Technology Development and Exchange, 10*(1), 27–40.

Zia, M. Q., Naveed, M., Bashir, M. A., & Iqbal, A. (2022). The influence of servant leadership on employees' outcomes via job embeddedness in hospitality industry. *Journal of Hospitality and Tourism Insights, 5*(3), 612–628. doi:10.1108/JHTI-01-2021-0003

Zia-ud-Din, M., Shabbir, M. A., Asif, S. B., Bilal, M., & Raza, M. (2017). Impact of Strategic Leadership on Employee Performance. *International Journal of Academic Research in Business & Social Sciences, 7*(6), 8–22. doi:10.6007/IJARBSS/v7-i6/2938

Zopiatis, A., & Constanti, P. (2010). Leadership styles and burnout: Is there an association? *International Journal of Contemporary Hospitality Management, 22*(3), 300–320. doi:10.1108/09596111011035927

Zopiatis, A., & Constanti, P. (2012). Extraversion, openness and conscientiousness The route to transformational leadership in the hotel industry. *Leadership and Organization Development Journal, 33*(1), 86–104. doi:10.1108/01437731211193133

Zorlu, Ö., Baytok, A., & Avan, A. (2016). The effect of transformational leadership behaviours on knowledge management practices: A study about hotel chains. *The Journal of Academic Social Science, 4*(35), 209–236. doi:10.16992/ASOS.6577

Compilation of References

Zwingmann, I., Wegge, J., Wolf, S., Rudolf, M., Schmidt, M., & Richter, P. (2014). Is transformational leadership healthy for employees? A multilevel analysis in 16 nations. *German Journal of Research in Human Resource Management*, *28*(1–2), 24–51. doi:10.1177/239700221402800103

About the Contributors

Ahmet Baytok is the head of department at the Tourism Management department at Afyon Kocatepe University and has received his associate professorship in Tourism. He currently interests in the research of leadership in hospitality, organizational behavior, management and sustainability in tourism.

Özcan Zorlu is the co-head of Tourism Guidance department at faculty of Tourism at Afyon Kocatepe University. He received his bachelor's degree inhospitality and tourism management at Balıkesir University and his master's degree in tourism management from Balıkesir University. He has received his associate professorship in tourism and written widely on specifically organizational behavior, knowledge management and alternative tourism activities in tourism.

Ali Avan is the vice dean of Faculty of Tourism at Afyon Kocatepe University. He received his bachelor's degree in hospitality and tourism management at Mersin University, his master's degree in tourism management from Afyon Kocatepe University and his Ph.D. in business administration from Afyon Kocatepe University. He is associate professor in Tourism Management department now, and his areas of research include consumer behavior in tourism, services marketing, tourism marketing and sustainability in tourism.

Engin Bayraktaroğlu received PhD degree in Tourism Management from Anadolu University Graduate School of Social Sciences, Turkey in 2019. He is currently working as Assistant Professor at Anadolu University Faculty of Tourism. His research interest includes destination value, destination development, tourist mobility, philosophy of tourism.

* * *

Muhammad Junaid Ahsan is doing a Ph.D. in Business and Management studies from the Department of Economics and Management at the University of Pisa, Italy. His research interests are sustainability, leadership, CSR, and organization management.

Seza Aksoy was born on July 3, 1995 in Çorlu, Tekirdağ. She completed her education from primary to high school in Çorlu. After graduating from Çanakkale Onsekiz Mart University, Department of Tourism Management, she completed her master's degree in Tourism Management at Kırklareli University dissertation. She received her specialization in tourism management with her thesis titled "The Role

About the Contributors

of Transformational Leadership and Resilience Capacity in Reducing the Negative Impact of Crises in Hotel Businesses".

Keziban Avci is Associate Professor in Department of Health Management, Faculty of Health Sciences at Ankara Yıldırım Beyazıt University. At the same time, Dr. Avcı has been working as a researcher of Quality Management and Improvement Department at Türkiye Health Care Quality and Accreditation Institute in Health Institute of Türkiye. Her specialties are human resources management in health care, performance management, quality, and accreditation in health care. Her scholarly work is in the areas of health services productivity, performance evaluation, health quality, patient safety and medical errors, and resource planning.

Onur Çakır received his Bachelor of Science degree in Tourism and Hospitality Management from the Bilkent University in 2007. His professional career in tourism began with internships during high school education and later he worked at international hotel chains such as Dedeman Blue Waters Side, Sheraton Hotel Ankara, Intercontinental Hotel Istanbul and Remington Hospitality Management Orlando between 2001 and 2008. In 2009, he began his academic career as a lecturer at Erzincan University Vocational School of Tourism and Hospitality. He received his MSc in Tourism Management from Sakarya University in 2011, and he completed his PhD in Anadolu University in 2015. Currently, he is working as an Associate Professor in Department of Tourism Management at Kırklareli University. His research interests include tourism and hotel management, sustainable tourism, rural tourism, tourism education, and tourism history.

Fatma Doğanay Ergen graduated from Tourism Management and Hotel Applied Sciences of Abant İzzet Baysal University in 2010. She completed her master's degree in Tourism and Hotel Management at Afyon Kocatepe University in June 2013. In 2014, Ergen started to work as a lecturer and as the head of Tourism and Hotel Management program at Nisantasi University. She completed her PhD in Tourism and Hotel Management at Balıkesir University. After completing her PhD's, she was appointed as assistant professor to the Department of Tourism Guidance at Nişantaşı University and continued working at Nişantaşı University. In 2019, she was appointed as a professor assistant and head of the Department of Tourism Guidance at Isparta University of Applied Sciences. She is currently working at Isparta University of Applied Sciences. She works on alternative tourism types, health tourism and tourism management.

Ozan Güngör is a lecturer in the Food and Beverage Management, Adnan Menderes University Aydın, Turkey. He is a PhD student in tourism management. He mainly teaches issues related to gastronomy and culinary arts. His research focuses on tourism marketing, tourism and gastronomy. He has authored, co-authored and book chapters, articles and proceedings on tourism and gastronomy.

Mert Gürlek, Ph.D., is an associate professor at the Burdur Mehmet Akif Ersoy University, Turkey. He holds two PhDs, one in Management & Organization and one in Tourism Management, both from Gazi University, Turkey. His studies has been published in top-tier journals such as The Service Industries Journal, Social Responsibility Journal, Tourism Management Perspectives, Kybernetes, Ethics & Behavior, Journal of Management & Organization, Journal of Hospitality Marketing & Management, Current Issues in Tourism, Journal of Hospitality and Tourism Management, and Journal of Destina-

About the Contributors

tion Marketing & Management, Journal of Cleaner Production, and Business Ethics, the Environment & Responsibility.

Stefanie Haselwanter, MA works as research assistant and lecturer at the Tourism department of Management Center Innsbruck (MCI), Austria. Her research focuses on the intersection of Entrepreneurship and Leadership as well as on leadership, governance and management of tourism destinations. She writes her doctoral thesis in the field of entrepreneurial leadership in the context of tourism destinations at the Catholic University of Eichstätt-Ingolstadt.

Muhammad Hasham Khalid has done Masters in Engineering Management from Riphah International University, Pakistan. Prior to this, he has done Bachelor's of Science in Mechanical Engineering. He has Participated & Presented in International Joint e – Conference at Centre of Industrial Revolution and Innovation, held by Taylor's University and the University of Kelaniya, Kuala Lumpur Malaysia. His research has also been accepted in 6th International Conference on Banking, Insurance & Business Management, Hailey College of Banking & Finance, University of The Punjab, Lahore, Pakistan. His research was also included in 8th Global Conference on Business Management and Social Sciences UK (8TH GCBM). His research interests are supply chain management, leadership behaviors, sustainability, green practices, lean practices & reverse logistics.

İlker Kılıç, Ph.D., is an assistant professor in Eskişehir Osmangazi University, Turkey. He holds PhDs, tourism management from Eskişehir Osmangazi University, Turkey. He has published in leading tourism journal including Current Issues in Tourism. He has experience in, Influencer Marketing, Corporate Social Responsibility and Carrying Capacity in tourism.

Shilpi Sarna is currently working as Professor (HR & Law), Lloyd Business School, at Lloyd Group of Institutions, Greater Noida. She has completed her Ph.D. in Labour Laws from Jiwaji University and having 19 years of experience in the field of Teaching, Training, Banking & Insurance. She is HR Analytics certified by IIM Rohtak, and expert in the areas of organizational Behavior, Human Resource Management, Performance Management, Strategic HR and Stress Management and Labour Laws. She has numerous publications in national, international, and Scopus indexed Journals. She has good experience of organizing FDP, workshops, seminars, and conferences.

Julia Unterlechner, MA is a graduate of the Master's programme "Entrepreneurship and Tourism" at Management Center Innsbruck (MCI), Austria. For her Master thesis, she researched in the field of transformational leadership with special focus on small and medium-sized enterprises (SMEs). Today she works in Public Relations and Communication at one of the top-sights in Tyrol "Schloss Ambras Innsbruck", which is part of the museum group and research institution "KHM-Museumsverband Wien".

Bahar Urhan works at Akdeniz University, Faculty of Communication, Department of Public Relations and Publicity. She has works in the fields of Interpersonal Communication, Intercultural Communication, New Media, Soft Skills, and Nonverbal Communication.

Hakan Yılmaz is an Associate Professor in the Department of Gastronomy and Culinary Arts, Anadolu University Eskişehir, Turkey. He received his Ph.D. Anadolu University from the department of

About the Contributors

Public Relations and Advertising. He mainly teaches issues related to marketing communication and media in tourism and gastronomy. His research focuses on tourism marketing, media and communication in tourism and gastronomy. He has authored, co-authored and edited several books, book chapters, articles and proceedings on marketing communication and media in in tourism, and gastronomy.

Sinan Yılmaz is an Assistant Professor of Management and Organization at the Business Administration Department in Zonguldak Bülent Ecevit University. He received hid Ph.D. in Management and Organization from Anadolu University Graduate School of Social Sciences. He teaches general business, international business and strategic management and business policy.

Index

A

Agile Leaders 179
Alpine Tourism Industry 155-156, 161-164, 167, 170-173, 176
Asian Countries 119, 143, 187

B

Behavioral Leadership Approach 40, 43-44, 55
Best Worst Method 73-74, 87
BWM 73-75, 77-78, 80-81, 85-87, 90

C

Camping 173, 263-264, 267-269
Change Management 12, 23, 30, 59, 71, 178
Charismatic Leadership 10, 74-77, 83, 85-86, 89, 91-108, 132, 138, 147, 152, 154, 178, 200-201, 256-257
Chef 246, 250-255, 258
Collaborative Leadership 13, 205-206, 212, 215-216
Consequences of Transformational Leadership 110, 112, 117-121, 128
Consistency Degree 80, 90
Crisis Management 18, 23, 30, 32, 35, 76, 84, 86, 131, 144, 146, 186, 192, 212

D

Digital Leadership 9, 13, 74-75, 83, 85, 88, 90, 179, 181, 183-188, 191-192, 194-198
Directive Leadership 77, 183, 199, 205-206, 212, 215, 217

E

Entrepreneurial Leadership 90, 101, 155, 176-177
Evidence-Based Knowledge 121, 128

H

Hospitality 20, 36, 40-43, 46-49, 51-53, 55-59, 76-77, 84, 86-92, 99-112, 114, 116, 119-131, 133, 139, 143-153, 162, 175-178, 180-184, 186-188, 190-197, 208-210, 214, 216, 218-219, 221-230, 232, 259, 279
Hospitality Industry 40-43, 46-49, 51-53, 55, 57, 59, 76, 86-90, 101, 103-104, 108, 110, 119-120, 125-128, 143, 147-153, 176-177, 179-183, 186-187, 190-192, 195, 197, 209-210, 216, 218-219, 221-227, 229, 259
Hotel Industry 20, 59, 73-78, 80, 83-86, 88, 90, 100, 116, 125-126, 147-149, 151-152, 154, 180, 182, 187-188, 190, 194-196, 198, 210, 213, 223, 227, 243

I

Incubator Leadership 205-206, 212, 217

K

Kitchen 100, 246-247, 250-258
Knowledge-Oriented Leadership 230-233, 241-245

L

Laissez-Faire 9, 12, 50-51, 54, 62-68, 70-72, 76-77, 100-101, 134, 157-159, 165, 167, 170, 173, 228, 256
Leader Behaviors 40, 44, 53-54, 151
Leader-Member Exchange (LMX) 148, 179, 182
Leadership 1-6, 8-24, 27-40, 42-53, 55-62, 66-78, 80-81, 83-115, 117-119, 121-160, 162-179, 181-239, 241-252, 254-267, 275-279
Leadership and Personality 1
Leadership Approaches 1-2, 10, 18-19, 23, 41-43, 54-56, 93, 95, 103, 137, 163, 200-201
Leadership Competencies 1, 3, 6-7, 18-22, 27, 100, 108, 195, 267, 275

Leadership Development 1, 5, 19, 21, 49, 69, 90, 102, 105-106, 174, 198, 267
Leadership Dimensions 155-156, 158, 163, 171, 173, 219
Leadership in Tourism 90, 98, 104, 106, 108, 129, 131, 139-142, 155, 166, 171, 199, 208, 211-212
Leadership Perspective in the Hospitality and Tourism Industry 181
Leadership Skill 23, 27
Leadership Team 1, 15-17, 20
Leadership Types 73-77, 80, 83-86, 90, 134, 143, 200, 205-206

M

Management 2, 4-5, 7-10, 12-14, 17-24, 27, 30, 32, 34-43, 47, 50-60, 63, 66-67, 69, 71-74, 76, 78, 84-90, 92-96, 99-106, 108, 111-112, 114, 119-131, 133-135, 139, 143-144, 146-156, 174-179, 182, 186-187, 189-195, 197-199, 202-204, 207-217, 223-229, 231, 233-235, 240, 242-252, 255-259, 262-265, 267, 275, 277-279
Meta-Analysis 36, 58, 71, 110, 119, 121, 123, 128, 139, 147, 276
Multi-Criteria Decision Making (MCDM) 73-75, 77-78, 80, 84-86, 88, 90

N

Non-Systematic Literature Review 218

O

Organizational Behavior 14, 37, 41, 57-58, 71, 104-105, 122, 124, 126, 129, 214, 226, 259, 275, 278
Outdoor Recreation Activities 263-264, 267

P

Perceived Challenges 263-264, 266-269, 271-272, 274-275
Proactive Measures 23

R

Rock-Climbing 264, 267-269
RSLQ 263, 268

S

Self-Leadership 263-269, 274-278

Servant Leadership 11, 18-20, 58, 74-75, 77, 83, 85-88, 95, 105-106, 110, 200-201, 214-215, 218-229
Small and Medium-Sized Enterprises 78, 87, 155-156, 161, 175
Social Learning Theory 61, 223
Soft Skills 23-25, 28, 30, 34-39
Specialization in Tourist Guidance 230, 237-239
Strategic Leadership 12-13, 18, 21, 93-94, 192, 199-200, 202-217
Strategic Management 12, 120, 199, 204, 207, 209-217
Strategy 61-62, 66, 94, 102, 122, 172, 176, 181, 192, 199, 204, 206, 208, 210, 214-217, 226, 250
Systematic Literature Review 20, 110, 112, 121, 123-125, 139, 141
Systematic Review 57, 89-90, 109, 124, 127-128, 224

T

Team Members 11-12, 15-16, 43, 46, 52-53, 61-62, 66-68, 95, 102, 201, 221, 234, 254-255
Theoretical Perspective 112, 116, 119, 128
Tourism 2, 20, 27, 47, 55, 57, 59, 74, 76-77, 84, 86, 88-92, 99-108, 111-112, 114, 122-127, 129-131, 133, 139-153, 155-156, 161-167, 169-184, 186-199, 208-214, 216-217, 223, 225-232, 236, 239, 241-245, 275, 278-279
Tourism Enterprises 104, 199, 208, 217, 227
Tourist Guidance 230-232, 235, 237-245
Transformational Leadership 19, 32-37, 39, 57, 69, 73-74, 76-77, 83-86, 89, 95-96, 107, 109-114, 117-160, 162-163, 165, 167-168, 170-176, 178, 181, 183, 190, 192-195, 200-201, 211, 213, 256, 259

V

Visionary Leadership 73-75, 77, 81, 83-85, 88, 101-102, 199, 205, 212, 216-217, 233

Recommended Reference Books

IGI Global's reference books are available in three unique pricing formats:
Print Only, E-Book Only, or Print + E-Book.

Shipping fees may apply.

www.igi-global.com

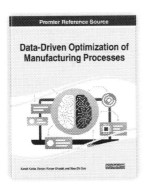

Data-Driven Optimization of Manufacturing Processes

ISBN: 9781799872061
EISBN: 9781799872085
© 2021; 298 pp.
List Price: US$ 225

Emerging Materials and Advanced Designs for Wearable Antennas

ISBN: 9781799876113
EISBN: 9781799876120
© 2021; 210 pp.
List Price: US$ 225

Emerging Applications and Implementations of Metal-Organic Frameworks

ISBN: 9781799847601
EISBN: 9781799847618
© 2021; 254 pp.
List Price: US$ 225

5G Networks and Advancements in Computing, Electronics, and Electrical Engineering

ISBN: 9781799869924
EISBN: 9781799869948
© 2021; 522 pp.
List Price: US$ 295

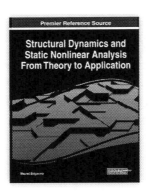

Structural Dynamics and Static Nonlinear Analysis From Theory to Application

ISBN: 9781799843993
EISBN: 9781799844006
© 2021; 347 pp.
List Price: US$ 195

Developing and Monitoring Smart Environments for Intelligent Cities

ISBN: 9781799850625
EISBN: 9781799850632
© 2021; 367 pp.
List Price: US$ 215

Do you want to stay current on the latest research trends, product announcements, news, and special offers?
Join IGI Global's mailing list to receive customized recommendations, exclusive discounts, and more.
Sign up at: www.igi-global.com/newsletters.

Publisher of Timely, Peer-Reviewed Inclusive Research Since 1988

www.igi-global.com   Sign up at www.igi-global.com/newsletters   facebook.com/igiglobal   twitter.com/igiglobal   linkedin.com/igiglobal

Ensure Quality Research is Introduced to the Academic Community

Become an Evaluator for IGI Global Authored Book Projects

 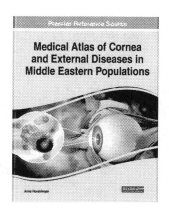 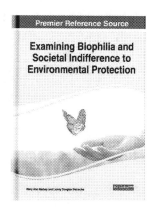 

The overall success of an authored book project is dependent on quality and timely manuscript evaluations.

Applications and Inquiries may be sent to:
development@igi-global.com

Applicants must have a doctorate (or equivalent degree) as well as publishing, research, and reviewing experience. Authored Book Evaluators are appointed for one-year terms and are expected to complete at least three evaluations per term. Upon successful completion of this term, evaluators can be considered for an additional term.

If you have a colleague that may be interested in this opportunity, we encourage you to share this information with them.

Easily Identify, Acquire, and Utilize Published Peer-Reviewed Findings in Support of Your Current Research

IGI Global OnDemand

Purchase Individual IGI Global OnDemand Book Chapters and Journal Articles

For More Information:
www.igi-global.com/e-resources/ondemand/

Browse through 150,000+ Articles and Chapters!

Find specific research related to your current studies and projects that have been contributed by international researchers from prestigious institutions, including:

- Accurate and Advanced Search
- Affordably Acquire Research
- Instantly Access Your Content
- Benefit from the InfoSci Platform Features

> *It really provides* **an excellent entry into the research literature of the field.** *It presents a manageable number of* **highly relevant sources** *on topics of interest to a wide range of researchers. The sources are* **scholarly, but also accessible** *to 'practitioners'.*
>
> - Ms. Lisa Stimatz, MLS, University of North Carolina at Chapel Hill, USA

Interested in Additional Savings?

Subscribe to
IGI Global OnDemand *Plus*

Learn More

Acquire content from over 128,000+ research-focused book chapters and 33,000+ scholarly journal articles for as low as US$ 5 per article/chapter (original retail price for an article/chapter: US$ 37.50).

6,600+ E-BOOKS. ADVANCED RESEARCH. INCLUSIVE & ACCESSIBLE.

IGI Global e-Book Collection

- **Flexible Purchasing Options** (Perpetual, Subscription, EBA, etc.)
- Multi-Year Agreements with **No Price Increases** Guaranteed
- **No Additional Charge** for Multi-User Licensing
- No Maintenance, Hosting, or Archiving Fees
- Transformative **Open Access Options** Available

Request More Information, or Recommend the IGI Global e-Book Collection to Your Institution's Librarian

Among Titles Included in the IGI Global e-Book Collection

Research Anthology on Racial Equity, Identity, and Privilege (3 Vols.)
EISBN: 9781668445082
Price: US$ 895

Handbook of Research on Remote Work and Worker Well-Being in the Post-COVID-19 Era
EISBN: 9781799867562
Price: US$ 265

Research Anthology on Big Data Analytics, Architectures, and Applications (4 Vols.)
EISBN: 9781668436639
Price: US$ 1,950

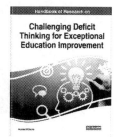

Handbook of Research on Challenging Deficit Thinking for Exceptional Education Improvement
EISBN: 9781799888628
Price: US$ 265

Acquire & Open

When your library acquires an IGI Global e-Book and/or e-Journal Collection, your faculty's published work will be considered for immediate conversion to Open Access *(CC BY License)*, at no additional cost to the library or its faculty *(cost only applies to the e-Collection content being acquired)*, through our popular **Transformative Open Access (Read & Publish) Initiative**.

For More Information or to Request a Free Trial, Contact IGI Global's e-Collections Team: eresources@igi-global.com | 1-866-342-6657 ext. 100 | 717-533-8845 ext. 100

Have Your Work Published and Freely Accessible
Open Access Publishing

With the industry shifting from the more traditional publication models to an open access (OA) publication model, publishers are finding that OA publishing has many benefits that are awarded to authors and editors of published work.

Freely Share Your Research

Higher Discoverability & Citation Impact

Rigorous & Expedited Publishing Process

Increased Advancement & Collaboration

Acquire & Open

When your library acquires an IGI Global e-Book and/or e-Journal Collection, your faculty's published work will be considered for immediate conversion to Open Access *(CC BY License)*, at no additional cost to the library or its faculty *(cost only applies to the e-Collection content being acquired)*, through our popular **Transformative Open Access (Read & Publish) Initiative**.

Provide Up To 100% OA APC or CPC Funding

Funding to Convert or Start a Journal to Platinum OA

Support for Funding an OA Reference Book

IGI Global publications are found in a number of prestigious indices, including Web of Science™, Scopus®, Compendex, and PsycINFO®. The selection criteria is very strict and to ensure that journals and books are accepted into the major indexes, IGI Global closely monitors publications against the criteria that the indexes provide to publishers.

Learn More Here:

For Questions, Contact IGI Global's Open Access Team at openaccessadmin@igi-global.com

Are You Ready to Publish Your Research?

IGI Global offers book authorship and editorship opportunities across 11 subject areas, including business, computer science, education, science and engineering, social sciences, and more!

Benefits of Publishing with IGI Global:

- Free one-on-one editorial and promotional support.
- Expedited publishing timelines that can take your book from start to finish in less than one (1) year.
- Choose from a variety of formats, including Edited and Authored References, Handbooks of Research, Encyclopedias, and Research Insights.
- Utilize IGI Global's eEditorial Discovery® submission system in support of conducting the submission and double-blind peer review process.
- IGI Global maintains a strict adherence to ethical practices due in part to our full membership with the Committee on Publication Ethics (COPE).
- Indexing potential in prestigious indices such as Scopus®, Web of Science™, PsycINFO®, and ERIC – Education Resources Information Center.
- Ability to connect your ORCID iD to your IGI Global publications.
- Earn honorariums and royalties on your full book publications as well as complimentary copies and exclusive discounts.

Join Your Colleagues from Prestigious Institutions, Including:

Learn More at: www.igi-global.com/publish
or Contact IGI Global's Aquisitions Team at: acquisition@igi-global.com